# THE GRAMMAR OF RAISING AND CONTROL

For *Billy*, *Kate*, *Elijah*, and *Isaac*

Who we hope to teach so much,
But from whom we learn so much more

WILLIAM D. DAVIES AND STANLEY DUBINSKY

# THE GRAMMAR
## OF RAISING
# AND CONTROL

A COURSE IN SYNTACTIC ARGUMENTATION

© 2004 by William D. Davies and Stanley Dubinsky

BLACKWELL PUBLISHING
350 Main Street, Malden, MA 02148-5020, USA
108 Cowley Road, Oxford OX4 1JF, UK
550 Swanston Street, Carlton, Victoria 3053, Australia

The right of William D. Davies and Stanley Dubinsky to be identified as the Authors of this Work has been asserted in accordance with the UK Copyright, Designs, and Patents Act 1988.

All rights reserved. No part of this publication may be reproduced, stored in a retrieval system, or transmitted, in any form or by any means, electronic, mechanical, photocopying, recording or otherwise, except as permitted by the UK Copyright, Designs, and Patents Act 1988, without the prior permission of the publisher.

First published 2004 by Blackwell Publishing Ltd

*Library of Congress Cataloging-in-Publication Data*

Davies, William D., 1954–
The grammar of raising and control: a course in syntactic argumentation / William D. Davies and Stanley Dubinsky.
    p.   cm.
Includes bibliographical references and index.
ISBN 0-631-23301-6 (hardcover : alk. paper) — ISBN 0-631-23302-4 (pbk. : alk. paper)
1. Grammar, Comparative and general—Syntax.  2. Generative grammar—History. I. Dubinsky, Stanley, 1952– II. Title.

P291.D38 2004
415—dc22
2003025118

A catalogue record for this title is available from the British Library.

Set in 10/12 pt Palatino
by Graphicraft Limited, Hong Kong
Printed and bound in the United Kingdom
by TJ International Ltd, Padstow, Cornwall

The publisher's policy is to use permanent paper from mills that operate a sustainable forestry policy, and which has been manufactured from pulp processed using acid-free and elementary chlorine-free practices. Furthermore, the publisher ensures that the text paper and cover board used have met acceptable environmental accreditation standards.

For further information on
Blackwell Publishing, visit our website:
http://www.blackwellpublishing.com

# CONTENTS

| | |
|---|---|
| Preface | vii |
| Acknowledgments | x |

## Unit I  Classical Transformational Grammar — 1

| | |
|---|---|
| Introduction:   Building the Foundations of a Syntactic Analysis | 1 |
| 1  Laying the Empirical Groundwork | 3 |
| 2  Transformational Grammar and Rosenbaum's Analysis | 17 |
| 3  Postal's *On Raising* | 30 |
| Reading from Postal (1974) | 35 |
| 4  Extended Standard Theory: Chomsky's "Conditions on Transformations" | 60 |
| Reading from Chomsky (1973) | 62 |
| 5  The *On Raising* Debates: Bresnan, Postal, and Bach | 89 |

## Unit II  Extensions and Reinterpretations of Standard Theory — 105

| | |
|---|---|
| Introduction:   Branching Paths of Inquiry | 105 |
| 6  Relational Grammar: Perlmutter and Postal's "The Relational Succession Law" | 107 |
| Reading from Permutter and Postal (1972/83) | 108 |
| 7  Revised Extended Standard Theory: Chomsky and Lasnik's "Filters and Control" | 137 |
| Reading from Chomsky and Lasnik (1977) | 138 |

## Unit III  Government and Binding Theory — 175

| | |
|---|---|
| Introduction:   The Interaction of Principles and Possible Analyses | 175 |
| 8  Chomsky's *Lectures on Government and Binding* and the ECM Analysis of Raising | 177 |

| | | |
|---|---|---|
| 9 | Development of and Problems for the ECM Account: Kayne (1981) and Cole and Hermon (1981) | 200 |
| | Reading from Cole and Hermon (1981) | 209 |
| 10 | Are All These Really Raising Constructions? Cross-Linguistic Issues | 243 |

## Unit IV  The Minimalist Program  273

| | | |
|---|---|---|
| Introduction: Neo-Raising, Neo-ECM, and the Raising/Control Distinction | | 273 |
| 11 | Functional Projections and the Rise of the Minimalist Program | 275 |
| 12 | The Return to a Raising-to-Object Analysis | 299 |
| | Reading: Lasnik and Saito (1991) | 300 |
| 13 | The Separation/Unification of Raising and Control | 332 |
| References | | 363 |
| Name Index | | 374 |
| Subject Index | | 377 |

# PREFACE

(1) Barnett seemed to understand the formula.
(2) Barnett believed the doctor to have examined Tilman.
(3) Barnett tried to understand the formula.
(4) Barnett persuaded the doctor to examine Tilman.

The sentences in (1) and (2) and their relationship to the sentences in (3) and (4) form the thematic core of this book. Inasmuch as understanding the analysis of (3) and (4) is important to understanding the analysis of (1) and (2), this book is about them as well. Sentences (1) and (2) are examples of Raising – Raising-to-Subject (sometimes Subject-to-Subject Raising) and Raising-to-Object (sometimes Subject-to-Object Raising), to be more precise. Sentences (3) and (4) are examples of Control, Subject Control, and Object Control, respectively. Raising and Control are among a handful of syntactic phenomena (including anaphora and question formation) which have been central concerns of generative syntax since the 1960s and must be factored into every instantiation of a comprehensive model. In many instances understanding the analysis of these constructions in a particular framework requires understanding the key assumptions underlying that framework, which leads to a general understanding of the framework itself. Thus, Raising and Control provide an excellent window into generative theories of syntax.
    Starting with the classical transformational argumentation relating to Raising and Control, this book traces the development of analyses within the Chomskyan tradition from Standard Theory to the Minimalist Program, with some consideration of other generative alternatives along the way. Through a close examination of the development of analyses of this particular data domain one may gain insights into the interaction between data and theory. The shifts in the analyses of Raising and Control dramatically illustrate how theoretical models at times drive the perception of data, and how linguistic facts at other times force the restructuring of linguistic models. An understanding of the phenomena themselves and how data drive analyses and analyses are driven by theory are what we most hope you will get from this book.

Examining the development of the analyses of Raising and Control may also provide a sense of how the theory has evolved since the Standard Theory of Chomsky's *Aspects*-model. To the extent that it does, this is an added bonus. However, such an understanding most likely requires the assistance of volumes more focused on this topic, such as Newmeyer (1986). So, with any luck at all, this book will serve multiple functions.

The book is divided into four units, each consisting of two to five separate chapters. Unit I, "Classical Transformational Grammar," provides an introduction to the empirical domain of the book, an examination of one of the earliest transformational treatments of the constructions (Rosenbaum 1967), a look at two contrasting theoretical perspectives (those of Postal 1974 and N. Chomsky 1973), and a depiction of the mid-1970s debate on the issue of Raising. Unit II, on "Extensions and Reinterpretations of Standard Theory," provides two distinct theoretical perspectives of the late 1970s and early 1980s, those of Relational Grammar and of Revised Extended Standard Theory (REST). In Unit III, "Government and Binding Theory" is the focus. There we introduce the theoretical principles that drive the Exceptional Case Marking (ECM) analysis of Raising-to-Object constructions, consider the theoretical innovations that are necessitated in attempting to extend the ECM analysis beyond its English model, and explore the raising construction in a range of languages that ultimately might not have it. Finally, Unit IV "The Minimalist Program," begins with a look at the theoretical revisions of the early 1990s, revisions which motivate an abandonment of the ECM analysis and a return to a "Raising"-like account of these constructions. The last chapter of this unit brings the discussion into the present tense, examining recent attempts to collapse the Raising/Control distinction in favor of unitary analyses of them.

The subtitle of this book is *A course in syntactic argumentation*, and this is due to our belief that it is suitable material for a course in syntactic theory. The book contains six readings, drawn from the literature, which are intended to provide the student/reader with a feel for the literature that would necessarily be lacking from a pure summary of it. At the same time, we have endeavored to provide explanation and discussion of these passages, so as to make them accessible to one who is not familiar with the theoretical contexts in which they were written. We think that a course based on this book could profitably use the content of the book to avoid the alternative of reading the source materials for all the different analyses presented here. This enables students to go off on their own to explore other readings on the topic and perhaps on some topics other than the ones presented in this book. Note that the sources cited in the six readings are listed at the end of each reading; all other sources cited are listed in references at the end of this book.

Having successfully taught some version of such a course on four distinct occasions at two universities, the authors can attest to its success. By restricting the data domain to Raising and Control, as we have done in this book, the empirical focus acts as a lens through which students may examine the development of theoretical models of syntax. And while it would be difficult to devise a comprehensive course covering 35 years of generative theory in a single semester, a course based on this book makes such an endeavor quite feasible. While students do not come away from this course with a thorough knowledge of each model, they do achieve a deep understanding of the basic premises that underlie the conceptual distinctions among them. They also develop, through their exposure to the various models and analyses, a faculty for "theoretical translation" – that is, an ability to grasp the intent of differing theoretical models, notational conventions, and innovations, without getting lost in or discouraged by the often confusing details. In this regard, the students who have passed through such a course have all become better practitioners of syntactic analysis, and more critical consumers of linguistic theory.

At the same time, there are a number of things that we do not intend the reader to derive from this book. First off, this is not a comprehensive treatment of the full range of constructions that might be grouped under the rubric of "Raising" or "Control." The constructions that occupy the central focus of this book, as noted above, are Subject-to-Subject Raising and Subject-to-Object Raising, alongside the parallel Subject and Object Control constructions. The book makes little to no mention of non-obligatory Control, of Control by constituents other than subjects and objects, of *"tough"* constructions (sometimes classed as Object-to-Subject Raising), of Possessor Raising, of *"seems like"* Copy Raising, of a construction named "Richard" (Rogers 1971, 1972, 1974; Potsdam and Runner 2001), of Super Equi, or of Hyper Raising. Nor is this volume intended to be a history or compilation of all generative approaches to Raising and Control. It should be made clear at the outset that the volume does not do justice to the many non-MIT-oriented theoretical models (such as Categorial Grammar, G/HPSG, and LFG) that all have much to say regarding Raising and Control. Finally, this book does not provide a full and comprehensive understanding of any of the theories or theoretical models actually covered in this volume. There are many other volumes devoted to introducing MIT-oriented generative syntax, Relational Grammar, or other theories touched on here. Of course, readers who are truly interested in understanding the workings of a particular model are best advised to consult the primary sources, many of which are included in the references to this volume.

With this in mind, we hope that the reader will find the ensuing pages useful and informative.

# ACKNOWLEDGMENTS

Any large endeavor requires the goodwill and support of many people. This book is no exception. We would like to thank the anonymous referees who read the initial book proposal and all who patiently listened to our developing idea and enthusiastically encouraged us to attempt this. Among them there are some who deserve special mention.

Frederick Newmeyer, Paul Postal, Roumyana Slabakova, and an anonymous reader for Blackwell carefully read the manuscript and offered excellent suggestions that strengthened the volume you now hold in your hands. Despite the fact that some suggestions were not followed up on, all were greatly appreciated.

A number of native speakers provided grammaticality judgments for some of the non-English data included here, and we extend our thanks to Surachman Dimmyati, Annie Dumenil, Hasan, Masharudin, Ruskawi, Sugiyono, Apolonia Tamata, and Rowena Torrevillas.

This volume developed out of several classes we have taught since the spring 1999 semester. The questions, comments, puzzlements, perceptions, and outrage of the students in those classes helped shape the book and gave us confidence that the project was worth trying. Thanks to the students of syntactic theory classes and the syntax seminar at the University of South Carolina: Raquel Blazquez-Domingo, Carla Breidenbach, Craig Callender, Lori Donath, Cheryl Fitzgerald, Angie Green, Rachel Hayes, Claudia Heinemann-Priest, Won-yoo Kim, Denis Kopyl, Larry LaFond, Rulai Li, Changyong Liao, Theresa McGarry, Robert Moonan, Heather Myers, Mila Tasseva-Kurktchieva, Leticia Trower, Cherlon Ussery, Chalmers Van Deusen, Kristen Vanheest, and Lan Zhang. And thanks to the students of the University of Iowa syntax seminar: Judit Balassa, Susanna Bauer, Jane Gressang, Dongmei Li, Lixia Ma, Danielle Seager-Frerichs, and Yuping Zhou.

Thanks to Tami Kaplan, formerly of Blackwell, for encouraging us to pursue the project and shepherding us most of the way through it, and Sarah Coleman for her editorial and logistical help. Thanks also to Craig Callender, Craig Dresser, Fiona Sewell, Zara Wanlass, and Lan Zhang for assistance in preparing and proofreading the manuscript.

Financial assistance for various aspects of the work was provided by the University of Iowa Arts and Humanities Initiative, the University of Iowa College of Liberal Arts and Sciences, the Obermann Center for Advanced Studies, and the University of South Carolina Department of English Language and Literature. Work on Madurese was supported in part by the National Science Foundation through grant SBR 98-09044 to the University of Iowa.

As always our families provided a lot of support but more importantly a great deal of tolerance through many disruptive visits and absences over the past year and a half, always providing the right balance of inspiration and exasperation. So our special thanks to Melissa and Elijah and Patty, Billy, and Kate.

The editor and publisher gratefully acknowledge the permission granted to reproduce the copyright material in this book:

1  Paul Postal, sections 4.2, 4.3, 4.6, 4.8, and 4.10 (pp. 95–102, 118–24, 125–9, 132–4) from *On Raising: One rule of English grammar and its theoretical implications* (Cambridge, MA: MIT Press, 1974). Reprinted by permission of MIT Press.
2  Noam Chomsky, sections 1–3 (pp. 232–44) from "Conditions on transformations" in *A festschrift for Morris Halle*, eds Stephen Anderson and Paul Kiparsky (New York: Holt, Rinehart, and Winston, 1973).
3  David Perlmutter and Paul Postal, editor's foreword and sections 1, 2, 3.1, 5.1, and 7 (pp. 30–9, 42–3, 49–52) from "The Relational Succession Law" in *Studies in relational grammar, vol. 1*, ed. David Perlmutter (Chicago: University of Chicago Press, 1972 [1983]). Reprinted by permission of University of Chicago Press.
4  Noam Chomsky and Howard Lasnik, sections 0 and 1.1 (pp. 425–33) and 1.3 (pp. 439–44) from "Filters and Control" in *Linguistic Inquiry* 8:3 (Summer 1977). © 1977 by the Massachusetts Institute of Technology. Reprinted by permission.
5  Peter Cole and Gabriella Hermon, sections 1–6.3 (pp. 1–19) from "Subjecthood and islandhood: Evidence from Quechua" in *Linguistic Inquiry* 12:1 (Winter 1981). © 1981 by the Massachusetts Institute of Technology. Reprinted by permission.
6  Howard Lasnik and Mamoru Saito, pp. 324–43 from "On the subject of infinitives" in *Papers from the 27th Regional Meeting of the Chicago Linguistic Society*, eds Lise M. Dobrin, Lynn Nichols, and Rosa M. Rodriguez (Chicago: Chicago Linguistic Society, 1991). © 1991 by Chicago Linguistic Society. Reprinted by permission.

Every effort has been made to trace copyright holders and to obtain their permission for the use of copyright material. The publisher apologizes for any errors or omissions in the above list and would be grateful if notified of any corrections that should be incorporated in future reprints or editions of this book.

# UNIT I
# CLASSIC TRANSFORMATIONAL GRAMMAR

## INTRODUCTION: BUILDING THE FOUNDATIONS OF A SYNTACTIC ANALYSIS

This unit traces the developments in the treatment of Raising and Control in early generative syntax. The distinction between Raising and Control is robust in early transformational grammar, the Standard Theory as delineated in Noam Chomsky's 1965 *Aspects of the theory of syntax*. But as with other grammatical features, developments in this area were many and rapid, in part fueled by the exuberance of the early practitioners of generative linguistics and in part by the developing rift between interpretive semantics and generative semantics.

Chapter 1 examines the grammatical characteristics of Raising and Control, outlining the empirical distinctions between these constructions which every analysis in the generative era must deal with in developing an adequate analysis. As the course of the book shows, the same distinctions that fueled the initial Standard Theory analyses drive the proposals of the 2000s.

Chapter 2 provides an overview of Standard Theory and lays out Rosenbaum's (1967) classic analysis of both Raising and Control. In Rosenbaums's analysis, both Raising-to-Subject (RtoS), as in *Barnett seemed to understand the formula*, and Raising-to-Object (RtoO), as in *Barnett believed the doctor to have examined Tilman*, include movement of the subject of the embedded clause into a position in the matrix clause. Although Raising and Control are unified in a single rule in Rosenbaum's analysis, reaction to and evaluation of his proposal often led to the splitting of these constructions into separate structures. And the movement analysis of RtoO later became controversial.

The classic transformational work on Raising is Postal's (1974) tome *On Raising*. Chapter 3 outlines a number of Postal's many and varied data arguments for recognizing a movement analysis of both RtoS and RtoO and includes reading selections from that work. Postal's treatment emerged roughly simultaneously to Chomsky's (1973) "Conditions on transformations," which includes Chomsky's shift from deep structure semantics to interpretive semantics and the concomitant repudiation of the movement analysis of RtoO. Chapter 4 details these developments and includes a selection from "Conditions on transformations."

In some ways the Raising-to-Object transformation was a rallying point for the so-called "linguistic wars" (Harris 1995; Huck and Goldsmith 1995) between generative semantics, as embodied in Postal (1974), and interpretive semantics, represented by Chomsky (1973). As generative semanticists sought to generalize syntactic operations throughout the grammar, introducing levels of abstract representation deep into the lexicon, Chomsky's interpretivist endeavors were aimed at drawing clear distinctions between the lexical and syntactic components of the grammar (as epitomized in N. Chomsky 1970), and constraining what the syntactic component of the grammar could do.[1] The combative nature of this debate is evident in Bresnan's (1976) review of Postal, which lays out objections to nearly every one of Postal's empirical arguments for movement in RtoO, and Postal's (1977) uncompromising response to that review. This material is the subject of Chapter 5.

## Note

1 Needless to say, initial theoretical stances can be poor predictors of theoretical evolution, and as will be seen in unit IV, some of the theoretical repositioning in Chomsky's 1990s Minimalist Program involves the adoption of assumptions that would have been deemed generative semantic heresy in the 1970s.

# CHAPTER 1

# LAYING THE EMPIRICAL GROUNDWORK

## 1 Constructions and labels

A primary motivation for the attention given to Raising and Control in generative syntax is the striking similarity of the constructions in English. This is obvious in the data in (1) and (2), which illustrate Raising-to-Subject and Subject Control.

(1) Barnett seemed to understand the formula.

(2) Barnett tried to understand the formula.

The surface strings in (1) and (2) are identical: an intransitive matrix clause with an infinitival complement, NP-V-to-VP. The sole surface difference is the choice of the matrix verb, *seem* vs. *try*. However, as will be seen in the following section, there are fundamental differences between the two sentences that center on the subject of the matrix clause. In the Raising construction in (1), the subject *Barnett* is semantically linked only to the embedded verb *understand*, while in (2) it is semantically linked to both the matrix verb *try* and the embedded verb. For this reason, the subject in (2) is said to "control" the reference of the subject of the embedded clause and the construction has come to be referred to as "Subject Control."

Parallel data are found with transitive matrix verbs where the locus of these differences is the immediately postverbal NP.

(3) Barnett believed the doctor to have examined Tilman.

(4) Barnett persuaded the doctor to examine Tilman.

Again, the surface strings are (virtually) identical, but there are fundamental differences in the characteristics of the NPs immediately following the matrix verbs. In (3), *the doctor* is semantically linked only with the embedded verb *examine*, while in (4) *the doctor* is semantically linked to both the matrix verb *persuade* and the embedded verb. The construction in (3) is referred to as Raising-to-Object and that in (4) as Object Control. Additionally, there are constructions such as (5) that parallel the surface strings (3) and (4).

(5)   Barnett promised the doctor to examine Tilman.

In (5), the subject *Barnett* but not the object *the doctor* is semantically linked to the embedded predicate, and the sentence, like (2), is a case of Subject Control.

Whether or not the structures in (1–5) are Raising or Control depend on properties of the matrix verb, that is, the Raising and Control that are examined here are lexically governed. In other words, while some syntactic rules apply independent of lexical selection (e.g., SUBJ-AUX Inversion applies in questions regardless of the main verb of the sentences), other rules apply only in the context of particular lexical items. Being marked for Raising may have nothing to do with the argument structure of a verb or the thematic roles it assigns. It will be seen below that there are large classes of "raising predicates" and "control predicates," and their structure will be examined in the course of our discussion. However, we first turn to diagnostics for distinguishing the two constructions.

## 2   Empirical distinctions between Raising and Control

Despite the superficial similarities in word order and morphology, raising and control constructions differ in a variety of ways, many of them related to meaning. This section outlines the traditional arguments for distinguishing Raising and Control.

### *Thematic roles*

Raising and control structures have distinct thematic structures; that is, the roles of the participants in the state of affairs described in the sentence are distinct. In the case of intransitive verbs, the matrix subject appears to have a role only in the action of the complement. Note that (1) is truth-conditionally equivalent to (6).

(6)   It seemed that Barnett understood the formula.

In (6), *Barnett* is assigned the thematic role of "experiencer" as the subject of *understand*. *It*, on the other hand, as a pleonastic (or semantically empty) element, receives no thematic role, showing that the predicate *seem* need not assign a thematic role to its subject. The thematic structure of (1) is identical to (6). *Barnett* is understood to be an experiencer, but has no other thematic role assigned. Conversely, in (2), *Barnett* appears to have two roles in the sentence, one as experiencer of *understand* and one as agent of *try*. The control verb *try*, unlike the raising verb *seem*, assigns a thematic role to its subject. Thus, intransitive raising and control verbs have different thematic structures.

Transitive raising and control verbs exhibit a similar difference, with the difference residing in the postverbal argument. In (4), *Barnett persuaded the doctor to examine Tilman*, *the doctor* plays two roles in the sentence: one as the agent of the embedded verb *examine* (i.e., the examiner) and the other as the object of persuasion (i.e., the persuadee) of the verb *persuade*. *Persuade* assigns three thematic roles: agent, persuadee, thing persuaded of (the clausal complement). In (3), *Barnett believed the doctor to have examined Tilman*, *the doctor* plays a single role, that of agent or examiner. That is, (3) is truth-conditionally equivalent to (7).

(7)  Barnett believed that the doctor had examined Tilman.

In (7), as in (3), *believe* has two thematic roles to assign: agent to its subject and theme to the clausal complement. Thus, transitive raising and control predicates have distinct thematic structures, just as intransitives do.

## *Embedded passive*

Raising and control structures can be distinguished by their behavior when the complement clause is passive (Rosenbaum 1967:59–61). For raising predicates such as *seem*, a sentence with a passive complement is synonymous with the same sentence with an active complement. This is illustrated in (8).

(8) a.  Barnett seemed to have read the book.
    b.  The book seemed to have been read by Barnett.

With an intransitive control verb, the sentences with embedded passive are not synonymous with the active, and, in fact, an embedded passive is not always possible.

(9) a.  The doctor tried to examine Tilman.
    b.  Tilman tried to be examined by the doctor.

(10) a.  Barnett tried to read the book.
     b.  #The book tried to be read by Barnett.

The sentences in (9) are not synonymous. In (9a), it is the doctor who attempts the examination; however, the attempt may fail for some reason, be it Tilman's refusal to be examined or some other circumstance. On the other hand, in (9b), it is Tilman who makes the attempt, but may be unsuccessful due to the doctor's refusal or some other circumstance. (10) shows that the passive is not possible when the object of the embedded clause is an inanimate entity such as a book. This relates to the thematic structure of *try*, which assigns the agent role to its subject, and so in the normal state of affairs requires a sentient, volitional entity as subject.

The same situation is encountered with transitive raising and control predicates. With raising predicates, sentences with embedded passive and active are truth-conditionally equivalent; so, (11) and (3) are synonymous.[1]

(11)  Barnett believed Tilman to have been examined by the doctor.

In both (3) and (11), Barnett's belief is that the doctor examined Tilman. In contrast, with a matrix control predicate, the embedded passive and active are not synonymous. The state of affairs expressed in (12) is not the same as that expressed in (4).

(12)  Barnett persuaded Tilman to be examined by the doctor.

In (12), Barnett must persuade Tilman of the need for the examination, while in (4), it is the doctor that must be persuaded. The synonymy or non-synonymy of sentences with active and passive complements thus provides a second diagnostic for distinguishing Raising and Control.

## Selectional restrictions

Another diagnostic distinguishing raising and control constructions is available from selectional restrictions imposed by embedded predicates. For semantic reasons, many predicates require that one argument or another have particular properties. This is illustrated in (13).

(13)  a.  The rock is granite.
      b.  #The rock understands the important issues of the day.

(13a) is a perfectly well-formed sentence; the predicate *be granite* selects for a subject that can in fact be granite. (13b), on the other hand, is pragmatically odd; the predicate *understand* requires that its subject be sentient. Since rocks do not have this property, (13b), while syntactically well-formed, is semantically ill-formed.

The influence of the selectional restrictions of predicates of complement clauses provides a diagnostic for distinguishing Raising from Control. The data in (14, 15) illustrate.

(14)  a.  The rock seems to be granite.
      b.  #The rock seems to understand the important issues of the day.

(15)  a.  #The rock tried to be granite.
      b.  #The rock tried to understand the important issues of the day.

Looking first at (14), we see that (14a) is perfectly well-formed, while (14b) is semantically odd. The data precisely parallel the situation in (13). In (14a), the embedded predicate is *be granite*, and *the rock* can be the subject of the entire sentence, while in (14b), the embedded predicate is *understand*, and having *the rock* as subject of *seem* is semantically ill-formed. Thus, it is possible to account for the judgments in (14) on the basis of the semantics of the embedded predicate. With the control predicate *try*, the situation changes. Both sentences in (15) are semantically ill-formed, the embedded predicate having no influence over the judgments of acceptability. In fact, the oddness in (15a) and (15b) results from the semantic requirements of *try*; *try* assigns the agent role to its subject, which requires an entity capable of volition. The sentences in (15) are ill-formed precisely because rocks violate this selectional restriction. Raising constructions can thus be distinguished from control constructions on the basis of whether or not the selectional restrictions of the **embedded** predicate can determine the semantic well-formedness of the sentence.

The sentences in (16) and (17) show that the situation is similar with transitive raising and control predicates. With raising predicates such as *believe*, when the selectional restrictions of the embedded predicate are satisfied, the sentence is well-formed (16a), but when they are violated, the sentence is semantically ill-formed (16b). As (17) shows, with control verbs such as *persuade* the situation changes. Despite the fact that the selectional restrictions of the embedded predicate are satisfied in (17a), this sentence is as semantically ill-formed as (17b). The reason is that *persuade* requires a sentient object, an object that is capable of being persuaded; *the rock* satisfies this requirement in neither (17a) nor (17b).

(16) a. Barnett believed the rock to be granite.
b. #Barnett believed the rock to understand the issues of the day.

(17) a. #Barnett persuaded the rock to be granite.
b. #Barnett persuaded the rock to understand the issues of the day.

## *Pleonastic subjects*

As seen in the preceding sections, the fact that control predicates assign a thematic role to the controller while raising predicates assign no thematic role to the corresponding argument provides an explanation for the distinct behaviors of the two classes with respect to embedded passive and selectional restrictions. A further diagnostic where this is relevant involves the *it* of meteorological expressions and existential *there*. While either can be the subject of an intransitive raising predicate such as *seem* (18), neither is possible with control predicates (19).

(18) a. It seemed to be raining.
b. There seems to be a unicorn in the garden.

(19) a. *It tried to be raining.
b. *There tried to be a unicorn in the garden.

Since pleonastic elements are semantically empty, they can be assigned no thematic role. Therefore, they are not possible subjects for verbs such as *try*, which assign thematic roles to their subjects, in this case agent, and the sentences in (19) are ungrammatical. Conversely, as was seen above, intransitive raising verbs do not assign a thematic role to their subjects and so pleonastic elements are semantically allowable subjects. As the sentences in (18) show, as long as the pleonastic subjects are sanctioned by the predicates of the embedded clause, they are possible subjects of intransitive raising predicates.

Again, parallel data are found with transitive raising and control predicates.

(20) a. Barnett believed it to have rained.
b. Barnett believed there to be a unicorn in the garden.

(21) a. *Barnett persuaded it to rain.
b. *Barnett persuaded there to be a unicorn in the garden.

Raising predicates such as *believe* accept meteorological *it* or existential *there* as postverbal NPs (20), while control predicates such as *persuade* do not (21). Again, the ungrammaticality of the sentences in (21) is attributable to the fact that *persuade* has a thematic role to assign to its object, and this role cannot be assigned to semantically empty elements such as *it* and *there*.

### *Idiom chunks*

A final diagnostic for distinguishing raising from control constructions comes from the behavior of idiomatic expressions. In (22), *the cat* can take on a special meaning.

(22) The cat is out of the bag.

The sentence in (22) is ambiguous. When interpreted literally it describes a situation in which a particular feline is not in a particular container, and *the cat* denotes that feline. As an idiom, (22) means that a one-time secret is no longer a secret, and *the cat* denotes that secret. Clearly this is an unusual meaning of *the cat* and is only possible when *the cat* occurs in this particular idiomatic expression.

As (23) and (24) show, the possibility of idiomatic interpretations distinguishes Raising from Control.

(23) a. The cat seemed to be out of the bag.
b. ?The cat tried to be out of the bag.

(24) a. Tina believed the cat to be out of the bag by now.
b. ?Tina persuaded the cat to be out of the bag.

With raising predicates, expressions can retain their idiomatic interpretation: (23a) and (24a) can still be interpreted as describing situations in which *the cat* can refer to a secret. On the contrary, with control predicates, the idiomatic interpretation is no longer possible: in (23b) and (24b) *the cat* can only be interpreted as referring to a particular feline.[2]

## 3 Where things get fuzzy

There are verbs in English which seem to occur in both raising and control structures, albeit with slightly different meaning. One such predicate is *begin*, as described in detail by Perlmutter (1970).

(25)  The street sweeper began to work.

(25) can be viewed as either a raising or a control structure, and this can be made clear with the addition of further context as in (26).

(26)  a.  The street sweeper began to work, once we replaced the spark plugs.
      b.  The street sweeper began to work, as soon as he got to the park.

In (26a), *the street sweeper* is clearly a machine, and *begin* functions only as an aspectual raising verb, assigning no thematic role to its surface subject. In (26b), though, *the street sweeper* denotes a person. Here the NP is assigned the thematic role of agent by the embedded verb *work*, but additionally, the commencement of the activity is a volitional act, in which case *the street sweeper* is also assigned an agent role by the matrix verb *begin*. As Perlmutter shows, *begin* displays some of the behaviors typical of raising predicates.

(27)  It began to rain.
(28)  Headway began to be made toward a solution.

In (27), the subject is meteorological *it*, which (as shown previously) is possible with Raising but not Control, and in (28), *headway* is sanctioned in the idiomatic expression *make headway*, but not as a possible agent of *begin*. On the basis of evidence such as this, Perlmutter argued for two thematically distinct verbs *begin*, one a raising verb and the other a control verb.[3]

Two other English verbs which show the characteristics of both raising and control predicates are *promise* and *threaten*. In each case, the distinction depends on whether the subject of the verb is an agent. When the subject is non-agentive, the verb takes a single argument, which may be propositional as in (29a) or nominal as in (29b).

(29)  a.  Rain threatened to fall.
      b.  Rain threatened.

When the subject is agentive, the verb takes two arguments, an agent and a theme, which is generally propositional, (30a). (30b) is a control construction.

(30)  a.  Sandra threatened that she would leave.
      b.  Sandra threatened to leave.

These raising/control distinctions are illustrated in (31) and (32).

(31) a. The boy promises to be a gifted musician.
    b. The boy promised to pick up a quart of milk on the way home.

(32) a. Several downtown businesses threaten to go bankrupt.
    b. Several downtown businesses have threatened to take the city to court over the new parking regulations.

In (31b), the boy has clearly made a verbal commitment to perform a task, a volitional act. Thus, here *promise* assigns the role of agent and the structure is Control. In contrast, (31a) describes someone's assessment of whether or not the boy will become a gifted musician; the boy is not making a verbal commitment and is not a participant in the event of promising. In (32), *threaten* shows the same contrast. In (32b), a conscious threat has been made by the representatives of these businesses, while (32a) simply describes a likely scenario which imputes no volition to the businesses or their representatives. As with *begin*, the volitional uses of *promise* and *threaten* are control constructions and the non-volitional uses are raising constructions.

As (33) and (34) illustrate, both verbs can take pleonastic subjects when they are licensed by the embedded predicates, indicating their status as possible raising predicates.

(33) a. There promises to be trouble at the concert.
    b. It promises to be a beautiful day.

(34) a. There threatens to be a revolution in San Marino.
    b. It threatens to be a hard winter.

Finally, Postal (1974:ch. 11) discusses other cases in English in which the distinction between Raising and Control is blurred. There are cases that would be analyzed as Raising-to-Object/Object Control, with predicates such as *allow*, *find*, *permit*, and others. On the one hand, these predicates behave as raising predicates exhibiting the property of allowing pleonastic elements (35a, b) and idiom chunks (35c).

(35) a. I allowed **there** to be a unicorn in the garden.
    b. The president will not permit **it** to seem that he is hiding something from the public.
    c. Hoover allowed **tabs** to be kept on Jane Fonda.

On the other hand, these predicates display the control-type behavior of not preserving meaning when the complement is passive.

(36) a. Barnett permitted the doctor to examine Tilman.
    b. Barnett permitted Tilman to be examined by the doctor.

Clearly, in (36a) Barnett has given the doctor permission to do the examination, while in (36b), Barnett has given Tilman permission to undergo the examination. See Dowty (1985) for an examination of the semantics of these predicates.

## The lists of verbs

Thus far, our illustrations of Raising and Control have involved very few predicates. There are, however, extensive numbers of both raising and control predicates in English. Here we provide lists compiled from other sources.

*Intransitive raising predicates* (Postal 1974:292)

a. *Adjectives*

| | | | |
|---|---|---|---|
| about | certain | likely | sure |
| apt | going | set | unlikely |
| bound | liable | supposed | |

b. *Verbs*

| | | | |
|---|---|---|---|
| appear | fail | promise | stop |
| become | get | prove | strike |
| begin | grow | quit | tend |
| cease | happen | resume | threaten |
| chance | impress | seem | turn |
| come | keep (on) | stand | turn out |
| commence | need | start | were |
| continue | persist | start out | wind up |
| end up | proceed | stay | |

c. *Auxiliaries*

| (Modals) | may | should | (Non-modals) |
|---|---|---|---|
| can | might | will | be |
| could | must | would | have |
| ought | shall | | used |

*Transitive raising predicates* (Postal 1974:305, 308)

| | | | |
|---|---|---|---|
| acknowledge | determine | intuit | rule |
| admit | discern | judge | specify |
| affirm | disclose | know | state |
| allege | discover | note | stipulate |
| assume | feel | posit | suppose |
| believe | figure | presume | surmise |
| certify | gather | proclaim | take |
| concede | grant | reckon | think |
| declare | guarantee | recognize | understand |
| decree | guess | remember | verify |
| deduce | hold | report | |
| demonstrate | imagine | reveal | |

*Subject control predicates*
a. *Adjectives*

| | | |
|---|---|---|
| careful | eager | reluctant |

b. *Verbs*

| | | | |
|---|---|---|---|
| attempt | endeavor | hope | promise |
| condescend | fail | intend | refuse |
| continue | forget | learn | remember |
| dare | help | manage | try |
| desire | | | |

*Object control predicates*

| | | | |
|---|---|---|---|
| allow | force | permit | tell |
| cause | let | persuade | urge |
| coax | order | | |

## Ruwet (1991)

In his consideration of raising and control structures in French, Ruwet (1991) points to the apparent difficulty in determining precise syntactic diagnostics for distinguishing the two classes that are applicable in all cases. He takes as his starting point the generally accepted notion that *sembler* 'seem' is a raising predicate and *prétendre* 'claim' is a control verb. The particular syntactic test for Raising in French that he examines is *en*-cliticization on the embedded verb.

A restricted set of verbs (perhaps a subset of unaccusative verbs[4]) allows the subjects to optionally take the partitive clitic *en* as complement.

(37) a. La préface de ce livre est trop longue.
       'The preface of this book is too long.'
   b. La préface (en) est trop longue.
       'The preface (of it) is too long.'

In (37b) the subject *la préface* optionally takes the clitic *en* as a pronominal complement, substituting for the PP complement *de ce livre* found in (37a).

French raising verbs such as *sembler* 'seem' can be distinguished from control verbs such as *prétendre* 'claim' by means of the *en* clitic. As (38b) shows, *en* can cliticize to the embedded verb in a raising construction, although it is associated with the subject of the matrix clause.

(38) a. L'auteur de ce livre semble être génial.
       'The author of this book seems to be brilliant.'
   b. L'auteur semble **en** être génial.
       'The author of it seems to be brilliant.'

On the contrary, *en* cannot cliticize to the embedded verb in a control construction, as in (39b).

(39) a. L'auteur de ce livre prétend être génial.
       'The author of this book claims to be brilliant.'
   b. *L'auteur prétend **en** être génial.
       (The author of it claims to be brilliant.)

(39b) is ungrammatical precisely because of the presence of *en*. Thus, *en*-cliticization is taken to be a syntactic diagnostic for Raising in French.

Ruwet further shows that *promettre* 'promise' and *menacer* 'threaten' are ambiguous between Raising and Control in the same way as for English. For example, (40) can mean either that the young boy gives a verbal promise that he will become a great musician or that his chances of becoming a great musician are promising.

(40)  Ce jeune garçon promet de devenir un grand musicien.
      'The young boy promises to become a great musician.'

Likewise, (41) can mean either that the terrorists verbally threaten to break everything or that there is a good chance that they will do so.

(41)  Les terroristes menacent de tout casser.
      'The terrorists threaten to break everything.'

Thus, it seems that *promettre* and *menacer* are clear examples of verbs that take either raising or control structures.

However, Ruwet demonstrates that the *en*-cliticization facts seem to cast doubt on the status of these verbs. If *en*-cliticization is a marker of Raising, and if these two verbs both possess a raising and a control variant, then one would expect that *en*-cliticization would provide a means for clearly distinguishing the raising senses of (40) and (41) from the control interpretations. However, with this class of "ambivalent" verbs, Ruwet finds that *en*-cliticization on the embedded verb is only possible when the subject is non-human. Compare (42b) and (43b) with (38b) above.

(42)  a.  La préface menace de ne jamais **en** être publiée.
          'The preface of it threatens to never be published.'
      b.  ??L'auteur menace de ne jamais **en** devenir célèbre.
          (The author of it threatens to never become famous.)

(43)  a.  Les conditions promettent d'**en** être satisfaisantes.
          'The conditions of it promise to be satisfactory.' (e.g., treaty)
      b.  *Les représentants promettent d'**en** être intègres.
          (The representatives of it promise to be upright.)

Thus, with the class of verbs that includes *promettre* 'promise' and *menacer* 'threaten', the distinction between raising and control structures is fuzzy. While raising predicates are supposed to exert no influence on the selection of their subjects, this does not seem to be the case with this class of verbs. Ruwet goes on to demonstrate that not only are there "ambivalent" raising and control verbs that disallow *en*-cliticization with a human subject, but also that there are certain "pure" control verbs such as *prétendre* 'claim' and *exiger* 'demand' which allow *en*-cliticization on the embedded verb provided the matrix subject is non-human.

(44) La liste ne prétend pas **en** être exhaustive.
'The list of them does not claim to be exhaustive.'

Ruwet successfully demonstrates the fact that identifying Raising and Control is not always a black and white issue. Regrettably, it is not always the case that syntactic diagnostics are available as reliable tests for Raising and/or Control.

## A third class

As outlined above, there is a large class of raising predicates and a large class of control predicates. And for the most part, the membership of the two classes is mutually exclusive, notable exceptions to this being *begin*, *promise*, and *threaten*. There is a third class of verbs, exemplified by *want* and *prefer*, which at first blush also appear to belong to both classes.

Notice first that when *want* and *prefer* are followed by an infinitival complement, the infinitive can have an overt accusative subject, or not, as seen in (45) and (46).

(45) a. She wanted them to be nice.
 b. She wanted to be nice.

(46) a. Barnett would prefer the doctor to examine Tilman.
 b. Barnett would prefer to examine Tilman.

Example (45a) seems to have more in common with the Raising (-to-Object) sentence in (47a) than with the Object Control sentence in (47b). At the same time, (45b) has more in common with the Subject Control sentence in (48b) than with the Raising (-to-Subject) sentence in (48a).

(47) a. She believed them to be nice.
 b. She persuaded them to be nice.

(48) a. She seemed to be nice.
 b. She tried to be nice.

These superficial observations are supported by some of the diagnostics developed earlier in this chapter. According to these diagnostics, (45a) and (46a) appear to be cases of Raising, as they pattern like *believe*: for example, the postverbal NP can be existential *there* (49) and idioms can have their idiomatic interpretation (50).

(49) a. I want there to be fried squid at the reception.
 b. Fillmore would prefer there to be a unicorn in the garden.

(50) a. I want the fur to fly at next week's meeting.
 b. Tina would prefer the cat to be out of the bag.

As (45b) and (46b) show, however, verbs of the *want*-class also appear to occur in control constructions. The sentences seem to be examples of intransitive control constructions such as were seen with verbs like *try*. Note that like *try*, in (45b) *she* appears to be assigned two thematic roles, one as subject of *want* and one as subject of *be nice*. Likewise, in (46b) *Barnett* is assigned a thematic role by *prefer* as well as by *examine*. Further, pleonastic subjects are excluded (51) and idioms lose any idiomatic interpretation (52) (or are just completely ungrammatical (52a)).

(51)   a. *There wants to be fried squid at the reception.
       b. *There would prefer to be a unicorn in the garden.

(52)   a. *The fur wants to fly.
       b. The cat would prefer to be out of the bag.

What distinguishes verbs of the *want*-class from others examined thus far is their ability to occur with the complementizer *for*, as illustrated in (53).

(53)   a. Terry wants very much for Ashley to arrive on time.
       b. The administration would prefer for all professional staff to agree to a furlough.

This is possible neither with "pure" raising predicates (54) nor with "pure" control predicates (55).

(54)   a. *Barnett believes (very much) for the doctor to have examined Tilman.
       b. *Terry proved (very convincingly) for Ashley to be an idiot.

(55)   a. *Barnett persuaded (very strongly) for the doctor to examine Tilman.
       b. *Tina forced (very strongly) for the author to rewrite the introduction.

Verbs that may also belong to this class include *hate, intend, like, mean,* and others.

## Notes

1   As Postal (p.c.) points out, the synonymy of the embedded actives and passives under Raising holds only of specific/non-quantificational nominals. In (i) and (ii), which are parallel to (3) and (11), the relative scope of the quantified expressions affects interpretation and obviates the synonymy referenced by this diagnostic.

   (i)   Barnett believed no doctor to have examined many students.

   (ii)  Barnett believed many students to have been examined by no doctor.

   (i) is true just in case there is no single doctor who has individually examined many students, while (ii) is true just in case there are many students who did not receive an examination by a doctor.

2 (23b) is somewhat degraded syntactically and (24b) is acceptable only to the degree that one believes that cats can be persuaded of anything. However, it remains clear that *the cat* can only denote an animal in these sentences.
3 Contra Perlmutter, Newmeyer (1969) argues that *begin* is only an intransitive verb.
4 Unaccusative verbs are a subset of intransitive verbs, and are in complementary distribution with unergative (intransitive) verbs. Where transitive verbs are characterized by having a subject and an object, intransitive verbs fail to have one of these. A verb that has (underlyingly) a subject but no object is termed unergative, and a verb that has an object (underlyingly) but no subject is termed unaccusative. The "unaccusative hypothesis" was most fully developed by David Perlmutter and Paul Postal in the mid-1970s, in the context of their Relational Grammar theory. The terminology was struck by Geoffrey Pullum. For a detailed and entertaining tale about the origin of this notion, see Pullum (1991).

# CHAPTER 2

# TRANSFORMATIONAL GRAMMAR AND ROSENBAUM'S ANALYSIS

The fuzzy data not withstanding, there are clear cases of the distinction between Raising and Control and we now turn to examining the theoretical treatment of these differences from Standard Theory on.

## 1 Standard Theory

The *Aspects*-model of Chomsky (1965), referred to as "Standard Theory," consisted of various components, the most important for the syntax being:

1. Phrase Structure – generates the constituent structure;
2. lexicon – lexical insertion rules that insert lexical items into the constituent structure, resulting in Deep Structure;
3. transformations – insertion, movement, deletion rules that derive Surface Structure.

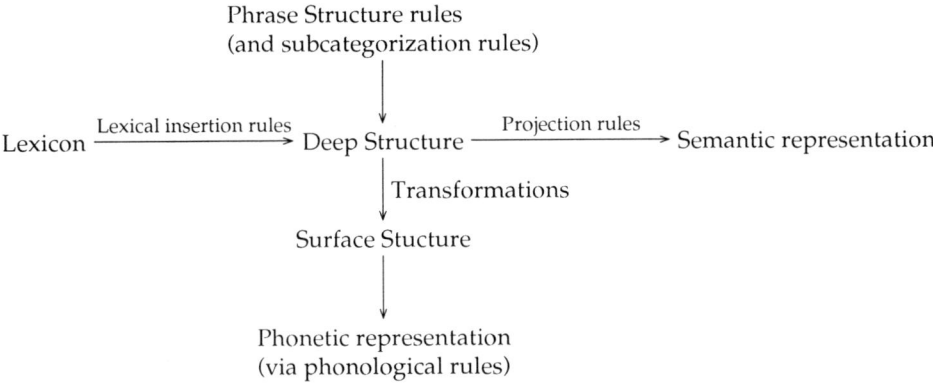

*The Standard Theory (ST) model*

## Phrase Structure rules

Phrase Structure (PS) rules were unrestricted rewrite rules of the form

$a \rightarrow b\ c$    "*a* rewrites as *b c*"

the application of which resulted in the structure

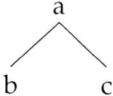

The most important PS rules for understanding the Standard Theory treatment of Raising and Control are:

S → NP (Aux) VP

VP → V (NP) (PP) {S/PP}

NP → DET N (S)

In Standard Theory complementizers were not contained in Deep Structure but were inserted via transformational rules, so that the Deep Structure of (1a) would be (1b).

(1) a. They believe that Haskins left.
    b. they [$_{AUX}$TENSE] believe [$_S$Haskins [$_{AUX}$TENSE] leave]

The complementizer *that* is inserted during the syntactic derivation via the *Complementizer Insertion* transformation. Within Standard Theory non-lexical categories such as complementizers could be inserted or deleted by transformation since these elements do not affect meaning, which is read off Deep Structure.

## Transformations

Transformations were very construction-specific, language-specific rules which took as their input a Phrase Structure, and then performed movement, insertion, and deletion operations, the output of which was a new Phrase Structure. Transformations consisted of three parts: the structural description (SD), the structural index (SI), and the structural change (SC). The Passive transformation was formalized along the following (simplified) lines (adapted from Akmajian and Heny 1976:153):

(2) Passive (optional)

| | SD: | X | NP | Aux | V | NP | | | Y |
|---|---|---|---|---|---|---|---|---|---|
| | SI: | 1 | 2 | 3 | 4 | 5 | | | 6 |
| | SC: | 1 | 5 | 3 | be | 4-en | by | 2 | 6 |

This transformation would be part of the derivation of

(3)  Tilman was examined by the doctor.

Deep Structure (and factoring of SD) for (3):

(4)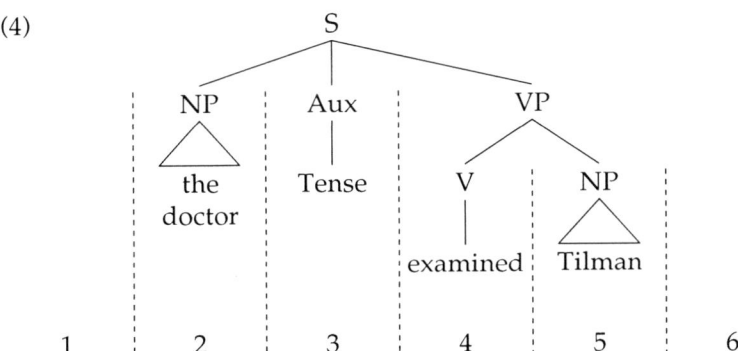

This diagram shows how the tree is factored to satisfy the SD of the Passive transformation, a point that will become important later in the discussion of Chomsky (1973).

Reflexives were also formed via transformation. Unlike the optional Passive, Reflexivization was an obligatory transformation; failure to apply the transformation derives an ungrammatical sentence. A statement is given in (5).

(5)  *Reflexivization (obligatory)*
```
     SD:   X    NP   Aux   V    Y    NP   Z
     SI:   1    2    3     4    5    6    7
     SC:   1    2    3     4    5    6    7
                                          [+reflexive]
```
Conditions: (i) 2 = 6; (ii) 2 and 6 must be in the same clause

(5) would apply to a structure for the string

(6)  Mary [tense] look at Mary

to derive the output

(7)  Mary [tense] look at herself

as part of the derivation of the sentence

(8)  Mary looked at herself.

Transformations were responsible for inserting pronouns, complementizers, and various other types of lexical material, moving elements in sentences, deleting material, and deriving some word forms (including deverbal nominals, such as *destruction* from *destroy*). Some of the common transformations included:

1 Dative Movement (for the derivation of double object sentences such as *Kerry gave Lynn the book*);
2 Subject–Auxiliary Inversion (for the derivation of questions);
3 *do*-Support (for the insertion of *do*);
4 *there*-Insertion (for the derivation of sentences with existential *there*).

## 2 Lees (1960) and Rosenbaum (1967)

One of the initial treatments of Raising was in Lees (1960:63). Lees wished to account for data similar to those in (9).

(9) a. I said that he is rich.
  b. That he is rich was said by me.
  c. He was said to be rich by me.

Lees noted that while (9b) could be derived from (9a) via a regular application of Passive, (9c) could not. For Lees, this was because (i) Passive was understood to be a clause-bounded rule that could not apply to the subject of a complement clause, and (ii) the complement clause subject in (9a) is separated from the main verb by a complementizer *that*. Nor, argued Lees, could (9c) be derived by Passive from **I said him to be rich* since the latter is not a well-formed sentence. Lees proposed that (9c) was in fact derived through the application of a Second Passive transformation which applied directly to (9a). In deriving (9c) from (9a), Second Passive moves the subject of the complement clause *he* into the matrix subject position and the matrix first person singular subject into a *by*-phrase; it also converts the matrix predicate into a passive and the complement residue into an infinitival.[1]

Rosenbaum (1967) sought a more general analysis with a wider domain of data. He was interested in examining the entire complementation system in English and provided Standard Theory analyses of both Raising and Control. Rosenbaum distinguished two types of sentential complements: what he referred to as NP complements and VP complements, which had the following structures within the VP:

(10) NP complements        VP complements

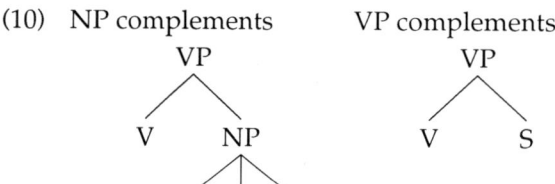

These two structures distinguished the sentential complements in (11) and (12).

(11) They doubt [$_{NP}$that you will go]            NP complement

(12) The doctor condescended [$_{VP}$to examine John]            VP complement

Rosenbaum argues that an NP node dominates the complement clause in (11) on the basis of (i) the possible occurrence of *it*, as in (13), and (ii) the fact that the complement can be passivized, as in (14), where the Passive transformation could only move an NP to subject position.[2]

(13) They doubt it (very much) that you will go.

(14) That you will go is doubted by them.

On the other hand, neither of these facts is true of *condescend*.

(15) *The doctor condescended it (last week) to examine John.

(16) *To examine John was condescended by the doctor.

Thus, Rosenbaum used the distinction between NP and VP complements to distinguish the two cases. A sentence such as (11) would be derived through a number of transformations as follows:

(17) they doubt [$_{NP}$[it] [$_S$you will go]]   Deep Structure
$$\Downarrow$$
they doubt [$_{NP}$[it] [$_S$that you will go]]   Complementizer Insertion
$$\Downarrow$$
they doubt [$_{NP}$[$_S$that you will go]]   Pronoun Deletion

Rosenbaum also analyzed sentential subjects as NP complements because (i) the PS rule for S requires an NP subject and (ii) *it* appears in an extraposition construction such as (18b).[3]

(18) a. That Barnett won surprised me.
 b. It surprised me that Barnett won.
 c. For Barnett to win surprised me.

Since they are synonymous, the sentences in (18) are assigned the same Deep Structure (ignoring irrelevant details):

(19) [$_{NP}$[it] [$_S$Barnett won]] surprised me

(18a) is derived using the same transformations as (17): Complementizer Insertion for *that* and Pronoun Deletion to remove *it*. (18b) is derived as follows:[4]

(20) [$_{NP}$[it] [$_S$Barnett won]] surprised me   Deep Structure
$$\Downarrow$$
[$_{NP}$[it] [$_S$that Barnett won]] surprised me   Complementizer Insertion
$$\Downarrow$$
[$_{NP}$it] surprised me [$_S$that Barnett won]   Extraposition

Sentential complements with the prepositional complementizer *for* are handled in the same way as tensed complements. The insertion of *to* along with *for*, in (21), is accomplished by the Complementizer Insertion rule, which treats *for-to* as a single morphological expression.

(21)   [$_{NP}$[it] [$_S$Barnett won]] surprised me         Deep Structure
         ⇓
       [$_{NP}$[it] [$_S$for Barnett to win]] surprised me   Complementizer Insertion
         ⇓
       [$_{NP}$[$_S$for Barnett to win]] surprised me        Pronoun Deletion

## Raising

In Rosenbaum's treatment of Raising, all the complements that he took to involve this rule were analyzed as NP complements. In each case, the complements can take *it*, and in the case of object complements, passivization is possible.

(22)   a.  The students seem to have gone.
       b.  It seems that the students have gone home.

(23)   a.  Everyone expected Dana to win the election.
       b.  Everyone expected that Dana would win the election.
       c.  Everyone expected it very much that Dana would win the election.
       d.  That Dana would win the election was expected by everyone.

In (22) the deep structure is:

(24)   [$_{NP}$[it] [$_S$the students have gone home]] seem

(22b) is derived via Complementizer Insertion of *that* and Extraposition.

To handle Raising, Rosenbaum proposed a transformation that he referred to as Pronoun Replacement. In this transformation, the subject of the embedded clause replaces the pronoun *it* as the matrix clause subject. Thus (22a) has the following derivation:

(25)   [$_{NP}$[it] [$_S$the students have gone home]] seem         Deep Structure
         ⇓
       [$_{NP}$[it] [$_S$for the students to have gone home]] seem   Complementizer Insertion
         ⇓
       [$_{NP}$it] seem [$_S$for the students to have gone home]     Extraposition
         ⇓
       [$_{NP}$the students] seem [$_S$for to have gone home]        Pronoun Replacement
         ⇓
       [$_{NP}$the students] seem [$_S$to have gone home]            Complementizer Deletion

In (25), the underlying subject of *seem* is the complex NP, *it the students have gone home*. After Complementizer Insertion, the sentential constituent of this complex NP is extraposed to the end of the matrix sentence. The subject of the extraposed sentence, *the students*, then moves to replace the pronoun *it*. In Rosenbaum's formulation of the Pronoun Replacement transformation, Extraposition must already have taken place, so that the indefinite pronoun *it* is the sole element in the matrix NP when the Pronoun Replacement rule is applied. Thus the raised NP moves into an existing NP node that was left behind after Extraposition. Additionally, since Raising is not triggered by all complement-taking predicates, Rosenbaum includes a lexical feature [+PR] in the structural description of the Pronoun Replacement transformation indicating that the transformation can apply only to sentences with predicates having this diacritic. The inclusion of this annotation rules out the possibility of deriving (26) by the application of the same rules, since *surprise* lacks the [+PR] feature.[5]

(26) *Barnett surprised me to win.

The sentence in (26) would be derived as in (27). However, the derived sentence is ungrammatical inasmuch as the application of Pronoun Replacement is illicit since *surprise* does not govern this transformation, and hence is marked [−PR].

(27) [$_{NP}$[it] [$_S$Barnett win]] surprise me     Deep Structure
⇓
[$_{NP}$[it] [$_S$for Barnett to win]] surprise me     Complementizer Insertion
⇓
[$_{NP}$it] surprise me [$_S$for Barnett to win]     Extraposition
⇓
[$_{NP}$Barnett] surprise me [$_S$for to win]     *Pronoun Replacement
(*surprise*[−PR]) ⇓
[$_{NP}$Barnett] surprise me [$_S$to win]     Complementizer Deletion

Rosenbaum analyzed Raising-to-Object (RtoO) in the same way, proposing no new transformations. The derivation of (23a) is given in (28).

(28) everyone expected [[$_{NP}$it [$_S$Dana win the election]]     Deep Structure
⇓
everyone expected [[$_{NP}$it [$_S$for Dana to win the election]]     Complementizer Insertion
⇓
everyone expected [$_{NP}$it] [$_S$for Dana to win the election]     Extraposition
⇓
everyone expected [$_{NP}$Dana] [$_S$for to win the election]     Pronoun Replacement
⇓
everyone expected [$_{NP}$Dana] [$_S$to win the election]     Complementizer Deletion

In (28), the complex NP, *it Dana win the election*, is the underlying **object** of the raising verb, *expect*. After Complementizer Insertion, the sentential constituent of this complex NP is extraposed to the end of the matrix sentence. Note that, in this case, the application of Extraposition is "string vacuous," i.e., it results in no linear reordering of any constituents. The subject of the extraposed sentence, *Dana*, then moves to replace the pronoun *it*. As before, the raising predicate, *expect*, must carry the feature [+PR]. Thus, in his analysis of raising structures, Rosenbaum provided a unified treatment of both Raising-to-Subject (RtoS) and RtoO.

## *Control*

In Standard Theory, sentences with Control were derived through the application of a transformation referred to as Equivalent Noun Phrase Deletion, which came to be known as Equi NP Deletion or simply Equi. In this transformation, a coreferent subject of an embedded complement is deleted in the course of the derivation provided the appropriate conditions obtain. For Rosenbaum, other than Equi itself, no other additional transformations were required. The sentence *The doctor condescended to examine John* had the derivation given in (29).

(29)  the doctor condescended [$_S$[$_{NP}$the doctor]          Deep Structure
examine John]
⇓

the doctor condescended [$_S$for [$_{NP}$the          Complementizer Insertion
doctor] to examine John]
⇓

the doctor condescended [$_S$for to examine          Equi NP Deletion
John]
⇓

the doctor condescended [$_S$to examine John]   Complementizer Deletion

Again, an object control sentence, such as

(30)  Barnett persuaded the doctor to examine Tilman

would have essentially the same derivation:

(31)  Barnett persuaded [$_{NP}$the doctor] [$_S$[$_{NP}$the      DS
doctor] examine Tilman]
⇓

Barnett persuaded [$_{NP}$the doctor] [$_S$for          Complementizer Insertion
[$_{NP}$the doctor] to examine Tilman]
⇓

Barnett persuaded [$_{NP}$the doctor] [$_S$for          Equi
to examine Tilman]
⇓

Barnett persuaded [$_{NP}$the doctor] [$_S$to          Complementizer Deletion
examine Tilman]

In both derivations, (29) and (31), the Equi transformation operates to erase the subject NP of the complement clause when it is identical to the subject (*condescend*) or object (*persuade*) of the matrix verb. The Equi rule requires that the complement clause be either infinitival or a gerund (thus keeping it from applying to a sentence with a tensed complement, such as *Barnett persuaded [NPthe doctor] [Sthat [NPthe doctor] should examine Tilman]*). Rosenbaum's Equi transformation, unlike the Pronoun Replacement (i.e., Raising) rule with its [+PR] feature, involves no lexical trigger. He also does not distinguish in this rule between object control verbs such as *persuade*, and subject control verbs such as *promise*.

## The Standard Theory typology of transformations and evidence for Raising

Within Standard Theory there were three recognized domains for transformations. First, there were "unbounded" transformations, such as *wh*-Fronting, Topicalization, and others that were able to move constituents over any number of sentence nodes. Second, there were transformations that moved or deleted elements over precisely one sentence node, e.g., Raising and Equi. Finally, there were clause-bounded transformations that could only affect elements within the domain of a single sentence node; these included transformations such as Passive, Dative Movement, Reflexivization, and Reciprocal Formation. The last two of these provided Standard Theory with theory-internal arguments for the raising analysis with verbs like *expect*.

It was generally assumed that Reflexivization and Reciprocal Formation were subject to a clausemate condition, that is, the antecedent and the anaphor had to be members of the same clause. This accounted for the difference in grammaticality between (32) and (33) and (34) and (35).

(32)   Mary looked at herself.

(33)   *Mary expects [S(that) herself would finish soon].

(34)   The children talked to each other.

(35)   *The children believe [S(that) each other is intelligent].

With verbs such as *expect* and *believe*, it is possible for the postverbal NP to be a reflexive (36) or a reciprocal (37) under the appropriate conditions of co-reference.

(36)   Mary expects herself to finish soon.

(37)   The children believe each other to be intelligent.

Under the assumption that both Reflexivization and Reciprocal Formation are clause-bounded transformations, data such as (36) and (37) can be taken to provide evidence for Raising. In order to account for the well-formedness of these sentences, the embedded subject NPs which surface as *herself* and *each other* must raise into the matrix clause, thereby satisfying the clausemate condition on antecedent and anaphor.

## 3  Responses to Rosenbaum

Following Rosenbaum, there were attempts to refine the raising analysis, much of which resulted in analyses that treat RtoS and RtoO as separate transformations. This resulted from some direct critiques of Rosenbaum's proposal.

### *Lakoff (1967) and Ross (1967)*

In separate work Lakoff (1967) and Ross (1967) objected in particular to the move in Rosenbaum's analysis that required Raising (his Prounoun Replacement transformation) to apply to the output of Extraposition. The majority of their objections consisted of theory-dependent arguments. For example, it was assumed at the time that Extraposition was a postcyclic rule, that is, a transformation that applies only after the application of all cyclic transformations (such as Passive, Reflexivization, and so on) and last cyclic transformations (such as *wh*-Fronting and Topicalization). Notice, however, than in Rosenbaum's account of Raising in (25) and (27), Extraposition (a postcyclic transformation) is assumed to precede Pronoun Replacement (a cyclic transformation). This ordering is crucial for Rosenbaum, because the application of Extraposition relies on the presence of a pronoun. Accordingly, the extraposition of the sentence in (38b) is possible, while the extraposition in (39b) is not, since the extraposed clause is moved away from the full NP, *the fact*.

(38) a. [ it [that Kelly left]] surprised me
     b. [ it ] surprised me [that Kelly left]

(39) a. [ the fact [that Kelly left]] surprised me
     b. *[ the fact ] surprised me [that Kelly left]

Given this, the interaction of Extraposition and Reflexivization creates problems for the derivation of (36). In (36), the raised argument *herself* can only be reflexivized by the matrix subject after the application of Pronoun Replacement (i.e., Raising), which itself must follow Extraposition. An analysis that crucially depends on the application of a postcyclic rule prior to cyclic rules violates the theory and thus cannot be correct (under the rule-ordering assumptions crucial to the theory). Other theory-internal arguments based on ordering paradoxes were also presented.

There was also a metatheoretical objection based on the undesirability of "string vacuous movement." It was noted that in case of RtoO, the output of Extraposition yielded no change in the order of constituents, simply a readjustment of the constituent structure (moving the S node out of the containing NP node), as in the derivation of *Everyone expected Kerry to win the election*, the relevant steps given in (40).

(40)   everyone expected [[$_{NP}$it [$_S$for Dana to   Complementizer Insertion
win the election]]
⇓
everyone expected [$_{NP}$it] [$_S$for Dana to   Extraposition
win the election]

It was argued that a theory that banned string vacuous operations would be a more restrictive theory; thus, analyses that crucially depended on such operations should be avoided. This is a position that is echoed in Chomsky (1973) (see chapter 4).

The critiques also included a strong empirical argument against the application of Extraposition in the raising analysis. Under Rosenbaum's analysis the sentences in (41) both involve Extraposition of the clausal complement; in fact, (41b) is derived from (41a) (data from Postal 1974:21).

(41)   a.   It is widely believed that Melvin is an ex-priest.
       b.   Melvin is believed to be an ex-priest.

In (41a), Extraposition results in a structure with a major constituent break between *believed* and *that Melvin is an ex-priest*; this accounts for the possibility of an intonation break between *it is widely believed* and *that Melvin is an ex-priest*. In (41b), the application of Extraposition should result in a similar structure. However, an intonation break between *Melvin is believed* and *to be an ex-priest* is highly unnatural. Therefore, the analysis of Raising that crucially depends on the application of Extraposition makes the wrong predictions about the data.

### *English as a VSO language (McCawley 1970)*

Since in Rosenbaum's analysis Pronoun Replacement always operated on the output of Extraposition, it was possible to account for RtoS and RtoO with a single rule. With that portion of the analysis discredited, RtoS and RtoO were taken to be two similar but distinct processes, and new approaches to a unitary rule of Raising were entertained. One such attempt is embodied in McCawley's (1970) proposal that underlyingly English is a VSO language.

McCawley (1970) argued that the grammar of English can be greatly simplified under the assumption that the deep structure is VSO and that there is a postcyclic rule of V–NP inversion which moves the subject in front of the verb, much along the lines of contemporaneous accounts of verb-second languages such as German. McCawley argued that 10 of 15 cyclic transformations he considered were no more complex under the VSO hypothesis than under the accepted SVO formulations. But more importantly, the other five cyclic transformations, which included both Passive and *there*-Insertion, were actually simpler to formalize in the VSO formulation.

Under the assumption of underlying VSO order, a unitary rule of Raising was possible. As Postal (1974:26) illustrates, with a VSO structure Raising derives the phrase marker in (42b) from that in (42a).

(42)

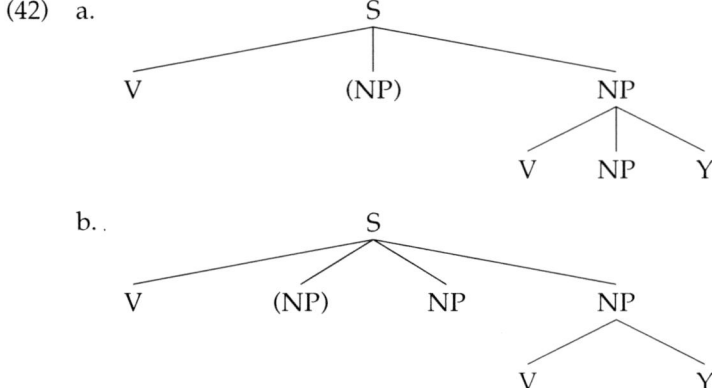

When the optional NP in (42) is not present, the matrix verb is intransitive (e.g., *seem, appear*) and the structures represent RtoS, as exemplified in (43a, b).

(43)  Leslie seems to have escaped.

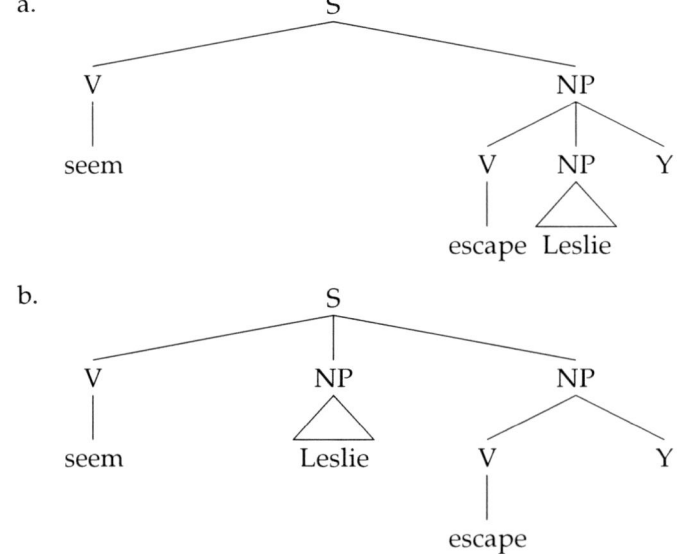

When the optional NP is present, the matrix verb is transitive (e.g., *expect, believe*), and the structures represent RtoO, as exemplified in (44a, b).

(44)   We expect Leslie to have escaped.

a.
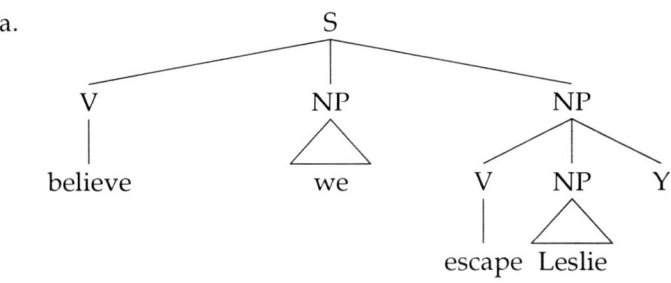

b.
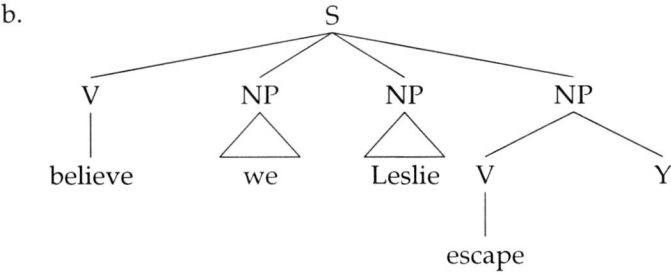

**Notes**

1  Later it will be seen that Lees's proposal for the derivation of (9c) is very close to the proposal Chomsky makes in (1973), in that Passive is permitted to operate cross-clausally.
2  Note that this second argument is an appeal to economy, since an alternative might be to have two separate rules of Passive: rule (2) plus a rule in which the element #5 is an S.
3  Again, theoretical economy plays a role, in preferring one PS rule (S → NP AUX VP) over two (S → NP AUX VP and S → S AUX VP).
4  The ungrammaticality of *It that Barnett won surprised me*, as an alternative to (18a), is accounted for by having the Pronoun Deletion rule be obligatory when the pronoun is immediately followed by an S constituent.
5  Obviously, the use of a lexical diacritic such as [+PR] might be considered ad hoc. As will be seen further along in the book, lexical diacritics of one sort or another are often found to be necessary for any adequate theory of these constructions.

# CHAPTER 3

# POSTAL'S *ON RAISING*

Reflexives, reciprocals, pleonastic pronouns, idiom chunks, and semantic equivalence were among the most widely accepted types of evidence for Raising within Standard Theory. In his voluminous 1974 tome, *On Raising: One rule of English grammar and its theoretical implications*, Paul Postal provided the most far-ranging and detailed examination of Raising that exists, attempting to motivate the existence of the transformation with a preponderance of data. Here Postal presents arguments that support the spirit of a Rosenbaum-type analysis which recognizes a raising transformation, but given the problems discussed by Lakoff and Ross for the role of Extraposition, Postal adopts McCawley's V-initial analysis of English in order to formulate a single rule for both RtoS and RtoO.[1] In *On Raising*, Postal reviews the "traditional" arguments for Raising, and adduces an additional 14 arguments focusing on Raising with transitive verbs, along with one "seductive non-argument." Postal goes on to consider some additional "potential arguments" and reflect on the place of Raising as a rule of grammar and its implications for linguistic theory. The purpose of the current section is to survey some of the additional arguments that Postal presents. Although he ultimately rejects the role of constituent structure in the formulation of Raising (in favor of a grammatical relations-based approach), the arguments that he puts forth in favor of a raising rule are based on data that any complete and adequate analysis of Raising must provide an account for.

While standing on its own as an investigation of Raising, Postal motivates a raising analysis against the backdrop of arguing against Chomsky's (1973) theory, which rejects RtoO (while recognizing RtoS). While a full consideration of Chomsky's approach in "Conditions on transformations" is left until chapter 4, it is helpful to contrast the two positions with respect to the relevant verbs. The two competing grammar fragments differ in many ways, but crucially they differ in the surface structure assigned to infinitival complements of these verbs.

(1) Raising: (Postal 1974)

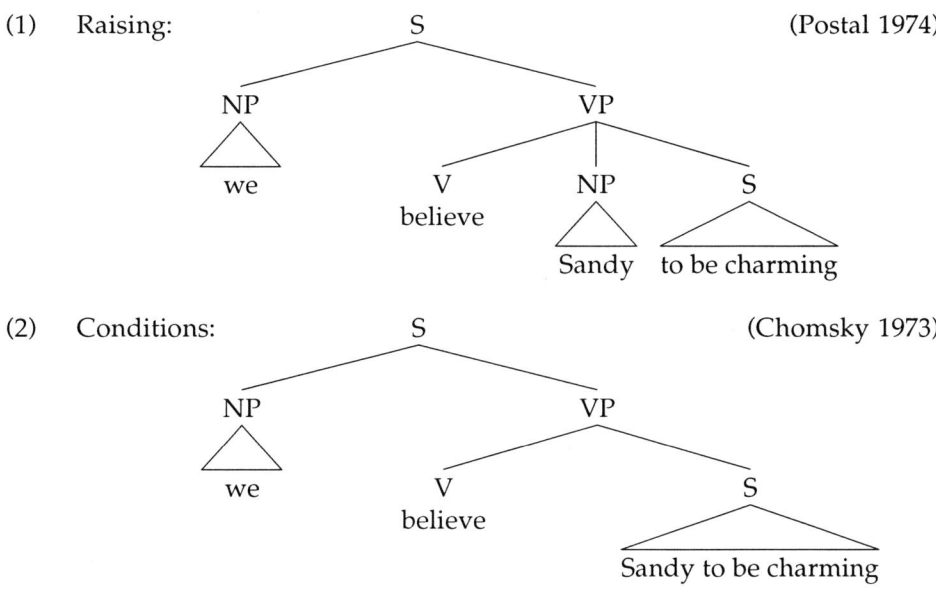

(2) Conditions: (Chomsky 1973)

In (1) is the familiar raising analysis in which the Deep Structure subject *Sandy* is a surface direct object. In Chomsky's "Conditions" approach, *Sandy* is not only a Deep Structure subject but also a Surface Structure subject.

In chapters 3 and 4 of *On Raising*, Postal's basic strategy is to show that the "Conditions" grammar, by treating the string *Sandy to be charming* as contained within the sentential complement, makes incorrect predictions about a range of data that the Raising grammar accounts for. His arguments are of basically three types:

1 The "subject" of the infinitive does not behave like a subject.
2 The "subject" and the infinitive do not behave as a single constituent.
3 The "subject" of the infinitive behaves like an object.

## 1 Arguments from Heavy NP Shift and adverbs

One of Postal's "new" arguments for Raising comes from the interaction of what he refers to as "Complex NP Shift" (generally referred to as Heavy NP Shift) and raising predicates. The point of this argument is that the Deep Structure embedded subject does not behave like a subject at the point of the derivation in which Heavy NP Shift operates on the matrix clause.

The sentences in (3) and (4) illustrate Heavy NP Shift. (For the most part, Postal's example sentences are used here.)

(3) a. Jack bought a book from Melvin.
    b. *Jack bought from Melvin a book.
    c. Jack bought from Melvin – a book which taught him organic knitting.

(4) a. I showed the cookies to Jack.
    b. *I showed to Jack the cookies.
    c. I showed to Jack – all of the coffee grounds and lettuce cookies.

In (3c, 4c), Heavy NP Shift has taken a long or complex direct object NP and postposed it over a PP. When the object is not sufficiently heavy, this shift results in ungrammaticality (or at least severe degradation of grammaticality), (3b, 4b).[2]

Postal (1971) had proposed that Heavy NP Shift is subject to the constraint in (5).

(5) Heavy NP Shift does not operate on NPs that are subjects at the point of application.

The constraint in (5) is suggested by Postal to account for the ungrammaticality of the examples in (6).

(6) a. *Are happy – all of the men who recovered from mononucleosis.
       (from: All of the men who recovered from mononucleosis are happy.)
    b. *That retired too soon – the man who founded this company – is obvious.
       (from: That the man who founded this company retired too soon is obvious.)

In (6a), the heavy NP subject of the main clause, *all of the men who recovered from mononucleosis,* is shifted, and in (6b) the heavy NP subject of the embedded clause, *the man who founded this company,* is shifted. If Heavy NP Shift is constrained as in (5), the sentences in (6) are predicted to be ungrammatical.

If (5) is correct, the raising analysis predicts that a heavy NP should be able to shift when the complement clause is an infinitive, since the NP is not a subject but an object at this point in the derivation. The raising analysis therefore predicts the ungrammaticality of (7a, 8a) and the grammaticality of (7b, 8b).

(7) a. *I believe (that) were tortured by Brazilians – the priests who are going to speak today.
    b. I believe to have been tortured by Brazilians – the priests who are going to speak today.

(8) a. *Sam expected (that) were missing from class – only those students who had caught the Friday flu.
    b. Sam expected to be missing from class – only those students who had caught the Friday flu.

In (7a), *the priests who are going to speak today* is uncontroversially the subject of the embedded tensed complement clause. Under the raising analysis, *the priests who are going to speak today* in (7b) is the direct object of the matrix clause when

Heavy NP Shift is applied. The facts are the same with respect to *only those students who had caught the Friday flu* in (8). Postal points out that the difference between a tensed clause and an untensed clause cannot explain the difference in (7, 8) because a heavy NP subject of an infinitive clause cannot shift.

(9) a. For all of the girls who got pregnant to have abortions would be tragic.
 b. *(For) to have abortions – all of the girls who got pregnant – would be tragic.

One might attempt to explain the data in (9) by an ad hoc constraint banning Heavy NP Shift in infinitival sentential subjects; (9b) is ungrammatical because the heavy NP, *all of the girls who got pregnant*, is shifted in an infinitival clause. However, as (10b) shows, Heavy NP Shift is possible in an infinitival sentential subject; here the NP object, *the letter which came yesterday*, is shifted over the prepositional phrase, *to Sam*.

(10) a. For Kelly to show the letter which came yesterday to Sam would be tragic.
 b. For Kelly to show to Sam – the letter which came yesterday – would be tragic.

Postal provides additional evidence for (5) by examining a number of other contexts, including gerundive complements and nominative absolutes. While it is possible to reorder the subject leftward out of a gerundive complement (11b), the subject cannot undergo Heavy NP Shift (11c).

(11) a. I don't favor that sort of person being allowed to join.
 b. That sort of person, I don't favor being allowed to join.
 c. *I don't favor being allowed to join that sort of rude, uncouth, ill-behaved person.

Neither can the subject of a nominative absolute undergo Heavy NP Shift (12b).

(12) a. All of the beer being gone, we had to drink 7-UP.
 b. *Being gone – all of the beer which we had smuggled into the country from Bavaria, we had to drink 7-UP.

Postal argues that in these contexts one finds subjects of non-finite clauses that are unable to undergo Heavy NP Shift. Therefore, an attempt to account for the difference in grammaticality between (7a) and (7b) and (8a) and (8b) in terms of tensed versus untensed clauses cannot account for all of the data, and formulating the constraint on Heavy NP Shift in terms of subjects is supported. The fact that the heavy NPs in (7b, 8b) can be shifted argues for the raising analysis of these verbs because the Deep Structure subject of the complement behaves like an object, not a subject.

Postal attributes his second argument to Kuno (1972). This argument, based on adverbs, purports that the NP + infinitive complement of verbs like *believe* and *expect* does not behave as a single constituent (as it would in the analysis represented by the structure in (2)). Consider the data in (13, 14).

(13) a. I believed that Nixon, foolishly, was interested in ending the war.
     b. I believed Nixon, foolishly, to be interested in ending the war.

(14) a. I have found that Bob recently has been morose.
     b. I have found Bob recently to be morose.

In (13) and (14) both sentences in each pair are grammatical, but the meaning is different. In the (a) sentences, the adverb can only be understood as modifying the complement clause. In the (b) sentences, the interpretation of the adverb is ambiguous.[3]

Postal proposes to account for this difference in terms of a constraint on the placement of "sentential" adverbs, which he formulates as (15).

(15) A "sentential" adverb can*not* be inserted in a complement clause.

The constraint in (15) would allow main clause adverbs to occur between dependents of the main clause node but would prohibit them from occurring in complement clauses.

If (15) is correct, it provides an argument for the raising analysis by showing that the NP + infinitive string does not constitute a clausal constituent. Note that (15) straightforwardly accounts for the lack of ambiguity in (13a), since the adverb *foolishly* occurs inside the sentential complement of *believe* and cannot modify the matrix predicate from that position. The ambiguity of (13b), on the other hand, is allowed by (15), on the assumption that the NP *Bob* has raised out of the complement clause into object position and that the string *Bob to be morose* is not a single constituent at the relevant level of structure. The lack of ambiguity in (14a) is also consistent with the constraint in (15): while *recently* might a priori modify either the act of finding out that Bob is morose or the fact of his being morose, here it can only refer to the latter. The fact that (14b) is ambiguous thus provides an argument for Raising. Under the raising analysis, ignoring the adverb, (14b) has the structure in (16).

(16)

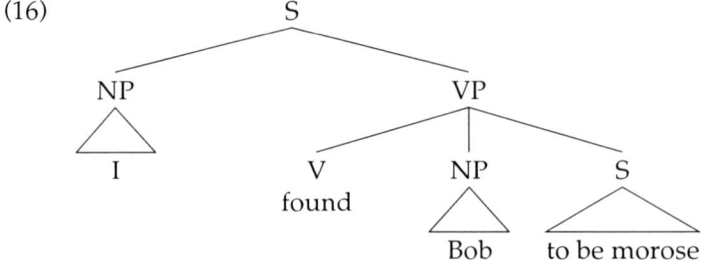

If *recently* is the leftmost dependent of the embedded S-node, then the interpretation is that Bob's being morose is a recent state of affairs. If *recently* is a dependent of the matrix VP, then the interpretation of the sentence is that it was recently that I found out what I did.

Postal notes that it is not always possible to interpolate a sentential adverb between an NP and an infinitive. When the NP + infinitive string is clearly part of the same constituent, the result is ungrammaticality, as in (17), or can only be construed as modifying the embedded clause (18b).[4]

(17) *Harry would prefer for Bob, unfortunately, to marry Sheila.

(18) a. I recently arranged for Bob to meet my niece.
     b. I arranged for Bob recently to meet my niece.

In the excerpt that follows here, the reader will examine five additional arguments for Raising, as presented in Postal (1974). (NB: In the excerpt the term "B-verb" refers to the *believe* class of raising verbs.)

# READING FROM POSTAL (1974)

Paul Postal, sections 4.2, 4.3, 4.6, 4.8, and 4.10 (pp. 95–102, 118–24, 125–9, 132–4) from *On Raising: One rule of English grammar and its theoretical implications* (Cambridge, MA: MIT Press, 1974). Reprinted by permission of MIT Press.

## 4.2 *Not*-initial NPs [pp. 95–8]

Certain NPs in English can occur with an initial morpheme *not*. These are to be distinguished from NPs beginning with *no* (*nobody*, *nothing*, *no peaches*, etc.):

(25) a. Not many gorillas have learned to tap-dance.
     b. Not much sense can be made out of that proposal.
     c. Not many Turks speak Yiddish.
     d. Not many Albanians have been interviewed by Sevareid.
     e. Not many farmers are easy to convince.

The *not*-initial NPs in (25) all occur as superficial subjects. It turns out that other functional positions in which NPs occur do not permit *not*-initial NPs:

(26) a. *Joe kissed not many models.
     b. *Jane earns not much money.
     c. *Sally talked to Bob about not many problems.
     d. *I bought kangaroos from not many Australians.

The generalization seems to be as follows:

(27) *Not*-initial NPs occur only in (derived) subject positions.

Principle (27) surely requires refinements.[1] It is, for instance, only a necessary condition.[2] Note the ill-formedness of all of the following examples, in which

---

[1] It should be stressed that (27) does not hold for NPs of the form *not* $\begin{Bmatrix} one \\ a\ single \end{Bmatrix}$:

(i) a. I met not $\begin{Bmatrix} one \\ a\ single \end{Bmatrix}$ doctor.
  b. He found not $\begin{Bmatrix} one \\ a\ single \end{Bmatrix}$ jar of chocolate butter.

Nor does it hold for those of the type cited in the text when these are *parts of adverbs*:

(ii) a. Not three hours ago, I saw Melvin over there.
  b. I met him not many years before that.

Next, *not*-initial NPs can occur as parts of conjunct NPs forming a coordinate subject:

(iii) a. Not many colonels and not many majors were demoted yesterday.
   b. Not much wheat and not much barley was sold to the Turks.

The whole must, however, be a subject:

(iv) a. *They demoted not many colonels and not many majors yesterday.
   b. *They sold not much wheat and not much barley to the Turks.

Furthermore, the *many* or *much* preceded by *not* need not be an immediate constituent of a subject NP but can be an immediate constituent of a preposed genitive NP that is part of a subject NP:

(v) a. Not many people's mothers are movie stars.
  b. Not many citizens' passports were seized by the police.

However, the genitive NP must be part of a subject and must be preposed:

(vi) a. *I called not many people's mothers.
   b. *Friends of not many people('s) are outside.

Thus the constraint would appear to be, if adverbs and conjoined cases are ignored, that *not* be the leftmost constituent of a subject NP. It should be emphasized that none of the further statements about *not*-initial NP distribution just made have any real bearing on the argument in the text. For these refinements do not alter the fact that *not*-initial NPs distinguish subject from nonsubject positions.

The notion of derived subject relevant for principle (27) is not entirely clear. In general, I should like to maintain a universal notion of subject something like the following:

(vii) For any clause C (at any level of derivation), the subject NP of C is that NP, N which is the leftmost immediate constituent NP of C.

This would be supplemented by the notion "subject of verb," to say that N is the subject of that verb V which is the immediate constituent of C. These accounts need considerable refinement,

subject NPs remain postverbal, owing to the regular failure of Subject Formation to apply in certain classes of environments:

(28) a. *Are not many policemen corrupt? (Note the necessity in a–d of reading *not* as part of the NP.)
  b. *Are there not many bars in Paris?
  c. *Did not many kangaroos eat the poisoned grain?
  d. *Will not much rice be imported by Greenland?
  e. *Were not many girls to come, I would be sad.

This will have no real bearing on the present discussion, however. The key point is that *not*-initial NPs are banned from derived nonsubject positions. It

---

though. For instance, one must guarantee that rules deleting subject NPs do not have the effect of turning objects into subjects under (vii), which we can do in terms of a global theory by restricting (vii) to just those NPs which are corresponding constituents of subject NPs – by (vii) – in cycle-final structures. In other words, an NP is a subject if it both meets (vii) and corresponds to a cyclic subject.

In these terms, then, it is probably possible to say that condition (27) refers to surface subjects, a claim that is consistent with Gapping cases like (viii) and (ix), since the *not*-initial NPs in the gapped cases meet both (vii) and the condition requiring correspondence to cyclic subjects.

(viii) a. Not many Greeks speak Turkish, and not many Turks speak Greek.
  b. Not many Greeks speak Turkish, and not many Turks Greek.

(ix) a. Many Greeks speak Spanish, but not many Spaniards speak Greek.
  b. Many Greeks speak Spanish, but not many Spaniards Greek.

It might be thought that a surface account of (27) fails because any definition that makes *not many Indians* a subject in (x)a will make *not many Indians* a subject in (x)b:

(x) a. Many Pakistanis were captured, but not many Indians (were captured).
  b. They captured many Pakistanis but not many Indians.

This is wrong, however. First, *not many Indians* in (x)a corresponds to a cyclic subject, while that in (x)b does not. But even more fundamentally, there is no reason to think that *not many Indians* is a constituent in (x)b, in contrast to (x)a. That is, we find also such cases as (xi), where the sequences *not* + X can never occur as constituents elsewhere.

(xi) a. They captured Tom but not Bob.
  b. They investigated Melvin's return but not mine.

I think, then, that so far, nothing precludes an account of (27) in terms of surface subject.

[2] Kayne has supplied the following examples, which illustrate further the lack of sufficiency of principle (27):

(i) *You'll soon know whether not many people like her.

(ii) *I'm in favor of not everyone leaving immediately.

(iii) *We were talking about not everybody's having registered.

Curiously, (iii), but not (ii), becomes well-formed when *many people* replaces *everybody*.

might be thought that such examples as (29) are counterexamples:

(29) There are not many blacks on the White House staff.

However, as Ross observes, the *not* here is not part of the NP, as proved by modal analogues like (30), contrasted with (31):

(30) There may not be many blacks on the White House staff (but . . . )

(31) *There may be not many blacks on the White House staff.

Hence, the generalization holds.

Together with the Raising analysis, (27) predicts a contrast between B-verb complements of the *that* and infinitival varieties. And just such a contrast exists:

(32) a. Harry believes (that) not many pilots are familiar with Racine.
b. *Harry believes not many pilots to be familiar with Racine.

(33) a. Harry proved (that) not many of those formulas were theorems.
b. *Harry proved not many of those formulas to be theorems.

(34) a. Harry found (that) not much grain was stored in telephone booths.
b. *Harry found not much grain to be stored in telephone booths.

With respect to the distribution of *not*-initial NPs, the postverbal NPs in the infinitival complement cases behave like nonsubjects, just as the Raising analysis predicts. An account like Chomsky's offers, on the contrary, no basis for the contrasts between pairs like those in (32)–(34).

No appeal to the tensed versus untensed clause distinction can rescue a non-Raising analysis here, since *not*-initial NPs can occur as derived subjects in several types of untensed clauses:

(35) a. Not many guests having arrived, Melvin poured a stiff drink.
b. For not many of you to pass would be tragic.
c. It would be normal for not much to be done about that.
d. I would prefer $\begin{Bmatrix} \text{for not much} \\ \text{*not much} \end{Bmatrix}$[3] to be said about this.

---

[3] I shall return to contrasts between *prefer* NP/*prefer for* NP several times later on [see (41), (101) and n. 11 in this reading]. In general, it turns out that, in the former, the NP behaves like a member of the main clause and, in the latter, like part of the complement. I take this to indicate that Raising operates optionally for *prefer*, similar to the way it works for *wish* and *desire*, as described in Section 4.16. If so, the grammar predicts that, by and large, the *for* cases will work like *that* clauses in contrast to the others without *for*. Comparison of (35)d with (i) is an initial indication that this is correct.

(i) I would prefer that not much be said about this.

e. ?Joan prayed for not many of them to be convicted.
f. ?I am in favor of not many of them being released.

Thus a non-Raising treatment of B-verb complements is disconfirmed by the behavior of *not*-initial NPs.[4]

## 4.3 *Alone*-final NPs [pp. 99–102]

Certain NPs can end with the form *alone* expressing essentially the meaning 'only':

(36) a. Gronzmeyer alone can help you.
b. Jones alone knows the secret formula.
c. My uncle alone was able to survive.
d. Matilda alone is easy to seduce.
e. Harrison alone can be forced to resign.

(37) a. *Call Bob alone.
b. *I talked to Smith alone about the wombat question.

---

[4] Baker observes that in his idiolect examples like the following are well-formed:

(i) Not many girls would Jack dance with.

(ii) Not many people can I think of who would put up with Oscar's manners.

He thus suggests that the proper condition on *not*-initial NPs is not that they be subjects, but rather that they be clause-initial. This would automatically account for facts like (v) and (vi) in footnote 1. However, I find examples like (i) and (ii) somewhat ill-formed. But, in support of Baker's contention, the following is well-formed, probably for everyone:

(iii) those girls, not many of whom the judge is willing to parole,

If, then, a clause-initial proposal is to be adopted, it must be stated in such a way as to be consistent with examples like (35)b, c, d. It must also be compatible with examples like (iv) presumably only by a view of Adverb Preposing as involving Chomsky adjunction.

(iv) a. Ten years ago, not many people were eating soyburgers.
b. Under those conditions, not many doctors will volunteer.

I shall make no decision here as to whether a clause-initial account is ultimately preferable to a subject one. Observe that this choice has no bearing at all on the validity of the argument for B-verb Raising. This follows since, in a non-Raising grammar, not only is the italicized NP in (v) not a derived subject, but there is also a clause boundary after *believes*, just as in (vi).

(v) *Jack believes *not many people* to be happy.

(vi) Jack believes not many people are happy.

Thus a non-Raising system is equally incompatible with a clause-initial account of *not*-initial NPs.

c. *Melvin hires those plumbers alone.
d. *We were freed by the soldier alone.
e. I believe $\begin{Bmatrix} \text{*that alone} \\ \text{only that} \end{Bmatrix}$.
f. Jim $\begin{Bmatrix} \text{proved} \\ \text{expected} \end{Bmatrix}$ $\begin{Bmatrix} \text{*that result alone} \\ \text{only that result} \end{Bmatrix}$.
g. *I refuse to work with her alone.

The generalization seems to be similar to that for *not*-initial NPs:

(38) *Alone*-final NPs can occur only in (derived) subject positions.[5]

Thus, parallel to the situation with *not*-initial NPs, principle (38) predicts, given the Raising analysis of B-verb infinitival complements, contrasts between pairs like (39):

---

[5] I would propose, of course, that the notion of subject defined in footnote 1 is also appropriate here.
 Like principle (27), governing *not*-initial NPs, principle (38) is not strictly true. It seems that *alone* meaning 'only' can also occur in certain kinds of adverbial NPs:

(i) a. In that way alone can we be sure of winning.
    b. ?Under those conditions alone will I agree to do it.

Moreover, Plath points out that there is a usage of *alone* in emphatic coordinate contexts:

(ii) a. I will tell this to you and to you alone.
     b. The car was stolen by Jim and by Jim alone.

Even more peculiarly, it seems to me that *alone* can occur on the predicate NPs of cleft sentences:

(iii) It was the Germans alone who started doing that.

Amazingly, as pointed out by McCawley, this is apparently possible only when the predicate NP corresponds to the subject of the embedded sentence:

(iv) a. *It was the Germans alone who we defeated.
     b. *It was the Germans alone who they sent money to.
     c. *It was the Germans alone who they were contacted by.

These points have no real bearing on the argument in the text, however, since it remains true that such NPs cannot occur in normal object positions.
 In some respects, *alone*-final NPs are freer than *not*-initial NPs. For example, they can occur in *unfronted* subjects:

(v) a. Did Bob alone call Sally on time?
    b. Under no circumstances would she alone be chosen.
    c. Were Tom alone to come, I would call Jack.

In others, however, as pointed out by Kayne, they are more restricted:

(vi) a. Bob alone studied organic knitting, and Tom alone studied conceptual art.
     b. *Bob alone studied organic knitting, and Tom alone conceptual art.

(39) a. Larry found (that) Bob alone had drunk the bourbon + vinegar mixture.
 b. *Larry found Bob alone to have drunk the bourbon + vinegar mixture.
 c. They proved (that) Martha alone had been at the scene.
 d. *They proved Martha alone to have been at the scene.

The fact that predicted contrasts exist would again be evidence that the post-main-verb NP in infinitival B-verb complements is not a derived subject. Principle (38) predicts directly the parallelism between such pairs as (40):

(40) a. *Larry believes that alone to be possible.
 b. *Larry believes that alone.

Once more, this is a conclusion that cannot be undermined by appeal to the properties of untensed clauses generally. For *alone*-final NPs can occur as the derived subjects of untensed clauses:

(41) a. Harry alone having been arrested, I called his wife.
 b. For Harry alone to be sent there would be unfair.
 c. I would prefer $\begin{Bmatrix} \text{for Harry alone} \\ \text{*Harry alone} \end{Bmatrix}$ to be arrested.
 d. It would be strange for you alone to be nominated on the first ballot.
 e. I arranged for Tony alone to receive a secret message.

Thus the properties of *alone*-final NPs also at once support a Raising analysis and disconfirm an analysis like Chomsky's, which assigns subject status to the relevant NPs not only in underlying structures but throughout derivations.

It is worth remarking briefly on the logic of the three arguments given so far in this section. In the case of Complex NP Shift, we discovered a restriction that blocks a certain operation from applying to subjects. Since the two grammatical proposals in competition make contrasting claims about the subject status of certain NPs in derived structures, such a restriction permits differentiation of the two positions. Similarly, in the case of both *not*-initial and *alone*-final NPs, we discovered that these can occur only in derived subject positions. This kind of generalization also interacts with the difference between the competing positions to permit their empirical separation. We have seen in all three cases that the Raising analysis correctly predicts the nonsubject status of those NPs which behave as nonsubjects, while a non-Raising system like Chomsky's gives the wrong answer in all three, predicting in each case that the NPs in question should behave like derived subjects, when they do not.

It follows that in searching for further empirical bases for distinguishing the consequences of Raising and non-Raising grammars of B-verb constructions, one should attempt, among other things, to find restrictions that are sensitive to derived subjects. It would be equally relevant to discover properties that were restricted to nonsubjects, or to derived objects. Such cases will be considered later.

## 4.6 A fundamental pronominalization constraint
## [pp. 118–24]

It has been known since late 1966 that a basic constraint on stipulated coreferential pronominalization in English (and, no doubt, other languages) is the following:

(68) A pronoun cannot both precede and command its antecedent NP.[6]

Recall that one constituent, which it neither dominates nor is dominated by, A, commands another, B, if the first S node above A also dominates B. Hence, in the configurations of (69) there are the command relations among non-S nodes given in (70).

(69)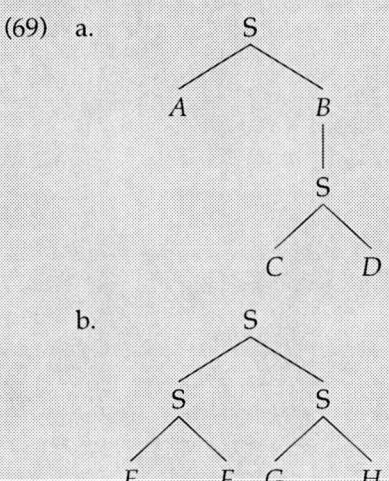

(70) a.  A commands B.
     b.  A commands C.
     c.  A commands D.
     d.  B commands A.
     e.  C commands D.
     f.  D commands C.
     g.  E commands F.
     h.  F commands E.
     i.  G commands H.
     j.  H commands G.

The principle in (68) accounts for an enormous range of facts, briefly and inadequately indicated by the following narrow selection:

---

[6] This formulation is due to Langacker (1969). See Ross (1969) and Postal (1970, 1971) for further discussion.

(71) a. *He$_i$ wants Jane to kiss Bob$_i$.
  b. *They$_{i,j}$ didn't believe I would help the employees$_{i,j}$.
  c. *She$_i$ called the man who annoyed Joan$_i$.
  d. *He$_i$ visited Jane, who used to know Bob$_i$.

While the exact point or points in derivations where (68) is applicable have never been specified precisely,[7] it seems clear that these must include a stage after the application of cyclic NP reordering rules (like Passive), for reasons such as (72):

(72) a. *He$_i$ called all of the girls who Bob$_i$ knew.
  b. ?All of the girls who Bob$_i$ knew were called by him$_i$.

While sentences like (72)b are less than perfect for many speakers, they do not manifest the complete block on coreferential linkages found in those like (72)a. Hence, the constraint in (68), which is responsible for the character of (72)a, must be sensitive to the structures produced by a rule like Passive in order to prevent the assignment of the status of examples like (72)a to passive sentences like (72)b.

One of the most obvious properties of raising operations is that *they alter command relations*. In particular, if there is a raising operation associated with B-verb infinitival complements, this operation permits the raised NP to command certain elements after it is raised which it did not before, since it is moved into a higher clause. Consequently, the way is open in principle for the Raising analysis, in conjunction with principle (68), to generate certain pronominalization contrasts that a system without Raising in these cases would not predict. In short, (68) offers another empirical possibility for differentiating Raising versus non-Raising grammars for B-verb complements.

Moreover, some sentences discovered by Bach (1970) turn the theoretical possibility into an actuality. Bach notes that in his speech and that of many others (myself included) the following sorts of contrasts exist:

(73) a. Joan believes (that) he$_i$ is a genius even more fervently than Bob$_i$ does.
  b. *Joan believes him$_i$ to be a genius even more fervently than Bob$_i$ does.
  c. Tom proved (that) she$_i$ was telepathic just as easily as Joan$_i$ did.
  d. *Tom proved her$_i$ to be telepathic just as easily as Joan$_i$ did.

That is, if we choose the first pair for discussion, *he* and *Bob* can be stipulated coreferents in (73)a, but *him* and *Bob* cannot be in (73)b. Under the Raising analysis of B-verb infinitival complements, this is an automatic consequence of principle (68),[8] since after application of Raising *him* will command *Bob*,

---

[7] This question is considered in Postal (to appear), where it is argued that the constraint must be defined at more than one stage of derivation and is, consequently, global.

[8] That is, automatic under the assumption that the constraint is sensitive to the output of Raising. However, since it has already been seen that the constraint is sensitive to the output of Passive,

although before application it would not have. These characteristics would follow from tree structures something like those shown in (74). Here (74)a represents the *that*-clause case and (74)b the infinitival structure *after* Raising has applied. It can be seen that, while in (74)a the first S node ($S_1$) above *he* does not dominate *Bob* and hence *he* does not command *Bob*, in (74)b the first S node ($S_0$) above him does dominate *Bob*, and hence *him* does command *Bob*. Therefore, it would follow from principle (68) that *him* and *Bob* cannot be coreferential in (73)b, while (68) is inapplicable in the case of *he* and *Bob* in (73)a, accounting for their possible coreferentiality. However, this contrast depends on the difference in command relations generated by Raising application in the infinitival cases and its non-application in the *that*-clause case.

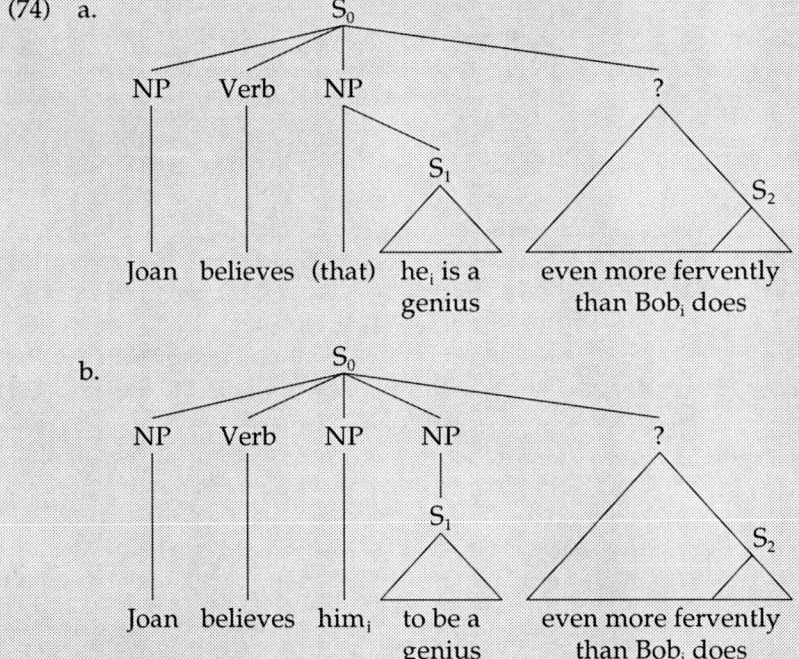

(74) a.

b.

I can think of one possible objection to this argument, which would take advantage of the fact that our knowledge of the constituent structures of comparative clauses is far from definitive. A critic might then claim that there is no basis for attaching the unlabeled nodes in (74) to the node $S_0$. He might claim that these are actually attached at some higher point, so that the structure would be the one shown in (75) rather than (74)b.

---

and since Passive operates, in a system with B-verb Raising, on the output of Raising, it follows that the constraint must consider the output of Raising. Parallel to (72) is the case of (i) and (ii):

(i) *$He_i$ believed all of the girls who knew $Bob_i$ were happy.

(ii) All of the girls who knew $Bob_i$ were believed by $him_i$ to be happy.

(75)

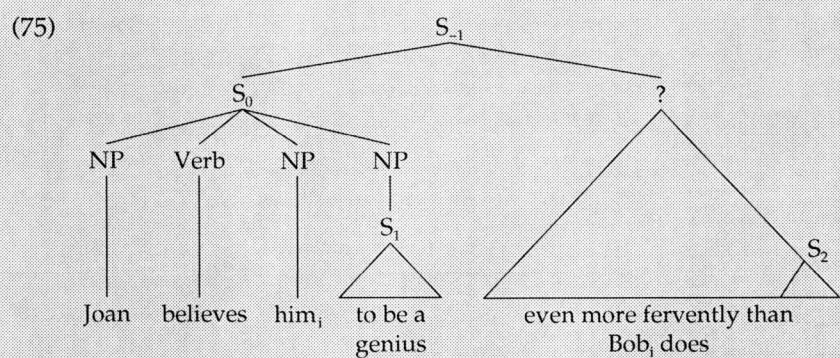

If this were the case, then, even in (73)b, *him* would not command *Bob*, and principle (68) would not be relevant to the example. The critic might then claim, weakly to be sure, that some as-yet-unknown principle blocks the coreference linkage in sentences like (73)b,d. Because of the loss of generality in the description of pronominalization constraints, and because (75) is not motivated, this objection seems to me to have at worst little force. However, even this problem can, I think, be eliminated by embedding sentences like (73) as *gerundive nominals*:

(76) a. Joan's believing (that) $he_i$ is a genius even more fervently than $Bob_i$ does worries me.
 b. *Joan's believing $him_i$ to be a genius even more fervently than $Bob_i$ does worries me.

For here it is known independently that a verb like *worries* determines gerundive form for the main verb of its complement subject. But if the appropriate structure for the relevant cases were like (75) instead of (74), the structure of a sentence like (76)b would be like (77).

(77)

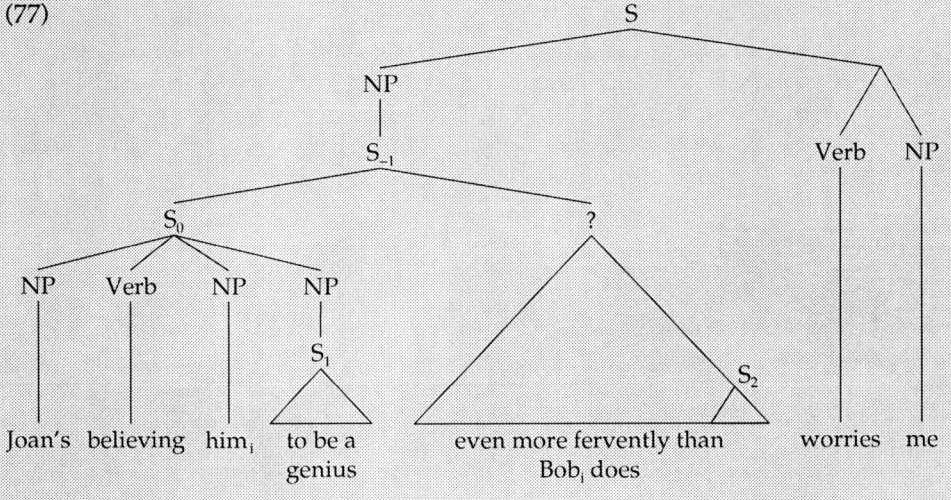

But in such a structure, *believing* is not the main verb of the complement clause but rather of a clause embedded within that. The complement clause itself, $S_{-1}$, does not even have a main verb in any accepted sense. Hence, given structures like (77), the rules determining the relation between main verbs like *worry* and the gerundive form of their complement subjects would be unnecessarily complicated. Thus (75) is not an appropriate structure, and the objection to the argument collapses.

In conclusion, the sentences observed by Bach reveal a contrast in terms of principle (68) which is a direct consequence of the Raising analysis. Chomsky's system, on the other hand, assigns both B-verb infinitival and *that*-clauses structures that differ at no point in command relations, and thus it predicts that contrasts like those in (73) and (76) do not exist. Any such non-Raising system is thus falsified by Bach's observations.

It is, of course, possible that an opponent of Raising might suggest ad hoc constraints as the basis for contrasts like those in (73) and (76), constraints having nothing to do with the general principle (68). One further thing should be said about this. Clearly, examples like (73) and (76) are extremely marginal – in the sense that a speaker could naturally live his entire life without ever encountering this particular example of backward pronominalization. Far from weakening the argument for Raising derivable from such examples, this type of marginality greatly strengthens it. Because of the marginality, it follows that the linguistic experience of speakers will not dependably provide them with the opportunity to come in contact with the relevant examples. Thus they would, in general, have no basis for adding to their grammars any special constraints designed to handle contrasts like those in (73) and (76) independently of principle (68). Consequently, the definite judgments available to English speakers about such cases must follow from general principles that are internalizable independently of such marginal sentences, principles like (68), which are either universal and innate or at least capable of being induced on the basis of a wide variety of not-at-all-marginal examples. Thus, while it is conceivable that ad hoc constraints for examples like those underlying the present pro-Raising argument could achieve descriptive adequacy, they could never provide any basis for justifying their own incorporation into the grammar; that is, explanatory adequacy would be impossible. This general form of argument, in which the marginality of a phenomenon actually strengthens the force of evidence for Raising, can be applied to many of the other phenomena found relevant in this study to justifying the choice of a Raising system.

## 4.8 Right Node Raising [pp. 125–9]

There is a rule in English and many other languages that I shall refer to as Right Node Raising (henceforth: RNR).[9] Its operation is illustrated by such examples as these:

---

[9] For discussion, see Hankamer (1971), and Maling (1972), who independently show that RNR is actually the rule involved in what had previously been called Backward Gapping (Ross, 1970).

(82) a. Jack may be – and Tony certainly is – a werewolf.
 b. Tom said he would – and Bill actually did – eat a raw eggplant.
 c. Tony should have – and Pete probably would have – called Grace.
 d. Terry used to be – and George still is – very suspicious.

Roughly, given certain paired sequences of identical constituents in disjoint clauses, RNR places a double of the sequence on the right, by Chomsky adjunction, and deletes all original occurrences.[10] Note the characteristically extremely sharp intonation breaks at the points of deletion indicated by dashes in (82). Hence, schematically (82)a would be derived as shown in (83). While there are myriad problems in achieving a precise formulation of RNR, its crucial feature for the present discussion is, fortunately, simply the property that the identical sequences, a copy of which is added on the right, *are always constituents* – in fact, I think, even in examples like (82)b–d, NP constituents, but this does not matter here.

(83) a.

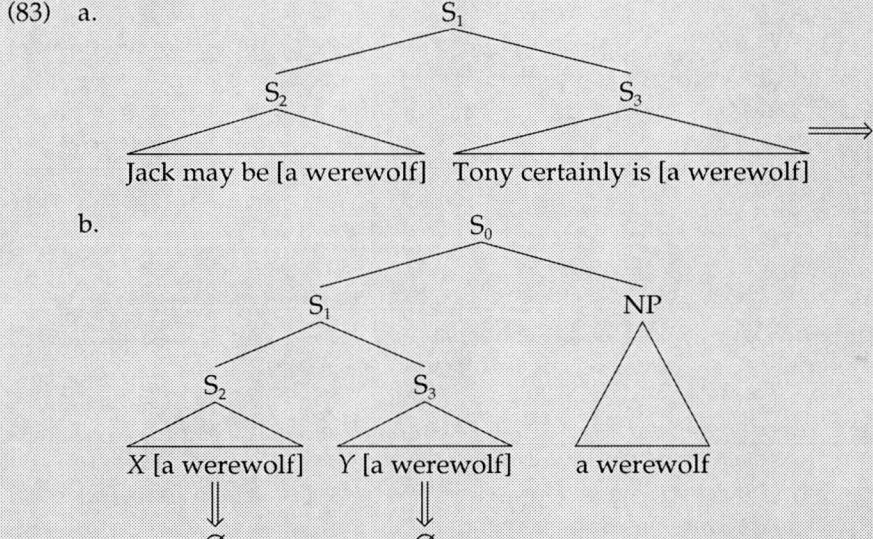

 b.

Since *that* clauses are constituents, one is not surprised that these undergo the rule, as shown in (84).

---

RNR has also often been called Conjunction Reduction, which, I think, amounts to a confusion between the rule operative in (82) and that involved in the derivation of such examples as the following:

(i) a. Joe and Tom weigh, respectively, 150 and 200 pounds.
 b. Harry danced and sang.

Notice these involve no sharp intonational marking and no requirement that the identical sequences be on right branches, both typical features of RNR derivations.

[10] Alternatively, but less plausibly, one might argue that one of the original sequences is adjoined, with the other(s) deleted.

(84) a. Harry has claimed – but I do not believe – that Melvin is a communist.
b. The *News* may have reported – but I do not accept – that Nixon did that.
c. Harry may have believed – but I certainly don't believe – that the war is justified.
d. Henry claimed – but nobody has so far proved – that Mu-grammars are recursive.

Note further that the *that* clauses undergoing RNR include those forming the complements of B-verbs.

As we have seen, in Chomsky's system, the basic structure of infinitival and *that*-clause complements for B-verbs is the same. Both are simply S, with all further distinctions being clause internal. No raising operation affects either. There is, then, nothing to predict any contrast in behavior under RNR operation. In a descriptive system that involves a raising operation for B-verb infinitival complements, however, the situation is different. Here, (cyclic) Raising operation guarantees that, at the earliest point where RNR might apply, the original single constituent clause has been broken apart in the infinitival cases. That is, at the point where RNR might apply, a Raising system claims, in contrast to a system like Chomsky's, that examples such as (85) do not have a derived structure in which *Bill to be a spy* is a constituent.

(85) Harry believes Bill to be a spy.

If so, then a Raising analysis necessarily predicts that such sequences cannot undergo RNR, in contrast to *that*-clause complements which, not undergoing Raising, remain constituents. And this prediction is borne out:

(86) a. I find it easy to believe that Tom is dishonest, but Joan finds it hard to believe that Tom (he) is dishonest.
b. I find it easy to believe Tom to be dishonest, but Joan finds it hard to believe Tom (him) to be dishonest.

(87) a. I find it easy to believe – but Joan finds it hard to believe – that Tom is dishonest.
b. *I find it easy to believe – but Joan finds it hard to believe – Tom to be dishonest.

The sharp contrast in behavior is exactly that predicted by the Raising analysis of B-verb infinitival complements, but not predicted at all by a non-Raising system, which makes only clause-internal distinctions between the relevant infinitival and *that*-clause complements.

Moreover, adding some ad hoc condition on RNR referring to the internal structure of the relevant constituents, that is, distinguishing tensed from untensed clauses, not only would be lacking in generality in comparison with the automatic predictions of the Raising analysis but also would not be empirically viable. In fact, nontensed, infinitival clauses can undergo RNR when they clearly meet the condition of constituency:

(88) a. I think it would be unwise for John to marry Laura, but Tom feels it would be clever for him to marry her.
b. I think it would be unwise – but Tom feels it would be clever – for John to marry Laura.

(89) a. I like to visit new places, but Tom doesn't like to visit new places.
b. I like – but Tom doesn't like – to visit new places.

I conclude that the contrast in RNR behavior between B-verb infinitival and *that*-clause complements is at once a strong argument in favor of the Raising conception of English grammar and a critical counterexample to a non-Raising grammar like that advocated by Chomsky. The facts follow directly from an interaction of the constituent condition on RNR plus the Raising analysis but are in conflict with the predictions of Chomsky's system.[11]

---

[11] One possible line of defense for a non-Raising system has been suggested to me by Howard Lasnik. He notes that while RNR operates on *that* clauses, it does so only correlated with the actual surface occurrence of the *that*. Hence, compare (87)a in the text with (i), which seems no better than the infinitival case (87)b.

(i) *I find it easy to believe – but Joan finds it hard to believe – Tom is dishonest.

A non-Raising defender might argue then that what is wrong with (i), and also with (87)b, is not incorrect application of RNR but occurrence of a clause in a certain position without a complementizer required in that position. As support, note that well-formed untensed clause examples like (88)b have the element *for* in clause-initial position.

So far, however, this approach has not developed to the point where it forces abandonment of the argument in the text. Crucially, it has not been shown that the suggested constraint is independently motivated. To account for the contrast between (87)a and (i), it would suffice to specify precisely the possible conditions for deletion of the *that* of a *that* complement, which, with a few exceptions like (ii), require as a necessary (but not sufficient) condition that the *that* clause directly follow the verb of which it is the complement.

(ii) It seems to me (that) Bill is unhappy.

Moreover, examples like (89)b and (iii) show that clauses, with or without subjects, can occur in the position in question without explicit clause-initial complementizer.

(iii) Harry wanted to discuss–but we didn't actually discuss–(Tom's) dating Greta.

Nor is this conclusion avoidable by an even further extension of nonhomogeneity in the notion of complementizer by trying to extend it to genitives. For observe (iv):

(iv) Harry may not resent – but I do resent – that sort of thing going on.

Finally, note such contrasts as the following:

## 4.10 Pseudocleft sentences [pp. 132–4]

An argument parallel to the previous two, but closer to that involving RNR, can be formulated on the basis of the pseudocleft sentence construction, illustrated by sentences like (94):

(94) a. What I want is to become a millionaire.
 b. What he doesn't seem to understand is that money doesn't grow on trees.
 c. What Melvin proved is that there is a proof of every set of proofs.

Here what is crucial is the sequence after the main verb *be*. While the overall derivation of these sentences is unclear, complex, and controversial, one thing seems evident, as with the sequences operated on by RNR. Namely, the post-*be* sequence is a constituent in derived structure.

Compare (95), on the one hand, with (96), on the other.

(95) a. What I believe is that Bill is intelligent.
 b. What Harry proved is that Tony was a Venusian.
 c. What Joan found was that Barbara was pregnant again.

(96) a. *What I believe is Bill to be intelligent.
 b. *What Harry proved is Tony to be a Venusian.
 c. *What Joan found was Barbara to be pregnant again.

That is, pseudocleft sentences can be based on B-verb complements only when these are *that* clauses, not when they are infinitival. Under the Raising analysis of B-verb infinitival complements, this can be taken to follow automatically from the fact that under such an analysis in examples like (97) the italicized string of elements does not form a derived constituent, a direct consequence of the deformation produced by Raising.

(97) I believe *Bill to be intelligent*.

Under a conception like Chomsky's, however, the external structures of the two types of complement in (95) and (96) do not differ, and the contrast between them is unexplained.

---

(v) a. I didn't think I would prefer for Wallace to win, but Tom said I would prefer for Wallace to win.
 b. I didn't think I would prefer – but Tom said I would prefer – for Wallace to win.

(vi) a. I didn't think I would prefer Wallace to win, but Tom said I would prefer Wallace to win.
 b. *I didn't think I would prefer – but Tom said I would prefer – Wallace to win.

So, all in all, I see little hope of anyone succeeding in attributing the ill-formedness of examples like (87)b to the absence of a complementizer, which is what would be required to overthrow the argument for Raising along the lines suggested by Lasnik.

Similar to the previous two arguments, questions of complementizers arise again. As discussed in footnotes 35 [footnote 11 in this reading] and 39 for the relevant contexts of those arguments, the *that* is not deletable in examples like (95):

(98) a. *What I believe is Bill is intelligent.
 b. *What Harry proved is Tony was a Venusian.
 c. * What Joan found was Barbara was pregnant again.

Again, however, I attribute this to the same condition blocking *that* deletion when the *that* clause does not immediately follow the verb of which it is the complement.[12] Examples like the following show that a complementizer is not uniformly required for clauses in the position of the pseudoclefts in (98):

(99) a. What I resented most was there being no beer.
 b. What I am in favor of is Nixon being shipped to Pakistan.
 c. What I hate is to miss obscenity trials.

Therefore, the contrast between examples like (96) and sentences such as (100) favors Raising.

(100) a. What I arranged (for) was for Bob to come in last.
 b. What I prayed for was for Sally to return.

Note also example (101):

(101) a. I would prefer Bob to win.
 b. I would prefer for Bob to win.
 c. *What I would prefer is Bob to win.
 d. What I would prefer is for Bob to win.

Here the contrast can be naturally explained by recognizing Raising application in (101)a, its absence in (101)b, as in several earlier cases of *prefer NP*, *Prefer for NP* contrasts. See Section 4.16 [not reproduced here].

# References

Bach, Emmon (1970) "Anaphoric Pronouns and the Theory of Binding," presented at the Seminar on the Construction of Complex Grammars, sponsored by the

---

[12] That is, I assume that underlying (98)a, for example, is something like this:

(i) [the thing which I believe is *I believe* that Bill is intelligent]

Deletion of the italicized material then blocks *that* deletion, as in the RNR and Gapping cases. Evidently, this restriction on deletion is sensitive to surface structure, at least in a system with no extrinsic rule-ordering statements.

Mathematical Social Sciences Bound, Center for Advanced Study in the Behavioral sciences, held at Haward University, Cambridge, Mass.

Bierwisch, Manfred, and Karl E. Heidolph, eds. (1970) *Progress in Linguistics*, Mouton and Co., The Hague.

Hankamer, Jorge (1971) "Constraints on Deletion in Syntax" Yale University Doctoral Dissertation, New Haven, Conn.

Langacker, Ronald W. (1969) "On Pronominalization and the Chain of Command," in Reibel and Schane, eds. (1969).

Maling, Joan (1972) "On 'Gapping and the Order of Constituents,'" *Linguistic Inquiry* 3, Number 1.

Postal, Paul M. (1970) "On Coreferential Complement Subject Deletion," *Linguistic Inquiry* 1, Number 4.

Postal, Paul M. (1971) *Cross-Over Phenomena*, Holt, Rinehart and Winston, New York.

Postal, Paul M. (to appear) "A Fundamental Pronominalization Constraint."

Reibel, David A., and Sanford A. Schane, eds. (1969) *Modern Studies in English*, Prentice-Hall, Englewood Cliffs, N.J.

Ross, John R. (1969) "The Cyclic Nature of English Pronominalization," in Reibel and Schane, eds. (1969).

Ross, John R. (1970) "Gapping and the Order of Constituents," in Bierwisch and Heidolph, eds. (1970).

## 2 Evidence from other languages

As stated above, Postal ultimately rejects a configurational approach to Raising (and grammar in general) in favor of a theory that takes grammatical relations as primitive rather than derived notions, and he sketches a rough idea of the rule of Raising in section 4 of chapter 8.[5] In this regard he states (1974:288): "If anything along the lines of the account in this section is correct, it follows that in studying English Raising we have actually been studying Raising in every other language that contains it as well." While this may be true, data from languages with other morphological and syntactic properties provide additional types of evidence for Raising.

### *Niuean case marking*

Seiter (1983) shows that Niuean, a Polynesian language spoken in New Zealand and Niue Island, has a rule of Raising triggered by the epistemic modal *maeke* 'can, be possible' and the aspectual *kamata* 'begin,' in addition to some other predicates. Niuean offers evidence of Raising from case marking. Niuean has ergative case morphology, subjects of transitive clauses being marked for ergative case and subjects of intransitive clauses and direct objects being marked for absolutive case, as in (19).

(19) a. Nofo e taokete haana he māga ha mautolu.
 live ABS brother his in village of us
 'His brother lives in our village.'

b. Ne kai he pusi ia e moa.
   PAST eat ERG cat that ABS chicken
   'That cat ate the chicken.'

In (19) ergative case is marked by the particle *he* and absolutive case by the particle *e*. For a variety of reasons, Seiter (1983) argues that the clauses in (20) are related by a rule of Raising.

(20) a. To maeke ke lagomatai he ekekafo e tama ē.
        FUT possible SBJ help ERG doctor ABS child this
        'The doctor could help this child.'
     b. To maeke e ekekafo ke lagomatai e tama ē.
        FUT possible ABS doctor SBJ help ABS child this
        'The doctor could help this child.'

Evidence for Raising includes the fact that the embedded subject in (20a), *ekekafo* 'doctor,' precedes the subjunctive marker *ke* in (20b). Additionally, as subject of the transitive embedded clause in (20a), *ekekafo* takes the ergative case particle, while in (20b) it takes the absolutive case particle. This absolutive case marking provides evidence that the embedded subject has raised to be subject in the matrix intransitive clause.

Seiter (1983) also presents evidence for Raising from quantifier float. The quantifier *oti* 'all' normally occurs in final position in the NP that it modifies, as in (21).

(21) Kua tele tuai [$_{NP}$e lautolu **oti** ] a au.
     PERF kick PERF ERG they all ABS me
     'All of them have kicked me.'

However, quantifiers may "float" from the subject and direct object NPs that they modify to an immediate postverbal position, as in (22).

(22) Kua tele **oti** tuai [$_{NP}$e lautolu ] a au.
     PERF kick all PERF ERG they ABS me
     'They've all kicked me.'

In raising structures, the quantifier of the raised subject may float to immediate postverbal position in the matrix clause, (23b).

(23) a. Kua kamata tuai [$_{NP}$e tau tagata **oti** ] nā ke fia-momohe.
        PERF begin PERF ABS PL person all that SBJ want-sleep-PL
        'All of those people have begun to get sleepy.'
     b. Kua kamata **oti** tuai [$_{NP}$e tau tagata ] nā ke fia-momohe.
        PERF begin all PERF ABS PL person that SBJ want-sleep-PL
        'Those people have all gotten sleepy.'

In (23b), the fact that *oti* immediately follows the matrix verb *kamata* shows that the NP *e tau tagata* is a dependent of the matrix clause (i.e., its subject) at the relevant level of structure.

At the same time, the quantifier may also occur in floated position in the embedded clause, even when the embedded NP it quantifies occurs as the matrix subject, as in (24).

(24) Kua kamata tuai [<sub>NP</sub>e    tau tagata ] nā  ke fia-momohe   **oti.**
     PERF begin   PERF   ABS PL person  that SBJ want-sleep-PL all
     'Those people have all begun to get sleepy.'

In (24), *oti* immediately follows the embedded verb *fia-momohe*, which it could not do unless the NP *e tau tagata* was also at some point a dependent (i.e., subject) of the embedded clause. Quantifiers that modify matrix NPs cannot normally be floated into complement clauses. This is illustrated by the ungrammaticality of (25b).

(25) a. Kua manako [<sub>NP</sub>a    lautolu **oti** ] ke  mohe a    Pita.
        PERF want          ABS they    all   SBJ sleep ABS P
        'All of them want Pita to sleep.'
     b. *Kua manako [<sub>NP</sub>a    lautolu ] ke  mohe **oti** a    Pita.
        PERF want          ABS they     SBJ sleep all  ABS P
        (All of them want Pita to sleep.)

Given this restriction on quantifier float, the fact that the quantifier *oti* may occur in the embedded clause in (24) is an indication that the matrix subject *tau tagata* 'those people' is originally a dependent of the embedded clause that has been raised.

## *Icelandic case marking*

Icelandic provides another quite unique example of case morphology providing evidence of Raising. In Icelandic, while subjects typically take nominative case and direct objects accusative case, many verbs assign idiosyncratic or "quirky" case to their arguments. Thus, the object of 'rescue' occurs in the dative case rather than accusative case (26a), and the subject of 'recover from' occurs in the dative case rather than nominative case (26b) (Andrews 1982).

(26) a. Þeir      björguðu   stúlkunni.
        they.NOM  rescued    the.girl.DAT
        'They rescued the girl.'
     b. Barninu        batnaði          veikin.
        the.child.DAT  recovered.from   the.disease.NOM
        'The child recovered from the disease.'

In Icelandic, quirky case is preserved when the NP moves, as the passive counterpart of (26a) shows.

(27) Stúlkunni    var   bjargað.
    the.girl.DAT was rescued
    'The girl was rescued.'

As (26a) shows, the subject of 'rescue' normally occurs in the nominative case. There, the subject *þeir* 'they' is nominative. But in the passive clause (27), *stúlkunni* 'the girl' retains the dative case it is assigned as the object of 'rescue.' Of course, when the object is not assigned quirky case as in (28a), the corresponding passive takes a nominative subject, as in (28b).

(28) a. Ég      leyndi     hana    staðireyndanna.
        I.NOM concealed her.ACC the.facts.GEN
        'I concealed the facts from her.'
     b. Hun      var    leynd    staðireyndanna
        she.NOM was concealed the.facts.GEN
        'She was concealed the facts.'

In (28a), the object of 'concealed' is the accusative pronoun *hana* 'her,' and in (28b), the subject of the passive sentence is the nominative pronoun *hun* 'she.'

These case facts interact in an interesting way to provide evidence for Raising in Icelandic. As in English, the verb 'believe' occurs with both a tensed complement (29a) and an infinitive complement (29b).

(29) a. Þeir      telja    að   Maria  hafi skrifað ritgerðina.
        they.NOM believe that M.NOM has written the.thesis.ACC
        'They believe that Mary has written her thesis.'
     b. Þeir      telja   Maríu  hafa      skrifað ritgerðina.
        they.NOM believe M.ACC to.have written the.thesis.ACC
        'They believe Mary to have written her thesis.'

As in English, the Deep Structure subject of the embedded complement occurs not in the nominative case but in the accusative case in Icelandic, *Maríu* in (29b). However, when the embedded predicate assigns quirky case to its subject, as does 'recover from' (26b), this case is preserved in the raising structure, whether the matrix predicate is active (30a) or passive (30b).

(30) a. Hann    telur    barninu     í     barnaskap sínum hafa
        he.NOM believe the.child.DAT in foolishness his    to.have
        batnað             veikin.
        recovered.from the.disease.NOM
        'He believes, in his foolishness, the child to have recovered from the disease.'
     b. Barninu       er talið  hafa      batnað             veikin.
        the.child.DAT is believed to.have recovered.from the.disease.NOM
        'The child is believed to have recovered from the disease.'

The Icelandic case data provide evidence for Raising in two ways. First, assuming that case is assigned locally, the fact that the matrix clause NP, *barninu* 'child,' in (30) occurs in the dative case under the influence of the predicate of the complement clause supports an analysis in which the argument is base generated in the complement. Second, inasmuch as the subject in (30b) is not assigned the case which is normal with passives of the verb 'believe,' *barninu* 'child' must have raised into this position.

## *Object agreement in Kipsigis*

Languages in which objects as well as subjects trigger agreement morphology on predicates provide yet another type of language-particular evidence for Raising. One such language is Kipsigis, a Nilotic language. Jake and Odden (1979) motivate a raising analysis for a subset of Kipsigis verbs (including *mac* 'want,' *yay* 'make,' and *ri:p* 'watch') in part based on object agreement. The sentences in (31) illustrate object marking with first and second person singular pronouns; third person subjects trigger no overt morphology.

(31) a. kà-tíl-ân.
       PAST-cut–1SG.OBJ
       'He cut me.'
   b. kà-tíl-ín.
       PAST-cut-2SG.OBJ
       'He cut you.'

The sentences in (32) illustrate the raising construction.

(32) a. mócè Mú:sá [á-lápát ].
       want M     1SG.SUBJ-run
       'Musa wants that I run.'
   b. móc-ó:n    Mú:sá [à-lápát ].
       want–1SG.OBJ M    1SG.SUBJ-run
       'Musa wants me to run.'

(32a) is an example of a matrix verb taking a clausal object complement. However, in (32b), the subject of the embedded complement triggers first person singular object morphology on the verb. Jake and Odden argue that the object agreement in (32b) provides evidence that the embedded subject has raised to object of the matrix clause.[6]

Raising in Kipsigis is what is referred to as "Copy Raising," that is, although an element has raised out of a complement clause, a pronominal copy (or resumptive pronoun) is left in the embedded clause. Joseph (1976) has proposed that Raising in Greek is an example of Copy Raising. Note that Copy Raising provides evidence of both embedded and matrix positions of the raised NP. The sentences in (33) provide an additional example in Kipsigis.

(33) a. kà-yây    Mú:sá [à-tíl        péndó].
       PAST-make M     1SG.SUBJ-cut meat
       'Musa made that I cut the meat.'

b.  kà-yáy-ân         Mú:sá [à-tíl       péndɔ́].
    PAST-make-1SG.OBJ  M     1SG.SUBJ-cut meat
    'Musa made me cut the meat.'

## Question formation in Chamorro

Chamorro, an Austronesian language spoken on Saipan and Guam, offers yet another type of evidence for Raising. According to Gibson (1980), RtoO is limited to a relatively small number of verbs. One verb that governs Raising is *ekspekta* 'expect.'

(34) a.  Si Lucy ha  ekspekta na    si Miguel pära      u    konni'
         the L  3SG expect   COMP  the M     IRREALIS  3SG  take
         i famagu'un pära eskuela.
         the children to   school
         'Lucy expects that Miguel will take the children to school.'
     b.  Si Lucy ha  ekspekta si Miguel pära      u    konni' i famagu'un
         the L  3SG expect   the M     IRREALIS  3SG  take   the children
         pära eskuela.
         to   school
         'Lucy expects Miguel to take the children to school.'
     c.  In-ekspekta si Miguel as  Lucy pära      u    konni' i
         PASS-expect the M     OBL L    IRREALIS  3SG  take   the
         famagu'un pära eskuela.
         children  to   school
         'Miguel is expected by Lucy to take the children to school.'

In (34a), the complementizer *na* occurs on the left edge of the complement clause. Complementizers are obligatory with the complements of most Chamorro verbs, so the absence of one in (34b) is unexpected, and Gibson proposes that *si Miguel* has raised into the matrix clause. In (34c), *si Miguel* is definitely a matrix clause dependent as it precedes the matrix agent *as Lucy* and is the subject of the passive clause. So, it is clear that (34c) is an example of Raising in Chamorro.

Gibson adduces evidence that (34b) may actually be a case of Raising as well. Yes/no questions in Chamorro can only be formed on intransitive clauses. This is illustrated by the pair of sentences in (35).

(35) a.  *Kao ha  li'li' hao     si Juan nigap?
         ?    3SG see   2SG.ABS the J   yesterday
         (Did Juan see you yesterday?)
     b.  Kao ni-li'li'  hao     as  Juan nigap?
         ?   PASS-see   2SG.ABS OBL J    yesterday
         'Were you seen by Juan yesterday?'

(35a) is a transitive clause: *si Juan* is the subject and the second person absolutive pronoun *hao* the direct object. A yes/no question with the question particle *kao* is impossible, as the ungrammaticality of the sentence shows. In order to form a licit yes/no question with *kao*, the sentence must be intransitive. If the clause is passivized, which results in an intransitive structure, a grammatical question can be formed, as in (35b). Results with the raising verb *ekspekta* are similar. When the matrix clause is active and transitive, the yes/no question is ungrammatical, (36a). When the matrix verb is passivized, a grammatical question can be formed, (36b).

(36) a. *Kao ha ekspekta hao i ma'estra pära un na'-funhayan
? 3SG expect 2SG.ABS the teacher IRREALIS 2SG CAUS-finish
esti na lebblu?
this of book
(Does the teacher expect you to finish this book?)
b. Kao in-ekspekta hao ni ma'estra pära un na'-funhayan
? PASS-expect 2SG.ABS OBL teacher IRREALIS 2SG CAUS-finish
esti na lebblu?
this of book
'Are you expected to finish this book by the teacher?'

In (36a) *hao* 'you,' the complement subject, occurs as an absolutive pronoun in the matrix clause, between the matrix verb and the matrix subject *i ma'estra* 'the teacher.' Since the matrix clause is transitive, the *kao* yes/no question is not possible; hence the ungrammaticality of (36a). The matrix clause is transitive because the embedded subject has raised to object. Once the matrix is passivized, and this element becomes the matrix subject, the yes/no question can be formed.

## Notes

1 It should be noted that although Postal adopted McCawley's position vis-à-vis underlying VSO word order for English, he was no longer (at this point in his theoretical evolution) much concerned with details of underlying precedence relations. The reason for this is that Postal (together with David Perlmutter) was already formalizing Relational Grammar, in which there are no underlying precedence relations at all, and in which surface precedence is read off from relational structure.
2 (3b, 4b) improve with a very long and dramatic pause before the postposed NP. But note that a pause of this duration is unnecessary in (3c, 4c).
3 Postal's judgments of these data are slightly at variance with our own, and somewhat controversial. For instance, he takes as unambiguous certain sentences that we (and others) feel to have at least two interpretations. In all of these cases, however, Postal's arguments are adequately supported without resorting to controversial empirical claims.
4 Postal (p. c.) suggests that these examples are structurally ambiguous. In one structure, in which the claims related to (17) and (18b) would be true, *for* is a complementizer and the entire string following the main verb is an infinitival constituent clause. In the other structure, *for* is a preposition and forms a surface PP in the matrix clause, preceding the subjectless infinitival complement clause. Our discussion here obviously pertains only to the first structural interpretation.

5   The theory Postal envisions is Relational Grammar, which he developed with David Perlmutter and which is taken up in unit II.
6   Notice here in (32), as with Niuean (above) and Chamorro (below), that Raising applies optionally with finite complements of raising predicates. This is significant in that the data support Postal's view of how Raising is triggered, over that of Rosenbaum. For Rosenbaum, a raising predicate such as *believe* can have either a finite or non-finite complement. If an infinitival complement is selected, the [+PR] feature on the verb triggers an obligatory rule of Raising. Rosenbaum's obligatory raising rule would have to be made optional for Kipsigis, since the determination of finiteness does not determine the application of the rule. For Postal, Raising is always optional, and in English it is the application of Raising that determines the non-finiteness of the complement clause. For Postal then, the application of Raising in Kipsigis simply fails to determine the finiteness of the complement clause.

# CHAPTER 4

# EXTENDED STANDARD THEORY: CHOMSKY'S "CONDITIONS ON TRANSFORMATIONS"

## 1 Introduction to the early Extended Standard Theory (EST) model

The framework of "Conditions on transformations" represents a major departure from the Standard Theory (ST) of the *Aspects*-model in which Rosenbaum made his proposals regarding Raising and in which the types of arguments made by Postal in favor of Raising were rooted. As seen in previous chapters, a large number of transformations were posited within ST which had very specific types of effects and very specific types of conditions. For example, the Reflexivization transformation includes the insertion of a reflexive pronoun, the specification that term 2 = 6 in the structural description, and the clausemate condition on terms 2 and 6 (see chapter 1, (5)). One focus within ST was the enumeration of particular transformations and discovery of why particular constructions are licensed in grammars of particular languages. While some relatively specific transformations were still important to the theory, a focus of the developing framework, what Chomsky (and those following) referred to as the Extended Standard Theory (EST), was on reducing the number of transformations and much of their specificity and sharpening the conditions on their application. In "Conditions," Chomsky pursues this, stating transformations such as Passive in a maximally general way and proposing a set of conditions (Tensed-S Condition, Specified Subject Condition, and Subjacency) as constraints on the application of these generalized and generic transformations. These revisions in the theory had major implications for the treatment of Raising and Control, perhaps most notable being the elimination of Raising-to-Object (as will be seen below).

Conceptually, EST represented a move toward lexicalism. Within ST, there were category-changing syntactic transformations; for example, deverbal nouns were derived from related verbs, e.g., *destruction* from *destroy*, *denial* from *deny*, and so on. In "Remarks on nominalization," Chomsky (1970) argued against such analyses, claiming that relationships between such words were the domain of the lexicon, and that they should be stated in terms of lexical redundancy rules. Additionally, based on quantifier scope facts and anaphoric relations, it was argued that deep structure alone did not determine the semantic representation of a sentence. Rules of interpretation for anaphora and quantification applied to surface structure and contributed to building the semantic interpretation of a sentence. Both of these changes are emblematic of constraining the power, hence the role, of syntactic transformations, a major theme of "Conditions on transformations." In it, Chomsky assumes a theory organized as follows:

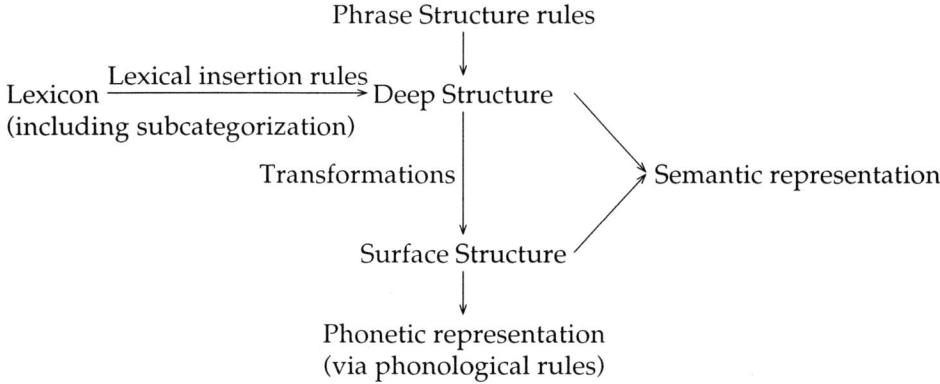

*The Extended Standard Theory (EST) model*

This model differs from the ST of the *Aspects*-model (see section 1 of chapter 2) in two important respects. In ST, the base component consisted of "branching" rewrite rules (such as S → NP Aux VP) and "subcategorization" rewrite rule (such as [+Det___] → ±Count]). In EST, subcategorization information was contained only in the lexicon. The other major change from ST was the involvement of Surface Structure in the determination of semantic representations. In ST, all semantic representations were read off from Deep Structure, and transformations did not affect meaning. A rule of Reflexivization, for instance, took the Deep Structure *John likes John* and replaced the second occurrence of *John* with the reflexive pronoun *himself*. In the EST model, however, reflexive interpretations were derived through coindexation, and the availability of these interpretations could only be determined after the application of all transformations (since intervening phrasal nodes can determine whether a given coindexation of an NP and a reflexive pronoun is licensed). Thus, Surface Structure was taken to play a role in semantic representations.

# READING FROM CHOMSKY (1973)

Noam Chomsky, sections 1–3 (pp. 232–44) from "Conditions on transformations" in *A festschrift for Morris Halle*, eds Stephen Anderson and Paul Kiparsky (New York: Holt, Rinehart, and Winston, 1973).

1 From the point of view that I adopt here,[1] the fundamental empirical problem of linguistics is to explain how a person can acquire knowledge of language. For our purposes, we can think of a language as a set of structural descriptions of sentences, where a full structural description determines (in particular) the sound and meaning of a linguistic expression. Knowledge of a language can be expressed in the form of a system of rules (a grammar) that generates the language. To approach the fundamental empirical problem, we attempt to restrict the class of potential human languages by setting various conditions on the form and function of grammars; the term "universal grammar" has commonly been used to refer to the system of general constraints of this sort. With a narrow and restrictive formulation of the principles of universal grammar, it may become possible to account for the remarkable human ability, on the basis of limited and degenerate evidence, to select a particular grammar that expresses one's knowledge of language and makes possible the use of this knowledge.

For heuristic purposes we may distinguish two aspects of universal grammar: (a) conditions on form, and (b) conditions on function – that is, (a) conditions on the systems that qualify as grammars, and (b) conditions on the way the rules of a grammar apply to generate structural descriptions. In the terminology of Chomsky (1965, Chapter 1) and earlier work, these are, respectively, conditions on the class $G_1, G_2, \ldots$ of admissible grammars and on the function f that assigns the structural description $SD_{f(i, j)}$ to the sentence $S_i$ generated by the grammar $G_j$. The distinction is one of convenience, not principle, in the sense that we might choose to deal with particular phenomena under one or the other category of conditions. The distinction might be carried over to particular grammars as well. That is, while it has generally been assumed that particular grammars contain specific rules whereas conditions on the functioning of rules are assigned to universal grammar, there is no logical necessity to make this assumption. It is possible that particular grammars differ in conditions of application, just as it is possible that some specific rules actually belong to universal grammar.[2]

---

[1] For very helpful comments on an earlier draft of this paper, I am indebted to Ray Dougherty, Morris Halle, Richard Kayne, and Howard Lasnik, among others. I am indebted to the Guggenheim Foundation for a fellowship grant that enabled me to complete the work presented here.
[2] For discussion of limited generality of conditions, see Ross (1967), Chomsky (1968), and Postal (1971).

To illustrate, we can consider the enumeration of distinctive features or the specification of the form of phonological rules to be conditions of the first sort, that is, conditions on the form of grammars. Or consider the definition of a grammatical transformation as a structure-dependent mapping of phrase markers into phrase markers that is independent of the grammatical relations or meanings expressed in these grammatical relations. This definition makes certain operations available as potential transformations, excluding others. Thus an operation converting an arbitrary string of symbols into its mirror image is not a grammatical transformation, and transformations generally apply to phrase markers that meet some condition on analyzability with no regard to other associated properties.

To take a standard example, the Passive transformation (reducing it to essentials) applies to any phrase marker that can be "factored" into five successive substrings in such a way that the second and fourth are noun phrases, the third a verb of a particular category (perhaps determined by some semantic property), and the first and fifth anything at all (including nothing). Thus the structural condition defining the transformation can be given in the form $(Z, NP, V_x, NP, Y)$. The transformation rearranges the noun phrases in a fixed way. It will, therefore, apply to the phrase markers underlying the sentences of (1), converting them to the corresponding passive forms:

(1) a. Perhaps–John–read–the book–intelligently
 b. John–received–the book
 c. John–regards–Bill–as a friend
 d. John–painted–the wall–gray
 e. John–expects–the food–to be good to eat

Evidently, the semantic and grammatical relation of the main verb to the following noun phrase varies in these examples (there is no relation at all in (e)), but these relations are of no concern to the transformation, which applies blindly in all cases, producing *Perhaps the book was read intelligently by John, The book was received by John, Bill is regarded as a friend by John, The wall was painted gray by John, The food is expected to be good to eat by John*. By requiring that all transformations be structure-dependent in this specific sense, we limit the class of possible grammars, excluding many imaginable systems.

I will presuppose here, without further discussion, a set of additional conditions on the form of grammar constituting what I have called the "extended standard theory" (see Chomsky (1970b; 1972)). Other conditions on the choice of possible transformations that also seem to me plausible and suggestive, if controversial, are outlined in Emonds (1970).[3]

The conditions on the form of grammar mentioned so far are quite abstract and still permit much too wide a range of potential grammars. One might

---

[3] As already noted, the distinction between conditions on form and conditions on function is, in part, one of convenience. Thus Emonds' constraints could be formulated as conditions on the applicability of arbitrarily chosen transformations.

therefore look for much more specific restrictions. An example, to which I return, is the "Complementizer Substitution Universal" in (2):[4]

(2) Only languages with clause-initial COMP permit a COMP-substitution transformation

This principle presupposes that COMP is a universal element that may appear in various sentence positions and asserts that an item can be moved into COMP position only when COMP is initial. In particular, "*wh*-words" – the relativized constituents in relative clauses or questioned constituents in interrogatives – can be moved only to the left, such movement being permitted only when there is an initial COMP in the phrase to which the transformation is being applied.

It would be quite natural to explore further along these lines. Thus one might try to enumerate "major transformations" such as Question Formation, Imperative, and so on from which languages may draw, with some permitted variation and minor "housekeeping rules" (Bach (1965; 1971)). It may well be that transformations fall into various categories meeting quite different conditions. By constructing a more intricate, more highly articulated theory of grammar in such ways as these, we can perhaps move toward a solution of the fundamental empirical problem.

A second approach attempts to constrain the functioning of grammatical rules and thereby to limit the generative power of grammars of a given form. The earliest suggestions appear in Chomsky (1964)[5] (namely, the condition of "Recoverability of Deletion,"[6] the "*A*-over-*A* Condition," and so on). Another example, to which I will return, is the Insertion Prohibition suggested in Chomsky (1965), which prevents transformations from inserting morphological material into sentences that have already been passed in the cycle. Many examples are discussed in a very important study by Ross (1967), where a number of specific conditions are proposed. These conditions are formulated in such a way as to restrict severely the operation of the rules of grammars while not affecting their form. Thus such conditions contribute toward a solution of the fundamental empirical problem.[7]

---

[4] J. Bresnan's reformulation (1970) of L. Baker's "Q-Universal" (Baker (1970)).

[5] This work appears in three versions, which differ in their treatment of these problems. The first is in H. G. Lunt, ed. (1964), *Proceedings of the Ninth International Congress of Linguists, 1962*, The Hague: Mouton; the second is in J. A. Fodor and J. J. Katz, eds (1964), *Structure of Language*, Englewood Cliffs, NJ: Prentice-Hall; the third is listed in the bibliography. A further revision, in lectures given at Berkeley in January, 1967, appears in Chomsky (1968).

[6] On the difficulty of defining this properly and the importance of the issue, see Peters and Ritchie (1973).

[7] Another approach toward solving this problem would be to refine the evaluation measure for grammars. As explained in Chomsky (1965), it seems to me that only limited progress is likely along these lines. It has been suggested in recent work that no evaluation measures are necessary, and this is surely a logical possibility (see Chomsky (1965, pp. 36–7)). Those who offer this suggestion, however, typically propose theories of grammar that make infinitely many grammars available compatible with any imaginable data, so that an evaluation measure is necessary in these cases. The point is, I suspect, that "natural" evaluation measures are generally presupposed, without analysis.

In this paper I want to consider conditions on the functioning of grammars once again, specifically, conditions on how transformations apply. As noted, I assume here the general framework of the extended standard theory and, in particular, the lexicalist theory of base structures and nominals discussed in Chomsky (1970a). The work leading to the extended standard theory suggested constraints on base structures and on the relations between derivations and semantic representations but said little about transformations. Here, I will explore some conditions on the application of transformations within the framework of the extended standard theory.

As an example of a possible condition on transformations, consider the "A-over-A" principle, stated in (3):[8]

(3) If a transformation applies to a structure of the form
$[_\alpha \ldots [_A \ldots ] \ldots ]$
where $\alpha$ is a cyclic node, then it must be so interpreted as to apply to the maximal phrase of the type $A$

Consider again the Passive transformation with a structural condition imposing a factorization into (X, NP, V, NP, Y). So formulated, the rule would apply to the examples in (4), with the factorization indicated by –, giving the impossible forms in (5):

(4) a. John and–Bill–saw–Mary
    b. The man who saw–Mary–bought–the book
    c. John's winning–the race–surprised–me

(5) a. *John and Mary was seen by Bill
    b. *The man who saw the book was bought by Mary
    c. *John's winning I was surprised by the race

But the misapplication of the rule in these cases is blocked by the A-over-A Condition (3). This principle requires that *John and Bill*, *the man who saw Mary*, and *John's winning the race* are the factors selected by the first NP in the structural condition of the Passive in the case of (a), (b), and (c), respectively.

Notice that the condition (3) does not establish an absolute prohibition against transformations that extract a phrase of type $A$ from a more inclusive phrase of type $A$. Rather, it states that if a transformational rule is nonspecific with respect to the configuration defined, it will be interpreted in such a way as to satisfy the condition. Thus it would be possible to formulate a (more complex) rule with a structural condition imposing the factorization indicated by – in (4); such a rule might extract *Bill*, *Mary*, and *the race*, respectively. Alternatively, one might interpret the A-over-A constraint as legislating against any rule that extracts a phrase of type $A$ from a more inclusive phrase $A$. The

---

[8] This is the formulation in Chomsky (1968), where a number of examples and problems are discussed. We may assume here that the cyclic nodes are S and NP.

former interpretation, which in effect takes the *A*-over-*A* Condition to be an integral part of an evaluation measure, is perhaps more natural, and I will adopt it tentatively here, for this and other conditions to be discussed. Thus the *A*-over-*A* Condition as interpreted here does not prevent the application of *wh*-Movement to form (6) from (7), or the application of Pseudo-Cleft Formation to form (8) from (9), or the application of Conjunct Movement to form (10) from (11):[9]

(6) Who would you approve of my seeing

(7) You would approve of [my seeing who][10]

(8) The only person John admires is himself

(9) [The only person [John admires himself]] is Predicate

(10) John met Bill

(11) [John and Bill] met

In contrast, we interpret the Complementizer Substitution Universal (2) as imposing an absolute restriction against rules that move an item to the right to a COMP position. But the *A*-over-*A* principle, rather than legislating against the existence of certain rules, permits an ambiguous and unspecific formulation of such rules as Passive, constraining their application in a specific way. The logic of this approach is essentially that of the theory of markedness.

Suppose that we were to formulate the Passive with the structural condition (12):

(12) (X, NP, VY, NP, Z)

Then the rule will apply to either of the italicized noun phrases in (13) to give (14a) or (14b):

(13) PRO took *advantage* of *Bill*

(14) a. Advantage was taken of Bill
b. Bill was taken advantage of

---

[9] In principle. On the dubious status of this rule, see Dougherty (1970). We will return briefly to such examples as (6) and (8).

[10] The impossibility of *\*Whose would you approve of seeing John* from *You would approve of whose seeing John* can perhaps be attributed to a principle that requires that if the specifier of a noun phrase or adjective phrase (in the sense of Chomsky (1970a)) is extracted, then the whole phrase must be extracted: thus the same principle would prevent the formation of *\*Which did you see books* from *You saw which books*, or *\*How is John tall* from *John is how tall*. See Ross (1967) for relevant discussion.

The *A*-over-*A* Condition does not prevent the desired ambiguous application in this case. The same formulation of Passive[11] permits "pseudo-passives" such as *The plan was argued about all day* and *The brat insists on being given in to*. For this formulation of the rule to apply correctly, it is necessary to add the condition that the third term in the factorization (12) be a semantic unit. For example, the sentence *England was lived in by many people* is more natural than *England was died in by many people*, but only when *live in* is interpreted as "reside" and not as in "we really lived in England" in the sense of "in England, we really lived."[12]

Quite generally, the terms of the structural condition of a transformation are either variables or single nonterminals, the case in question being one of the rare exceptions. A single nonterminal is a semantic unit – it has a "reading," in the sense of Katz and others. Thus we might consider the general condition (15):

(15) Each factor imposed by a transformation either is a morphological or semantic unit or corresponds to a variable in the structural condition of the transformation.

This condition, along with the *A*-over-*A* Condition (3), permits Passive to be formulated with the structural condition (12), constraining the application of the rule properly in quite a range of cases.

2 To pursue the matter further, let us assume (following, in essentials, Bresnan (1970)) that there is a universal element COMP and that the base system of English includes the rules in (16):[13]

(16) a. $S \rightarrow COMP\ NP \begin{Bmatrix} T(M) \\ (for)\text{-}to \\ \text{'}s\text{-}ing \end{Bmatrix} VP$

b. $COMP \rightarrow P\ NP\ \pm WH$

---

[11] Again, oversimplified, overlooking auxiliaries, the agent phrase, and the composite nature of the rule discussed in Chomsky (1970a). Using the terminology suggested there, the structural condition should contain a term after the first NP which can be an arbitrary sequence of specifiers.
[12] See Chomsky (1965, pp. 104, 218). Recall that although transformations are independent of grammatical or semantic relations, they do, of course, reflect properties of lexical items and lexical categories.
[13] More precisely, these "rules" may be factored into several rules that provide intermediate structures that need not concern us here. Much of what we shall suggest will hold under certain other assumptions about English grammar as well; I give these, without further justification, for concreteness. In (16), P stands for "Preposition," T for "Tense," M for "Modal"; and *to* and *ing* are the items that appear (excluding tense and modal), respectively, in *for him to remain is a nuisance*, *his remaining is a nuisance* (where *for* and possessive, respectively, are assigned to the accompanying noun phrases, the presence of *for* depending on the main verb). We may assume that one realization of M is the element *subjunctive* discussed in Culicover (1971) in his analysis of imperatives and related structures (and thus subjunctives are assumed here to be tensed). We return to some more specific rules later.

We assume that the NP or P NP of COMP can be replaced by the *wh*-phrase of questions and relatives (Emonds' structure-preserving hypothesis determines which of these positions is filled). Following Baker (1970), I assume that +WH (essentially, his "Q") underlies direct and indirect questions, while −WH underlies relatives.[14] We impose the condition that no lexical item can be inserted into COMP by base rules; that is, we require that the terminal string dominated by COMP in the base is null. If a −WH COMP is not filled by a *wh*-phrase, it will optionally be realized as *that* (otherwise null) if the auxiliary contains Tense. We may assume that *whether* derives from *wh*-Placement on *either* and *wh*-Movement (see Katz and Postal (1964)) and that free relatives such as *I read what he gave me* derive from full relatives with unspecified heads (*I read* [$_{NP}$PRO[$_S$*he gave me it*]] − see Bresnan (1972) for a detailed analysis). Further details and appropriate rules will be given as we proceed.

Let us return to the Passive transformation which, reduced to essentials, applies to a phrase marker of the form NP–V–NP–X, rearranging the NPs. Consider the sentence (17):

(17) I believe the dog is hungry

This can be analyzed into the successive substrings *I*, *believe*, *the dog*, *is hungry*, which are NP, V, NP, X, respectively, so that the transformation should yield \**The dog is believed is hungry (by me)*. In exactly the same way, the sentence *The dog is believed to be hungry (by me)* derives from (18), with the analysis indicated:

(18)  [$_S$[$_{NP}$I] [$_{VP}$[$_V$believe] [$_S$[$_{NP}$the dog] [$_{VP}$to be hungry]]]]

Notice that there is no problem in explaining why the Passive transformation, with its domain defined in terms of a structural condition on phrase markers in the conventional way, applies to (18); the problem, rather, is to explain why it does not apply to (17).[15]

---

[14] Presumably, *either* may underlie nominal complements, as in *the idea that S*, *the question whether S*. Conditions for *wh*-Movement vary slightly, particularly in appositive clauses. See Postal (1971, pp. 71–2) for some discussion.

[15] Under any formulation of the theory of transformations so far proposed, it would require an extra condition on the transformation to exclude (18) from the domain of the Passive with the structural condition (X, NP, V, NP, Y). One might imagine a different theory in which the domain of a transformation is defined not by a structural condition of the familiar sort but rather by a condition on grammatical relations: thus "Passive" in this theory might be defined not in terms of the structural condition (X, NP, V, NP, Y), but in terms of the total configuration which expresses subject and object as relational terms. Under this revised theory, Passive would not apply to (18) unless the configuration were modified by a transformation raising the subject of the embedded sentence to the object position in the matrix sentence. There is, however, no empirical motivation for such a revision of the theory of transformations. It would, furthermore, be ill-advised in the case of Passive because of pseudo-passives (see the discussion following (14)), double passives such as (14), indirect object constructions, and so on.

Note that COMP will not block factorization of (18) in accordance with the structural condition of the Passive transformation if the terminal string dominated by COMP is null, as we have assumed.

The most obvious distinction between (17) and (18) is that the embedded sentence in (17) is tensed (finite) while the corresponding sentence of (18) is nontensed. Suppose, then, that we propose the tentative principle in (19):

(19) Items cannot be extracted from tensed sentences

The principle of Insertion Prohibition mentioned earlier states that morphological material cannot be inserted into sentences that have been passed in the cycle. If, in fact, Insertion Prohibition is restricted to tensed sentences, we can generalize (19) to incorporate this principle.

Let us restrict our attention initially to rules of extraction that move an item to the left (as in the case of Passive) and to rules of insertion that move an item from the left into an embedded phrase. With this restrictive assumption, we can generalize (19) to (20), incorporating the Insertion Prohibition; we henceforth refer to (20) as the "Tensed-S Condition":[16]

(20) No rule can involve $X, Y$ in the structure
$$\ldots X \ldots [_\alpha \ldots Y \ldots ] \ldots$$
where $\alpha$ is a tensed sentence.

To understand the application of the Insertion Prohibition as a special case of this principle, consider the sentences in (21):

(21) a. The candidates each hated the other(s)
 b. The candidates each expected the other(s) to win
 c. The candidates each expected that the other(s) would win

Dougherty (1970) has argued that such a sentence as *The men hated each other* derives from *The men each hated the other(s)* (ultimately, from *Each of the men hated the other one(s)*) by a rule that moves *each* into the determiner position in *the other(s)*.[17] Assuming this, note that the sentences of (21) should be transformed into those of (22):

(22) a. The candidates hated each other
 b. The candidates expected each other to win
 c. *The candidates expected that each other would win

---

[16] A weaker assumption would be that $\alpha$ is a language-specific parameter in the condition. In this exploratory study I will do no more than suggest a number of possibilities and investigate their consequences in English.

Notice that one rule that obviously does not satisfy the condition is Coreference Assignment (however it is formulated). Thus the pronoun can be anaphoric in *John said that he would leave*, for example. The same rule also applies within coordinate structures (for example, *John said that he and Bill would leave*) and others that block various other types of rules.

[17] I presuppose Dougherty's work (1970) here with no further specific reference. Notice that if one were to accept the alternative analysis of Jackendoff (1969), principle (20) would again apply – in this case, not to a movement rule but to a rule of interpretation.

Only the first two cases are permitted; (22c) is blocked, as required, by the Tensed-S Condition.

Before turning to other examples, let us consider some facts that lead us to a supplementary principle. Suppose that (23b) derives from the underlying form (23a):

(23) a. John expected [$_S$PRO to win]
     b. John expected to win

Now notice that from (24a) we can derive (24b), whereas from (25a) we cannot derive (25b):

(24) a. The candidates each expected [$_S$PRO to defeat the other]
     b. The candidates expected to defeat each other
(25) a. The men each expected [$_S$the soldier to shoot the other]
     b. *The men expected the soldier to shoot each other

To account for this difference, let us postulate a second principle, the "Specified Subject Condition" (26), where by "specified subject" we mean a subject NP that contains either lexical items or a pronoun that is not anaphoric:

(26) No rule can involve $X$, $Y$ in the structure
     $\ldots X \ldots [_\alpha \ldots Z \ldots - WYV \ldots ] \ldots$
     where $Z$ is the specified subject of $WYV$ in $\alpha$

We shall return to this principle later to give a more careful formulation. As set forth here, it suffices to distinguish (25), with the specified subject $Z =$ *the soldier* in the embedded sentence $\alpha$, from (23) and (24), which have no specified subject in that position.[18]

Within the extended standard theory, as developed in the references cited earlier, both NP and S are nodes to which cyclic operations apply, and the notion "subject of" is defined not only in S but also in such NPs as (27), where *John*, in all cases, is the "subject," in an extended sense of this term:

(27) a. John's refusal to leave
     b. John's picture of Bill
     c. John's strategy for victory

---

[18] Helke (1971) observes that *each*-Movement is not permitted in such cases as *The candidates each expected the others to clash* (*The candidates expected each other to clash*), *The candidates each expected the others to work together* (*The candidates expected each other to work together*). However, it seems that this results from the operation of independent rules that also exclude *The men walked between each other* from *The men each walked between the others*. What seems to be involved is a restriction on *each*-Movement in the case when the NP *the other* has the features [+totality, −individual] in the system of Dougherty (1970), where some relevant examples are discussed.

Correspondingly, in (26) α can be either NP or S. Examples (24) and (25) illustrate the application of (26) where α = S. The examples in (28)–(31) illustrate the application of this condition where α = NP:

(28) a. The men each saw [$_{NP}$pictures of the other]
     b. The men saw pictures of each other

(29) a. The men each saw [$_{NP}$John's pictures of the other]
     b. *The men saw John's pictures of each other

(30) a. COMP you saw [$_{NP}$pictures of who]
     b. Who did you see pictures of

(31) a. COMP you saw [$_{NP}$John's pictures of who]
     b. *Who did you see John's pictures of

The rule of *each*-Insertion applies to (28a) but is blocked by the Specified Subject Condition in (29). The rule of *wh*-Movement applies to (30a) but is blocked by the same condition in the case of (31).[19]

Let us next turn to the rule of *it*-Replacement that produces such sentences as *John is easy to please*. Consider the examples in (32) and (33):

(32) a. It is pleasant for the rich for poor immigrants to do the hard work
     b. It is a waste of time for us for them to teach us Latin

(33) a. It is pleasant for the rich to do the hard work
     b. It is a waste of time for us to learn Latin
     c. It is easy for us to learn Latin

The rule of *it*-Replacement applies to the examples of (33) to give the corresponding forms in (34), but it does not apply to (32) to give (35):

(34) a. The hard work is pleasant for the rich to do
     b. Latin is a waste of time for us to learn
     c. Latin is easy for us to learn

(35) a. *The hard work is pleasant for the rich for poor immigrants to do
     b. *Latin is a waste of time for us for them to teach us

---

[19] Some speakers (myself included) find a three-way gradation of acceptability, with (30b) better than *Who did you see the pictures of*, which is in turn preferable to (31b). A refinement of condition (26) incorporating the feature [definite] as well as the property of lexical specification might be proposed to accommodate these judgments. Specified subjects in NPs are [+definite]. If (26) is revised to include [+definite] as well as specified subjects, then (31b) will involve a double violation and *Who did you see the pictures of* only a single violation. This might account for the gradation of acceptability.

These data follow from our previous assumptions if we suppose that the phrases *for the rich* and *for us* in (32) and (33) form part of the predicate of the matrix sentence, with the subject PRO of the embedded sentence deleted in (33), exactly as in the case of (23). (The lexical item *easy* differs from *pleasant* and *waste of time* in that the rule of deletion is obligatory in the case of *easy* in this context.) Thus we take the structures underlying (33) to be of the form (36), as is clearly true (under our general assumptions) in the case of (32):

(36)    It–is Predicate for NP–[$_S$NP–VP]

This assumption is not unnatural on other grounds as well. Thus the leftmost *for*-phrase in all the cited examples is more readily detachable than the *for*-phrase in (37), for example:

(37)    It is intolerable for John to have to study Latin

Compare the variants (38) with (39):

(38)    a.  For the rich, it is pleasant for poor immigrants to do the hard work
        b.  For us, it is a waste of time to learn Latin
        c.  Latin is a waste of time to learn, for us
        d.  Latin is easier to learn for us than for John
        e.  It is easier to learn Latin for us than for John

(39)    a.  For John, it is intolerable to have to study Latin
        b.  It is intolerable to have to study Latin, for John
        c.  It is more intolerable to have to study Latin for us than for John

The examples in (39), if acceptable at all, are interpreted somewhat differently from (37): in (39), it must be understood that John finds it intolerable to have to study Latin, but this is not the case in (37). On the other hand, such examples as (38) seem true stylistic variants of the corresponding forms of (32)–(34). We might capture this fact by limiting stylistic inversion to a *for*-phrase of the predicate of the matrix sentence.

There are, moreover, selectional relations between a predicate that appears in the matrix form (36) and the subject of the embedded S, a property that further differentiates these structures from (37). Compare (40) and (41):

(40)    a.  It is intolerable for there to be snow in June
        b.  It is intolerable for the car to be so poorly constructed

(41)    a.  *It is easy for there to be snow in June
        b.  *It is easy for the car to be so poorly constructed

These facts, too, might be expressed by assigning the *for*-phrase to the matrix sentence in the examples (33), with deletion of the subject PRO of the embedded S after it is assigned coreference with the NP of the matrix *for*-phrase. (In such cases as *It is easy to learn Latin*, we might assume that the matrix predicate contains a nonspecified phrase *for*-Δ which is deleted, as is the nonspecified agent in agentless passives.) We can then restrict the selectional features to the predicate phrase of the matrix sentence.

We return to these structures later.

Consider next the "Unlike Person Constraint" discussed by Postal (1966; 1969). We might formulate this as a rule that assigns the feature * (deviant) to a sentence S dominating $PRO_i$ V–$PRO_j$–X, where $PRO_i$ and $PRO_j$ are both first person or both second person. Thus we cannot have such sentences as (42):

(42) a. *I saw me
 b. *I watched us leaving (in the mirror)
 c. *We watched me leaving
 d. *You (all) noticed you standing there (by yourself)

The point is clearly more general (see Postal (1969)). Thus in (43) we interpret the two pronouns as different in reference, and in (44) we interpret the NPs as nonintersecting in reference; that is, we assume that the officers are not included among the soldiers doing the shooting (we do not interpret this sentence as referring to a situation in which some of the officers shot others):

(43) He saw him

(44) The soldiers shot the officers (among them)

The point seems to be that a rule of interpretation RI applying to the structure NP–V–NP (among others) seeks to interpret the two NPs as nonintersecting in reference,[20] and where this is impossible (as in the case of first and second person pronouns – see (42)), it assigns "strangeness," marking the sentence with *. But consider the sentences in (45):

(45) a. We expect them to visit *me*; I expect them to visit *us* (*me*)
 b. *We expect *me* to visit them; I expect *us* (*me*) to visit them
 c. *We expect *me* to be visited by them; I expect *us* (*me*) to be visited by them
 d. We believe I may still win; I believe *we* (*I*) may still win

In (45a) and (45d), the rule RI is blocked (by the Specified Subject Condition and the Tensed-S Condition, respectively). Therefore in these sentences the pair of italicized NPs may intersect in reference; the sentences are not marked with * by RI. But the rule RI applies to (45b) and (45c), assigning *, just as it

---

[20] This particular formulation presupposes the analysis of reflexives in Helke (1971) His approach to reflexives and inherent anaphora (*John lost his mind, John craned his neck*, and so on) fits very well into the present framework.

applies to the examples of (42). Although the matter is more complex, this appears to be a plausible first approximation to a correct analysis. Notice that it is difficult to see how RI can be construed naturally as anything other than a rule of semantic interpretation, operating at a fairly "superficial" level (at or close to surface structure), at least if we wish to incorporate (44) and (45) under the generalization. Exactly the same considerations apply if we restrict our attention to the Unlike Person Constraint.

Observe that we have now applied the principles to two kinds of rules, namely, syntactic operations moving constituents and rules of semantic interpretation. Some further possibilities are suggested by observations of Lasnik (1971). He points out that the sentences (46a,b) are ambiguous in a way in which (47) is not:

(46) a. I didn't see many of the pictures
b. I didn't see pictures of many of the children

(47) I didn't see John's pictures of many of the children

The first (more normal and less sophisticated, I believe) interpretation of (46a) in colloquial English associates *not* and *many*; under this interpretation, the sentence means "I saw few of the pictures," "Not many of the pictures are such that I saw them." Thus the sentence would be false, under this interpretation, if I had seen 50 of the 100 pictures (assuming 50 pictures to be "many" under the contextual conditions of the utterance), while it would be true if I had seen only 3 of the 100 pictures. Some speakers also accept a second interpretation of (46a), with the meaning "Many of the pictures are such that I didn't see them." Under this interpretation, which associates *not* with *see*, the sentence would be true if I had seen exactly 50 of the 100 pictures, since there would be 50 that I hadn't seen.

The same ambiguity arises in the case of (46b). Under the interpretation which associates *not* with *many*, the sentence means "I saw pictures of few of the children," "Not many of the children are such that I saw pictures of them." It would be false if I had seen pictures of 50 of the 100 children, true if I had seen pictures of 3 of the 100 children. Under the second interpretation, the sentence means "Pictures of many of the children are such that I didn't see them," which is true if I had seen pictures of 50 of the 100 children. For speakers who do not accept the second interpretation of (46a) and (46b), it seems that (47) is unacceptable. For speakers who assign both interpretations to the sentences of (46), (47) is acceptable with the unique interpretation that associates *not* with *see*; thus it means "John's pictures of many of the children are such that I didn't see them." The sentence (47), then, has no interpretation under which it is false, given that I had seen John's pictures of exactly 50 of the 100 children.

The observations are moderately subtle, but I believe that Lasnik's judgments are correct. Notice that the facts, as stated, follow from the Specified Subject Condition, which does not permit association of *not* with *many* in

(47). If (following Lasnik) we regard the assignment of scope of negation as a matter of semantic interpretation, the Specified Subject Condition again blocks a semantic rule. If, on the other hand, it is claimed that a rule of *not*-Movement extracts *not* from the NP object to give the first (normal) interpretation of the sentences of (46), this syntactic rule is blocked in (47) by the same condition.

Lasnik suggests also the following, slightly different example. Consider the sentences in (48):

(48) a. You didn't understand the proofs of enough of the theorems (for me to be justified in giving you an A)
 b. You didn't understand Euclid's proofs of enough of the theorems (for me to be justified in giving you an A)

The word *enough* differs from *many* in that *not* must be associated with it (rather than with *understand*) in (48a). That is, only what I have called the "normal" interpretation is possible in the case of (48a), which must mean something like "You understood proofs of some (but not enough) of the theorems..." It follows, then, that (48b) receives no direct interpretation at all (though an interpretation can be forced, as it can also be, say, in (31b)), just as (47) receives no interpretation for speakers who accept only the "normal" interpretation of (46). This appears correct and is a further example of the application of the Specified Subject Condition.

3 Consider next the sentence (49) which, we assume, derives from (50) by *wh*-Placement (on *something*), *wh*-Movement, and Auxiliary Inversion:

(49) What did you tell me that Bill saw

(50) COMP you told me [$_S$COMP Bill saw something]

The rule of *wh*-Movement in this case appears to violate both the Tensed-S Condition and the Specified Subject Condition.

Before turning to the problem posed by *wh*-Movement, let us consider the notion "transformational cycle" somewhat more carefully. The Insertion Prohibition, now sharpened as a special case of the Tensed-S and Specified Subject Conditions, is a step toward a stricter interpretation of the cycle: it asserts that once a stage of the cycle has been passed, we cannot introduce material into it from the outside under the stated conditions. To further sharpen the notion "transformational cycle," suppose that we impose the general condition (51):[21]

---

[21] The condition should perhaps be restricted to major transformations in the sense of Bach (1965; 1971), excluding his "housekeeping rules." A slightly different formulation of (51) would make it impossible for a rule applying to the domain dominated by $A$ to affect solely items that were originally dominated by $B$. These alternatives lead to slightly different empirical consequences in areas that do not concern us here.

(51) No rule can apply to a domain dominated by a cyclic node A in such a way as to affect solely a proper subdomain of A dominated by a node B which is also a cyclic node.

In other words, rules cannot in effect return to earlier stages of the cycle after the derivation has moved to larger, more inclusive domains. We will refer to (51) as the "Strict Cycle Condition."

From this condition it follows that *wh*-Movement must be a cyclic rule, since it applies in indirect questions and relatives.[22] The condition (51) seems fairly natural, and we will proceed to investigate its consequences.

Returning now to (50), we first assign *wh* and apply *wh*-Movement on the innermost cycle, which gives (52):

(52) COMP you told me [$_S$[$_{COMP}$what] Bill saw]

On the next cycle, we want to move *what* to the COMP position of the matrix sentence, to give (49).[23] The Specified Subject Condition is no longer a barrier, but we are left with a violation of the Tensed-S Condition. An investigation of the conditions of the violation indicates that they are quite narrow: an item can "escape" from a tensed sentence if it has been moved into the COMP position on an earlier cycle and is moving into the COMP position on the present cycle. Furthermore, in no case does an item in COMP position move to anything other than the COMP position.[24] These specific properties of COMP may be considered alongside the property formulated as the Complementizer Substitution Universal. With the appropriate reformulation of our conditions (which we give as (55)), *wh*-Movement can apply to (52), giving (53), which becomes (49) by Auxiliary Inversion and *that*-Insertion:

(53) What you told me [$_S$COMP Bill saw]

Suppose now that we replace some of the base rules in (16) to obtain the more detailed analysis (54) (following Bresnan (1970)):

(54) S → COMP S'
S' → NP Aux VP
⋮

Suppose further that we continue to take S (but not S') to be the domain of cyclic rules. Under this assumption we can reformulate the Tensed-S and

---

[22] It has been argued repeatedly that *wh*-Movement cannot be a cyclic rule, but I am aware of no conclusive arguments. To my knowledge, none of the arguments that appear in the literature apply to the formulations given here. However, at a later point I will deal with some considerations that might suggest that *wh*-Movement is post-cyclic.

[23] We shall return to the rule for inserting *that* in (49) [not reproduced here].

[24] In fact, this must be stipulated, quite apart from the Tensed-S Condition, to prevent improper passivization of, for example, *John asked what to read* to **What was asked to read by John*. On the other hand, *What did John ask to read* is permitted by the conditions.

Specified Subject Conditions, together with the narrow restrictions on COMP, as in (55):

(55) No rule can involve X, Y in the structure
...X...[α...Z...-WYV...]...
where (a) Z is the specified subject of WYV
or   (b) Y is in COMP and X is not in COMP
or   (c) Y is not in COMP and α is a tensed S

This modification of the conditions in effect asserts that an item can be extracted from a tensed sentence or across a specified subject only if there is a rule that moves it into the COMP position. Thus a *wh*-word can be extracted, as in (49)–(50), but the subject of the embedded sentence cannot be passivized in *I believe the dog is hungry*. Notice, however, that *wh*-Movement will not be permitted across a specified subject in (31a), which we restate here as (56), to give the ungrammatical *\*Who did you see John's pictures of*:

(56) COMP you saw [$_{NP}$John's pictures of who]

The relevant difference between (56) and (50) is that (56) has no COMP node in an NP. Therefore the *wh*-word in (56) cannot escape from the NP.

It is observed in Chomsky (1964) that *wh*-Movement can be applied only once to a constituent of the form S. We cannot, for example, question (or relativize) an item that is within an indirect question to derive (57) from (58):[25]

(57) *What did he wonder where John put

(58) COMP he wondered [$_S$COMP John put what where]

To derive (57) from (58), we must first place *where* in the COMP position of the embedded sentence. But in that case, *what* cannot enter the COMP position, which is filled by *where*, and thus cannot be extracted on the next cycle. The principles of the cycle presupposed so far in this discussion permit no other ordering of rule applications to give (57).

## References

Bach, E. (1965), "On some recurrent types of transformations," in C. W. Kreidler, ed., *Sixteenth Annual Round Table Meeting on Linguistics and Language Studies*, Georgetown University Monograph Series on Languages and Linguistics 18.

---

[25] Some speakers seem to accept such forms as *What did he wonder whether John saw*, *What crimes did he wonder how they solved*. For me, these are unacceptable. It would be possible to add special rules to allow for these examples by a complication of the particular grammar, given the suggested interpretation of the conditions.

Bach, E. (1971), "Questions," *Linguistic Inquiry* 2, 153–66.
Baker, C. L. (1970), "Notes on the description of English questions: the role of an abstract question morpheme," *Foundations of Language*, 6, 197–219.
Bresnan, J. (1970), "On complementizers: towards a syntactic theory of complement types," *Foundations of Language*, 6, 297–321.
Bresnan, J. (1972), "The theory of complementation in English syntax," PhD dissertation, MIT.
Chomsky, N. (1964), *Current Issues in Linguistics Theory*, The Hague: Mouton.
Chomsky, N. (1965), *Aspects of the Theory of Syntax*, Cambridge, MA: MIT Press.
Chomsky, N. (1968), *Language and Mind*, New York: Harcourt Brace Jovanovich.
Chomsky, N. (1970a), "Deep Structure, Surface Structure, and semantic interpretation," in R. Jakobson and S. Kawamoto, eds, *Studies in General and Oriental Linguistics* (Commemorative Volume for Dr Shiro Hattori), Tokyo: TEC Corporation for Language Research.
Chomsky, N. (1970b), "Remarks on nominalization," in R. Jacobs and P. Rosenbaum, eds, *Readings in English Transformational Grammar*, Waltham, MA: Ginn.
Chomsky, N. (1972), "Empirical issues in the theory of transformational grammar," in S. Peters, ed., *Goals of Linguistics Theory* (Proceedings of the Linguistics Conference at the University of Texas, Oct. 1969), Englewood Cliffs, NJ: Prentice-Hall.
Culicover, P. (1971), "Syntactic and semantic investigations," unpublished PhD dissertation, MIT.
Dougherty, R. (1970), "A grammar of coordinate conjoined structures: I," *Language*, 46, 850–98.
Emonds, J. (1970), "Root and structure-preserving transformations," unpublished PhD dissertation, MIT.
Helke, M. (1971), "The grammar of English reflexives," unpublished PhD dissertation, MIT.
Jackendoff, R. S. (1969), "Some rules of semantic interpretation for English," unpublished PhD dissertation, MIT.
Katz, J. and P. Postal (1964), *An Integrated Theory of Linguistic Descriptions*, Cambridge, MA: MIT Press.
Lasnik, H. (1971), "A general constraint: some evidence from negation," *Quarterly Progress Report of the Research Laboratory of Electronics*, 101, MIT, 215–17.
Peters, S., and R. W. Ritchie (1973), "On the generative power of transformational grammars," *Information Sciences*, 6, 49–83.
Postal, P. (1966), "A note on 'understood transitively,'" *IJAL*, 32, 90–3.
Postal, P. (1969), Review of A. McIntosh and M. A. K. Halliday, *Papers in General, Descriptive and Applied Linguistics*, in *Foundations of Language*, 5, 409–39.
Postal, P. (1971), *Cross-Over Phenomena*, New York: Holt, Rinehart and Winston.
Ross, J. R. (1967), "Constraints on variables in syntax," unpublished PhD dissertation, MIT.

# 2 Discussion of Chomsky (1973)

As stated previously, the intent of the framework developed in "Conditions" is to reduce the power of grammars by constraining the functioning of transformations while at the same time stating these transformations in the most general terms possible. Formulating the structural description of Passive as *X, NP, V, NP, Y* (as Chomsky does) and permitting it to operate unconstrained would result in the generation of many ungrammatical sentences. However, Chomsky shows that a constraint on rule application such as the *A*-over-*A* Condition allows such a general statement and rules out a number of illicit sentences, including the derivation of his (5a) *\*John and Mary was seen by Bill* from (4a) *John and Bill saw Mary*. To see precisely how this works, consider that the Passive rule could, in principle, apply to the string *Bill saw Mary* (within (4a)) to produce *Mary be+en see by Bill*. One would therefore expect (5a) to be grammatical, wherein the string *John and* corresponds to the factor labeled *X* in the Passive rule. The *A*-over-*A* Principle is invoked here to prevent Passive from applying to the NP *Bill* where it is immediately contained within the larger NP *John and Bill*.

At the heart of the article is the abandonment of the typology of transformations referred to above which categorizes transformations into *unbounded* (such as *wh*-movement, Topicalization, and others) and *bounded*, including transformations that affect elements separated by precisely one clause node (Raising, Equi) and those that apply within a single clause (Passive, Reflexivization). In the "Conditions" framework, such distinctions are irrelevant and certain constituent relations are ignored. For example, in an ST treatment, the ungrammaticality of (1b) is due to the fact that the domain of Passive is a single clause.

(1) a. I expect the doctor is examining the patient.
    b. *The doctor is expected by me is examining the patient.

Under "Conditions," (1b) is instead ruled out by the Tensed-S Condition (TSC). Although the string *I–expect–the doctor* meets the structural description of Passive, application of the transformation is illicit since *the doctor* is contained in a tensed clause that does not include *I* and *expect*.

The Specified Subject Condition (SSC) has the same effect, as illustrated with reflexives. Consider the ungrammatical sentence in (2).

(2)    *Marge expected Ted to vote for herself.

In the ST account, (2) is ungrammatical because the clausemate condition on Reflexivization would not be met by the relevant input structure. In that framework, the object NP *Marge* in the lower clause (which is input to the Reflexivization rule) is in a distinct clause from the matrix subject NP *Marge*. In the "Conditions" account, the clause node is irrelevant. Instead, (2) is ruled out because the reflexive interpretive rule cannot take *Marge* as antecedent of *herself*, the embedded specified subject *Ted* blocking application.

These different accounts highlight a key difference between ST and EST, one which is seen below to be related to the treatment of Raising. ST and EST make very different assumptions about the structure that (2) takes as its input. Within ST, the input to Reflexivization takes *Ted* to be a constituent of the matrix clause, having moved to that position by an application of Raising.

(3) [$_S$Marge expected Ted [$_S$to vote for Marge]]

EST, on the other hand, takes *Ted* to be the subject of the embedded clause, as in (4). Hence it qualifies as a specified subject and blocks the reflexive interpretive rule.

(4) [$_S$Marge expected [$_S$Ted to vote for herself]]

Within EST, "subject" is defined as "the NP immediately dominated by a cyclic node," where the cyclic nodes were S and NP. So, rather than have "rules" reference such nodes, it is the "conditions" which do so. Thus, the SSC can account for the ungrammaticality of reflexives in certain NPs that have a subject (5).

(5) *Marge was interested in Ted's story about herself.

Once again, *Ted* acts as a specified subject and blocks the reflexive.[1]

There are a number of cases of rule application that do not fall under the scope of the TSC and the SSC. For example, neither the TSC nor the SSC seems to apply to certain instances of *wh*-movement or other "unbounded" transformations such as Topicalization. Chomsky points to data such as the following:

(6) a. What did you tell me [$_S$that Terry saw]?
    b. What did you expect [$_S$Terry to see]?

Clearly, (6a) should be ruled out by the TSC (as well as by the SSC) since the embedded clause is tensed, and (6b) should be ruled out by the SSC since there is a specified subject, *Terry*. Therefore, in §3 Chomsky introduces what became known as the "COMP escape hatch," which stipulates that elements in COMP fall outside the scope of the two conditions (55).

Chomsky proposes the Subjacency Condition to account for data not handled by the TSC and SSC in an attempt to subsume Ross's (1967) various island constraints under a single condition. Ross's constraints, which include the Complex NP Constraint, the Sentential Subject Constraint, and others, are constraints on movement rules that apply to particular constructions. The Complex NP Constraint basically states that no element can be moved from a "complex NP," that is, either a relative clause or an NP with a head such as *fact* or *rumor* and a sentential complement. Thus, *the rumor that Pat talked to whom* in (7a) is a complex NP, and *wh*-movement is blocked, hence the ungrammaticality of (7b).[2]

(7) a. Chris believes [$_{NP}$the rumor [$_S$that Pat talked [$_{PP}$to whom]]]
    b. *To whom does Chris believe [$_{NP}$the rumor [$_{S'}$that [$_S$Pat talked]]]

Similarly, to account for the ungrammaticality of sentences such as (8b), Ross proposed the Sentential Subject Constraint, which stated that movement out of a sentential subject is prohibited.

(8) a. [$_{S'}$That [$_S$Stacy read what]] is unfortunate
 b. *What is [$_{S'}$that [$_S$Stacy read]] unfortunate?

Chomsky states the Subjacency Condition as follows (1973:247):

(9) No rule can involve X, Y, X superior to Y, if Y is not subjacent to X.

Here X is *superior* to Y refers to the fact that X is higher in the phrase marker than Y (specifically every *major* category containing Y contains X but not vice versa), and Y is *subjacent* to X if not more than one cyclic node intervenes between them. So, stated succinctly, the Subjacency Condition rules out movement over more than one NP or S node, what came to be referred to as *bounding nodes*. Accordingly, movement from Y to X violates subjacency in (10a), where S and NP are crossed, but not in (10b).

(10) a. ... X ... [$_S$ ... [$_{NP}$ ... Y ... ]] ...
 b. ... X ... [$_S$ ... Y ... ] ...

Subjacency straightforwardly accounts for the Complex NP facts. Consider again the ungrammatical (7b) and the associated structure in (7c).

(7) b. *To whom does Chris believe the rumor that Pat talked?
 c. to whom [$_{S2}$does Chris believe [$_{NP}$the rumor [$_{S'}$___ that [$_{S1}$Pat talked ___]]]]

The movement of *to whom* from the lower S' to the highest COMP position crosses two bounding nodes, NP and S2, a violation of the Subjacency Condition. Thus, (7b) cannot be derived and is ungrammatical.[3]

Subjacency can account for a larger array of data, but only provided certain crucial assumptions are made. First, it is necessary to invoke the COMP escape hatch so that *wh*-movement is not ruled out from sentential complements, as in (11).

(11) a. Who do you think that Ashley saw ___?
 b. who do [$_S$you think [$_{S'}$___ that [$_S$Ashley saw ___]]

As long as *who* moves first to the COMP of the embedded S' and movement to COMP is not subject to the Tensed-S Condition, the movement in (11) is not blocked. This analysis actually requires an additional assumption: there is no NP node dominating the clausal complement. Recall that under ST analyses such as Rosenbaum's and Postal's, sentential complements are analyzed as NPs (recall Rosenbaum's argument from Passive). If that analysis were adopted in EST, movement out of object complement clauses would be impossible, as (11c) shows.

(11) c. who do [$_{S2}$you think [$_{NP}$[$_{S'}$___ that [$_{S1}$Ashley saw ___]]]

Movement out of S' violates Subjacency inasmuch as two bounding nodes NP and S2 are crossed. Therefore, sentential objects cannot be dominated by an NP node, and (11b) is the necessary and accepted analysis.

Sentential subjects require an entirely different assumption in order for the Subjacency account to work. Chomsky must assume that unlike sentential objects, sentential subjects are dominated by NP. Consider (8) once more in light of this.

(8) b. *What is that Stacy read unfortunate?
     c. what is [$_{S2}$[$_{NP}$[$_{S'}$___ that [$_{S1}$Stacy read ___ ]]] unfortunate

Wh-movement is blocked in (8) because movement from the embedded COMP position crosses two bounding nodes, NP and S2. Were the NP dominating the sentential subject missing, only a single bounding node, S2, would be crossed and movement would not be blocked. So, in order for Chomsky to ensure that his proposal accounts for this range of data, he is forced to maintain the ST analysis of sentential subjects as NPs while abandoning the analysis of sentential objects as NPs. This is an issue that he does not address in "Conditions."[4]

## Raising

EST represents a seismic shift in the analysis of Raising: Raising-to-Object (RtoO) was eliminated and Raising-to-Subject (RtoS) took on a somewhat different look. In "Conditions," Chomsky adopted Rosenbaum's pronoun replacement analysis (referring to the *it*-Replacement transformation, following Ross 1967), although the extraposition structure was base-generated. Thus, (12b) was derived from (12a) and (13b) from (13a):

(12) a. It is likely [$_S$COMP John to leave]
     b. John is likely to leave.

(13) a. It seems [$_S$COMP John to be a nice fellow]
     b. John seems to be a nice fellow.

The analysis is different from the ST analysis in two important ways. First, the type of complementizer insertion that was part of Rosenbaum's analysis has been abandoned. While surface structures were still derived from deep structures via transformations, transformations inserting lexical material (such as pronouns and complementizers) were in many cases eliminated in favor of base generation and rules of semantic interpretation. This limited the power of transformations, but required enrichment in terms of interpretive rules (such as establishing coreferentiality of pronouns and their antecedents). Thus, rather than base-generated sentential subjects that are underspecified for tense and complementizers, the Deep Structures in RtoS include base-generated infinitival complements. Second, transformations must observe Emonds's (1976) Principle of Structure Preservation; that is, the output of a transformation must be identical to a structure that could be generated by the base Phrase Structure rules. Thus, with the exception of some "root" transformations (transformations that apply to the highest sentence in a phrase marker), transformations did not build structure. The effect of this was that all moved elements had to be moved to an existing node of the same type.

However, Emonds's notion of structure preservation carried with it the hypothesis that empty nodes could be generated in a Phrase Structure. These nodes were necessary to ensure that elements would have a position to which movement would be sanctioned. For example, Passive in EST came to be analyzed as involving two processes, postposing of the original subject and preposing of the object. In order for the Deep Structure subject to have an NP position to move to, it was necessary to generate an empty NP node in an agentive prepositional phrase, so (abstracting away from verbal morphology) the sentence in (14b) was derived from a structure such as (14a), where the Δ represents the empty node.

(14)  a.  the police arrest Kelsey by [$_{NP}$Δ]
      b.  Kelsey was arrested by the police.

With the admission of base-generated empty nodes, an analysis of RtoS that eschewed *It*-Replacement was available, and eventually the accepted EST analysis of Raising made use of this. Thus, (15b) was derived from (15a).

(15)  a.  [$_{NP}$Δ] seem [$_S$Terry to be completely incompetent]
      b.  Terry seems to be completely incompetent.

Within EST, RtoS was the only type of Raising recognized. RtoO was eliminated as a transformation.[5] Chomsky states this quite explicitly: "As already noted, under the analysis proposed here there is no necessity for a rule raising the subject of an embedded sentence to the object position of the matrix sentence (and, furthermore, it is questionable whether such a rule could even be added)" (1973: 254). With transformations no longer being restricted to a single clause, reflexive data such as (16), which once provided a key argument for RtoO, no longer do so.

(16)  Marge expected [$_S$herself to win the election].

Lacking a clausemate condition on Reflexivization, the reflexive in (16) can be interpreted as coreferent with the matrix subject *Marge* since there are no violations of the Tensed-S, Specified Subject, or Subjacency Conditions. Because (16) can be accounted for without resorting to Raising, within EST Reflexivization no longer serves as an argument for RtoO.

Chomsky considers the elimination of RtoO desirable on theoretical grounds as well. First of all, he considers RtoO to be a "string vacuous operation." That is, he contends that while RtoO alters the Phrase Structure, it does not reorder the terminal string.[6] Chomsky hypothesizes that eliminating string-vacuous movement strengthens the restrictiveness of the theory: "One might then raise the question whether cyclic transformations should not be constrained so as to forbid operations that never change the terminal string of a phrase marker but only its structure, as in the original formulations of subject raising to object position" (1973: 254). Second, as was seen previously, the typology of transformations expounded by Rosenbaum and generally accepted in ST was abandoned in EST, transformations being allowed to apply more generally but with their application restricted by universal conditions. Chomsky again takes this to be theoretically desirable in that rule-particular restrictions can be eliminated in favor of more general principles, and so reducing the types of grammars that the theory sanctions as well-formed: "Furthermore, it would be highly undesirable to extend the general theory of transformations so as to permit transformations to be restricted to a single clause, and so far as I can see, there are no strong empirical reasons motivating such an elaboration of the theory, given the general framework that we are exploring here" (1973:255).

### Control

Within EST, the treatment of Control changed significantly. Rather than having a Deep Structure along the lines of (17b), in which the embedded clause contained a lexically filled equivalent NP, the Deep Structure of (17a) included a base-generated null pronoun PRO, as in (17c).[7]

(17) a. Jackson tried to remain calm.
 b. Jackson tried [Jackson to remain calm]
 c. Jackson tried [PRO to remain calm]

A rule of interpretation applying to surface structure assigned the appropriate reference to PRO, which was then said to be "controlled."[8] Although attempts at a general rule of interpretation were made, for the most part it was assumed that the element that controlled PRO was stipulated in the lexical entry of the relevant verb. So, *try* is a subject-control predicate, as is *promise* (18), while *persuade* is an object-control verb (19).

(18) Jackson promised [PRO to make things right]

(19) Dana persuaded Jackson [PRO to make things right]

## 3 Postal's critique

In *On Raising*, Postal responds directly to Chomsky's proposals in "Conditions" as they relate to the issue of RtoO. Postal contends that eliminating the typology of transformations and allowing all rules to essentially be unbounded weakens the theory and allows generation of larger numbers of grammars. We will not evaluate this claim here but simply keep in mind that this assumption forms the backdrop of Postal's arguments and is a position that he wishes to defend. Postal's arguments from reflexives and reciprocals contend that

Chomsky's proposal cannot handle all of the data that a clausemate condition can. However, some of the data are somewhat marginal (or idiolectal, as Postal puts it) and we will not go into these here. His two other arguments are of some interest.

## Passive

Postal notes the problem for the generation of certain passives given the lack of an NP node dominating the complement of *believe*-type verbs. Postal cites the sentences in (20).

(20) a. It was believed by everyone that Melvin was an addict.
  b. That Melvin was an addict was believed by everyone.
  c. Everyone believed that Melvin was an addict.

Under the ST account advocated by Postal, (20b) is derived from (20c) via the regular application of Passive and (20a) is derived from (20b) by Extraposition.

In EST, the structural description of Passive still includes an NP following the verb. Thus, a different analysis is required. Emonds (1970, 1976) suggests that there are two distinct parts of Passive: one which postposes the preverbal NP to the empty NP in the agentive *by* phrase, [$_{PP}$by [$_{NP}$Δ]], and one which preposes the postverbal NP to the empty subject position. The derivation of (20a) proceeds by inserting expletive *it* following postposing the underlying subject. (20b) is derived not by applying Passive to the complement *that Melvin was an addict* (since it is not an NP) but by a special rule of *It*-Replacement that allows the sentential complement to substitute for the NP expletive.

Although seemingly troubled by this special rule of *It*-Replacement, Postal does not see this as a fatal problem "since the question of how to generate the expletive *it* has no well-founded answer in any other system" (1974: 59). The problem lies in accounting for a wider range of data. In particular, Postal notes that analogues of (20a, b) with infinitival complements are ungrammatical.

(21) a. *It was believed by everyone (for) Melvin to be an addict.
  b. *(For) Melvin to be an addict was believed by everyone.

Within Postal's approach, the sentences in (21) are ruled out by a statement like (22) (Postal's (14)).

(22) A complement whose subject is raised is marked infinitival.

Postal assumes that infinitival complements are possible with Raising verbs **only** if Raising has occurred. Given this assumption, the sentences in (21) cannot be derived since the infinitival complements would be illicit. Once Raising has occurred and the infinitival complement sanctioned, only (23) can be derived via Passive.

(23) Melvin was believed by everyone to be an addict.

According to Postal, within Chomsky's proposal it should be possible to derive the sentences in (21) in the same way as those in (20) since both complements (*that Melvin is an addict* and *(for) Melvin to be an addict*) are generated as Ss, that is, without a dominating NP node. As Postal admits, the ad hoc statement required in the EST account is no more costly to the grammar than the stipulation in (22). However, Postal notes that the statement in (22) has broader applicability: it can account for the paradigm in (24).

(24) a. It seems that Melvin is an addict.
 b. *It seems (for) Melvin to be an addict.
 c. Melvin seems to be an addict.

Since *seem* is a raising verb, (24b) is ruled out under the assumption that infinitival complements of raising verbs only arise if Raising has applied, which it clearly has not in (24). The ad hoc statement ruling out the generation of (21a, b) will presumably not apply in the case of (24). There is no application of Passive (or one of its subparts) in (24); therefore, a different explanation is required here and thus the analysis of these data requires more machinery.

### The Inclusion Constraint

Postal's last argument specifically directed against Chomsky's proposals in "Conditions" involves the Inclusion Constraint. Postal (1966, 1969) noted that pairs of NPs in certain configurations cannot overlap in reference. In *On Raising*, Postal exemplifies this with the paradigm in (25).

(25) a. *I like us.
 b. *We like me.
 c. *He$_i$ praised them$_{i+j}$.
 d. *They$_{i+j}$ criticized him$_i$.

Postal hypothesizes that there is a clausemate condition on the Inclusion Constraint such that it does not apply when the NPs are not clausemates, citing the data in (26).

(26) a. I believe [$_S$that we can win].
 b. They$_{i,j}$ both claimed [$_S$he$_i$ was innocent].
 c. We must call the girl [$_S$who saw me].

He then argues that if this is correct the Inclusion Constraint provides evidence for Raising with *believe*-type verbs since the raised subject cannot overlap in reference with the subject of the matrix clause (27a), while it can if Raising does not take place (27b).

(27) a. *I believed us to be right.
 b. I believed that we were right.

Chomsky's conditions can account for these data. As was seen in his discussion of such data in his (42–5), Chomsky posits a rule of interpretation he refers to as RI that marks as ungrammatical any sentence in which two non-reflexive, non-reciprocal NPs are interpreted as coreferent or intersecting in reference. RI correctly and straightforwardly marks all the sentences in (25) as ungrammatical. The Tensed-S Condition prevents RI from being applied to the sentences in (26), just as in Chomsky's (45d). This explanation accounts for (27b) as well. However, since *us* is not contained in a tensed sentence and there is no specified subject intervening between *I* and *us* in (27a), RI applies freely and the sentence is marked ungrammatical.

Postal introduces the data in (28) (Postal's (51)), in which subjects of infinitives appear to be immune from RI.

(28) a. I arranged for us to dine with Sally.
 b. I prayed for us to be allowed to marry.
 c. He$_i$ planned for them$_{i,j}$ to live in Persia.
 d. They$_{i,j}$ prayed for him$_i$ to get better.

Since in each example the underscored pronouns are subjects of infinitive clauses and there is no specified subject intervening between the two NPs with overlapping reference, rule RI should apply just as it does in (27a) and the sentences should be ungrammatical. Postal argues that the "Conditions" account makes the wrong prediction here and can only account for the data with an additional ad hoc statement. The analysis that incorporates the Inclusion Constraint with the clausemate condition predicts the grammaticality of these sentences, analyzing them in the same way as the sentences with tensed complements in (26). Postal therefore contends that the Inclusion Constraint data provide an argument for RtoO.

## Notes

1 As general conditions on transformations the TSC and SSC were intended to apply not only to a subset of rules but to all transformations and rules of interpretation. Thus, the Specified Subject Condition was alleged to account for the impossibility of *wh*-movement in some cases, as in Chomsky's data in (30–1). While this account was generally accepted, the data are actually more complex than this, the SSC excluding some data that it should not, as in (i).

(i) a. *Who did Ted write your book about?
 b. Who did Ted$_i$ write his$_i$ book about?

On the one hand, (ia) is ruled ungrammatical because *who* has moved out of the NP containing the pronominal subject *your*. On the other hand, this movement is not illicit when the pronominal subject is coreferent to the clausal subjects (ib). If the Specified Subject Condition were at work here, the two sentences should be equally ungrammatical. (See Davies & Dubinsky 2003 for an explanation of these facts.)

2 Note that since it is a PP that has been moved in (7b) the A-over-A Condition (see Chomsky 1973 excerpt example (3)) is not violated.

3 At the same time, it is worth noting that the Subjacency Condition did **not** subsume all of the attested island conditions. Consider, for example, the extraction in (i), which involves coordinated PPs.

(i) *[what door]$_1$ did the bird fly [$_{PP}$[$_{PP}$in the window] and [$_{PP}$out of t$_1$]]

Here, the extracted NP *what door* only crosses one bounding node, the matrix S. Thus, a constraint blocking extraction out of a coordinate structure is independently needed. Similarly, the extraction in (ii) shows the continued need for a separate *A-over-A* Condition.

(ii) *[$_{PP}$to what age]$_1$ can you ride for free [$_{PP}$up t$_1$]

Again, the extracted element (the PP *to what age*) only crosses one bounding node, and is not ruled out by the Subjacency Condition.

4 For some compelling evidence that this move is actually empirically justified, see Davies and Dubinsky (1999, 2001a).
5 Recall from section 2 that in *it*-Replacement the raised NP replaces an NP, thus moving to an NP position. In this way, Rosenbaum's early formulation of the raising transformations were more in keeping with Emonds's notions of structure preservation than were later formulations (such as Postal's) in which the raised element (at least in the RtoO case) was assumed to occupy an NP node created in the derivation.
6 While this came to be an often-cited reason for the non-existence of RtoO, especially in later formulations of Chomsky's, this position is a troubled one, both empirically and theoretically. First of all, Postal (1974) discusses cases such as (i), in which Raising does indeed reorder the terminal string.

(i) a. Herb figured out [that it is impossible to square a circle]
    b. Herb figured it out to be impossible to square a circle.

In (ib), the raising case, the raised subject of the complement clause *it* appears before the particle *out*. Second, the undesirability of string-vacuous operations seems to have been overlooked by Chomsky himself in certain cases. For example, the string-vacuous movement of a subject *wh*-expression to COMP, as in (ii), remained a part of the EST (and later, the Government and Binding) model.

(ii) [$_{S'}$who$_1$ [$_{S}$t$_1$left]]

This sort of vacuous movement is not seriously questioned by Chomsky until the introduction of the Barriers model (N. Chomsky 1986a).

7 Postal (1970) first proposed the formalism of a base-generated null pronoun, using the terminology of a pronoun marked with the feature [+doom].
8 Jackendoff (1969, 1972) argues for this position in detail.

# CHAPTER 5

# THE *ON RAISING* DEBATES: BRESNAN, POSTAL, AND BACH

## 1   Bresnan (1976)

Bresnan (1976) was one of the first, and perhaps most influential, replies to the claims made in Postal (1974).[1] The article sets out to attack Postal's arguments for the Raising-to-Object (RtoO) analysis of infinitival complements of *believe*-type and *want*-type verbs, and thereby (indirectly) to diminish the stature of Postal's rule-based approach as an alternative to Chomsky's (1973) conditions-based approach to grammar. Inasmuch as Postal (1974) is heavily focused on data, with one empirical argument following another for hundreds of pages, Bresnan's critique takes on the empirical core of Postal's volume and considers, one by one, each of the fifteen arguments presented in Postal's chapter 4.

### Argument I: Constraint on Heavy (i.e., Complex) NP Shift

Postal claims that complex NPs cannot be subjects at the time they undergo shift. Under the RtoO account, the NP *those friends who pestered him for money* is a derived object in (1a) but is a subject at all levels in (2a). For this reason, Heavy NP Shift is only possible in (1b) and not in (2b).

(1) a.   Melvin showed those friends who pestered him for money to be inconsiderate boors.
    b.   Melvin showed to be inconsiderate boors, those friends who pestered him for money.

(2) a.   Melvin showed that those friends who pestered him for money were inconsiderate boors.
    b.   *Melvin showed were inconsiderate boors, those friends who pestered him for money.

Bresnan's objection to this argument takes two forms. First, she tries to show that some subjects can in fact undergo Heavy NP Shift, thereby casting doubt on Postal's explanation for the ungrammaticality of (2b). Presenting cases of Locative Inversion, she shows that the heavy NPs in question are subjects in Postal's terms, pointing to subject–verb agreement of these NPs with the matrix verbs in (3) and (4) as evidence for this.

(3) a. An old castle that had been abandoned was situated near that town for many years.
    b. Near that town was situated an old castle that had been abandoned for many years.

(4) a. An entire army of ants climbed over my windowsill every day.
    b. Over my windowsill climbed an entire army of ants every day.

In (3b), for example, the postverbal NP *an old castle that had been abandoned for many years* triggers subject agreement on the verb. Thus, according to Bresnan, this NP is a sentential subject which has undergone Heavy NP Shift. Example (3b) thus stands as a counterexample to Postal's claim that subjects cannot undergo Heavy NP Shift. Postal's explanation for the ungrammaticality of (2b), i.e., that the heavy NP is a subject, is therefore suspect.

Second, she tries to show that some non-subjects cannot undergo Heavy NP Shift, thereby weakening Postal's claim that (1b) counts as evidence for the object status of its postposed NP. Bresnan presents the data in (5) and (6) to show the existence of non-subjects that do not undergo Heavy NP Shift.[2]

(5) a. I forced all the rowdy boys to leave.
    b. *I forced to leave all the rowdy boys.

(6) a. I convinced all of the antifeminist candidates to disqualify themselves.
    b. *I convinced to disqualify themselves all of the antifeminist candidates.

In (6b), the postposed heavy NP *all of the antifeminist candidates* is an object of the verb *convinced*. The ungrammaticality of this sentence leads Bresnan to claim that object status is not a sufficient condition for the application of Heavy NP Shift (as Postal claims for (1b)).

By showing that some surface subjects can undergo Heavy NP Shift and that some surface objects cannot undergo the rule, Bresnan tries to show that Heavy NP Shift facts cannot provide an argument for RtoO, since the "subject" NP of an infinitival complement could be postposed without having to raise to object position of the matrix clause.

*Evaluation of Bresnan's argument*

With regard to (3) and (4), the locative inversion evidence, one might question whether these cases involve the same operation of Heavy NP Shift implicated in (1b). Recall Lakoff's and Ross's assertions regarding the prosody associated with extraposition, where they demonstrated that extraposed phrases are preceded by a major intonation break (see example (41), chapter 2). One might wonder whether Bresnan's Locative Inversion examples would not be subject to the same criticism. (1b) certainly involves a clear intonation break, as shown here,

(1b)  Melvin showed to be inconsiderate boors // those friends who pestered him for money

It is not apparent that the same could be said of (4b),

(4b)  ??Over my windowsill climbed // an entire army of ants.

Given that Bresnan offers no formal account of Locative Inversion in this work (but see Bresnan 1994), one must asssume that she intends the postverbal subjects in (3b) and (4b) to be derived in the same manner as the clause-final NP in (1b), that is, via extraposition. The lack of an intonation break in (4b) is thus troublesome for her argument. That is, the subjects in (3b) and (4b) that she claims to have undergone Heavy NP Shift may not have done so at all, given their failure to be preceded by an intonation break. With regard to the ungrammatical cases in (5–6), notice that these involve putative control verbs as opposed to raising verbs. The postposed NPs are thus in some sense objects and subjects simultaneously (i.e., Equi NPs) rather than "derived" objects.

## Arguments II and III: Not-initial and alone-final NPs can only be subjects, not objects

Postal says the difference in grammaticality between (7a) and (7b) is predicted by Raising. The ungrammaticality of (7b) is attributed to the *not*-initial NP, *not many of those formulas*, being a surface (i.e., raised to) object.

(7)  a. Harry proved (that) not many of those formulas were theorems.
     b. *Harry proved not many of those formulas to be theorems.

Similarly, Postal claims that *alone*-final NPs can only occur in surface subject positions. The ungrammaticality of (8b) is, once again, attributed to the NP in question's being a surface object.

(8)  a. Michael thought (that) George alone was an idiot.
     b. *Michael thought George alone to be an idiot.

Bresnan's criticism of both of these arguments is parallel. She points to cases in which an uncontroversial surface subject **cannot** be *not*-initial or *alone*-final, and then suggests that surface subjecthood is only a necessary (but not a sufficient) condition to account for their distribution.

(9)  a. *Harry debated whether not many of those formulas were theorems.
     b. *George disapproved of Sheila alone taking the test.

The data in (9) are meant to show that *not*-initial or *alone*-final NPs may be in subject positions and still be ungrammatical, thus casting doubt on Postal's account for (7b) and (8b). Bresnan then goes on to show that *alone*-final NPs can indeed appear in positions that Postal would analyze as being surface objects. She notes that, in the same position, *not*-initial NPs are excluded.

(10) a. Michael wanted George alone to win the race.
b. *Michael wanted not many of those students to win the race.

From data like (10a), Bresnan casts doubt upon Postal's explanation for the ungrammaticality of (8b) and for its being evidence in favor of RtoO. From (10b), Bresnan casts doubt on Postal's use of *not*-initial and *alone*-final NPs as parallel arguments.

### Evaluation of Bresnan's argument

Bresnan's data in (9) do indeed show that *not*-initial and *alone*-final NPs may be excluded from some subject positions. These data do not, however, undermine Postal's explanation for the ungrammaticality of (7b) and (8b), but simply show the explanation of their distribution to be more complex than he supposed. One might wonder, for instance, whether the *wh*-property of the complement in (9a) is a factor, or whether subjects of gerunds such as in (9b) are different in this regard. The data in (10), though, do pose a challenge to Postal's claims. If the infinitival complements of *want* have the same analysis as those of the verb *believe* (that is, if the subjects of these complements undergo RtoO), then Postal's *alone*-final test is defective (but the *not*-initial test is unaffected). One cannot rule out (8b) on account of *George alone* being a surface object, if it is assumed that the same NP is a surface object in (10a). If, on the other hand, *want* verbs have a different analysis than *believe* verbs, then this argument in favor of RtoO might still be valid. In other words, Postal may simply be wrong about *want* being an RtoO verb. In such case, (10a) would be grammatical precisely because the NP *George alone* is not a surface object. The ungrammaticality of (10b) would then require further explanation. As shall be seen when we consider Kayne (1981), there are good reasons for concluding that the complements of *want* have a different analysis and that it may not be an RtoO verb.

### Argument VI: Pronominalization constraint

A pronoun cannot both precede and command its antecedent NP. Postal claims this explains the contrast between (11a) and (11b), under a raising analysis of (11b).

(11) a. Joan believes (that) he$_1$ is a genius even more fervently than Bob$_1$ does.
b. *Joan believes him$_1$ to be a genius even more fervently than Bob$_1$ does.

In (11a), the pronoun *he* can (but need not) be coindexed with *Bob*. This is not the case in (11b), where coreference between *him* and *Bob* is ungrammatical. Postal's explanation for this, as seen earlier, is as follows. In (11a), the pronoun *he* precedes the NP *Bob*, but does not command it. In (11b), because the pronoun *him* raises to the object of the matrix clause, it both precedes and commands the NP *Bob*, resulting in ungrammaticality if the two are coindexed.

In Bresnan's objection to this argument, she suggests that the ungrammaticality of (11b) has nothing to do with the position of the pronoun *him* relative to the NP *Bob*, but is the result of clause-internal ungrammaticality preceding the operation of VP ellipsis, as discussed below regarding (13). First of all, taking (11a) to be the result of VP ellipsis, its source is something like (12), where the VP *believes he is a genius* is replaced by the auxiliary *does*. Analogously, the source of (11b) would be something like (13), where the VP *believes him to be a genius* is replaced by the auxiliary *does*.

(12)  Joan believes he$_1$ is a genius even more fervently than Bob$_1$ believes he$_1$ is a genius.

(13)  *Joan believes him$_1$ to be a genius even more fervently than Bob$_1$ believes him$_1$ to be a genius.

Notice that (13) is itself ungrammatical, due to the coindexation of *Bob* and *him* in the second clause. If the pronoun *him* in the second clause were replaced by the reflexive *himself*, the sentence would be grammatical. However, in that instance, VP ellipsis could no longer apply, since the deleted constituent must be identical in order to be recoverable.

### Evaluation of Bresnan's argument

This argument is very compelling because it demonstrates the ungrammaticality of (11b) to plausibly have nothing to do with the application of Raising in that sentence. Thus, it shows that Postal's pronominalization constraint evidence is indeed potentially irrelevant to the debate between the raising and non-raising approaches to the construction. However, we will return to this paradigm when we consider Lasnik and Saito's (1991) analysis of these constructions, in which they bring further evidence to bear on this argument and demonstrate that pronominalization constraint data do indeed present a cogent argument in favor of a raising-style analysis.

### Argument VIII: Right Node Raising

In support of his analysis, Postal compares the interaction of Right Node Raising as in (14) with RtoO, as shown in (15).

(14)  a.  Joseph thinks that she is the burglar, but he cannot prove that she is the burglar.
      b.  Joseph thinks, but cannot prove, that she is the burglar.

(15)  a.  Joseph believes her to be the burglar, but he cannot prove her to be the burglar.
      b.  *Joseph believes, but he cannot prove, her to be the burglar.

In (14b), the identical complement of the two matrix verbs in (14a) is extraposed to the end of the sentence. According to Postal, (15b) is ungrammatical because the right node raised string, *her to be the burglar*, is not a unit constituent. This is taken as evidence for the raising analysis in which *her* moves out of the embedded complement. Similar contrasts can be seen in (16).

(16)  a.  Joseph thinks (that) she is the burglar, and Marge, that she is not the burglar.
      b.  *Joseph believes her to be the burglar, and Marge, her not to be the burglar.

According to Bresnan's critique of Postal, (15b), (16b), and other data like them are not a reflection of unit constituency so much as the result of the absence of an overt complementizer. Data such as (17) show this.

(17)  a.  *Joseph thinks (that) she is the burglar, and Marge, she is not the burglar.
      b.  Jack has wanted desperately for some time, *(for) his son to win a tournament.

Comparing (16a) and (17a), it would appear that an extraposed complement clause requires a complementizer. In (17b), it is seen that this constraint also applies to infinitival complement clauses, calling into question Postal's unit constituent explanation for the contrast in (16).

### *Evaluation of Bresnan's argument*

Once again, Bresnan has presented a compelling argument and shown that Postal's evidence is potentially irrelevant to the debate between the raising and non-raising approaches to the construction.

### **Argument XIII: Gerundive complements**

Rosenbaum hypothesized that gerundives such as (18) might have a raising analysis, and this position is adopted by Postal.

(18)  Judy prevented there from being a riot in the school cafeteria.

This position is supported by the typical range of criteria. The logical subject of the gerund may undergo passive, as in (19). It preserves the meaning of idiom chunks, as in (20). And the subject of the gerund may be a reflexive or a reciprocal, suggesting that it is a clausemate with the matrix subject, as in (21).

(19)  a.  Sandy prevented Ashley from running off the road.
      b.  Ashley was prevented from running off the road by Sandy.

(20)  a.  Headway was prevented from being made on the problem.
      b.  Tabs were prevented from being kept on JFK.

(21) a. Megan prevented herself from going off the deep end.
b. They prevented one another from losing control.

Some other putative raising verbs that take gerundive complements are *prevent, stop, keep, prohibit, dissuade, deter, restrain,* and *discourage*. Bresnan suggests that a raising analysis is indeed plausible for (18).

## *Methodological objections*

In a closing note, Bresnan faults Postal for not having articulated, or even attempted to articulate, a "formulation of the rule of Raising," a precise description of "the structures to which the rule applies," or a "systematic analysis of . . . constraints, conditions, and rules that . . . interact with [the rule]." She attributes this omission, plausibly, to a position staked out in Postal (1972:168), where he contends that explicit grammar construction is an unrealistic goal at this stage, and that generative research should first consist "in the construction and validation of arguments supporting . . . [claims] about particular grammars." For Bresnan, this position is faulty and presents (in her terms) "a defeatist and unscientific recommendation."

## *Evaluation of Bresnan's criticism*

To what extent is this criticism well founded? It is certainly true that Postal (1974) omits a precise characterization of the raising rule, as well as of the formal mechanisms that might be involved in such a rule. In its defense, it is worth pointing out that Postal wrote and published this book at a time when his own theoretical outlook was undergoing a major revolution. He alludes to this in his first chapter, where he suggests that a theory utilizing grammatical relations as underlying primitives might in fact be preferable to one based on configurational ones. In this context, it made no sense for Postal to adopt a Transformational Grammar (TG)-based formalism (which he no longer believed in). At the same time, his theory of grammatical relations was not sufficiently developed for use in the 1974 volume.

It is also important to consider the differences in methodological attitude which led Postal to his research program, and Bresnan to hers. Postal, for his part, believes that generative research must first build a formidable empirical basis before it can hope to put forward any truly useful and valid analyses. He argues for an empirical approach in our search to understand the structure of language, going meticulously through all the data and argumentation for one process (such as Raising), and then another, before positing entire grammars. In his valuation of empirically oriented research, Postal is right. The lasting value of his 30-year-old research on Raising is testimony to this. Bresnan, adopting Chomsky's viewpoint, believes that it is worthwhile to construct grammatical theories and formalisms at the outset, working out their internal logic and modifying them as empirically necessary, realizing that our initial assumptions will often turn out to be wrong. In this regard, Bresnan also has a very valid point, since most of the theoretical advances in generative grammar have come as the result of the empirical testing of formal hypotheses. It is worth trying, so long as one is prepared to be wrong a lot of the time.

## 2  Postal (1977)

Postal's (1977) reply to Bresnan's (1976) reply to Postal's (1974) book takes the following form. He first questions the overall success of her primary endeavor, pointing out that she has, crucially, failed to prove that RtoO is an unnecessary rule in the grammar. He then examines in great detail the substance of her empirical objections to one of his arguments (Complex NP Shift). In the last (short) section, he responds to her criticism of his methodology.

### Postal on the overall success of Bresnan's reply

Buried in the middle of Bresnan (1976) are four lines in which she admits the plausibility of a raising analysis for sentences such as *He prevented there from being a riot* (Postal's "argument 13"). Given that no "alternatives [to a raising analysis of these] are even plausible," Postal suggests that Bresnan has no choice but to admit a (string-vacuous) rule of RtoO into the grammar. Once Bresnan tacitly accepts Raising as the likely analysis for the gerundive complements of certain verbs, then (Postal insists) Chomsky's (1973) claim that there is no RtoO is undermined. One cannot now claim that Raising is "an unnecessary rule" and that it should "be dispensed with in favor of . . . general conditions." Given Bresnan's failure to rule out a raising analysis generally, her article is no longer about the existence of a raising rule, but about (the much less interesting question of) the extent of its application in English. That is, once RtoO is admitted as a necessary rule, it is not much of a cost to allow it to apply more widely.

### Postal on Bresnan on Heavy NP Shift

Postal rebuts the Heavy NP Shift argument, questioning whether the data that Bresnan reports are actually instances of Heavy NP Shift. Recall that Postal's account for the contrast in (22) is that the shifted NP in (22a) is not a surface subject, while the one in (22b) is so.

(22)  a.  Melvin showed to be inconsiderate boors, those friends who pestered him for money.
  b.  *Melvin showed were inconsiderate boors, those friends who pestered him for money.

Bresnan's point in introducing evidence such as (23) is to argue that some surface subjects (namely those involved in Locative Inversion) can indeed undergo Heavy NP Shift.

(23)  Near the fountain sits a large friendly gorilla.

Bresnan's contention that the NP *a large friendly gorilla* is a subject rests on the observation that it controls agreement with the matrix verb.

Postal's response involves rejecting Bresnan's claim that the postverbal NP in Locative Inversion (example (23)) is a subject at the relevant level of structure (thereby eliminating its relevance as a counterexample to (22b)). He presents several arguments in support of this, some more compelling than others. We will recite only some of them here. First of all, he points out that Locative Inversion constructions, such as (23), (nearly) always allow *there*-Insertion into subject position (following the locative PP). Postal's crucial Heavy NP Shift data, such as (22a), do not. This is seen in the contrast shown in (24).

(24) a. Near the fountain (there) sits a large friendly gorilla.
 b. Melvin showed (*there) to be inconsiderate boors, those friends who pestered him for money.

Postal's claim regarding (24a) is that *there* is the surface subject, and that the NP *a large friendly gorilla*, while possibly a subject at some level of structure, is not a surface subject. Agreement in these cases is not a reliable test for surface subjecthood, for the simple reason that sentences with *there* subjects normally have agreement controlled by a postverbal (non-subject) NP.

Second, Postal shows that the distribution of postverbal NPs in Bresnan's Locative Inversion data is subject to lexical constraints. Only a subset of intransitive verbs allows it, as (25) shows.

(25) a. Near the fountain sits/lives/*eats/*burps/*spits a large friendly gorilla.
 b. *Near the fountain kissed everyone in sight a large friendly gorilla.

In (25a), only certain intransitive verbs occur in Locative Inversion contexts, and (25b) is ungrammatical on account of the verb being transitive. Heavy NP Shift is not constrained in this way, as seen in (26).

(26) a. Melvin showed to be sitting/living/eating/spitting near the fountain, those derelicts who had been pestering him for money.
 b. Melvin showed to be kissing everyone in sight, those derelicts who had taken Love Potion #9.

Postal shows that the verbs which can appear in Locative Inversion constructions are exactly the same verbs as license *there*-Insertion, thereby reinforcing his argument that (24a) has a *there* subject (which may subsequently be deleted by the application of an additional rule).

Another argument against surface subjecthood of a postverbal NP in a Locative Inversion structure comes from control of the deleted subject of certain adverbial expressions. Example (27) presents the case of *without* + gerund phrases.

(27) a. Travis tricked Melba without deceiving himself/*herself.
 b. Melba was tricked by Travis without deceiving herself/*himself.

As (27) shows, only the surface subject can be identified as the subject of the gerund *deceiving*. In contrast, the postposed NP in a Locative Inversion structure cannot control a *without* + gerund clause.

(28) a. *Near the fountain (there) sat a large friendly gorilla without moving.
     b. Near the fountain, a large friendly gorilla sat without moving.

Example (28a) is ungrammatical on account of the NP *a large friendly gorilla* being postverbal, and thereby unable to control the gerund *moving* (cf. (28b) where it is preverbal). This all suggests that the postverbal NP in a Locative Inversion is not a subject and that these constructions are not relevant counterexamples to Postal's Heavy NP Shift argument.

### *Postal on Bresnan on Postal on methodology*

Here Postal responds to Bresnan's criticism regarding his failure to formalize the rule of Raising. First, he states, her objection is not altogether legitimate. He has in fact provided a formal structural description for the rule, and (he claims) the required structural change should be "obvious to the reader." Be this as it may, Postal contends that Bresnan has failed to demonstrate how (further) formalization of Raising might have avoided any of the problems that she raises in her critique. Finally, he asserts, the absence of formalization could not be a "research defect" of *On Raising*, if it is not also held to be a shortcoming of Chomsky's own writing (e.g., N. Chomsky 1970) or of Bresnan's critique itself, both of which have less formalization than Postal (1974).

While Postal's objections to Bresnan's criticism here are generally justified, his comparison of Postal (1974) with Chomsky (1970) is slightly less than appropriate. Chomsky (1970) sets out to motivate the exclusion of certain phenomena from syntax, and though it does not present a formalization of the implicated lexical representations of nominalizations, such a formalization does lie outside the purpose of the article. Postal (1974), on the other hand, does present syntactic argumentation for a rule of syntax without articulating the precise syntactic operation of the purported rule. While under other circumstances this might have been a methodological shortcoming (as Bresnan claims), Postal wrote *On Raising* during a period of major transition in his own theories of syntax. In 1974, the formal transformations of Standard Theory were no longer relevant and the formalizations of (the developing) Relational Grammar were not yet in place. Rather than labeling it "defeatist and unscientific," it would be more accurate to say that Postal's argumentation was designed to motivate his analysis under any possible formalization that could then have been imagined.

## 3   Bach (1977)

To this point, two views of RtoO have been presented. Postal's asserts that an RtoO syntactic rule must apply to such structures (in order to preserve the coherence of other parts of the grammar, such as Reflexivization), while Chomsky denies the existence of an RtoO rule (contending that the work of Postal's RtoO rule is better done by a set of general conditions). At the same time, Postal and Chomsky do agree on the Deep Structure (DS) of these constructions. That is, they both understand the postverbal, preinfinitival NP in (29) to be the underlying syntactic subject of the infinitival complement clause.

(29)   Harry believes them to have left.

Enter Bach.

Bach presents a third, alternative view of these constructions that he calls the "No-Rule Hypothesis" (and which he entertains as a plausible analysis, though not necessarily the correct one).[3] On the one hand, he agrees with Chomsky that (29) is not derived through the application of a syntactic rule. On the other, he thinks that Postal has got the Surface Structure (SS) right. That is to say, Bach suggests that *them* in (29) could be the underlying and surface object of the verb *believe*. These three positions can be compared in (30), abstracting away from these authors' particular views of the Phrase Stucture (PS) component and grammatical primitives.

(30)   a.   DS:    [$_{VP}$believe [$_S$them to have left ]]           Postal 1974
             SS:    [$_{VP}$believe [$_{NP}$them ] [$_S$ to have left ]]
         b.           [$_{VP}$believe [$_S$them to have left ]]           Chomsky 1973
         c.           [$_{VP}$believe [$_{NP}$them ] to [$_{VP}$have left ]]   Bach 1977

In elaborating his position, Bach admits that Postal's arguments concerning the constituent structure of (29) are compelling. In particular, he thinks that Postal has successfully shown the following: (i) the NP-to-VP string in (30) is not a constituent (e.g., Postal's Right Node Raising argument), (ii) the preinfinitival NP is not a subject (e.g., the Heavy NP Shift evidence), and (iii) the preinfinitival NP is an object (e.g., the distribution of adverbs). This said, Bach claims that these arguments in no way compel an analysis in which Raising has applied. As Bach states, Postal's "arguments show that Chomsky's surface structure is wrong; but they do not show that this must result from the operation of a rule, rather than being directly generated in the base" (1977:625).

This creates the possibility of a "No-Rule Hypothesis" in which *believe* and *persuade* in (31) have identical syntactic complement structure.

(31)   a.   We believed Paul to be nice.
         b.   We persuaded Paul to be nice.

Under this view, the difference between (31a) and (31b) is mediated through the addition in the latter instance of a semantic rule that causes the NP *Paul* to be interpreted as a thematic complement of the verb *persuade* (in addition to being the subject of the following infinitive).

In posing this alternative (in which the syntax of *believe* and *persuade* is identical), Bach points out a fundamental flaw with Postal's motivation for asserting

[$_{VP}$believe [$_S$them to have left]] as the DS for (29). At least in part, the DS in (31a) and the structure in (31b) are motivated (for both Postal and Chomsky) by a theory in which two clauses with logically equivalent meaning are assumed to share a common underlying structure. In this instance, Postal would point to underlying synonymy of (29) and (32).

(32) Harry believes they have left.

If (29) and (32) are logically equivalent and if (32) must have an S-complement in Deep Structure, then so must (29). However, evidence in Bresnan (1970, 1972) (as well as in Postal 1974) suggests that finite and non-finite complements are not equivalent in meaning. Consider (33).

(33) a. We found Hillary to be very alert.
b. We found that Hillary was very alert.

Bach points out that "a *for*-clause denotes the kind of thing that a *that*-clause names an instance of" and is an EVENTUALITY, and to the extent that finite and infinitival clauses have distinct meanings, it would be fair to say that they need not have a common underlying structure. Thus, one might conclude that there is no more (or less) motivation to provide (29) and (32) with a common Deep [syntactic] Structure than there is to provide (31a) and (31b) with one.

One therefore can, if one chooses to, provide (31a) and (31b) with the same underlying and surface syntactic representation, as in (34).

(34) [$_S$we [$_{VP}$believed/persuaded [$_{NP}$Paul ] to [$_{VP}$be nice ]]]

Both clauses will require a semantic rule by which *Paul* is interpreted as the logical subject of *be nice*, and in the latter case, an additional rule will require that *Paul* also be interpreted as the logical object of *persuade*. As Bach states, this solution while simplifying the syntax requires powerful semantic machinery, e.g., one would now need a meaning postulate for *believe* to guarantee the equivalence of (29) and (32), which no longer have the same underlying structure. So, plausibly the cost of each analysis is the same, and decisions must be based on other factors.

The "No-Rule Hypothesis" presented in Bach is in fact related to an entire family of non-derivational syntactic solutions, including Montague Grammar and its derivatives (Categorial Grammar and Generalized Phrase Structure Grammar (GPSG)) along with Lexical Functional Grammar (LFG) and Head Driven Phrase Structure Grammar (HPSG). An LFG analysis (see Bresnan 1982) for a sentence such as (31a) is in fact quite similar, in its fundamental conceptualization, to Bach's partial formalization above. As is true of the theory as a whole, the LFG account eschews rule application such as that found in Postal or Chomsky. LFG representations encode surface c(onstituent)-structure and assume predicates to possess underlying a(rgument)-structure (responsible for the articulation of semantic relations between constituents). These two types of information can be represented as in (35) (note that this is not the formal

LFG notation but is rather an attempt to convey informally these aspects of the analysis).

(35) c-structure: [$_S$we [$_{VP}$believed [$_{NP}$Paul ] [$_{VP}$to be nice ]]]
   a-structure: believe < (we)$_{EXP}$(Paul be nice)$_{THEME}$ >
   be-nice < (Paul)$_{THEME}$ >

The c-structure in (35) is similar to Bach's proposal in (34). The a-structure establishes that *believe* expresses a semantic relation between the EXPERIENCER *we* and the propositional THEME *Paul be nice*, and additionally that *Paul* is the THEME of the predicate *be nice*. Crucially, the NP *Paul* is not an independent semantic argument of *believe*, even though it stands in the c-structure as its complement.

This would presumably be sufficient, were it not for the fact that semantic relations (i.e., a-structure) cannot tell the entire story. Recall from chapter 3, section 2, the discussion of case preservation in Icelandic raising constructions as reported in Andrews (1982). The crucial example is repeated here in (36).

(36) Hann    telur    barninu    í   barnaskap sínum
    he.NOM  believe  the.child.DAT in foolishness his
    hafa     batnað             veikin.
    to.have  recovered.from     the.disease.NOM
    'He believes, in his foolishness, the child to have recovered from the disease.'

In (36), the logical subject of the infinitival complement and surface object of the verb *telur* 'believe' is *barninu* 'the child,' an NP having dative case. Normally, the raised NP in an Icelandic raising construction is accusative. However, here the embedded verb is *batnað* 'recover from,' which requires that its syntactic subject be dative. The preservation of dative case on the raised NP (even when this NP undergoes subsequent passivization) is evidence that this NP is a syntactic subject of the embedded verb, even while it functions as the syntactic object of the matrix raising verb *telur*. This relation, called "structure sharing," is expressed in LFG as "functional control." Adding the f(unctional)-structure to (35) yields a representation that encodes the additional information expressed in (37).

(37) c-structure: [$_S$we [$_{VP}$believed [$_{NP}$Paul ] [$_{VP}$to be nice ]]]
   a-structure: believe < (we)$_{EXP}$(Paul be nice)$_{THEME}$ >
   be-nice < (Paul)$_{THEME}$ >
   f-structure: PREDICATE    = believe
                SUBJECT      = we
                OBJECT       = Paul ←
                COMPLEMENT = [ PREDICATE = be nice ]
                             [ SUBJECT   = ──────── ]

As the f-structure representation in (37) shows, *Paul* functions simultaneously as the object of the matrix clause and the subject of the complement. This structure sharing is graphically represented in (37) by the line connecting the f-structures for the matrix object and the embedded subject. In this way, the NP *Paul* can be seen to possess two grammatical functions (or relations) in (31a), even while it only has one semantic role in the a-structure. By introducing grammatical functions into the representation, supplementing the a-structure and c-structure (which is all that Bach finds necessary), LFG effectively admits a largely syntactic solution to the problem of Raising, one that has more in common with Postal's syntactic proposal than with the wholly non-syntactic solution offered in Bach.

It is significant, and important to mention here, that the LFG representation of Control is syntactically identical to Raising, with regard to the c-structure and f-structure portions of the representation. Arguments for this approach are provided in Bresnan (1982), and empirical evidence from Russian in Neidle (1982).[4] Accordingly, example (31b) with the control verb *persuade* is taken to have the structure sketched out in (38).

(38)  c-structure: [$_S$we [$_{VP}$persuaded [$_{NP}$Paul ] [$_{VP}$to be nice ]]]
      a-structure: persuade < (we)$_{EXP}$(**Paul**)$_{GOAL}$ (Paul be nice)$_{THEME}$ >
                   be-nice < (Paul)$_{THEME}$ >
      f-structure: PREDICATE   = persuade
                   SUBJECT     = we
                   OBJECT      = Paul
                   COMPLEMENT  = [ PREDICATE = be nice ]
                                 [ SUBJECT   = ─────── ]

Notice that the only salient difference between the two structures involves the addition of an extra semantic role for *Paul* in the a-structure of *persuade*. This syntactic assimilation of raising and obligatory control structures (i.e., complements of Subject Control verbs such as *try* and Object Control verbs such as *persuade*) is fully in keeping with the proposals of Bach, above, and quite distinct from the typical treatment of obligatory Control in the Chomskyan tradition (which is taken to involve a phonologically null category PRO in the subject position of the lower infinitival clause that is associated with a matrix NP via an interpretive rule). Chapter 13 will explore much more fully the relationship of Raising to Control, along with arguments for treating them together and for treating them separately.

## Notes

1  Lightfoot (1976) was another pro-Chomsky critique of Postal (1974), but it is fair to say that Bresnan's review generated more discussion.
2  The ungrammaticality of (5b) and (6b), as instances of illicit Heavy NP Shift, is potentially subject to debate. These sentences do improve somewhat when particularly heavy NPs are so displaced, as in (i).

   (i)  I convinced to disqualify themselves, all of the antifeminist candidates who voted against the organization's basic charter.

3   A good deal of Bach's discussion is devoted to an understanding of how differing initial assumptions (i.e., theories) lead directly to distinct (and distinctly plausible) analyses. So as not to misrepresent Bach, then, it must be noted that his "No-Rule Hypothesis" is presented as one potentially attractive analysis of these constructions. His overall conclusion, though, is that "there is a lot of work left to do" before the correct analysis can be identified.

4   Davies (1988) demonstrates that "structure sharing" cannot work as an account for these structures in all languages. In particular, where Icelandic raising clauses and passives are shown to exhibit case preservation and case preservation is taken as evidence for the necessity of functional Control, Quechua raising structures exhibit properties that suggest that functional Control cannot always be right. The relevant evidence comes from the grammatical case on the derived subject of experiencer predicates. As Davies shows, these verbs require their subjects to have accusative case. Unlike Icelandic, though, the lexically governed case of these subjects is not preserved when these subject NPs undergo derivations such as Raising. Specifically, when they undergo RtoS, they occur in nominative case. Therefore, Davies concludes, it is not the case that all instances of Raising involve functional Control (but that is all that LFG theory allows as a mechanism to derive these).

# UNIT II

# EXTENSIONS AND REINTERPRETATIONS OF STANDARD THEORY

## INTRODUCTION: BRANCHING PATHS OF INQUIRY

The 1970s brought increasing theoretical innovations which centrally affect the analyses of Raising and Control. Syntactic theory became more fragmented than it was during the heyday of Standard Theory with many generative-based approaches emerging, in part as a reaction to developments with the Extended Standard Theory. By the end of the decade there were a large number of competing frameworks, which in part may have inspired James McCawley's selection for the title of his 1982 book, *30 million theories of grammar*. In 1979, the University of Wisconsin-Milwaukee hosted a conference of invited proponents of 14 distinct frameworks to present analyses of a common data set and outline the major assumptions and theoretical devices of these frameworks. The resulting volume, *Current approaches to syntax*, was published in 1980 (Moravcsik and Wirth 1980). So the 1970s saw the rise of competing theories sometimes with very different analyses of the same phenomena.

This unit examines the state of syntactic theory from two distinct perspectives that evolved in the mid to late 1970s, the first being that of Perlmutter and Postal's Relational Grammar Theory and the second being that of Chomsky's Revised Extended Standard Theory. Hence the subtitle here, "branching paths of inquiry." These paths of inquiry, as we have seen, began to diverge a few years earlier with the publication of Postal (1974) and Chomsky (1973), and here they seem to bear less resemblance to one another than they did in unit I.

As one of the more popular and influential of the alternative theories of this period, David Perlmutter and Paul Postal's Relational Grammar (RG) is a framework that assumed that grammatical relations such as subject, direct object, and so on were the basic building blocks of syntactic analyses, a break from the Transformational Grammar (TG) assumption that grammatical relations could be configurationally defined on the basis of phrase structure. The RG approach falls into a more populous class of rule-based approaches to grammar, in which the goal of syntactic inquiry was understood to be that of uncovering grammatical universals and thereby achieving the broadest empirical coverage that a theory might offer. In this sense, RG exemplifies an inductive (i.e., bottom-up) theory of grammar, in which the theoretical hypotheses are applied to empirical cross-linguistic evidence to achieve universally and typologically valid generalizations about syntactic structure. Lexical Functional Grammar (LFG) also fits this model. Chapter 6 includes a sketch of RG along with a reading from Perlmutter and Postal's seminal work, "The Relational Succession Law," which postulates a cross-linguistic generalization regulating raising constructions. Their chapter is typical of the RG program, which primarily focused on abstracting away from the morphosyntactic idiosyncracies of particular languages in order to uncover general rules that could apply cross-linguistically.

Chapter 7 examines the continuing developments of the Extended Standard Theory as embodied in Chomsky and Lasnik's "Filters and Control," parts of which are included in a reading. In general, in this framework there is a move away from conditions on rules to conditions on representation, so that movements are more freely allowed but ill-formed structures are filtered or ruled out as semantically uninterpretable at a level of Logical Form (LF). In contrast with RG, Revised Extended Standard Theory (REST) is a deductive (i.e., top-down) theory of grammar, positing (plausible) linguistic generalizations and universals and seeking to confirm these with empirical data. We shall see in chapter 7's discussion of Chomsky and Lasnik that the central idea behind their approach was to attain a level of computational simplicity and generality that would suffice to account for the universal faculty of language and would accommodate a theory of linguistic innateness. While the REST framework still eschews a movement analysis for RtoO (as Chomskyan theory continued to do until 1990), these further refinements in the determination of and interpretation of anaphoric relations leads to motivation for movement in RtoS, lacking in Chomsky (1973). Additionally, the framework includes both interpretive rules for obligatory control of PRO and a rule of Equi-NP Deletion to handle verbs such as *want*.

In this unit, the differences between these two approaches are made salient. Postal's (1974) rule-based approach to raising constructions is seen to stand at the beginning of a long quest for universal rules. Chomsky's (1973) striving for simplicity in the transformational component, by invoking conditions on transformations, can be taken to lead naturally to the transposition of such mechanisms out of the transformational component entirely, and to their articulation as filters and rules of construal.

# CHAPTER 6

# RELATIONAL GRAMMAR: PERLMUTTER AND POSTAL'S "THE RELATIONAL SUCCESSION LAW"

## 1  Background to "The Relational Succession Law"

In "The Relational Succession Law," Perlmutter and Postal (P&P) present an early glimpse into Relational Grammar (RG), the theory to which Postal refers in *On Raising* (see chapter 3). This chapter will briefly set the context for the Relational Succession Law (RSL) proposal, and then (following the reading) critically examine some of the assertions set forth in the article. Following that, it will lay out the RG model for raising and control structures, as it developed subsequently. The purpose of these last two sections will be to familiarize the reader with the incorporation of RSL into a larger, relationally based theory of syntax.

The RSL represents one attempt to abstract away from language-specific particulars of transformations and present a principle that constrains the application of a particular set of transformations, namely raising transformations. In this regard the RSL bears some similarity to principles such as Subjacency, but importantly it differs from such a principle by being limited to a subdomain of rules, namely raising rules. Crucially, the RSL is stated in terms of grammatical relations. Informally, the RSL states that an element raised out of a (clausal) constituent will come to have the same grammatical relation as that of the constituent out of which it was raised. Thus any NP raised out of a clausal subject will be a subject, and any NP raised out of a clausal object will be an object.

The RSL is devised to apply cross-linguistically, and its applicability to Raising in other languages should be apparent. Although there are differences in word order and morphological effects among Icelandic, Chamorro, Niuean, and other languages, if the analyses of Raising are correct, they follow the RSL. Consider first the Niuean data from chapter 3.

(1) a. To maeke ke lagomatai he ekekafo e    tama ē.
       FUT possible SBJ help      ERG doctor  ABS child this
       'The doctor could help this child.'
    b. To maeke e   ekekafo ke lagomatai e    tama ē.
       FUT possible ABS doctor  SBJ help      ABS child this
       'The doctor could help this child.'

In (1a), the complement clause is the subject of the modal predicate *maeke* 'be possible.' In (1b), the embedded subject, *ekekafo* 'doctor,' has raised into the matrix clause and is the subject of the matrix intransitive clause. Note that this NP occurs in canonical subject position, immediately following the verb in this VSO language, and takes the absolutive case one expects on intransitive subjects. Thus, *ekekafo* appears to have raised out of a subject complement and assumed the subject relation, in accordance with the RSL. Raising in Icelandic also appears to conform to the principle, (2).

(2) a. Þeir    telja   að  Maria  hafi skrifað ritgerðina.
       they.NOM believe that M.NOM has written  the.thesis.ACC
       'They believe that Mary has written her thesis.'
    b. Þeir    telja   Maríu hafa      skrifað ritgerðina.
       they.NOM believe M.ACC to.have written  the.thesis.ACC
       'They believe Mary to have written her thesis.'

In (2b), the subject of the embedded object complement, Mary, has raised to become the object of the matrix clause. Not only is it in immediate postverbal position, as expected in this SVO language, but it is marked with the structural case assigned to Icelandic direct objects, namely accusative. Thus, these Icelandic data are consistent with the prediction of the RSL. The following excerpt presents empirical support for the RSL and provides a theoretical rationale for adopting it as a cross-linguistic universal.

# READING FROM PERLMUTTER AND POSTAL (1972/83)

David Perlmutter and Paul Postal, editor's foreword and sections 1, 2, 3.1, 5.1, and 7 (pp. 30–9, 42–3, 49–52) from "The Relational Succession Law" in *Studies in relational grammar, vol. 1*, ed. David Perlmutter (Chicago: University of Chicago Press, 1972 [1983]). Reprinted by permission of University of Chicago Press.

## Editor's foreword [pp. 30–1][1]

The paper published here is a somewhat abridged version of a manuscript left unfinished in December 1972.[2] The basic framework and orientation of the paper are transformational throughout. As it was nearing completion, however, the authors' theoretical orientation began to change – most significantly in regarding grammatical relations as primitives of grammatical theory rather than as concepts defined in terms of other notions and in conceiving of the structures on which cyclical rules operate as representing grammatical relations but not the linear order of elements. The discrepancy between this view of linguistic structure and the transformational framework in which the paper was written led the authors to decide not to publish it at that time.

The paper consists of one basic idea – the Relational Succession Law – and a partial working out of its consequences. This idea, when pushed to the limit, had many more consequences than the authors saw at the time. In a sense, much of the subsequent development of relational grammar consisted of a further working out of the consequences of ideas that appear for the first time in this paper. Thus, although the paper is written in a transformational framework and although the authors saw themselves as advocating a more significant role for grammatical relations within transformational grammar rather than a new theory, in retrospect this was the first paper in relational grammar.

There are two reasons for including the paper in this volume [i.e., in Perlmutter, *Studies in relational grammar 1*]. First, it gives a view of the earliest stage in the development of relational grammar. It argues that the *effect* of certain transformations is determined by grammatical relations. The subsequent attempt to make some of the ideas in this paper precise led us to abandon the transformational framework in which it is embedded. Second, this paper makes some theoretical claims that have played an important role in relational grammar but have not previously appeared in print.

The paper shares most of the basic assumptions of transformational grammar. The conception of sentence structure is that of a derivation (a sequence of structures), with transformations mapping one structure in the derivation onto

---

[1] The editor is indebted to Judith Aissen, Sandra Chung, and Carlota Smith for discussion of the original manuscript and to Judith Aissen, Terry Klokeid, Stephen Marlett, Paul Postal, Geoffrey Pullum, Eduardo Raposo, and Carol Rosen for comments on the first draft of the Editor's Foreword and Afterword. Work on the Foreword and the Afterword was supported in part by the National Science Foundation through Grant No. BNS 7817498 to the University of California, San Diego.

Most of the substantive points in this paper were presented by Perlmutter in talks at the University of London and Cambridge University in November 1972, by Postal at the Université de Paris VIII (Faculté de Vincennes) in February 1973, and by Perlmutter at the University of Tokyo in June 1973.

[2] The terminology of the paper has been changed to conform to more recent usage.

the next. The structures themselves are constituent structure trees, with VSO constituent order assumed for English under the influence of the arguments in McCawley 1970 and Postal 1974. (The paper was written before Berman's [1974] now classic critique of the VSO hypothesis.) Consistent with its assumption of derivations and sequential rule application, the paper assumes a cyclical theory of grammar and a division of syntactic rules into (at least) two groups – cyclical and postcyclical.

The conception of ascensions in the paper is that of rules that move constituents, and there is considerable discussion of the derived constituent structure produced by such rules. This discussion is in tune with the transformational approach to grammatical relations which, following Chomsky 1965, conceived of grammatical relations as derivative concepts defined in terms of the positions of NPs in trees. The paper follows that tradition in speaking of raising "into subject position" and "into object position," "subject" and "object" being conceived of as terms referring to NPs occupying particular *positions* in trees.

The paper is also transformational in addressing itself to a number of issues that arise internal to a transformational framework, e.g., whether various sentential complements are dominated by NP-nodes, what is the relative order of application of Passive and Extraposition. Like most other transformational works at that time, it deals primarily with data from English. Examples from French and Portuguese are cited to show that the generalizations established for English are not confined to that language, and a construction in Malagasy is used to illustrate the generalizations' validity for a non-Indo-European language [not reproduced here]. The Afterword reexamines the paper from the perspective of current relational grammar.

# The Relational Succession Law

## 1 Some Concepts defined [p. 32]

Languages (may) contain, we claim, a subset of cyclic rules which we will refer to as 'Ascension Rules'. An ascension rule is a cyclic rule which takes some NP constituent, $NP_a$, from a position within some immediate constituent, A,[3] of an S, $S_1$, in an input tree, $T_j$, and, operating on the $S_1$ cycle, makes the correspondent of $NP_a$ an immediate constituent of the correspondent of $S_1$ in the output tree, $T_{j+1}$.[4] Schematically:

---

[3] A stronger definition would result if constraints were provided on the categories to which A could belong. We return to this below, arguing that A can be NP and nothing else.

[4] This account is vague in not specifying whether an ascension rule is a pure movement rule or a doubling rule (leaving a pronominal 'copy' in the original position). We suggest that ascension rules can be of either type, and further that the contrast between the two may be at least partly predictable from the structure of the constituent A (e.g., where A is an island in the sense of Ross 1967, any ascension from A must be a doubling rule).

(1)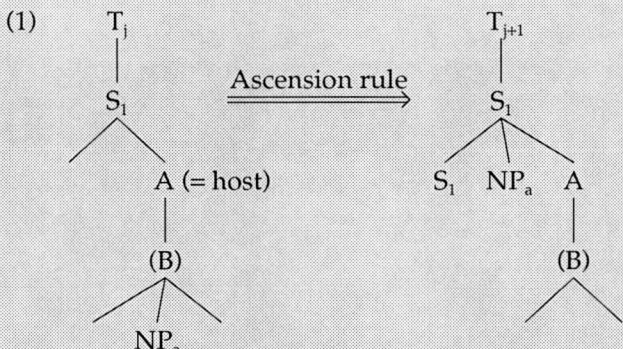

The NP (NP$_a$) that is moved by an ascension rule we will refer to as the 'ascendee'. The constituent A in (1) out of which the ascendee ascends we will call the 'host' constituent. Finally, we assume a linguistic theory in which grammatical relations such as 'subject of', 'direct object of', and 'indirect object of' are defined.[5] We will use the term 'object' as a cover term for both direct and indirect objects.

The schematization of ascension rules in (1) contains several so far unjustified assumptions – in particular, the asymmetry that the ascendee ends up *to the left* of its host. We return to this point below, suggesting, first, that this asymmetry is a characteristic of all ascension rule derivations and, second, that it is a consequence of the principle governing ascension rules that this paper proposes.

It should also be stressed that we are assuming that rules like Topicalization and WH-Movement are not cyclical and hence not even possible candidates for inclusion in the set of ascension rules.[6]

## 2 A generalization governing well-known ascension rules in English [pp. 33–6]

In English, the best-known ascension rules are unquestionably the rules which have been called variously 'IT-Replacement', 'Pronoun Replacement', or '(Subject)-Raising',[7] on the one hand, and 'Tough Movement' or 'Object

---

[5] Grammatical relations are fundamental to our account. We claim that they play a key defining role for cyclic rules. However, our conception of grammatical relations differs considerably from that in most past generative work, specifically in that we claim that derived structures play a basic role in characterizing such relations.

[6] It is worth noting that our view that such rules are not cyclic follows not only from particular empirical considerations (see Postal 1972) but from a general theory of the cyclic–postcyclic contrast according to which it is impossible for unbounded rules of this sort to be cyclic. [Editor's note: The allusion here is to the 'Cyclicity Law', which was stated in Perlmutter and Postal 1974 as follows: "If a rule creates or destroys termhood, it is a cyclical rule." In later versions of relational grammar, in which the notion of rules converting one structure into another was abandoned, the cycle, and hence the Cyclicity Law, ceased to have any meaning.]

[7] See the discussion in Rosenbaum 1967, Ross 1967, Postal 1971, Perlmutter 1971, Kiparsky and Kiparsky 1970.

Shift',[8] on the other. We refer to these respectively as 'Subject Raising' and 'Object Raising'. The former has for some time been taken to be involved in the derivations of the b-examples of:

(2) a. It turns out that Melvin is incoherent.
    b. Melvin turns out to be incoherent.

(3) a. It happens that I am leaving.
    b. I happen to be leaving.

The latter has for some time been taken to be involved in the derivations of the b-examples in:

(4) a. It is easy to please John.
    b. John is easy to please.

(5) a. It will be a cinch to solve that problem.
    b. That problem will be a cinch to solve.

Subject Raising also operates, we claim, in the derivations of the b-examples in:

(6) a. Harry believes (that) Joan is pregnant.
    b. Harry believes Joan to be pregnant.

(7) a. Harry expects (that) Joan will return.
    b. Harry expects Joan to return.

This latter claim is challenged by Chomsky (1971, 1973) but defended at great length by Postal (1974). We are assuming here that the rule operative in (6b) and (7b) is the same as that operative in (2b) and (3b), an assumption now traditional (since Rosenbaum 1967), outlined by McCawley (1970) and discussed by Postal (1974). There is nothing in the present discussion, however, that hinges on this assumption. Our remarks here would remain unaffected if it were assumed that there are two distinct rules, Subject Raising$_1$, operative in (2) and (3), and Subject Raising$_2$, operative in (6) and (7).

If one takes these assumptions as given, there is a regularity in the derivations sanctioned by the English rules Subject Raising and Object Raising which we believe has not previously been made explicit, a regularity governing the relations between the position which an ascendee assumes in the $S_1$ of $T_{j+1}$ of (1) and the position of the constituent A of $T_j$ from which the ascendee is removed. It is our purpose here to uncover this regularity and to suggest the hypothesis that it is the direct consequence of an invariant principle of Universal Grammar, which we will take steps toward formulating precisely.

---

[8] See the discussion in Postal 1971 and Bresnan 1971.

Let us begin with the sentences in (2a) and (3a). We assume, as has been traditional in generative work and unchallenged until recently,[9] that sentences like (2a) and (3a) are derived by application of Extraposition,[10] and hence that *underlying these constructions are sentential subject NPs*. From this, together with the assumption that structures essentially like those underlying (2a), (3a), etc., also underlie respectively (2b), (3b), etc.,[11] it follows that in these cases an ascendee moves out of a sentential subject NP into subject position, or, put differently, that Subject Raising in these cases has the effect of mapping a tree with a main verb *turn out, happen*, etc., and a sentential subject into a derived tree in which these main verbs have ascendees as subjects. The operation performed by Subject Raising in these examples, then, is:[12]

(8)

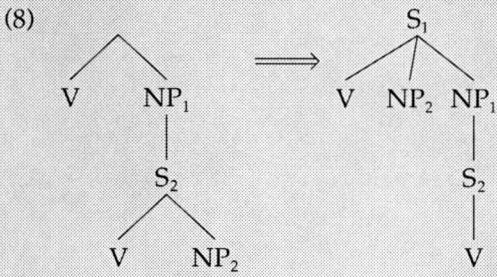

Turning next to (4) and (5), we also assume (as has been standard) that the a-examples involve application of Extraposition, and hence that these examples have underlying sentential subjects. It follows that, just as in the Subject Raising cases in (2) and (3), Object Raising has the effect of moving the ascendee out of a sentential subject into subject position. Thus, the operation performed by Object Raising is:

---

[9] Emonds (1970, 1972) argues that the complements in such cases are generated directly at the right end of verb phrases, so that such sentences never involve sentential subjects. The development of the present argument provides one objection to this analysis. See also Higgins 1973 and Postal 1974. [Editor's note: Generating such complements at the right end of verb phrases was also proposed by Kajita (1966) and Bresnan (1972), and by Gross (1968) and Ruwet (1972) for French. This analysis was subsequently adopted in a number of other studies.]

[10] For extensive discussion of this rule and its role in such derivations see Rosenbaum 1967 and Ross 1967.

[11] This assumption is challenged by Bresnan (1971), who argues in an analysis partially similar to but distinct from that of Emonds (1970, 1972) that sentences like (2b) and (3b) are generated by a rule operating not on a sentential subject but rather on a complement generated directly at the extreme end of verb phrases. Again, the argument presented in the present paper provides an objection to that analysis.

[12] We adopt here underlying structures in which English has verb-initial structure, as proposed by McCawley (1970) and further supported by Bach (1971), Ross (1970), and Postal (1974). The argument of the present paper would be unaffected, however, if the underlying order of major constituents in English should turn out not to be VSO. In the absence of any evidence for a VP constituent, we assume that no such constituent exists. Subjects, direct objects, and indirect objects of a verb are thus its sisters.

(9)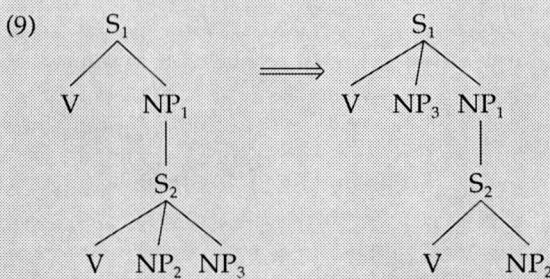

Finally, consider (6) and (7). Here the a-examples have 'sentential objects' and Subject Raising makes the ascendee a derived object, performing the operation:[13]

(10)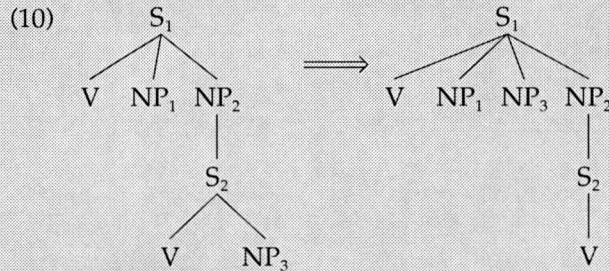

The table in (11) summarizes those aspects of Subject Raising into subject position, Object Raising, and Subject Raising into object position with which we are concerned here.

(11)

|  | GR of ascendee before ascension | GR of ascendee after ascension | GR of host NP before ascension |
|---|---|---|---|
| Subject Raising into subject position | Subject | Subject | Subject |
| Object Raising | Nonsubject | Subject | Subject |
| Subject Raising into object position | Subject | Direct Object | Direct Object |

The table in (11) shows that there is no correlation between the grammatical relation of the ascendee after ascension and its grammatical relation before

---

[13] In (10), as in (8), the embedded sentence contains an intransitive verb. Nothing of relevance to the argument is changed if the embedded verb is transitive.

ascension. Strikingly, however, the grammatical relation of the ascendee after ascension is always the same as that of its host NP prior to ascension. If an NP ascends out of a (sentential) NP that is in subject position, it becomes a subject, and if it ascends out of a (sentential) NP that is in object position, it becomes an object.

Assuming that the constituent A in (1) is in all cases an NP, we can state the generalization:

(12) *The Relational Succession Law*
An ascendee assumes within the clause (S1 in (1)) into which it ascends the grammatical relation of its host NP (the NP (A in (1)) out of which it ascends).

Under the assumptions we have made, the Relational Succession Law is true of all derivations involving Subject Raising and Object Raising in English.[14]

We now go one step further. We propose that the Relational Succession Law is not just a generalization about certain derivations in English, but rather a constraint on possible rules in human languages. That is, the Relational Succession Law is a principle of Universal Grammar to which all ascension rules in human languages conform. In §3, we examine some consequences of the incorporation of this principle into linguistic theory.

## 3 Some consequences of the Relational Succession Law

### 3.1 *Some impossible rules [pp. 36–9]*

An immediate consequence of the Relational Succession Law is that it rules out in principle certain rules that would otherwise be potential rules of human languages.

Consider first Subject Raising into subject position in English, as illustrated in (8). It is possible a priori that there could be a language just like English except that it has a Subject Raising rule which, instead of placing the raised NP to the left of the clause out of which it is promoted, as in (8), places it to the right of it, as in:

---

[14] If it were possible for Object Raising to raise NPs in embedded objects in subject clauses, deriving (i-b) from the structure underlying (i-a):

(i) a. It will be a cinch to say you solved that problem.
    b. That problem will be a cinch to say you solved.

*that problem* would still be moving out of a sentential subject: *to say you solved that problem*. As ascension rules are sketched in (1), the ascendee becomes the sister of the host constituent A. Since we find sentences like (i-b) of doubtful well-formedness, the point may be academic.

(13)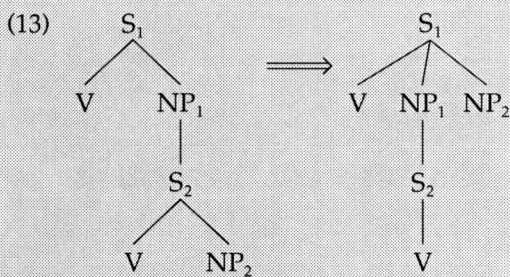

Call this rule 'Subject Raising 1A'. Subject Raising 1A would derive (14b) and (15b) from the structures that underlie (14a) and (15a), respectively.

(14) a. It turns out that Melvin is incoherent.
b. *To be incoherent turns out Melvin.

(15) a. It happens that I am leaving.
b. *To be leaving happens me.

Subject Raising 1A is easily formulable as a transformation, and no constraints on transformations have yet been established that would rule it out in principle.[15] Yet we claim that no language can have Subject Raising 1A in its grammar. The Relational Succession Law predicts just this.

Turning now to Object Raising, it is possible a priori that natural languages could have rules which promote the object of the complement in (9) by placing it under $S_1$ immediately to the *right* of the host NP, $NP_1$. Call such a rule 'Object Raising A'. It would perform the operation:

(16)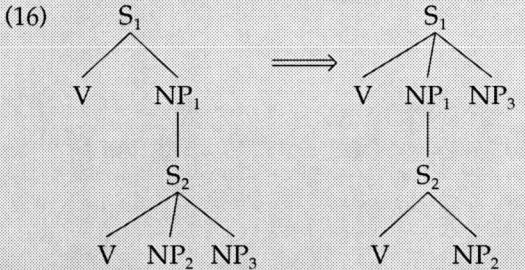

Thus, Object Raising A would derive (17b) and (18b) from the structures underlying (17a) and (18a), respectively.

(17) a. It is easy to please John.
b. *To please is easy John.

---

[15] Emonds (1970, 1972) makes a proposal to this effect. Emonds' proposal, however, works only within his system, which requires that *that*-clauses and infinitives *not* be dominated by NP. However, Higgins 1973, Postal 1974, and the present paper present evidence that this aspect of Emonds' system is incorrect. His proposal to rule out transformations like (13) falls with it.

(18) a. It will be a cinch to solve that problem.
b. *To solve will be a cinch that problem.

Object Raising A is easily formulable as a transformation, but we claim that no such rule will be found in any natural language because any such rule would violate the Relational Succession Law.

Finally, consider Subject Raising into object position. Instead of putting the ascendee, $NP_3$ in (10), immediately to the left of the host NP, it is a priori possible that Subject Raising could place the ascendee to the right of the host NP, performing the operation:

(19)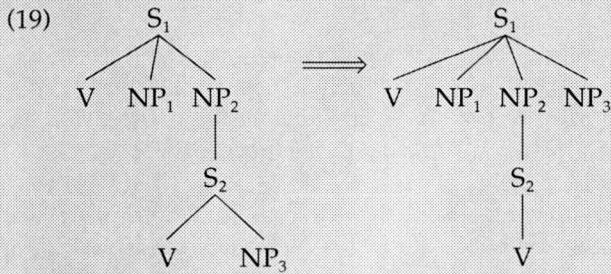

Call this rule 'Subject Raising 2A'. It would convert the structures underlying (20a) and (21a) into (20b) and (21b), respectively.

(20) a. Harry believes (that) Joan is pregnant.
b. *Harry believes to be pregnant Joan.

(21) a. Harry expects (that) Joan will return.
b. *Harry expects to return Joan.

There is also another possibility – a rule of Subject Raising that places the subject of the object complement in subject position in the matrix. Call this rule 'Subject Raising 2B'. It would perform the operation:

(22)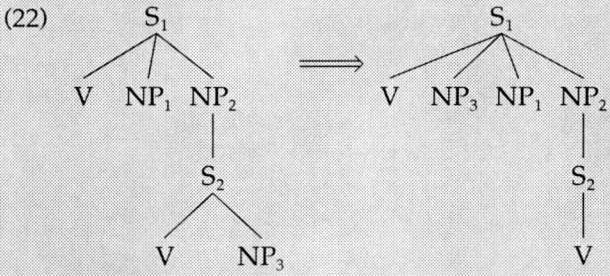

Subject Raising 2B would thus derive (23b) and (24b) from the structures underlying (23a) and (24a), respectively.

(23) a. Harry believes (that) Joan is pregnant.
     b. Joan believes Harry to be pregnant.

(24) a. Harry expects (that) Joan will return.
     b. Joan expects Harry to return.

Note that Subject Raising 2B would also generate (25b) from the structure underlying (25a).

(25) a. Jim expects (that) I will contradict myself.
     b. *I expect Jim to contradict myself.

Although Subject Raising 2A and Subject Raising 2B are formulable as transformations, both of these hypothetical rules violate the Relational Succession Law. They would therefore be impossible in any grammar constructed in accordance with a theory of Universal Grammar that incorporates the Relational Succession Law. Since such rules cannot, we claim, exist in any natural language, we propose that some appropriately precise formulation of the Relational Succession Law is a part of the theory of Universal Grammar.

In brief, the incorporation of the Relational Succession Law into Universal Grammar rules out in principle such hypothetical rules as Subject Raising 1A, Object Raising A, Subject Raising 2A, and Subject Raising 2B, while allowing the rules of Subject Raising 1, Object Raising, and Subject Raising 2.

## 5 Some ascension rules in other languages

### 5.1 Analogues of the English rules discussed [pp. 42–3]

If the Relational Succession Law is a part of Universal Grammar, then we expect to find in other languages rules like Subject Raising 1, Object Raising, and so on, but never rules like Subject Raising 1A, Subject Raising 2A, Subject Raising 2B, or Object Raising A. While we have made no large-scale investigation of this matter, our general experience with languages supports it. For instance, the Romance languages have analogues of both the English rules Subject Raising and Object Raising. This can be seen for French, for example, from such pairs as[16]

(29) a. Il semble que la porte de la cathédrale est fermée.
        'It seems that the door of the cathedral is closed.'
     b. La porte de la cathédrale semble être fermée.
        'The door of the cathedral seems to be closed.'

---

[16] For arguments supporting the analogue of Subject Raising 1 in French, see Ruwet 1970, 1972. For discussion of the analogue of Object Raising, see Kayne 1975, esp. pp. 16–17, and Gaatone 1970. For some further discussion of both rules in French, see Fauconnier 1971.

(30) a. Il est difficile de lire ces livres.
'It is difficult to read these books.'
b. Ces livres sont difficiles à lire.
'These books are difficult to read.'

In Portuguese, we also find analogues of Subject Raising and Object Raising, which relate such pairs as[17]

(31) a. Parece que os brasileiros têm ganho o jogo.
'It seems that the Brazilians have won the game.'
b. Os brasileiros parecem ter ganho o jogo.
'The Brazilians seem to have won the game.'

(32) a. Ele considera que essas pessoas são importantes.[18]
'He considers that those people are important.'
b. Ele considera essas pessoas importantes.
'He considers those people important.'

(33) a. É impossível ler estes livros.
'It is impossible to read these books.'
b. Estes livros são impossíveis de ler.
'These books are impossible to read.'

The Relational Succession Law provides an essential link in explaining why French and Portuguese can have the rules needed to generate (29b), (30b), (31b), (32b), and (33b), but not those to generate the c-sentences below from the corresponding a-sentences.

(29) c. *Etre fermé semble la porte de la cathédrale.
'To be closed seems the door of the cathedral.'

(30) c. *A lire est difficile ces livres.
'To read is difficult these books.'

(31) c. *Ter ganho o jogo parece os brasileiros.
'To have won the game seems the Brazilians.'

(32) c. *Essas pessoas consideram ele importantes.
'Those people consider him important.'[19]

---

[17] For evidence in support of the analogue of Subject Raising 1 in Portuguese, see Quícoli 1972, chap. 2.
[18] Speakers of Portuguese differ on whether *considerar* takes *que*-complements in surface structure, as in (32a).
[19] The English gloss is grammatical with a different meaning, derived from 'those people consider that he is important' rather than 'he considers that those people are important.' This confusion does not arise in Portuguese because of the plural ending on *importantes*.

(33) c. *De ler é impossível estes livros.
'To read is impossible these books.'

We suggest, then, that many languages will contain analogues of Subject Raising and/or Object Raising, since the Relational Succession Law permits these and in each case makes it possible to state the rule with a minimum of language-particular apparatus. Rules which ascend an NP from a sentential subject into superordinate object position or from a sentential object into superordinate subject position, however, will never be found.

## 7 The syntax of the host NP after ascension [pp. 49–52]

The Relational Succession Law states that each ascension rule has the effect of substituting for the term T of some grammatical relation of a verb an NP which was formerly a constituent of T. The question then naturally arises as to the status of the correspondent of the former term in the resulting structure. In other words, when part of a subject becomes the new subject, what is the relational status of (the remnant of) the old subject, and similarly for objects? This question takes on special importance in the context of attempts to define grammatical relations configurationally. For instance, if it is claimed that the direct object relation involves configurations like:

(47)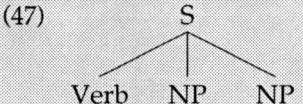

then application of an ascension rule to the sentential subject of an intransitive verb might turn the resulting verb into a transitive. Thus, given an underlying structure like:

(48)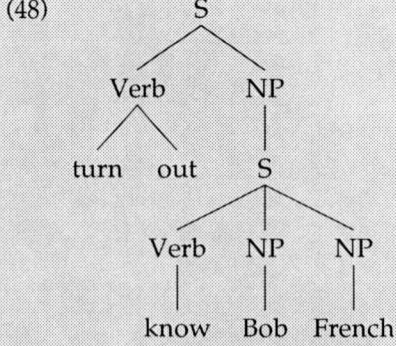

application of Subject Raising would generate:

(49)

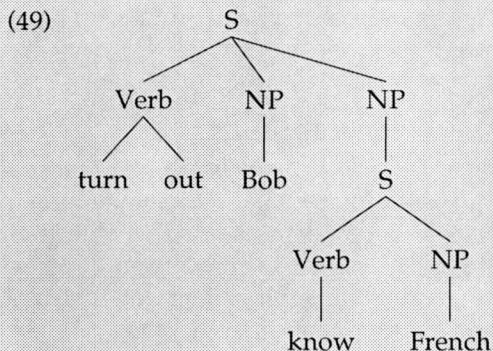

which has the form of (47), suggesting that the sentential remnant is now the direct object of *turn out*.

Such a result not only seems intuitively incorrect, there are certain grammatical facts which suggest that it is simply wrong. For instance, there is nothing to predict that Passive cannot apply to structures of the type (49). But it never can:

(50) a. *To know French was turned out by Bob.
 b. *To lie and cheat is tended by our president.
 c. *To be dead was happened by Napoleon.

Appeals to the stativity of the main verbs in such cases will not suffice, since many stative verbs permit passivization:

(51) a. That was understood by the researchers.
 b. That was believed by the troops.
 c. Tea parties are adored by little children.

We conjecture that the failure of passivization in such cases is a function of two principles: (i) Passive is inherently defined as applying to the direct object of a verb; (ii) the host NP ceases to be the term of any grammatical relation. If (ii) is the case, and if (i) is not only true but a consequence of general principles defining cyclic rules, then we not only predict the facts in *(50) with no special statements, but we arrive at the stronger prediction that parallel sentences in any other language will be ill-formed.

Let us make a further conjecture. Suppose not only that (ii) is valid, but that it is itself a consequence of an even deeper principle which says that if any rule on a cycle $S_j$ 'replaces' the term of one of the NP–verb relations, the NP bearing that relation then not only ceases to bear this relation, but cannot assume any new relation either. One consequence of this would be that in a case-marking language, where nominative is the case of the subject, accusative that of the direct object, operation of a rule like Passive could never turn the former subject into a direct object. This would mean that the analogue of Passive never functions in such a way that the former subject ends up marked accusative. Thus we do not expect to find paired sentences in any language of the form:

(52) a. wrote Bill/$_{NOM}$the letter/$_{ACC}$
b. written the letter/$_{NOM}$Bill/$_{ACC}$

Rather, we expect the former subject to be either marked with some oblique case (as in Russian) or else fitted with a special prepositional or postpositional marker, as in English, French, or German. From this relational point of view, Passive is seen as a rule which creates new derived subjects and one which is prevented by a universal principle from creating new direct objects.

This means that Passive is properly looked upon as a rule whose nature is to create new subjects (out of direct objects), rather than to create new objects. This contrasts with the apparently symmetrical situation possible for a statement of this rule in a nonrelational theory of grammar, in which, for instance, given a structure of either the forms:

(53) a. V NP NP
b. NP NP V

it seems quite arbitrary whether one says that the subject moves to the right or the object to the left. Our account leads us to a nonsymmetric statement of the form:

(54) The direct object becomes the subject.

Given the Relational Succession Law governing ascension rules, a priori there are many possibilities as to the syntax of the host NP after ascension:

(55) a. When the ascendee becomes superordinate subject, there will be two superordinate subjects; when it becomes superordinate object, there will be two superordinate objects.
b. After ascension, the host NP assumes a different grammatical relation.
c. After ascension, the host NP cannot bear any grammatical relation at all.
d. After ascension, the ascendee assumes a different grammatical relation if there is an independently motivated rule in the grammar to achieve this effect, e.g., a rule that changes a direct object into an indirect object if there is more than one direct object. Otherwise, ascension entails no additional changes in grammatical relations, both the host and the ascendee bearing the same relation after ascension.
e. After ascension, the host NP assumes a different grammatical relation if there is an independently motivated rule in the grammar to achieve this effect, e.g., a rule that changes a direct object into an indirect object if there is more than one direct object. Otherwise, the ascendee and the host NP both bear the grammatical relation to the verb borne by the host NP prior to ascension.

These are only some of the possibilities. We have conjectured that (55c) is the case on the basis of rather slim evidence because (55c) makes the strongest possible claim that is consistent with the data we are familiar with. We hope that this claim will stimulate research into the question, so that data from a variety of languages can be brought to bear on the issue.

## References

Anderson, Stephen R., and Kiparsky, Paul, eds. 1973. *A Festschrift for Morris Halle*. New York: Holt, Rinehart, & Winston.
Bach, Emmon. 1971. "Questions." *Linguistic Inquiry* 2:153–66.
Berman, Arlene. 1974. "On the VSO Hypothesis." *Linguistic Inquiry* 5:1–37.
Bresnan, Joan W. 1971. "Sentence Stress and Syntactic Transformations." *Language* 47:257–81.
Bresnan, Joan W. 1972. "Theory of Complementation in English Syntax." PhD diss., MIT.
Chomsky, Noam. 1965. *Aspects of the Theory of Syntax*. Cambridge: MIT Press.
Chomsky, Noam. 1971. *Problems of Knowledge and Freedom*. New York: Pantheon.
Chomsky, Noam. 1973. "Conditions on Transformations." In Anderson and Kiparsky, 1973.
Emonds, Joseph. 1970. "Root and Structure-Preserving Transformations." PhD diss., MIT.
Emonds, Joseph. 1972. "A Reformulation of Certain Syntactic Transformations." In Peters, 1972.
Fauconnier, Gilles. 1971. "Theoretical Implications of Some Global Phenomena in Syntax." PhD diss., University of California at San Diego.
Gaatone, David. 1970. "La Transformation impersonnelle en français." *Le Français moderne* 38:389–411.
Gross, Maurice. 1968. *Grammaire transformationnelle du français: Syntaxe du verbe*. Paris: Larousse.
Higgins, Roger. 1973. "On J. Emonds' Analysis of Extraposition." In John Kimball, ed., *Syntax and Semantics*, vol. 2. New York: Academic Press.
Kajita, Masaru. 1966. *A Generative-Transformational Study of Semi-Auxiliaries in Present-Day American English*. Toyko: Sanseido.
Kayne, Richard. 1975. *French Syntax: The Transformational Cycle*. Cambridge: MIT Press.
Kiparsky, Paul, and Kiparsky, Carol. 1970. "Fact." In Manfred Bierwisch and Karl E. Heidolph, eds, *Progress in Linguistics*. The Hague: Mouton & Co.
McCawley, James D. 1970. "English as a VSO Language." *Language* 46:286–99.
Perlmutter, David M. 1971. *Deep and Surface Structure Constraints in Syntax*. New York: Holt, Rinehart, & Winston.
Perlmutter, David M., and Postal, Paul M. 1974. Lectures on Relational Grammar, Summer Linguistic Institute of the Linguistic Society of America, University of Massachusetts, Amherst.
Peters, Stanley, ed. 1972. *Goals of Linguistic Theory*. Englewood Cliffs, NJ: Prentice-Hall.
Postal, Paul M. 1971. *Crossover Phenomena*. New York: Holt, Rinehart, & Winston.
Postal, Paul M. 1972. "On Some Rules That Are *Not* Successive Cyclic." *Linguistic Inquiry* 3:211–22.
Postal, Paul M. 1974. *On Raising*. Cambridge: MIT Press.
Quícoli, António Carlos. 1972. "Aspects of Portuguese Complementation." PhD diss., State University of New York at Buffalo.

Rosenbaum, Peter. 1967. *The Grammar of English Predicate Complement Constructions.* Cambridge: MIT Press.
Ross, John R. 1967. "Constraints on Variables in Syntax." PhD diss., MIT.
Ross, John R. 1970. "Gapping and the Order of Constituents." In Manfred Bierwisch and Karl E. Heidolph, eds, *Progress in Linguistics.* The Hague: Mouton & Co.
Ruwet, Nicolas. 1970. "Note sur la syntaxe du pronom *en* et d'autres sujets apparentés." *Langue française,* 6. Revised version in Ruwet, 1972.
Ruwet, Nicolas. 1972. *Théorie syntaxique et syntaxe du français.* Paris: Editions du Seuil.

## 2  A closer look at the claims in "The Relational Succession Law"

Although couched in the general terms of the Standard Theory analysis of raising constructions, P&P formulate their generalization regarding raising constructions in terms of grammatical relations, which are primitive constructs in Relational Grammar. While basing their principle on English data, they show it is equally applicable to other languages, such as French and Portuguese. In section 5.2, which is not included here, they also show its applicability in Malagasy, an Austronesian language of Madagascar. "The Relational Succession Law" provides an explanation for the fact that certain transformations that could be written are unattested in human language.

In "The Relational Succession Law," P&P have begun to offer the rationale for their developing theory, Relational Grammar. (Another important paper from the time is Keenan and Comrie 1977, which was also written around 1972, on relativization and the Accessibility Hierarchy.) In part, the effort grew out of an interest in formulating cross-linguistic generalizations, an attempt to set the boundaries of linguistic variation in pursuit of identifying those elements that belong to the hypothesized innate language endowment of humans. One form this took was an examination of particular constructions (such as Passive, Raising and so on) across languages. Thus, this chapter and Relational Grammar theory itself might be seen as following a tradition (see McCawley 1970) of recognizing superficially distinct operations (both cross-linguistically and within a single language) and reducing them to single rules. As has already been seen, there are some broad similarities in raising constructions across languages, and thus Raising (like Passive) was brought forward as a phenomenon which might be explained in a fashion that abstracts away from the morphological details of the individual languages that exhibit it. However, one encounters some significant difficulties in attempting to formulate such generalizations in terms of universal rule statements within the Standard Theory conception of transformations, since transformations were stated in terms of linear order and dominance relations, which on the surface vary considerably in the world's languages. Languages with different word orders have distinct structural descriptions and distinct structural changes, and virtually every transformation has language-specific morphological changes. It is this view which led directly to theories of syntax (such as Relational Grammar and Lexical Functional Grammar) whose primitive units of analysis are grammatical relations (or functions), rather than unit constituents or ordered strings.

This said, the chapter and its observations are not immune to criticism. Looking at examples (4) and (5) in section 2, one might reasonably suggest that P&P are over-reaching somewhat by including "Tough Movement" (i.e., *John is tough to get along with*) in the same class of constructions as the RtoS and RtoO structures that have concerned us to this point.[1] If "Tough Movement" (Object Raising in their terms) is taken off the table (that is, if subject but not objects of embedded clauses undergo Raising), then only the first and third rows of table (11) remain, from which to derive the RSL generalization.

(11')

|  | GR of ascendee before ascension | GR of ascendee after ascension | GR of host NP before ascension |
|---|---|---|---|
| Subject Raising into subject position | Subject | Subject | Subject |
| Subject Raising into object position | Subject | Direct Object | Direct Object |

This leaves RtoS ("Subject Raising into subject position") and RtoO ("Subject Raising into object position"). For these two rules, the RSL holds in the form given in the chapter. The NP raised out of a clausal subject is a surface subject and the NP raised out of a clausal object is a surface object.

If one looks further into the subsequent literature, we find that Raising turns out to be even more circumscribed than P&P initially thought. Twelve years after they wrote the initial version of the RSL chapter (but only a year after they published it), they published two chapters (Perlmutter and Postal 1984a, 1984b) in which they claim that clausal subjects of intransitive verbs are objects underlyingly. According to this hypothesis, the clausal subject of (3), *that Melvin is incoherent*, is an object that has undergone an object–subject revaluation (called Unaccusative Advancement).

(3) [that Melvin is incoherent] is likely

According to their account of these constructions (Perlmutter and Postal 1984a:153–4), the subject of (4), *Melvin*, is first raised out of the clausal object, the infinitival clause *Melvin to be incoherent*, and then promoted into subject position.

(4) Melvin is likely [to be incoherent]

The RSL would be invoked here to insure that the raised subject of *to be incoherent*, *Melvin*, inherits the object relation borne by the infinitival complement of *be likely*. Under this view, RtoO and RtoS are both instances of raising an NP out of an object clause to create a new object. If this is true and if "Tough Movement" is not Raising, then the correlations covered under the RSL can (de facto) be summarized by just the third row from table (11).

(11″)

|  | GR of ascendee before ascension | GR of ascendee after ascension | GR of host NP before ascension |
|---|---|---|---|
| Subject Raising into object position | Subject | Direct Object | Direct Object |

Additionally, there are suggestions in the literature that there may be exceptions to the RSL when the raised element is initially a possessor within an NP (see Aissen 1979 and Davies 1981 on Possessor Ascension in Tzotzil and Choctaw, respectively). The RSL, given all this, still holds and is a correct generalization, even though its coverage is less than what was first envisioned.

Criticisms aside, "The Relational Succession Law" was the first of a large body of work developing the theory of Relational Grammar and applying the framework to analyses of a wide variety of the world's languages. There is a sizeable literature on Raising in the world's languages written within the RG framework, as attested in the bibliography created by Dubinsky and Rosen (1987). An understanding of the theory (as sketched out in the following sections) will enable one to profitably consult this literature.

## 3 Relational Grammar as a formal theory of syntax

### *The representation of clause structure*

As stated above, RG takes grammatical relations (GRs) to be undefined linguistic primitives used in the formulation of universal grammar and language-particular grammars. Representations are taken to be sets of *linguistic states*, defined as the GR holding between two entities at some level or levels. To represent clause structure, the theory requires:

(i)   a set of primitive linguistic elements: phrases, words, sounds;
(ii)  a set of *relational signs (R-signs)*, the names of primitive GRs: 1 = subject, 2 = direct object, 3 = indirect object, P = predicate . . . ;
(iii) levels, indicated by *coordinates*: the indices that identify the level of structure at which a particular GR holds.

The means for representing a linguistic state is the *arc*. Arcs are made up of three types of entities: (i) *nodes*, which can have grammatical category names (e.g., N, V . . . ), essentially as in Standard Theory (ST) and Extended Standard Theory (EST), (ii) *R-signs*, the name of the GR holding between two nodes, and (iii) *coordinates*. Thus, an individual arc is made up of four components: the *dependent (head) node*, the *governor (tail) node*, the *R-sign*, and the *coordinate*. If node *a* is the head and node *b* the tail, the GR that *a* bears to *b* is represented by the R-sign, with which the arc is labeled. Finally, since RG posits GRs at multiple levels of structure (in the same way as ST and EST include multi-level derivations), the level at which the GR holds is indicated by the *coordinate* assigned to the arc, coordinates being assigned sequentially starting with 1, which is taken to be the *initial* level. Thus, the representation that *a* bears the 1-relation to *b* at the initial level is as in (5).

(5)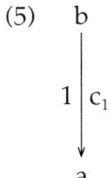

So in (5), *a* heads a 1-arc with tail *b* at the $c_1$ level.

The notion of linguistic level is reconstructed as the notion *stratum* in RG. A stratum consists of all arcs with the same tail which have the same coordinate. A simple transitive clause (one without relation-changing operations) would consist of all the initial-stratum arcs that depend on the clause node. The sentence in (6a) would have the representation in (6b).

(6) a. The doctor examined Hasan.
    b.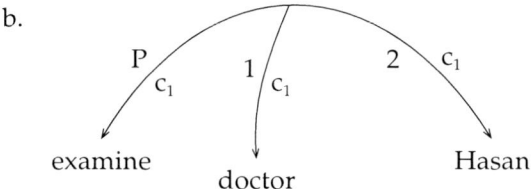

The representation in (6b), referred to as a *relational network (RN)*, abstracts away from the internal structure of nominal and verbal nodes as well as linear order and other language-particular aspects. All of this information can be included in a fully specified RN, e.g., linear precedence is represented by arcs relating the nodes at the heads of the arcs in (6b), as in Johnson and Postal (1980). However, one of the main goals of RG was to identify cross-linguistic generalizations regarding constructions sanctioned by universal grammar, and stripped down RNs such as (6b) facilitate cross-linguistic comparison. So, apart from the lexical items representing the nodes at the head of the arcs in (6b), the Javanese and Choctaw sentences in (7) and (8), respectively, would be represented by the same RN.

(7) Dhokter iku mriksa Hasan.
    doctor that examine H
    'The doctor examined Hasan.'

(8) Alikchi-at Hasan pisa-tok.
    doctor-NOM H see-PST
    'The doctor examined Hasan.'

RG took the cyclic transformations of ST/EST to be relation-changing operations. Thus, as the Passive transformation for English replaced the preverbal subject NP with the postverbal direct object NP and moved the subject NP into a postverbal PP, within RG, the initial-stratum 2 was promoted to 1 and the initial-stratum 1 was demoted. Thus, the English clause in (9a) was represented by the RN in (9b).

(9) a. Hasan was examined by the doctor.
    b.

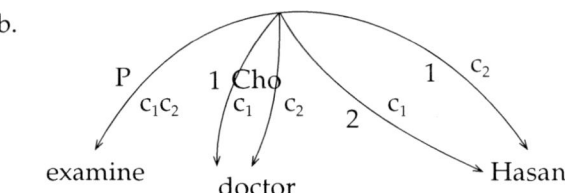

In (9b), *Hasan* advances to 1 in the $c_2$ stratum, and *the doctor* demotes to bear the *chômeur (Cho)* relation. Taken from the French for 'unemployed,' the chômeur relation indicates that the element that bears it is inert in the clause. Chômeur is the relation that an element normally bears when another element in the clause takes on its GR.[2] As strata in a representation increase, the RN becomes somewhat difficult to read and so an alternative but equivalent *stratal diagram* representation is often used. (10) is the stratal diagram for (9a).

(10)

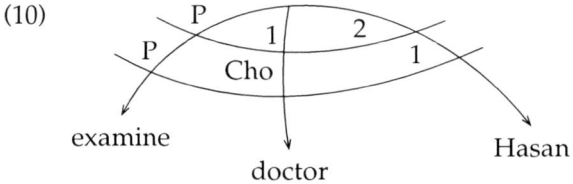

In (10), the lines intersecting the arcs represent individual strata, with the R-signs above indicating the GR that the element at the head of that arc bears in that stratum. As indicated in (10), the first line indicates the $c_1$ or initial stratum and the second the $c_2$ stratum, which here is the *final* stratum. As before, language-particular aspects of the English passive are abstracted away from in the representations for (9a). The same representations would be used for the Javanese clause in (11).

(11) Hasan di-priksa karo dhokter iku.
    H ov-examine by doctor that
    'Hasan was examined by the doctor.'

As is evident in the representations for passive clauses, the RNs of RG bear some resemblance to the transformational derivations of ST/EST. However, unlike ST/EST, RG is a non-derivational theory. One structure is not derived from another in the same way as a transformation derives one phrase marker from another. In the representations in (9b) and (10), all of the GR information for all levels exists in the static representation; thus, all the information in an RN is available for language-particular statements of morphosyntactic rules, linear ordering, and so on.[3] Whether it is a well-formed structure in a particular language is a matter of whether the RN meets all universal and language-particular well-formedness conditions.

## *Rules, constructions, and universal laws*

RNs are freely generated objects. The grammar of a particular language determines whether a given RN is an admissible representation in the language on the basis of language-particular and universal well-formedness conditions, which serve to filter out ill-formed representations (in the same spirit as the filters of Chomsky and Lasnik 1977).

### *Language-particular well-formedness conditions*

Lexical entries and morphosyntactic and interpretive rules make up part of the grammar of a language that act as well-formedness conditions on RNs. For example, in English the lexical entry for the verb *examine* will include the subcategorization information that *examine* must co-occur with a 1 and a 2 in the initial stratum of structure, i.e., that it must be transitive. Any RN that contains a P-arc with *examine* as its head but does not contain an initial 1-arc and an initial 2-arc will be ill-formed.

Case marking, verb agreement, and other morphosyntactic rules also act as well-formedness conditions. For example, the grammar of English contains the specification that the final subject of a finite clause occurs in nominative case. An RN for the clause *Him was examined by the doctor* will be marked as ill-formed since there is an NP that heads a final-stratum 1-arc which appears in objective case.

Finally, certain interpretive rules, such as those for bound anaphors, are stated as well-formedness conditions. For example, in Japanese, as in many other languages of the world, only subjects can bind reflexive anaphors, as shown by the interpretation of (12).

(12) John ga Mary o   zibun no  uti   de        = [Kuno 1973:293, (11a)]
     NOM    ACC self  GEN home LOC
 korosita.
 killed
 'John killed Mary in his/*her own home.'

Here in (12), only the subject *John* can antecede the reflexive *zibun*, even though another candidate, the object nominal *Mary*, is in an appropriate position to do so, configurationally. Thus, in the grammar of Japanese is a rule stating that only a nominal heading a (final) 1-arc can bind a reflexive. Any RN in which a reflexive is bound by a nominal that does not meet this condition will be filtered out as ill-formed.

## Constructions

One of the goals of RG was to identify a universal inventory of relation-changing structures which categorized the clausal constructions possible in human languages. These consisted of *advancements*, *demotions*, *ascensions*, and *births*. Advancements were structures in which an element revalued to a GR higher on the hierarchy of GRs (1 > 2 > 3 > Oblique). One example of this is Passive, which in RG was characterized universally as the advancement of a 2 in a transitive stratum to 1 (Perlmutter and Postal 1977). Other advancements included 3-2 Advancement (dative shift) and Unaccusative Advancement (2 of an intransitive stratum to 1). As seen in the RSL, ascensions were those constructions such as Raising in which an element raises or ascends out of one structure to bear a GR in a higher structure. These are examined in more detail below in section 4. Demotions were structures in which an element revalued to a GR lower on the hierarchy and births were insertions of elements in a non-initial stratum, such as posited in the RG analysis of *there*-Insertion. (For more details, readers are referred to Perlmutter and Postal 1983a and the extensive literature cited in Dubinsky and Rosen 1987.)

Grammars of individual languages selected a subset of the identified constructions as part of the language-particular component of the grammar. Thus, in languages such as English and Javanese the sub-RN associated with Passive (2 to 1 Advancement from a transitive stratum) was well-formed and any RN containing this sub-RN and not violating any other conditions would be a well-formed structure. Conversely, in a language such as Choctaw, there is no Passive structure and so the grammar of Choctaw would contain a well-formedness condition that marked as ill-formed any RN that included the sub-RN associated with Passive.

## Laws

The laws of RG are universal, inviolable conditions on RNs. The laws represent empirically based cross-linguistic generalizations which aim to address the question of how languages are alike. The RG laws are independent of one another and constrain the inventory of possible RNs. They thus do not have to be repeated in grammars of individual languages. The Relational Succession Law represents one such universal. Others of relevance to our discussion of Raising include the Final 1 Law and the Stratal Uniqueness Law.

The *Final 1 Law* states that every well-formed clause must contain an element heading a 1-arc in the final stratum, in other words, every clause must contain a subject. Thus, even clauses such as the seemingly subjectless sentence from Italian in (13a) must contain a 1-arc.

(13) a. È piovuto.
is rained
'It rained.'

b.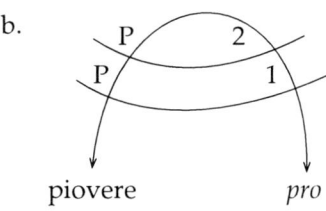

piovere    pro

c. *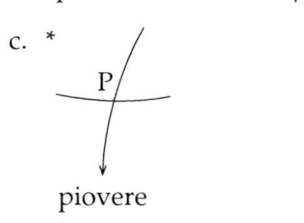

piovere

In the representation in (13b), a pleonastic pronoun lacking a phonetic matrix, *pro*, enters the structure in the second stratum as a 2 and advances to 1 via Unaccusative Advancement (see Rosen 1981 for arguments that *piovere* is an Unaccusative predicate). This structure satisfies the Final 1 Law (and all other RG laws) and is well-formed. However, the representation in (13c) is ruled out inasmuch as it does not contain a 1-arc in the final stratum, running foul of the Final 1 Law.

The *Stratal Uniqueness Law* states that there may be at most one 1, one 2, and one 3 (collectively referred to as the *term* relations) in any given stratum. Thus, as the representations of Passive in (9b) and (10) show, when the initial 2 advances to 1, the initial 1 demotes to chômeur. If the initial 1 were to retain its GR, the structure would be ill-formed, as in (14).

(14)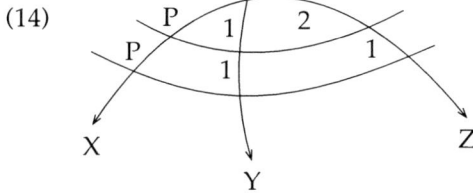

(14) violates the Stratal Uniqueness Law since there are two 1-arcs in the $c_2$ stratum. The Stratal Uniqueness Law also comes into play in the RG analysis of dative shift, illustrated by the Madurese clause in (15b).

(15) a. Bambang ngerem buku dha' Ita.
B         send    book   to    I
'Bambang sent a book to Ita.'
b. Bambang ngerem-e Ita buku.
B         send-E      I    book
'Bambang send Ita a book.'

c.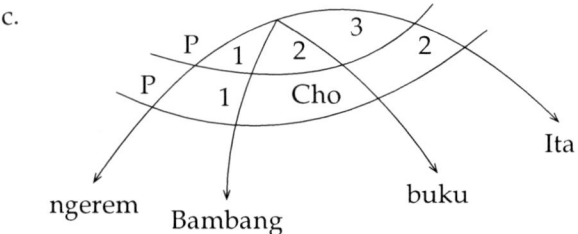

In the representation of (15b) given in (15c), when the initial 3, *Ita*, advances to 2 in the second stratum, it usurps the GR of the initial 2, *buku*, which demotes to chômeur. (15c) is in compliance with the Stratal Uniqueness Law (and all other RG laws) and is thus a well-formed RN. A discussion of these laws and others is found in Perlmutter and Postal (1983a).

## 4 Raising and Control in Relational Grammar

In RG, clausal complements contain a clause node and its dependents as heading an arc whose tail is the matrix clause node. Thus, (16a) has the representation in (16b).

(16) a. I expect that Claire won.

b.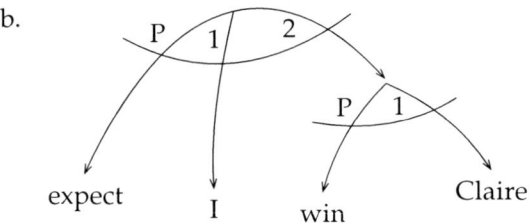

In the stratal diagram (16b), the predicate *win* and the nominal *Claire* bear the P relation and the 1-relation (respectively) to the embedded clause (represented above the line). The embedded clause *win Claire* itself bears a 2-relation in the matrix clause (presented below the line).

Raising is represented by indicating that the raised element bears a GR to the matrix clause. Thus, (17a) has the representation in (17b).

(17) a. I expect Claire to have won.

b.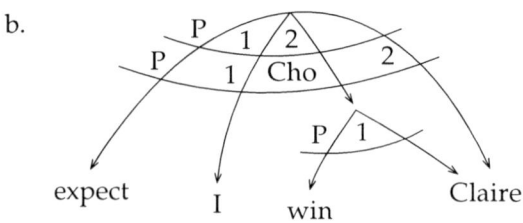

In (17b) the final 1 of the embedded clause, *Claire*, raises to bear the 2-relation in the matrix clause. Owing to the Stratal Uniqueness Law, the embedded clause, which bears the 2-relation in the initial stratum of the matrix clause, can no longer bear this relation and is demoted to chômeur. Note that the structure in (17b) obeys the Relational Succession Law: the clausal host of the raising bears the 2-relation and the raised NP bears the 2-relation in the stratum in which it raises.

This is true of RtoS as well. Abstracting away from the complex nature of the embedded predicate, the sentence in (18a) is analyzed as in (18b).

(18) a. Barnett seems to have won.

b.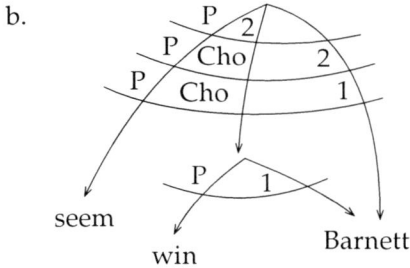

In (18) *seem* is analyzed as an unaccusative predicate, and so in the representation the complement clause bears the 2-relation in the initial stratum. The embedded subject *Barnett* raises to 2 and then advances to 1 via Unaccusative Advancement, thereby satisfying the Final 1 Law. As before, the clause demotes to chômeur in the stratum in which the raised NP first bears a GR in the matrix clause. Perlmutter and Postal (1984a) provide (theory-internal) arguments that all intransitive raising predicates are unaccusative that need not concern us here.

The cases of Raising that are seen in other languages will receive the same kind of analysis as the cases of English Raising. This harks back to Postal's (1974) assertion that in exploring Raising in English one is essentially exploring Raising in human language in general.

### *Possessor Raising*

Another type of Raising that first received widespread attention in the RG literature is that in which an NP that bears a GR in a clause is understood to be the possessor of another NP in that clause. While not a part of English grammar, Possessor Raising is found in a wide variety of the world's languages. Kinyarwanda, a Bantu language of Rwanda, illustrates this construction, (19b) (Kimenyi 1980).

(19) a. Ingurube z-a-ri-iye ibíryo by'ábáana.
   pigs they-PST-eat-ASP food of.children
   'The pigs ate the children's food.'

b. Ingurube z-a-ri-ir-iye          ábáana  ibíryo.
   pigs    they-PST-eat-APP-ASP children food
   'The pigs ate the children's food.'

In (19a), *ábáana* 'children' occurs as a prepositional modifier of the head noun of the direct object *ibíryo* 'food.' In (19b), *ábáana* occurs as a bare NP in direct object position. Additionally, the verb is marked with the applicative affix *-ir* and *ibíryo* occurs in sentence-final position. The Possessor Raising structure is represented as in (20).

(20)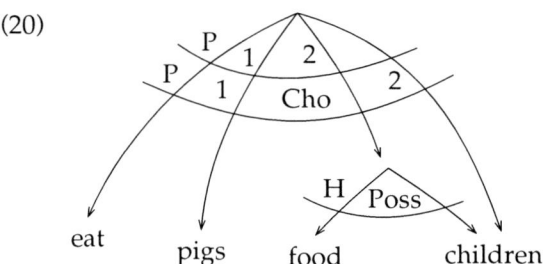

In (20), the possessor *ábáana* has raised out of the NP and bears the 2-relation to the clause; the remnant of the raising host, *ibíryo*, is demoted to chômeur (thus the Stratal Uniqueness Law is observed).

Kimenyi (1980) provides evidence for this analysis beyond the mere change in word order and morphological marking. He shows that in the possessor raising structure the possessor behaves as a direct object under Passive, pronoun incorporation, and relativization, and the remnant NP does not. Only the case of Passive is illustrated here.

(21) a. Abáana ba-a-ri-ir-iw-e          ibíryo n'îngurube.
        children they-PST-eat-APP-PASS-ASP food   by.pigs
        'The children were eaten (their) food by the pigs.'
     b. *Ibíryo by-a-ri-ir-iw-e          ábáana n'îngurube
        food   it-PST-eat-APP-PASS-ASP children pigs
        (The food of the children was eaten by the pigs.)

Note that in (21) the applicative suffix *-ir* occurs, signaling that these clauses are instances of Possessor Raising. (21a), where the possessor *ábáana* has been passivized, is grammatical, while (21b), in which the host *ibíryo* has been passivized, is not.

Possessor Raising has been documented in a number of languages, including Cebuano (Bell 1983), Choctaw (Davies 1986), Japanese (Dubinsky 1985, 1997), Malagasy (Perlmutter and Postal 1983b), Southern Tiwa (Allen et al. 1990), and Tzotzil (Aissen 1990).[4]

## Control

The precise analysis of Control (referred to as Equi) was not a topic of great concern within RG, and a number of different representations can be found in the literature. Most widely used, however, were RNs in which the controller and controllee were a single NP heading arcs with two different clause nodes as tails, as in (22b).

(22) a. Tilman tried to understand.
b.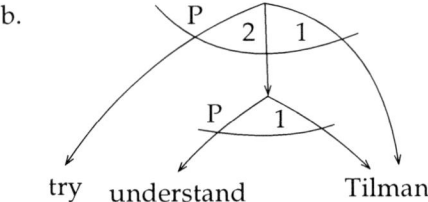

In (22b), *Tilman* heads a 1-arc in the matrix clause and a 1-arc in the embedded clause and is assigned a thematic role by both the matrix verb *try* and the embedded verb *understand*. The embedded clause *Tilman understand* itself heads a 2-arc in the matrix clause.

Note that the RG analyses of Raising and Control bear some resemblance to the structure-sharing analysis discussed in chapter 5 (section 3). Specifically, in both, a single NP bears GRs in more than one clause. However, there are obvious differences as well. In the raising structure, the shared NP does not bear a GR in the initial stratum of the matrix clause (and hence cannot be assigned a thematic role by the matrix predicate) and the complement clause bears the chômeur relation in the final stratum. In the control structure, the shared NP bears GRs in the initial strata of both clauses and the complement clause is not demoted to chômeur. The RG analysis of these structures thus does not make the same prediction regarding the universality of case preservation as the LFG analysis does (chapter 5, section 3).

## Notes

1 Chomsky (1977) asserts that *tough* constructions involve some sort of *wh*-movement, and are in this way distinct from raising constructions. Evidence in support of this involves, among other things, the fact that *tough* constructions are subject (like other *wh*-movement structures) to the *wh*-island constraint of Ross (1967). Compare (i) and (ii).

(i) *who are the presents fun (for us) [to give to]

(ii) *who did you wonder [what to give to]

The ungrammaticality of (i) is attributed to the presence of a phonologically null *wh*-operator in the infinitival clause that blocks the extraction of the *wh*-object of the preposition *to*. This view is further supported by the fact that *tough* movement constructions, in contrast with Raising, may involve tensed embedded clauses. Compare (iii) and (iv).

(iii)  a. That violin is easy for us to believe Dale to be able play a sonata on ____.
       b. That violin is easy for us to believe Dale can play a sonata on ____.

(iv)   a. John seems likely ____ to have left town.
       b. *John seems likely ____ left town.

The grammatical (iiib), which some consider to be ill-formed, contrasts with the ungrammatical (ivb), and (iii) is therefore consistent with the hypothesis that *wh*-extraction is involved in its lowest clause.

2   This notion (i.e., chômeur) is prefigured in the RSL chapter, in P&P's discussion of their examples (50) and (51). There, they suggest that the clausal host of ascension "cannot bear any grammatical relation at all" after Raising has taken place. The evidence for this claim, as seen in the excerpt, is that the clausal object can no longer undergo Passive (an operation that affects active objects). In their formalization of RG, the notion "cannot bear any grammatical relation" was replaced by an inactive (or inert) grammatical relation, the chômeur.

3   The device of traces of EST and later forms of Chomskyan models perform a similar task to the multiple strata of RG. The traces allow the tracking of structural information from previous phrase markers, information that in pre-trace versions of Transformational Grammar would otherwise be lost when a phrase marker undergoes a transformation, which creates a new phrase marker.

4   While ST and EST provided no analysis of Possessor Raising, Baker (1988) provides an analysis within Chomsky's Government and Binding framework for Possessor Raising and a number of the other relation-changing constructions explored in depth in RG.

# CHAPTER 7

# REVISED EXTENDED STANDARD THEORY: CHOMSKY AND LASNIK'S "FILTERS AND CONTROL"

## 1 Background and introduction to "Filters and Control"

This article represents a general move by Chomsky and Lasnik (C&L) from the articulation of conditions on rules to the articulation of conditions on representations. Here, rather than restricting movement as done in "Conditions on transformations," the Tensed-S Condition and Sentential Subject Condition (and their like) act at a level of Logical Form to render certain interpretations ill-formed, if illicit movement has applied. This approach anticipates the (later) Government and Binding Theory approach of treating all violations of movement conditions as binding theory violations. As a "theory building" article, it attempts to make transformations as general as possible and have them be optional, as well. The goal in this regard is to get rid of the convoluted rule statements of Standard Theory (and to a somewhat lesser degree those of "Conditions on transformations"). Also, by making all transformations optional, C&L do away with the necessity of having rules that must be marked in the grammar as optional or obligatory. This all makes for a more general theory. Also presented here is the first statement of the T-model of grammar (that is, a model in which surface structure is input to separate phonetic and semantic representations – the PF and LF of Government and Binding Theory).

"Filters and Control" is essentially presented in two parts. Part 1 lays out some fundamental changes to the Extended Standard Theory (of Chomsky 1973), explores the possibility that some syntactic rules are motivated by perceptual, psycholinguistic factors, proposes an analysis for control constructions, and provides an overview of the complementizer system in English. Parts 2, 3, and 4 are concerned with demonstrating how the particular surface filters proposed for English work to eliminate the need for "ordering, obligatoriness, and complex contextual dependencies in the transformational system," and with providing a formalization of the general properties of surface filters.

In the extract that is presented here, only the introductory pages of the article and two subsections of part 1 are presented (sections 1.1 and 1.3), the sections dealing with changes to the theory and with the analysis of control constructions. This choice reflects the primary focus of the present volume (namely, the manner in which theoretical innovations affect analyses of Raising and Control, and the ways in which the empirical facts constrain such theoretical innovations). Although there will indeed be some discussion of the sections omitted from the following excerpt, it is far beyond the scope of this volume to explore the mechanics of each of the proposed surface filters or, for that matter, to examine the formalism invoked to represent these.

# READING FROM CHOMSKY AND LASNIK (1977)

Noam Chomsky and Howard Lasnik, sections 0 and 1.1 (pp. 425–33) and 1.3 (pp. 439–44) from "Filters and Control" in *Linguistic Inquiry* 8:3 (Summer 1977). © 1977 by the Massachusetts Institute of Technology. Reprinted by permission.

## 0 Introductory comments[1] [pp. 425–6]

The questions that we want to consider here have arisen in a number of different contexts in recent work on the nature and use of language. Among these are the following:

(1)   a.  Restricting the options for transformational grammar (TG) (discussed in section 1.1 below);
       b.  Perceptual strategies and syntactic rules (section 1.2 [not reproduced here]);
       c.  Problems of obligatory control (section 1.3);
       d.  Properties of the complementizer system (section 1.4 [not reproduced here]).

A number of questions that arise in these domains seem to fall together. In each case, we find that it is necessary to develop some notion of well-formedness for surface structures. We call a condition of this sort a "(surface) filter". The notion is proposed in a limited way in Chomsky (1965) as a device to simplify and restrict the theory of transformations. The relevant considerations here were those of (1a). There is a much more far-reaching investigation and analysis of filters in Perlmutter (1968; 1971). The topic is taken up again in Chomsky (1973).[2]

---

[1] We are indebted to Alan Prince and Edwin Williams for helpful suggestions and comments.
[2] Cf. as well Ross (1973); also Hudson (1972), for a proposal dealing with one of the phenomena we will discuss. Lasnik has proposed a surface filter requiring that a complement sentence with a subject begin with an overt complementizer if it is separated from its governing verb. Postal (1974, 128) discusses a version of this filter. Below, we consider various filters related to this one.

We will suggest that with an appropriate concept of "surface filter", the program that falls under (1a) can be substantially advanced.

Turning to (1b), the idea that syntactic rules may serve the function of facilitating perceptual strategies has been advanced in recent work in psycholinguistics (cf. Bever (1970), Bever and Langendoen (1971), Fodor, Bever, and Garrett (1974)). Here too, it has been suggested that the point of contact may be, in part, at the level of surface filters (cf. Chomsky (1973)).

Among the filters that have been proposed, we find, for example, one that prevents the occurrence of a lexical noun phrase (e.g. *Bill*) in the context left vacant in (2):

(2)  It is unclear what____to do.

We will propose that it is correct to block such constructions at the surface level, but that the appropriate device is not a surface filter but rather a rule of obligatory control of the sort that assigns either *John* or *Bill* as the subject of the verb *leave* in such constructions as (3a,b):

(3)  a.  John persuaded Bill to leave.
     b.  John promised Bill to leave.

Filters and rules of obligatory control impose well-formedness conditions on surface structures, as do properties of logical form.

Since the important work of Bresnan (1971; 1972), the structure of complementizers has been the subject of much study and controversy. We assume, following Bresnan, that the basic structure of the sentence is COMP+S, where COMP is a category that includes the italicized "sentence-introducers" in (4):

(4)  a.  [$_{\bar{S}}$[$_{COMP}$*for*][$_S$John to leave]] ____ would be a mistake
     b.  [$_{\bar{S}}$[$_{COMP}$*that*][$_S$John has left]] ____ is obvious
     c.  [$_{\bar{S}}$[$_{COMP}$*whether*][$_S$John left]] ____ is unclear

We will use the conventional device of labeled bracketing, as in (4), to represent phrase markers. We assume that COMP+S is of the category $\bar{S}$, as indicated in (4). The italicized items are complementizers; the category to which they belong is COMP.[3]

A system of surface filters to account for some of the properties of complementizers is proposed in Chomsky (1973). Lasnik and Bresnan have studied the interaction of complementizers and verbal categories, bringing to light properties that relate directly to the theory of Equi NP Deletion and Raising.[4] We will modify and extend these ideas below.

We will begin by discussing each of the topics (a), (b), (c), and (d) of (1), indicating the role to be played by the notion "surface filter". We will then

---
[3] Note that these notions are not to be confused with the notion "complement" as when *that John left* is called a complement to the verb *think* in *I think that John left*.
[4] Cf. Bresnan (1972), Chomsky (1974), for various interpretations of these results.

turn to the problem of devising an appropriate system of filters as a preliminary to developing a general theory relating to this aspect of grammar.

## 1 Background considerations

### 1.1 Restricting the options for transformational generative grammar (TG) [pp. 426–33]

The earliest work on TG had several goals: (A) to develop a set of concepts rich enough to permit the expression of linguistic processes that escaped any natural formulation within the theory of phrase structure, but that seemed to involve operations that map phrase markers into phrase markers; (B) to show that this enrichment of grammatical theory laid the basis for a more adequate account of the meaning of linguistic expressions; (C) to show that the theory of TG could provide explanations for some of the formal properties of natural language. For examples of work motivated by these goals, see Chomsky (1955; 1957) and the papers in Fodor and Katz (1964).

The first two goals, (A) and (B), have to do with descriptive adequacy; the third, (C), with explanatory adequacy (cf. Chomsky (1964; 1965)). But there is a certain tension between these two pursuits. To attain explanatory adequacy it is in general necessary to restrict the class of possible grammars, whereas the pursuit of descriptive adequacy often seems to require elaborating the mechanisms available and thus extending the class of possible grammars.

We may think of the theory of grammar T as consisting of two parts: a universal grammar UG that determines the class of possible grammars and the way they operate, and a system of evaluation that ranks potential grammars in terms of "optimality" or "simplicity". We have a genuine explanation for a class of phenomena P when we can show that given T and certain "boundary conditions" E provided by experience, the phenomena P follow from the optimal grammar consistent with UG and E. Then we can say that the phenomena P are explained by the theory T. Looking at the same matter from a different point of view, we can say that a child equipped with T and presented with E will construct the grammar G as a representation of his knowledge of language, where G entails P. The grammar G is embedded in a performance system that enables knowledge of language (competence) to be put to use in speech and understanding.

To attain explanatory adequacy the theory T must be sufficiently restricted so that relatively few grammars are available, given a reasonable amount of experience E, to be submitted to evaluation; otherwise, the burden on the evaluation procedures is intolerable. A reasonable project for linguistic theory, then, is to attempt to constrain UG so that potential grammars are "scattered" in terms of a measure of optimality; only a few grammars need be considered, given experience. If such a UG can be constructed, we may reasonably attribute it to the organism as a species-specific innate property. We can then account for the remarkable rapidity, facility, and uniformity of language acquisition on the assumption that the child in effect knows the class of potential grammars and must simply determine to which of these he is exposed. Correspondingly, we can account for the familiar fact that knowledge of language extends far beyond available experience and we may hope to explain the curious arrangement of complex phenomena that we typically find in studying a particular language. For discussion, cf. Chomsky (1965; 1975), and many other sources.

Early work in pursuit of descriptive adequacy led to an extremely rich theory of TG. For a formalization that encompasses much descriptive practice, cf. Peters and Ritchie (1973). Even this extremely rich theory does not encompass such devices as structure-building rules, global rules, transderivational constraints, and others that have often been proposed. Any enrichment of linguistic theory that extends the class of possible grammars requires strong empirical motivation. We feel that this is lacking in the case of devices that exceed the framework of Chomsky (1955), Peters and Ritchie (1973), and comparable work; cf. Dougherty (1973), Chomsky (1972), Brame (1976).

If this judgment is correct, then the problem we face is to restrict the options that are available in this narrower, but still overly permissive framework, so that we may approach the basic goals of linguistic theory: to provide explanations rather than descriptions and to account for the attainment of grammatical competence, so-called "language learning", or "language growth", to use what may be a less misleading term.

As a point of departure, we assume the general framework of the extended standard theory (EST).[5] Specifically, we assume that the grammar consists of a base with a categorial component and a lexicon, a transformational component, and two systems of interpretive rules, a phonological and a semantic component. The categorial component of the base is a context-free grammar generating an infinite class of abstract phrase markers. The lexicon, incorporating word formation and redundancy rules, determines the class of lexical items.[6] Inserting lexical items in abstract phrase markers, we derive base phrase markers (but see note 19). Rules of the transformational component apply to these to yield surface structures.

Surface structures must meet certain well-formedness conditions. Some of these, though not all, are stated as surface filters. Others may be imposed by the interpretive rules. Base phrase markers that map into well-formed surface structures we will call "deep structures".[7]

The rules of the phonological and semantic components apply to surface structures to yield representations in universal phonetics (UP) and logical form (LF), respectively. We will not be concerned here with phonology or UP.[8]

---

[5] Cf. Jackendoff (1972), Chomsky (1972).
[6] Cf. Aronoff (1976).
[7] We note that the notion "deep structure" is to be understood as a technical term within the context of EST. For discussion of some confusions about this notion, see Chomsky (1975).
[8] We will also not consider here the question of whether phonological rules are interspersed among transformations, as proposed by Bresnan (1971). If this conclusion is correct, then some modifications (though not essential ones) are required in the formulation presented here.

We understand LF to be a universal system of representation that incorporates whatever aspects of meaning are strictly determined by sentence grammar, not involving situational context, background beliefs, speaker's intentions, etc. To determine the properties of LF is an empirical problem, exactly as in the case of UP.[9]

Representations in UP and LF provide the "interface" between linguistic structures and the performance systems. Thus we assume that all aspects of phonetic form and meaning determined strictly by sentence grammar are indicated in the representation in UP and LF, respectively. The grammar, then, determines a sound–meaning relation; more accurately, it determines a pairing of conditions-on-sound and conditions-on-meaning, each of which may be further specified by the interaction of grammar and other systems.

We assume further that semantic relations such as Agent, Goal, Instrument, etc. (what have been called "thematic" or "case" relations in various theories) are determined by the interaction of deep structure configurations and lexical properties. Under the trace theory of movement rules, which we assume here,[10] surface structures suffice to provide the relevant configurations, carried over under transformation from deep structures. The rules giving LF can therefore be assumed to apply strictly to surface structures. Note that these rules in effect determine the syntax of LF, yielding structures that remain to be interpreted, strictly speaking. If general conditions on LF are not satisfied, the underlying base-generated structure is, by definition, not a deep structure. The well-formedness conditions on LF, which we will not discuss here in any detail, derive ultimately from the theory of interpretation of representations in LF: for example, the representation must be of a sentence, not an open sentence with free variables; referential phrases must be in argument positions; etc.

Certain aspects of what is often called "meaning" or "sense" may be determined by interactions of LF and other cognitive systems. There is, we believe, some empirical support for the belief that the syntax of LF is close to that of standard forms of predicate calculus and that familiar interpretive principles may then be appropriate to LF.

Assuming this much, the problem is to restrict further the options available within this general framework without sacrificing descriptive adequacy, so that we can further the goals set above. Several significant steps have been taken in this direction in recent years.

The theory can be constrained at the level of the base, the transformational component, the surface filters, or the interpretive rules; or by general conditions on rule application such as, for example, the A-over-A (A/A) Condition. The contribution of general conditions of the latter sort is indirect, but significant. Where general conditions of application can be stated, the rules themselves need not build in these conditions. Therefore, the format for rules can

---

[9] Cf. Chomsky (1977a, chapter 4).
[10] Cf. Chomsky (1975; 1977a). We adopt here the form of trace theory presented in Chomsky (1977b). Cf. also the references of note 15.

be restricted in expressive power, with a consequent limitation of the class of possible rules and possible grammars.

In our opinion, the most promising approach to constraining the theory of the base is offered by the X-bar ($\bar{X}$) theory.[11] As for transformational rules, an important contribution is that of Emonds (1970; 1976), who proposed that all such rules fall into one of a few restricted types: root transformations, minor movement rules, stylistic rules, and cyclic rules (the latter, structure-preserving). The cyclic rules, to which we restrict attention, are the most important category. We return to further reductions of the theory of transformations. Among the rules of interpretation, the most important, for present purposes, are the rules of construal that relate antecedents and anaphors.[12] The pairing of antecedent and anaphor is subject to a number of general conditions; among them, those related to "command"[13] and the Tensed-S (propositional island) and (Specified) Subject Conditions.[14]

We make the natural assumption that the relation between a phrase that has been moved by a transformation and its trace is a relation of bound anaphora. Many of the properties of movement rules now follow at once from the independently motivated conditions on anaphora; for example, the asymmetries between "raising" and "lowering" rules, object-to-subject and subject-to-object rules, etc. Others can be explained by simplifying the general principle that rightward movement rules are "upward-bounded" in the sense of Ross (1967) to the principle of subjacency, which takes upward-boundedness to be a general property of movement rules. In particular, several of the "island conditions" proposed in Ross (1967) and subsequent work can be explained in these terms.[15]

In the light of this and related work, we feel that it is possible to put forth some very restrictive hypotheses concerning the various components of the grammar and their interactions. We will assume that UG is not an "undifferentiated" system, but rather incorporates something analogous to a "theory of markedness". Specifically, there is a theory of core grammar with highly restricted options, limited expressive power, and a few parameters. Systems that fall within core grammar constitute "the unmarked case"; we may think

---

[11] See references in Chomsky (1975); also Jackendoff (forthcoming) and several papers in Akmajian, Culicover, and Wasow (1977).

[12] Among the rules of construal are the rules of control, the rules assigning antecedents to bound anaphors (reflexives, reciprocals, etc.), and the rule of disjoint reference. Interpretive rules include also rules of focus, rules assigning quantifier scope and interpretation, etc. Cf. Chomsky (1977a,b) for some indication of what we have in mind. We assume that the rules governing quantifiers are clause-bound in the unmarked case. Cf. May (1977).

[13] Cf. Lasnik (1976), Reinhart (1976).

[14] Cf. Chomsky (1975; 1977a,b). It is quite natural to regard these conditions as, in effect, late rules of interpretation that mark certain positions within cyclic categories as "opaque" to anaphoric connections outside these categories; specifically, positions in the domain of a subject (the subject condition) and tense (the propositional island condition). We omit further elaboration here. See below, [original] p. 440 [not reproduced here].

[15] Cf. Fiengo (1974; 1977), and the references of note 10.

of them as optimal in terms of the evaluation metric. An actual language is determined by fixing the parameters of core grammar and then adding rules or rule conditions, using much richer resources, perhaps resources as rich as those contemplated in the earlier theories of TG noted above. These added properties of grammars we may think of as the syntactic analogue of irregular verbs. We believe, however, that the theory of core grammar covers quite an extensive range, including many of the well-studied constructions of recent linguistic work.[16]

The base component of core grammar will be a system falling within an appropriate version of the X-bar theory. We assume that the basic features will be as indicated in (5):[17]

(5)

|      | +N        | −N          |
|------|-----------|-------------|
| +V   | Adjective | Verb        |
| −V   | Noun      | Preposition |

The major categories (NP, VP, etc.) will be "projected" from these, in accordance with the principles of X-bar theory.

The transformational rules of the core grammar are unordered and optional. Structural conditions are severely restricted. Neither truth functions (*or*, *not*, etc.) nor quantification is permitted. Multiple conditions are also excluded: for example, rules that apply to a factorization in which factor sequences simultaneously meet several conditions. A transformational rule will apply in a certain domain (e.g. sentence, noun phrase); it will then do something to a category in that domain. Adjacency of categories cannot be stipulated and no more than one element of the context in which the operation applies may be specified. The operations are restricted to movement, left- and right-adjunction, and substitution of a designated element. In addition, there may be deletion rules subject to a recoverability condition; we distinguish these operations from transformations here. Only a finite and quite small number of transformations are available in principle. For a formalization of a theory of the sort we have in mind, cf. Lasnik and Kupin (1976). It may be that the rules can be restricted even more narrowly in format, as suggested in the references of note 10.

The rules of construal simply associate two categories (say, by coindexing), one an antecedent, the other an anaphor (e.g. a plural noun phrase as antecedent and the reciprocal *each other* as anaphor), subject to the conditions on anaphora (cf. note 13). Recall that the relation of a moved category to its trace is regarded as a special case of anaphora, and is thus subject to the conditions on anaphora.

We will assume that the various components of the grammar are related as indicated in (6):

---

[16] For some indication of the scope, for one rule of core grammar, cf. Chomsky (1977b). See also Quicoli (1975a; 1975b; 1976), extending the very important work of Kayne (1975).
[17] In more or less traditional terms, we may think of [+N] as "substantive" and [+V] as "predicable". For a different theory of category features, cf. Jackendoff (forthcoming).

(6) 1. Base
2. Transformations (movement, adjunction, substitution)

3a. Deletion        3b. Construal
4a. Filters         4b. Quantifier interpretation, etc.
5a. Phonology
6a. Stylistic rules

The rules of the base generate base structures, which are converted to surface structures by the transformations of 2. These surface structures then undergo semantic interpretation by the rules 3b, 4b, etc. Independently, they are mapped into UP by the rules 3a, 4a, 5a, 6a. We assume that deletion does not precede construal, etc., since deleted elements must undergo semantic interpretation.[18] We also assume that the "deletion transformations" follow all others, and are, in fact, of a rather different sort. We will continue to use the term "surface structure" for the forms given prior to deletion, as above; this is one of several departures from conventional usage, which we will note as we proceed.

Let us now consider the interaction of these components in slightly more detail.

The rules of the base, optional and unordered, generate deep structures with lexical items as terminal nodes.[19] Where no rule applies to expand some category, we will assume that it is "expanded" to the terminal symbol $e$ (identity). We may then have such base structures as (7) and (8) (omitting details, here and below):

(7) $[_{\bar{S}}[_S[_{NP}\text{John}][_{VP}[_V\text{persuaded}][_{NP}\text{Bill}][_{\bar{S}}[_S[_{NP}e][_{NP}\text{to leave}]]]]]]$

(8) $[_{\bar{S}}[_S[_{NP}e][_{VP}\text{was }[_{AP}\text{en }[_{VP}[_V\text{hit}][_{NP}\text{Bill}]]]]]]$

Structure (7) is a deep structure, underlying the sentence (7'):

(7') John persuaded Bill to leave.

The element $[_{NP}e]$ in (7) is what is conventionally represented PRO, a position that must undergo control.

Structure (8), though base-generated with the subject NP unexpanded, is not well-formed as a surface structure. The reason is that it violates a condition on LF, since it has a free variable in the subject position, there being no rule of

---

[18] The assumption is not without empirical consequences, and alternatives are easily imagined, but we will not pursue this interesting question here.

[19] In fact, there is little reason to suppose that lexical items are inserted in base structures, in this theory. For some arguments to the contrary, see Otero (1976), den Besten (1976). We will continue to accept this assumption here for ease of exposition, but everything we say can be translated into an alternative theory in which lexical insertion takes place in surface structure and only abstract features are generated in the base (which is now limited to the categorial component) in positions to be filled by lexical items.

control for this case. If there were no transformational rule that could overcome this defect, converting (8) into a well-formed surface structure, it would not be a deep structure, by definition. There is such a rule, however.

Transformational rules apply to the base-generated structures, as indicated in (6). Given the base-generated structure (8), we can apply the transformation (9) to yield the derived structure (10):

(9) Move NP

(10) $[_S[_S[_{NP}Bill][_{VP}was [_{AP}en [_{VP}hit [_{NP}e]]]]]$

We refer to the element $[_{NP}e]$ of (10) as the "trace" of $[_{NP}Bill]$. We assume that a movement rule always leaves a trace, in this sense; that is, though the category and its contents are moved by the transformation, the category remains with null content, possibly to be filled by a later rule. Cf. references cited above, where it is noted, among other things, that this is a fairly conventional, if implicit, assumption in much work in TG. We may assume that the trace of $[_{NP}Bill]$ is coindexed with $[_{NP}Bill]$, by convention, so as to preserve antecedent–trace relations.

Note that the trace in (10) is indistinguishable from PRO in (7), apart from the fact that the trace in (10) is coindexed with an NP by virtue of a movement rule, whereas the PRO element $[_{NP}e]$ in (7) has no index.

Application of base and transformational rules yields a surface structure. Note that the notion "surface structure" as we employ it here is more abstract than in other presentations of TG, because of the presence of trace and PRO and because we are abstracting away from the effect of deletion and stylistic rules.

Continuing with the analysis of (6), we turn to the two independent systems of rules below the horizontal line. On the left, we have a series of rules that provide ultimately the representation in UP. Deletion rules may remove certain elements, under quite stringent conditions, which we will not explore here. We will see below that there is good reason to have the filters that determine surface structure well-formedness apply after deletion. Phonological rules then assign a representation in UP. Stylistic rules (scrambling, etc.), may then apply. We have nothing to say about these, though we assume that they may refer to phonetic properties. One might just as well say that sentence grammar, or at least core grammar, abstracts away from these phenomena.

On the right below the horizontal line in (6), we have the interpretive rules that map surface structures to LF. The rules of construal associate antecedents and anaphors, let us say by the device of coindexing. For example, since PRO = $[_{NP}e]$ in (7) is in a position subject to control, a construal rule will assign an index to PRO. The index will be that of the object of the matrix sentence in this case; had the matrix verb been *promise*, the index would have been that of the matrix subject. Control depends on the properties of the matrix verb.[20] Note that we have been assuming tacitly that lexical NPs are indexed in surface

---

[20] For an account of control and thematic relations, cf. Jackendoff (1972). For some critical discussion, cf. Freidin (1975) and Hust and Brame (1976).

structure. These and other details that we have omitted here pose no problems of principle, to our knowledge.

The distinction between trace and PRO lies in the manner of indexing: in one case, by a movement rule; in the other, by a rule of construal. Since movement rules and rules of construal have somewhat different properties, there are a number of respects in which the NP–trace relation differs from the NP–PRO relation. For some discussion, see Chomsky (1977a, introduction).

We have as yet said nothing about the filters that determine well-formed surface structures. These will have to bear the burden of accounting for constraints which, in the earlier and far richer theory, were expressed in statements of ordering and obligatoriness, as well as all contextual dependencies that cannot be formulated in the narrower framework of core grammar. Our hypothesis, then, is that the consequences of ordering, obligatoriness, and contextual dependency can be captured in terms of surface filters, something that surely need not be the case in principle; and further, that these properties can be expressed in a natural way at this level. We return to this component of the grammar, having indicated here the role we expect it to play in terms of the considerations of (1a).

### 1.3  Problems of obligatory control [pp. 439–44]

We noted above that there are certain positions subject to control, citing examples (2), (3), and (7), repeated here as (27) and (28):

(27)  it is unclear [$_S$what [$_S$ ___ to do]]   (= (2))

(28)  a.  John persuaded Bill [$_S$[$_S$ ___ to leave]] (= (3a), (7))
      b.  John promised Bill [$_S$[$_S$ ___ to leave]]  (= (3b))

Alongside (27) we have (29):

(29)  a.  John told Bill [$_S$what [$_S$ ___ to do]]
      b.  John asked Bill [$_S$what [$_S$ ___ to do]]

Case (29a) is analogous to (28a): the object of the matrix verb, *Bill*, controls the embedded subject marked with ___; case (29b) is correspondingly analogous to (28b).

We see, then, that there are two factors that enter into obligatory control. In the first place, certain structures are "structures of obligatory control", for example, (30), where +WH is the mark for a (direct or indirect) interrogative:

(30)  [$_S$[$_{COMP}$what +WH][$_S$ ___ to VP]]

In the second place, certain verbs require that an embedded subject be controlled either by the matrix subject or matrix object,[21] as determined by properties

---

[21] Or matrix indirect object, as in *They appealed to John to leave*. We might argue that in (28b) the object is actually indirect, as in *John's promise to Bill to leave*.

of the matrix verb, as in (28). Where these two factors interact, we have the paradigm exhibited by (27) and (29). Note that in (27) we understand the "controlled" embedded subject to be arbitrary in reference.[22]

We can express these facts by making use of the base-generated element PRO, which we have taken to be [$_{NP}$e], i.e. an unexpanded NP in the base. Thus we assume that (30), as in (27) and (29), is base-generated in the form (31), and that (28a,b) are base-generated in the form (32):

(31) [$_S$[$_{COMP}$+WH][$_S$ NP to do what]]

(32) John (persuaded, promised) Bill [$_S$[$_{COMP}$−WH][$_S$NP VP]]

We take −WH to be the complementizer category that marks noninterrogatives, contrasting with +WH. Thus, we take the rule expanding COMP to be (33), where −WH can then be either *that*, *for*, or nothing:

(33) COMP → ±WH

If *Wh* Movement applies in (31), in accordance with the principle (16), we derive (30), with a trace in the vacated position.

We now formulate a rule that requires control in the structure (30). If (30) is embedded as in (29), control will be assigned by virtue of properties of the matrix verb; that is, the NP subject of the embedded sentence will be assigned either the index of the matrix object (as in (29a)) or of the matrix subject (as in (29b)). If, on the other hand, there is no governing verb that assigns control, the embedded subject is assigned an arbitrary index. We understand [$_{NP}$e] with an index that is not coindexed to an antecedent to be arbitrary in reference.

It is a general property of control rules that they can apply only to appropriate anaphoric elements, in this case, PRO = [$_{NP}$e]. Therefore, if any NP other than PRO were generated in the base – that is, if the optional base rules had expanded NP in the subject position of (31) – the rule of control could not apply. Since (30) (hence (31)) is a structure of obligatory control, there will be no well-formed output and the underlying base-generated structure is not a deep structure. Thus, we cannot have such sentences as (34):

(34) a. *It is unclear what John to do.
 b. *I told Bill what John to do.
 c. *Who did you tell Bill what *t* to do?

In (34c), *t* represents the trace of the displaced *who*; i.e. *it is* [$_{NP}$e], where the index *i* is that of *who*. The rule of control cannot apply in this case, since the

---

[22] More specifically, an arbitrary agent. Working within a somewhat different framework, Lasnik and Fiengo (1974) discuss this aspect of predicates requiring obligatory control. They suggest that the understood missing subject of a complement of *want* can bear any subject relation to the complement VP, while the understood subject of the complement of (e.g.) *force* must bear the agent relation.

NP already has an index. Therefore (34c) is excluded by inapplicability of an obligatory rule of control, as are (34a,b). We may assume that all rules of control are obligatory.

The preceding discussion illustrates a rule of control (one of the construal rules, we assume; cf. note 12) that applies, obligatorily by general convention, in a particular structural context. As stated above, there are also rules of control associated with particular verbs. Thus, *persuade, promise, tell*, and *ask* require control of the subject of an embedded infinitive;[23] control is exercised by the matrix subject or object as determined by the properties of the verb. Since control is obligatory, we cannot have (35), analogous to (34):

(35) a. *John persuaded Bill [Tom to leave]
 b. *who did John persuade Bill [t to leave] ($t$ = trace of *who*)
 c. *John promised [Bill to leave] (*Bill* the subject of *leave*)[24]
 d. *who did John promise [t to leave] (trace of *who* the subject of *leave*)

Notice that in this case, we cannot attribute obligatoriness of control entirely to the structural position, as in the case of (30) and (31). With a different choice of matrix verb, sentences with the structure of (35c) are quite possible; e.g. (36):

(36) a. John believed [Bill to be incompetent]
 b. who did John believe [t to be incompetent] (trace of *who* the subject of *be*)

It is true, however, that verbs that take an NP or PP complement along with a "bare" infinitival complement (an infinitive with no complementizer) are verbs of obligatory control. Thus no verb can appear in the structure (37a) unless NP' = PRO; we have (37b–d) but not (37e–g):

(37) a. NP ____ (P) NP [$_S$[NP' to VP]]
 b. we informed (proved to) Bill [that Harry was here]
 c. we pleaded with Bill [for Harry to be admitted]
 d. we persuaded (appealed to) Bill [PRO to leave)
 e. *we informed (appealed to) Bill [Harry to leave]
 f. *we pleaded with Bill [Harry to leave]
 g. *who did we persuade (appeal to, plead with) Bill [t to leave] ($t$ the trace of *who*)

---

[23] This property of control follows from the Tensed-S Condition (which blocks any anaphoric relation between an anaphor in a tensed sentence and an antecedent outside it) and the Specified Subject Condition (which permits only the subject of an embedded sentence or NP to be related anaphorically to an antecedent outside). Cf. note 14. Therefore, from these conditions, which are quite independently motivated, it follows that only the subject of an infinitive or gerund is susceptible to control.

[24] Note that the sentence (35c) is grammatical but not the structure indicated.

No special stipulations are required in the lexicon to account for these facts. They follow from a filter that is motivated independently. Infinitival constructions are blocked after NP or PP on independent grounds; as we will see.

Note that infinitival constructions with PRO subject are permitted in such constructions. The filter blocking constructions of the form [NP to VP] in certain constructions thus excludes PRO. We might take it to be a general principle that such filters apply only to indexed NPs; i.e. lexical NPs (which we assume to be indexed in surface structure; cf. [p. 146 of this chapter]) and trace (which is coindexed by a movement rule; cf. p. 432 [in C&L]). Recall that filters apply independently of construal rules; cf. (6). Therefore the indexing assigned by construal is "invisible" to filters. This amounts to treating "bound variables" (trace) on a par with the lexical NPs that bind them.

Note also that in the case of such structures as (37a) with NP' = PRO, we never have the analogue of (27), with PRO understood as arbitrary in reference. This follows at once from the fact that the governing verb assigns control, just as in the case of (34b,c).

It follows from this analysis of control that PRO and lexical NPs (including trace) are in complementary distribution in surface structures.[25] Where we find PRO, we can find neither a lexical NP nor a trace, and conversely. This property of control, stipulated in some earlier work,[26] follows, as we see, from a more principled treatment of the problem of control.

From these considerations, it follows also that obligatory control is to be distinguished from the phenomenon of Equi NP Deletion, as in (38):

(38) a. we want very much [for Bill to win]
　　　b. we want [Bill to win]
　　　c. We want (very much) to win.
　　　d. ?We want very much for ourselves to win.
　　　e. ?We want ourselves to win.

From (38a), we see that *want* (like *prefer*, etc.) takes the complementizer *for* in an embedded complement, as distinct from *believe*, *think*, and epistemic verbs in general, which require a null complementizer in an infinitive complement. From (38b), we see that the *for* complementizer may delete (and in some dialects, must delete) immediately after the verb. Since a lexical NP can appear in the subject position of the complement infinitive, it follows that PRO cannot appear there. Consequently, (38c) cannot be a case of control.[27]

---

[25] Given other properties of the grammar, it also follows, though not from the considerations presented here alone, that they are in complementary distribution in deep structures, though the class of relevant contexts is more complex in structure.

[26] E.g. Chomsky (1977a, chapter 4).

[27] Unless, of course, we were to assume a dual selectional classification for all of the *want*-type verbs, assigning them as complement both null-complementizer + PRO + VP and *for* + lexical – NP + VP. This would require a redundancy rule in the lexicon, a complication of the grammar that calls for empirical motivation, lacking in this case, since there is a simpler explanation, as we see directly. Furthermore, under this alternative analysis we would be forced to complicate the theory

Since NPs can appear freely in the subject position of the infinitival complement, there is nothing to prevent the reflexive forms from appearing, as in (38d,e). These, in fact, are dialectal variants. The obvious conclusion, then, is that the reflexive forms delete in the context (39), obligatorily in some dialects and optionally in others, leaving (40a,b) corresponding to (38d,e), respectively:

(39) [$_S$ for ___ to ... ]

(40) a. we want very much for to win
 b. we want for to win

Note that this rule, involving a high degree of uncertainty and variation, is outside the framework of core grammar. Expressions with the structure of (40b) are dialect variants, but are excluded in Standard English by the filter (41) that blocks *for-to* constructions:

(41) *[for-to]

Since *for* can delete by the rule of free complementizer deletion noted above, we derive (38c) as the variant, optional or obligatory depending on dialect, of (38d,e).

Equi, then, is simply a matter of reflexive deletion. It follows too that we cannot have Equi with *believe*-type verbs; these do not permit *for* complementizers so that deletion of reflexive cannot apply in the context (39). Thus we have neither (42), analogous to (38a), nor (43), analogous to (38c):

(42) *John believes sincerely [for Bill to be incompetent]

(43) *John believes (sincerely) to be incompetent

Rather, we can only have (44), which is permitted in all dialects, analogous to (38e):[28]

(44) John believes himself to be incompetent.

The phenomena of Equi and related matters thus fall out very simply, with no unmotivated rules.[29] The crucial observation is the distinction between *want*-type and *believe*-type verbs, noted earlier [p. 139]. And, as we see, Equi and control are quite different phenomena.[30]

---

of control. Verbs would no longer be categorized as assigning control (presumably, by virtue of their semantics), since there would be nothing then to prevent the control rule from applying to *want* in cases (38a,b), blocking the sentence as ill-formed for the same reasons that blocked (35).

[28] We cannot have *John believes sincerely himself to be incompetent*, analogous to (38d), for independent reasons to which we return below.

[29] Cf. Chomsky (1974; 1977a, chapter 4).

[30] Careful analyses restricted to Equi have characteristically noted that there are two quite different processes of Equi NP Deletion, corresponding to our distinction between Equi and control. Cf. Kayne (1975).

Given this framework, we can eliminate a gap in an independent argument in favor of a reflexive-deletion analysis for Equi advanced by Fodor (1975). He points out that in the sentence (45), as the meaning makes clear, the element deleted in the position of ___ cannot be either *Churchill* or *he* (plus possessive):

(45) Only Churchill remembers ___ giving the speech about blood, sweat, toil and tears.

He concludes, then, that it must be *self* that deletes in this position. Another possibility would be that PRO is what appears in this position, and that the structure is one of control.[31] However, this is excluded under the present analysis, since we see that lexical NPs can appear freely in the position marked by ___.

The rules of control, which fall under (6-3b), play a role somewhat analogous to that of surface filters in that they block derivations leading to ill-formed surface structures. The failure of well-formedness, in this case, is semantic in origin.[32] It is not unreasonable to suppose that the rules of control, or at least significant aspects of these rules, belong to UG. Thus, obligatoriness of control in such structures as (30) seems quite general across languages, and presumably has to do with the semantics of infinitival constructions, an interesting though poorly understood question. Similarly, we would expect that in other languages, verbs with semantics similar to the English verbs of obligatory control would also require control in analogous contexts (necessarily infinitives or gerunds; cf. note 23). The rules of control just discussed are extremely simple, and in fact, may not even have to be stated in particular grammars. They are somewhat analogous in their effects to surface filters, though with the added property that they also assign indices that determine semantic properties.

## References

Akmajian, A., P. Culicover, and T. Wasow, eds (1977) *Formal Syntax*, Academic Press, New York.

Aronoff, M. (1976) *Word Formation in Generative Grammar*, Linguistic Inquiry Monograph 1, MIT Press, Cambridge, Massachusetts.

Besten, H. den (1976) "Surface Lexicalization and Trace Theory," in H. van Riemsdijk, ed. (1976).

Bever, T. G. (1970) "The Cognitive Basis for Linguistic Structures," in J. R. Hayes, ed., *Cognition and the Development of Language*, Wiley and Sons, New York.

Bever, T. G. and D. T. Langendoen (1971) "A Dynamic Model for the Evolution of Language," *Linguistic Inquiry* 2, 433-63.

Brame, M. K. (1976) *Conjectures and Refutations in Syntax and Semantics*, American Elsevier, New York.

Bresnan, J. W. (1971) "Sentence Stress and Syntactic Transformations," *Language* 47, 257-81.

---

[31] See Lightfoot (1977).
[32] This is loosely put. As noted earlier, the rules of "semantic interpretation" applied to surface structures relate to the syntax of logical form.

Bresnan, J. W. (1972) "Theory of Complementation in English Syntax," unpublished Doctoral dissertation, MIT, Cambridge, Massachusetts.
Chomsky, N. (1955) *Logical Structure of Linguistic Theory*, Plenum, New York, 1975.
Chomsky, N. (1957) *Syntactic Structures*, Mouton, The Hague.
Chomsky, N. (1964) *Current Issues in Linguistic Theory*, Mouton, The Hague.
Chomsky, N. (1965) *Aspects of the Theory of Syntax*, MIT Press, Cambridge, Massachusetts.
Chomsky, N. (1972) *Studies on Semantics in Generative Grammar*, Mouton, The Hague.
Chomsky, N. (1973) "Conditions on Transformations," in S. Anderson and P. Kiparsky, eds, *A Festschrift for Morris Halle*, Holt, Rinehart, and Winston, New York; reprinted in Chomsky (1977a).
Chomsky, N. (1974) *The Amherst Lectures, Documents Linguistiques*, Université Paris VII.
Chomsky, N. (1975) *Reflections on Language*, Pantheon, New York.
Chomsky, N. (1977a) *Essays on Form and Interpretation*, American Elsevier, New York.
Chomsky, N. (1977b) "On Wh-Movement," in A. Akmajian, P. Culicover, and T. Wasow, eds (1977).
Dougherty, R. C. (1973) "A Survey of Linguistic Methods and Arguments," *Foundations of Language* 10, 432–90.
Emonds, J. E. (1970) "Root and Structure-Preserving Transformations," unpublished Doctoral dissertation, MIT, Cambridge, Massachusetts.
Emonds, J. E. (1976) *A Transformational Approach to English Syntax*, Academic Press, New York.
Fiengo, R. W. (1974) "Semantic Conditions on Surface Structure," unpublished Doctoral dissertation, MIT, Cambridge, Massachusetts.
Fiengo, R. W. (1977) "On Trace Theory," *Linguistic Inquiry* 8, 35–62.
Fodor, J. A. (1975) *The Language of Thought*, Crowell, New York.
Fodor, J. A. and J. Katz, eds (1964) *The Structure of Language*, Prentice-Hall, Englewood Cliffs, New Jersey.
Fodor, J. A., T. G. Bever, and M. F. Garrett (1974) *The Psychology of Language*, McGraw-Hill, New York.
Freidin, R. (1975) Review of Jackendoff (1972), *Language* 51, 189–205.
Hudson, R. A. (1972) "Why it is that that that that Follows the Subject is Impossible," *Linguistic Inquiry* 3, 116–18.
Hust, J. and M. Brame (1976) "Jackendoff on Interpretive Semantics," *Linguistic Analysis* 2, 243–77.
Jackendoff, R. S. (1972) *Semantic Interpretation in Generative Grammar*, MIT Press, Cambridge, Massachusetts.
Jackendoff, R. S. (forthcoming) [1977] $\bar{X}$ *Syntax: A Study of Phrase Structure*, Linguistic Inquiry Monograph 2, MIT Press, Cambridge, Massachusetts.
Kayne, R. S. (1975) *French Syntax: The Transformational Cycle*, MIT Press, Cambridge, Massachusetts.
Lasnik, H. (1976) "Remarks on Coreference," *Linguistic Analysis* 2, 1–22.
Lasnik, H. and R. Fiengo (1974) "Complement Object Deletion," *Linguistic Inquiry* 5, 535–71.
Lasnik, H. and J. Kupin (1976) "A Restrictive Theory of Transformational Grammar," [*Theoretical Linguistics* 4, 173–96].
Lightfoot, D. (1977) "On Traces and Conditions on Rules," in A. Akmajian, P. Culicover, and T. Wasow, eds (1977).
May, R. (1977) "Logical Form and Conditions on Rules," in J. Kegl, D. Nash, and A. Zaanen, *Papers from the Eighth Regional Meeting of the North Eastern Linguistic Society*.

Otero, C. (1976) "The Dictionary in a Generative Grammar," mimeographed paper, UCLA, Los Angeles, California.
Perlmutter, D. M. (1968) "Deep and Surface Constraints in Syntax," unpublished Doctoral dissertation, MIT, Cambridge, Massachusetts.
Perlmutter, D. M. (1971) *Deep and Surface Structure Constraints in Syntax*, Holt, Rinehart and Winston, New York.
Peters, P. S. and R. W. Ritchie (1973) "On the Generative Power of Transformational Grammars," *Information Sciences* 6, 49–83.
Postal, P. M. (1974) *On Raising*, MIT Press, Cambridge, Massachusetts.
Quicoli, A. C. (1975a) "Conditions on Quantifier Movement in French," mimeographed paper, MIT, Cambridge, Massachusetts.
Quicoli, A. C. (1975b) "Clitic Movement in French Causatives," mimeographed paper, MIT Cambridge, Massachusetts.
Quicoli, A. C. (1976) "Conditions on Clitic Movement in Portuguese," *Linguistic Analysis* 2, 199–223.
Reinhart, T. (1976) "The Syntactic Domain of Anaphora," unpublished Doctoral dissertation, MIT, Cambridge, Massachusetts.
Ross, J. R. (1967) "Constraints on Variables in Syntax," unpublished Doctoral dissertation, MIT, Cambridge, Massachusetts.
Ross, J. R. (1973) "The Same Side Filter," in C. Corum et al., eds, *Papers from the Ninth Regional Meeting of the Chicago Linguistic Society*, University of Chicago, Chicago, Illinois.
van Riemsdijk, H. C., ed. (1976) *Green Ideas Blown Up*, University of Amsterdam, Publiharies van het Instituute voor Algemene Taalwetenschap, No. 13.

## 2 A closer look at the content of "Filters and Control"

In our discussion of C&L, this section will first present some exegesis of section 1.1 of the article, examining C&L's goals for linguistic theory and their conceptualization of the components of the grammar. It will also take a closer look at their treatment of Passivization, insofar as it is a model for the later discussion of their analysis of RtoS. The section will then move to a brief synopsis of section 1.2, wherein C&L provide psycholinguistic motivation for (some of) the filters that they propose. A detailed examination and evaluation of their proposals for control (section 1.3) will be taken up in section 3 of this chapter, preceded here by a brief synopsis of some of the more relevant content in the remainder of the article.

### *Restricting the options (section 1.1)*

Although Chomsky (1965) only names two levels of adequacy (descriptive and explanatory) where the construction of grammars is concerned, linguists have come to recognize three levels of adequacy. The first, OBSERVATIONAL ADEQUACY, involves the not always trivial task of determining which are the well-formed expressions in a language, and which are not (and presumably being able to state whether the ill-formedness, where it occurs, is syntactic, semantic, or pragmatic). The second level of adequacy (the first that C&L refer to in their article) is DESCRIPTIVE ADEQUACY. Traditionally, a descriptively adequate grammar is one that generates all and only the grammatical sentences of a language, and which provides a principled account for native speakers' intuitions about the structure of these. In other words, having determined what the facts are (i.e., which sentences are grammatical), the linguist must then provide an analysis (e.g., a set of rules) that will generate all these sentences and no others, and which accords with native speakers' perception of their structure.

Since descriptively adequate grammars can be constructed with a range of initial hypotheses and formal mechanisms (that is, a number of "theories of grammar"), C&L articulate the notion EXPLANATORY ADEQUACY as a metric for evaluating **theories** of grammar (as opposed to the grammars themselves). Thus, among the various theories used to construct descriptively adequate grammars of languages (e.g., Relational Grammar, the Revised Extended Standard Theory, Categorial Grammar, etc.), we might expect that one of these is, in C&L's terms, "optimal." At its core, an explanatorily adequate theory is supposed to be the one which can account for a child's acquisition of his or her language. Assuming that the particular grammar of a language is constructed as a response to linguistic stimuli, C&L would say that the explanatorily adequate theory of grammar is the one which will successfully predict, given the linguistic experience of the child, the grammar that the child does in fact construct (i.e., "the attainment of grammatical competence").

Two points might be made here, regarding the discussion of adequacy. First, C&L explicitly assume that grammatical competence involves a UG (universal grammar), which is taken to be a universal set of boundaries on possible human grammars that is a "species-specific innate" attribute of the human mind. It should be noted that this is not a necessary assumption for there to be an explanatorily adequate theory of grammar, since one might imagine a theory of grammatical acquisition which successfully predicts the grammar to be acquired, solely on the basis of linguistic input. In fact, assuming certain properties of language to be innate may in fact make explanatory adequacy more easily attainable, since any inexplicable property of the grammar can be off-loaded onto UG (and one would not know, a priori, whether this property is truly a UG property or whether it is simply a property that the linguist is unable to account for). The second point worth making concerns the connection between the discussion of adequacy and the rest of the paper. As lofty as the goals of this discussion may be, and as closely it may be followed by a description of the (Revised) Extended Standard Theory of grammar, there is no explicit claim that (R)EST represents a model that has attained (or that is about to attain) explanatory adequacy. In this regard, the rhetorical device of presenting one discussion adjacent to the next creates the tacit impression that they are in fact linked (even though C&L make no such claim). The reader should realize, then, that C&L's goals are indeed legitimate, and that these goals form a basis for some of the principles articulated in the article, but that the remainder of the paper does not presume to present a (testable) explanatorily adequate theory of grammar.

This said, the changes that C&L propose for the EST model, often referred to as REST, involve two principles that are indeed aimed at (eventually) arriving at a theoretical model that will ultimately possess explanatory adequacy. First and foremost, they propose to simplify and generalize the transformational component of the grammar, reducing rules to simple operations that are freely applied at any point in the derivation. Done away with are construction-specific rules, rule ordering, and obligatory transformations, as well as the formerly favored "conditions" on transformations, i.e., those of Chomsky (1973). Restrictions on generative capacity are now apportioned to the previously articulated (see chapter 4, section 1) modules of the grammar. Input to Deep Structure is now constrained by X-bar theory (Jackendoff 1977). The mapping from Deep Structure to Surface Structure (derived through simplex movement operations) is limited by principles of structure preservation (Emonds 1970, 1976). Mapping from Surface Structure to Universal Phonetics (i.e., phonetic representation) is limited by (language-specific) filters, and mapping from Surface Structure to Logical Form (i.e., semantic representation) is restricted by (possibly universal) principles governing the construal of one constituent with another.

Presented here is a schematic diagram of the REST model of grammar, as described in C&L. This diagram is modeled after the one presented in section 1 of chapter 4, and incorporates the numbered components provided by C&L in (6) in the excerpt.

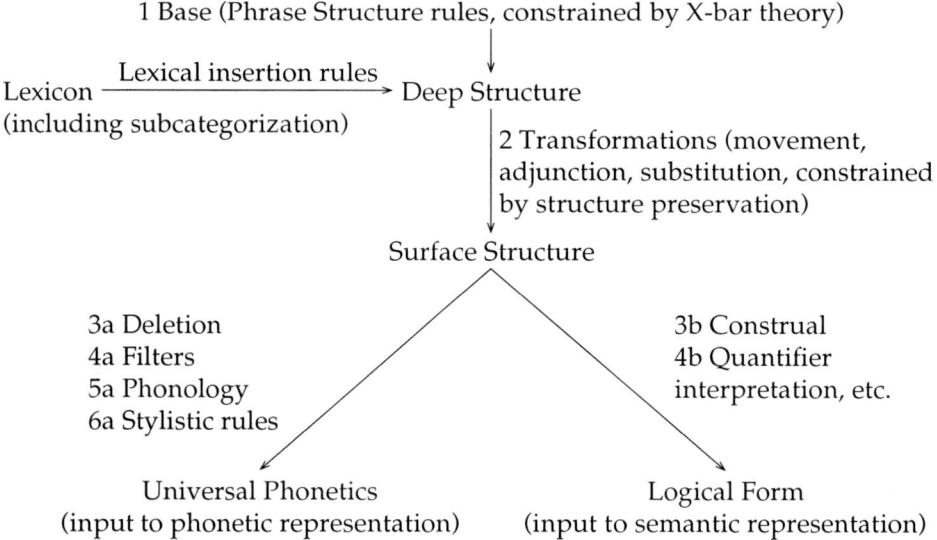

*The Revised Extended Standard Theory (REST) Model*

One of the most salient differences between EST and REST is the repositioning of the semantic representation module (now Logical Form, LF). Phonetic and semantic representations are now both taken to be mapped directly from Surface Structure, and to be parallel with one another. The mechanisms constraining this mapping are in keeping with nature of the modules themselves.

On the Universal Phonetics (UP) side, ungrammatical outputs are thrown out by filters, such as *[wh comp], which are appropriately language particular. This "language-particular" space is, as should be expected, the repository of those aspects of grammar which do not interface with meaning. On the LF side, ungrammatical outputs are ruled out by rules of construal, e.g., the obligatory binding of variables, which are presumed to be universal in nature. Expectedly, this "universal" space is precisely where one would seek to impose universal principles, on the understanding that such principles are motivated by universal aspects of language meaning. The Tensed-S Condition, for example, is transformed here from being a condition on movement rules into a condition on the interpretation of indices.

Working backwards through the model, we find that transformations have now been simplified to a set of very general operations (movement, adjunction, and substitution). Movement is most readily exemplified as part of the Passive rule, wherein the object NP moves into subject position. Adjunction involves adding material to an existing constituent in order to create a larger constituent of the same category. Finally, substitution involves the insertion of material into an empty node. These transformations are unlinked to any rule (i.e., are context free) and they apply freely (i.e., they are neither obligatory or inherently conditioned). They are also unordered with respect to one another (e.g., adjunctions are not applied before/after substitutions). Finally, they obey principles of structure preservation (which set limits on the permutation of base-generated structure). At the top of the model, we find the Base component, which generates phrase markers in the Deep Structure via a set of Phrase Structure rules. C&L assume a (universal) set of category features, out of which the major categories (for a given language) are composed. These PS rules are constrained, as we have already noted, by principles of X-bar theory. Of course, the insertion of lexical items into the Deep Structure is constrained (as in EST) by subcategorization features on these items.

Summing up, the REST model includes a different sort of constraint mechanism for each mapping relation between its component modules. These are shown here in (1).

(1) 
| Mapping from: | to: | is mediated by: |
|---|---|---|
| Base | DS | X-bar theory |
| Lexicon | DS | Subcategorization features |
| DS | SS | Structure preservation |
| SS | UP (PF) | Filters |
| SS | LF | Rules of construal and quantifier interpretation |

In a system where all movement is optionally and freely applied, overgeneration inevitably results. Having taken the diacritics away from the transformational component, overgeneration must now be "cured" elsewhere. C&L's treatment of the passive construction, as outlined in section 1.1, provides a window onto how this system works. As C&L point out, the DS for the passive sentence *Bill was hit* is as shown here in (2) (with some orthogonal structure omitted).

(2) [$_{NP}$e] [$_{VP}$was [$_{AP}$-en [$_{VP}$hit [$_{NP}$Bill]]]]

In mapping from DS to SS, application of the rule "move NP" moves *Bill* from the verb complement NP position into the subject NP slot, leaving behind an empty node. According to C&L, "move NP" results in coindexation of the two NPs involved in the rule, as shown in (3). The two NPs are now in what has come to be known as an "antecedent–trace" relation.

(3) [$_{NP}$Bill]$_i$ [$_{VP}$was [$_{AP}$-en [$_{VP}$hit [$_{NP}$e]$_i$ ]]]

Under this model, the application of "move NP" is in every instance optional. What forces movement in passive structures is that (2) would violate a constraint at LF if movement did not apply. The subject element [NP e] in (2) is unindexed without movement, there being no rule of control to provide it with an interpretation. If it remains empty, it will be a free (and uninterpreted) variable at LF. Hence, although "move NP" itself is optional and although nothing in DS or SS requires object–subject movement in passives, the derivation is necessary to preserve well-formedness in the (later) LF module.

## *A teleology for (aspects of) syntax (section 1.2)*

In this section, C&L suggest a possible "functional explanation" to explain the existence of certain filters, such as the *[$_{NP}$NP tense VP] filter. According to their account, this filter rules out sentences such as (4a), on the (tacitly retained) assumption that sentential subjects are NPs.

(4) a. *He left is a surprise.
 b. That he left is a surprise.

Here, the sentential subject *he left* has the structure given in (5), and (5) violates the *[$_{NP}$NP tense VP] filter.

(5) [$_{NP}$[$_S$[$_{NP}$he] PAST [$_{VP}$leave]]]

The sentential subject in (4b), on the other hand, contains additional structure that prevents the filter from applying, as shown in (6).[1]

(6) [$_{NP}$[$_{S'}$that [$_S$[$_{NP}$he] PAST [$_{VP}$leave]]]]

C&L suggest that this filter is linked to a perceptual strategy that would initially lead one to interpret the sentential subject of (4a) as a main clause (i.e., if something looks like a main clause, treat it so), and would thereby force the reader/hearer to reanalyze the sentence midway. Thus, the filter's function is to avoid such perceptually difficult constructions, in favor of ones that are easier to process.

The presentation in this section of ("speculations about") teleology is initially surprising, given C&L's stand on innateness, until we understand how this teleology is (tacitly) limited. While such teleological explanations for grammatical principles are most often the province of functionally oriented theories of grammar, C&L invoke teleology here as a possible explanation for the evolution of the child's innate language capacity. Thus, for them, the filter is the outcome of an evolutionary process in which perceptual strategies have led to UG principles that would make such a filter the unmarked case. Their point here is that the child language learner will never be presented with the kind of negative evidence (e.g., grammatical correction) which would allow the filter ruling out (4a) to be learned.

C&L's point about learnability is well-taken, but is the filter universal? The evolutionary pressures leading to the expression of the filter in English would presumably act on all languages. If we consider only English and a few other (similar) languages, we might be led to think that it is a universal. But the perceptually based teleology invoked here becomes somewhat suspect when it is observed that some languages (such as Madurese) do not have a filter that reflects such a strategy.

(7) a. [Hasan ngeco' sepedha] ma-sossa Siti
 Hasan AV.steal bicycle AC.cs-sad Siti
 'Hasan stole the bicycle made Siti sad.'
 b. [Ja' [Hasan ngeco' sepedha]] ma-sossa Siti
 COMP Hasan AV.steal bicycle AC.cs-sad Siti.
 'That Hasan stole the bicycle made Siti sad.'

The Madurese examples in (7a,b) are parallel to the English sentences in (4a,b), with the obvious exception that (7a) is grammatical despite not having an overt complementizer in its sentential subject, showing that Madurese does not have the relevant filter (even though the sentence presents the same perceptual difficulties as does (4a)). Of course, C&L note that these perceptual strategies are assumed to facilitate, but not to guarantee, the existence of the appropriate filters in a given language/dialect. But one might expect nonetheless to find such an important perceptual strategy as cited above to result in very few exceptions.

## Sections 1.3 and 1.4

Section 1.3 of C&L (presented in the excerpt) is principally concerned with the analysis of obligatory control structures. The content of this, together with an examination of C&L's analysis of raising and Equi constructions, will be taken up in section 3 of this chapter.

Section 1.4 of C&L discusses the properties of the English complementizer system. Here they present in some detail the PS rules (e.g., S'→COMP S), the selectional restrictions imposed from the lexicon (e.g., [$_{AP}$illegal [$_{S'}$for NP to VP]]), and the filters (e.g., *[for-to]) that generate the desired results. Of note in this section is their assumption that all complementizers must carry a WH feature (i.e., COMP→±WH). Complementizers that do not carry this feature are deemed "uninterpretable." So, while these base rules are optional in principle, interpretability at LF may play a role in forcing their operation (as we saw with NP movement in Passive). Also worth pointing out is the heavy reliance in this model on selectional restrictions that refer to grammatical categories. Category selection (C-selection) in this model is the unremarkable associate of semantic selection (S-selection), and is needed to distinguish between predicates (such as *likely* and *possible*) that are semantically indistinguishable, but which select for distinct complements as shown in (8).

(8) a. That I will win is likely/possible.
　　b. It is likely/possible that I will win.
　　c. I am likely/*possible to win.

The grammaticality of (8c) with *likely* is determined in C&L's model by its being subcategorized for a [$_S$NP to VP] complement (while *possible* is not so subcategorized). As unremarkable and sensible as all this may seem, Chomsky proposes ten years later (Chomsky 1986b:90) to do away with c-selection, in favor of pure s-selection (basing this proposal on what he says were observations by David Pesetsky). Needless to say, a great number of intractable problems for the analysis of complements has ensued in its wake (see Grimshaw 1979 and Newmeyer 2001).

## *Filters, and more filters (section 2, etc.)*

At 34 pages, section 2 at the core of the C&L paper presents a very detailed elaboration of some particular filters that are claimed to play a central role in the syntax of English. The shorter of the subsections (2.1) presents the "*that*-trace" filter, *[that [$_{NP}$e]], showing how it serves to block the extraction of embedded subjects across an overt complementizer, as in (9b).

(9) a. who do you think [[$_{NP}$e] saw Bill]
　　b. *who do you think [that [$_{NP}$e] saw Bill]

C&L make two key points in this section. First, the filter must be refined. In this regard, they show that on the one hand the filter does not just reference the complementizer *that* (that is, extraction from embedded subject position is also prohibited when a +WH complementizer is present) as in (10),

(10) *who do you wonder [whether [$_{NP}$e] saw Bill]?

and on the other hand the filter does not apply to relative clauses, as shown in (11).

(11) do you know [$_{NP}$the man [that [$_{NP}$e] saw Bill]]?

Taken altogether these facts motivate a filter that has the form given in (12).[2]

(12) *[$_{S'}$ ±WH [$_{NP}$e] ... ], unless S' or its trace is in the context: [$_{NP}$NP ____ ... ]

Second, C&L argue in favor of incorporating this filter into UG, despite apparent cross-linguistic evidence to the contrary, as seen in the Spanish example (13).

(13) quién creiste [que [___ vio a Juan]]?
 who you(SG).believed that saw DAT John
 'Who did you believe that saw John?'

Their motivation for doing this is to counter the otherwise plausible position taken by Perlmutter (1968) that the filter in (12) is language specific and only works in languages that do not have Subject Deletion (which in (13) would involve the absence via deletion of the matrix subject *tú* 'you'). On C&L's account though, the apparent violations of (12) that occur in Subject Deleting languages actually involve structures which the filter in (12) cannot apply to. For them, the process of subject deletion applies to the underlying structure for (13) given in (14a), yielding the structure in (14b).

(14) a. quién tú creiste [que [[$_{NP}$e] vio a Juan]]?
 b. quién ___ creiste [que [___ vio a Juan]]?

Since deletion eliminates the "category with null content" following *que*, and replaces it with "nothing," the filter in (12) does not apply. Note here that "deletion" in the REST model is an operation that is part of the mapping from surface structure to universal phonetics, and the trace [$_{NP}$e] would still be present in the mapping from surface structure to logical form. This is important, because without the trace [$_{NP}$e] of *quién* in the embedded clause, the *wh* expression would be rendered uninterpretable.

As feasible and coherent as C&L's proposal may seem, it is important to examine their arguments for claiming (12) to be part of UG. As one can see, their solution is dependent on the particular structure of the REST model. For instance, it crucially relies on syntactic deletion being restricted to the mapping between surface structure and universal phonetics. For example, if one were to assume that logical form were a deeper part of the structure (i.e., that the interpretive module for quantifier-variable relations was not where REST has it, cf. Lakoff 1971), then part of the motivation for distinguishing between traces [$_{NP}$e] and "nothing" would be lost. Second, the reader might (and should) find it to be curious that the distinction between "empty categories" and "deleted categories" is crucially important at the Surface Structure – universal phonetics interface. On the one hand, it makes perfect sense for operations that do not affect interpretation to be situated in the interface between surface structure and universal phonetics, such as the optional deletion of otherwise recoverable elements (e.g., *that*-deletion, and subject pronoun deletion in languages having robust agreement inflections on the verb). This said, it is unclear why (or how) a distinction between two sorts of phonologically null outputs ("trace" vs. "nothing") could possibly be relevant to this mapping. In contrast with the Surface Structure–LF mapping, where (null) categories might profitably be distinguished by the sort of element that binds them, the distinction here seems contrived only to drive the conclusion that the relevant filter is universal. In this regard, the reader can only grant the coherence (within the assumptions of the REST model) of the claim that the filter in question is part of UG. Empirical arguments would need to be found in order to go further.

C&L's section 2.2 is primarily focused on an account for the distribution of infinitival constructions of the form [NP to VP], where the NP is lexical. As the reader may recall from section 1.3 (of the excerpt), C&L note that interrogative infinitival constructions with lexical NPs cannot appear in the immediate scope of a +WH element. This accounts for the ungrammaticality of (15a) in contrast with (15b), where (15b) involves a PRO subject in the infinitive.

(15) a. *We wondered [whether [Sally to leave]]
　　　b. We wondered [whether [____ to leave]]

Here, C&L discuss the distribution of declarative infinitival constructions. They observe that the [NP to VP] construction is unacceptable in the domain of nouns (16a), adjectives (16b), adverbs (16c), and in sentence-initial position (16d).

(16) a. *we discussed [our plan [Sally to win]]
　　　b. *it is [forbidden [your child to drive after dark]]
　　　c. *they want desperately [their candidate to win]
　　　d. *[Bob to finish on time] would be a miracle

Conversely, as seen here in (17), the construction is well-formed in the domain of verbs and the prepositional complementizer *for* (note that the examples in (16) are all rendered grammatical by the insertion of *for* before the infinitival clause).

(17) a. we all want [Bob to finish on time]
　　　b. [for [Bob to finish on time]] would be wonderful

From this range of facts, C&L distill the filter in (18).[3]

(18) *[$_\alpha$NP to VP], unless $\alpha$ is adjacent to and in the domain of [−N]

Turning to infinitival relative clauses, C&L observe that the filter (18) helps to predict their form and distribution as in (19), where the infinitival relative clause is ungrammatical unless adjacent to and preceded by *for*.

(19) a plan *(for) [you to consider [$_{NP}$e]]

However, when the target of relativization is the subject of the infinitival clause, things get a little confusing.

(20) a. *a student for [[$_{NP}$e] to help with the report]
　　　b. a student [[$_{NP}$e] to help with the report]

While it is clear that (20a) is ruled out by C&L's separately posited *[for-to] filter (example (41) in the excerpt), it is not so apparent for C&L why (20b) is not ruled out by (18). Note in this regard that [$_{NP}$e] in (20) is the trace of a deleted relative pronoun, and as such, is considered by C&L to be on a par with "lexical NP" (in contrast with PRO). To accommodate this state of affairs, C&L suggest that (20b) presents the filter with an ambiguous structure. It can be regarded as "[[$_{NP}$e] to VP]" in the context of *a student*, a structure that would be ruled out by (18). Alternatively, it can be factored into "[$_{NP}$[$_{NP}$a person] to VP]" as in (21).

(21) [$_{NP}$[$_{NP}$a student] to [$_{VP}$help with the report]]

Assuming that the factorization in (21) properly contains the factorization in (20b), and that the *A-over-A* Condition (or its "spirit") requires that the filter apply to the larger category, C&L propose revising (18) to (22), where the boldfaced phrase admits the apparent exception.

(22) *[$_{\alpha}$NP to VP], unless α is adjacent to and in the domain of [–N] **or α = NP**

Their analysis of these constructions and the filter that they distill for them present a profusion of problems, both theoretical and empirical, such that this discussion can only touch upon a few of them. The most obvious empirical difficulty for C&L, one acknowledged in the article, concerns the distribution of phrases such as (21). Having initially ruled out infinitival constructions such as (16d) from subject position with the filter in (18), they have now readmitted a subclass of these. The revised filter (22) should not care about the context for (21), since the phrase is admitted by virtue of its being an NP. Unfortunately for their analysis, subject–object asymmetry is still observed, as in (23).

(23)  a.  We interviewed a student to help with the report.
      b.  *A student to help with the report was interviewed by Margo.

The contrast in (23) suggests that the infinitival construction is still sanctioned as a verb complement and ruled out as a subject (even though the revised filter (22) can no longer accommodate that fact). Other facts further cloud the issue (cf. C&L 1977:464–6), and C&L admit that they "have no serious proposal to make" regarding the problematic cases.[4]

Their solution is problematic on theoretical grounds as well. The factorization of (20b) that is devised to satisfy the (revised) filter is one that renders "invisible" several crucial bits of structure (shown in boldface in (24)).

(24) [$_{NP}$[$_{NP}$a person] [$_{COMP}$**(who)**] [$_{S}$[$_{NP}$**e**] to [$_{VP}$clean the pool]]]

Even admitting the operation of deletion on the relative pronoun *who*, it is still unclear how these (empty) categories are rendered invisible to the filter. Recall that [$_{NP}$e] is a "trace", and was previously argued by C&L to be "visible" and to be distinguished from "nothing". Further, in order to successfully predict that the filter will choose (21) over (20b) as the relevant structure, C&L resurrect the "spirit" of the *A-over-A* Condition. However, conditions on representations such as this are ordinarily taken to rule out the "relatedness" of two categories (such as an NP and its trace) across a boundary defined by the condition. It is unclear here exactly how this condition (or its "spirit") would choose between the two structures in contention. Acknowledging some of the empirical uncertainty regarding the proper characterization of the [NP to VP] filter, C&L are ultimately indecisive as to whether (18) or (22) is the more appropriate characterization. This will become an issue when their analysis of RtoO constructions is examined in section 3.

C&L turn next to the case of the null (Ø)-complementizer and its interaction with RtoS adjectives. C&L claim that the complement structure of a typical RtoO sentence involves the Ø-complementizer in the base, as shown in (25).

(25)  They believe Ø him to be a fool.

Having posited earlier (in their section 1.4) that complementizer deletion may freely apply, the deletion of Ø leaves the [NP to VP] complement adjacent to and in the domain of the verb *believe*, and sanctioned by filter (18)/(22). In the case of an RtoS verb such as *seem*, C&L assume the same underlying complement structure prior to movement. That is, *seem* is followed by a Ø-complementizer and a [NP to VP] category. Following movement, the structure in (26) obtains, where [$_{NP}$e] is the trace of *Terry*.

(26)  Terry seems Ø [$_{NP}$e] to be a fool.

Again, the Ø-complementizer may freely delete, leaving the [NP to VP] category adjacent to and in the domain of a verb, *seems*. Less tractable is the case of a RtoS adjective such as *likely*. Consider (27), which is analogous to (26).

(27)  Terry is likely Ø [$_{NP}$e] to be a fool.

Here, if the Ø-complementizer deletes (as posited for (26)), the [NP to VP] constituent will be adjacent to and in the domain of the [+N] adjective *likely*, and should be ruled out by filter (18)/(22). In order to accommodate this well-populated class of cases, C&L propose a rule whereby the Ø-complementizer acquires a [−N] feature when it follows a [+V] element. Simply put, the Ø-complementizer becomes an element that will satisfy filter (18)/(22) whenever it follows a verb or an adjective. Since complementizer deletion is free **and optional**, (27) can be saved from the filter if deletion does not apply. The requisite input to the filter (with features indicated) is shown in (28).

(28)  Terry is likely$_{[+N]}$ Ø$_{[-N]}$ [$_{NP}$e] to be a fool.

In the cases of RtoS and RtoO verbs, (25) and (26), complementizer deletion is still free to apply, or not, since the outcome in either case will satisfy filter

(18)/(22). Regarding their somewhat ad hoc move to save RtoS adjective constructions from the filter, C&L rightly note that it is somewhat odd in the mapping to universal phonetics to have "a rule adding a phonetically unrealized feature" to a phonologically null category. They suggest here that the rule may be the result of a principle that guarantees at least one (and perhaps only one) permissible outcome from a given base structure.[5] In their (very informal) terms, there is a principle that insures that "you should be able to say what you think." However, while their solution is compatible with the data at hand, there is clearly a host of other options that remain unexplored, and one might say that the analysis is not motivated so much by the data as by a desire to maintain what has been proposed to this point.

Another issue taken up in this section is a crucial difference between lexical NPs and traces. To this point, C&L have argued that they are alike and to be distinguished from (controlled) PRO. Here, they note that there is after all a difference between the two categories. Using data such as (29), they make the case that lexical NPs may not be separated from their preceding complement-taking verb by an adjunct.

(29) a. *We all believe sincerely him to be the best choice.
  b. Who do you all believe sincerely [$_{NP}$e] to be the best choice?
  c. We believe (*sincerely) Joseph.

To accommodate these facts they propose the filter given here in (30),

(30) *[V adjunct NP], NP lexical

and apply the results of this filter to the [NP to VP] filter proposed earlier.[6]

The remainder of the article consists of: (i) a short section 3 in which C&L refine the filter for tensed clauses from section 1.2, ending up with a revision that parallels the [NP to VP] filter (18)/(22); a brief discussion of the general formal properties of filters (section 4); and three appendices that take up, in some detail, issues that were deemed orthogonal to the main body of the article.

## 3   Raising and Control (and Equi) in REST

This section will review C&L's analysis of obligatory control structures, Raising (both RtoS, which is a simple case of NP movement, and RtoO, which is assumed not to involve any movement), and Equi NP Deletion. These will be discussed in turn.

### *Obligatory Control*

Section 1.3 elaborates C&L's account of Control. Here, the analysis of Control (a rule of construal) is dependent on two things: (i) certain structures or verbs that require Control, and (ii) a special category, PRO, that is distinguished from lexical NP and trace and is able to avoid the filter (18)/(22). As they show in the excerpt, there are two classes of control structures that must be accounted for, +WH infinitival clauses such as (31a) and (31b),

(31) a. I don't know [what [[$_{NP}$e] to say]]
  b. [what [[$_{NP}$e] to say]] often depends on the situation

and −WH infinitival complements of particular verbs (e.g., *try* and *persuade*) as in (32a,b).

(32) a. You tried [[$_{NP}$e] to be nice]
  b. You persuaded him [[$_{NP}$e] to be nice]

C&L stipulate that the +WH infinitive structure, [+WH [$_S$NP to VP]], is subject to obligatory Control independent of context (provided that it passes the [NP to VP] filter (18)/(22), as we shall see shortly). A key feature of C&L's account is the generation of an empty NP category [$_{NP}$e] that bears no index in Surface Structure (i.e., PRO). Control is here understood to be a rule of construal that applies in the mapping from Surface Structure to Logical Form and assigns an index to this null NP. In (31a), Control assigns coindices to the matrix subject and the embedded controlled subject [$_{NP}$e], in accordance with the meaning of the matrix verb. In (31b), Control assigns an index to the subject of the infinitive [$_{NP}$e], as it occurs in a "structure of obligatory control," but since there is no external antecedent, its reference is arbitrary.

To understand this, consider +WH cases in which obligatory Control is violated, as in (33). These data have either a lexical NP or a trace as the subject of the embedded infinitive.

(33) a. *[what [anyone to say]] often depends on the situation
  b. *You don't know [what [anyone to say]]
  c. *who don't you know [what [[$_{NP}$e] to say]]

The sentences in (33a) and (33b) are ruled out for two reasons. First of all, *anyone* is a lexical NP that is already indexed by Surface Structure (presumably at the point of insertion). And since the NP already carries an index, Control cannot apply to it. The same can be said of [$_{NP}$e] in (33c), since the trace of *who* is indexed in the application of the movement rule. These are thus obligatory control structures that are unable to undergo obligatory control. Further, the [NP to VP] structures *anyone to say* and [$_{NP}$e]$_{TRACE}$ *to say* both violate the filter (18)/(22), being "adjacent to and in the domain of" a +WH NP.[7]

In contrast, a −WH infinitive, [−WH [$_S$NP to VP]], will only undergo obligatory Control when it is the complement of a "control" verb, which determines whether the infinitival subject of the complement is to be coindexed with the matrix subject (as with *try* or *promise*) or the matrix object (as with *persuade*). In (32a), above, the infinitive is not a "structure of obligatory control," but the matrix verb forces the coindexation of *you* and [$_{NP}$e] (likewise for the coindexation of *him* and [$_{NP}$e] in (32b)).

The ungrammatical −WH cases, such as in (34), again have either a lexical NP or a trace as the subject of the embedded infinitive.

(34) a. *You tried [Bill to be nice]
b. *who did you try [[$_{NP}$e] to be nice]
c. *You persuaded Bill [Hillary to be nice]
d. *who did you persuade Bill [[$_{NP}$e] to be nice]

The sentences in (34) are also ruled out for their failure to undergo Control. Here, the −WH infinitivals are complements of obligatory control verbs, *try* and *persuade*, and the subjects of the infinitival clauses are, in each case, preindexed and unable to undergo Control. In (34c,d), the infinitivals also violate the [NP to VP] filter, being "adjacent to and in the domain of" the NP *Bill*. Note that the [NP to VP] filter does not apply in the case of (34a,b), since the infinitival is "adjacent to and in the domain of" the verb *try*. Here, *try* could be replaced with *believe*, making the sentences grammatical. This, C&L point out, shows that the obligatoriness of Control lies with the choice of verb, and that the ungrammaticality of (34a,b) cannot be ascribed to its structure alone.

### Raising (RtoS)

As already noted, movement (like all syntactic rules in the mapping from Deep Structure to Surface Structure) applies freely and is not obligatory. The free application of "move NP" in derivation of (35) is analogous to that of Passive (seen in (3) above).

(35) [$_{NP}$Bill]$_i$ appears [$_S$[$_{NP}$e]$_i$ to [$_{VP}$be nice]]

The indices on the NP *Bill* and its trace are assigned in the application of "move NP," and are interpreted at LF via construal. As long as the subject of *appear* is base-generated as [$_{NP}$e], construal will rule out cases in which *Bill* is not moved, since failure to apply movement will result in a free variable that is uninterpretable. C&L (in section 1.4 of their article) consider the several structures hypothetically available for RtoS predicates, shown in (36), and discuss how to rule out the impossible ones (i.e., (36c,d)).

(36) a. John$_i$ is likely [$_{S'}$Ø [$_S$[$_{NP}$e]$_i$ to leave]]
b. it is likely [$_{S'}$(that) [$_S$John will leave]]
c. *John$_i$ is likely [$_{S'}$(that) [$_S$[$_{NP}$e]$_i$ will leave]]
d. *it is likely [$_{S'}$Ø [$_S$John to leave]]

While the movement of *John* in (36c) can be ruled out by the Tensed-S Condition (TSC), accounting for the ungrammaticality of (36d) is not as straightforward. There is no filter (such as [NP to VP]) that could rule out the complement of (36d) without also ruling out the complement of (36a), since lexical NPs and traces are treated equivalently in the REST model.[8] In order to contend with facts such as these, C&L (their p. 449) posit an "obligatory lexical insertion rule" that inserts pleonastic *it* into the subject position of certain verbs (such as *seem*, *appear*, and *be*) whenever they have a clausal (i.e., S′) complement, except when the complementizer is Ø. Accordingly, (36c) would be blocked even without the involvement of the TSC, since the base would have the matrix subject position already filled by *it*, as in (36b). In the case of (36d), *it*-Insertion cannot apply (since the complement is a bare infinitive), and the structure will always have an empty NP subject in the base, as in (37).

(37)  [$_{NP}$e] is likely [$_{S'}$Ø [$_S$John to leave]]

In this circumstance, movement is motivated by the need to avoid an uninterpretable variable.

## *Raising (RtoO)*

C&L present no elaborated analysis of RtoO constructions for the simple reason that they are taken to be constructions involving no movement at all.

(38)  a.  Julian believes [$_S$[$_{NP}$them] to [$_{VP}$be nice]]
      b.  who$_i$ does Julian believe [$_S$[$_{NP}$e]$_i$ to [$_{VP}$be nice]]

As illustrated in (38), RtoO clauses are assumed to have the same structure as the ungrammatical control examples (34a,b). The "account" for these is simply that: (i) *believe* is subcategorized for a bare infinitival S complement (alternatively, an S′ infinitival complement with a Ø-complementizer, which may delete or not); (ii) the complement does not violate the [NP to VP] filter; and (iii) the matrix verb does not require obligatory control. These complements, having no tense, are not constrained by the TSC. Accordingly, nothing blocks operations such as reflexive interpretation (39a) and "move NP" (39b) from "relating" the embedded and matrix subject positions.

(39)  a.  Julian$_i$ believes [$_S$himself$_i$ to be nice]
      b.  Julian$_i$ is believed [$_S$[$_{NP}$e]$_i$ to be nice]

While C&L's analysis of RtoO is internally consistent, the interaction of this analysis with their [NP to VP] filter leaves unanswered questions. Any analysis of RtoO must necessarily block passivization of the entire infinitival complement in (38a), as shown in the ungrammatical example (40).

(40)  *[them to be nice] is believed by everyone who knows them

In contrast, notice that tensed sentential complements can certainly be passivized, as in (41).

(41)  [that they are nice] is believed by everyone who knows them

Recall first that C&L implicitly assume subject clauses to be NPs in their presentation of the filter that accounts for the contrast in (4), repeated here.

(4) a. *He left is a surprise.
    b. That he left is a surprise.

This filter, the "[$_{NP}$NP tense VP] filter," rules out (42) along with (4a), on the understanding that the subject clause is itself an NP and that tensed NP clauses cannot fail to have a complementizer.

(42) *[$_{NP}$they are nice] is believed by everyone who knows them

We will therefore assume, with C&L, that the infinitive *them to be nice* is an NP in (40).

Now in the distillation of the [NP to VP] filter, C&L are somewhat uncertain whether to claim that an [NP to VP] structure is grammatical in any context, provided that the clausal constituent is itself an NP, as in (22),

(22) *[$_\alpha$NP to VP], unless $\alpha$ is adjacent to and in the domain of [–N] **or $\alpha$ = NP**

or whether to dispense with this qualification, as in (18).

(18) *[$_\alpha$NP to VP], unless $\alpha$ is adjacent to and in the domain of [–N]

Either proposal leads to empirical problems. Consider the contrast in (43), in which (40) is paired with example (111e) from C&L's article.

(43) a. *[$_{NP}$them to be nice] is believed by everyone who knows them [= (40), above]
    b. [$_{NP}$someone to fix the sink] was finally found [= C&L (111e)]

If (22) is adopted, the grammaticality of (43b) can be accounted for, but there is then no way to block (43a). In order to block (43a), one would have to adopt (18) as the correct version of the [NP to VP] filter, but then the filter will block (43b) as well. Thus, analyzing the subject of the embedded infinitive as remaining in the infinitival clause at Surface Structure leaves at least one seemingly insoluble problem for the REST account.

## *Equi*

Having determined that lexically triggered control of PRO is "obligatory", C&L must now contend with the class of verbs represented by *want*. As shown in (44), *want* appears to take both infinitival "control" complements and infinitival RtoO complements.

(44) a. Greg wants to be nice.
    b. Judy wants Greg to be nice.

In prior accounts, such as that of Postal, individual syntactic rules were held to apply when the conditions for triggering them were met. Under such assumptions, it would be fairly easy to claim that *want* was marked as both an RtoO verb and a control verb. In C&L's article, however, this option is no longer available. For them, if (44a) is a control structure involving a control verb *want*, then it is a "structure of obligatory control" and (44b) should be ungrammatical. That is, if *want* is like *try*, then (44b) should be no better than (34a), repeated here.

(34) a. *you tried [Bill to be nice]

To maintain the principle of "obligatory control," C&L propose that *want* is just like *believe*, excepting that *want* selects a *for* complementizer (where *believe* selects for a Ø-complementizer, if it does so at all). Since the *for* complementizer may delete, the underlying structure of (44b) includes this complementizer and (44b) will be rendered as (45) if deletion does not apply.[9]

(45) %Judy wants for Greg to be nice.

When the infinitival subject is null, as in (44a), the underlying structure is claimed to involve a reflexive pronoun, as in (46).

(46) Greg$_i$ wants [$_{S'}$for [$_S$himself$_i$ to be nice]]

This structure (46) is subject to a rule (i.e., Equi NP Deletion) that deletes a reflexive pronoun in the context [S' for ____ to ... ], optionally in some instances and obligatorily in others. This rule, combined with optional *for* deletion, can produce the following structures in (47).

(47) a. %Greg wants for himself to be nice.  [no application of deletion]
 b. %Greg wants himself to be nice.  [*for* deletion only]
 c. *Greg wants for to be nice.  [Equi NP Deletion only]
 d. Greg wants to be nice.  [*for* deletion and Equi NP Deletion]

In this paradigm, we see that the two deletion rules apply optionally and that (47c) is ruled out by the *[for-to] filter. The verb *believe*, in contrast, does not select for a *for* complementizer at all. Compare the paradigm in (48) with (47), where *want* is replaced by *believe*.

(48) a. *Greg believes for himself to be nice.  [*believe [S' for ... ]]
 b. Greg believes himself to be nice.
 c. *Greg believes for to be nice.  [*believe [S' for ... ]]
 d. *Greg believes to be nice.  [context for Equi NP Deletion not available]

Thus, C&L's account claims that (i) *want* is not an "optional" control verb, (ii) *want* is subcategorized for a *for-to* infinitival complement, and (iii) complements of *want* may undergo Equi NP Deletion.

## Concluding points

"Filters and Control" aspires at the outset to simplify the syntactic component of language by generalizing to the maximum extent possible, and thereby moving closer to a theory of grammar that is modeled on universal principles and the assumption of innateness (i.e., a theory that is explanatorily adequate). In this regard, C&L wish to eliminate construction-specific or context-dependent rules, along with rule ordering, preferring instead a theory in which rules are general and optional, and in which conditions on rule application are replaced with conditions on representations. As much as possible, they also seek to move language-particular constraints either into lexical representations (at one end of the derivation) or into the interface between Surface Structure and Phonetic Form (at the other). Everything else (including constraints on the base, on the Deep Structure–Surface Structure interface, and on the Surface Structure–Logical Form interface) is assumed to be part of UG, and the innate language faculty. This idealization yields the following split:

(49) *Language-particular aspects of syntax:*
  i. subcategorization properties of individual lexical items
  ii. rules deleting/inserting individual words
  iii. filters sensitive to particular configurations of words/structure

(50) *Language-universal aspects of syntax:*
  i. constraints on PS-rules (e.g., X-bar theory)
  ii. syntactic operations (e.g., movement, adjunction)
  iii. rules interpreting coindexation (e.g., construal, quantifier interpretation)
  iv. conditions constraining the form of representations (e.g., Tensed-S Condition)

Comparing the idealization with its implementation, we find that C&L have achieved modest success, but that the devil is clearly in the details. As with any attempt at massive generalization and idealization in the application of a theory, trade-offs are unavoidable. Among these are (i) the necessity of maintaining a rule of Equi NP in order to maintain the "obligatory" property of Control; (ii) the failure to fully accommodate the interaction of RtoO structure and Passive in the attempt to devise a singular filter for [NP to VP] constructions; (iii) the need to assert (at least) three formal classes of phonologically null category (indexed, unindexed, and deleted) in order to properly restrict the application of the (very general) filters that are proposed; etc.

### Notes

1 It should be noted at this point that the filters present a very powerful (perhaps overly powerful) mechanism of the grammar. Not only is the structure of filters quite unconstrained (a point made fairly clear in C&L's discussion of "general

properties of filters," section 4, (184), not reproduced here), but they apply in a manner that appears to ignore dominance (constituency) relations. For instance, the operation that filters out (4a) clearly ignores the intervening S-node (under the higher NP). This same filter is shown to rule out sentences such as (i).

(i)  *The man met you is my friend.

Here, the filter applies to an NP subject with the structure shown in (ii) in which the *wh* element *who* is deleted (see Chomsky 1977:98).

(ii)  [$_{NP}$[$_{NP}$**the man**] [$_{S'}$(who) [$_{S}$e PAST [$_{VP}$**meet you**]]]]

Here, the elements that the filter reacts to are in boldface, and it is clear that the filter does not require the NP element to belong to the same constituent as "tense VP." To be fair to C&L, they appear to acknowledge (tacitly but not explicitly) the expressive power of filters, when they say that they have tried to keep filters from proliferating, restricting them to "the direct expression of language specific idiosyncracies".

2  For C&L, the −WH complementizer is realized as *that* and the +WH complementizer is *whether*. For reasons made clear in the article, the filter does not reference the null complementizer or the prepositional *for* complementizer.
3  This formulation takes advantage of the feature-based view of category labels, in which V and P are both [−N]. They are somewhat ambivalent about the formulation of this filter, suggesting (i) as an alternative.

(i)  *[$_{\alpha}$NP to VP], unless α is adjacent to and in the domain of a verb or *for*

The reasons for this ambivalence lie in their uncertainty regarding the status of complementizer *for* as a prepositional element (tentatively assuming for (18) that complementizer *for* shares properties with the preposition *for*).
4  C&L point to examples such as (i), for which they correctly observe that the infinitival phrase appears to be more properly associated with the adjective *good* rather than with the NP *a good man*.

(i)  A good man to fix the sink is at the front door.

C&L's comments here echo (but do not cite) observations first made in Wells (1947) regarding what he called "discontinuous constituents." In Dubinsky (1999), these constructions are analyzed as complements of a degree phrase (DegP) rather than as infinitival relative clauses.
5  The view expressed by C&L here appears rather compatible with current Optimality Theoretic (OT) views of syntax. It is no accident, we think, that OT principles have been applied by Pesetsky (1997) to the same grammatical phenomena (the distribution of overt and null complementizers) considered in this article.
6  They note that the term "adjunct" must be defined so as to exclude the first NP of a ditransitive double-NP complement, such as *give the boy a book*. C&L also observe that the filter (30) is distinct from all the others discussed in their article in that it does not reference any aspect of the complementizer system. (30) here anticipates the "Case filter" of Government and Binding theory (to be discussed in unit III).
7  In this regard, it is important to recall that C&L assert that the [NP to VP] filter cannot apply to [PRO to VP]. Their logic is that filters apply only to "indexed" NPs

(in their terms, NPs already indexed by Surface Structure, but not NPs indexed via rules of construal, such as Control). We now have two varieties of null NPs that are invisible to filters: (i) unindexed NPs (i.e., PRO), since they receive their indices in another module of the grammar (LF) where filters do not operate; and (ii) indexed but "deleted" NPs (C&L's "nothing," discussed in the previous section) whose indices must presumably be erased by deletion. It would thus appear that filters are "ordered" with respect to deletion (and that the ordering complexities lifted out of the transformational component have been moved into the relationships among intermodule mapping functions (e.g., deletion, filters, construal, etc.).

8   Recall from the previous section that adjectives such as *likely* require that their infinitival complements be embedded within an S' that contains a Ø complementizer, so as not to run foul of the [NP to VP] filter.

9   While some speakers find (45) to be ill-formed, others deem it to be perfectly grammatical. This is indicated here with "%."

# UNIT III

# GOVERNMENT AND BINDING THEORY

## INTRODUCTION: THE INTERACTION OF PRINCIPLES AND POSSIBLE ANALYSES

(Extended) standard transformational grammar focused on the articulation of rules and the conditions constraining them, so rendering constructions ill- (or well-)formed on the basis of whether rules did (or did not) violate them. In this respect, it was deemed by some to be superior to grammars that were not so constrained.[1] The 1980s brought with them another evolution of Chomsky's theoretical program. The so-called Government and Binding (GB) Theory (Chomsky himself prefers to call it Principles and Parameters Theory) focused on the articulation of levels of representation and the theoretical modules (that is, sets of related conditions) which would act to filter out entire derivations. Rules, such as "Move NP," were rendered yet more general, and their application was assumed to transcend particular levels of structure. On the other hand, conditions on such representations, such as the set of "Binding Conditions" which serve to limit the distribution of referentially distinct classes of NPs, were grouped into functionally coherent modules and were made more precise in their application. The debate over which of the Binding Conditions applied at which levels of representation is indicative of this set of circumstances.

In building a syntactic theory in which particularized rules could not and ought not to be articulated, Chomsky's GB theory sought to predict the application of these generalized rules through condition-mediated motivations. Thus, rather than allow a morphologically passive verb form to trigger a "passive" rule, the passive verb is deemed to have (or not have in this case) particular properties that force its object to move into subject position. Having all such particular structures determined by a set of motivating (and universal) principles yielded a particular formalization of Chomsky's earlier analysis of RtoO constructions, which was now undergirded by a whole set of theoretical imperatives. Chapter 8 of this unit outlines some of the fundamental bases of GB Theory, such as are necessary to an understanding of the GB analysis of

RtoO and Exceptional Case Marking (ECM), and lays out the GB approach to the construction.

Chapter 9 examines the difficulties that can arise in applying the ECM analysis to RtoO constructions in other languages, focusing particularly on French (Kayne 1981) and Quechua (Cole and Hermon 1981). As shown there, employing an analysis designed for one language can necessitate modifying the theory, sometimes dramatically, to accommodate seemingly recalcitrant data. Chapter 10 explores the difficulties that can arise from assuming too quickly that RtoO-like constructions in given languages, particularly Madurese and Japanese in this case, are indeed RtoO structures. As demonstrated there, at times a radically distinct analysis better captures the facts and at others the constellation of facts is such that a satisfying analysis proves elusive.

## Note

1 A number of syntacticians took just the opposite view, asserting that grammatical rules are of necessity language and construction specific. Various construction grammar analyses, typified in Shibatani and Thompson (1996), bear witness to the continuing viability of such approaches.

# CHAPTER 8

# CHOMSKY'S *LECTURES ON GOVERNMENT AND BINDING* AND THE ECM ANALYSIS OF RAISING

## 1 The Government and Binding model and its components

Government and Binding Theory (GB) as set out in *Lectures on Government and Binding* (Chomsky 1981) represents Chomsky's next major theoretical development. First publicly enumerated in Chomsky's 1979 lectures at the Generative Linguistics in the Old World (GLOW) conference and workshop held at the Scuola Normale Superiore in 1979, and refined during class lectures at MIT the following academic year, GB was heralded as a major theoretical advance and generated great excitement among syntacticians (not to mention spawning a vast literature). Because of changes in the theoretical perspective and apparatus, the accounts of particularly Raising but also Control take on new dimensions.

GB represents a modular approach in which the grammar is made up of a set of semi-autonomous subsystems which interact to account for the complexity of language. While the basic components of the grammatical rule system remain the same from REST to GB (i.e., the lexicon, the base, transformations, PF, and LF), the implementation of those components and the principles governing them change dramatically. The subsystems of principles included:

- Binding theory;
- Bounding theory;
- Case theory;
- Control theory;
- Government theory;
- θ-theory;
- X-bar theory.

For the most part, the principles that govern any one of these subsystems do not directly govern the others. Part of the vast GB literature has touched on the issue of which levels of representation particular subsystems are relevant to and debates about the precise formulations of the various principles. In what follows here, the principles are presented and explained in the most general and commonly accepted terms, avoiding (in some instances) intricate debates about precise formulations.

The basic T-model of grammar remained the same in GB as was outlined in Chomsky & Lasnik (1977). While the diagram in (1) is somewhat of a simplification, the basic form of the grammar as outlined here (with the primary grammatical modules governing each level indicated) can be usefully compared with the REST model diagramed in chapter 7.

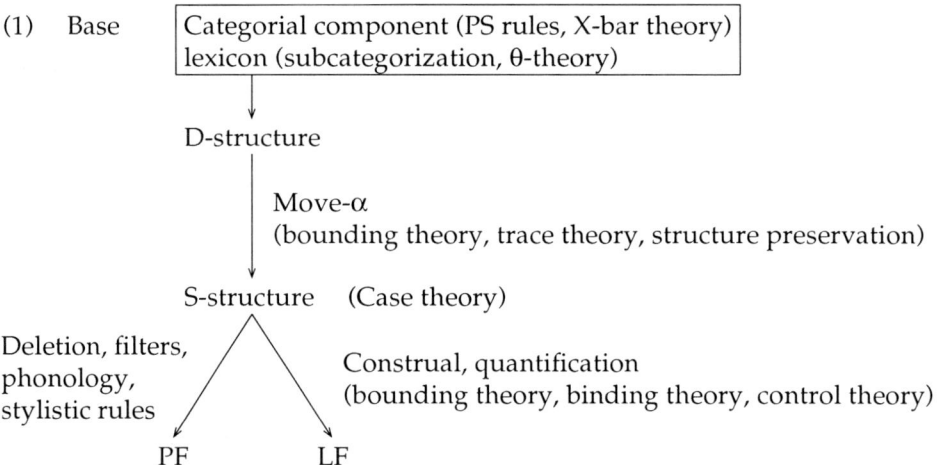

The Government and Binding (GB) model

While the form of the model remains the same, GB represents a seismic shift from the REST perspective. Its theoretical devices and their implementation are markedly different from what we saw in chapter 7. As alluded to above, the GB model consists of a number of subtheories, each with a distinguishing principle or set of principles that constrain the form of representations. As we will see in this chapter, each of these subtheories, while specifically formulated to apply to a particular module of grammar, is able to affect the form of representations at more than one level of a derivation.

**D-structure**: As in the REST model, the base consists of a categorial component and lexicon, which combine to form D-structures. D-structure is viewed as a projection of the subcategorization requirements of lexical items, determined in large part by their thematic structure. Thematic roles (such as discussed in Gruber 1965 and Jackendoff 1972) have a much more important place in GB than in previous Chomskyan models of grammar. Where they had previously figured prominently only in other theories, such as Fillmore's (1968) Case Grammar, thematic roles are put to work in GB in an attempt to place strict limits on the role of categorial subcategorization specifications in the lexicon.

**The transformational component**: In keeping with the move (already seen in the REST model) to make rules maximally simple, general, and optional, all movement and adjunction is reduced to the single rule "Move-α." "Move-α" allows any element to be moved to any position. As before, the output of the rule is constrained by restrictive conditions on representations (at various levels). However, in GB, these representational restrictions consist of the subtheories, including: (i) structure preservation, (ii) bounding theory (which is the module containing the Subjacency condition), (iii) trace theory (which ensures that the application of Move-α coindexes the moved element and its trace), (iv) Case theory (which forces the application of Move-α in certain contexts), and (v) binding theory (which governs the distribution of anaphors, pronominals, and referring expressions).

**S-structure**: As indicated above, the output of the transformational component (Move-α) is constrained by Case theory. Case theory requires that all NPs be assigned Case, and thus forces the application of Move-α to any NP that does not occupy a Case position. Since the Case Filter operates in the PF component, Case must be assigned by S-structure, i.e., prior to the mapping from S-structure to PF.

**PF**: The mapping from S-structure to PF in GB is largely unchanged from the REST model and is made up of deletion rules, filters, phonology, and stylistic rules. Note that stylistic rules, which are a distinct rule type in the REST model, are in GB just the instantiation of Move-α in the PF component. The Case Filter, which constrains the distribution of NPs in representations, is the PF principle that garners the most interest in the GB literature. Outside of it, the PF component is not a primary focus of innovation in the GB model.

**LF**: The mapping from S-structure to LF receives greater attention in GB. As in REST, rules of construal and quantifier interpretation operate in the LF component. However, in keeping with the move toward generalized rules, quantifier raising is just an instantiation of Move-α in that module. Move-α also applies at the S-structure/LF interface to ensure that *wh*-operators are moved to scopal positions in languages that do not have overt *wh*-movement (thus insuring for them proper interpretations). Bounding theory (as one of the subtheories that restricts representations) will rule out outputs of Move-α that violate Subjacency. As all indexing of NPs takes place by S-structure, indices are no longer introduced at this level in the interpretation of PRO. Rather, control theory operates in this module to judge the well-formedness of representations provided by S-structure. Binding theory, responsible for judging the well-formedness of coindexing relations between NPs in representations, operates in this component to ensure appropriate antecedent–anaphor relations, supplanting the role outlined by Chomsky and Lasnik for Tensed-S Condition and the Specified Subject Condition.

So, as in REST, the principles of GB are constraints on the well-formedness of representations. The modules of the grammar, while principally thought of as applying to particular components of the model, actually have effects reaching beyond a particular component. This is because of the inclusion of the Projection Principle, an overarching constraint ensuring that D-structure, S-structure, and LF are structurally identical. The operation of the Projection Principle and the interaction of the various subtheories of GB are explicated in the discussion that follows.

## 2 The subtheories and principles of the GB model

### *Government*

A fundamental notion cutting across many of the grammatical subtheories is government. Informally speaking, *government* is the relation that holds between a lexical head and all the nodes contained within its maximal projection that are not separated from it by another maximal projection. For example, a verb governs its complements. However, a verb does not govern elements in a complement S', since S' is a maximal projection. Likewise, a preposition governs its complement but nothing that is wholly contained in that complement. Government plays a crucial role in θ-theory, case theory, binding theory, and control theory, so it is worth a more detailed consideration.

Government can be defined as in (2).

(2) *Government:*
α governs β if and only if:
i. α is an $X^0$,
ii. α c-commands β, and
iii. there is no YP γ that dominates β but does not dominate α.

So, a head X governs any element contained in its maximal projection XP that is not contained in another maximal projection YP. Further, governors are limited by stipulation to the categories N, V, A, P, and INFL (excluding untensed INFL). To see how government works, consider the structure in (3).

(3)
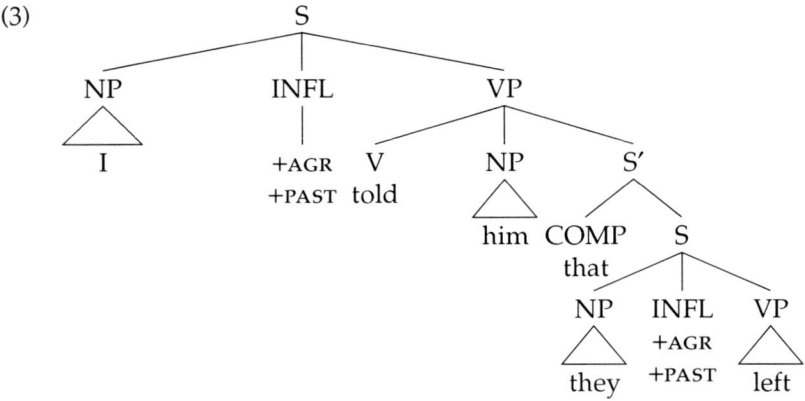

In (3) the INFL of the matrix clause governs the matrix subject *I* and the VP *told him that they left* since (i) INFL is an $X^0$ category and a governor, (ii) it c-commands both the NP and the VP, and (iii) there is no maximal projection that dominates either the NP or VP but not INFL. The same situation obtains in the complement clause, so the embedded INFL governs the embedded subject *they* and the VP *left*. The other government relation obvious in (3) is that between the verb *tell* and its complements. Here *tell* governs both the NP *him* and the S' *that they left*, since V is a governor, V c-commands NP and S', and there is no maximal projection that dominates NP or S' that does not dominate

V. Importantly, the V *tell* does not govern any element of the complement clause: the NP *they*, the embedded INFL, or the VP *left*. This is because S′ is taken to be a maximal projection (Chomsky 1981:164) and thus blocks government, since provision (iii) of definition (2) is not satisfied. Maximal projections are said to *block* government. While S′ is a maximal projection (taken to be the maximal projection of INFL), S is assumed not to be a maximal projection and will not block government. This proves crucial in the analyses of Raising and Control.

## The Projection Principle and θ-theory

One of the foundational principles in GB is the Projection Principle, an overarching constraint on the form of syntactic representations. Representations at all levels of syntactic structure must conform to the Projection Principle, stated simply and straightforwardly in (4) (Chomsky (1981:29)):

(4) *Projection Principle:*
Representations at each syntactic level (i.e., LF, and D- and S-structure) are projected from the lexicon, in that they observe the subcategorization properties of lexical items.

The Projection Principle is interpreted as ensuring that the representation of a particular sentence will be identical at each level of syntax, encompassing the prohibition against structure-building first hypothesized in Emonds's notion of structure preservation. That is, no transformational process other than adjunction can insert nodes into a structure. All nodes must be in the representation starting with D-structure. It further ensures that most aspects of syntactic structure exist to satisfy the subcategorization requirements of some lexical item contained in the structure. Thus, mapping from D-structure to S-structure and from S-structure to LF is tightly constrained. For example, the subject and direct object in the sentence in (5) exist in the syntactic structure because the verb, *examine*, requires both a subject and an object.

(5) Ashley examined Dana.

And so the structure in (6) results from the projection of the argument structure of *examine* from the lexicon into D-structure constrained by the principles of X-bar theory.

(6)
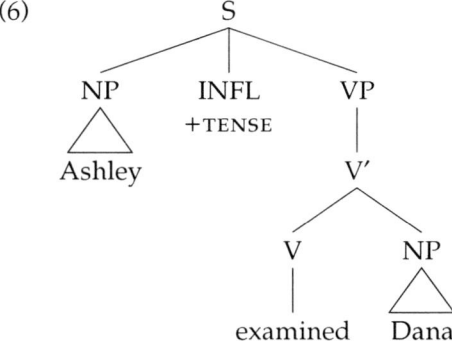

Basically speaking, the structure in (6) serves as D-structure, S-structure, and LF representations of (5).

However, as Chomsky (1982) notes, it is only complements that are always projected from the lexical requirements of heads. While the subject NP in a sentence like (5) is in this instance projected due to the argument structure of the verb *examine*, not all subjects result from the lexical requirements of verbs. Pleonastic subjects as found with meteorological verbs and other constructions in English are not arguments but are nonetheless required. To account for this, Chomsky proposes that all clauses must have subjects independent of lexical requirements, combining this requirement with the Projection Principle into what he refers to as the *Extended Projection Principle* (EPP). The subject requirement is built into the expansion of the S node; of this, Chomsky (1981:71) states that "the projection principle and the analysis of S as NP–INFL–VP" are "assumptions which seem to be near optimal." The subject requirement of the EPP proves crucial to the analysis of Raising (and Passive).

X-bar theory and the Projection Principle are key ingredients in generating the D-structure representation of a sentence, but equally important is θ-theory. θ-theory is the module governing the assignment and tracking of θ-roles, the names of the roles identifying the arguments of a verb in a particular state of affairs, roles such as agent, theme, and so on. The θ-roles are determined by the semantics of the lexical item licensing the arguments and are part of the subcategorization information of that lexical item (Chomsky would argue that they **are** the subcategorization information). In (5), *examine* licenses the arguments X and Y, and assigns them the agent and theme θ-roles, respectively.[1] The chief principle of θ-theory is the θ-criterion, stated in (7).

(7) θ-*criterion (Chomsky 1981:36):*
Each argument bears one and only one θ-role, and each θ-role is assigned to one and only one argument.

The θ-criterion ensures that all of the arguments required by a lexical item are included in the representation and that no extraneous arguments are included. A structure that does not include all of the required arguments will be ill-formed since there will be unassigned θ-role(s) and the θ-criterion provision that each θ-role is assigned will be violated. A structure that includes unsubcategorized arguments will include arguments that are not assigned a θ-role and the θ-criterion will be violated.

Clearly, then, the θ-criterion interacts crucially with the generation of D-structure. However, since the Projection Principle states that the subcategorization requirements of lexical items must be satisfied at all syntactic levels, the θ-criterion is relevant to S-structure and LF as well. In fact, Chomsky considers LF the level at which θ-roles are assigned, and defines the notion θ-*position* as "a position in LF to which a θ-role is assigned" (1981:35). For this reason, Chomsky (1981:335) eventually revises the θ-criterion to apply to *argument chains* rather than simply to arguments, a *chain* being comprised of all lexical items and traces bearing the same index.

θ-roles are assigned to arguments such as subject, object, and others. Structural positions that contain arguments that can be assigned a θ-role are referred to as argument (A-)positions, and this term applies whether or not a θ-role is in fact assigned. For instance, subject position is always considered an A-position, even when a pleonastic NP such as *it* or *there* occupies it. All other positions are referred to as non-argument or A-bar (A'-)positions. So, on the one hand, positions in phrase structure trees can be categorized as A- or A'-positions. (θ-roles are never assigned to A'-positions.)

On the other hand, structural positions can also be categorized in terms of whether or not a θ-role is assigned. θ-positions are D-structure positions to which a θ-role is assigned at LF, and non-θ-positions are D-structure positions which never receive a θ-role in the derivation. Given the θ-criterion's prohibition on any argument being assigned more than one θ-role, movement of arguments must be to non-θ-positions. This has implications for the GB analysis of Raising and is explored in later sections.

## *Movement*

The transformational component of GB brings to its logical conclusion the program of reducing the specificity of transformations begun in "Conditions" and continued in REST (as in Chomsky and Lasnik 1977). The sole movement rule in GB is Move-α. Essentially this means "move any category to any position." This maximally general statement is possible because the principles of the various grammatical modules serve to constrain the representations arising from movement.

The modules most directly relevant to constraining and motivating movement are bounding theory and Case theory. Part of bounding theory, Subjacency is the principle which most directly restricts movement. As formulated in Chomsky (1973), movement may cross at most one bounding node. As before, the bounding nodes in English are S and NP. Thus, any element moved by the transformation Move-α may cross no more than one S or NP node.

Although there is a single rule of movement subject to the same constraints, subtypes of movement can be identified on the basis of the landing site of the moved element, that is, the type of position to which the element moves. Movement to A-positions is generally referred to as NP-movement inasmuch as such movement is largely restricted to NPs. Movement to A'-positions has different characteristics than NP-movement. The prototypical instance of this is the *wh*-movement of question and relative clause formation.[2] The motivation for each subtype of movement is different. On the one hand, *wh*-movement is driven by a +*wh* feature in COMP which must be satisfied by a *wh*-phrase or empty operator residing in COMP. On the other hand, NP-movement is motivated by the requirement that all NPs be Case marked by S-structure for a Phrase Structure to be well-formed. NP-movement and Case theory are what are relevant to the GB analysis of Raising.

## *The Case Filter*

The notion of Case in GB is based on the familiar notion of morphological case in languages with a system of case marking NPs in clauses. However, the Case of GB (crucially, with a capital "C") is abstract Case, meaning that even though there may be no overt morphological manifestation, NPs are always marked for Case. This notion is developed in Rouveret and Vergnaud (1980). The principle of chief importance to Case theory is the Case Filter, stated as in (8).

(8) *Case Filter (Chomsky 1981:49):*
 \*NP if NP has phonetic content and has no Case.

The Case Filter disallows any structure that contains an overt NP that has not been assigned Case by S-structure. Empty categories such as PRO, *pro*, and trace are exempt from the Case Filter; all other NPs must be Case marked.

As with θ-marking, structural Case is normally assigned under government; that is, the element that assigns Case to an NP must govern that NP.[3] Chomsky proposes the Case assignment rule for English in (9).

(9) *Case assignment in English:*
 a. INFL containing the feature [+TENSE] assigns nominative Case.
 b. Case-assigning V assigns objective Case.
 c. Case-assigning P assigns oblique Case.

Importantly, only tensed INFL assigns Case (9a); the infinitival INFL *to* does not. The structure in (10) illustrates these Case assignment configurations.

(10)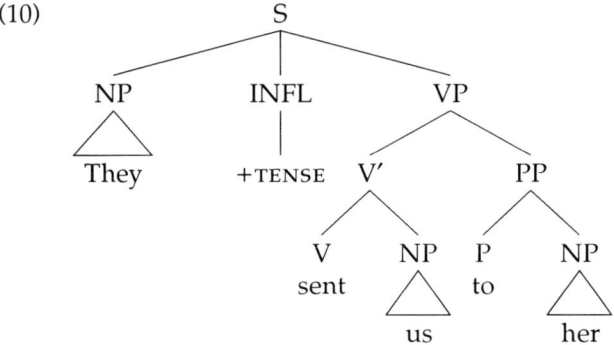

In (10), the nominative Case on the subject *they* is assigned by INFL, the objective Case on the direct object *us* is assigned by the governing verb *send*, and oblique Case on the object of the preposition *her* is assigned by the governing preposition *to*. While Case is overtly manifested on the NPs in (10) because they are pronouns, full NPs that show no case distinctions in English are assigned the same abstract Case in precisely the same way in the sentence in (11).

(11) The philanthropist sent a large check to the refugee fund.

In GB, NP-movement is motivated by the Case Filter. Any structure that contains an overt NP that is not Case marked by S-structure is proclaimed ill-formed. Thus, any NP that is generated in a position where it cannot receive Case must move to a position in which it does receive Case. One example of this type of motivated movement comes from unaccusatives. Recall from chapter

6 that in Relational Grammar, unaccusatives are analyzed as intransitives that contain a direct object rather than a subject. This is operationalized in GB by what Burzio (1981) dubbed the "ergative analysis." In Burzio's analysis, an unaccusative clause such as (12a) is associated with the D-structure in (12b).

(12) a. Ashley slipped.
    b.

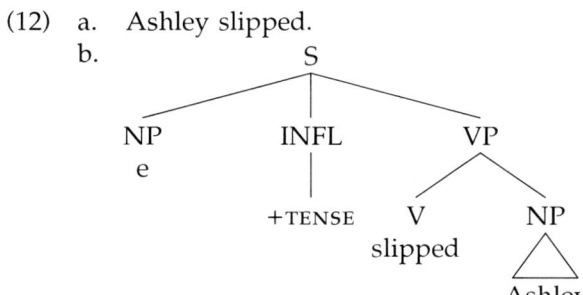

The verb *slip* takes a theme complement as its sole argument, here *Ashley*, which is projected in its complement position in the VP. As it is a complement, *slip* assigns it its θ-role. However, as an intransitive predicate, by definition *slip* has no Case to assign. So, in its D-structure position, the complement NP cannot receive Case. Following the Extended Projection Principle (EPP), the subject position must be generated since all clauses must have subjects; so an empty subject position must projected at D-structure. An NP in the subject position will be assigned nominative Case because the clause contains a tensed INFL and thus provides a landing site for the complement to move to to receive the Case it requires. Movement of the NP *Ashley* in the transformational component yields the S-structure in (12c).

(12) c.

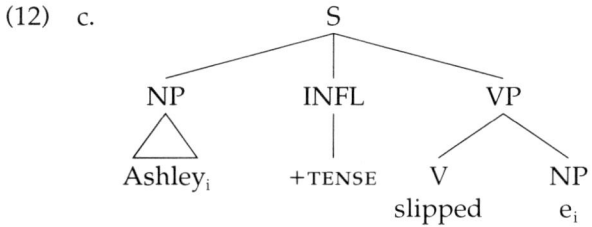

In (12c), the NP *Ashley* receives nominative Case from the tensed INFL and is coindexed with its trace in complement position. Movement in unaccusatives thus can be seen to be motivated by the need of the complement to be assigned Case and so pass the Case Filter.

NP-movement in passives has a similar motivation. The passive sentence in (13a) is associated with the D-structure in (13b) and the S-structure in (13c).

(13) a. Dana was arrested.
    b. [$_{NP}$e] was arrested Dana.
    c. Dana$_i$ was arrested e$_i$.

The NP *Dana* moves from its D-structure object position in (13b) to the subject position in (13c). *Dana* is assigned its THEME θ-role on the basis of its status as complement of *arrested*. However, although the passive participle *arrested* governs the NP and assigns the θ-role, it has no Case to assign. Within GB it is assumed that the Case that the verb *arrest* would assign its object in a sentence such as *The police arrested Dana* has been absorbed by the passive participle, given the adjectival nature of passive participles. Thus, in a passive the object NP moves to subject position so that it can be assigned Case by the tensed INFL.

NP-movement in the unaccusative sentence in (12) and the passive sentence in (13) share another property: in both the NP moves to a non-θ-position. The unaccusative predicate *slip* has a single θ-role to assign to its complement and does not assign a θ-role to the subject position, which is projected to satisfy the subject requirement of the EPP. The passive auxiliary *be* has no θ-role to assign, and again the empty subject position is generated to satisfy the EPP. Note that this is consistent with the θ-criterion. Since *Ashley* in (12a) and *Dana* in (13a) are both assigned a θ-role on the basis of their complement position, if the subject position in either (12) or (13) were a θ-position, the condition that each argument receive one and only one θ-role would be violated. In this way, all NP-movement is movement to a non-θ-position, a point that will figure prominently in the GB analysis of RtoO structures.

The θ-criterion serves to rule out the derivation in (14).

(14)  D-structure: [$_{NP}$e] said Terry to understand the problem.
      S-structure: Terry$_i$ said e$_i$ to understand the problem.

In (14), an embedded subject *Terry* has moved to the empty matrix subject position. The NP has moved from a Caseless position to a position where it can be Case marked. Thus, the structure is not illicit due to a Case Filter violation. Rather, the NP has moved from a position in which it would be assigned the θ-role of experiencer to a position where it will be assigned the θ-role of agent. Thus, in (14), the chain of (*Terry$_i$*, e$_i$) is assigned two θ-roles and thereby violates the θ-criterion, and the structure is ill-formed.

## *Binding theory*

Binding theory is the module of grammar whose principles account for the distribution of anaphors, pronouns, lexical arguments and variables, and the relations that can exist between each of these and potential antecedents in sentences. One basic fact that binding theory attempts to explain is the near complementary distribution of anaphors (reflexives and reciprocals) and pronouns, as illustrated in (15).

(15) a.  The children$_i$ soiled themselves$_i$.
     b.  *The children$_i$ soiled them$_i$.
     c.  *The children$_i$ claimed that the teacher scolded themselves$_i$.
     d.  The children$_i$ claimed that the teacher scolded them$_i$.

Recall that in Standard Theory, the distribution of the reflexives and pronouns in (15) are accounted for in terms of the clausemate condition on the Reflexivization transformation. The transformation applies obligatorily in (15a, b), accounting for the grammaticality of (15a) and ungrammaticality of (15b). The ungrammaticality of (15c) is due to the fact that the clausemate condition on Reflexivization is not satisfied and the rule cannot apply. Such an approach is not available within the GB framework. Within GB, arguments are assigned a referential index at S-structure. This indexation (represented by the subscripts) is "free," that is, it operates without constraints. It is the binding theory that evaluates the structures and filters out any illicit indexation.

Binding refers to the coindexation of two constituents that stand in a c-command relationship. The notions *bound* and *free* can be defined informally as in (16) and (17), respectively.

(16) α is *bound* by β if and only if:
   a. α and β are coindexed, and
   b. β c-commands α.

(17) α is *free* only if it is not bound.

Following (16), if β is in an A-position, α is said to be *A-bound* by β, and if β is in an A'-position, α is said to be *A'-bound* by β. These concepts are illustrated in the structures in (18).

(18)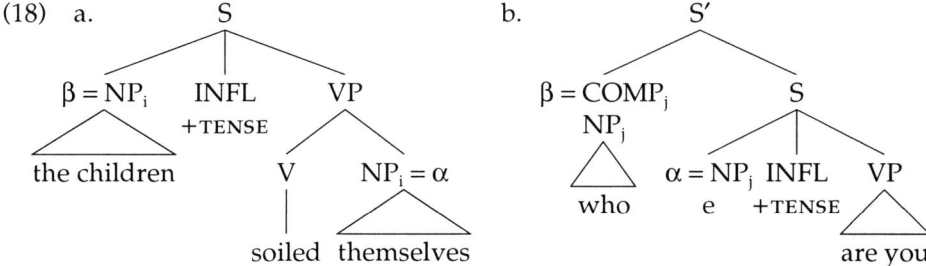

In (18a), the object NP, *themselves*, is A-bound by the subject NP, *the children*, since (i) the two NPs are coindexed, (ii) *the children* c-commands *themselves*, and (iii) *the children* is in an A-position. In (18b), the structure for the question *Who are you?*, the trace *e* in subject position is A'-bound by the NP *who* since the two are coindexed, *who* c-commands the trace, and *who* is in an A'-position, contained within COMP.

In all of the sentences in (15) then, *the children* A-binds *themselves* and *them*. The principles of the binding theory, given in (19), are responsible for evaluating the well-formedness of these binding relationships.

(19) *Binding theory (Chomsky 1981:188):*
   (A) An anaphor is bound in its governing category.
   (B) A pronominal is free in its governing category.
   (C) An R-expression is free.

The locality condition (clausemate condition) on reflexives from Standard Theory is reconstructed within GB using the notion *governing category*, initially formulated by Chomsky as in (20).[4]

(20) *Governing category (Chomsky 1981:188)*:
α is the governing category for β if and only if α is the minimal category containing β and a governor of β, where α = NP or S.

So, the governing category for any phrasal node β is the smallest NP or S that contains it and its governor.

Taking (19) and (20) together, it is possible to provide an account of the distribution of *themselves* and *them* in (15). First, consider the structure for the doublet in (15a, b).

(21)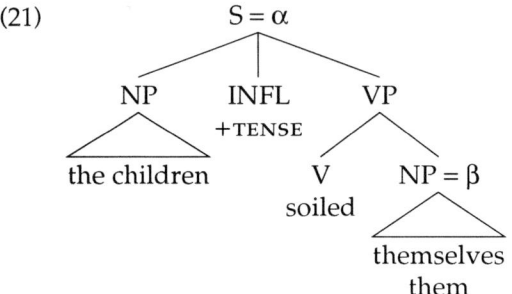

In (21), the governing category for the object NP (*themselves/them*) is the entire S, as it is the smallest NP or S containing the NP and its governor (here the V *soil*). Therefore, it is within this S that the anaphor *themselves* and the pronominal *them* must be evaluated by the binding principles. The coindexation of *themselves* with the NP *the children* in the representation satisfies principle A since the anaphor is bound in its governing category; therefore, (15a) is well-formed. However, in the representation in (21), coindexation of the pronominal *them* with *the children* results in a violation of principle B since the pronominal is not free in its governing category; therefore, (15b) is ungrammatical.

Now consider the structure for the doublet in (15c, d).

(22)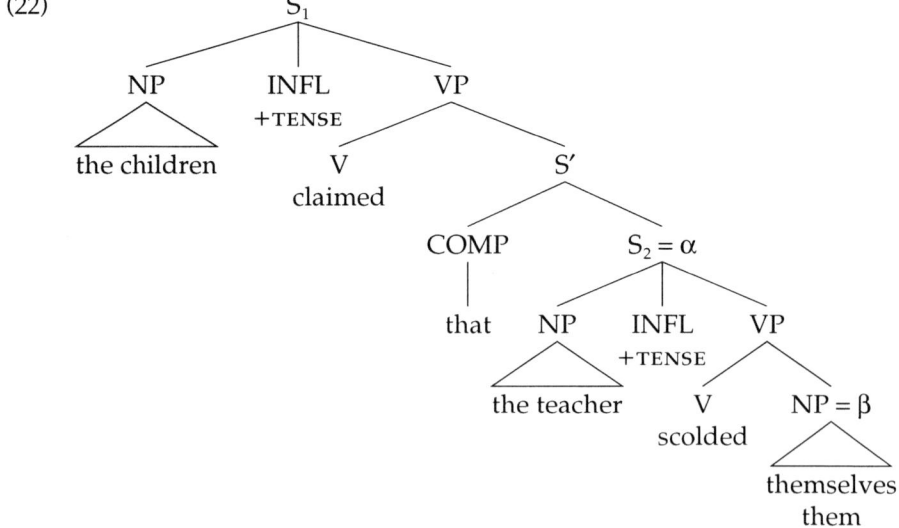

In (22), $S_2$ is the governing category for the NP *themselves/them*; it is the minimal NP or S containing the NP and its governor, *scolded*. When the NP is *themselves*, even if *themselves* is coindexed with *the children*, the structure violates principle A of the binding theory since the anaphor is not bound by an antecedent contained within its governing category. Thus, the sentence in (15c) is ungrammatical. However, coindexation of *them* with *the children* does not result in a violation of principle B. Even though the pronominal is bound by *the children*, it is free in its governing category $\alpha$ since its binder is an element not contained in $\alpha$. Thus, (15d) is grammatical.

A final consideration is the place of empty categories in the binding theory. Traces of NP-movement are taken to be anaphors inasmuch as like anaphors NP-traces must be coindexed with another element in the appropriate local domain in the sentence; this coindexation is a by-product of the rule Move-$\alpha$. What is more, since NP-movement is movement to an A position, like reflexive and reciprocal anaphors, NP-traces must be A-bound. As anaphors, traces of NP movement are subject to principle A of the binding theory. The applicability of principle A is apparent in unaccusative and passive structures. Consider again the unaccusative and passive sentences in (12a) and (13a) repeated in S-structure configurations in (23a) and (23b), respectively.

(23) a. [$_S$Ashley$_i$ slipped e$_i$ ].
 b. [$_S$Dana$_i$ was arrested e$_i$ ].

In (23a), the governing category of the trace *e* is the sentence since the S is the minimal S containing *e* and its governor, *slipped*. Additionally, *e* is coindexed with a c-commanding element in an A-position, the subject *Ashley*. Thus, the trace is bound by *Ashley* and the configuration in (23a) satisfies principle A of the binding theory. The situation is similar in (23b), where the trace is bound by *Dana* in the minimal NP or S containing it and its governor, *arrested*.

In some instances, the ungrammaticality of a sentence is accounted for by the failure of an NP-trace to satisfy principle A, for example, (24).

(24) *Dana is thought was arrested.

The S-structure for (24) in (25b) is derived from the D-structure in (25a).

(25) a. *e* is thought [$_S$*e* was arrested Dana]
 b. Dana$_i$ is thought [$_S$*e* was arrested e$_i$]

*Dana* has moved from its D-structure position as complement of *arrested* in (25a) directly to the matrix subject position (25b). Note that this structure violates neither the $\theta$-criterion nor the Case Filter. The chain including *Dana* and its coindexed trace receive a single $\theta$-role; the complement of *arrested* is a $\theta$-position but the subject position of the matrix clause is not. The NP *Dana* is assigned nominative Case by the matrix tensed INFL only. However, the governing category of the trace of NP-movement is the embedded S (since its governor is *arrested*) and the trace is not bound in this S. This results in a principle A violation, which accounts for the ungrammaticality of (24).[5]

## 3 Raising-to-Subject

As in its theoretical predecessors, the analysis of RtoS sentences involves movement. However, GB principles determine that the analysis takes on particular characteristics. First consider the sentences in (26).

(26) a. It seems that Lee is having a bad day.
     b. Lee seems to be having a bad day.

The analysis of (26a) does not differ too radically from that of the REST theory. The D-structure is as in (27).

(27)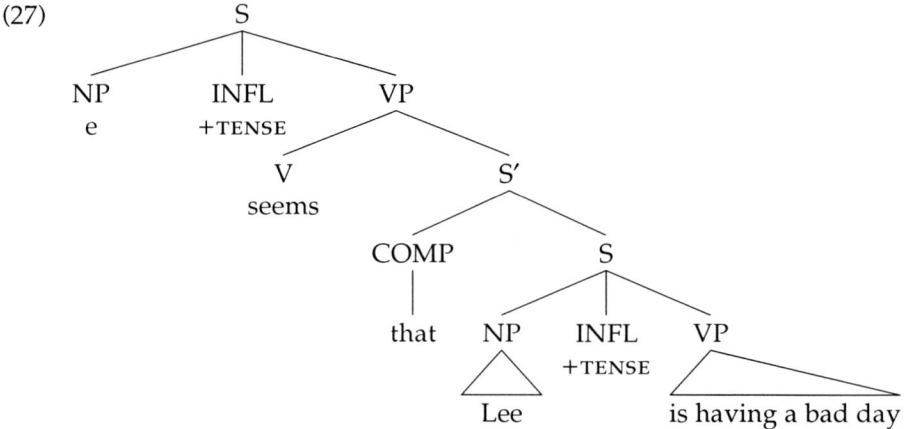

The verb *seem* selects for a single propositional complement. The empty subject position in the matrix clause is projected in conformity with the EPP. (26a) is derived through a late rule of *it*-Insertion.[6]

It seems reasonable to expect that the propositionally related (26b) would be derived from a very similar D-structure, although one without an overt complementizer and with an untensed *to* INFL, as in (28).

(28)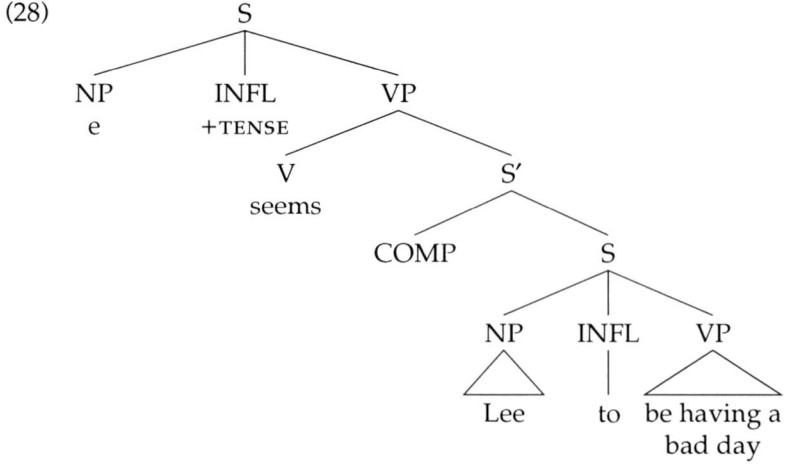

Unlike (27), insertion of *it* into matrix subject position does not yield a well-formed structure. Simply inserting *it* would result in the ungrammatical (29).

(29) *It seems Lee to be having a bad day.

(29) violates the Case Filter since *Lee* is not assigned Case. Given the D-structure in (28), *Lee* must move to a Case-marked position. This can be accomplished by movement to the matrix subject position, where *Lee* can receive nominative Case from the tensed INFL. Applying this movement to (28) results in the structure in (30).

(30)
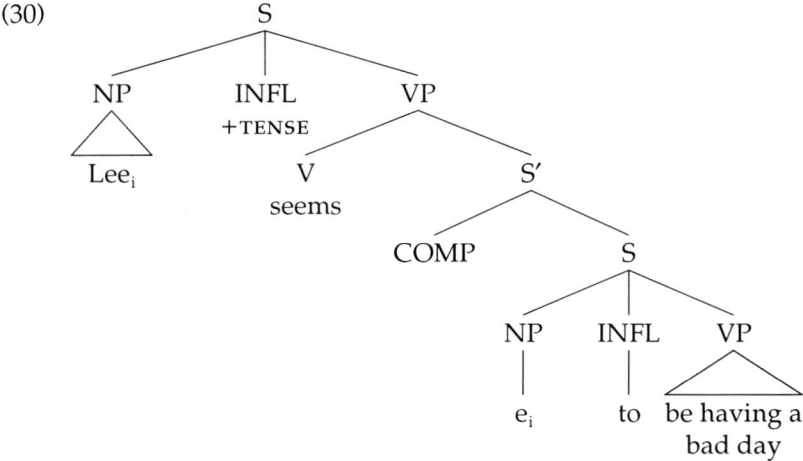

However, (30) is ill-formed. Following principle A of the binding theory, the trace $e_i$, as an anaphor, must be bound in its governing category. But the trace has no governing category in (30) because it has no governor. Recall that the untensed INFL *to* is not a governor. And although the matrix verb *seem* is a potential governor, government is blocked by the S', a maximal category that dominates the trace but does not dominate *seem*.

A potential solution to this problem is the removal of the S'. This removes the barrier to government of the trace by *seem*, giving an S-structure like that in (31).

(31)
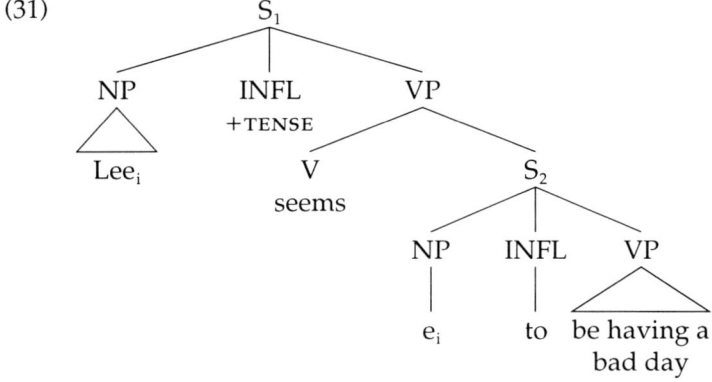

In (31), the governing category for the trace $e_i$ in the embedded clause is $S_1$ as that is the minimal NP or S that contains the trace and its governor *seem*. Under this set of assumptions, (31) does not constitute a principle A violation: the trace is bound by *Lee* in $S_1$.

The removal of the S' leads to the question of whether (a) the S' occurs in D-structure (as in (28)) and is deleted or (b) the complement clause is simply generated as a plain S in the D-structure, as in (32).

(32)  *e* seems [$_S$Lee to be having a bad day]

Chomsky (1981) assumes that English includes a marked rule of S'-deletion, specified for particular matrix predicates that makes it possible for those predicates to govern the subject position of a complement clause.[7] All predicates previously assumed to govern RtoS are assumed in Chomsky's analysis to govern S'-deletion. This analysis, as opposed to the base-generated S complement analysis, gains support from sentences such as (33).

(33)  What$_j$ does Leslie seem to be reading $e_j$?

In order for *wh*-movement to apply in (33) without violating Subjacency, there must be a COMP position for the *wh*-phrase to move through on its way to the matrix COMP, just as has been assumed for *wh*-movement since "Conditions." Base-generation of an S complement to *seem*, while allowing *seem* to govern the embedded subject position, would thus render *wh*-movement problematic.[8]

So, the difference between a raising predicate such as *be likely* and a semantically similar non-raising predicate such as *be possible* is that one triggers S'-deletion and the other does not. Thus (34) is grammatical because the trace $e_i$ is governed by *likely*, while (35) is ungrammatical since the trace $e_i$ is ungoverned, resulting in a principle A violation.

(34)  Leslie$_i$ is likely [$_S$e$_i$ to be reading].

(35)  *Leslie$_i$ is possible [$_{S'}$[$_S$e$_i$ to be reading]].

## 4  Raising-to-Object

The GB analysis of RtoO structures continues the precedent begun in "Conditions" of eschewing a movement analysis. As with RtoS, the theoretical principles introduced in GB have significant implications for the analysis in terms of both the devices needed for the account and the justification for an analysis that includes no movement.

Consider first non-RtoO and RtoO sentences with the verb *believe*.

(36)  a.  Lynn believes (that) Lee and Leslie like lemons.
      b.  Lynn believes Lee and Leslie to like lemons.

The essentially identical D-structure and S-structure for the non-RtoO sentence in (36a) is given in (37).

(37)  Lynn believes [$_{S'}$(that) [$_S$Lee and Leslie like lemons]]

Clearly the complement of *believe* here should be an S' with the overt complementizer *that*. As with the analysis of RtoS structures, the structure for RtoO sentence faces difficulties if the complement is S', as evident in (38).

(38)  Lynn believes [$_{S'}$[$_S$Lee and Leslie to like lemons]]

As it stands, (38) cannot be the S-structure for (36b). In (38), there is no way for the embedded subject *Lee and Leslie* to be assigned Case. The untensed INFL *to* cannot assign Case and the potential Case-assigner *believe* does not govern the NP because the maximal projection S' blocks government. Thus, (38) is ruled out as a violation of the Case Filter.

As the D-structure subject in RtoO is assigned objective Case and this Case is clearly assigned by the verb *believe* in (36b), it is necessary to create the proper structural relationship between the matrix verb and the embedded subject. Here again, Chomsky invokes the rule of S'-deletion. Assuming (38) to be the D-structure for (36b), application of S'-deletion yields the S-structure in (39).[9]

(39)  Lynn believes [$_S$Lee and Leslie to like lemons]

Now, the embedded subject *Lee and Leslie* is in a government relationship with *believe*; thus *believe* can Case mark the NP. That *believe* has a Case to assign to its complement (while an RtoS predicate like *seem* does not) is evident from its ability to occur in simple transitive sentences such as (40), in which it assigns objective Case to its complement *them*.

(40)  Lynn believes them.

Because it is the exception rather than the rule for a matrix predicate to Case mark the subject of a complement clause, the type of Case marking exhibited in RtoO structures is referred to as *Exceptional Case Marking* or *ECM*. Verbs with the lexical property of inducing S'-deletion and assigning Case to the subjects of their complements are referred to as ECM verbs. (This designation has remained among many linguists despite the fact that in the current Minimalist framework there is no exceptional Case marking and movement has returned as the analysis of choice.)

The S'-deletion analysis with *believe* allows an account of sentences such as (41) in which the D-structure subject of the complement of *believe* is the matrix clause subject at S-structure.

(41)  Lee and Leslie are believed to like lemons.

The derivation of (41) parallels derivations with RtoS predicates such as *seem*.

(42) a. D-structure: [~NP~e] are believed [~S'~[~S~Lee and Leslie to like lemons]]
     b. S-structure: [Lee and Leslie]~i~ are believed [~S~e~i~ to like lemons]

S'-deletion in the derivation allows proper structural relationship for the NP trace $e_i$ to be bound by its antecedent *Lee and Leslie* in its governing category, thereby satisfying Principle A of the binding theory.

It should be clear that S'-deletion is not the only means by which the D-structure subject of an RtoO sentence can be brought into the proper structural relationship with the matrix verb so that it can be assigned Case by that verb. Movement into the matrix clause, as in the classical Standard Theory analysis, is an obvious alternative. Under such an analysis, the RtoO sentence in (36a) would have the D-structure in (43a) and the S-structure in (43b).

(43) a. D-structure: Lynn believes [~NP~e] [~S'~[~S~Lee and Leslie to like lemons]]
     b. S-structure: Lynn believes Lee and Leslie~i~ [~S~e~i~ to like lemons]

The analysis in (43) includes an empty NP complement in the matrix VP and application of the S'-deletion rule. The empty position in D-structure (43a) is required to satisfy the Projection Principle: since the NP *Lee and Leslie* occupies this position at S-structure (43b), the Projection Principle induces its existence at D-structure. S'-deletion is necessary for the same reason as with RtoS: the matrix verb must govern the trace so that it can be bound in its governing category, thus satisfying Principle A.

The movement analysis just sketched is rejected as an unnecessary complication of the theory. Not only is S'-deletion required in the movement analysis, the empty D-structure complement position must be a non-θ-position. If it were a θ-position, the movement of *Lee and Leslie* to this position would induce a violation of the θ-criterion inasmuch as the NP is assigned a θ-role as subject of the embedded verb *like*. However, the theory stipulates that all complement positions are θ-positions. Chomsky (1981:37) states this explicitly, claiming that "if α subcategorizes the position β, then α θ-marks β." The movement analysis of RtoO would require an exception to some aspect of the theory as developed: allowing exception to the Projection Principle or exception to θ-theory. Proponents of GB thus considered a non-movement ECM analysis of RtoO structures to be derived from the principles of the theory.[10]

## 5 *Want*-type verbs

We turn now to a consideration of *want*-type verbs. A partial paradigm is given in (44).

(44) a. Leslie wants very much for Lee to have a good day.
     b. Leslie wants Lee to have a good day.
     c. *Lee is wanted by everyone to have a good day.

In (44a), the complement clause takes the prepositional complementizer *for*, and so must be of the category S', as in the structure in (45).

(45)  Leslie wants very much [$_{S'}$for [$_S$Lee to have a good day.]]

In (45), the prepositional complementizer *for* governs and assigns Case to *Lee* inasmuch as S is not taken to be a maximal category and thus does not block government. Based on the ECM analysis of *believe* and the analysis of (44a), one possibility for the derivation of (44b) is (46).

(46)  a.  D-structure:  Leslie wants [$_{S'}$[$_S$Lee to have a good day.]]
      b.  S-structure:  Leslie wants [$_S$Lee to have a good day.]

S'-deletion allows the NP *Lee* to be governed and assigned Case by *want*. However, the ungrammaticality of (44c) poses problems for such an analysis. As shown previously in (41), *believe* permits the D-structure subject of its complement to move to matrix subject position in passives. If *want* triggers S'-deletion as in (46), (44c) is predicted to be grammatical, with a derivation as in (47), where $e_i$ is bound by *Lee* in its governing category.

(47)  a.  D-structure:  [$_{NP}$e] is wanted by everyone [$_{S'}$[$_S$Lee to have a good day]]
      b.  S-structure:  Lee$_i$ is wanted by everyone [$_S$e$_i$ to have a good day]

Thus *want* is not open to the ECM/S'-deletion analysis of *believe*-type verbs.

Chomsky proposes that *want* cannot trigger S'-deletion but that there is a rule of *for*-deletion in the PF component (optionally triggered in immediate postverbal position with selected predicates). Thus, at S-structure, *for* still resides in COMP and governs and Case marks *Lee*. (44b) thus has the S-structure in (48a) and a PF output along the lines of (48b).

(48)  a.  S-structure:  Leslie wants [$_{S'}$for [$_S$Lee to have a good day.]]
      b.  PF output:   Leslie wants [$_{S'}$[$_S$Lee to have a good day.]]

## 6  Control

On p. 55 of *Lectures on Government and Binding*, Chomsky states "there is an intrinsic fascination in the study of properties of empty categories." One of these empty categories is the PRO of control constructions. Just as considerations of thematic structure provide early arguments for the Equi NP analysis of control, θ-theory provides a rationale for positing PRO in control constructions such as:

(49)  They tried to understand that theory.

In (49) *they* bears two θ-roles, the agent role associated with *try* and the experiencer role associated with *understand*. The θ-criterion prohibits any one argument from bearing more than one θ-role. Thus, an argument distinct from the matrix subject *they* must exist in the structure for (49) in order to accept the experiencer role. Additionally, the EPP requires a subject position to be projected in all clauses. Thus, if the infinitival complement of *try* is a full clause, there must be an empty subject projected in the complement of (50). PRO, of course, is the element that fills these two requirements.

But what are the properties of the empty category PRO? In part PRO is similar to the empty category NP trace, and in part it is different. On the one hand, PRO is like an anaphor; in obligatory control, it is bound and gets its reference from an antecedent argument just like anaphors. On the other hand, PRO is like a pronominal. PRO can be locally free:

(50)  She$_i$ said [that [PRO$_i$ to extricate herself from that relationship] would be judicious].

In (50), *she* is coindexed with a PRO in subject position of the sentential subject of a complement clause. Additionally, like a pronominal, PRO need not take an overt antecedent in its sentence:

(51)  [PRO to perjure oneself] would be unwise.

In (51), PRO takes arbitrary reference, as indicated by the form of the anaphor that it binds, *oneself*.

Thus, PRO is claimed to have characteristics of both anaphors and pronominals. As an anaphor, it should be subject to Principle A of the binding theory, and so it should be bound in its governing category. As a pronominal, it should be subject to Principle B and so should be free in its governing category. This contradiction leads to the conclusion that PRO must be ungoverned. The deduction that PRO must be ungoverned is referred to in the GB literature as the PRO Theorem.[11]

It follows from the PRO Theorem and the theory of government that the distribution of PRO is limited to subjects, since complement positions are always governed by the lexical head that selects them. Further, since tensed INFL is a governor of subject position, it follows that PRO can only occur as subject of infinitives and gerunds. Given this, (49) must have the structure in (52).

(52)  They tried [$_{S'}$[$_S$PRO to understand this theory]].

The complement of *try* is an S′ with an empty COMP rather than simply S. As a maximal projection, S′ blocks government of PRO by *try*, ensuring that PRO is ungoverned.

What remains of control theory is assigning reference to PRO. As Chomsky states, "this theory involves a number of different factors: structural configurations, intrinsic properties of verbs, other semantic and pragmatic considerations" (1981:78–9). It is sufficient for present purposes to note that precise formulations of rules of construal for PRO were not a central concern in GB. The importance of control theory lies in accounting for the distribution of PRO and the manner in which it interacts with the other subsystems of grammar.

## 7 Summary: *want* and *expect* and the variety of verb specifications

In addition to the structure in which *want* occurs with a *for* S' complement (either overt or deleted in PF), *want* occurs in control constructions, as in:

(53)  Lee$_i$ wants [$_{S'}$[$_S$PRO$_i$ to understand that theory]].

As in standard cases of obligatory control, the complement is S', ensuring that PRO is ungoverned. Thus, the *want*-class of verbs is, as we have seen, distinct from obligatory control verbs such as *try* in allowing lexical material in the subject of the complement S'. This class of verbs is thus often referred to as optional control verbs. But importantly, the complement of these verbs must always be S'.

Yet another pattern emerges with the verb *expect*. Like *want*, *expect* is an optional control verb. The complement of *expect* can take a lexical NP as D-structure subject, as in (54a, b), and can have a PRO subject (54c).

(54)  a.  Terry expects confidently [for Kelsey to challenge the incumbent].
      b.  Terry expects [Kelsey to challenge the incumbent].
      c.  Terry expects [to challenge the incumbent].

Based on the proposed account of *want*, the complements of *expect* in (54) can be analyzed as S' and not bare S, with *for* in COMP in (54a), with the *for* complementizer deleted at PF in (54b), and an empty complementizer in (54c). However, *expect* allows a structure unavailable with *want*. It is possible for the D-structure subject of the complement of *expect* to surface as the matrix subject in a passive, as in (55).

(55)  Kelsey$_i$ is expected [e$_i$ to challenge the incumbent].

Since this raising structure is possible, *expect* must be an S'-deletion trigger. Otherwise the trace in (55) could not be properly bound by *Kelsey*. Recognizing that *expect* can trigger S'-deletion makes available a second option in the analysis of (54b). This structure can receive the same type of ECM analysis as *believe* and similar verbs, as in the S-structure in (56).

(56)  Terry expects [$_S$Kelsey to challenge the incumbent].

In previous chapters, we have seen that the particular characteristics of the lexical items involved in Raising must be marked lexically as either participating in particular transformations or requiring specific types of complements. GB is no exception to this: the properties of particular verbs must be lexically specified. Predicates such as *seem* and *likely* trigger S'-deletion, and since they have no external argument and assign no structural accusative Case, they trigger RtoS. Verbs such as *believe* are also lexically marked to trigger S'-deletion but have an external argument and therefore assign structural accusative Case to an infintival subject via ECM. Verbs of the *want* class subcategorize for a *for* complement but do not trigger S'-deletion. And verbs such as *expect* are both subcategorized for a *for* complement and marked as S'-deletion triggers. This is sketched in (57).

(57) a. *seem* [ ____ S'], +S'-deletion
　　 b. *believe* [ ____ S'], +S'-deletion
　　 c. *want* [ ____ for S]
　　 d. *expect* [ ____ S'/for S], +S'-deletion

The level of detail needed in (57) is neither an advantage nor a disadvantage for the GB approach inasmuch as any approach requires this level of detail. However, the facts in (57) reveal an interesting property of the GB analysis. Movement is the feature shared by RtoS and RtoO in the Standard Theory analysis (recall that Rosenbaum 1967 proposed a single Raising transformation) and the RG analysis. In GB the common feature that these constructions share is S'-deletion. While this is perhaps a minor point, RtoS and RtoO shared no particular feature in Chomskyan theory after "Conditions." So, in GB the two constructions are again in a sense unified.

## Notes

1 　In fact, the assignment of the θ-role of subjects is mediated by the VP, i.e., determined by the verb in combination with its complements, but this detail is unimportant here.
2 　Chomsky (1977) identifies a number of different construction types that he argues exhibit characteristics of *wh*-movement, including *tough* movement, topicalization, comparative formation, and others.
3 　An exception to this is the assignment of genitive Case, which is assigned in the structure [$_{NP}$ ___ X]. Genitive Case falls outside the scope of present concerns.
4 　The notion of governing category went through revisions by Chomsky (1986a) and others, e.g., Rizzi (1990). The relatively simple, straightforward formulation in (20) is sufficient for understanding the role of the binding theory in the determination of analyses of Raising and Control.
5 　Here, we can clearly see that binding theory supplants the Tensed-S Condition (TSC), in filtering out bad representations. In this regard, the move to binding theory represents a simplification of conditions. Just as conditions on rules were supplanted in C&L (1977) by conditions on representations, the TSC and the Specified Subject Condition (SSC) are supplanted in GB by principle A of the binding theory. The intention here is to gain the greatest empirical coverage from the fewest theoretical principles. Thus, not only does binding theory lead to the invocation of one condition (principle A) where two (TSC and SSC) were previously needed. At the same time, note that principle A only filters the output of Move-α as applied to NP-movement structures. The interaction of Move-α and *wh*-elements is still governed by separate principles, i.e., bounding theory and Subjacency.
6 　In "Filters and Control" it is inserted by an early lexical insertion rule. This rule is triggered when *seems* has an S' complement with a *that* complementizer. Failure to apply the rule would leave the matrix subject empty and uninterpretable.

7   Chomsky's rule of S'-deletion is not a deletion rule of the ordinary type. Deletion rules such as Equi, gapping, complementizer deletion and others target words and phrases. S'-deletion targets a nonterminal node *a* and at the same time reattaches the dependents of that node as dependents of the node immediately dominating *a*. Therefore, S'-deletion is, in fact, a tree-pruning rule of the type discussed by Ross (1967) and employed by Postal (1974) in his analysis of Raising. It is unclear how S'-deletion interacts with the notion of structure preservation.

8   If Emonds's notion of structure preservation encompasses deletion of existing nodes, S'-deletion is incompatible with a strict notion of structure preservation since this is a rule that affects nonroot nodes. It should also be noted that there is an intrinsic ordering of *wh*-movement and S'-deletion since the movement of the *wh*-element requires the existence of the COMP position which is lost after the deletion.

9   Recall that in the REST movement Case was not the issue. Rather concern for the distribution of [NP to VP] led to the [$_{S'}$ complement analysis in which the null complementizer Ø licensed the infinitive. Remember that while the V *believe* could take the bare S complement, the A *likely* could not have a bare [$_S$NP to VP] complement.

10  Postal and Pullum (1988) argue that the assertion that a movement analysis of RtoO is impossible does not derive directly from the principles of the theory, or at least that it should not, citing structures which include pleonastic, hence non-θ complement positions. Their work is taken up in chapter 12.

11  In Hornstein (1999), which will be discussed in chapter 13, a movement approach to Control is offered. This account is justified on the grounds that PRO has distinct distributions depending on whether it is in an "obligatory control" (OC) context or a "non-obligatory control" (NOC) context. Williams (1980) first argued for the interpretive differences between these two types of Control. Hornstein presents data from Lebeaux (1985), which show that OC PRO (but not NOC PRO) is like an anaphor in that it requires a c-commanding antecedent. NOC PRO, in contrast, does not require any antecedent, and if it does have an antecedent, it can be neither c-commanding nor local. On this basis, Hornstein (1999:74) suggests that PRO is structurally ambiguous ("an anaphoric expression in OC configurations and a pronominal in NOC structures"), rather than being "simultaneously" an anaphor and a pronominal in accordance with the PRO Theorem.

# CHAPTER 9

# DEVELOPMENT OF AND PROBLEMS FOR THE ECM ACCOUNT: KAYNE (1981) AND COLE AND HERMON (1981)

The ECM account developed for English in Chomsky (1981) is challenged in this chapter by analogous data from other languages. The first part of the chapter examines Kayne's (1981) article in which the application of an ECM-style analysis to French leads to a revision of the general analysis of ECM constructions. Kayne's revised analysis of ECM attempts to incorporate otherwise problematic French data into a GB model, and to extend this revised and generalized ECM account to both languages. The second part of the chapter presents an excerpt from Cole and Hermon's (1981) article on raising constructions in Imbabura Quechua. The facts that they present can be accounted for within the ECM analysis, but not without some cost to the grammar.

## 1 French ECM and control cases: Kayne (1981)

In his 1981 article "On certain differences between French and English", Kayne shows, on the basis of data such as (1) and (2), that *believe* verbs in French do not have the equivalent of the English ECM construction.

(1) a. I believe John to be intellegent.
 b. *Je crois Jean être intelligent
(2) a. *I believe to have made a mistake.
 b. Je crois avoir fait une erreur.

This contrast is considered together with some other differences, including: (i) the absence of preposition stranding in French (vs. English) as in (3), and (ii) the appearance of *de* in apparent control clauses (where English would forbid *for*) as in (4).

(3) a. Which candidate have you voted for? [= Kayne 1981:(2)]
 b. *Quel candidat as-tu voté pour?

(4) a. *John tried for to cross the river.
    b. Jean a essayé de traverser le fleuve.

Kayne relates the ungrammaticality of (1b) and (3b) to the grammaticality of (2b) and (4b), proposing that French prepositions cannot govern their complements in the same manner as verbs (in contrast with English, in which V and P govern in the same way). He goes on to provide an analysis in which *believe* (i.e., RtoO) verbs of English and French have identical complement structure, and the differences between the two languages reside in the ability of certain constituents to govern. The summary that follows here focuses on Kayne's account of raising constructions (and its implications for the analysis of Equi and Control), and does not present his analysis of preposition stranding (i.e., his account of the contrast in (3)). The interested reader is encouraged to examine his discussion of preposition stranding in section 4 of the article.

Kayne's argument proceeds in the following manner. He first shows that French *de* is a (prepositional) complementizer analogous to the *for* complementizer in English (and unlike the English (prepositional) infinitival marker *to*). He then lays out the distributional differences between the prepositional complementizers in the two languages. Following that, he presents an account for these differences, which involves some revision to the (standard) GB analysis of ECM constructions.

In order to adopt his proposed analyis, Kayne must first demonstrate that French *de* and English *for* both fill a complementizer position before an infinitival clause. This is not immediately obvious. Consider (5).

(5) a. Jean a essayé de traverser le fleuve.
    b. John tried to cross the river.
    c. *John tried for to cross the river.

At first glance, it would appear to make sense to equate the preposition *de* in (5a) with the preposition *to* in (5b), since prepositional complementizers are ungrammatical with bare infinitives. This would assume that some version of the English **for-to* filter also applies in French.

Kayne presents several arguments to show that French *de* is a complementizer, three of which are considered here. First, he shows that *de* is like *for* (and unlike *to*) in that it cannot appear in a +WH infinitival complement. Consider the contrast between (6) and (7), where the examples in (7) are both ungrammatical on account of the presence of *de* (here *d'*) and *for*, respectively.

(6) a. Je lui ai dit où aller.                [= Kayne 1981:(7)]
    b. I told him where to go.

(7) a. *Je lui ai dit où d'aller.              [= Kayne 1981:(8)]
    b. *I told him where for to go.

Kayne suggests that assuming *de* to be a complementizer (like *for*) allows the ungrammaticality of (7a) and (7b) to both be explained as due to violations of doubly filled COMP. In other words, *ou* and *d'* in (7a) and *where* and *for* in (7b) are in competition for the same syntactic position.

Kayne's next arguments take into account ways in which French *de* and Italian *di* display similar behavior. One of these arguments concerns the impossibility of these prepositional elements in RtoS clauses. Examining here only the English and French facts, consider the contrast in (8) and (9).

(8) a. Jean semble être parti.  [= Kayne 1981:(28)]
    b. John seems to have left.

(9) a. *Jean semble d'être parti.  [= Kayne 1981:(28)]
    b. *John seems for to have left.

Again, examples (9a) and (9b) are ill-formed on account of the presence of *de* and *for*, respectively. If *de* and *for* are assumed to be complementizers, then, Kayne suggests, both cases might be explained in terms of the impossibility of "extracting subjects across an adjacent complementizer" (Kayne 1981:352).

Another sort of argument presented to support the assertion that *de* is a complementizer draws from the linear distribution of complementizers and negation. Kayne first points out that verbal negation in English cannot precede the complementizer *that* or the complementizer *for*, as shown in (10) and (11).

(10) a. *We persuaded him not that he should come.
     b. We persuaded him that he should not come.

(11) a. *We would prefer not for him to come.
     b. We would prefer for him not to come.

At the same time, negation can precede the infinitival marker *to* (although the reverse order is also possible). This is illustrated in (12), where (12a) is somewhat more natural.

(12) a. We would prefer not to come.
     b. We would prefer to not come.

Similarly, in French, the negative clitic *ne* cannot precede the complementizer *que*, as shown here in (13).

(13) a. *Je lui ai dit ne qu'il devrait voir personne.  [= Kayne 1981:(53)]
     b. Je lui ai dit qu'il ne devrait voir personne.

Given that the negative clitic *ne* cannot precede *de*, as in (14), it is clear that its distribution is consistent with its being a complementizer.

(14) a. *Je lui ait dit ne de voir personne.  [= Kayne 1981:(50)]
     b. Je lui ait dit de ne voir personne.  [= Kayne 1981:(48)]

If *de* were the French analog of the English infinitival marker *to*, then there would be no straightforward explanation for the contrast between grammatical (12a) and ungrammatical (14a), in which the negative element precedes the item in question.[1]

Having established that *de* and *for* both occupy the COMP position in an infinitival complement clause, Kayne next turns his attention to the important difference in their distribution. As seen above in (4), repeated here, *for* cannot precede an infinitival complement with a null subject (4a), while *de* can do so (4b).

(4) a. *John tried for to cross the river.
    b. Jean a essayé de traverser le fleuve.

Conversely, *de* cannot precede an infinitival complement clause with an overt subject NP (such as *quelque chose* in (15b)), while *for* can do so (appearing before the subject *something* in (15a)).

(15) a. It would be a pity for something to happen to him.
     b. *Ce serait dommage de quelque chose lui
        arriver.                                          [= Kayne 1981:(56)]

Assuming (as Kayne does) that the structure of null subject infinitivals involves PRO, the differences can be expressed structurally as follows in (16).

(16) a. *[$_{S'}$for [$_S$PRO to VP]]                    [= (4a)]
     b.  [$_{S'}$de [$_S$PRO -er VP]]                    [= (4b)]
     c.  [$_{S'}$for [$_S$something to VP]]              [= (15a)]
     d. *[$_{S'}$de [$_S$quelque chose -er VP]]          [= (15b)]

On the assumptions that the subject position of infinitivals is ungoverned within S (in both English and French) and that PRO is licensed only in ungoverned positions, the most reasonable account of the difference between *for* and *de* is that the former governs and assigns case to the subject of S, while the latter does not. Accordingly, (4a) is ungrammatical because *for* governs and assigns Case to PRO, and (15b) is ungrammatical because *de* does not govern or assign Case to *quelque chose*.

Kayne generalizes from these empirical facts to make the general proposal that French prepositions are unlike verbs in that they assign oblique Case only to those complements for which they are subcategorized and cannot structurally govern the specifier of their complement. In contrast, English prepositions (like English verbs) are said to assign accusative Case and govern the specifier position of their complements. This clearly accounts for the contrast in (4), repeated from above:

(4) a. *[$_S$John tried [$_{S'}$for [$_S$PRO to cross the river]]
    b.  [$_S$Jean a essayé [$_{S'}$de [$_S$PRO traverser le fleuve]]

Here, *for* governs and assigns Case to the PRO subject of its S complement. In (4a), PRO is governed in the matrix S and bound by *John* in this domain, causing a Principle B violation. In (4b), on the other hand, the prepositional COMP *de* does not govern PRO, and PRO is left ungoverned as required by the PRO Theorem. The contrast in (15) is also provided an expanation under this analysis.

(15) a. It would be a pity [$_{S'}$for [$_S$something to happen to him]]
 b. *Ce serait dommage [$_{S'}$de [$_S$quelque chose lui arriver]]

Here, the subject of the infinitival complement is an overt NP which needs Case. This is provided in (15a), where *for* governs and assigns accusative Case to *something*. In (15b), though, *quelque chose* is not assigned Case and violates the Case Filter.

In taking up the contrast seen above in (1), Kayne adopts the notion of a prepositional null complementizer Ø (from Chomsky and Lasnik 1977) and proposes that all *believe* verbs select an S' complement with this complementizer. The structures are elaborated here in (17).

(17) a. I believe [$_{S'}$Ø [$_S$John to be intellegent]]
 b. *Je crois [$_{S'}$Ø [$_S$Jean être intelligent]]

Under this account, there is no S'-deletion or S'-transparency in English. Rather the difference between the English and the French facts lies in the assertion that French prepositions (including null ones) do not govern or assign Case across an S-boundary. In English, the null complementizer assigns Case in the same way as *for*, making the grammaticality of (15a) and (17a) completely parallel.

## 2 Discussion of issues raised in Kayne (1981)

There are a number of empirical factors that complicate the implementation of Kayne's proposal. Some of these are discussed in the article, while others emerge from a look at data not considered there. The first complication in Kayne's account concerns the fact that alongside the ungrammatical (17b) above, in which an overt NP cannot appear as the subject of a *believe* verb infinitival complement, French has (18), in which a *wh*-element appears to have originated in the banned position.

(18) Quel garçon crois-tu ____ être intelligent?
 'Which boy do you believe to be intellegent?'

Comparing (17b) and (18), it would appear that the same position from which lexical NPs are prohibited is a position that can contain a *wh*-trace of such NPs. Kayne suggests that there are two ways in which to approach these facts. One way, he says, might be to decide that the output of Raising (i.e., RtoO) in

French must obligatorily undergo further movement. In other words, the subject of the infinitival complement of *believe* must either be PRO (as in (2b) above) or +WH (as in (18) here). This solution, of course, provides no way to explain the distribution of these elements in Case-theoretic terms. PRO, as we have seen, must be ungoverned and not receive Case. The *wh*-element in (18), *quel garçon*, moves cyclically to a Caseless A' position, and (according to Case theory) must be Case marked prior to reaching its S-structure position. Accordingly, Kayne proposes a solution that takes advantage of the cyclic nature of *wh*-movement, and proposes (19) as the structure for (18).

(19) [$_{S'}$quel garçon$_1$ crois-tu [$_{S'}$t$'_1$ [$_S$t$_1$ être intelligent]]]

On the assumption that a V can govern across one S-type boundary (but not across two such boundaries), Kayne proposes that the verb *croire* Case marks the intermediate trace of *quel garçon*, $t'_1$. Although the solution does indeed solve the empirical problem at hand, it is not without shortcomings. In particular, assigning Case to an intermediate *wh*-trace begs the question of how this is to be constrained. Presumably all *wh*-elements move in the same manner through the embedded S'. Assuming this, questioning the object in (2b) should have the derivation shown here in (20).

(20) [$_{S'}$quelle erreur$_1$ crois-tu [$_{S'}$t$'_1$ [$_S$PRO avoir fait t$_1$]]]
 'What error do you believe yourself to have made?'

Under Kayne's account, the lower clause object in (20), *quel erreur*, would be assigned accusative Case twice (once by *faire* in the lower VP, and once by *croire* across S'). While this may not pose a problem in this particular instance, as the two Cases are of the same type, it is generally assumed in GB theory that an NP-chain (i.e., the NP and all its traces) can have exactly one Case and one θ-role.

Another, potentially more intractable, problem for this account involves the application of passives to English RtoO constructions. Consider (21).

(21) a. Judy believes [$_{S'}$Ø [$_S$him to be nice]]
 b. He$_1$ is believed by Judy [$_{S'}$Ø [$_S$t$_1$ to be nice]]

Under Kayne's preliminary account (as noted above), *him* in (21a) is assigned (accusative) Case by the prepositional null complementizer Ø. Since nothing in this lower S' is changed by the passivization of *believe*, it must be assumed that the null complementizer continues to assign Case to this position in (21b). If this is so, then the NP-chain of A-movement {$he_1$, $t_1$} is assigned two Cases (nominative in the matrix S and accusative in the lower S) and the Case motivation for NP-movement in the passive construction is lost. Kayne anticipates this difficulty in appendix 2 of the article (his pp. 366–7), and suggests that Ø has the property of "transmitting" government and Case. He posits a principle of transitivity of government, given here in (22).

(22) If X governs Ø and Ø governs β, then X governs β.

Here, since *believe* governs Ø (across one S-type node) and Ø governs *him* (across one S-type node), *believe* is said to govern *him*. This principle allows *believe* to "transmit" its Case to *him* (rather than have the infinitival subject directly Case marked by Ø).[2] On the standard assumption that the passive form *believed* has no Case to assign, there is no Case to be transmitted through Ø in (21b) and movement is once again motivated. In adopting this Case transmission solution, Kayne's account appears to predict the ungrammaticality of (23), which would otherwise be unexplained under the first solution proposed in the article.

(23) *[Ø [him to be nice]] is believed by everyone

If Ø assigns Case directly to *him*, then there is nothing to rule out (23) other than that the movement is not Case motivated. However, if Ø "transmits" government and Case, then moving the infinitive into the subject position leaves Ø without a governor and with no way to transmit Case (accusative or nominative) to the subject of the infinitive.

Another empirical complication for Kayne's approach is presented by the *want* class of verbs in English. Consider (24).

(24) a. Joshua wants him to leave.
 b. Joshua wants to leave.

Under the "Filters and Control" account, *want* (unlike *believe*) selects an S' complement with a *for* complementizer. In (24a), *for* is deleted, and (24b) involves *for* deletion and Equi NP Deletion. In Chomsky (1981), the account for (24a) remains essentially analogous. There, *want* selects an S' with *for*, which assigns Case to the infinitival subject and then deletes at PF. (24b), on the other hand, is claimed by Chomsky to have an empty complementizer, as in (25).

(25) Joshua wants [$_{S'}$e [$_S$PRO to leave]]

Since *want* does not trigger S' transparency (or deletion) and since there is no complementizer to assign Case to the subject position through the S node, PRO is licensed as a subject. Kayne, in discussing the structure of English subject control verbs such as *try* (his p. 362), also assumes selection of an S' complement with an empty (as opposed to "null") complementizer. If *try* (or *want* in (25)) were to select a null Ø complementizer, the government and Case properties of the matrix verb would be transmitted to the subject position. Kayne does not discuss the derivation of (24a), but we might imagine two possible D-structures, given here in (26).

(26) a. Joshua wants [$_{S'}$for [$_S$him to leave]]
 b. Joshua wants [$_{S'}$Ø [$_S$him to leave]]

Either *want* selects a *for* complementizer, which Case marks *him* and deletes at PF as in (26a), or *want* selects a Ø complementizer, which transmits the Case assigned by *want* through S to the complement subject *him* as in (26b). Notice, however, that (24a) cannot passivize, in contrast with (1a).

(27) a. *He is wanted by Joshua to leave. (passive of (24a))
b. John is believed by me to be intelligent. (passive of (1a))

The ungrammaticality of (27a) is a good indication that *want* cannot have the same complement structure as *believe* (that is, cannot select a Ø complementizer). Unfortunately, while the choice of (26a) over (26b) explains the contrast in (27), the analysis has no account for the ungrammaticality of (28).

(28) *[him to leave] is wanted by everyone (cf. (23))

Given that *want* can passivize (e.g., *that car is wanted by everyone*), there should be nothing to rule out (28), since *him* receives Case from the (deleted) complementizer *for*.

Turning to *expect*, we recall from chapter 8 that it exhibits the same basic complement paradigm as *want*, here in (29).

(29) a. Joan expects for him to leave.
b. Joan expects him to leave.
c. Joan expects to leave.

Unlike *want*, though, (29b) can passivize. Compare (30) and (27a).

(30) He is expected by Joan to leave.

This suggests that *expect* can have the complement structure of both *want* and *believe*, with (29b) being ambiguous between *for*-deletion (which would not allow (30)) and a Ø complementizer (which would allow it).

Incorporating Kayne's Ø complementizer proposal into the standard GB approach, the subcategorization frames available to the three verb classes discussed here are given in (31).

(31) a. believe: [ that [NP Tense VP]]
 [ Ø [NP to VP]]
b. want: [ for [NP to VP]]
 [ e [PRO to VP]]
c. expect: [ that [NP Tense VP]]
 [ Ø [NP to VP]]
 [ for [NP to VP]]
 [ e [PRO to VP]]

Kayne's analysis of the English facts would require three sorts of phonologically unrealized complementizers with different properties: deleted, empty, and "null." Also, his "null" Ø complementizer proposal, as a replacement for S'-deletion or transparency, does little to improve upon Chomsky's approach once government and Case transmission are incorporated into the account. In some ways, having government transmitted from *believe* though Ø to the infinitival subject appears to be no more than a notational variant of S'-transparency.[3]

Kayne's real contribution lies not in the mechanics of his proposal so much as in his incorporation of the French facts into the GB account, by reducing these differences to a simple difference in the properties associated with prepositions in each language. The differences might be summed up as in (32).

(32) Properties of complementizers

|  | *French* | *English* |
|---|---|---|
| Overt prepositional complementizers (French *de*, English *for*) | Block government | Properly govern |
| Null prepositional complementizers (French, English Ø) | Block government | Transmit? government |
| Empty complementizers ($C^0$ as an empty node) | Block government | Block government |

What we see in (32) is that the complementizer position in French has identical properties with respect to government whether empty or filled and whether overt or null. It is this property which explains the observed fact that "lexical subjects of infinitives are normally impossible in French" (Kayne 1981:355). In contrast, English prepositional complementizers have properties which allow the subject position of infinitives sometimes to be filled.

## 3  A consideration of Quechua ECM cases: Cole and Hermon (1981)

In "Subjecthood and islandhood: Evidence from Quechua," Cole and Hermon (1981) examine the RtoO construction in Imbabura Quechua, a language of Ecuador, attempting to apply Chomsky's (1980) "On binding" (OB) framework. Inasmuch as OB is the immediate theoretical precursor of GB (in a sense an early form of the theory or a transition between REST and GB), many of the issues Cole and Hermon (C&H) raise are directly relevant to GB. In this extremely lucid and well-argued paper, C&H outline an analysis of Imbabura Quechua RtoO structures that seriously challenges any theory that disallows movement in RtoO. In the excerpt which follows, C&H provide arguments based on the linear order of constituents, the relationship of morphological case to tense and agreement, and the differential behavior of nominative and accusative NPs as evidence that the proper analysis of Imbabura Quechua RtoO must include movement of the embedded subject to an object position in the matrix clause. This poses a serious challenge to some central tenets of GB, most notably the impossibility of movement to any argument position other than subject.

In the article, C&H refer to the Nominative Island Condition (NIC), which can be simply formulated as in (33).

(33) *Nominative Island Constraint:*
A nominative anaphor must be bound in its S'.

Since the nominative position is the subject position of a tensed clause (an assumption carried over into GB), the intent of the NIC is to constrain the distribution of anaphors in subject position. The NIC bans reflexive and reciprocal anaphors and traces of NP-movement from the subject position of tensed clauses. Thus, the NIC represents an attempt to collapse the Tensed-S Condition and Specified Subject Condition into a single constraint, which in REST had become well-formedness conditions on coindexation. In this way, the NIC represents a stage in the development of the binding principles of GB.

The excerpt from the C&H article is followed by a discussion of the issues that the article raises.

# READING FROM COLE AND HERMON (1981)

Peter Cole and Gabriella Hermon, sections 1–6.3 (pp. 1–19) from "Subjecthood and islandhood: Evidence from Quechua" in *Linguistic Inquiry* 12:1 (Winter 1981). © 1981 by the Massachusetts Institute of Technology. Reprinted by permission.

## 1 Introduction[1]

The purpose of this article is to examine the implications for linguistic theory of certain aspects of the structure of complement clauses in the Quechua languages, focusing particularly on Imbabura Quechua.[2] Our aim is to compare the

---

[1] We would like to thank Leland George, Polly Jacobson, Chuck Kisseberth, Jaklin Kornfilt, Peter Landerman, Jerry Morgan, Geoff Pullum, Henry Thompson, David Weber, Edwin Williams, and two anonymous LI [*Linguistic Inquiry*] reviewers for their comments on earlier versions of this article. This research was supported in part by grants from the National Science Foundation (grant number BNS 77-27159) and by the Research Board, the Center for Advanced Study, and the Center for International Comparative Studies of the University of Illinois. An earlier version of this article was presented at the Brown University Conference on the Nature of Syntactic Representation, May, 1979.

[2] This article is part of an ongoing study of the structure of IQ and other Quechua languages. The facts given here are based on information provided by Carmen Chuquín, Mariana Chuquín, and Emilia Chuquín, native speakers of IQ, whose generous assistance is gratefully acknowledged. Special thanks are due to Carmen Chuquín for her help in many aspects of this study.

crosslinguistic adequacy of two approaches to object complementation which we shall refer to as the *raising* and the *nonraising analyses*. We shall argue that the raising analysis may be generalized to languages that are structurally quite different from English. This, however, is not true with regard to the nonraising analysis. Thus, we argue for the adoption of the raising analysis crosslinguistically. A major goal of the article is to examine the implications for the Extended Standard Theory (EST) of Subject-to-Object Raising. We shall show that the incorporation of Raising requires modifications in several of the central tenets of EST. In particular, we argue that the explanation of islandhood in terms of conditions on binding proposed in "On Binding" (Chomsky (1980)) requires major modification.

## 2  Object complementation in English

There are certain syntactic properties associated with sentences like (1) in English.

(1)  Frank believes $\begin{Bmatrix} \text{Charles} \\ \text{him/*he} \end{Bmatrix}$ to be asleep.

Sentences like (1) differ from those like (2) in a number of ways.

(2)  Frank believes $_S$[that $\begin{Bmatrix} \text{Charles} \\ \text{he/*him} \end{Bmatrix}$ is asleep]

First, the underlying complement subject of (2) is an island with respect to a variety of syntactic rules, while that of (1) is not. Some examples of this difference are given in (3)–(6).

(3) *Passivization*
  a. Charles is believed by Frank to be asleep.
  b. *Charles is believed by Frank that is asleep.

(4) *Reciprocal Interpretation*
  a. Charles and Frank believe each other to be asleep.
  b. *Charles and Frank believe that each other are asleep.

(5) *Disjoint Reference*
  a. Charles$_i$ believes $\begin{Bmatrix} \text{*him}_i \\ \text{him}_j \end{Bmatrix}$ to be asleep.
  b. Charles$_i$ believes that he$_{i,j}$ is asleep.

---

IQ is a dialect of Highland Ecuadorian Quechua, a member of the northern group of Quechua A languages (Parker (1963)), and has 40,000 to 60,000 speakers in the Province of Imbabura, Ecuador. For further information on IQ, see Stark and Carpenter (1973), Cole, Harbert, and Hermon (1978), Cole and Jake (to appear), and Cole (forthcoming). A Spanish-based orthography is employed for IQ examples.

(6) *Reflexive Interpretation*
   a. Charles believes himself to be asleep.
   b. *Charles believes that himself is asleep.

Second, the complement clause in (1) is nonfinite, untensed, and lacking verb agreement, while the one in (2) is finite. Third, the underlying complement subject in (1) appears in the accusative case, while the one in (2) is in the nominative case.

Within generative syntax, there have been two widely accepted explanations proposed for the differences between (1) and (2). In the Standard Theory, the properties of (1) have been analyzed as resulting from the application of Subject-to-Object Raising (SOR). This rule is claimed to map an underlying structure like (7) onto a derived structure roughly like (8).

(7) s[$NP_1$ V s[$NP_2$ VP]]

(8) s[NP V $NP_2$ s[Ø to VP]]

It is claimed that the differences between (1) and (2) arise because (1) has a derived structure like (8), while the derived structure of (2) is like (7). The rules in (3)–(6) are assumed to be clause-bounded.[3] Thus, they apply to the raised (accusative) NP, but not to the unraised (nominative) NP.

In contrast to the raising analysis, within the framework of the EST, it has been proposed that (1) has a structure like (7) in both underlying and derived structure. According to this approach, the differences between (1) and (2) do not arise from the derived constituency of the complement subject (which is claimed to be the same in both sentences), but rather from differences in the internal structure of the complement clause. The rules involved in (3)–(6) and similar examples are presumed not to be clause-bounded. Rather, the failure of these rules to apply to the complement subject in sentences like (2) is explained as resulting from the Tensed-S Condition (Chomsky (1973) and elsewhere), according to which no rule may involve two elements X and Y in the structure ... X ... [$\alpha$ ... Y ... ] ..., where $\alpha$ is a tensed sentence. In later work, Chomsky ((1977) and elsewhere) has made it clear that, although the language-particular realization of finiteness may vary, the general principle of islandhood of finite clauses is claimed to hold crosslinguistically.[4]

In the most recent version of EST, the version proposed by Chomsky (1980) in "On Binding", the immediate determining factor is not finiteness, but rather

---

[3] In the sections which follow, we show that a raising analysis for IQ is necessary even within the EST framework. In such an analysis, it is not immediately obvious that rules like those in (3)–(6) must be clause-bounded. An alternative to clause-boundedness which we consider is a condition rather analogous to the Nominative Island Condition (Chomsky (1980)) which has the effect of making complement subjects islands with respect to rules like those in (3)–(6). See section 6 and following sections [not reproduced here] for further discussion of alternatives to clause-boundedness.
[4] See Cole and Hermon (1979a) for a crosslinguistic discussion of the finiteness hypothesis.

the case-marking of the complement subject. More specifically, the finite nature of the complement clause determines the (nominative) case of the complement subject. Nominative case, in turn, causes the complement subject to be an island (the Nominative Island Condition (NIC)).[5] The mechanism employed by the NIC is as follows: according to the NIC, a nominative anaphor cannot be free in S̄ in logical form. This condition has the effect of blocking bound anaphoric relations between subjects of tensed clauses and antecedents in a higher clause.[6] The overall effect is similar to that of the Tensed-S Condition.

The raising and nonraising approaches make radically different claims regarding the structure of complex sentences and the conditions on rule application. How might the approaches be distinguished? One possibility is to look at the implications of the two analyses for other aspects of English grammar. Although promising in principle, in practice it has been impossible to reach a definitive resolution to the controversy in this way. Both analyses appear to account for roughly the same range of data in English. (See Postal (1974) and (1977), Bresnan (1976), and Bach (1977).)

A more practical way to distinguish between the two analyses is crosslinguistic. Do other languages exhibit an array of facts similar to those found in English? If so, can one of the approaches be generalized crosslinguistically while the other cannot? If it can be shown that one approach explains similar data in a broad range of languages, while the other is linked to peculiarities of English, the approach with wider crosslinguistic application is clearly to be preferred.

In sections 3–6 we examine certain aspects of complementation in Imbabura Quechua. We show that data analogous to those in sentences (3)–(6) cannot be explained either by the finiteness of the complement clause or by case-marking. Rather, they would appear to be a result of the derived constituency of the underlying complement subject. Crucial to our argument is the existence of a class of experiencer verbs in IQ, the subjects of which are accusative. These accusative subjects, in contrast to accusatives analogous to the under-

---

[5] Chomsky is not explicit about the relationship between abstract case, which is relevant for the NIC and superficial case-marking. Clearly, some degree of abstraction in case categories is necessary in order to accommodate languages like English in which case-marking is often neutralized on the surface. We shall assume, however, that in a language with overt case-marking, like IQ, the superficial case is the case relevant for the NIC. We take this position because the theory of case would be vacuous if there were *no* correspondence between abstract case and actual morphological case. It *is* our assumption that case theory does, in fact, make falsifiable claims about language.

This assumption becomes crucial in section 6, in which we discuss the islandhood properties of certain accusative experiencer subjects in IQ. We show there that these NPs display the same islandhood properties as nominative NPs. and argue for a reformulation of the NIC in terms of subjecthood rather than nominative case. Our arguments clearly depend on the supposition that the superficial accusative case of the subjects in question is a reliable indicator that these NPs are accusative rather than nominative in logical form.

[6] As in earlier versions of EST, Comp-to-Comp *Wh* Movement is not affected. The NIC fails to block movement from Comp to Comp because the nominative trace left in S by *Wh* Movement is bound by the trace left in Comp. Chomsky's case-marking rule is written in such a way as to prevent the trace in Comp from receiving nominative case. Thus, *Wh* Movement does not cause an NIC violation.

lying complement subject of (1), have a distribution with respect to islandhood identical to that of nominative complement subjects. These data suggest that it is subjecthood rather than nominative case which is crucial for islandhood in IQ. This is compatible with the raising analysis, but not with an analysis in terms of the NIC.

In section 7 [not reproduced here], we argue that the analysis proposed for IQ must be extended crosslinguistically to all other languages exhibiting island phenomena. In sections 8–10 [not reproduced here], we examine the implications of SOR for EST. We show that the description of IQ appears to require major modifications in the "On Binding" framework, among them the substitution of a Case-marked Subject Island Condition (CSIC) for the NIC. Even with these modifications, IQ presents certain serious theoretical problems for the "On Binding" framework which remain unresolved. We shall now turn to the arguments in favor of a raising analysis in IQ.

## 3  A brief introduction to Quechua morphology and syntax

In sections 4–6, we shall present a variety of arguments in favor of a rule of SOR in IQ. A brief description of some of the salient syntactic and morphological properties of the Quechua languages, and of IQ in particular, is desirable before the arguments themselves are presented.

The Quechua languages exhibit many of the morphological and syntactic characteristics associated with OV languages (Greenberg (1963) among others). The preferred word order is SOV, although in matrix clauses SVO occurs freely as well. Nouns are marked for case (-Ø 'nominative', -ta 'accusative'), and matrix clause verbs agree with the subject in person and, in some instances, in number. This is illustrated in (9).

(9) a. *SOV Order*
    Juan aicha-ta micu-rca
    Juan meat-acc eat-past-3

   b. *SVO Order*
    Juan micu-rca aicha-ta
    Juan eat-past-3 meat-acc
    'Juan ate meat.'

In addition to Subject–Verb Agreement, there is also a rule of Object Agreement, an example of which is given in (10).

(10) *Matrix Clause Verb Agreement*
    Can uya-wa-ngui
    you hear-1-2
    'You hear me.'

The morphology of matrix clauses differs from that of complements. Complement clauses in Quechua are typically nominalized. In Imbabura, nominalization is obligatory in almost all environments. Therefore, we shall limit our discussion of complementation to nominalized clauses. There is a strong tendency toward OV order within the nominalized complement clause. Nominalizing suffixes indicating tense are added to the complement verb,[7] and the nominalized verb receives a case marker determined by the grammatical relation of the complement clause to the matrix verb, as illustrated in (11).

(11) [Juan chaya-shca-ta] yacha-ni
Juan arrive-past Nom-acc know-1
'I know that Juan has arrived.'

As seen in (11), the complement clause as a whole receives accusative case because it is the object of the matrix verb *yachana* 'to know'. In IQ, and in Ecuadorian Quechua generally, there is no verb agreement in nominalized clauses:

(12) Francisco cri-n [ñuca Quito-man ri-shca-ta]
Francisco believe-3 I Quito-to go-past Nom-acc
'Francisco believes that I went to Quito.'

In the examples given above, the subject of the complement clause appears in the nominative case. In addition to this pattern, complement subjects may appear in the accusative:

(13) a. *Complement Subject in Nominative Case*
Maria-ca cri-n Francisco cay-pi ca-j-ta
Maria-topic believe-3 Francisco this-in be-pres Nom-acc
'Maria believes that Francisco is here.'
b. *Complement Subject in Accusative Case*
Maria-ca Francisco-ta cri-n cay-pi ca-j-ta
Maria-topic Francisco-acc believe-3 this-in be-pres Nom-acc
'Maria believes Francisco to be here.'

The complement subjects in (13) show islandhood properties parallel to those found in English ((3)–(6)), as is shown in (14)–(16).

(14) *Disjoint Reference*
a. Juzi$_i$ cri-n $\begin{Bmatrix} \text{*pay-ta}_i \\ \text{pay-ta}_j \end{Bmatrix}$ cayna shamu-shca-ta
Jose believe-3 he-acc yesterday come-past Nom-acc
'Jose$_i$ believes him$_j$ to have come yesterday.'
b. Juzi$_i$ cri-n pay$_{ij}$ cayna shamu-shca-ta
Jose believe-3 he-nom yesterday come-past Nom-acc
'Jose$_i$ believes that he$_{ij}$ came yesterday.'

---
[7] See section 5 for details.

(15) -llataj *Reflexivization*
   a. Juzi$_i$ cri-n    pay-lla-to-taj$_i$ wasi-ta    randi-shca-ta
      Jose believe-3 himself-acc    house-acc buy-past Nom-acc
      'Jose$_i$ believes himself$_i$ to have bought the house.'
   b. *Juzi$_i$ cri-n    pay-lla-taj$_i$    wasi-ta    randi-shca-ta
      Jose believe-3 himself-nom house-acc buy-past Nom-acc
      ('Jose$_i$ believes that himself$_i$ bought the house.')

(16) *Object–Verb Agreement*
   a. Juzi ñuca-ta yacha-wa-n Maria-ta    juya-j-ta
      Jose I-acc    know-1-3    Maria-acc love-pres Nom-acc
      'Jose knows me to love Maria.'
   b. *Juzi yacha-wa-n ñuca    Maria-ta    juya j-ta
      Jose know-1-3    I-nom Maria-acc love-pres Nom-acc
      ('Jose knows me that I love Maria.')

Examples (14)–(16) show that in IQ, just as in English, nominative subjects are islands. Example (14) shows that nominative subjects, in contrast to accusatives, do not undergo Disjoint Reference. Sentence (15) shows that nominatives are islands with respect to -*llataj* Reflexivization, while (16) shows the islandhood of nominatives with regard to Object–Verb Agreement. There are, in fact, no rules which would be expected to distinguish between nominative and accusative noun phrases for which the nominatives do not constitute islands.[8]

---

[8] For a number of rules, there is no way to determine whether the rule has applied to a nominative or an accusative NP. This is because the effect of the rule is to eliminate the evidence for the previous case marking of the NP.
  One class of cases involves incorporation into the verb. For example, in -*ri* Reflexivization (though *not* in -*llataj* Reflexivization) and Reciprocal Formation a reflexive (-*ri*) or reciprocal morpheme (-*naju*) is added to the verb, as in (i)–(ii):

(i) -ri *Relexivization*
    Wawa-ca    ricu-ri-rca    espejo-pi
    child-topic see-reflex-past 3 mirror-in
    'The child saw himself in the mirror.'

(ii) *Reciprocal Formation*
     Wambracuna maca-naju-rca
     boys    hit-recip-past 3
     'The boys hit each other.'

When the reflexive or reciprocal morpheme refers to a complement subject, there is no way to tell whether the subject is nominative or accusative:

(iii) *Reflexivized Complement Subject*
      Ñuca yacha-ri-rca-ni    Quito-pi ca-j-ta
      I    know-reflex-past-1 Quito-in be-pres Nom-acc
      'I know myself to be in Quito.'

In the pages that follow, we shall argue that (13b) and similar examples involve SOR. Within the "On Binding" framework, SOR is an instance of a more general rule, Move α, an assumption which we shall for the time being accept since its correctness is largely irrelevant to our claims (but see section 9 [not reproduced here]). Thus, we shall contend that the properties of sentences like (13b) are due, not to the internal structure of the complement clause, but rather to the application of Move α and the resulting change in constituent structure. We shall now turn to the arguments for this claim.[9]

## 4 Argument one: linear order

In English, the putative rule of SOR has the effect of changing grammatical structure, but not the linear order of the words in the sentence. Compare (17) and (18), the alleged derived and underlying structures for (1) in the raising analysis.

(17) Frank believes Charles $_S$[to be asleep]

(18) Frank believes $_S$[Charles to be asleep]

Because there is no overt change in word order, the English data are susceptible to an analysis in which no rule like SOR applies. In the EST nonraising analysis, *Charles* is simply the subject of an infinitival clause in (1) and a finite clause in (2) (repeated).

---

(iv) *Reciprocal Complement Subject*
Wambrecuna cri-naju-rca     Quito-pi ca-j-ta
boys     believe-recip-past 3 Quito-in be-pres Nom-acc
'The boys believed each other to be in Quito.'

Note that there is nothing about the structure of the complement clause (e.g. finite versus nonfinite verb form) which might let us know whether the complement subject was nominative or accusative. This aspect of Quechua is discussed in section 5.
What is important to note here is that for all rules that do not obscure the nominative–accusative distinction, the nominatives are islands while the accusatives are not. Hence, there is no evidence whatsoever that Quechua does not manifest the same islandhood constraints found in English. (For discussion of whether these constraints are due to nominative case, as Chomsky (1980) has claimed, or to some other principle such as subjecthood, see section 6 and following [not reproduced here].)

[9] We shall assume in what follows that *Francisco-ta* in (13b) originates as complement subject rather than as matrix direct object in underlying structure. While IQ does not provide the full range of arguments available in English (for instance), there are good language-internal grounds for positing such a deep structure. For example, complement passivization of (13b) results in a synonymous sentence. This is not true in "Equi" sentences like (60) [not reproduced here]. Although nonsynonymy is not always an indicator that the structure involves control rather than NP movement, there appear to be no well-documented cases of control structures in which synonymy under passivization obtains. Thus, we shall assume that sentences like (13b) are not control structures.

(1) Frank believes $\begin{Bmatrix} \text{Charles} \\ \text{him/*he} \end{Bmatrix}$ to be asleep.

(2) Frank believes $_s$[that $\begin{Bmatrix} \text{Charles} \\ \text{he/*him} \end{Bmatrix}$ is asleep].

Were there an overt change in word order, a raising analysis would be uncontroversial, and the alternation would be attributed to the application of Move $\alpha$, as is the alternation observed in Subject-to-Subject Raising (SSR):

(19) It seems that Charles is asleep.

(20) Charles seems to be asleep.

IQ manifests just such an alternation as was seen in (13) (repeated).

(13) a. *Complement Subject in Nominative Case*
Maria-ca    cri-n    Francisco cay-pi ca-j-ta
Maria-topic believe-3 Francisco this-in be-pres Nom-acc
'Maria believes that Francisco is here.'
b. *Complement Subject in Accusative Case*
Maria-ca    Francisco-ta cri-n    cay-pi ca-j-ta
Maria-topic Francisco-acc believe-3 this-in be-pres Nom-acc
'Maria believes Francisco to be here.'

This alternation parallels what we find with SSR, and appears to be a straightforward application of Move $\alpha$. Because *crin* 'believes' intervenes between *Francisco* and *caypi cajta* 'to be here', there is no possibility that *Francisco* is the derived subject of the complement clause.

Furthermore, it should be noted that SOR in Quechua does not violate the hypothesis that Move $\alpha$ is structure-preserving. If (13b) is derived from a deep structure along the lines of (21), no violation would take place.

(21) NP $_{NP}\Delta$ V $_s$[NP VP]

In the derivation of (13b), Move $\alpha$ applies to the complement subject, moving it into the empty NP slot in the matrix clause, yielding a derived structure similar to (22):

(22) NP NP V $_s$[t VP]

Additional support for this derivation is provided by an examination of the full range of word order possibilities in IQ.

(23) a. *SOV Order in Main Clause with Underlying Subject Complement in Nominative*
Maria-ca   Francisco cay-pi ca-j-ta   yacha-n
Maria-topic Francisco this-in be-pres Nom-acc know-3
'Maria knows that Francisco is here.'

b. *SOV Order in Main Clause with Underlying Complement Subject in Accusative*
Maria-ca   Francisco-ta cay-pi ca j-ta   yacha-n
Maria-topic Francisco-acc this-in be-pres Nom-acc know-3
'Maria knows Francisco to be here.'

(24) a. *SVO Order in Main Clause with Underlying Complement Subject in Nominative*
Maria-ca   yacha-n Francisco cay-pi ca j-ta
Maria-topic know-3 Francisco this-in be-pres Nom-acc
'Maria knows that Francisco is here.'

b. *SVO Order in Main Clause with Underlying Complement Subject in Accusative*
Maria-ca   yacha-n Francisco-ta cay-pi ca j-ta
Maria-topic know-3 Francisco-acc this-in be-pres Nom-acc
'Maria knows Francisco to be here.'

(25) *Underlying Complement Subject Precedes Matrix Verb*
a. *Maria-ca   Francisco yacha-n cay-pi ca-j-ta
Maria-topic Francisco know-3 this-in be-pres Nom-acc
('Maria knows Francisco to be here.')

b. Maria-ca   Francisco-ta yacha-n cay-pi ca-j-ta
Maria-topic Francisco-acc know-3 this-in be-pres Nom-acc
'Maria knows Francisco to be here.'

In the sentences of (23) and (24), the word order is consistent with the appearance of *Francisco* either as derived complement subject or as derived matrix direct object. In these sentences, *Francisco* may appear in either nominative or accusative case. In contrast, in (25) the word order is consistent only with derived matrix direct objecthood. And in just this environment *Francisco* may appear only in accusative case. The facts suggest that the base rules of Imbabura allow the following structures.[10]

(26) a. NP S̄ V
b. NP V S̄

(27) a. NP $_{NP}\Delta$ V $_{\bar{S}}$[NP VP]
b. NP $_{NP}\Delta$ $_{\bar{S}}$[NP VP] V
c. NP V $_{NP}\Delta$ $_{\bar{S}}$[NP VP]

---

[10] Of course, these base rules also allow structures in which the object NP in (27) has undergone lexical insertion.

Move $\alpha$ applies to the subject NP of $\bar{S}$, yielding the range of data illustrated in (23) through (25). There would appear to be no reasonable explanation for these data that does not involve raising.

## 5  Argument two: case and the internal structure of the complement clause

As we discussed previously, there are two sets of facts for which both the raising and the nonraising analyses provide satisfactory accounts in English. These are the case-marking facts illustrated in (1) and (2) and the islandhood facts illustrated in (3)–(6). Both the raising and the nonraising analyses account for the core data with respect to the construction in English. We shall show in this section that for IQ the raising analysis accounts for both the case-marking and the islandhood facts, but even were we to assume that the nonraising analysis accounts for the islandhood facts, it provides no explanation for the distribution of case markers.[11]

The SOR account of case-marking and islandhood in IQ does not differ significantly from the account needed for English, so we shall only discuss it briefly. Raising results in accusative case because, in derived structure, the underlying complement subject has been moved by Move $\alpha$ into the object position in the matrix clause. The normal application of case-marking rules (e.g. rule (68b) of Chomsky (1980)) would mark the noun phrase accusative. The islandhood of the nominative subject could be accounted for in either of two ways: by conditions on binding (an analogue of the NIC (see the next section where this proposal is developed)), or by formulation of the rules in (14)–(16) and similar rules as clause-bounded. We shall assume the conditions-on-binding analysis of islandhood in order to deviate minimally from the model proposed in "On Binding".

To turn to the nonraising analysis, conditions on binding appear (at least at first glance) to provide an account for the islandhood facts, as they do in the raising analysis. However, no account is provided for case-marking itself. This is because the internal structure of the complement clause is the same regardless of the case-marking of the complement subject. Therefore, it is not possible to attribute complement subject case marking to the finiteness of the complement clause.

Two manifestations of finiteness have been cited in the EST literature: tense (Chomsky (1973), among others) and verb agreement (George and Kornfilt (1978)). We would like to show that neither of these is relevant to the choice of case for the complement subject.

As was seen in (12), nominalized clauses are tensed, the tense being expressed by the choice of nominalizer. The tense system found in nominalized clauses in IQ is given in (28).

---

[11] We shall show in the next section that the nonraising analysis cannot in fact account for the islandhood facts.

(28) *Nominalizers Used in Complement Clauses in IQ*
   a. Indicative Nominalizers
      i. Present: *-j, -y*
      ii. Past: *-shca*
      iii. Future: *-na*
   b. Subjunctive Nominalizers: *-chun, -ngapaj*

(The choice between subjunctive and indicative nominalizers is determined by the matrix verb in a manner familiar from Romance and other Indo-European language families: verbs of desire like *muna-* 'want', for example, govern subjunctive.) Since the same tense suffixes appear when the underlying complement subject is either accusative or nominative, it is clear that tense plays no role in case assignment.

Another possible realization of finiteness is verb agreement. It will be remembered that there is no verb agreement in nominalized clauses in IQ, as was illustrated in (12) (repeated).

(12) Francisco cri-n    [ñuca Quito-man ri-shca-ta]
     Francisco believe-3 I    Quito-to    go-past Nom-acc
     'Francisco believes that I went to Quito.'

Hence, the occurrence of verb agreement, like the occurrence of tense, fails to correlate with nominative case. Furthermore, in other dialects of Quechua in which nominalized clauses do manifest verb agreement (e.g. Ancash Quechua), the underlying complement subject may still appear in either the nominative or the accusative case. In fact, we have not been able to find any aspect of the internal structure of the complement clause to which case-marking might be attributed. But it would be incorrect to claim that case-marking is random and need not be explained. Rather, a pattern quite similar to that of English is found. For example, matrix subjects do not vary randomly between nominative and accusative. Rather, with the exception of certain experiencer nominals discussed in section 6, they appear invariably in nominative case. This is explicable if accusative case in sentences like (13b) is attributed to SOR, but it is inexplicable in a nonraising framework because the internal case-marking shows no correlation with any aspect of the internal structure of the complement clause.[12]

We have shown, then, that the nonraising analysis, unlike the raising analysis, fails to provide a descriptively adequate account of the case-marking of the complement subjects in Quechua. We conclude that the raising analysis is to be preferred.

---

[12] The only way to save the finiteness analysis in a language like Imbabura would be to make finiteness an entirely abstract property with no surface realization whatsoever. We believe that this possibility should be rejected because the claim of finiteness would then have no empirical correlates other than the phenomena it was postulated to "explain".

## 6 Argument three: nominative case and islandhood

### 6.1 Accusative experiencer subjects

We showed in the previous section that the nonraising analysis of (13) fails to provide an explanation for the distribution of complement subject case-marking. In contrast, SOR provides an adequate account of these facts. We will now turn to islandhood. As was shown earlier, nominative complement subjects are islands while accusative complement subjects in sentences like those of (14)–(16) are not. At first glance, these facts appear to be amenable to explanation by the NIC. We shall show, however, that this is not correct.

It will be recalled that, according to the NIC, it is case-marking which determines whether or not an NP is an island. An NP bearing nominative case is an island, but accusative and oblique NPs are not. It should be emphasized that the source of the case-marking is irrelevant to the operation of the constraint.

We shall show in this section that in IQ it is not case-marking, but rather derived constituency, which determines whether or not an NP is an island. There is a class of verbs the subjects of which receive accusative case. We shall show that these accusative subjects pattern with nominative subjects rather than with the accusative complement subjects in (14)–(16). This state of affairs is a direct counterexample to the NIC, which predicts that the accusative subjects would not be islands.[13] But it is entirely predictable if the accusative complement subjects in (14)–(16) have undergone SOR and, hence, are objects in derived structure, and if the conditions on binding involve subjecthood rather than nominative case.

There are two rather similar constructions in IQ in which the subject appears in accusative case. These constructions are illustrated in (29)–(30).

(29) -naya *Desiderative Experiencers*
 Juzi-ta puñu-naya-n
 Jose-acc sleep-desid-3
 'Jose wants to sleep/Jose is sleepy.'

(30) *Lexical Experiencers*
 Juzi-ta rupa-n
 Jose-acc be hot-3
 'Jose is hot.'

---

[13] The structure of the grammar in the "On Binding" model makes it impossible to save the NIC analysis by rule ordering. According to such a proposal, the relevant surface accusative NPs would be nominative at the point when the NIC applies, and would be changed to accusative at a later stage in the derivation. However, this cannot be correct because the NIC applies to logical form, which is determined by surface structure. Thus, any rule applying prior to surface structure would affect the input to the NIC. The only way to save the NIC would be to introduce accusative case in examples like (29) and (30) by means of a special case-marking rule in the phonological (deletion-filter) component that would change certain nominatives to accusative. Such a move should, of course, be rejected, since it would make the NIC totally unfalsifiable.

There are a variety of reasons to believe that the accusative NPs in (29)–(30) are subjects, at least in logical form. Some of these are discussed in detail in a previously written article (Cole and Jake (to appear)), but it may be useful to outline the arguments here. First, in so-called "Equi" constructions, as would be expected both in EST and in other varieties of generative syntax, only complement subjects are susceptible to control by a matrix constituent:

(31) *Control of Subject by Matrix Constituent*
Maria$_i$ muna-n $_S$[pro$_i$ Juan-ta ricu-na-ta]
Maria want-3 Juan-acc see-infin-acc
'Maria wants to see Juan.'

(32) *Failure of Control of Nonsubject by Matrix Constituent*
\*Maria$_i$ muna-n $_S$[Francisco pro$_i$ ricu-na-ta]
('Maria wants Francisco to see (her).')

In contrast to (32), accusative experiencers like those in (29)–(30) are susceptible to control by a matrix constituent:

(33) *Control of Desiderative Experiencer by Matrix Constituent*
Maria$_i$ muna-n $_S$[pro$_i$ puñu-naya-na-ta]
Maria want-3 sleep-desid-infin-acc
'Maria would like to want to sleep.'

(34) *Control of Lexical Experiencer by Matrix Constituent*
Maria$_i$ mana muna-n-chu $_S$[rupa-na-ta]
Maria not want-3-neg be hot-infin-acc
'Maria doesn't want to be hot.'

Thus, there is reason to believe that the accusative nominals in (29)–(30) are in fact subjects.

A second argument, one not found in Cole and Jake (to appear), has to do with a constraint against the extraction of complement subjects by *Wh* Movement. This constraint is discussed in detail in Cole and Hermon (1979b). The constraint in question is the IQ analogue of the constraint preventing the extraction of subject NPs in English sentences like (35a,b):

(35) a. *Who did you say that t left?
b. Who(m) did you say that he saw?

Similar constraints are found in a variety of languages. See Perlmutter (1971), Bresnan (1972), Chomsky and Lasnik (1977), and Pesetsky (1978a; 1978b), among others, for discussion. What is relevant here is the fact that crosslinguistically this is a constraint against the extraction of subjects and not other constituents.[14]

---

[14] This is not to say that the authors in question posit a constraint against the extraction of subjects per se. Rather, this falls out from other considerations: that is, the Fixed Subject Constraint in Bresnan (1972), the *that e* filter in Chomsky and Lasnik (1977), etc.

In IQ, a distribution similar to (35) is found:

(36) *Wh-Question Formation in IQ*
    a. *Pi-taj      Maria cri-n    t aicha-ta micu-shca-ta?
       who[nom]-wh q Maria believe-3 meat-acc eat-past Nom-acc
       ('Who does Maria think that ate meat?')
    b. Ima-to-taj     Maria cri-n     Jose t micu-shca-ta?
       what-acc-wh q Maria believe-3 Jose    eat-past Nom-acc
       'What does Maria believe that Jose ate?'

This pattern indicates that complement subjects, in contrast to other positions in the complement clause, may not be extracted by *Wh* Movement. Thus, extractability by *Wh* Movement constitutes a diagnostic for subjecthood in IQ.

To return to accusative experiencers like those in (29)–(30), the accusative experiencer may not be extracted by *Wh* Movement, though other positions within the complement clause may. Consider (37a) and (37b), which illustrate that an accusative desiderative experiences and an accusative lexical experiencer, respectively, cannot be extracted by *Wh* Movement.

(37)   a. *Pi-ta-taj      Maria Juzi-man ni-rca [t micu-naya-j-ta]?
       who-acc- wh q Maria Jose-dat   say-past eat-desid-pres Nom-acc
       ('Who did Maria say to Jose that wants to eat?')
    b. *Pi-ta-taj      Maria Juzi-man ni-rca [t rupa-j-ta]?
       who-acc-wh q Maria Jose-dat    say-past burn-pres Nom-acc
       ('Who did Maria say to Jose that is hot?')

Compare these sentences with (38a) and (38b), which show that direct objects in desiderative experiencer complement clauses and lexical experiencer complement clauses, respectively, may be extracted by *Wh* Movement.

(38)   a. Pi-ta-taj      Maria Juzi-man ni-rca [Juan-ta t
       who-acc-wh q Maria Jose-dat   say-past Juan-acc
       ricu-naya j-ta]?
       see-desid-pres Nom-acc
       'Whom did Maria say to Jose that Juan wants to see?'
    b. Pi-ta-taj      Maria Juzi-man ni-rca [Juan-ta t
       who-acc-wh q Maria Jose-dat   say-past Juan-acc
       muna-j-ta]?
       want-pres Nom-acc
       'Whom did Maria say to Jose that Juan wants?'

These examples, like the "Equi" sentences given earlier, indicate that the accusative experiencers in (29)–(30) are in fact subjects, at least in logical form.[15]

---

[15] Additional arguments in Cole and Jake (to appear) involve switch reference constructions that are sensitive to subjecthood and conditions on binding. These arguments are presented within the framework of relational grammar, but they are easily reformulated in EST.

For a more detailed discussion of the derivation of sentences like (29)–(30) from the perspective of EST, see Hermon (1979; forthcoming).

Further evidence for the subjecthood of accusative experiencers is provided by the Opacity Condition. At this point in the article, we shall limit our discussion of Opacity to showing that accusative experiencers behave like subjects with respect to that condition.

According to the Opacity Condition, if $\alpha$ is in the domain of the subject of $\beta$ ($\beta$ minimal) (where $\beta$ is NP or $\bar{S}$), then $\alpha$ cannot be free in $\beta$. That is to say, in effect, that an element $c$-commanded by a subject may not be related, by transformational or interpretive rules, to an element that is not also $c$-commanded by the subject.[16] What is significant here is that Opacity provides a diagnostic within the "On Binding" framework for determining whether a noun phrase is a subject. If the accusative experiencers of (29)–(30) cause other elements in their domain to be islands, the accusative experiencers must be subjects (but see footnote 17 below).

The sentences of (39) show that accusative experiencers do, in fact, cause Opacity.

(39) a. *Disjoint Reference with Desiderative Experiencer Subjects*
Juan$_i$ cri-n   Maria-ta  pay-ta$_{ij}$ ricu-naya-j-ta
Juan believe-3 Maria-acc he-acc  see-desid-pres Nom-acc
'Juan$_i$ believes that Maria wants to see him$_{ij}$.'
b. *Disjoint Reference with Lexical Experiencer Subjects*
Juan$_i$ cri-n   Maria-ta  mana pay-ta$_{ij}$ muna-j-ta
Juan believe-3 Maria-acc not   he-acc  want-pres Nom-acc
'Juan$_i$ believes that Maria doesn't want him$_{ij}$.'
c. *ri- Reflexivization with Desiclerative Experiencer Subjects*
*Juan$_i$ cri-n   Maria-ta  ricu-naya-ri$_i$-j-ta
Juan believe-3 Maria-acc see-desid-reflex-pres Nom-acc
('Juan believes that Maria wants to see himself.')
d. *ri- Reflexivization with Lexical Experiencer Subjects*
*Juan$_i$ cri-n   Maria-ta  mana muna-ri$_i$-j-ta
Juan believe-3 Maria-acc not   want-reflex-pres Nom-acc
('Juan believes that Maria doesn't want himself.')
e. *Reciprocal Interpretation with Desiderative Experiencer Subjects*
*Juan-pash Juzi-pash cri-n   Maria-ta
Juan-also  Jose-also  believe-3 Maria-acc
ricu-naya-naju-j-ta
see-desid-recip-pres Nom-acc
('Juan and Jose believe that Maria wants to see each other.')
f. *Reciprocal Interpretation with Lexical Experiencer Subjects*
*Juan-pash Juzi-pash cri-n   Maria-ta mana
Juan-also  Jose-also  believe-3 Maria-acc not
muna-naju-j-ta
want-recip-pres Nom-acc
('Juan and Jose believe that Maria doesn't want each other.')

---

[16] Except if it is so related by movement through Comp. The trace left by a movement rule in Comp provides an antecedent for the trace left in the complement clause within the domain of a subject. Thus, the trace left in the domain of the subject is not free in $\bar{S}$.

The examples of (39) show that accusative experiencers block Disjoint Reference, Reflexivization, and Reciprocal Interpretation with regard to nonsubject elements in the complement clause. This constitutes evidence within the EST framework that the accusative experiencers are subjects.[17]

## 6.2 Disjoint reference

We should like to turn now to evidence that accusative experiencers behave not merely like subjects, but like *nominative* subjects. As we saw, according to the NIC, nominative NPs not only have the effect of preventing nonsubjects in their domain from undergoing various rules (Opacity), but they are also islands themselves (NIC). We shall now show that accusative experiencer subjects in IQ are islands, just like nominative subjects. We shall first consider Disjoint Reference. Compare (40) and (41a,b), which illustrate the fact that this rule does not apply to nominative subjects, to desiderative experiencer subjects, or to lexical experiencer subjects, respectively.

(40)      Juzi$_i$ cri-n    pay$_{ij}$    micu-ju-j-ta
         Jose believe-3 he[nom] eat-prog-pres Nom-acc
         'Jose$_i$ believes that he$_{ij}$ is eating.'

(41) a.    Juzi$_i$ cri-n    pay-ta$_{ij}$ micu-naya-j-ta
            Jose believe-3 he-acc   eat-desid-pres Nom-acc
            'Jose$_i$ believes that he$_{ij}$ wants to eat.'
     b.    Juzi$_i$ cri-n    pay-ta$_{ij}$ rupa-j-ta
            Jose believe-3 he-acc   hot-pres Nom-acc
            'Jose$_i$ believes that he$_{ij}$ is hot.'

As predicted by the NIC, Disjoint Reference cannot apply to the nominative complement subject in (40). Thus, the complement subject is interpretable as having either the same reference as or a different reference from the matrix subject.

But the NIC makes the wrong prediction with regard to (41). According to the NIC, (41) should have the same pattern as (14a), repeated here as (42).

(42) *Disjoint Reference*

Juzi$_i$ cri-n    $\left\{\begin{matrix}\text{*pay-ta}_i\\ \text{pay-ta}_j\end{matrix}\right\}$ cayna    shamu-shca-ta
Jose believe-3 he-acc    yesterday come-past Nom-acc
'Jose$_i$ believes him$_j$ to have come yesterday.'

Because the complement subject is accusative in (42), Disjoint Reference is free to apply; and the matrix and complement subjects are interpreted as

---

[17] The Opacity facts are also consistent with an analysis in which sentences like (29)–(30) have dummy subjects. This analysis, however, is ruled out by the "Equi" and complement subject extraction facts described above.

noncoreferential. But in (41), Disjoint Reference mysteriously fails to apply, and despite the accusative case of the complement subject, the matrix and complement subjects may be interpreted as having either the same or different reference.

An additional fact for which the NIC provides no explanation is the contrast in possible interpretations between (41) and (43). (43a) and (43b) illustrate the application of Disjoint Reference with desiderative and lexical experiencer subjects, respectively, preceding the matrix verb.

(43) a. Juzi-ca$_i$ $\begin{Bmatrix} \text{*pay-ta}_i \\ \text{pay-ta}_j \end{Bmatrix}$ cri-n micu-naya-j-ta
 Jose-topic he-acc believe-3 eat-desid-pres Nom-acc
 'Jose$_i$ believes him$_j$ to want to eat.'

 b. Juzi-ca$_i$ $\begin{Bmatrix} \text{*pay-ta}_i \\ \text{pay-ta}_j \end{Bmatrix}$ cri-n rupa-j-ta
 Jose-topic he-acc believe-3 be hot-pres Nom-acc
 'Jose$_i$ believes him$_j$ to be hot.'

In (43), in contrast to (41), Disjoint Reference has applied. The NIC offers no account of why the complement subject of (41) is an island but that of (43) is not.

The islandhood of accusative experiencer subjects suggests that, in IQ at least, it is not nominative NPs that are islands, but rather subjects. The data would seem to show that, if conditions on binding are to account for the data, the NIC should be replaced by a condition which makes reference to subjecthood rather than to nominative case. As a first approximation, we shall replace the NIC by a Subject Island Condition (SIC). This condition would mimic Chomsky's NIC, but would refer to subjecthood rather than to nominative case:

(44) A subject anaphor in S cannot be free in $\bar{S}$ containing S.[18]

(For reasons to be discussed in sections 8 and 9 [not reproduced here], the SIC will have to be modified to account for the full range of data found.) If the NIC is to be replaced by the SIC, what is the explanation for the fact that *payta* in (43) is not an island? The raising hypothesis provides a ready answer: in

---

[18] Note that, according to the SIC, a subject anaphor in S cannot be free in $\bar{S}$. There is no such requirement for an anaphor in $\bar{S}$ but not in S: that is, a trace in Comp. This analysis is similar to Chomsky's original formulation of the NIC: A nominative anaphor in S cannot be free in $\bar{S}$.

Chomsky is able to revise the NIC to eliminate reference to S (according to his ultimate formulation of the NIC, a nominative anaphor cannot be free in $\bar{S}$) by avoiding the assignment of nominative case to traces in Comp. (See Chomsky (1980) for details.) Note, however, that this simplification of the NIC crucially depends on the claim that the islandhood of the subject of sentences like (13a) is due to nominative case. But, as we show in this section, nominative case is not in fact the determining factor in islandhood. Thus, the SIC must be stated along the lines of Chomsky's original formulation of the NIC.

derived structure, the underlying complement subject of (43) is no longer a subject. It is, as a result of SOR, the matrix direct object.

The SIC plus SOR also provide an account of the contrast between (41) and (43). The sentences of (41) are structurally ambiguous between a raised and an unraised reading. In the unraised reading, the complement subject is an island. Hence, the matrix and complement subject may be interpreted as coreferential. In contrast, the sentences of (43) are structurally unambiguous: they have only the raised reading. Thus, *payta* is interpretable only as a direct object, and is, therefore, not subject to the SIC. As a result, only the disjoint reference reading is available.

## 6.3 Validator placement

Our second argument for SOR is based on a constraint on validator placement. The Quechua languages make frequent use of a series of morphemes often referred to as *enclitics* or *validators*. The validators indicate the evidential status of the sentence: firsthand knowledge, hearsay, etc. The number and meaning of the validators vary from language to language. Those found in Imbabura are shown in (45).

(45) -ma(ri) 'emphatically asserted', -mi 'firsthand knowledge', -shi 'hearsay',[19] -cha(ri) 'doubtful information', -chu 'negation, yes-no question'

In general, the placement of validators is free.[20] There is, however, an important restriction on their placement which is illustrated in (46).

(46) a. Juan-mi cri-n Maria Juzi-ta ricu-shca-ta
Juan-valid believe-3 Maria Jose-acc see-past Nom-acc
'It is Juan who believes that Maria saw Jose.'
b. Juan cri-n-mi Maria Juzi-ta ricu-shca-ta
Juan believe-3-valid Maria Jose-acc see-past Nom-acc
'Juan believes [e.g. but doesn't know] that Maria saw Jose.'
c. *Juan cri-n Maria-mi Juzi-ta ricu-shca-ta
Juan believe-3 Maria-valid Jose-acc see-past Nom-acc
('It's Maria who Juan believes saw Jose.')
d. *Juan cri-n Maria Juzi-ta-mi ricu-shca-ta
Juan believe-3 Maria Jose-acc-valid see-past Nom-acc
('It's Jose who Juan believes Maria saw.')
e. *Juan cri-n Maria ricu-shca-mi Juzi-ta
Juan believe-3 Maria see-past Nom-valid Jose-acc
('Juan believes that Maria saw [e.g. not heard] Jose.')

---

[19] IQ speakers normally substitute *nin* 'says' for the validator *-shi*. *-Shi* is understood by IQ speakers, but not normally used.
[20] The placement appears to be determined by discourse factors.

As is shown in (46), the validator (in this case, -*mi* 'firsthand information') may not appear on constituents of the complement clause including nominative complement subjects. It may, however, be suffixed to accusative underlying subjects like the one in (47).

(47) a. Maria-ca    Francisco-ta-mi    yachan wasi-man
Maria-topic Francisco-acc-valid knows  house-to
shamu-shca-ta
come-past Nom-acc
'It is Francisco whom Maria knows to have come home.'
b. Maria yachan Francisco-ta-mi    wasi-man shamu-shca-ta
Maria knows Francisco-acc-valid house-to   come-past Nom-acc
'It is Francisco whom Maria knows to have come home.'

The facts given so far are compatible with both the raising and the NIC analyses. But the NIC analysis provides no explanation for the fact that the accusative experiencers in (48) cannot be validated.

(48) a. -*naya Desiderative Experiencer Subjects*
*Maria Juzi-ma ni-rca    paipaj wawa-ta-mi
Maria Jose-da say-past her     child-acc-valid
micu-naya-shca-ta
eat-desid-past Nom-acc
('Maria said to Jose that her child [e.g. not her husband] wanted to eat.')
b. *Lexical Experiencer Subjects*
*Maria Juzi-man ni-rca    Francisco-ta-mi    wasi-man
Maria Jose-dat   say-past Francisco-acc-valid house-dat
shamu-ngapaj        muna-j-ta
come-subjunc Nom want-pres Nom-acc
('Maria said to Jose that Francisco [e.g. not John] wants to come home.')

This state of affairs is predictable on the basis of the raising-SIC analysis. The accusative experiencers in (48a,b) are embedded beneath a matrix verb *ni*- which does not govern SOR (see (67 [not reproduced here])). Thus, they cannot be raised to the matrix clause. This explains their islandhood. In contrast, the matrix verb in (47) is a raising trigger (*yacha-* 'know'). The underlying complement subject has been raised into the matrix clause, which explains the possibility of validation.

## References

Bach, E. (1977) "Review of P. M. Postal, On Raising: One Rule of English Grammar and Its Theoretical Implications," *Language* 52, 621–54.

Bresnan, J. W. (1972) "Theory of Complementation in English Syntax," Doctoral dissertation, MIT, Cambridge, Massachusetts.
Bresnan, J. W. (1976) "Nonarguments for Raising," *Linguistic Inquiry* 7, 485-502.
Chomsky, N. (1973) "Conditions on Transformations," in S. R. Anderson and P. Kiparsky, eds, *Festschrift for Morris Halle*, Holt, Rinehart and Winston, New York.
Chomsky, N. (1977) "On *Wh*-Movement," in P. W. Culicover, T. Wasow, and A. Akmajian, eds, *Formal Syntax*, Academic Press, New York.
Chomsky, N. (1980) "On Binding," *Linguistic Inquiry* 11, 1-46.
Chomsky, N. and H. Lasnik (1977) "Filters and Control," *Linguistic Inquiry* 8, 425-504.
Cole, P. (forthcoming) *Imbabura Quechua*, Lingua Descriptive Studies, North-Holland, Amsterdam [pub. 1982 as *Imbabura Quechua*, North-Holland, Amsterdam].
Cole, P. and G. Hermon (1979a) "Complement Structure and Islandhood in EST: A Crosslinguistic Study," to appear in the proceedings of the Fifteenth Regional Meeting of the Chicago Linguistic Society, Chicago Linguistic Society, University of Chicago, Chicago, Illinois [pub. 1979 in *Papers from the Regional Meetings, Chicago Linguistic Society* 15, 60-9].
Cole, P. and G. Hermon (1979b) "A Constraint on the Extraction of Complement Subjects in Quechua," presented at the 1979 International Congress of Americanists.
Cole, P., W. Harbert, and G. Hermon (1978) "Headless Relative Clauses: Evidence from Quechua," *Studies in the Linguistic Sciences* 8, 26-41.
Cole, P. and J. Jake (to appear) "Accusative Subjects in Imbabura Quechua," to appear in *Folia Linguistica Historica* [pub. 1978 in *Studies in the Linguistic Sciences* 8(1), 72-96].
George, L. and J. Kornfilt (1978) "Finiteness and Boundedness in Turkish," to appear in the proceedings of the Third Generative Linguists of the Old World Conference, Amsterdam [pub. 1981 in F. Heny, ed., *Binding and Filtering*, Coomhelm, London].
Greenberg, J. H. (1963) "Some Universals of Grammar with Particular Reference to the Order of Meaningful Elements," in J. H. Greenberg, ed., *Universals of Language*, MIT Press, Cambridge, Massachusetts.
Hermon, G. (1979) "Non-nominative Subjects in an EST Framework: Evidence from Imbabura Quechua," presented at the 1979 International Congress of Americanists.
Hermon, G. (forthcoming) [1981] "Non-nominative Subject Constructions: A Crosslinguistic Analysis," Doctoral dissertation, University of Illinois at Urbana-Champaign, Illinois.
Parker, G. J. (1963) "Comparative Quechua Phonology and Grammar 1: Classification," *University of Hawaii Working Papers in Linguistics* 1, 65-88.
Perlmutter, D. (1971) *Deep and Surface Structure Constraints in Syntax*, Holt, Rinehart and Winston, New York.
Pesetsky, D. (1978a) "Complement Trace Phenomena and the Nominative Island Condition," presented at the Ninth Annual Meeting of the North Eastern Linguistic Society, and to be published in *CUNY Forum* 5/6 [pub. 1979 as "Complementizer-Trace Phenomena and the Nominative Island Condition," in E. Battistella, ed., *Proceedings of the Ninth Annual Meeting of the North Eastern Linguistic Society*, pt 2, Queens College Press, New York; expanded version pub. 1982 in *Linguistic Review* 1, 297-344].
Pesetsky, D. (1978b) "Complement Trace Phenomena and the Nominative Island Condition," unpublished Syntax Generals paper, MIT, Cambridge, Massachusetts (an extended version of Pesetsky (1978a)).
Postal, P. M. (1974) *On Raising*, MIT Press, Cambridge, Massachusetts.
Postal, P. M. (1977) "About a Nonargument for Raising," *Linguistic Inquiry* 8, 141-54.
Stark, L. and L. K. Carpenter (1973) *El Quichua de Imbabura: una gramatica pedagogica*, Instituto Interandino de Desarrollo, Otavalo, Ecuador.

## 4 Discussion of Cole and Hermon (1981)

The main conclusions that C&H wish to draw in the article are:

(i) RtoO in Imbabura Quechua (and other languages) must be analyzed as movement.
(ii) The NIC must be reformulated in terms of (case-marked) subjects because non-nominative subjects show the same behavior as nominative subjects.
(iii) Even with these revisions, the OB framework faces "a serious problem."

Because (ii) and (iii) represent points specific to a short-lived framework, transitional between REST and GB, the focus of the following discussion will be (i) and whether or not the IQ facts can be easily accommodated in the GB framework.[4]

In the preceding excerpt, C&H demonstrate that RtoO in IQ shows some of the same properties as does RtoO in English with respect to the distribution of reflexive and reciprocal anaphors and disjoint interpretation of pronouns. Following this, they provide three arguments for a movement analysis of RtoO.

- *Linear order*: The D-structure subject of a sentential complement of certain predicates, e.g., *cri* 'believe,' can occur in either nominative or accusative case. This D-structure subject can precede the matrix predicate, a canonical object position, while the rest of the complement follows the matrix predicate (13b). C&H reason that the linear order of elements can only be the result of movement to an object position in the matrix clause.
- *Case-marking*: In English there is a correlation between tense and the Case of the subject of the complement clause. In a finite clause, the subject is nominative since the +tense INFL assigns Case to the subject. With a nonfinite clause, the subject is assigned Case either through ECM or by a prepositional complementizer. In Imbabura Quechua, tense is marked overtly in the relevant complement clauses regardless of whether the embedded subject is nominative or accusative. Additionally, there is no verb agreement in these complement clauses. Since tensed INFL assigns nominative Case, there is no means of assigning accusative case to the embedded subject from properties of the embedded clause. Therefore, C&H reason, the assignment of accusative case to the embedded subject must be a result of its being an object in the matrix clause.
- *Subject properties*: Accusative subjects in RtoO sentences behave as though they are matrix clause dependents while embedded nominative subjects and accusative subjects in non-RtoO structures do not with respect to disjoint reference and the placement of validator morphology. This is most easily accounted for by the movement analysis in which the accusative NP has raised into the matrix clause.

On the basis of these facts, C&H propose an analysis of RtoO in which the raised NP moves from its D-structure complement subject position to an empty object position in the matrix clause. As they state, as long as the empty position in the matrix clause is generated in D-structure, no violation of structure preservation takes place. And to effect this, C&H propose the base rules in their (26) and (27), which include the possibility of empty NP positions as preverbal object (27a, b) and postverbal object (27c).

However, recall from the discussion in chapter 8 that empty complement positions are effectively ruled out by the stipulation that all complement positions are θ-positions. Movement from a D-structure θ-position to such an empty position would thus constitute a violation of the θ-criterion. Thus, C&H's proposal is unavailable in a GB analysis.

Of course, this does not automatically rule out the possibility of an analysis of the Quechua data consistent with GB principles. It may, in fact, be possible to propose an ECM analysis. Assuming a head-final structure for Quechua and taking SOV to be the basic word order of a clause, the SVO order of (34b) could be derived through extraposition of the NP object in the structure underlying (34a).

(34) a. Juan aicha-ta micu-rca.
       J     meat-ACC eat-PAST.3
       'Juan ate meat.'
    b. Juan micu-rca aicha-ta.
       J    eat-PAST.3 meat-ACC
       'Juan ate meat.'

In this analysis the D-structure of (34) would be:

(35)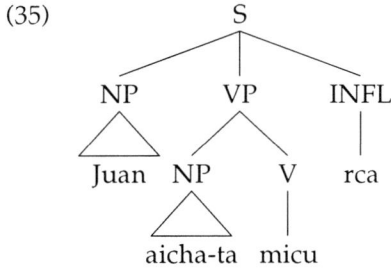

Nominative case on *Juan* is assigned by INFL and accusative case on *aicha* 'meat' by V. Thus, Case is assigned in a leftward direction under government. Extraposition of the object will not destroy the Case-marking relation between it and the verb.

What of complex clauses? Again, assuming a basic SOV structure, the sentence in (36a) (C&H's (23a)) has the structure in (36b).

(36) a. Maria-ca Francisco cay-pi ca-j-ta         yacha-n.
       M-TOP    F         this-in be-PRES NOM-ACC know-3
       'Maria knows that Francisco is here.'

b.

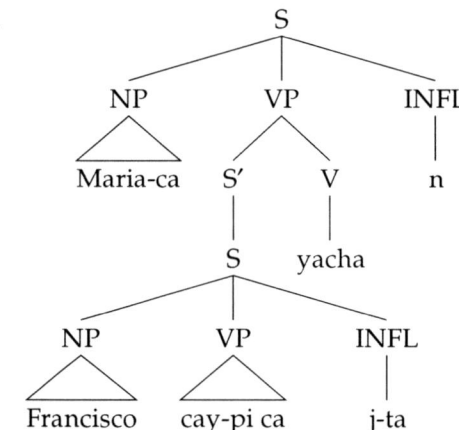

Case marking can proceed as before, with the matrix INFL assigning nominative Case to *Maria* and the INFL of the embedded clause assigning nominative Case to *Francisco*. And the alternative word order in which *Francisco caypi cajta* occurs postverbally (C&H (24a)) is accounted for by extraposition of the complement S'.

An ECM analysis might be invoked to account for the accusative case in (37) (C&H's (23b)).

(37) Maria-ca [Francisco-ta cay-pi ca-j-ta] yacha-n.
 M-TOP F-ACC this-in be-PRES NOM-ACC know-3
 'Maria knows Francisco to be here.'

Applying Chomsky's S'-deletion rule (or alternatively the equivalent notion of S'-transparency), the matrix predicate *yacha* 'know' could be a possible governor for the embedded subject *Francisco* since there would no longer be a maximal projection blocking government. Under such an analysis, (37) would have the structure in (38).

(38)

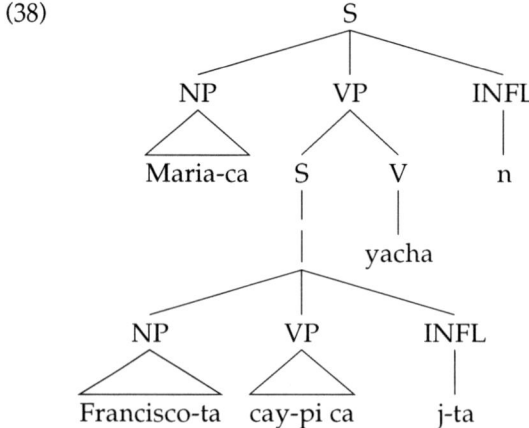

With *yacha* a possible governor of *Francisco*, it can assign accusative Case to the NP.

Notice that this analysis requires two unusual but crucial assumptions. First, Case assignment by the embedded INFL must be made optional. That is, the embedded INFL cannot assign Case to *Francisco* in (38). We know that this INFL must have nominative Case to assign since it is tensed and it assigns nominative Case in (36); but in (38), which has a structurally identical S, it does not discharge its Case. While this could seem somewhat questionable, it might be argued that since the embedded complements are actually nominalizations, the INFL operates in an unusual way. Hermon (1984) notes this unusual behavior of the complement subjects of S'-deleting verbs and suggests that a marked feature of Imbabura Quechua is that a non-local lexical governor (the matrix verb) can govern even when a more local non-lexical governor (i.e., INFL) is available; thus the non-local government overrides the local government.

Second, the verb *yacha* 'know' must be allowed to assign accusative Case twice, once to the complement clause and once exceptionally to the complement subject. This move is somewhat more suspicious and violates Aoun's (1979) *Biuniqueness Condition*, which states that a Case assigner may not assign Case to more than one nominal element. One might invoke some kind of inherent Case marking here, claiming that the verb *yacha* can assign structural Case via ECM to the complement subject and inherent accusative Case to the complement clause. Thus, in (37), repeated here, the boldfaced accusative Case on *Francisco* is structural and the italicized accusative Case on the clause is inherent, a special property of *yacha*.

(37) Maria-ca [Francisco-**ta** cay-pi ca-j-*ta*] yacha-n.
 M-TOP F-ACC this-in be-PRES-ACC know-3
 'Maria knows Francisco to be here.'

This would parallel the assignment of accusative Case twice in a double object construction such as with verbs like *cu* 'give' (from Jake 1985).[5]

(39) Warmi-ca jari-ta aswa-ta cu-rca-chu?
 woman-TOP man-ACC beer-ACC give-PAST.3-Q
 'Did the woman give the man beer?'

Within GB, the accusative Case on *aswa* 'beer' in (39) would be assigned as inherent Case by the verb *cu* while the accusative Case on *jari* 'man' is assigned by the accusative structural Case rule. If such an approach is admitted, under the ECM analysis of (37), the variant with the complement *Francisco-ta cay-pi ca-j-ta* (C&H's (24b)) can also be accounted for via extraposition of the complement S, as shown in (40).

(40) Maria-ca $t_i$ yacha-n [Francisco-**ta** cay-pi ca-j-*ta*]$_i$.
 M-TOP know-3 F-ACC this-in be-PRES-ACC
 'Maria knows Francisco to be here.'

The ECM analysis just sketched accounts for most of the behavior of the accusative subject in RtoO structures. The distribution of anaphors and pronominals (disjoint reference) follows from the established binding principles and the exceptional government of the embedded subject. With the deletion of the complement S' node, reflexives and reciprocals are sanctioned with a matrix antecedent because the governing category of the NP is the matrix S, since that is the S or NP that contains the anaphor and its governor. The validator facts might be similarly explained. The validator -*mi* can be exceptionally affixed to the accusative subject because the NP is governed by the main verb of the matrix clause, to which the validator is relevant, as proposed by Hermon (1984). In this way, an analysis of the Imbabura Quechua RtoO facts considered thus far might be made consistent with the principles of GB theory.

There is one set of facts yet to consider. These are the cases in which the complement subject precedes the matrix verb, but the remainder of the complement clause follows the main verb, C&H's (25), repeated here:

(41) a. *Maria-ca Francisco yacha-n cay-pi ca-j-ta.
       M-TOP    F         know-3   this-in be-PRES NOM-ACC
       (Maria knows Francisco to be here.)
    b. Maria-ca Francisco-ta yacha-n cay-pi ca-j-ta.
       M-TOP    F-ACC        know-3   this-in be-PRES NOM-ACC
       'Maria knows Francisco to be here.'

Recall that C&H account for the grammaticality of (41b) through the raising of *Francisco* to matrix direct object position, where it can receive accusative Case from the matrix verb *yacha* 'know.' Their analysis predicts and accounts for the ungrammaticality of (41a), in which *Francisco* occurs in nominative Case, by virtue of the fact that *Francisco* is in a structural position in which it should take accusative Case, but it does not.

However, this analysis is not available in GB so long as it is assumed that all complements of verbs are in θ-positions and movement into a θ-position results in a violation of the θ-criterion. Hermon (1984) proposes to account for this with a condition on word order. Within a clause, word order in Imbabura Quechua is relatively free: subjects may precede or follow the verb, and as we have seen (34), objects may also precede or follow the verb. As Hermon notes, in most instances dependents of tensed complement clauses may not reorder out of the complement into the matrix clause. Thus, (42), in which the embedded subject *Francisco* occurs before the matrix verb *ni* 'say' and the remainder of the complement follows the matrix verb, is ungrammatical.

(42) *Maria   Francisco ni-n   cay-pi ca-j-ta.[6]
      M.NOM  F.NOM      say-3  this-in be-PRES NOM-ACC
      (Maria says that Francisco is here.)

(42), then, is parallel to the ungrammatical (41a), in which the complement nominative subject cannot precede the matrix verb when the remainder of the complement clause follows the matrix verb. It is only embedded subjects of

S'-deletion predicates that can reorder in this way (embedded objects cannot), and only when they are in accusative Case. Hermon proposes that elements that occur in the same governing category can be freely ordered. Since the embedded subject is governed by the matrix verb after S'-deletion, it can be freely ordered with respect to any matrix element since its governing category is the matrix S. Thus, in the ECM analysis sketched here, both the word order and validator placement possibilities are attributable to the exceptional government of the embedded subject by the matrix verb.

While the analysis can be made to work in this way, it is important to note that two crucial assumptions about Imbabura Quechua must be made in addition to the regular assumptions of GB theory. First, it must be possible for government by INFL to be superseded by government by the matrix verb, and second, a subset of verbs must be allowed to assign more than one Case under specific circumstances. It is also important to note, however, that any account of the data must come to grips with these relatively idiosyncratic characteristics of the language.

As we see, Hermon's (1984) solution remains faithful to the θ-criterion under Chomsky's assumption that all complement positions are θ-positions. The accusative NP in (41b) is generated in an embedded θ-position and moves into some A'-position afterwards. It should be noted that four years later the assumption that all complement positions are θ-positions was challenged in Postal and Pullum (1988). There they present extensive empirically based arguments for the existence of subcategorized expletive objects. Among a range of other examples, Postal and Pullum cite structures in which clausal (43), gerundive (44), and infinitival (45) complements have been extraposed, leaving expletive *it* in a subcategorized position.

(43) a. I didn't suspect **it** for a moment *that you would fail.*
     b. I regret **it** very much *that we could not hire Mosconi.*

(44) a. I figured **it** out *to be impossible for us to get there by noon.*
     b. You owe **it** to yourself, in my opinion, *to get an annual checkup.*

(45) a. They kept **it** *from becoming too obvious that she was pregnant.*
     b. We can prevent **it**, I assure you, *from becoming known that we are here.*

In each of the examples in (43–5), the expletive *it* takes the place of the italicized phrase, which has been extraposed from its D-structure argument position. In many instances, matrix clause dependents and parentheticals intervene between the expletive and its associated phrase, showing that the phrases are no longer in the subcategorized position. On the basis of these and other example types, Postal and Pullum argue that the stipulation that expletives cannot occupy θ-positions, or at the very least subcategorized positions, cannot be maintained. From this it follows that non-thematic complement positions (including empty complement positions) must be sanctioned. Of course, if it is possible to generate empty complement positions in D-structure, C&H's

(1981) analysis, in which the accusative NP in (41b) moves from the embedded clause into an empty matrix clause object position, again becomes viable.

While it seems that few proponents of GB were persuaded by Postal and Pullum's arguments, as we see in chapter 12, the reintroduction of the Raising analysis of RtoO within the Chomskyan paradigm was a scant three years down the road.

## 5 The wider application of the ECM analysis

As developed in chapter 8, the ECM analysis is determined primarily by the assumptions made in the implementation of θ-theory and the Projection Principle. Since it was designed specifically with English data in mind, not unexpectedly application of the analysis to other languages raises various issues, and certain refinements prove necessary when confronted with data from other languages. Subtle differences in the details of each language test the strength and resilience of the framework.

The data Kayne discusses indicate that French differs crucially from English in not allowing ECM of a complement subject by a matrix verb. Thus, as shown in this chapter, French disallows lexical subjects in infinitives, and since the prepositional complementizer *de* is not a governor it can introduce control clauses, leaving PRO ungoverned. All of this makes the mechanism of S'-deletion irrelevant to French grammar. The Imbabura Quechua data present a different challenge. Since in Quechua RtoO involves tensed complement clauses, it is necessary to stipulate that a lexical governor (the matrix verb) overrides a more local, non-lexical governor (the tensed INFL of the complement clause). Here, S'-deletion comes into play, but special assumptions about government and Case assignment prove necessary.

While some languages allow the wholesale adoption of the core GB ECM proposal, there are other languages that require yet different modifications. For example, recall the Icelandic data from chapter 3, repeated here.

(46) a. Þeir    telja   [María hafa     skrifað ritgerðina].
        they.NOM believe M.ACC to.have written the.thesis.ACC
        'They believe Mary to have written her thesis.'
     b. Hann    telur   [barninu     hafa    batnað
        he.NOM believe  the.child.DAT to.have recovered.from
        veikin].
        the.disease.NOM
        'He believes the child to have recovered from the disease.'

Assuming S'-deletion to be operative, in (46a) 'believe' governs and assigns accusative Case to *María*, just as in English. However, in (46b), although 'believe' can still exceptionally govern, the accusative Case it would assign to the embedded subject is overridden by the 'quirky' Case that *batnað* inherently assigns to its subject. Thus, *barninu* 'the child' occurs in dative Case.

However, the most extensive examination of ECM and its application to a wide variety of languages is Diane Massam's (1985) MIT dissertation. Massam examines RtoO in a variety of languages (including English and Icelandic) and further modifies the theory and some analyses. Of particular interest are structures claimed to involve RtoO from finite complements.

Massam's work incorporates a number of innovations from Chomsky's (1986a) *Barriers* framework, many of which need not concern us here. However, one obvious difference is the elevation of the non-lexical categories INFL and COMP to heads of their own phrases, with IP replacing S and CP replacing S'. Thus, a sentence such as (47a) is given the structure in (47b).

(47) a. Ashley believes that Kelsey left.
　　 b.

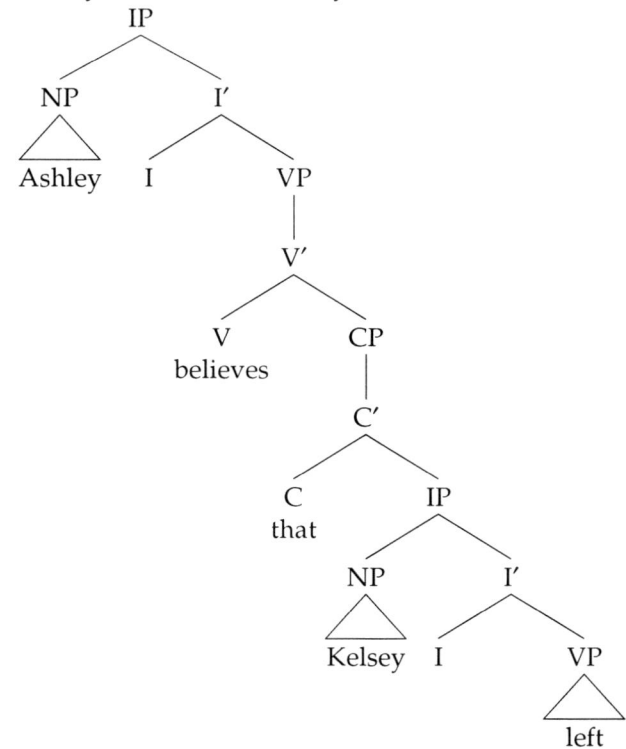

It should be noted that clausal subjects now occupy the specifier (SPEC) position of IP. In the *Barriers* framework, government is defined in such a way that if α governs β, then α also governs the SPEC of β, provided there is no closer governor. Using these innovations, Massam proposes an updated analysis of English ECM. Rather than triggering S'-deletion (now CP-deletion), a verb like *believe* is allowed to select an IP complement and can govern the complement subject when I is not finite (and hence not a governor). Thus, the RtoO sentence in (48a) has the structure in (48b), with *believe* assigning Case to *Kelsey*.

(48) a. Ashley believes Kelsey to have left.
    b.
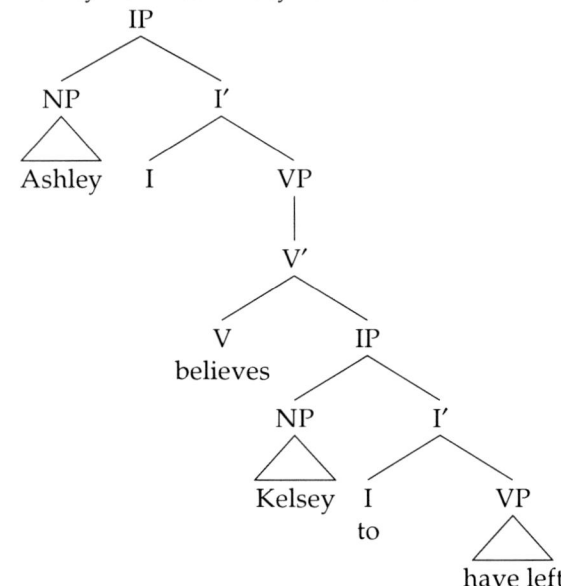

Massam goes on to examine purported RtoO structures in a variety of languages, particularly those with finite complements. These include among others Niuean (49), Kipsigis (50), and Bauan Fijian (51).[7]

(49) *Niuean:*
    a. To maeke [ke lagomatai he ekekafo e tama ē].
       FUT possible SBJ help ERG doctor ABS child this
       'The doctor could help this child.'
    b. To maeke e ekekafo$_i$ [ke lagomatai $t_i$ e tama ē].
       FUT possible ABS doctor SBJ help ABS child this
       'The doctor could help this child.'

(50) *Kipsigis:*
    a. mócè Mú:sá [á-lápát].
       want M 1SG.SUBJ-run
       'Musa wants that I run.'
    b. móc-ɔ́:n Mú:sá [à-lápát].
       want–1SG.OBJ M 1SG.SUBJ-run
       'Musa wants me to run.'

(51) *Bauan Fijian:*[8]
    a. Au$_j$ a vinakata [mo mokuti Timoci *pro*] *pro$_j$*.
       1SG PST want SUB.2SG hit T
       'I wanted you to hit Timothy.'

b. Au$_j$ a    vinakati **iko**$_i$ [mo        mokuti Timoci $t_i$] pro$_j$.
   1SG PST want     you  SUB.2SG hit     T
   'I wanted you to hit Timothy.'

The (b)-variants in these examples are the purported RtoO structures. In (49b) the matrix predicate *maeke* 'possible' assigns absolutive Case to *ekekafo* 'doctor,' in (50b) the matrix verb 'want' assigns accusative Case to the first person singular pronoun (realized as object agreement on the verb), and in (51b) *vinakati* 'want' assigns Case to *iko* 'you.' In addition to the fact that the complement clauses in these structures are finite, a number of properties distinguish them from the RtoO of English and Icelandic:

(i)   the raised NP occurs not in the canonical subject position but to the left of a complementizer in Niuean and Fijian or as object agreement on the matrix verb in Kipsigis,
(ii)  the trace of the raised NP is in a Case-marked position, and
(iii) RtoO is not restricted to subjects – Niuean and Kipsigis RtoO can apply to objects and Fijian RtoO can apply to objects, prepositional objects, and conjuncts, illustrated for Fijian in (52) and (53).

(52) Au kiliai **iko**$_i$ [ni       vinakata $t_i$ ko   Timaima].
     1SG think you  SUB.3SG want         ART T
     'I think Timaima likes you.'

(53) Au namaki **Bale**$_i$ [ni     damudamu na  **nona**$_i$ boto].
     1SG expect B    SUB.3SG red          ART her   boat
     'I expect Bale's boat to be red.'

In (52) the NP *iko* 'you' is the object of the embedded clause and in (53) the NP *Bale* is coreferent with the possessor of the embedded subject *nona* 'her.' Pronouns coreferent to the raised NP in Fijian are possible with objects and subjects as well, but are obligatory with NPs other than subjects or objects. In the GB analysis, the raised NPs in (49–53) receive ECM from the matrix verbs.

To accommodate these properties of Fijian, Niuean, and Kipsigis RtoO within the strictures of GB theory, Massam must propose some innovations. Since the complement clauses are finite, every position in the embedded clauses is Case marked. Therefore, since movement occurs from a Case-marked position, movement cannot be motivated by the need for Case. What is more, since the trace is in a Case-marked position, the movement is more like A'-movement than A-movement. Thus, Massam proposes that in these languages movement is to a second SPEC position in the complement CP, which she labels SPEC2 (the normal SPEC being reserved for *wh*-movement). In this analysis, the Fijian example (51b) has the structure in (54).

(54)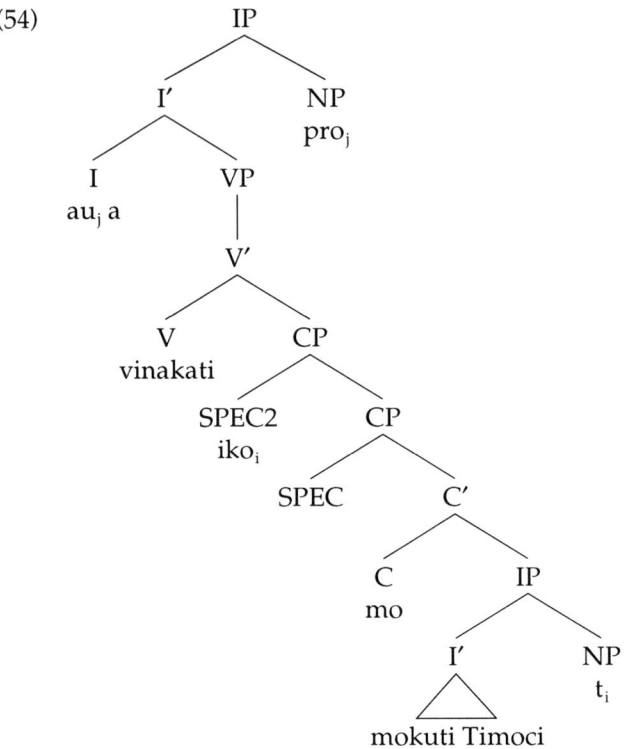

In (54), the D-structure subject of the complement clause *iko* 'you' has moved to SPEC2. Since the C *mo* is not a governor, the matrix verb governs *iko* and assigns it Case, thus avoiding a Case Filter violation. Massam gives a parallel analysis for Niuean and Kipsigis.

These data force a number of modifications to the theory, but most notable is the adoption of a second SPEC position in these embedded complements. As Massam states, this SPEC position has special properties, being "ambiguous in several respects as to whether it is an A-position or an A-bar position" (1985:110). The ambiguity is largely an issue in binding theory regarding the moved NP's relationship with its trace and the status of a trace in SPEC2 if there is subsequent movement. Additionally, elements in SPEC2 are full participants in morphological and syntactic processes of the matrix clause, including the possibility of moving to matrix subject position, as illustrated in the Fijian example in (55).

(55) **Au**$_i$ a tukuni [$t_i$ [ni'u a mokuti Mere]].
    1SG PST say.PASS   SUB.1SG PST hit  M
    'I was said to have hit Mary.'

The ability of the NP to move to SPEC2 (an A'-position) and then to subject position in the matrix clause (an A-position) is theoretically problematic. Movement from an A'-position to an A-position is an example of improper movement, ruled out in the theory since the trace of A'-movement is not supposed to be bound by an antecedent in an argument position. In argumentation too detailed for present concerns, Massam proposes that SPEC2 of CP has properties distinct from the SPEC position dedicated to *wh*-movement, properties which permit this movement to an A-position. Massam explores the theoretical implications of this at length in the concluding chapter of her thesis.

What is crucial to our understanding here is the need to further modify the theory to accommodate the special properties of RtoO constructions with finite complements. Apparent RtoO constructions from finite complements in Western Malayo-Polynesian languages and Japanese are explored in detail in the following chapter.

## Notes

1  This assumes, of course, that negation works the same in both languages. However, regardless of the language-particular properties of negation, Kayne's argument can stand if it is the case that negation can follow but not precede a complementizer in both languages. This would argue that *to* cannot be a complementizer, since negation can precede it, and that *de* is a complementizer, since negation cannot precede it.

2  In this regard, Ø must now be distinguished from *for* which governs and assigns Case on its own, as in (i).

   (i)   [$_{S'}$for [$_S$him to be late]] is truly irksome

   Here, *for* governs and assigns Case directly to *him*, there being no category from which government or Case could be transmitted.

3  Chomsky (1981:297–8) discusses the problem of accounting for sentences such as (i).

   (i)   *him to be here is hard to believe          [= Chomsky 1981:297 (31i)]

   He suggests (somewhat inaccurately, cf. chapter 7) that such sentences are accounted for under the *[NP to VP] filter of Chomsky and Lasnik (1977). But says that this "has now been eliminated." In order to maintain Kayne's Ø complementizer analysis and account for the different distribution of the Ø and *for* complementizers, Chomsky notes that one would have to stipulate that the Ø complementizer can assign Case only "in immediate post-verbal position." However, Chomsky notes this sort of solution "virtually amounts to accepting the S'-deletion hypothesis" for ECM verbs.

4  C&H argue that the NIC must be reformulated in terms of a Case-marked Subject Island Condition. They show on the basis of the accusatively case-marked subjects that what is relevant to the opacity of subjects of tensed clauses is not nominative case. This is because desideratives and some verbs (e.g., *rupa* 'be hot,' *muna* 'want') require accusative case marking on their subjects, and these accusative subjects behave exactly the same as nominative case-marked subjects in terms of disjoint reference and validator placement (cf. C&H's (43) and (48)). C&H also argue that even when the NIC is reformulated as their CSIC, problems accrue to the OB framework because of certain Imbabura Quechua passivization facts.

5 Lefebvre and Muysken (1982) posit a rule to account for a number of instances of double accusatives (including accusative Case on adverbs and double accusatives in causative constructions) that stipulates that any element in the domain of a Case-assigning V may be assigned Case by that V. Hermon (1984) counters that such a rule is unnecessary inasmuch as many instances of multiple accusative Case can be accounted for in other ways.

6 The orthography in (40) is consistent with that of C&H but differs from that used in Hermon (1984).

7 The Fijian data discussed here and by Massam are from Gordon (1980) or from our own consultation with a native speaker. In the Fijian data SUB means subordinating conjunction, to which a subject marker cliticizes. Recall also that SBJ in the Niuean gloss stands for subjunctive.

8 Fijian is a VOS language with pronominal subject clitics, which are coindexed with an empty pronoun (*pro*) in the canonical subject position. This is reflected in the data in (49) but is ignored in subsequent examples, as it is unimportant to present concerns.

# CHAPTER 10

# ARE ALL THESE REALLY RAISING CONSTRUCTIONS? CROSS-LINGUISTIC ISSUES

As seen in the previous chapter, raising phenomena in various languages may lead to modifications in details of the theory or may challenge the theory in more profound ways. But it is incumbent on the analyst to ensure that the data in question actually are what they seem to be. This chapter focuses on this issue, examining data of purported cases of Raising in Austronesian languages and Japanese, applying the kinds of diagnostics for Raising that we have seen applied in analyses of English and other languages. Here we see that in the first instance the purported raising construction might not be so, and in the second case the correct analysis is rather elusive.

## 1 "Raising" in Austronesian languages

Raising analyses have been proposed for a variety of languages in the Austronesian family, which ranges over Oceania and stretches from Easter Island to Madagascar. In Philippine languages such as Tagalog and Cebuano, RtoS has been proposed for sentences such as those in (1) and (2).[1]

(1) *Tagalog (Kroeger 1993:(17b))*:
Inasah-an ko         ang = pambansang.awit [na    awit-in  ni = Linda].
expect-DV 1.SG.GEN NOM = national.anthem COMP sing-OV GEN = L
'I expected the national anthem to be sung by Linda.'

(2) *Cebuano (Bell 1976:(119c))*:
Ang iho   na'alinggatan sa    mananagat nga    mibalik.
NOM shark notice.LV     GEN fisherman  COMP return
'That the shark has returned was noticed by the fisherman.'

In the Javanic languages of Indonesia, RtoO analyses have been proposed for Indonesian, Javanese, Balinese, and others.[2]

(3) *Indonesian (Chung 1976:(38)):*
Mereka anggap buku itu sudah di-baca oleh Ali.
they believe book that PERF PASS-read by A
'They believe this book to have been read by Ali.'

(4) *Javanese (Davies 1990:(30)):*
Amir ngarepna Musa wingi arep menyang dina Selasa.
A AV.expect M yesterday will to day Tuesday
'Yesterday Amir expected Musa to go Tuesday.'

(5) *Balinese (Wechsler and Arka 1998:(23d)):*
Polisi tawang=a lakar ngangkep Wayan.
police OV.know=3 FUT AV.arrest W
'He knew the police would arrest Wayan.'

There is, in fact, good reason to suspect that Raising (or ECM) is not involved in these cases. A close examination of data from Madurese, a Javanic language very closely related to Indonesian, Javanese, and Balinese, reveals the problems. The sentence in (6) is the Madurese counterpart to the structures in (3–5).

(6) Siti ngera Hasan bari' melle montor.
S AV.think H yesterday AV.buy car
'Yesterday Siti thought Hasan to have bought a car.'

Various syntactic tests reveal that *Hasan* is a constituent of the matrix clause, not the least of which is the fact that the matrix adverbial *bari'* 'yesterday' intercedes between it and the embedded clause. This is the kind of evidence that Postal (1974) brought forth in favor of the Raising analysis in English. There are some obvious differences between the Madurese structure and English RtoO, however.

Two important facts about Javanic languages are (i) there is no overt case morphology of any kind and (ii) there is no overt tense marking. Since there is no overt tense marking, there is no reason to suppose that in alleged RtoO/ECM constructions the embedded clause contains an untensed form of the verb. There is therefore no reason to suppose that subjects in these complement clauses are not assigned Case by INFL. Thus, the kind of Case facts that motivate Raising and ECM for English are of necessity not overt in Madurese. Consider first the simple clause in (7).

(7) Hasan melle montor.
H AV.buy car
'Hasan buys/bought a car.'

Since all NPs must be assigned Case, in (7), *Hasan* must receive Case by virtue of being in subject position, perhaps assigned by the INFL node. Consider now a potential RtoO/ECM structure.

(8) Siti ngera    [Hasan melle  motor].
    S   AV.think H       AV.buy car
    'Siti thought Hasan to have bought a car.'

In (8), the complement clause contains no complementizer, and one might propose that *Hasan* is assigned Case by the matrix verb *ngera* 'think' in the way that *believe* assigns Case to *Hasan* in a sentence like *Siti believes Hasan to have bought a car*. However, note that the complement clause has the exact same form as the simple clause in (7). There is no reason to assume that in (8) *Hasan* cannot receive Case from the embedded INFL. Therefore, an ECM analysis is not obviously required to account for the data. By the same token, there is no reason to assume Case-motivated movement in (9).

(9)  Hasan$_i$ e-kera   Siti bari'    [e$_i$ melle  motor].
     H      ov-think S  yesterday     AV.buy car
     'Hasan was thought by Siti yesterday to have bought a car.'

In (9), it appears that *Hasan* has moved from its position in the embedded clause to be subject of the matrix clause. It appears to receive its θ-role from the embedded predicate *melle* 'buy,' and appears to be unthematically related to the matrix verb *kera* 'think,' the kinds of facts that are taken as evidence for Raising. However, the movement is not obviously motivated by Case. *Hasan* can clearly receive Case by virtue of being the matrix subject, but again the embedded subject position is not obviously a non-Case-marked position, calling into some question the rationale for a movement analysis. Of course, while there is no positive evidence that Raising or ECM is required to account for the well-formedness of these sentences, neither are the data inconsistent with such an analysis. However, there are empirical arguments against a Raising analysis based on the variety of types of arguments that can raise, the possibility of resumptive pronouns, the interpretation of idioms in these structures, and other features.

First, the "raised" NP need not be a subject. In (6) *Hasan* does play the role of subject in the embedded clause. However, unlike RtoO in most languages, the "raised" element can bear any of a number of grammatical functions. In (10) *Hasan* is the possessor of the object of the embedded clause, *ana'* 'child,' and in (11) *Hasan* is the possessor of the subject of the embedded clause.

(10) Siti ngera     Hasan ja'   dokter juwa mareksa    ana'-eng.
     S   AV.think H        COMP doctor that AV.examine child-DEF
     'Siti thinks that the doctor examined Hasan's child.'

(11) Marlena a-bala-agi Hasan ja'    embi'-eng ngekke' Ali.
     M       AV-say-AGI H       COMP goat-DEF  AV.bite A
     'Marlena said that Hasan's goat bit Ali.'

More literal translations of (10) and (11) are 'Siti thinks about Hasan that the doctor examined his child' and 'Marlena said about Hasan that his goat bit Ali,' respectively. And in (12) the embedded direct object has "raised."[3]

(12) Siti ngera    Hasan ja'    dokter juwa mareksa.
     S   AV.think H    COMP doctor that  AV.examine
     'Siti thinks that the doctor examined Hasan.'

While there have been proposals that non-subjects can raise to object in a few languages (as in the raising of objects in Niuean, Kipsigis, and Fijian examples in the previous chapter), these cases are exceedingly rare and perhaps bear closer scrutiny. Additionally, these proposals never include the possibility of possessors raising directly from embedded clauses to matrix clauses.

Second, unlike familiar instances of RtoO, a pronoun coreferential with the "raised" NP can occur in the base position in the embedded clause, what has been referred to as "Copy Raising" in the literature. In (13–16), the raised element is coindexed with the pronominal *aba'eng* in the complement clause.

(13) Hasan ngera    Siti$_i$ ja'    aba'eng$_i$ melle  motor.
     H    AV.think S     COMP she       AV.buy car
     'Hasan thinks Siti bought a car.'
     lit.: 'Hasan thinks about Siti that she bought a car.'

(14) Siti ngera    Hasan$_i$ ja'    dokter juwa mareksa    aba'eng$_i$.
     S   AV.think H      COMP doctor that  AV.examine he
     'Siti thinks that the doctor examined Hasan.'
     lit.: 'Siti thinks about Hasan that the doctor examined him.'

(15) Siti ngera    Hasan$_i$ ja'    dokter juwa mareksa    ana'-eng aba'eng$_i$.
     S   AV.think H      COMP doctor that  AV.examine child-DEF he
     'Siti thinks that the doctor examined Hasan's child.'
     lit.: 'Siti thinks about Hasan that the doctor examined his child.'

(16) Marlena a-bala-agi Hasan$_i$ ja'    embi'-eng aba'eng$_i$. ngekke' Ali.
     M       AV-say-AGI H      COMP goat-DEF he            AV.bite A
     'Marlena said that Hasan's goat bit Ali.'
     lit.: 'Marlena said about Hasan that his goat bit Ali.'

The sentences in (13–16) would be instances of Copy Raising, as proposed for Greek by Joseph (1976). Just as with the raising of non-subjects, Copy Raising is quite rare in the world's languages and the data leading to such proposals may well be open to alternative analyses.[4] Additionally, it has been argued extensively that Copy Raising affects only complement subjects (Moore 1998; Potsdam and Runner 2001). Thus, a raising analysis of the Madurese data would be unusual on a number of counts.

Casting further doubt on the raising analysis is the behavior of idioms in this construction. As shown in chapter 1, idioms provide compelling evidence for RtoS and RtoO analyses since even when a part of the idiom has moved out of the clause containing it, the idiomatic meaning can be retained. This is not true of the Madurese construction. The sentence in (17) is an example of a Madurese idiom.

(17) Nase' la dhaddhi tajjin.
    rice PERF become porridge
    'It is too late to do anything about it.'
    lit.: 'The rice has become porridge.'

The idiomatic meaning of (17) derives from the fact that once rice has been overcooked to the point of becoming like porridge, there is no remedy for it. As (18) shows, when wholly contained in the complement clause, this string can be interpreted idiomatically.

(18) Siti ngera bari' ja' nase' la dhaddhi tajjin.
    S AV.think yesterday COMP rice PERF become porridge
    'Siti thought yesterday that it is too late to do anything about it.'
    'Siti thought yesterday that the rice had became porridge.'

However, when *nase'* 'rice' appears in the matrix clause, the idiomatic meaning is no longer available.

(19) Siti ngera nase' bari' ja' la dhaddhi tajjin.
    S AV.think rice yesterday COMP PERF become porridge
    'Siti thought about the rice yesterday that it became porridge.'

In (19), *nase'* precedes both the matrix adverb *bari'* 'yesterday' and the complementizer *ja'*, showing that it is a constituent of the matrix clause here. The sentence in (19) does not allow the idiomatic reading but admits only the literal interpretation. Thus, idiom chunks operate in a way inconsistent with the predictions of a raising analysis. The pair of sentences in (20) shows the same effect with the idiomatic expression *ajam atellor e beras* 'She or he has it easy' (lit.: 'A chicken laid an egg in the rice').

(20) a. Siti namto-agi ja' ajam a-tellor e beras.
        S AV.certain-AGI COMP chicken AV-egg at rice
        'Siti is certain that he or she has it easy.'
        'Siti is certain that the chicken laid an egg in the rice.'
    b. Siti namto-agi ajam ja' a-tellor e beras.
        S AV.certain-AGI chicken COMP AV-egg at rice
        'Siti is certain about the chicken that it laid an egg in the rice.'

In (20a), the referent of the idiom is established through discourse context. However, when *ajam* 'chicken' occurs in the matrix clause in (20b), it loses any idiomatic meaning.

The Madurese structure differs from RtoO proposed in other languages with respect to the kinds of embedded clauses that can participate in the construction. While RtoO involving tensed complement clauses has been proposed for a number of languages, it is not only complement clauses but some apparent adverbial clauses that are affected in Madurese. In (21), there is apparent raising out of a causal clause, introduced by *polana* 'because.'

(21) a. Ebu    manyessel polana na'-kana'-na  lo' patang a-caca.
        mother regret    because RED-child-DEF not RECIP AV-speak
        'Mother regrets that her children do not speak to each other.'
    b. Na'-kana'na  e-manyessel-le Ebu    polana lo' patang a-caca.
        RED-child-DEF ov-regret-E    mother because not RECIP AV-speak
        'Mother regrets that her children do not speak to each other.'
        lit.: 'The children are regretted about by mother because they don't speak to each other.'

In (21b), the subject of the adverbial clause in (21a), *na'kana'na* 'her children,' occurs as the subject of the matrix clause. If it has moved to this position, it has moved out of an adverbial clause. Movement out of adverbial clauses is ruled out by the Empty Category Principle. Therefore, an RtoO analysis of the Madurese structure is inappropriate.

In addition to adverbial clauses, the Madurese construction is not constrained by island effects. It is possible for the "raised" NP to refer to elements in coordinate structures (22) and complex NPs (23).

(22) Hasan ngera    Bambang ja'    Marlena ngerem paket    dha' Ali
     H     AV.think B         COMP M       AV.send package to    A
     bi' ana'-eng.
     and child-DEF
     'Hasan thought about Bambang$_i$ that Marlena sent a package to Ali and his$_i$ child.'

(23) Wati ng-enga'-e    Atin cereta-na ja'    lake-na      ng-angkep
     W    AV-remember-E A    story-DEF COMP husband-DEF AV-capture
     maleng.
     thief
     'Wati remembered about Atin$_i$ the story that her$_i$ husband captured the thief.'

In (22), the NP *Bambang* refers to the possessor of the second of two conjoined NPs that are the goal in the embedded clause. If this were movement, it would constitute a violation of the Coordinate Structure Constraint (Ross 1967). If movement were involved in making *Atin* a matrix clause dependent in (23), the sentence would violate the Complex NP Constraint. The fact that the RtoO analysis would have to countenance island violations is another strike against it.

Another problem for the RtoO analysis is the fact that the construction in Madurese is very productive. While RtoS and RtoO in English and other languages we have looked at is lexically circumscribed to include a relatively small number of predicates, the Madurese construction includes most (if not all) verbs which take sentential complements. Thus, alongside examples with the predicates *kera* 'think,' *bala* 'say,' and others already illustrated, the structure is possible with *yaken* 'sure,' *loppa* 'forget,' *lapor* 'report,' *kabarragi* 'spread the news,' *terrangngagi* 'explain,' *janji* 'promise,' *tao* 'know,' *koto* 'whisper,' *bukteyagi* 'prove,' and virtually any other non-control predicate that can take a clausal complement.

Finally, the embedded NP that occurs in the matrix in the Madurese construction can occur as a prepositional object in the matrix clause. In each case illustrated thus far, it is possible for the NP to occur as the object of the prepositions *parkara* or *halla* 'about' or in some instances *ka* 'to.'[5] Examples are given in (24–6).

(24) Siti ngera parkara Hasan$_i$ ja' dokter juwa mareksa aba'eng$_i$.
 S AV.think about H COMP doctor that AV.examine he
 'Siti thinks about Hasan that the doctor examined him.'

(25) Ali a-janji halla labang-nga ka Siti ja' e-pa-becce'-a are Sennen.
 A AV-promise about door-DEF to S COMP OV-CS-good-IRR day Monday
 'Ali promised about the door to Siti that it would be fixed by Monday.'

(26) Sengko' loppa ka Ita$_i$ ja' Hasan a-kerem bungkosan dha' aba'eng$_i$ dhari Kanada.
 I forget to I COMP H AV-send package to her from Canada
 'I forgot about Ita that Hasan sent a package to her from Canada.'

In each case here, the matrix prepositional object is coreferential with an embedded NP.

An RtoO analysis of the Madurese construction is rendered less convincing by the fact that (i) the targets of Raising are not exclusively subjects, (ii) embedded coreferent pronouns are possible in all cases, (iii) idiomatic meanings are not preserved, (iv) adjunct clauses as well as complement clauses may participate, (v) island constraints are violated, (vi) there is no apparent lexical restriction on matrix predicates, and (vii) the raised element may occur as a prepositional object in the matrix clause. The Madurese construction parallels the English construction in (27).

(27) Martin assumed about Frieda$_i$ that Melvin had warned her$_i$.

The English and Madurese constructions are akin to what has been referred to by Higgins (1981) and others as "prolepsis" – both typically require the matrix argument be coindexed with an embedded argument.[6] The appearance that the Madurese construction might be Raising is due to the possibility of zero pronouns in the language, an option unavailable in English.

Madurese freely admits zero pronominals in the appropriate discourse context, especially as subjects or possessors. The option is also available in direct object position, although there is some speaker variability in the acceptability of this. So when the embedded NP in prolepsis is a subject or possessor it looks very much like Raising, but in fact the structures with and without overt pronouns are precisely the same, as in the similarity between (28) and (29).

(28) Siti ngera Hasan₍ᵢ₎ [ja' dokter juwa mareksa ana'eng *pro*₍ᵢ₎]

(29) Siti ngera Hasan₍ᵢ₎ [ja' dokter juwa mareksa ana'eng aba'eng₍ᵢ₎]
'Siti thinks that the doctor examined Hasan's child.'
lit.: 'Siti thinks about Hasan that the doctor examined his child.'

In (28) a zero pronoun possessor is coindexed with the matrix NP *Hasan* and in (29) the overt pronminal *aba'eng* is coindexed with *Hasan*.

The fact that the matrix NP can occur as a prepositional object is the key to the full analysis of the Madurese. The base form of the structure includes matrix PPs. Base-generation of the NP in a PP not only accounts for the obvious cases in which these NPs occur as prepositional objects, but also accounts for verbal morphology. In Madurese the suffixes *-agi* and *-e* can occur in certain environments when a prepositional object surfaces as a bare NP, similar to the English double object construction. This is illustrated for *-agi* in (30) and *-e* in (31).

(30) a. Ita melle   buku kaangguy Bambang.
        I   AV.buy book for       B
        'Ita bought a book for Bambang.'
    b. Ita melle-**agi**  Bambang buku.
        I   AV.buy-AGI B        book
        'Ita bought Bambang a book.'

(31) a. Bambang ngerem paket    dha' Siti.
        B       AV.send package to   S
        'Hasan sent a package to Siti.'
    b. Bambang ngerem-**e** Siti paket.
        B       AV.send-E S    package
        'Hasan sent Siti a package.'

In (30a) the beneficiary *Bambang* occurs as the object of *kaangguy* 'for.' When it occurs as the bare NP in (30b), the verb must be suffixed with *-agi*. In (31b), the prepositional object of (31a), *Siti*, occurs as a bare NP and the verb obligatorily includes the suffix *-e*.

These same suffixes occur with some verbs when the matrix NP in the complex clauses occurs as a bare NP. This is obvious in the pairs in (32) and (33).

(32) a. Marlena a-bala parkara Hasan ja'  embi'-eng ngekke' Ali.
        M       AV-say about   H     COMP goat-DEF AV.bite A
        'Marlena said about Hasan that his goat bit Ali.'
    b. Marlena a-bala-**agi** Hasan ja'  embi'-eng ngekke' Ali.
        M       AV-say-AGI   H     COMP goat-DEF AV.bite A
        'Marlena said about Hasan that his goat bit Ali.'

(33) a. Sengko' loppa parkara Ita ja'   Hasasn ngerem paket   dha'
       I      forget  about  I  COMP H     AV.send package to
       aba'eng.
       she
       'I forgot about Ita that Hasan send a package to her.'
   b. Sengko' ng-loppa-e Ita ja'   Hasasn ngerem paket   dha'
       I      AV-forget-E I  COMP H     AV.send package to
       aba'eng.
       she
       'I forgot about Ita that Hasan send a package to her.'

With the predicate *bala* 'say,' when the matrix element is a bare NP, the suffix *-agi* occurs on the verb (32b). With predicate *loppa* 'forget,' *-e* is suffixed when the matrix element is a bare NP (33b). The use of these suffixes parallels their appearance in structures in (30b) and (31b). This is accounted for if the matrix object is generated as a matrix prepositional object and is not raised into this position.

There is thus strong evidence that the Madurese analogue of the construction that has been analyzed as RtoO for other Javanic languages is in fact not a raising construction at all and is most appropriately analyzed as a case of prolepsis. Parallel evidence for Javanese and Indonesian is available in Davies (2001).

## 2  "Raising" in Philippine languages

As noted above, some have claimed that Philippine languages such as Tagalog and Cebuano contain RtoS constructions, exemplified again for Cebuano in (34).

(34) a. Naka'linggat si   Lito [nga   nagpalit si   Linda ug   dulsi para
       AV.notice    NOM L      COMP AV.buy  NOM L       GEN candy for
       sa bata'].
       GEN child
       'Lito noticed that Linda had bought candy for the child.'
   b. Na'alingatan ni   Lito **si   Linda** [nga   nagpalit ug   dulsi para
       notice.LV   GEN L       NOM L        COMP AV.buy   GEN candy for
       sa  bata'].
       GEN child
       'Linda was noticed by Lito to have bought candy for the child.'

(34a) is the non-raising construction, with the matrix predicate in the actor voice and the subject *Lito* taking the nominative or topic marker *si*, used with proper nouns. (34b) is the alleged raising structure. Note the changes: the matrix verb is in the locative voice, *Lito* takes the non-topic marker *ni*, and the embedded subject from (34a), *Linda*, appears to the left of the complementizer, takes the topic marker, and no longer occurs in the embedded clause. To all intents and purposes, this looks like raising.

However, there is more to the construction than this surface appearance. First, as in Madurese, it is possible to have so-called "copy raising." Kroeger (1993) reports this for Tagalog, claiming that Copy Raising is restricted to embedded non-subject agents. It is indeed possible to get a pronominal copy in the embedded clause in Cebuano, but as (35) shows, it is not limited to non-subject agents.

(35) Na'alingatan ni Lito si Linda$_i$ [nga nagpalit **siya**$_i$ ug dulsi
     notice.LV GEN L NOM L COMP AV.buy 3.SG.NOM GEN candy
     para sa bata'].
     for GEN child
     'Linda was noticed by Lito to have bought candy for the child.'

In (35), *siya* is the subject of the embedded clause; so while it is an agent, it is also the subject. What is more, as in Madurese, there appears to be no restriction to subjects or agents; prepositional objects (36) and possessors (37) can also occur as resumptive pronouns in raising structures.

(36) Na'alingatan ni Lito si Maria$_i$ [nga nagpalit si Linda ug
     notice.LV GEN L NOM M COMP AV.buy NOM L GEN
     dulsi para niya$_i$].
     candy for 3.SG.GEN
     'Maria was noticed by Lito that Linda had bought candy for her.'

(37) Gihung-hongan nako si Lito$_i$ [nga nagpalit si Linda ug dulsi
     whisper.LV I.GEN NOM L COMP AV.buy NOM L GEN candy
     para sa iyang$_i$ anak].
     for GEN his child
     'Lito was whispered about by me that Linda had bought candy for his child.'

In (36), the matrix subject *Maria* is also the embedded prepositional object, signaled by *niya*. In (37), the matrix subject *Lito* is coreferent with the possessor *iyang* in the benefactive argument. So, as in Madurese, coreferential pronouns are possible and arguments bearing almost any grammatical function can be raised.

As in Madurese, the Cebuano construction does not obey the Coordinate Structure Constraint.

(38) Gimahayan nako si Lito$_i$ [nga gidakup siya$_i$ ug si Pedro
     regret.LV I.GEN NOM L COMP OV.arrest 3.SG.NOM and NOM P
     sa pulis].
     GEN police
     'Lito was regretted by me that he and Pedro were arrested by the police.'

(39) Na'alingatan ni Lito si Pedro$_i$ [nga nihatag ko ug kuwarta
notice.LV GEN L NOM P COMP AV.give I.NOM GEN money
kang Linda ug iyang$_i$ anak].
to L GEN his child
'Pedro was noticed by Lito that I gave money to Linda and his child.'

Here, the matrix subject is coreferent with an embedded pronoun contained in a coordinate NP: in (38) *Lito* is coindexed with *siya* in the embedded clause, and in (39) *Pedro* is coindexed with the possessive *iyang* in the goal NP.

An additional similarity to Madurese is the fact that in the Cebuano construction the matrix argument can occur as a prepositional object. This is illustrated in (40) and (41).

(40) Naka'linggat si Lito **kabahin ni** Linda$_i$ [nga nagpalit (siya$_i$)
AV.notice NOM L about GEN L COMP AV.buy 3.SG.NOM
ug dulsi para sa bata'].
GEN candy for GEN candy
'Lito noticed about Linda that she had bought candy for the child.'

(41) Naka'linggat si Lito **kabahin ni** Maria$_i$ [nga nagpalit si
AV.notice NOM L about GEN M COMP AV.buy NOM
Linda ug dulsi para niya$_i$ ].
L GEN candy for 3.SG.GEN
'Lito noticed about Maria that Linda had bought candy for her.'

(40) is the analog of (34b) and (41) the analogue of (36). It is thus clear that the Cebuano structure that has been identified as RtoS is actually completely analogous to the Madurese structure and is best analyzed as prolepsis, with the twist that the additional matrix argument is a subject rather than an object.

The Cebuano situation also parallels Madurese in terms of the argument from verb morphology. In each of the Cebuano instances in which the additional NP occurs not as a prepositional object but as the subject, the verb is in the locative voice. Thus far only the predicate *linggat* 'notice' has been illustrated. However, the data in (42) and (43) show the same thing.

(42) Gimahayan nako si Lito [nga nilakat (siya)].
regret.LV 1.SG.GEN NOM L COMP leave 3.SG.NOM
'I regretted about Lito that he left.'

(43) Gihung-hongan nako ang tubag [nga gihatag ni Linda kang
whisper.LV 1.SG.GEN NOM answer COMP give.OV GEN L to
Maria].
M
'I whispered about the answer that Linda gave it to Maria.'

In Cebuano, locative voice is also used when recipients and beneficiaries occur as subject, as in (44).

(44) Gisultian nako    si    Linda.
    talk.LV  1.SG.GEN  NOM   L
    'I talked to Linda.'

Thus, just as in Madurese, base generation of the extra argument as prepositional object accounts for the locative voice morphology used when the NP occurs as subject, and explains why no other voice morphology is used with other matrix predicates.

The data from these Austronesian languages underscore the need to closely examine the characteristics of structures posited, striving to ensure that analyses are not driven solely by the desire to find the familiar. We turn now to Japanese RtoO, for which a definitive analysis has proved elusive.

## 3 "Raising" in Japanese

Alongside the Austronesian cases just presented, there are other languages that appear to have (and might indeed have) RtoS and RtoO constructions, but whose properties differ in ways that trouble the traditional GB account of such structures. The Japanese example (45) has been assessed (first by Kuno 1976) as a RtoO clause, and is claimed to contrast with (46), which is a typical object control construction.

(45) Yamada wa Tanaka o    baka da to    omotteita. [= Kuno 1976:(17b)]
     TOP           ACC fool is  COMP thought
     'Yamada thought Tanaka to be a fool.'

(46) Yamada wa Tanaka ni   sore o   suru koto o    [= Kuno 1976:(63b)]
     TOP           DAT  that ACC do   NMNL ACC
     meizita.
     ordered
     'Yamada ordered Tanaka to do that.'

In (45), *Yamada* is the subject of the matrix verb *omotteita* 'thought,' and the accusative-marked noun *Tanaka* is the subject of the embedded predicate phrase *baka da* 'is a fool.'

Purported RtoO constructions in Japanese, such as example (45), distinguish themselves from their English counterparts in that (i) the embedded clause is tensed and (ii) the "raised" object can also optionally appear with nominative subject marking as in (47).

(47) Yamada wa Tanaka ga   baka da to    omotteita. [= Kuno 1976:(17a)]
     TOP           NOM  fool is  COMP thought
     'Yamada thought Tanaka to be a fool.'

As this chapter examines some of the analyses put forward for this construction, it will become clear that there are several possible (and a few plausible) analyses. Example (45) might be an RtoO construction, as Kuno claims. It might be some sort of control structure (similar to the Austronesian cases), as suggested by Saito (1983). It might be neither, and instead involve some novel way of getting accusative Case onto the noun, as Sells (1990) proposes. In the discussion that follows, we will first examine Kuno's (1976) arguments for taking (45) to be an RtoO construction and his arguments against analyzing it as a case of Control. This will be followed by an assessment of the theory-internal problems that such evidence and the accompanying analysis present to GB theory and its ECM approach to such phenomena. Then, the merits of Saito's and Sells's alternative analyses will be examined.

Kuno (1976) is primarily concerned with RtoO, on account of the fact that RtoS is difficult to argue for in SOV languages. This is because, in contrast with English, a Japanese RtoS clause would involve an NP that changes neither its position nor its grammatical function. To see why this is so, consider example (48).

(48) Taroo ga   kuru   koto   ga   kimatteimasu.              [= Kuno 1976:(14)]
     NOM   come   NMNL   NOM   is.determined
  i. 'It is determined that Taro will come.'
  ii. 'It is Taro for whom it is determined that he will come.'

In (48), *Taroo* is the thematic subject of the embedded predicate *kuru* '(will) come.' If it remains in situ then the entire clause *Taroo ga kuru koto* is the subject of the matrix verb *kimatteimasu* 'is determined' (having the interpretation shown in (48i)), and has the structure given in (49a). If, on the other hand, *Taroo* is moved out of the embedded clause (with the interpretation in (48ii)), then the sentence will have the structure shown in (49b).

(49) a. [Taroo ga kuru koto] ga kimatteimasu
        'It is determined that Taro will come.'
     b. Taroo ga [kuru koto] ga kimatteimasu
        'It is Taro for whom it is determined that he will come.'

Example (48) is in fact ambiguous in interpretation between *Taroo* being a main clause subject and it being an embedded clause subject. As (49) shows, there is nothing other than the presence or absence of the focus interpretation to mark the application of RtoS. As a consequence, Kuno devotes the majority of his chapter to an analysis of RtoO clauses.

### Evidence for RtoO in (45)

There are five explicit arguments presented in Kuno (1976) for an RtoO analysis of (42). These arguments are similar in form to some of those presented in Postal (1974). The first of these arguments involves the observation that accusative Case can be assigned to the embedded subject of a complement. Accordingly, in (45), *Tanaka* is marked with accusative *o* and appears to be a surface object of the verb *omotteita*. This contrasts with (47), in which *Tanaka* is marked with nominative *ga* and appears to be a surface subject of the predicate *baka da* 'is a fool'.

Another familiar sort of argument concerns the placement of adverbs relative to the logical subject of the embedded clause. The relevant contrast is seen here in examples (50–1).

(50) Yamada wa Tanaka o, orokanimo, tensai da    [= Kuno 1976:(22d)]
       TOP          ACC stupidly    genius is
     to     omotteita.
     COMP thought
     'Stupidly, Yamada thought Tanaka to be a genius.'

(51) *Yamada wa Tanaka ga, orokanimo, tensai da    [= Kuno 1976:(21d)]
       TOP          NOM stupidly    genius is
     to     omotteita.
     COMP thought
     (Stupidly, Yamada thought Tanaka to be a genius.)

In (50), the adverb *orokanimo* 'stupidly' is intended to modify the matrix verb *omotteita* 'thought.' Its placement after the accusative-marked *Tanaka o* is taken to be an indication that this NP has been raised out of the embedded complement clause. In contrast, when the logical subject of the embedded clause has nominative Case *Tanaka ga*, as in (47), the main clause adverb cannot follow it. The ungrammaticality of (51) is thus taken by Kuno to be an indication that *Tanaka ga* has not raised out of the embedded clause.

Another similar diagnostic concerns the possibility of word order inversions achieved by the movement (i.e., scrambling) of the embedded clause subject in front of the matrix subject. As seen in (52), the purported raised object *Tanaka o* may be scrambled to the beginning of the sentence, in front of the topic *Yamada wa*. This is not possible when the nominal has nominative *ga* marking, as in (53).

(52) Tanaka o, Yamada wa tensai da to    omotteita. [= Kuno 1976:(29b)]
       ACC       TOP genius is COMP thought
     'Tanaka, Yamada thought him to be a genius.'

(53) *Tanaka ga, Yamada wa tensai da to    [= Kuno 1976:(28b)]
       NOM       TOP genius is COMP
     omotteita.
     thought
     (Tanaka, Yamada thought him to be a genius.)

Kuno attributes this contrast to the application of RtoO in (52), on the assumption that the dependents of a given clause may be reordered within that clause. Example (53) is argued to be ungrammatical as a result of the attempted reordering of an embedded clause subject to a position outside of its clause.

Quantifier scope interpretations also contribute evidence for RtoO in Japanese, according to Kuno. In (54), the existential quantifier expression *dareka* 'someone' precedes the universally quantified *minna* 'everyone,' and the preferred interpretation is that in (54i) wherein the existential has scope over the universal. Still, it is in fact possible to interpret the sentence with universal > existential scope, as in (54ii).

(54) Dareka ga minna o baka da to     [= Kuno 1976:(39)]
someone NOM everyone ACC fool is COMP
omotteiru.
thought
    i. 'There is someone who thinks that everyone is a fool.'
    ii. ?'For each person, there is someone who thinks that person is a fool.'

(55) Dareka ga minna ga baka da to     [= Kuno 1976:(37)]
someone NOM everyone NOM fool is COMP
omotteiru.
thought
    i. 'There is someone who thinks that everyone is a fool.'
    ii. #'For each person, there is someone who thinks that person is a fool.'

This contrasts with (55), in which the second (55ii) interpretation is unavailable. Kuno points out that the scope ambiguity of (54) is consistent with both *dareka ga* and *minna o* being clausemates. In (55), the unavailability of the second interpretation is attributed to *minna ga* being a dependent of the embedded clause.

The final argument presented in favor of an RtoO analysis for (45) concerns the distribution of pronominals and reflexives. In Japanese, reflexive antecedence is not clause-bound in the same way as English (although the antecedents do need to be subjects at some level). Accordingly, the reflexive pronoun *zibun* 'self' may take a subject antecedent in the same clause or one in a higher clause. This said, the binding of pronouns in Japanese is similar to that in English, in that personal pronouns cannot have an antecedent in the same clause. Thus, the distribution of *kare* 'him' and *zibun* 'self' in (56) supports an RtoO analysis for the logical subject of *tensai da* 'is a genius.'

(56) Yamada$_1$ wa zibun$_1$/*kare$_1$ o tensai da to     [= Kuno 1976:(44)]
       TOP self/him ACC genius is COMP
omotteita.
thought
'Yamada$_1$ thought himself$_1$/*him$_1$ to be a genius.'

(57) Yamada$_1$ wa zibun$_1$/?kare$_1$ ga tensai da to     [= Kuno 1976:(43)]
       TOP self/him NOM genius is COMP
omotteita.
thought
'Yamada$_1$ thought himself$_1$/*him$_1$ to be a genius.'

In (56), *kare* is ungrammatical with the indicated indexation, supporting Kuno's contention that it is in the same clause as its intended antecedent. In contrast, *kare* can have *Yamada* as its antecedent in (57) when it is marked with *ga*. Kuno takes this fact to be an indication that the pronoun remains within the embedded complement clause.

### *Evidence against taking (45) to be Control*

Kuno notes that it is difficult, in general, to argue against a control (Equi-NP) analysis of sentences such as *I expect Mary to come*. And arguments that work for English have no parallel in Japanese. Thus, Kuno is forced to provide arguments against a control analysis of (45) that are particular to the grammar of Japanese.

One of the most obvious differences concerns the morphological marking of the raised nominal in an RtoO construction in contrast with that of the controller in an object control clause. Compare (45) and (46) above. As Kuno points out, the controller in a prototypical object control clause is marked with *ni*, and not accusative *o*.

Alongside the previous morphological argument, Kuno presents a semantic argument. He notes first of all that object controllers in Japanese must be sentient. In this regard, he observes the contrast in (58) and (59).

(58) Yamada wa Tanaka ni sore o site-kureru      [= Kuno 1976:(63a)]
     TOP          DAT      that ACC do-receive
     koto o    kitaisiteiru.
     NMNL ACC is.expecting
     'Yamada is expecting of Tanaka that he will do that.'

(59) *Yamada wa sono hon ni yoku ureru koto      [= Kuno 1976:(64a)]
      TOP      that book DAT well sell    NMNL
      o    kitaisiteiru.
      ACC is.expecting
      (Yamada is expecting of that book that it will sell well.)

In (58), *Tanaka* is a direct argument of the matrix verb *kitaisiteiru* 'is.expecting,' which controls the subject of *sore o site-kureru* 'will do that.' Example (59) shows what happens when the controller is non-sentient. Here *sono hon* 'that book' would be the controller, but as a non-sentient nominal cannot appear in this construction. These facts contrast with (60).

(60) Yamada wa sono hon o    tumaranai to      [= Kuno 1976:(64b)]
     TOP      that book ACC boring     COMP
     omotta.
     thought
     'Yamada thought that book to be boring.'

Here, the same nominal that could not serve as an object controller can indeed appear as the raised object in an RtoO clause. On the basis of this contrast, Kuno argues that (60) cannot be a control construction.

Another difference between object control and the purported RtoO construction concerns linear order possibilities. As shown in (61), compared with (58), the clausal complement of a control clause may precede the controller.

(61) Yamada wa sore o site-kureru koto o     [= Kuno 1976:(65a)]
       TOP that ACC do-receive NMNL ACC
      Tanaka ni kitaisiteiru.
       DAT is.expecting
      'Yamada is expecting of Tanaka that he will do that.'

Here, the controller *Tanaka ni* occupies a position between the clausal object *sore o site-kureru koto o* and the verb *kitaisiteiru*. This inversion of elements is not possible in clauses that Kuno has analyzed as RtoO constructions. Observe (62).

(62) *Yamada wa baka da to     Tanaka o     omotteita.     [= Kuno 1976:(66)]
       TOP fool is COMP            ACC thought
     (Yamada thought Tanaka to be a fool.)

In (62), *Tanaka o* intervenes between the complement clause *baka da to* and the verb *omotteita*, and the sentence is rendered ungrammatical. This difference in the linear distribution of the key constituents is presented as an argument against treating (45) as a control construction.

Kuno next points to the fact that the controlled pronoun in a control construction may be optionally overt. In this regard compare (46), repeated from above, with (63).

(46) Yamada wa Tanaka ni sore o suru koto o     [= Kuno 1976:(63b)]
       TOP           DAT that ACC do NMNL ACC
      meizita.
      ordered
      'Yamada ordered Tanaka to do that.'

(63) ?Yamada wa Tanaka$_1$ ni kare$_1$ ga sore o     [= Kuno 1976:(67b)]
       TOP           DAT he NOM that ACC
      suru koto o meizita.
      do NMNL ACC ordered
      'Yamada ordered Tanaka$_1$ that he$_1$ do that.'

In (63), which is regarded as slightly marginal but not ill-formed, the subject of the embedded clause has an overt subject *kare* 'he' that is coindexed with the matrix controller *Tanaka*. In this regard, examples such as (63) bear some resemblance to the Madurese examples (24–6) presented in section 1 of this chapter. In contrast with the attested control constructions, RtoO clauses such as (45) do not permit a resumptive subject pronoun in the embedded complement clause. Example (64) here is illustrative.

(64) *Yamada wa Tanaka₁ o    kare₁ ga  baka da to      [= Kuno 1976:(68)]
     TOP            ACC he    NOM fool is COMP
     omotteita.
     thought
     'Yamada thought of Tanaka that he is a fool.'

The insertion of *kare ga* after *Tanaka o* in (64) renders the sentence completely unacceptable, supporting Kuno's claim that it cannot be analyzed as a control construction.

In his last set of arguments, Kuno presents evidence from the unusual distribution of certain nominal adjectives (such as *syoojiki* 'honest(y)' and *kiyoo* 'adroit(ness)') and certain fossilized verbal expressions (such as *nigeru* meaning 'to run away'). Since the structure of both arguments is parallel, we will only present here the data representing the nominal adjectives. Nominal adjectives, such as *sizuka* 'quiet,' differ from regular adjectives in that they do not inflect and are supported in a predicate phrase with the copula verb *da* 'be' just as predicate nominals are. Accordingly, the syntax of the expression *sizuka da* 'is quiet' resembles that of *hon da* 'is a book' more than it does that of *aka-i* 'is red.' Kuno points out that some nominal adjectives can appear in predicate phrases as well as in thematic subject or object positions (*sizuka* is not one of these, being restricted to predicate phrases). Among those predicate adjectives that can appear in thematic argument (subject, object) positions, there are some (such as *hutyuui* 'careless(ness)') that can be either the subject or the object of a clause. Some others, such as *syoojiki* 'honest(y)' and *kiyoo* 'adroit(ness),' can occur as thematic subjects but not as thematic objects (in simple clauses). This fact is illustrated in (65).

(65) a. Syoojiki wa bitoku desu ka?
        honesty TOP virtue is   QUE
        'Is honesty a virtue?'
     b. *Syoojiki o   omonzimasu ka?
        honesty ACC treasure     QUE
        (Do [you] treasure honesty?)

It is this last group that Kuno is concerned with, because it turns out that members of this class of nominal adjectives can in fact appear with accusative Case in the RtoO construction. Example (66) illustrates.

(66) Yamada wa syoojiki ga/o    bitoku da to     kangaeteita
     TOP honesty NOM/ACC virtue is  COMP was.thinking
     'Yamada was thinking that honesty is a virtue.'

While the possibility of *ga* marking on *syoojiki* and *kiyoo* is expected in (66), the *o* marking is anomalous. One might explain, as Kuno does, that these nominal adjectives must be subjects underlyingly and that they can raise into a derived object position (and thereby get accusative Case in the RtoO construction). However, such an explanation would be unavailable if the nominal adjective were a matrix underlying object controller.

## The exceptional properties of Japanese RtoO constructions

As comprehensive as his arguments are, Kuno also points out a number of properties of Japanese RtoO constructions, which distinguish them from their English "counterparts" and which have left the door open for others to question his RtoO analysis. The three potential problems for the RtoO analysis involve: (i) the morphological attributes of the embedded clause; (ii) the distribution of "NP *no koto*" phrases, and (iii) the interaction of RtoO and passive.

It should already be obvious from the data presented thus far that Japanese RtoO constructions differ in one very salient way from English RtoO clauses. In English, the alternation of raised and non-raised nominals correlates with the presence or absence of tense, i.e., finiteness. That is, raising is only possible when the complement clause is infinitival, as in (67).

(67) a. Mark believes him/*he to be late.
     b. Mark believes he/*him is late.

In Japanese, as we have seen, the nominative/accusative alternation of the candidate for raising is essentially optional. Further, the complement clauses in question are all arguably finite. They have an overt complementizer *to*, and as Kuno points out, the embedded clause predicate can have tense, mood, or any number of sentence-final particles. Accordingly, the *da* 'be' in an RtoO clause can be augmented or replaced in any of the following ways: *da zo* 'be + ASSERTIVE'; *da ka* 'be + QUESTION'; *daroo* 'would be'; *hazuganai* 'could not be'; and (marginally) *datta* 'was.'

Now Kuno, taking as he does a Postal-like rule-oriented approach to grammar, should not be overly concerned about this fact. In fact, in a rule-based approach to grammar it might indeed be simpler to have a completely optional rule of RtoO, triggered by certain verbs, as in Japanese, than an optional RtoO rule that further requires the complement clause to be infinitival, as in English. However, for a Chomskyan principles-based approach the Japanese facts pose a dilemma. Under a Case-motivated approach to movement, there is no motivation for RtoO out of the complement clause, since the clause is finite and nominative Case is always available for the embedded subject. If *syoojiki* 'honesty' in (66) can get nominative Case in the lower clause (and it can), what would trigger it to move into the higher clause to get accusative Case (which it also can have)? An ECM solution fares no better. Consider a plausible (partial) constituent structure representation for (66), shown here in (68).

(68) Yamada wa [$_{CP}$[$_{IP}$syoojiki bitoku da] to] kangaeteita

The appearance of the complementizer *to* suggests that the complement of the verb *kangaeteita* 'thought' is a CP. Also, since the embedded clause is finite and can have a nominative subject, it is reasonable to assume that *to* is attached to a finite IP. Under these conditions, it is difficult to imagine what might allow *kangaeteita* to Case mark *syoojiki*. CP (i.e., S') deletion is implausible, given that the head of CP is overt. CP "transparency" is similarly problematic, since the finite head of IP presumably governs *syoojiki*. Hermon's (1984) approach to similarly problematic constructions in Quechua (as discussed in chapter 9, section 4) might have a place here. Recall that Hermon proposes that, under certain circumstances, government by a lexical governor (the higher verb *kangaeteita* in this case) would supercede government by a non-lexical governor (the embedded INFL). However, Hermon also assumed (for Quechua) that S' (CP) deletion would open the way to lexical government from outside the embedded clause. In Japanese, this solution is complicated by the fact that an overt complementizer *to* remains in the clause, suggesting that CP deletion cannot have taken place.

Given this theoretical dilemma, it is not surprising that linguists' attention has been drawn to the two other peculiar puzzles presented in Kuno's article (the distribution of "NP *no koto*" phrases in RtoO clauses, and the interaction of RtoO and passive), and that they have moved from these toward analyses of the construction that involve neither RtoO nor ECM.

We will first examine the facts that Kuno presents, and then move on to discuss two alternative analyses (Marantz 1983 and Saito 1983; Sells 1990) that are conceptually linked to them. The distribution of "NP *no koto*" phrases is rather restricted; *Tanaka no koto* 'Tanaka's matter' can appear optionally in place of *Tanaka* when it is the object of a verb of "feeling, thinking, or saying" (Kuno 1976:41). Thus, the alternation in (69) is observed.

(69)  Yamada wa  Tanaka (no  koto)  o    nikundeiru.    [= Kuno 1976:(92)]
      TOP           GEN matter ACC hates
      'Yamada hates Tanaka.'

The *no koto* alternation is not available in (70), even though *siranai* 'not know' is a verb which would license it. This is because *musuko* is not the object of this verb, but rather the subject of its object complement clause.

(70)  Yamada wa  musuko (*no  koto)  ga    baka na       [= Kuno 1976:(95)]
      TOP son           GEN matter NOM fool is
      koto  o    siranai.
      NMNL ACC not.know
      'Yamada didn't know that his son is a fool.'

In RtoO clauses, though, the embedded subject can indeed have *no koto* when it is accusative, but not when it is nominative. This contrast (noted by Masayoshi Shibatani [p.c. to Susumu Kuno], 1972) is given in (71).

(71)  a. *Yamada wa  musuko no  koto  ga    baka        [= Kuno 1976:(97a)]
            TOP son        GEN matter NOM fool
         da    to   omotteita.
         is    COMP thought
         'Yamada thought his son was a fool.'

    b. Yamada wa musuko no koto o baka    [= Kuno 1976:(97b)]
        TOP son    GEN matter ACC fool
      da to    omotteita.
      is COMP thought
      'Yamada thought his son was a fool.'

In (71a), *musuko no koto ga* is ungrammatical, while in (71b), *musuko no koto o* is fine. Given that *musuko no koto* could not have been base generated in the lower clause, Kuno is forced to say that *no koto* is added after the application of RtoO (a conjecture which would have fared well in 1976, but which is untenable under current theoretical assumptions). If anything, one would have to wonder whether *musuko no koto* is not base generated as the object of *omotteita* 'thought.' But if that were true, then (71b) is not an instance of Raising.

The interaction of passive and Raising, as discussed in Kuno (1976), raises further questions regarding the RtoO analysis. However, where the *no koto* facts suggest that a purportedly raised RtoO nominal might be a base-generated matrix object, the passive facts seem to suggest that such a nominal might not be raised at all (even at the surface). Before presenting the key evidence, it must be understood that "passive" is a multifaceted phenomenon in Japanese. In addition to constructions that are analogous in meaning and form to passives in English, Japanese also has a construction commonly referred to as an "adversative passive". Examples of these are given in (72).

(72) a. Sono biru wa Haruki-san ni       [= Dubinsky 1997:(21)]
     that bldg. TOP          DAT
     sekkei-sareta.
     design-was.done
     'That building was designed by Mr Haruki.'
   b. Tanaka wa basu ni doro o hanerareta.    [= Dubinsky 1997:(5)]
        TOP bus DAT mud ACC was.splashed
     'Tanaka was splashed mud by the bus.'
   c. Watasi wa ame ni hurareta.       [= Dubinsky 1997:(6)]
     I     TOP rain DAT was.fallen
     'I was fallen by rain.'

Example (72a) represents what is referred to as a "pure" or "direct" passive. In these, the surface subject is the underlying object of the transitive verbal base, the promoted object may be inanimate, and the sentence is logically equivalent to its active counterpart. In "adversative" passive, (72b) and (72c), the surface subject need not be the underlying object of the verb; in (72b) the verb *haneru* 'splash' still has its object *doro* 'mud' and in (72c) the verb *huru* 'fall/precipitate' is not even transitive. Adversative passive subjects must also be sentient. And, finally, adversative passive clauses carry the sense that the subject of the sentence was adversely affected by the event in question. Accordingly, (72c) actually means something like 'I was adversely affected by it having rained,' and does not entail that I actually got wet. Analyses of adversative passives (e.g., Akatsuka-McCawley 1972; Dubinsky 1997) typically involve an affixal predicate *(r)are* that introduces its own affected argument, as shown here in (73).

(73) [watasi [ame huru] rare ]  (cf. (72c) above)
     I      rain fall  be.affected

Kuno demonstrates that thinking and feeling verbs (of the RtoO variety) can be passivized as in example (74).

(74) Yamada ga   Tanaka o    korosita to           [= Kuno 1976:(106a)]
       NOM         ACC killed   COMP
     sinzirareteiru.
     is.believed
     'It is believed that Yamada killed Tanaka.'

Kuno points out that the "pure" passive equivalent of (60) is ungrammatical, as shown here in example (75).[7]

(75) *Sono hon  wa  Yamada ni   tumaranai to      omowareta.
     that book TOP         DAT boring    COMP was.thought
     'That book was thought by Yamada to be boring.'

Now alongside ungrammatical passives such as (75), one finds grammatical constructions such as (76) which appear to be passives of RtoO sentences.

(76) Tanaka wa  Yamada ni   baka da to           [= Kuno 1976:(101b)]
          TOP         DAT fool  is  COMP
     omow-areta.
     thought-affected
     'To Tanaka's chagrin, Yamada thought that he (Tanaka) was a fool.'

However, as Kuno explains, sentences such as (76) are demonstrably adversative passives. Thus, according to the analysis given for these above, *Tanaka* is introduced as an argument of *(r)are* and is coindexed with a null pronominal subject of the complement clause *baka da* 'is a fool.' Proof that there is no pure passive of RtoO nominals rests on the fact that sentences such as (73) must have sentient subjects and must always involve an adversative interpretation. Thus, (75), in contrast with (76), could only be a "direct" passive and not an "adversative" passive. The ungrammaticality of (75), then, contrasts with the English facts in (77).

(77) a. Yamada believes that book to be boring.
      b. That book is believed by Yamada to be boring.

The ability of an RtoO nominal (*that book* in (77a)) to undergo passivization is one of the key diagnostics brought to bear in proving that it has raised into a matrix object position (or that it is governed and Case marked by the matrix verb in an ECM analysis). Thus, the ungrammaticality of (75) as a passive of

(60) calls into question the notion that the purported RtoO nominals in Japanese are ever raised, and suggests that they do not have the same syntactic status as their English counterparts.

## Alternative analyses

The overt CP structure in Japanese RtoO constructions, combined with the fact that the embedded clauses are finite, presented overwhelming difficulties for any GB-based RtoO or ECM account of these constructions. This led to two distinct types of alternative proposals during the 1980s: one in which the accusative NP is claimed to be an underlying direct object in the base, and one in which the accusative Case on the RtoO nominal is claimed to arise from within the complement clause itself. We will examine both of these approaches in turn.

### Marantz (1983) and Saito (1983)

Recall from the above discussion that the distribution of *no koto* expressions (typified in example (71)) raises the possibility that (some) purported RtoO clauses may involve a surface direct object that is base generated in its higher position and has not undergone syntactic movement. While not explicitly referring to these data as an argument, Marantz suggests that Japanese has what he terms "unmarked raising." Agreeing with Kuno that the accusative nominal in RtoO is a matrix object, he suggests that the peculiarities of the "Japanese raising constructions are actually to be expected, given the correct theory of syntax" (Marantz 1983:31). Although the details of his proposal are at times unclear (he does not, for instance, provide a derivation for a simple RtoO clause), parts of Marantz's proposal bear similarities to Bach's (1977) suggestions.

In Marantz's view, there appear to be two ways in which an "NP *o* S" configuration can arise. One way is for the complement S to be preceded by an NP object of the matrix verb (one which is predicated by and which gets its thematic role from the adjacent S), as shown here in (78), where Marantz's analysis is inferred from the text.

(78)

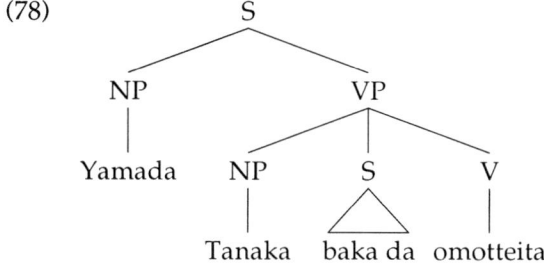

Yamada wa Tanaka o baka da to omotteita               [= (45)]

Here, *Tanaka* gets accusative Case from *omotteita*, but receives a semantic role from the embedded S.[8] Marantz points to the fact that there are other constructions in which a sentence predicates a nominal adjoined to its left. Non-argument focus constructions, as in (79), exemplify this.

(79) [$_S$John ga [$_S$atama ga warui]]
       NOM      head  NOM is.bad
    'It is John, who is stupid [lit.: whose head is bad]'

Marantz suggests that some RtoO clauses involve the embedding of focus structures into clauses headed by raising verbs, as in (80).

(80) Mary wa [$_S$John (no koto) o            [= Marantz 1983:(31a)]
       NOM         GEN matter ACC
    [$_S$doosiyoomonaku atama ga warui]] to omotteiru
      hopelessly       head  NOM is.bad  COMP thinks
    'Mary thinks that, as for John, he is hopelessly stupid.'

In this construction, it is presumed that *John (no koto)* is governed from outside and assigned Case by the matrix verb *omotteiru*.

The structures in (78) and (80), while similar in some respects, have a very distinct status in the GB theory. In (80), we see an approach to ECM which is similar, if not identical, to Massam's (1985) "SPEC2" analysis (discussed in chapter 9). In this regard, (80) falls into a general class of "movement to 'edge'" approaches to such constructions. The derivation in (78), to the extent that it accurately represents Marantz's thinking, is more problematic for the GB theory. In fact, the notion of having a syntactic (or functional) direct object be semantically linked to a lower clause is the hallmark of theories (such as Lexical Functional Grammar) which directly provide for such "structure sharing."

However, in the GB model, Marantz's proposal violates the θ-criterion limitation on the Projection Principle. Recall (from chapter 8) that the theory presented in Chomsky (1981, 1982) stipulates that all VP complement positions are projected from the lexicon and further that all such complement positions must be θ-positions. This means that the VP-internal NP in (78) must be base generated and subcategorized for by the verb, and assigned a θ-role by that verb. It would appear, with regard to (78), that Marantz's analysis does not respect this last requirement.

Without addressing the Projection Principle/θ-criterion issue explicitly, Saito's (1983) commentary on Marantz's paper presents a hypothetical alternative that would in fact rescue the construction from its clash with GB theory. In particular, he questions the assumption that the matrix accusative "RtoO" receives its θ-role from the embedded predicate, and offers example (81) as evidence.

(81) Mary wa John$_1$ no koto o [kurasu no       [= Saito 1983:(30)]
       NOM       GEN matter ACC class   GEN
    nakade kare$_1$ ga itiban baka da to] omotteiru
    within  he    NOM most fool is COMP thinks
    'Mary thinks of John that he is the most stupid in his class.'

In (81), the semantic subject of the embedded clause is realized as a resumptive pronoun *kare ga* 'he,' which is coindexed with the matrix nominal *John*.[9] Saito's suggestion, only hinted at in his paper, is that RtoO constructions might actually involve a null pronominal in the embedded clause. Under such an account, neither NP movement nor structure sharing would be needed to account for the facts, and the matrix object position would be projected as a semantically selected complement of the matrix verb. However, Saito does not address the fact that resumptive pronouns are generally ungrammatical in RtoO constructions, as Kuno (1976) shows (see example (64) above).

## Sells (1990)

Sells 1990 presents one of the more intriguing alternatives to Kuno's RtoO analysis, which involves an account in which the accusative nominal gets Case from the embedded predicate (rather than from the matrix verb) and is then scrambled out of the lower clause. In this regard, Sells's non-movement account is an inversion of Saito's suggestion, but (as will become clear) it is not an ECM-type analysis in the traditional GB sense.

Sells initially focuses on three properties of the Japanese RtoO construction: (i) the complement clause is not an infinitival; (ii) the presumed derived object nominal is unable to undergo simple passivization (differing from Marantz 1983 on this point); and (iii) Japanese has a double object constraint. As pointed out above, it is problematic that Japanese RtoO constructions have a tensed clause in which the subject can readily get nominative Case. The fact that the derived nominal cannot undergo passive would also weigh against a derived object RtoO analysis of (45). Further, Sells points out, Japanese has a prohibition on two objects in the same clause. This is traditionally known as the "double *o* constraint" (S. L. Harada 1973), which rules out two nominals having accusative Case marking as in (82).

(82) John ga    Mary ni/*o    hon o    yomaseta.          [= Sells 1990:(3)]
     NOM          DAT/ACC  book ACC made.read
    'John made/let Mary read the book.'

Example (82) can be rescued by having the causee nominal *Mary* marked with dative (*ni*), as shown. Without delving deeply into the details, Sells goes on to point out (on the basis of observations in Poser 1983) that the "double *o* constraint" is really a constraint on having two direct objects in a single transitive clause. Then, after showing that complement clauses are indeed direct objects, he claims that the accusative nominal in the Japanese RtoO construction cannot be a derived object, since that would violate the double object prohibition.

Sells makes the following proposal: the accusative nominal in the RtoO construction gets its accusative Case in the embedded clause, and it undergoes (optional) scrambling out of that clause. In support of this analysis, Sells must show (i) that scrambling of these is indeed possible, and (ii) how the "subject" of the embedded clause might wind up with accusative Case. He begins by showing that a direct object may be scrambled out of an embedded object phrase, presenting the data in (83) as evidence of this.

(83) [Kaiketu no hookoo o]₁ sono hookokusyo ga        [= Sells 1990:(17)]
　　　solution GEN direction ACC this  report         NOM
　　　Mary ni [_NP t₁ sisa]  o    siteiru
　　　　　DAT       suggest ACC does
　　　'It is the direction of the solution that this report suggests to Mary.'

In (83), the fronted nominal *kaiketu no hookoo* 'the direction of the solution' is the object of the predicate nominal *sisa* 'suggestion' (and *sisa* is itself an object of the light verb *siteiru* 'does').

Sells goes on to point out that the distribution of accusative RtoO nominals is affected by the choice of embedded predicate. He notes that RtoO complement clauses are restricted to those headed by predicate nominals (such as *baka* 'fool' and *hannin* 'culprit') and that these predicate nominals are arguably unaccusative (that is, their single argument is underlyingly a direct object). If the embedded predicates are indeed unaccusative and their nominal arguments are initially direct objects, one might think of the accusative Case option in (84) as being an instance of "semantic" Case marking.

(84) Yamada wa Tanaka ga/o   baka da to    omotteita.
　　　　　　TOP        NOM/ACC fool is COMP thought
　　　'Yamada thought Tanaka to be a fool.'

That is, *Tanaka* might show up with accusative Case in (84) if it were base generated as the semantic theme and syntactic direct object of *baka*, and did not surface as a subject.

In support of this conjecture, Sells provides a number of examples of nominals expressing "semantic" Case when they are in an embedded clause. In (85b), for instance, we find a Case alternation involving nominative *ga* and source *kara*.

(85) a. Taroo ga/*kara  tegami o   dasu.             [= Sells 1990:(24)]
　　　　　NOM/from    letter  ACC will.send
　　　　'Taroo will send a letter.'
　　 b. [Taroo ga/kara  tegami o   dasu]   koto wa yoku nai
　　　　　　NOM/from   letter  ACC will.send fact TOP good is.not
　　　　'The fact that Taroo will send a letter is not good.'

Note that "semantic" Case *kara* is not an option for the subject of a matrix clause, as (85a) illustrates. These facts are in accord with Shibatani's (1978) observation that "an independent sentence [i.e., a matrix clause] in Japanese requires at least one nominative NP."[10]

According to Sells, once the embedded nominal in (84) has been assigned accusative Case, it is free to scramble out of the embedded clause, just as other objects may do (cf. (83)). In this regard, Sells's analysis can claim to account for many of the diagnostics presented in Kuno (1976) that show the accusative RtoO nominal as being outside of the embedded clause. On his account, the reason that nominative nominals may not appear outside of the embedded clause is due to the simple fact that embedded subjects are generally not allowed to undergo scrambling. Since the accusative nominal gets out of the embedded clause via scrambling (an A′-movement operation), the failure of this nominal to undergo simple passive is accounted for under the familiar assumption that movement to A′-positions cannot be followed by A-movement (which passive is assumed to be).

Sells's account also solves one otherwise curious constraint on the ordering of the accusative nominal and the embedded clause in RtoO constructions. As Kuno pointed out (see (52)), it is possible for the accusative RtoO nominal to be scrambled away from the embedded clause. At the same time, the embedded clause itself may not appear in front of the RtoO nominal (see (62)). Consider the structures for these sentences under Sells's account, given in (86).

(86) a. [Tanaka o]$_1$ Yamada wa [t$_1$ tensai da to]   [= Sells 1990:(52)]
         ACC             TOP       genius is COMP
      omotteita
      thought
      'Tanaka, Yamada thought him to be a genius.'
    b. *Yamada wa [t$_1$ baka da to ]$_2$ [Tanaka o]$_1$ t$_2$   [= Sells 1990:(62)]
         TOP        fool is COMP            ACC
      omotteita
      thought
      (Yamada thought Tanaka to be a fool.)

In (86a), *Tanaka* has been scrambled out of the lower clause, leaving an A′-trace. In (86b), the same scrambling of the object has taken place, followed by scrambling of the clause itself away from the verb. Scrambling of the clause is, in principle, allowed (as we saw with control constructions in (61) above). However, in this instance, the second scrambling operation raises the trace of *Tanaka* into a position where it is no longer c-commanded by its antecedent, resulting in a violation on the proper binding condition on traces (see Saito 1985). At the same time, Sells's analysis fails to account for (56), repeated here.

(56) Yamada$_1$ wa zibun$_1$/*kare$_1$ o tensai da to   [= Kuno 1976:(44)]
        TOP self/him           ACC genius is COMP
     omotteita.
     thought
     'Yamada$_1$ thought himself$_1$/*him$_1$ to be a genius.'

Recall that in the RtoO analysis of (56), *kare* is ungrammatical because a pronoun cannot be bound by an antecedent in the same clause. Example (56) with *kare* violates condition B of the binding theory. However, Sells claims that the accusative nominal gets accusative "semantic" Case in the lower clause and **optionally** scrambles out of the complement clause. If it is possible for it to stay in situ, then (56) with *kare* should be grammatical under Sells's account.

## 4 Conclusion

The Madurese and Cebuano constructions and the Japanese construction point to the difficulties that can arise in trying to formulate the most appropriate analysis for a given set of data. While on the surface the data from these languages appear to have all the earmarks of Raising, closer examination reveals the insufficiency of applying the familiar raising (or ECM) analysis in these cases. As demonstrated throughout this book, changes in theory can bring a new face to familiar data, which makes the data relevant for analysis over many decades. By the same token, the same structures in particular languages can be the subject of analysis over many decades not because of theoretical shifts but because of the subtlety of the data themselves. Therefore, one can reasonably ask in a number of instances: are these all really raising constructions or is a closer look necessary? As we see in the next two chapters, both sides of this coin are still relevant, as another theoretical shift changes the face of the analysis of RtoO, and the debate about the most appropriate analysis of the data (and the Japanese data in particular) continues up to the present.

### Notes

1 The following abbreviations are used in the morphemic glosses of the non-English data in this chapter: ACC = accusative, AGI = *agi*, AV = actor voice, COMP = complementizer, CS = causative, DAT = dative, DEF = definite, DV = dative voice, E = *e*, FUT = future, GEN = genitive, LV = locative voice, IRR = irrealis, NMNL = nominalization, NOM = nominative, OV = object voice, PASS = passive, PERF = perfective, RECIP = reciprocal, RED = reduplication, TOP = topic.
2 The spelling in the Indonesian and Javanese examples has been changed from the original to conform to current spelling practices.
3 There is speaker variability with respect to the grammaticality of (11). As shown shortly, all speakers will accept the sentence with a pronoun coreferential with *Hasan* in the embedded object position.
4 In recent work, Kotzoglou (2002) argues that the Greek construction be given the same analysis argued for here for Madurese.
5 There is some speaker variation regarding the choice of preposition with particular predicates. However, all predicates allow the NP to occur as a prepositional object.
6 *Prolepsis* refers to the anticipation of some not yet existent state being true. The matrix object is thus a "proleptic" object inasmuch as it anticipates the existence of the element in the embedded clause.
7 The facts in (71–3) are complicated by the fact that sentences like (71) "become ungrammatical if their matrix predicates represent non-generic actions" (Kuno 1976:47). Accordingly, with the overt agentive phrase *Hanako ni* and a simple past tense verb *sinzirareta*, (i) is ungrammatical.

(i) *Yamada ga Tanaka o korosita to Hanako ni [= Kuno 1976:(108a)]
   NOM      ACC    killed  COMP         DAT
   sinzirareta.
   was.believed
   (It is believed by Hanako that Yamada killed Tanaka.)

At the same time, if the agent phrase is removed from (75) and the matrix verb is present progressive (i.e., *omowareteiru*), the resulting sentence is grammatical.

(ii) Sono hon wa tumaranai to omowareteiru.
 that book TOP boring COMP is.thought
 'That book is thought to be boring.'

With regard to these, Kuno presents arguments to show that (ii) is not derived by passiving an RtoO object. Rather, he suggests, (ii) involves passivization of the entire embedded clause *sono hon ga tumaranai* 'that book is boring,' followed by the Topicalization of *sono hon*. The discussion he presents (Kuno 1976:44–9) is far too elaborate to introduce here.

8 In making his case, Marantz takes a different view from that of Kuno on the passivization facts. According to Marantz, passivization of an "RtoO" nominal is possible, taking data such as example (ii) in note 7 to be an example of such. He would then rule out cases such as (75) on the grounds that "the Japanese passive affix demands a certain generic interpretation of verbs taking modifier and propositional arguments" (Marantz 1983:42).

9 It is rather significant, we believe, that the RtoO construction which allows a resumptive pronoun is one involving a *no koto* phrase, which itself cannot appear as a nominative subject of the embedded clause. This leads to the reasonable conjecture that the *no koto* construction is distinct from the RtoO construction, and it is the former alone that does not involve Raising, leaving the latter still open to a raising analysis.

10 Shibatani's observation has often been misinterpreted to mean that all finite clauses must have a nominative NP (with this reason, or some version of it, given as explanation for the ungrammatical NP *ni* NP *o* V case-marking pattern in potential constructions). For further discussion of this, see Dubinsky (1992:889–92).

# UNIT IV

# THE MINIMALIST PROGRAM

## INTRODUCTION: NEO-RAISING, NEO-ECM, AND THE RAISING/CONTROL DISTINCTION

In the early 1990s, Chomskyan theory took a turn that might be considered rather radical, when contrasted with the GB/Principles and Parameters (P&P) context in which it arose. After solidifying a model of grammar that views nearly all important principles and parameters as applying at various levels of representation (DS, SS, LF, and PF), Chomsky determined the optimal theory of grammar to be one in which no intermediate levels of representation would be relevant. In this Minimalist Program, there is a lexicon out of which items are selected, there are generalized operations for assembling these into structures, and there are levels (two to be precise) where a representation must interface with phonetic principles, so that the sentence can be pronounced, and with interpretive principles, so that it may be understood. Minimalism, in addition to explicitly doing away with the DS and SS levels of representation, also reduced the distinctions between lexical and syntactic information in part by adopting the assumption that structurally relevant features have meaning (are interpretable). This issue, which is still not completely resolved, led back to analyses that bear more than a passing resemblance to structures proposed by the Generative Semanticists of the 1970s. This radical reformulation of syntactic theory in the Minimalist Program is described in chapter 11.

One unintended outcome of the shift from GB to Minimalism is that a previously discarded analysis of RtoO, the movement account of Postal (1974), is once again relevant and theoretically attractive. Among the first to propose the revived movement analysis were Lasnik and Saito in their presentation at the 1990 meeting of the Chicago Linguistic Society (Lasnik & Saito 1991), which is included in its entirety in chapter 12. This proposal is examined there along with a number of other approaches to raising constructions which have developed since.

Chapter 13 examines the shifting division between the syntactic and semantic accounts of raising and control phenomena. Some of this debate typifies a more general tendency in linguistic theory to argue over the relative domain of the particular subfields of syntax and semantics (and pragmatics). Attempts to provide a unified syntactic treatment for both raising and control, and relegate the differences to lexico-semantic distinctions, are compared with the more standard approaches which deem the two constructions to be syntactically distinct.

# CHAPTER 11

# FUNCTIONAL PROJECTIONS AND THE RISE OF THE MINIMALIST PROGRAM

Two major subjects must be addressed in order to provide an understanding of the Minimalist Program (MP), of its relationship to its GB antecedents, and of the theoretical developments that led to a reconsideration of the raising analysis of RtoO constructions (the last to be explored fully in chapter 12). The first of these is the evolution of the phrase structure (PS) component of the grammar, beginning with the pre-MP development of an X-bar theoretic model of functional projections in the (Chomsky 1986a) *Barriers* model and the VP-internal subject hypothesis. The second is understanding the MP model through an examination of the ways in which it is different from and similar to the Chomskyan models that precede it.

## 1  The evolution of phrase structure from GB to MP

The nature of the phrase structure (PS) component of the grammar evolved considerably during the mid-1980s through the early 1990s. One marked development, seen in section 5 of chapter 9, was the replacement of S with IP and S′ with CP (Chomsky 1986a:2–4). The intent and immediate result of this innovation was to extend the familiar X-bar system of phrase structure to "non-lexical categories." Clausal Phrase Structure, previously represented as in (1a), was now articulated as in (1b).

(1)  a.

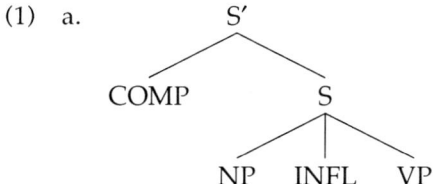

b.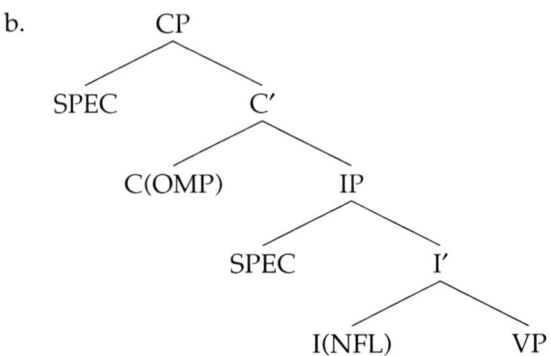

In (1b), the new nodes CP and IP are each endocentric (i.e., have a head), in contrast with the S' and S nodes of the old system. Second, binary branching is maintained where possible in this system, eliminating the ternary branching NP-INFL-VP structure of S, which had previously been assumed to be "near optimal" (Chomsky 1981:71). Further, there is a regular head-complement and head-specifier configuration. The phrasal complement of each head (C and I) is a sister of the head; and the specifier of each projection is the daughter of its XP and a sister to X'. In this system, the configurational position of subjects (in Spec,IP) and moved *wh*-elements (in Spec,CP) is made parallel. Similar innovations in the articulation of NP and DP (determiner phrase) structure were introduced around this time in Abney (1987).

While these innovations enhanced the regularity of the PS system and solved some puzzles, they also engendered new problems. For instance, under the old S'-S model, the ungrammaticality of (2) was accommodated by the Doubly Filled Comp Filter.

(2) *This is the reason why that I shouldn't have to serve.

Under that account, both *why* and *that* competed for space under the single COMP node in (1a). In the (1b) model, though, *why* would move to Spec,CP and *that* would be inserted under the now distinct node C, and no node would be "doubly filled" any longer. While this does indeed necessitate a new solution to the problem of "Doubly Filled Comp" violations, the new model did have the obvious advantage of separating the distribution of heads and phrases. Thus, Spec,CP is a position into which phrasal categories might be inserted, while C (head of CP) is a position reserved for phrasal heads. A full discussion of the advantages and disadvantages of these innovations is quite beyond the scope of this chapter, but it is clear from the wide-spread adoption of this system that it was considered attractive to many syntacticians at the time of its introduction.

## *The deconstruction of "subject"*

Establishing, as Chomsky did in 1986, a structurally analogous X-bar theoretic model for the phrasal projections of lexical categories and functional categories had the effect of more clearly distinguishing between the grammatical function SUBJECT and other (presumably VP-internal) argument positions. It also set the stage for what McCloskey (1997) terms the "deconstruction" of the notion of a unitary subject.

In the literature of the mid-1980s, it is clear that NP-of-S (or Spec,IP) is considered at once to be both a thematic position (the target for the assignment of subject thematic roles) and a position structurally determined by the grammar. The latter position is taken by Chomsky himself (1982), when he offers an "extension" to the Projection Principle. Recall from chapter 8 that the Projection Principle requires NP positions to be projected from the lexicon (i.e., that they be argument positions). It is this principle, in combination with the θ-criterion, which precludes RtoO in favor of the ECM account in the GB model on the understanding that a non-thematic object position could not be generated for a raised object to be moved into. RtoS contructions are not so constrained, their movement involving the obvious reordering of an embedded subject into a matrix subject position. In recognition of this (among other things), Chomsky suggests that "the requirement that a clause have a subject position is independent of the Projection Principle" (Chomsky 1982:10). This "Extended Projection Principle" was considered by Chomsky to be a language universal.[1]

At the same time, NP-of-S (or Spec,IP) was taken to be the grammatical position to which subject thematic roles were assigned. Marantz (1984) claims that semantic roles are assigned directly to constituents, and rejects the notion of a parallel level of predicate-argument structure wherein semantic roles might be articulated in a predicate calculus-like representation. He criticizes such approaches (e.g., Jackendoff 1976; Williams 1981; Dowty 1982) on the grounds that they fail to recognize the asymmetry inherent in subject semantic roles versus those of other (VP-internal) arguments. Thus, in a predicate calculus representation of the argument structure of the verb *like*, the subject and object arguments have equal status in an argument list (e.g., *like'* $(x, y)$ taken to mean '$x$ likes $y$'). Marantz (1984:23 ff) claims that it is the entire predicate, namely the VP with all its complements, that assigns a semantic role to the subject, rather than the verb itself. In his demonstration of this, he points out that the subject semantic role associated with a verb such as *throw* is dependent on the choice of object, as in (3).

(3)   a.   throw a baseball                                                    [= Marantz 1984:25 (2.19)]
      b.   throw support behind a candidate
      c.   throw a boxing match (i.e., take a dive)
      d.   throw a party
      e.   throw a fit

In (3), Marantz argues, various predicates all containing the same head verb *throw* assign distinct semantic roles to subjects (e.g., Agent in the case of (3a) and Theme in the case of (3e)). This "indirect" assignment by a verb of a semantic role to its VP-external subject was codified into the notion "external thematic role," and was claimed to be a syntactic, structural fact about sentences that correlates with other grammatical features. In Burzio (1981, 1986), for instance, "external thematic role" was operationalized into his generalization concerning the distribution of structural (accusative) Case assignment by verbs. There Burzio suggests that verbs which do not assign an "external theta role" also do not assign Case to their complements. For passives, the failure to assign the subject thematic role external to the VP correlates with the necessity of Case-motivated movement from object position. For unaccusative verbs (intransitive verbs having an underlying object rather than a subject), the movement of the single argument from object to subject position correlates with the failure of the verb to assign a thematic role VP-externally.

By the late 1980s, the notion of a single structural and thematic subject position had started to unravel. An early innovation leading in this direction was the VP-internal subject hypothesis, which suggests that the subject originates within the VP and then moves to Spec,IP in most (but not all) languages and entails positing two subject positions (see Zagona 1982; Kitagawa 1986; Sportiche 1988). Striking evidence for this hypothesis comes from Sportiche's (1988) analysis of quantifier float in French as shown in (4).

(4) a. Tous les enfants ont vu ce film.
       all  the children have seen this movie
    b. Les enfants (*tous) ont tous vu (*tous) ce film.
       the children        have all  seen         this movie

Sportiche posits a VP-internal position for subjects to explain the fact that the quantifier *tous* 'all' in (4b) can appear between the auxiliary and main verbs, but not in other plausible positions (such as before the auxiliary verb or after the main verb). He suggests that the NP complement of the quantifier may raise independently to Spec,IP, leaving the quantifier stranded as in (5).

(5) [$_{IP}$[$_{NP}$les enfants]$_1$ ont [$_{VP}$[$_{QP}$tous t$_1$] vu ce film]]

Of course, (4a) is derived by having the entire QP *tous les enfants* move from Spec,VP to Spec,IP. These facts, together with other considerations (e.g., adverb placement), provide evidence of a VP-internal position for the subject. Further evidence for a VP-internal subject position comes from languages for which it was argued that the subject of the sentence never raises to Spec,IP but remains in Spec,VP at S-structure. Such proposals include Kuroda (1988) for Japanese and McCloskey (1991) for Irish.

The notion of two subject positions was developed further in Guilfoyle, Hung, and Travis 1992 (GHT), which presents an analysis of Tagalog (and other Austronesian languages) that makes crucial use of the two subject positions, Spec,VP and Spec,IP, based on the insights of Schachter (1976). Schachter demonstrates that for Tagalog the properties most often associated with a single argument and identified as "subject properties" can sometimes be split between two argument positions in certain constructions. For example, in (6) [= GHT:(25)], *babae* 'woman' possesses all subject properties in (6a), while the subject properties are split in (6b) between *babae* and *bigas* 'rice.'[2]

(6) a. Mag-aalis   ng-bigas   sa-sako   para sa-bata'   ang-babae.
       AT-take.out ACC-rice OBL-sack   for   OBL-child   TOP-woman
       'The woman will take rice out of the sack for the child.'
    b. Aalisin       ng-babae    sa-sako   para sa-bata'   ang-bigas.
       TT-take.out GEN-woman OBL-sack   for   OBL-child   TOP-rice
       'The woman will take the rice out of the sack for the child.'

Under GHT's analysis, Tagalog has the phrase structure shown in (7), where Spec,IP is rightmost and Spec,VP is leftmost.

(7)
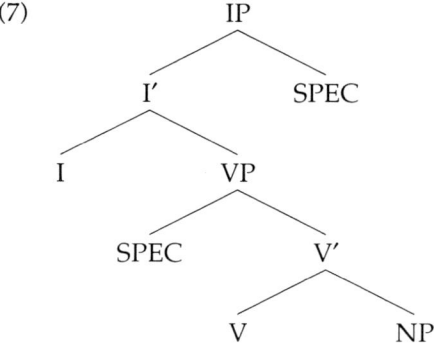

The derivations of (6a) and (6b) are shown in (8).

(8) a. [$_{IP}$mag-aalis$_2$ [$_{VP}$t$_1$    t$_2$ ng-bigas sa-sako para-sa-bata']
       ang-babae$_1$ $_{IP}$]
    b. [$_{IP}$aalisin$_2$   [$_{VP}$ng-babae t$_2$ t$_1$    sa-sako para-sa-bata']
       ang-bigas$_1$ $_{IP}$]

In (8a), the VP-internal subject *babae* moves from Spec,VP (on the left edge of VP) to Spec,IP (at the end of the clause), thus filling both subject positions. In (8b), *babae* remains in the Spec,VP subject position, while the theme *bigas* moves to Spec,IP. Under GHT's analysis, Schachter's "role-related properties," properties such as reflexive antecedence and being controlled, are characteristic of the Spec,VP position, while Schachter's "reference-related properties," such as floating quantifiers and extraction, associate with Spec,IP. When a single argument fills both positions (via movement), as is the case for *babae* in (8a), that argument exhibits all subject characteristics. In (8b), however, the deep subject *babae* originates in Spec,VP and remains there at S-structure, while the object *bigas* moves out of the VP complement position coming to occupy the surface subject position Spec,IP at S-structure. Accordingly, the subject properties in (8b) are split between these two arguments.

Such proposals as these, calling for multiple "subject" positions and for the parcelling out of "subject" properties among them, bear more than a passing similarity to RG conceptions of grammatical structure. The VP-internal subject position has its analogue in the RG concept "initial subject." Analogous to the derived "subject positions" (in the inflectional layer of the clause), the distinct status of "final subjects" is recognized in RG theory in triggering agreement and feeding word order rules (among other things). For example, Bell (1976) proposed distinct grammatical properties for initial and final subjects in Cebuano, a proposal quite similar to that offered (in the current model) by GHT for other Austronesian languages.

This resemblance to RG notions aside, the dissection of "subject" into thematic and functional positions (i.e., Spec,VP and Spec,IP) had the effect of eliminating the previously useful distinction between VP-internal and VP-external semantic roles. Also, to the extent that all subjects are initially projected within VP, it also means that all arguments appearing in Spec,IP are derived (i.e., moved there). The VP-internal subject hypothesis also opened the door to the speculation (alluded to above, with respect to Japanese and Irish) that not all languages have a functional subject position to move into.

## The unpacking of functional structure

Alongside the above developments, which involved the splitting of the thematic and functional domain of syntax vis-à-vis subjects, the functional domain itself was opened up for "deconstruction" with the publication of Pollock (1989), which re-examined observations about English and French verbal inflection in Emonds (1978, 1985). In a re-examination of INFL, Pollock suggests that a better account of the distribution of verbs (in relation to adverbials and negation) can be attained by positing two distinct syntactic projections, Agr (i.e., agreement) and T (i.e., tense) in its place. His proposal for the structure of English and French (negative) sentences is shown in (9).

(9) [= Pollock 1989:397 (77)]

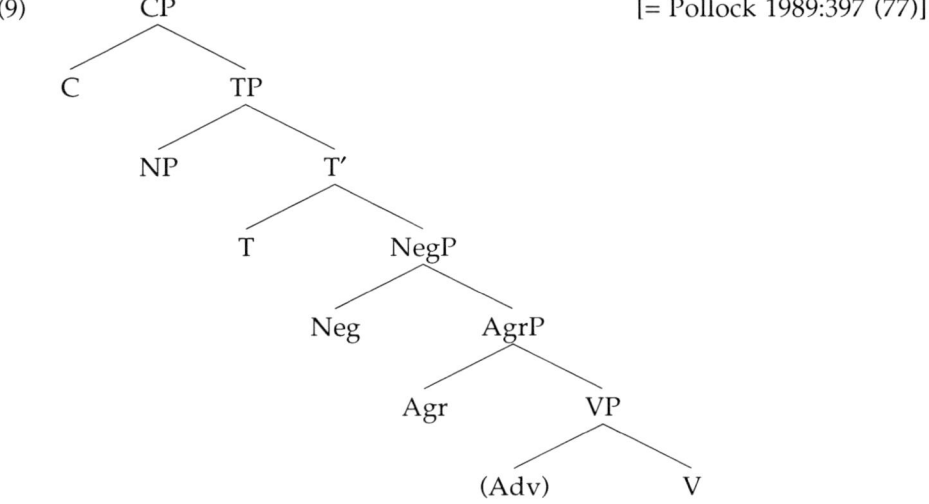

For Pollock (who was not concerned with multiple subject positions), the surface subject position is in Spec,TP (in place of Spec,IP). The verb, under certain circumstances, may move from V through Agr to T.³ In French, as opposed to

English, a tensed verb appears before the negation element in NegP (i.e., *pas* in French and *not* in English) and before an adverbial such as *souvent* or *often*. This is illustrated in (10), which can be contrasted with (11) (Pollock 1989:367).

(10) a. Jean (n') aime pas Marie.
     b. *John likes not Mary.
     c. Jean embrasse souvent Marie.
     d. *John kisses often Mary.

(11) a. *Jean souvent embrasse Marie.
     b. John often kisses Mary.

On Pollock's account, tensed lexical verbs in French (such as *aime* and *embrasse*) must move out of VP (where English requires the insertion of auxiliary verbs, e.g., *does not like*). In making a case for the separation of T and Agr, Pollock asserts that infinitival verbs in French are not required to move, and may thus optionally appear on either side of a VP adverb, as in (12).

(12) a. Souvent paraître triste pendant son     [= Pollock 1989:(24b)]
       often   to.look sad during one's
       voyage de noce, c'est rare.
       honeymoon   that.is rare
       'To often look sad during one's honeymoon is rare.'
    b. Paraître souvent triste pendant son     [= Pollock 1989:(27b)]
       to.look often  sad during one's
       voyage de noce, c'est rare.
       honeymoon   that.is rare
       'To often look sad during one's honeymoon is rare.'

In (12), the infinitive *paraître* appears alternately before or after the VP-adverb of frequency *souvent*. In (12a), *paraître* is assumed to be VP-internal, while in (12b), it is claimed to have moved out of the VP. At the same time, Pollock notes, these infinitives may not appear in front of the negation element *pas* (in contrast with tensed verbs, which can do so, cf. (10a) above). This is illustrated in (13).

(13) a. Ne pas regarder la télévision consolide     [= Pollock 1989:(16d)]
       l'esprit critique.
       '*ne* not to.watch the television strengthens one's independence.'
    b. *Ne regarder pas la télévision consolide     [= Pollock 1989:(16e)]
       l'esprit critique.

Here, in (13), the infinitive *regarder* is only grammatical following *pas*, and not before it. On the basis of this, and much other evidence, Pollock argues for an intermediate landing site for the verb which is VP-external and subordinate to the head of TP. This position, between *pas* and the adverbial (e.g., *souvent*), is the target of "short verb movement," and is formalized as the head of the agreement projection AgrP shown in (9).[4]

Note that (9) posits only one VP-external subject position, as AgrP is claimed by Pollock not to project a specifier. However, once empirical motivations were provided for disassembling INFL into TP and AgrP, it was a relatively short step to hypothesize additional, functional subject positions (i.e., Spec,TP and Spec,AgrP). In work on Icelandic transitive expletive constructions, Bobaljik and Jonas (1996) reverses the order of AgrP and TP (making TP the subordinate functional category) and argues for two VP-external subject positions, Spec,AgrP and Spec,TP. Example (14) illustrates this.

(14)  $[_{AgrP}$Það klaruðu$_1$ $[_{TP}$margar mýs$_2$   [= Bobaljik and Jonas 1996:(27)]
      there finished      many mice
      alveg    $[_{VP}$t$_2$ t$_1$ ostinn]]]
      completely   the.cheese
      'There finished many mice the cheese completely.'

In (14), Spec,AgrP is occupied by the subject expletive *það* and Spec,TP is occupied by the thematic subject *margar mýs*. The latter appears to the left of the VP peripheral adverb *alveg*, having moved out of its initial VP-internal subject position. As McCloskey (1997) points out, with two subject positions in the inflectional layer, this either brings to three the number of identified subject positions or casts doubt on the status of the VP-internal subject position itself.

## *A proliferation of agreement*

Unlike subject, the definition of the notion of direct object was less troublesome to Chomsky's transformational theory at the outset. It was, by and large, assumed that direct objects of simple clauses (such as *her* in (15a)) are not derived. Subsequently, Chomsky's (1981) adoption of the Projection Principle and the θ-criterion entailed that no surface direct object can be derived from any other position, since such a derivation would involve either the insertion of a phrase into an existing thematic object position, in violation of the θ-criterion, or the creation of a new (empty) object position in the course of the derivation, in violation of the Projection Principle. As we have seen (see chapter 8, section 4), this helped provide justification for the Exceptional Case Marking (ECM) analysis of accusative infinitival subjects, by which *him* in (15b) is a deep and surface subject despite its accusative case.

(15)  a.  James saw her.
      b.  Garth wants [$_S$him to leave]

Thus, the Projection Principle divided the class of apparent surface direct objects into true direct object complements (15a) and accusative infinitival subjects

(15b). Under these assumptions, direct object is trivially defined as the NP sister of V.

This situation changed with the publication of Larson (1988), in which the thematic position of a direct object is said to be dependent upon the valency of the verb. As shown here in (16), the direct object of a transitive verb is the NP sister of V, while the direct object of a ditransitive verb occupies Spec,VP (of a lower VP). Thus, under Larson's account, object properties do not correlate with a unified configurational notion of direct object.

(16) a. Green kissed Smith.

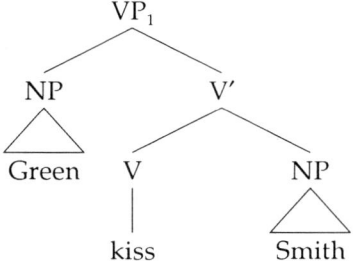

b. Green sent a letter to Smith.

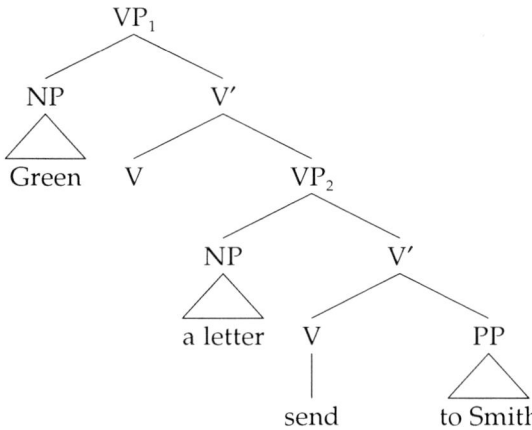

In (16b), the verb *send* is assumed to move to the head of $VP_1$ in order to assign Case to the object NP *a letter* as the specifier of its complement, $VP_2$ (in much the same manner as verbs were assumed to assign Case to the embedded subject in an ECM infinitival complement). Notice in (16b) that the direct object and the subject of a ditransitive verb each occupy a Spec,VP position, thus somewhat muddying any configurational definition of deep subject. Chomsky (1995:315–16) adopts and revises Larson's proposal concerning VP-shells, suggesting that a "Larsonian shell" is present not only when the transitive verb has multiple VP-internal arguments (as in 16b), but whenever the verb is transitive. Chomsky proposes that a (light) vP shell is present whenever the verb is transitive or assigns an agent role to its subject.[5] Under this assumption, (16) would be reanalyzed as in (17).

(17) a. Green kissed Smith.

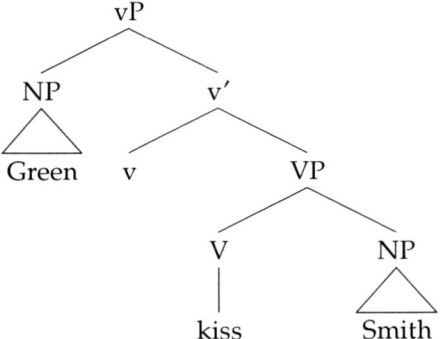

b. Green sent a letter to Smith.

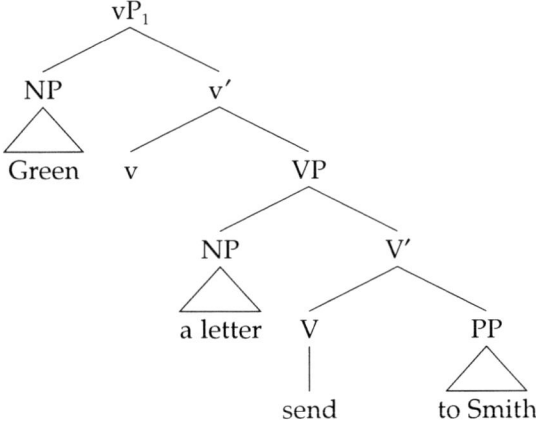

Chomsky's position here is that the causative or agentive thematic role of the external argument is assigned through the v-VP configuration, and he goes on to suggest that the configurational difference between an unergative verb (such as *run*) and an unaccusative verb (such as *arrive*) would be represented as in (18).

(18) a. Smith ran.

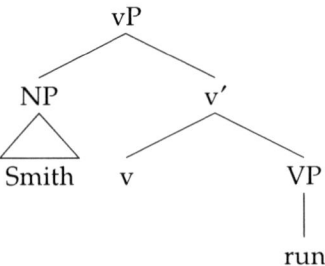

b. Smith arrived.

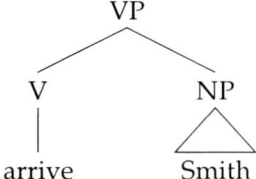

In this fashion, Chomsky is able to reintroduce the notion of subjects as "external" arguments, without invoking a grammatical position in the inflectional layer of the clause.[6]

Larson's approach does leave intact the notion that direct objects are not derived, in contrast to the VP-internal subject hypothesis which held that subjects occupy distinct thematic and inflectional positions. However, following the Pollock (1989) division of INFL into distinct Agreement and Tense components, Chomsky (1989) proposes an inflectional position for objects parallel to that of subjects. On the basis of observations in Kayne (1989), Chomsky takes Pollock's Agr to be a "subject-agreement element" (AgrS), and suggests that there is an "object-agreement element (AgrO) ... [that has] VP as its complement." On this view, (15a) has the representation at LF given in (19).

(19)   [$_{AgrSP}$James$_1$ saw$_2$ [$_{TP}$ ... [$_{AgrOP}$ her$_3$ [$_{VP}$t$_1$ t$_2$ t$_3$]]]]

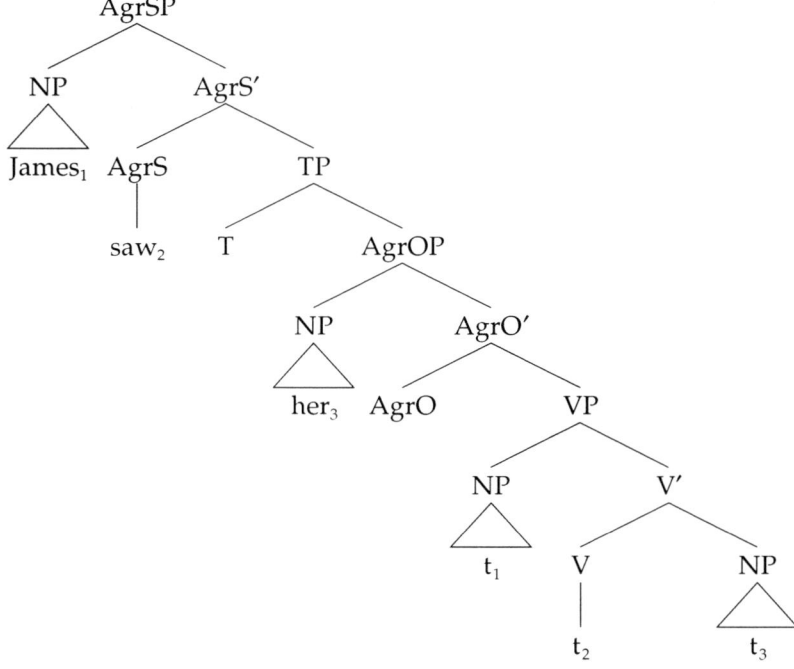

In (19), the verb *saw* moves from V through AgrO and T to AgrS. The subject *James* moves from Spec,VP to Spec,AgrSP, and the object *her* moves from

NP complement of V to Spec,AgrOP. It is assumed in this derivation that Case features are "checked" in a Spec-Head (specifier–head) configuration with the relevant category (e.g., accusative Case is checked by means of *her* occupying the Spec position of AgrOP). As (19) illustrates, the multiple Agr-projection hypothesis of Chomsky (1989) coupled with the VP-internal subject hypothesis claims that subjects and direct objects are all derived (at least by LF).

This representation presents a uniform approach to the functional relationship between a given phrasal element and the head of the functional category that it interacts with, as suggested with respect to *wh-* and negation features in Rizzi (1991) (this issue will be examined further in section 2 of this chapter). Where previously nominative Case was mediated through a specifier–head relation and accusative Case through a head–complement configuration, both are now operationalized as Spec–Head relations. With both subjects and objects each moving into the specifier position of their respective functional categories, the multiple Agr proposal does away with the traditional configurational difference between subjects and objects and replaces this with a difference that resides either in the labeling function (i.e., AgrS vs. AgrO) or in the relative superiority of the two functional projections. Other proposals (Franco 1993; Koizumi 1995; Runner 1995; Sportiche 1996) went further, providing for an additional agreement projection for indirect objects (AgrIO or $AgrO_2$). Thus, by 1993 we find proposals that collectively introduce projections corresponding to the grammatical functions of subject, direct object, and indirect object, something that had been explicitly rejected as part of Phrase Structure beginning with Chomsky (1965).

## 2 The Minimalist Program model

Intended as a way of extending and developing the Principles and Parameters (i.e., GB) model of grammar, the Minimalist Program (MP) evolved in a series of papers and chapters by Chomsky, beginning with Chomsky (1989) and culminating in the fourth chapter of Chomsky (1995) (Chomsky 1989, 1992, 1994, 1995). The initial goal (as stated in Chomsky 1989) was to extract a set of more general guidelines (e.g. "least effort" and "full interpretation") out of the various named principles, concepts, and conditions of GB (e.g., the Empty Category Principle, government, and Subjacency), and develop these into principles which might be elevated to "actual principles of language." Also, as the title of Chomsky (1989) ("Some notes on economy of derivation and representation") suggests, one might imagine a desire on Chomsky's part to provide some principled means for constraining some of the unbridled developments in derivational and representational formalisms that had arisen in the years following the publication of Chomsky (1981, 1982). As we have seen before in this volume, there is a natural tendency for the empirical necessities of linguistic description and analysis to lead away from the initially simple and unadulterated assumptions of any theoretical model, toward ever more complex accounts and formalisms. In this regard, followers of the GB model were not exempt, and the MP might be thought of as an effort to rein them in, while attempting at the same time to make further strides toward the initial goals of GB theory.[7]

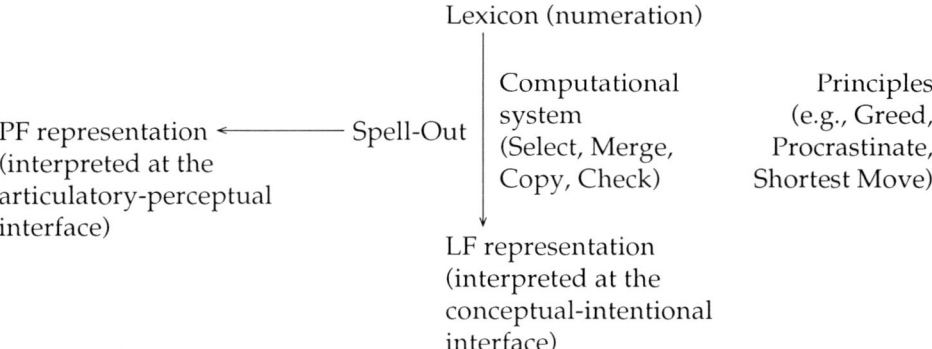

The Minimalist Program model of grammar

One of the most salient differences between this model and its antecedents is the elimination of autonomous levels of D- and S-structure representation. This is due in large part to the radically derivational character of the model. The MP model is explicitly not one in which representations are derived (or mapped) onto other representations. Rather, elements from the lexicon are collected and utilized step by step until a final representation is assembled (that of LF). This is an ongoing process and while a representation is, in principle, available after each step in the derivation, there are only two points at which any representation is relevant: once at the point that the derivation is interpreted at the articulatory-perceptual interface (i.e., at Spell-Out, which feeds a PF representation) and once again at the point that the derivation is completed, and the final (LF) representation interfaces with the conceptual-interpretive system. The difference between overt and covert movement of the GB model is captured here in the distinction between Spell-Out and post-Spell-Out representations. All movement operations accomplished "by" Spell-Out are overt (in much the same way as were movement operations effected between D-structure and S-structure in the GB model). Movement operations applied post-Spell-Out are covert in the same way as was (S-structure to) LF movement in GB.

## The computational component

Chomsky assumes there to be a single computational component (or system) for human language, $C_{HL}$, as he calls it. This is the machinery that drives the derivation and produces a representation out of the selected inventory of lexical elements. This computational system consists of a small number of elemental operations (e.g., Merge and Copy) and is constrained by general principles that ensure (i) that representations converge (i.e., are interpretable at the interface levels) and (ii) that they are derived "economically" (i.e., involve the "least effort").[8] In this respect, with the concomitant rejection of all levels of representation (save at the interfaces), the model moves squarely away from "conditions on representations" and toward "constraints on derivations."

Starting with a *numeration* (or selection) of lexical items out of the Lexicon, $C_{HL}$ constructs "syntactic objects" by the recursive application of a small set of operations. Two of these operations, Select and Merge, are in Chomsky's terms "costless," that is, they are not governed or constrained by considerations of convergence or economy. Select removes lexical items from the numeration and inserts them into the syntactic derivation. Merge takes two syntactic objects supplied by Select or previously derived and combines them to form a single new syntactic object with one of the two components being identified as the head of the newly formed object. In this view, A and B are merged to form a larger constituent of category A or B, so ensuring that all objects so derived are endocentric.

Other computational operations are driven and constrained by convergence or by economy principles. The first among these is Move, which is actually a combination of the operations Copy and Merge. Suppose, for instance, that constituent C' contains some constituent $A^{max}$, as in (20a), and $A^{max}$ needs to move to the specifier of C. Move will create a copy of $A^{max}$ and merge it with C', as shown in (20b).

(20) a.    b.

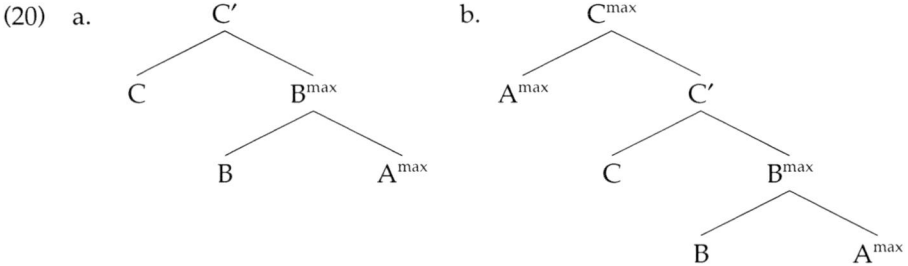

In this "copy theory of movement", all copies of $A^{max}$ are present in the representation until such time as output conditions require one or more to undergo deletion. Typically, in pre-Spell-Out applications of Move, the lower copy is deleted in deriving the PF representation and is thereby not pronounced, while the lower copy is retained at LF for the sake of interpretation.[9] Example (21) illustrates the application of both movement to Spec,XP and head movement in the unaccusative clause *he arrived*. (The distinction between Agr and T has been collapsed in this example just for the purpose of simplifying the illustration of the operation.)[10]

(21)

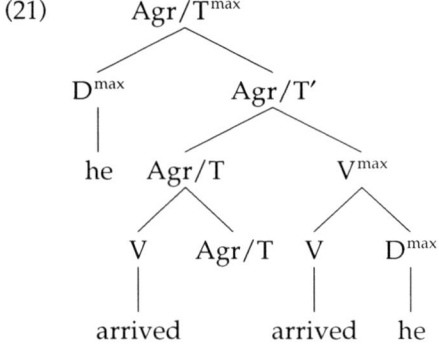

In (21), the lower copies of *arrived* and *he* would undergo deletion in the mapping between Spell-Out and PF.

Another operation utilized by the computational component is Feature Checking. Feature Checking is the operation that motivates movement in this system, and is itself a deletion operation, in that checked features are deleted (or rendered invisible in the relevant interface representation). Importantly, under Minimalist assumptions, lexical items come out of the lexicon fully inflected.[11] This is distinct from the approach in previous models, in which a lexical base form is inserted into a lexical category node, and inflectional affixes are inserted into inflectional category nodes with the items being merged via movement operations. Here, the inflected forms are assumed to have inflectional "features" which must be checked against an inflectional head that bears the requisite, matching features. Features are allowed to be checked only in two configurations: specifier–head and head–head. That is, a head (such as Agr/T in (21)) may check features of its specifier (such as *he* in (21)), and vice versa. In (21), *he* is in a Spec-Head configuration with Agr, and its nominative Case feature is checked by Agr in this configuration. Additionally, if a phrasal head undergoes movement and adjoins to a higher head, as the verb *arrived* does in (21), the moved head may have its features checked by the head that it adjoins to. Again in (21), *arrived* comes out of the lexicon bearing a "Tense feature" (i.e., it is lexically marked as +past), and this feature is checked by T (i.e., the node which actually carries the past tense interpretation) on the higher copy of *arrived* when it is an adjunct to T.

## Economy and interpretability conditions

While the operation Merge applies freely throughout the derivation (as indicated above), the operation Move does not. It is inherently uneconomical, in that it takes elements that have already been merged into the derivation and applies additional operations (Copy and Merge) to them. All other things being equal, the most economical thing is not to move. The driving force behind movement then is the requirement that (certain) features need to be checked (and erased) in order for a derivation to converge. Some principles, such as Greed, themselves promote convergence. For instance, if some constituent possesses a feature that must be checked, then Greed ensures that the constituent will move for its own sake, to have that feature checked.[12] This is the case in (21), where *he* must move to Spec,AgrP in order to have its nominative Case feature checked. Other principles inhibit movement.

The Last Resort principle, for example, precludes application of any extra operations (such as movement) unless there is no alternative. This is amply illustrated in (21), where Copy and Merge apply to *he* and *arrived* as a "last resort"; that is, they apply in order to make feature checking possible. If movement did not apply in this case, the derivation would "crash" (i.e., not converge). If movement were not necessary, then Last Resort would preclude it from applying. Last Resort thus determines that, if a derivation converges without the movement operation, then the operation is prohibited from applying.

In a similar vein, Procrastinate requires additional operations to be postponed as long as possible. By this principle, movement is postponed in cases where feature strength does not require it to be overt. This is illustrated in (19), where movement of the subject is claimed to be overt, while movement of the object to Spec,AgrO is assumed not to take place until after Spell-Out. Within the MP, features are assumed to be either "strong" or "weak," and which features are strong and which are weak varies from language to language. Chomsky (1995:232) suggests that strong features must be checked by Spell-Out, while weak features need only be checked by LF. In this context, Procrastinate dictates that weak feature checking must be postponed until after Spell-Out, because it can be. Chomsky (1995:198–9) claims that the EPP (or D-)feature of T in English is strong, and that this forces raising of the subject in (19) by Spell-Out to check this feature in the Agr/T complex. At the same time, Agr is hypothesized to be weak, and for this reason the raising of the object *her* to Spec,AgrOP is not accomplished until LF, as mandated by Procrastinate.

Another important principle of economy, Shortest Move, ensures that movement (when required) must take place across the shortest possible distance. Referring again to the derivation in (19), Shortest Move dictates that the NP object must move to Spec,AgrO rather than to the Spec,AgrS to check its Case feature. Thus, even if the subject position were empty and available at the point that movement of the object applies, it could not skip over AgrO and move into the AgrS projection.[13]

Finally, Full Interpretation is a condition that operates at the LF interface, and serves to "rule out the presence of 'excess' constituents in the structure, such as unbound variables or NPs without theta-roles" (Marantz 1995:353), which would presumably render it uninterpretable.

(22)   *there seems [that Harold left early]

The unacceptability of (22), on this view, is on account of the expletive NP *there* not having a θ-marked associate and thereby failing to be fully interpretable at LF.

### *The consequences of adopting MP concepts: commentary and comparisons*

As suggested above, the motivations for Chomsky's MP proposals were at once to make further progress in the direction of his long-standing conceptual goals for linguistic theory, and (perhaps) to encourage movement away from some of the more overarticulated aspects of GB theory as it had developed in the late 1980s. While the details of the MP appear to be radically different from its antecedents, the conceptual basis of this model is clearly in keeping with Chomsky's goals of: (i) bringing linguistics theory to a level of explanatory adequacy; (ii) eschewing rule-based approaches to syntax in favor of approaches founded on generalizable (UG) principles and constraints; and (iii) distilling the innate and autonomous syntactic basis for the language faculty.

This said, it is interesting to note that Chomsky's MP proposals both resuscitate ideas rejected long ago by Chomsky himself, and incorporate conceptually similar notions of other (current) approaches to syntax. By way of illustration, this discussion will examine (i) how the MP has adopted a view of grammar quite in keeping with Generative Semantics theory of the 1970s, a view that Chomsky (1971) argued forcefully against at that time (see Pullum 1996), and (ii) how closely it resembles Optimality Theoretic (Prince and Smolensky 1993) approaches to syntax.

While the operations performed by the computational system (e.g., Merge) are radically local, the evaluative principles (e.g., Last Resort) constraining the system are massively global. While the operation Merge applies to exactly two elements in the derivation, the Last Resort principle not only evaluates the entire derivation at hand, but evaluates this derivation in comparison with other (possible or actual) derivations. In this regard, the economy principles of the MP are even more global in nature than many of the "global rules" proposed by practitioners of Generative Semantics. Johnson and Lappin (1996:9) note in this regard that "global economy conditions bear an obvious resemblance to the transderivational constraints proposed by Generative Semanticists (see for example, Lakoff 1970 and 1971)."

Another facet of the MP also invites comparisons with Generative Semantics. Until the introduction of the MP model, Chomskyan theory relied on the Projection Principle (and versions of it) to ensure that lexical properties were projected into the syntax and uniformly maintained throughout a derivation. Complement positions bearing certain syntactic labels were either determined by the head of a phrase, or were not projected at all. From the outset, category (C-)selection was assumed by Chomsky to be predicted on the basis of semantic (S-)selectional properties (see Chomsky 1981:29, 1986b:82, 90–1; and see Grimshaw 1979 for a contrary view). Accordingly, the particular semantic/thematic properties of any given verb would be expected to unambiguously predict and restrict the phrase marker that it could be inserted into. These (Projection Principle) restrictions were invoked at the point of lexical insertion (D-structure), and were maintained throughout the derivation through adherence to principles of structure preservation (see Emonds 1976, and our discussion in chapter 4, section 2).

In the MP model, there is no D-structure, and no syntactic object for a Projection Principle to apply to. That is, lexical items are selected out of the numeration and merged one by one over the course of the derivation, and there is never a representation prior to Spell-Out that an evaluative metric like the Projection Principle might apply to. Thus, lexical insertion operates blindly without any mechanism to toss out subcategorization violations, until LF. There, the principle of Full Interpretation will rule out any derivation that has produced gibberish (inclusive of subcategorization violations). What this means is that the clause *why did Elmo put the keys?* will be uninterpretable at LF due to the failure of the verb *put* to assign one of its θ-roles, not because it failed to select a locative PP complement.

Because the former "subcategorization violations" are now ruled out post-Spell-Out, and because the principle invoked to do this is concerned with interpretation rather than structure, there is in this model little to constrain the final form of the derivation that is submitted to the LF interface. All sorts of previously unlicensed structures might be covertly constructed after Spell-Out, provided only that they are properly constructed by the computational system and that they are interpretable. In this regard, one might imagine that some analog of the highly articulated Deep Structures of Generative Semantics may very well be licensed at the LF end of MP derivations. While this is not to say that such representations should be ruled out a priori, it is not clear how the model would constrain these in a systematic way.

In basing well-formedness on "constraint satisfaction rather than rule application" (D. Johnson and Lappin 1996:2), both GB and MP resemble other constraint-based formalisms, including Arc Pair Grammar (D. Johnson and Postal 1980), Lexical Functional Grammar (Kaplan and Bresnan 1982), Functional Unification Grammar (Kay 1983), PATR-II (Shieber et al. 1983), GPSG (Gazdar et al. 1985), Categorial Unification Grammar (Uszkoreit 1986), and HPSG (Pollard and Sag 1987, 1994). However, the MP model seems to more clearly exhibit parallels with the Optimality Theory (OT) model of Prince and Smolensky (1993). As Prince and Smolensky (1993:2) suggest, "the proposals of Chomsky 1986[a], and especially 1989 [and] 1992, though very different in implementation, have fundamental similarities with our own."

To illustrate, the economy principles of the MP (e.g., Procrastinate and Last Resort) have the character of syntactic constraints, and as noted in Marantz (1995:353), all "involve implicit or explicit comparison of derivations" (or what might be thought of as "candidate sets" in OT), and suggest "a striving for the cheapest or minimal way of satisfying principles" (the best or "optimal" way?). One might also compare the principle of Full Interpretation in MP to that of Faithfulness in OT (i.e., a requirement that derivations (MP) or outputs (OT) match as closely as possible what they mean). Also, in that all movement operations are motivated by the need to satisfy feature checking, neither the MP model nor OT allow constraint satisfaction to be optional. Further, just as OT permits only one member of a candidate set to be "optimal," MP permits only the best derivation to "converge." And finally, one finds in MP that an explicit ranking of principles drives derivational outcomes in much the same manner as constraint ranking in OT determines the output. For instance, Shortest Move is ranked higher than Converge, forcing some otherwise convergent derivations to be ungrammatical, while convergence outranks Greed, Last Resort, and Procrastinate, causing them sometimes to be violated.

## 3  Bare Phrase Structure and uninterpretable features

Two developments of the mid-1990s complete the evolution of phrase markers in the MP, the first being the abandonment of X-bar theory (Chomsky 1994) and the second being the elimination of uninterpretable features and their associated categories from the numeration (Chomsky 1995).

As Chomsky (1994:395) notes, X-bar theory was motivated by a desire to eliminate redundancy between lexical properties and phrase structure rules, reducing the PS component to a set of UG X-bar theoretic principles. In the Minimalist model, Chomsky says, only minimal (i.e., terminal) elements and maximal projections (i.e., XPs) are relevant. Minimal elements are so because lexical items and their accompanying features are referenced by derivational operations and output conditions, and maximal elements are so because only XPs are relevant to LF interpretation. Thus, for purposes of computation and interpretation, X-bar categories are invisible. Chomsky then goes on to show that, in the MP, even the standard set of labels is irrelevant.

Central to the generation of phrase markers is the operation Merge. The label of this constituent is a term that identifies the "properties" or features relevant to its interpretation and its interaction with the larger phrase marker within which it is inserted. Chomsky asserts that Merge is asymmetric, so that the result of merging A and B must necessarily involve the projection of either A's or B's features, but not both and not neither.[14] Under this view, the phrase marker generated by Merge{A,B} would be either (23a) or (23b).

(23) a. 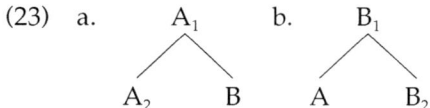 b.

Chomsky further asserts that, when the projecting element is a phrase (e.g., $A_2$ in (23a)), it is "natural . . . to take [its] label . . . to be not $A_2$ itself, but rather . . . the head of the constituent that it projects." Thus, on these assumptions, the phrase marker for *the tall unkempt lad* is (24b) rather than the familiar (24a). Note that, because phrase markers can only be constructed via Merge, there can be no non-branching nodes.

(24)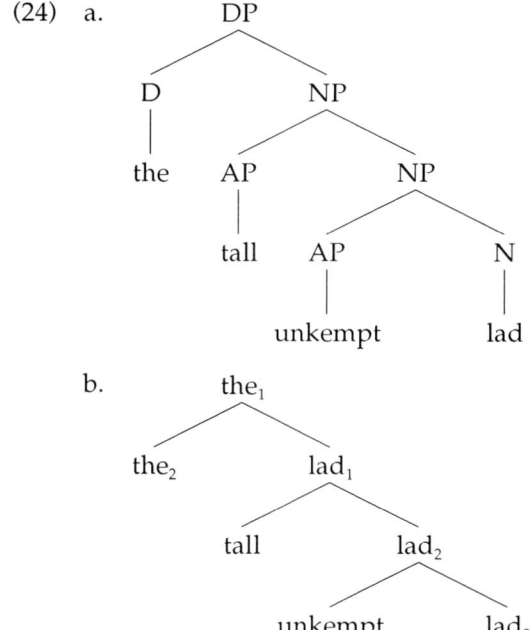

In this "bare" model of phrase markers, complement and specifier relations are defined in relation to the head of a phrase (where the head is a terminal element). The complement of a head is an element that combines with the projecting head of the phrase. In (23a), B is the complement of $A_2$ (if A is a terminal element) and in (23b) A is the complement of $B_2$ (if B is terminal). All other subsequently merged elements are understood as specifiers (multiple specifiers being possible, in principle). One consequence of this view of phrase markers is that a given element can be both a minimal and a maximal projection. Chomsky, however, sees this as an advantage, pointing out that bare phrase structure is thereby easily able to accommodate the distribution of clitics, which appear as both phrases (when they appear in θ-positions) and heads (when they adjoin to inflectional heads). The full details of Chomsky's bare phrase marker formalism are beyond the scope of this discussion, but it should be clear from this brief presentation how radical a revision it is, in comparison with its antecedents.[15]

Chomsky's assumption and development of the bare phrase structure model leads to one final, major revision in his theory of phrase markers and derivations, the elimination of Agr projections from the grammar (Chomsky1995:348 ff.). He notes first that Agr consists of formal features that are uninterpretable (i.e., that provide no "instructions" for the interpretation of the derivation at either the PF or LF interface), and second that it might be thought of as a category that has no features of its own, but instead is a location in which other features are checked. In particular, its Case features are assumed to be supplied by the V or the T that moves and adjoins to it, and its φ-features (person, number, gender features) are hypothesized to originate with the verbal or adjectival predicate as it is selected from the lexicon. That said, the only empirical evidence to support the existence of Agr comes from cases (such as the Icelandic transitive expletive construction) in which the relevant positions associated with it, $Agr^0$ or Spec,AgrP, are overtly filled. Alongside (14) above, Icelandic has sentences such as (25) in which Spec,AgrSP, Spec,TP, and Spec,AgrOP are overtly filled.

(25) [$_{AgrSP}$það  klaruðu$_1$]         [= Bobaljik and Jonas 1996:(28)]
         there  finished
    [$_{TP}$margar mý$_2$ [$_{AgrOP}$ostinn$_3$    alveg [$_{VP}$t$_2$ t$_1$ t$_3$]]]]
         many mice        the.cheese completely
    'There finished many mice the cheese completely.'

In (25), Spec,AgrSP and Spec,TP are each occupied by a subject (the first an expletive) and the object, having moved to the left of the adverb, occupies Spec,AgrOP. Since formal features must be checked and eliminated before Spell-Out and since pre-Spell-Out feature checking involves overt movement, it strikes Chomsky as a natural first hypothesis to assume that Agr is present in the structure only when it or its specifier is occupied by phonological material as in (25). This allows him to dispense with the notion that movement to Spec,AgrP is overt if the features are "strong" and covert if they are "weak." Rather, he suggests at first, Agr features are always "strong" or else they (and Agr) are not present.

Chomsky then goes on to question the need for an Agr projection even when it is associated with overt movement, as in (25). This move, in many respects, is an attempt to make the theory more coherent. Recalling the set of legitimate operations hypothesized for the computational component, it is clear that the only way for an element to be MERGED into the structure is for it to be SELECTED from the NUMERATION, and the elements in the numeration are claimed to be drawn from the lexicon. Thus, in this model, the source of an uninterpretable head such as Agr is not entirely clear.

In presenting his alternative to uninterpretable categories, Chomsky asserts that overt Raising can be forced by "strong" features that are assigned to a lexical category, such as light v, and that Agr itself can be dispensed with. Since multiple specifiers are available for the phrase markers generated by the Merge operation, Chomsky suggests that the stong (D-)features of v that motivate movement of *ostinn* in (25) are checked in an "outer" specifier position. The derivation of (the relevant part of) example (25) before movement of the subject is shown in (26).

(26)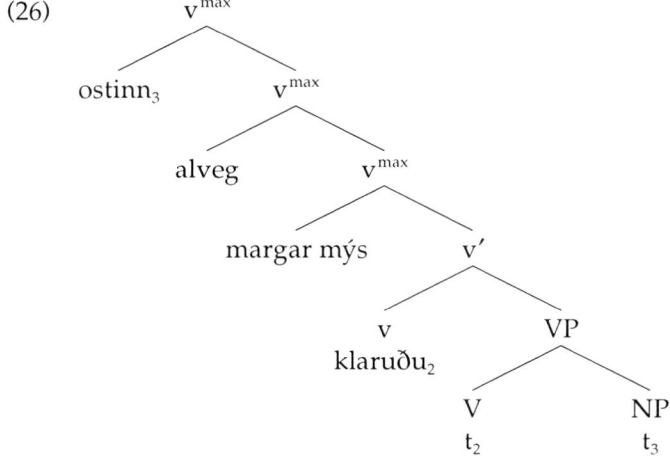

In (26), the subject *margar mýs* 'many mice' is merged with the v-VP constituent and assigned the external θ-role. The adverb *alveg* 'completely' is merged as a second specifier, and the object *ostinn* 'the cheese' is moved out of the lower VP to check Case and φ-features. Subsequent Raising of the verb *klaruðu* and the subject *margar mýs* yields the correct order. The formal definition of checking domains and the checking operation itself preclude any element other than *ostinn* from checking these strong features. Chomsky goes on to provide an analogous argument for the elimination of AgrS as a formal category.

Before concluding this section, it should be pointed out that acceptance of Chomsky's bare Phrase Structure innovations (over the previous mechanisms involving formal, functional categories such as Agr) is by no means universal among those who pursue research in what can be characterized as the Minimalist Program. Accordingly, some syntacticians remain concerned with such issues as: are functional projections universal? Are they universally projected in a fixed hierarchy? Are they projected outside of lexical projections (implying a parallel between D-structure/lexical and S-structure/functional), or are they interleaved?

On the issue of whether functional projections are instantiated in some fixed and universal hierarchy or whether the relative dominance of individual functional projections might vary parametrically from one language to another, there has been considerable discussion, and the positions taken vary widely. At one end of the spectrum is the view that the inventory of functional categories and their relative dominance are fixed by UG. At the other end is the idea that the inventory and their relative dominance vary from language to language. A good amount of discussion on this topic can be found in Davies and Dubinsky (2001b) (particularly in chapters by Davies and Dubinsky, Lasnik, Massam, McCloskey, and Travis).

## Notes

1 The analogous Final 1 Law (requiring that every "basic clause" have a surface subject) was by this time a well-established linguistic universal in RG theory (Perlmutter and Postal 1983a). Since this time, speculation has arisen regarding whether all languages obey the EPP and whether some languages satisfy the EPP in alternative ways. Additionally, developments in clausal architecture have radically reshaped the configurational definition of subject and, in fact, have cast doubt on whether a unitary notion of subject can be identified (see part III of Davies and Dubinsky 2001b).
2 In the glosses, AT stands for agent topic and TT stands for theme topic. The other abbreviations are: TOP(ic), ACC(usative), OBL(ique), and GEN(itive).
3 In Chomsky's (1986a:71) analysis, the requirement that the verb must move through Agr, rather than directly to T, is enforced by the Head Movement Constraint (HMC) (Travis 1984). Informally rendered, the HMC restricts the movement of a head (X) of XP to the head of the phrase superior to XP. In (9), the verb must move to Agr first, and then move to T (if it is not blocked by Neg).
4 The synopsis of Pollock (1989) given here does little justice to the complexity of the data and the rich, elaborated argumentation found therein.
5 Early on, those who adopted this idea were somewhat indecisive as to whether vP is simply a projection that facilitates the merging of an "external" argument (i.e., whether it correlates with transitivity), or bears semantic properties such as a CAUSE head that checks an agent θ-role. Insofar as it was implicated in the checking of accusative Case, the former view prevailed (since there are many transitive verbs that have non-agentive subjects and which check the accusative Case of their objects). On the other hand, for those who saw vP as a way to distinguish (thematically) unergative from unaccusative predicates (where intransitive unergatives have their single argument merged in vP), the latter view held sway. Recent work by Kratzer (1994, 1996), Marantz (1997), Pylkkänen (2001, 2002), and Son (2003) distinguishes between transitivity and agentivity by means of the additional functional categories of Voice (projecting VoiceP) and Appl[icative] (projecting ApplP).
6 The problem of re-establishing the external/internal argument distinction is also addressed in Bowers (1993) and in Kratzer (1994, 1996). Bowers and Kratzer each

introduce a functional projection (PredP/πP and VoiceP, respectively) designed to take the VP as its complement and assign the external θ-role to its specifier.
7  Further discussion of the MP can be found in Jackendoff (1995), Johnson and Lappin (1996), Lasnik (1993, 1999b), and Marantz (1995), in addition to Chomsky's own published work.
8  The operations of this computational component only apply to the derivation from the Lexicon (through Spell-Out) to LF. The operations that take the representation at Spell-Out and map to the PF representation are deemed by Chomsky to belong to the "phonological component" of $C_{HL}$ and to be somewhat different from those described here.
9  Note that deletion operates in the phonological component – between Spell-Out and PF – in much the same manner as it operated between S-structure and PF in the GB model.
10  In (21), a node is maximal if it does not project another node of the same category.
11  In the MP view, verbs come out of the lexicon fully inflected, but carry syntactic features that ultimately require them to move to higher head positions in the tree. In many respects, there might be little difference (other than a notational one) between this view of morphology and that of having verb stems and verb affixes inserted under separate nodes (as was the assumption in GB theory) and then combined via obligatory rules (such as the Stray Affix Filter).
12  A more "altruistic" version of this principle, called Enlightened Self-Interest, is proposed by Lasnik (1995, 1999b). By this principle, movement of some constituent A is driven by the need to check morphological features (of its own or of the constituent to which it moves).
13  This constraint on movement incorporates insights of Rizzi's (1990) (i.e., the principle of relativized minimality). The calculations of what counts as "shortest" are beyond the scope of this discussion. Chomsky (1992:14–19) and Marantz (1995:355–6) provide fuller explication of this principle. Chomsky (1992) discusses the competition in terms of economy between derivations having longer individual moves and fewer distinct (movement) steps, versus derivations having shorter moves and more steps. He concludes that distance is more relevant for computing economy than is the number of steps.

Shortest Move appears to stand in natural opposition to the tendencies of Procrastinate. Where Shortest Move seeks the smallest possible domain within which to apply the movement operation, Procrastinate seeks (by the need to wait) the largest possible domain.
14  This view of feature "percolation" is not a necessary assumption, even though it may initially seem intuitively correct. For one thing, Chomsky only considers four out of several possible ways of combining feature sets. Chomsky claims that combining categories A and B may pass either (i) all and only the features of A to the dominating phrasal node, or (ii) all and only the features of B to the dominating phrasal node. He further claims that the merger of A and B cannot project (iii) all of A and B's features (that is, the union of A and B) or (iv) none of A and B's features. There are other possibilities. The merger of A and B might also conceivably project (v) the features that are common to A and B (the intersection of A and B), (vi) the features of A that are not shared with B (the result of subtracting from A the intersection of A and B), or (vii) the features of B that are not shared with A (the result of subtracting from B the intersection of A and B). In addition to these basic, set-theoretic possibilities, there are other, complex ways of combining the features of A and B. In Generalized Phrase Structure Grammar and its successors (Gazdar et al. 1985), features of a given phrasal constituent may be inherited in

either from its "head" daughter (i.e., head features) or from its complement daughter (i.e., foot features). Another formal mechanism for combining feature sets, Unification, is described in Shieber (1986).

15  The radical nature of the proposal exemplified in (24b) is apparent when one considers that Chomsky himself, after introducing the notation on p. 247 of Chomsky (1995), does not use it again throughout the subsequent 150 pages of the book, preferring instead to retain the traditional phrase structure labels. While one might assume that he uses traditional labels, from this point, as a mere notional convenience, the fact may help explain why the proposal occurs only in chapter 4 of his book and has not, to our knowledge, been adopted anywhere else in the literature.

# CHAPTER 12

# THE RETURN TO A RAISING-TO-OBJECT ANALYSIS

*The Raising-to-Object transformation . . . was defended by Postal (1974). In the aftermath of the battle, which basically had already been won with the appearance of Chomsky (1973), Postal's book was reviewed.*
van Riemsdijk and Williams (1986:33)

The separation of thematic and inflectional layers in the more highly articulated Phrase Structure of MP created a whole array of non-thematic positions into which arguments typically move, in particular Spec,AgrSP and Spec,AgrOP. This move created a position in the matrix clause into which the embedded subject of RtoO could move without violating the θ-criterion, the principle that "explained" why RtoO was an illicit structure. Freed from this restriction, a number of linguists working in the basic framework of MP proposed neo-RtoO analyses, rehabilitating many of Postal's original arguments which had been previously discredited.

A mere five years after van Riemdijk and Williams's assertion, Johnson (1991) and Lasnik and Saito (1991) published proposals that incorporated movement of the infinitival subject out of the complement of an RtoO predicate to a position in the higher clause. Further, Runner (1995) resuscitated Postal's arguments from adverbs in arguing for Raising in the overt syntax, as did Zidani-Eroğlu (1997) in arguing for RtoO in Turkish.

This chapter examines some of this literature as well as further developments in proposals for ECM analyses (Bruening 2001a, 2001b, 2002; Hiraiwa 2001).

## 1 Neo-RtoO: A return to Raising

One of the first analyses to reintroduce a raising analysis of RtoO structures is Howard Lasnik and Mamoru Saito's. Presented at the spring 1990 meeting of the Chicago Linguistic Society and published in 1991, this work examines a number of phenomena showing that the infinitival subject of RtoO structures is in a position higher in the Phrase Structure than the subject of a tensed complement of the same predicate.

# READING: LASNIK AND SAITO (1991)

Howard Lasnik and Mamoru Saito, pp. 324–43 from "On the subject of infinitives" in *Papers from the 27th Regional Meeting of the Chicago Linguistic Society*, eds Lise M. Dobrin, Lynn Nichols, and Rosa M. Rodriguez (Chicago: Chicago Linguistic Society, 1991). © 1991 by Chicago Linguistic Society. Reprinted by permission.

## 1 Introduction

This paper is concerned with 'raising to object'. In the following section, we will examine a range of phenomena motivating the existence of an operation which raises the subject of an embedded infinitival to a position in the matrix clause, i.e., an operation which has the general effects of Postal's (1974) 'raising to object'. In Section 3, we will suggest that this operation must take place prior to S(urface)-structure, and hence, cannot be directly identified with the Logical Form (LF) movement of accusative NPs to SPECifier of AGR-O, proposed in Chomsky (1989). In Section 4, we will discuss some differences between *believe*-type and *want*-type verbs, and suggest that only the former trigger this operation. Finally, in Section 5, we will discuss some conceptual issues surrounding 'raising to object', including certain problems that arise if such an operation indeed exists.

## 2 Evidence for raising

Since the earliest detailed investigations of sentential complementation within a transformational framework, the dual nature of the immediately postverbal (underlined) NP in examples like (1) has been noted. In some respects, that NP behaves like the subject of the lower predicate, while in other respects, it behaves like the object of the matrix verb.

(1) I believe John to have convinced Bill

Rosenbaum (1967), for example, argues persuasively that at least in underlying structure, *John* in (1) must be a subject. He observes the synonymy between infinitival embedding and finite embedding, as in (2).

(2) I believe that John convinced Bill

As Rosenbaum notes, this will be expected if *John* is the subject of the lower clause in (1) as well as in (2). He also points out the contrast between *believe*-type constructions, on the one hand, and clear instances of NP + S complementation, on the other hand, with respect to semantic import of active vs. passive in the complement. (3) is synonymous with (1), but (5) is not synonymous with (4).

(3) I believe Bill to have been convinced by John

(4) I compelled the doctor to examine John

(5) I compelled John to be examined by the doctor

As noted in Rosenbaum (1967) and Bach (1974), the underlying subject status of the NP in question is confirmed by the fact that the existential *there* and idiom chunks associated with the embedded clause can appear in this position. Thus, (6)–(7) contrast with (8)–(9), which are instances of NP + S complementation.

(6) I believe there to be a man in the garden

(7) I believe advantage to have been taken of John

(8) *I forced there to be a man in the garden

(9) *I forced advantage to have been taken of John

Alongside these arguments for lower subject status, Postal (1974) lists three "traditional arguments" for higher object status, based on passivization, reflexivization, and reciprocal marking. All three of these processes typically establish a relation between an object position and a subject position in the same clause. But they can also establish a relation between the underlying subject of the complement clause and the subject of the matrix under certain limited circumstances including, in particular, the infinitival constructions under discussion. The following examples are from Postal (1974:40–2).

(10) a. Jack believed Joan to be famous
     b. Joan was believed to be famous by Jack

(11) a. *Jack$_i$ believed him$_i$ to be immoral
     b. Jack$_i$ believed himself$_i$ to be immoral

(12)     They believed each other to be honest

This class of arguments centrally involves the nature of the boundary separating the two linked NP positions. For Postal, any clause boundary would suffice to block the relevant relations, hence the second NP position must have become a clause-mate of the first (via 'raising to object'). Chomsky (1973) offered a somewhat different perspective on these phenomena. For Chomsky, the relevant structural property is not *whether* there is a clause boundary separating the two NPs, but rather *what sort* of clause boundary there is. Metaphorically, an infinitival clause boundary is weaker than a finite clause boundary. While the latter is strong enough to block the relations in question, the former is not. Chomsky formulated this relative inaccessibility of material in finite clauses (and of non-subjects of infinitives) in terms of his Tensed Sentence Condition (TSC) and Specified Subject Condition (SSC).

In addition to the much discussed phenomena alluded to above, where boundary strength at least potentially provides the needed distinctions, Postal sketches certain other arguments for raising in which the actual surface structure height of the deep structure subject is implicated. One argument is based on a scope difference between (13) and (14):

(13) The FBI proved that few students were spies

(14) The FBI proved few students to be spies

Postal indicates that *few students* can have wide or narrow scope in (13) while it can have only wide scope in (14), and that this distinction is best described in terms of the hierarchical notion 'command'. The precise semantic difference between (13) and (14) is not crystal clear, but there does seem to be some difference, and it is reasonable to assume that it has something to do with scope. Given this, it is plausible to reason, with Postal, that some sort of transformational reorganization is implicated. As Postal notes, notions of hierarchical clause membership, such as command, are independently known to play a role in describing quantifier scope.

Postal bases another similar argument on "a fundamental pronominalization constraint" due to Langacker (1969), which states that a pronoun cannot both precede and command its antecedent. There are a number of recent formulations of this constraint, including the noncoreference rule of Lasnik (1976) and Binding Condition C of Chomsky (1981). Any of these formulations can distinguish (15) from (16), but only if the embedded subject in (16) has raised into the higher clause.

(15) Joan believes he$_i$ is a genius even more fervently than Bob$_i$ does

(16) *Joan believes him$_i$ to be a genius even more fervently than Bob$_i$ does

Once again, hierarchical notions are known to play a role in determining such constraints on pronominal coreference, but if *him* in (16) remains in the lower clause, there cannot be a difference between (15) and (16) with respect to command, c-command, etc. The structural relation between *he* and *Bob* in (15) would be the same as that between *him* and *Bob* in (16) in relevant respects.

The logic of the argument based on (15)–(16) is compelling, but there is a potentially confounding factor in the specific examples Postal presents, namely, the VP ellipsis in the adverbial clause. If the elided VP is restored in (16), arguably we have (17).

(17) *Joan believes him$_i$ to be a genius even more fervently than Bob$_i$ believes him$_i$ to be a genius

But now notice that in (17), the illicit relation could be that between *Bob* and the second, rather than the first, *him*. And this relation falls into the category of those in (10)–(12) above, where boundary strength rather than height could be the determining factor. In fact, there is reason to believe that this potential complication does not seriously interfere. The noncoreference effects that would be expected if the constraints on pronominal anaphora applied to reconstructed VPs do not materialize in any strong way. For example, (18) is far better than (19), the latter displaying a clear Condition B effect.

(18) ?Mary believes him$_i$ to be a genius, and Bob$_i$ does too

(19) *Bob$_i$ believes him$_i$ to be a genius

Similarly, (20) displays little of the Condition C effect of (21).

(20) ?Mary believes Bob$_i$ to be a genius, and he$_i$ does too

(21) *He$_i$ believes Bob$_i$ to be a genius

But to control even for the slight residual effect displayed in (18), (15)–(16) can be modified as follows:

(22) Joan believes he$_i$ is a genius even more fervently than Bob's$_i$ mother does

(23) ?*Joan believes him$_i$ to be a genius even more fervently than Bob's$_i$ mother does

Postal's contrast still obtains, though in slightly weakened form. (23) does not seem quite as bad as (16). The important comparison is with (24), however, and (24) and (23) are quite close in acceptability.

(24) ?*Joan believes him$_i$ even more fervently than Bob's$_i$ mother does

Thus, as Postal indicates, the subject of the infinitival complement is patterning with objects in this regard: it seems to be approximately as high in the structure as an object.

Before exploring possible accounts of this property, we want to present several other paradigms displaying similar behavior. The first of these involves the distribution of reciprocal expressions. One aspect of this distribution constituted one of Postal's traditional arguments, as in (12) above, and was essentially neutral between a raising analysis and one in terms of boundary strength. The relative height of reciprocal and antecedent was not necessarily at issue in such constructions. But there is another aspect of the distribution where relative height is significant. Note that (25) is not significantly worse than (26).

(25) ?The DA proved [the defendants to be guilty] during each other's trials

(26) ?The DA accused the defendants during each other's trials

They both are considerably better than (27), the finite counterpart of (25).

(27) ?*The DA proved [that the defendants were guilty] during each other's trials

Given usual assumptions, the antecedent of a reciprocal must bear a command relation to the reciprocal, c-command, for example. But an embedded subject does not c-command an adverbial in the matrix clause. This indicates that at the point in the derivation relevant to the licensing of reciprocals, or anaphors in general, the structure of (25) has changed in such a way that the position of *the defendants* is comparable to what it is in (26).

Negative polarity item licensing is also known to display asymmetries characteristic of c-command determined relations. Thus, a negative subject of a simple sentence can license *any* in the object, but not vice versa:

(28) No one saw anything

(29) *Anyone saw nothing

Further, a negative object can, to a reasonably acceptable extent, license *any* in an adverbial:

(30) The DA accused none of the defendants during any of the trials

Now notice that to roughly the same extent, a negative subject of an infinitival can license *any* in an adverbial attached to the higher VP.

(31) ?The DA proved [none of the defendants to be guilty] during any of the trials

This is in rather sharp contrast to a corresponding finite complement:

(32) ?*The DA proved [that none of the defendants were guilty] during any of the trials.

Once again, there is reason to believe that at the relevant level of representation, the subject of the infinitival complement is approximately as high in the structure as an NP complement would be.

'Binominal each', a construction presented in Postal (1974) and explored in detail by Safir and Stowell (1988), also involves c-command relations (at least for many speakers). The 'antecedent' of *each* must c-command it:

(33) The students solved three problems each

(34) *Three students each solved the problems (i.e., on the reading 'The problems were solved by three students each')

Postal shows that there is what we have been calling a boundary strength effect with this *each*, presenting the following contrast, among others.

(35) *The students proved that three formulas each were theorems (i.e., on the reading 'Each of the students proved that three formulas were theorems')

(36) ?The students proved three formulas each to be theorems.

But there is an additional finite/non-finite asymmetry displayed by binominal *each*. Safir and Stowell present the 'small clause' in (37); the full infinitival in (38) seems equally good.

(37) Jones proved the prisoners guilty with one accusation each

(38) Jones proved the defendants to be guilty with one accusation each

(37) and (38) are comparable to (39).

(39) Jones prosecuted the defendants with one accusation each

However, the finite counterpart of (37) and (38) is degraded:[1]

(40) ??Jones proved that the defendants were guilty with one accusation each

In this paradigm, it is apparently not (just) boundary strength that is at issue, but, once again, structural height.

## 3   When does raising take place?

The examples discussed so far indicate that the subject of the embedded infinitival has roughly the height of the matrix object at some level of representation. And the level of representation in question must be where the possibility

---

[1] We are, frankly, puzzled by the fact that these finite complement are as good as they are. As far as we know, under no analysis do subjects of finite clauses undergo raising, so one would expect all such examples to be completely impossible.

of pronominal coreference is explained and where anaphors, negative polarity items and binominal *each* are licensed. According to Postal's (1974) 'raising to object' analysis, the relevant level is S(urface)-structure, since the subject becomes a structural object by the operation of a syntactic transformation. But there is an alternative possibility that we might consider.

Chomsky (1989) notes that structural Case assignment (or checking) appears to take place in two distinct basic configurations. Assuming that Agreement (or some related functional category) is responsible for nominative Case assignment/checking, such Case assignment can be regarded as an instantiation of Spec-Head agreement. Accusative Case assignment, on the other hand, is standardly viewed as arising from a government relation between a verb and the accusative NP. Chomsky speculates that the second type of Case assignment might be reducible to the first if, inside of the subject agreement (AGR-S) projection, there is an object agreement (AGR-O) projection. Then the structural relation necessary for accusative Case could once again be a Spec-Head relation, this time holding between the SPEC and head of AGR-O (with the contribution of V to the Case assignment process presumably following from the amalgamation of V with AGR-O). As Chomsky indicates, in a language like English, movement to SPEC of AGR-O does not take place between D(eep)-structure and S(urface)-structure. SPECs in English are phrase initial, but the accusative direct object of a verb follows the verb, hence follows the AGR head that takes the VP as its complement. But this leaves open the possibility that the movement takes place 'later', between S-structure and LF. Chomsky thus suggests the following phrase structure for sentences:

(41)
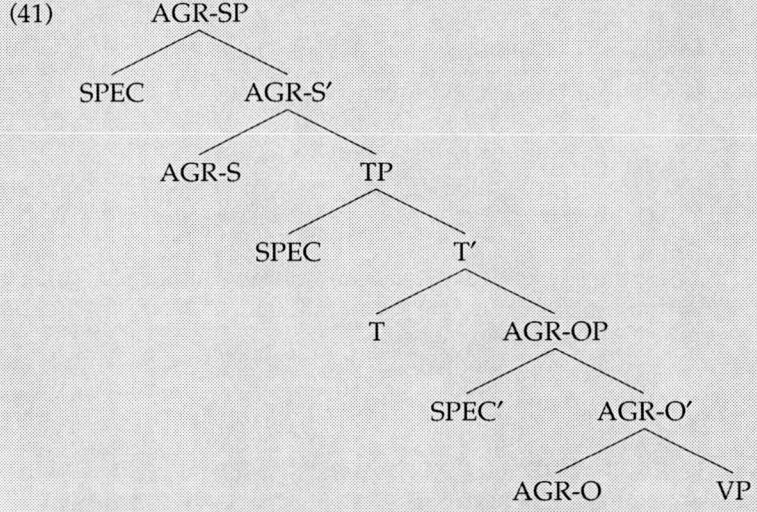

Assuming that in English, NPs with accusative Case must move to the SPEC position of AGR-OP in the LF Component for the purpose of Case assignment/checking, this hypothesis, then, implies that the subject of the embedded infinitival and the matrix object are in the same position at the level of LF.

Thus, a possibility arises that the subject is raised to the matrix not at S-structure but at LF.

In this section, we will explore the question of whether the raising that we have already seen evidence for takes place prior to S-structure, as Postal (1974) proposes, or after S-structure, along the lines of Chomsky's conjecture. We will find some reason to believe that the raising operation argued for in the preceding section is not LF movement to SPEC of AGR-O, but rather is an independent S-structure operation.

First, the parallelism between (23) and (24) indicates that the subject of the embedded infinitival assumes a position comparable in structural height with that of the matrix object at a level where the possibility of pronominal coreference is determined. Discussing the following examples, Chomsky (1981) argues that his Condition C must apply at S-structure:

(42) Which book that John$_i$ read did he$_i$ like

(43) *He$_i$ liked every book that John$_i$ read

The grammaticality of (42) shows that the condition does not apply at D-structure. (43), on the other hand, indicates that LF cannot be the only level where the condition applies: After quantifier raising (QR) applies in LF, (43) has roughly the same configuration as (42). Hence, Chomsky concludes that the condition applies at least at S-structure, and possibly also at LF.

If Condition C (or whatever the relevant disjoint reference condition is) applies at LF, in addition to S-structure, the parallelism between (23) and (24) can be accounted for at this level. Thus, it is immaterial whether the raising takes place at S-structure or LF. On the other hand, if the condition applies only at S-structure, the parallelism must be accounted for at this level. This implies that the embedded subject must be raised out of the embedded clause prior to this level, and hence, that the raising must be an S-structure operation. And there is a piece of evidence (although somewhat weak) that the disjoint reference condition applies only at S-structure.

It is shown in Saito (1986, 1989) that Japanese scrambling can move a WH-phrase out of the CP where it takes scope. (45) is slightly worse than (44), but is at worst only marginal.

(44) [$_{IP}$Kare-wa [$_{CP}$ [$_{IP}$Mary-ga  [$_{NP}$John-nituite-no dono hon]-o yonda]
    he -top           -nom     -about -gen which book-acc read
    ka] siritagatteiru]
    Q  want-to-know
    (He wants to know which book about John Mary read)

(45) ?[$_{IP}$[$_{NP}$John-nituite-no dono hon]-o$_i$ [$_{IP}$kare-wa [$_{CP}$[$_{IP}$Mary-ga $t_i$ yonda] ka] siritagatteiru]]

In both (44) and (45), the WH-phrase, *John-nituite-no dono hon*, takes embedded scope. Hence, the examples should both have the LF representation in (46).

(46) [IP Kare-wa [CP [NP John-nituite-no dono hon ] -o_i [C' [IP Mary-ga t_i yonda] ka]] siritagatteiru]

Now, it is pointed out in Saito (1986) that there is a difference between (44) and (45) in the possibility of coreference of *John* and *kare*: It is totally impossible in (44), but not in (45).[2] This difference is unexpected if the disjoint reference condition applies at LF (as well as at S-structure), since the two examples have the same LF representation, in which the pronoun clearly c-commands *John*. On the other hand, if the condition applies only at S-structure, the two examples can be correctly distinguished. Thus, the contrast between (44) and (45) suggests that the disjoint reference condition applies only at S-structure, and not at LF.

The argument above for raising as an S-structure operation was based on data that require rather subtle contrastive judgement, e.g., (23), (24) and (45). But it is possible to construct the same kind of argument on the basis of the licensing of anaphors, where the relevant facts are somewhat clearer. As pointed out in Barss (1986), and Lasnik and Saito (1990), examples such as the following indicate that anaphors cannot be licensed solely on the basis of an LF configuration:

(47) John$_i$ wonders which picture of himself$_i$ Mary showed to Susan

(48) *John$_i$ wonders who showed which picture of himself$_i$ to Susan

(47) shows that an anaphor within the embedded CP SPEC can be licensed by an antecedent in the matrix subject position. Given this fact, the ungrammaticality of (48) is surprising if anaphors can be licensed solely at LF. In LF, the WH-phrase in situ, *which picture of himself*, moves to the embedded CP SPEC position, where it takes scope. Thus, at LF, the configurational relation between *himself* and its antecedent is virtually identical in (47) and (48). Hence, the ungrammaticality of (48) shows that anaphors must be licensed at a level prior to LF, e.g., S-structure (and possibly at LF as well). (48) is ruled out because the reflexive fails to be licensed at that level.

Given the fact of anaphor licensing mentioned above, let us consider again the contrast between (25) and (26), repeated as (49) and (50), respectively.

(49) ?The DA proved [the defendants to be guilty] during each other's trials

(50) ?The DA accused the defendants during each other's trials

If the embedded subject in (49) moves to the matrix only in LF, then the anaphor, *each other*, can be licensed only at this level. We, then, predict incorrectly that the example has the status of (48). On the other hand, if the subject is raised to the matrix at S-structure, then the anaphor can be licensed already at this level, and we predict correctly that the example has the status of (47).

---

[2] It should be noted here that not all speakers agree on the improved status of (45) compared with (44). But the contrast between the two examples seems to us to be clear.

Hence, (49) indicates that the raising of the subject of an embedded infinitival must take place at S-structure, as proposed in Postal (1974).

Uriagereka (1988) suggests one further test to determine the level at which anaphors must be licensed, based on Chomsky's (1986) proposal that at LF, expletives are replaced by the arguments with which they are associated. For example, S-structure (51) becomes LF (52).

(51)  There arrived a man

(52)  A man arrived *t*

Based on the acceptability of (53), Uriagereka proposes that anaphors need not be licensed at S-structure, reasoning that the required c-command relation between *two knights* and *each other* holds at LF (54) but not at S-structure (53).[3]

(53)  There arrived two knights on each other's horses

(54)  two knights arrived *t* on each other's horses

However, this interesting argument is not entirely conclusive, since we have seen repeatedly that direct objects do, in fact, seem to c-command certain adjuncts. We defer to a later section discussion of how this could be possible, but given that it is, the anaphor in (53) could be licensed at S-structure. However, Uriagereka's test can be applied in less equivocal fashion to our central concern – the properties of raising constructions. As seen earlier, the subject of an infinitival can serve as the antecedent of a reciprocal within an adjunct in the higher clause. (55) is an example, similar to those above, of this phenomenon.

(55)  The DA proved [two men to have been at the scene] during each other's trials

However, (56), which should be identical to (55) at LF in relevant respects, under the expletive replacement hypothesis, is severely degraded.

(56)  *The DA proved [there to have been two men at the scene] during each other's trials

S-structure, rather than LF, is the level at which (55) can be appropriately distinguished from (56) with respect to anaphor licensing. Thus, this contrast implies that anaphors must be licensed at S-structure.

There is also some (slight) evidence that the licensing of negative polarity items is based on S-structure, rather than LF, configurations. May (1977)

---

[3] Actually, according to the specific analysis of expletive-argument pairs in Chomsky (1986), (53) would straightforwardly satisfy the binding requirement of the anaphor at S-structure, since Chomsky claimed that throughout the derivation expletives are coindexed with their associated arguments. But see Lasnik (in press) for arguments against this position.

discusses the ambiguity of sentences involving subject raising to subject position, such as (57).

(57) Some politician is likely to address John's constituency

He points out that the quantifier in subject position can have either wide or narrow scope with respect to the predicate *likely*. On the narrow reading, (57) is roughly synonymous with (58).

(58) It is likely that some politician will address John's constituency

May proposes that this reading of (57) is derived via the LF lowering of the quantifier to the embedded clause. Next, notice that while a negative raising predicate in a configuration like that in (58) can license *any*, as in (59), *any* is none-the-less impossible as the surface subject of the negative predicate, as shown in (60).

(59) It is unlikely that anyone will address the rally

(60) *Anyone is unlikely to address the rally

(59) is unsurprising: the negative predicate c-commands *anyone*. (60) is also unsurprising based on its S-structure configuration: *unlikely* does not c-command *anyone*. However, if quantifier lowering is possible, the LF of (60) should be like (59) in relevant respects. Thus, this is potentially a strong argument that such licensing must take place at S-structure, and consequently, that the licensing negative in examples like (31) above must have already raised by S-structure.

The one weakness in the argument above is that, for reasons that are unclear, quantifier lowering across a negative predicate is degraded. Thus, (61) does not readily permit the narrow scope interpretation.

(61) Someone is unlikely to address the rally

But if such lowering is barred, then even at LF *anyone* in (60) will not be in a licit configuration. The relevant factual question, then, is whether (60) is even worse than the narrow scope reading of (61). While the judgement is not as clear as one might hope, (60) does, in fact, seem to be worse. And just to the extent that it is worse, we have evidence that negative polarity items must be licensed at S-structure, and, hence, that raising must take place by S-structure.

## 4 Postal's B-verbs vs. W-verbs

Postal argues that despite the several differences between B(elieve)-type verbs and W(ant)-type verbs, raising to object position is equally applicable with both. Bach (1977) questions this, suggesting, with Bresnan (1972), that raising is limited to B-verb constructions. One of his arguments is of particular relevance to us since it belongs to the class of arguments implicating height of the subject of the infinitival complement. In particular, Bach indicates that the effects of the pronominalization constraint illustrated in (16) above are less clear with *want* than with *believe*. Continuing to control for potential interference from reconstruction of the elided VP, we can compare (62) with (23) above, repeated here as (63):

(62) ?Joan wants him$_i$ to be successful even more fervently than Bob's$_i$ mother does.

(63) ?*Joan believes him$_i$ to be a genius even more fervently than Bob's$_i$ mother does.

As Bach implies, there does seem to be at least something of a contrast.

Given the contrast between (62) and (23), it might be informative to insert *want* into other configurations examined above. In these, too, there is a consistent, though small, distinction. The reciprocal in (64) is slightly worse than the one in (65).

(64) ??*I wanted [those men to be fired] because of each other's statements.

(65) ?I believed [those men to be unreliable] because of each other's statements.

Similarly for the licensing of negative polarity *any*:

(66) ??*I wanted [none of the applicants to be hired] after reading any of the reports

(67) ??I believed [none of the applicants to be qualified] after reading any of the reports

Binominal *each* shows a similar pattern.

(68) ??*I wanted [them to be fired] for three reasons each

(69) ??I believed [them to be incompetent] for three reasons each

Note that, as would be expected under any existing account of raising phenomena, when the complement of *want* is introduced by the complementizer *for*, the subject of that complement does not behave at all like an object of *want*:

(70) ?*I wanted very much [for those men to be fired] because of each other's statements.

(71) *I wanted very much [for none of the applicants to be hired] after reading any of the reports.

(72) ?*I wanted very much [for them to be fired] for three reasons each.

In (70)–(72), it is clear that no syntactic raising has taken place, just as assumed by Postal. Evidently the presence of the complementizer *for* blocks raising, as suggested by Bresnan (1972). Even under Chomsky's LF approach (if a way can be found to maintain it), raising to higher SPEC of AGR-O will presumably not take place here, since *want*, the verb associated with that AGR-O, is not involved in Case assignment to the lower subject. Rather, it is *for* that determines the assignment of Case in this configuration. The situation is less straightforward for (64), (66), and (68), where there is no *for*. If we are to assimilate these to (70)–(72), we must postulate either that *for* is actually present at the point in the derivation where NP raising would take place, and is deleted later (as suggested in another context by Chomsky (1981)), or that there is a null version of the *for* complementizer that occurs with the W-verbs whenever *for* itself is absent.

## 5 Raising questions

We have seen several pieces of evidence for the existence of raising between D-structure and S-structure. The evidence was, if not overwhelming, at least suggestive. On the other hand, there are conceptual arguments in the literature to the effect that raising is not a possible operation. Chomsky (1981), for example, proposes that "each lexical element $\alpha$ assigns a $\theta$-role to every NP or clause in its complement..." [p. 93]. This would forbid an empty NP in the complement of *believe* into which the subject of the infinitival could raise. However, as noted by McCawley (1988), this constraint is not obviously crucial to Chomsky's theory. Chomsky further argues that if there is S'-deletion (a process weakening the strength of the clausal boundary) in these infinitival complements, then raising is superfluous [p. 146]. Note that while raising might indeed be superfluous with respect to boundary strength phenomena, the same is not true for height effects, as discussed above.

Thus far, then, there is no clearly compelling reason to reject syntactic raising. Chomsky (1986) pursues this issue further. Based on proposals of Pesetsky (1982), he suggests that 'c-selection' (subcategorization) might be eliminable, its effects deduced from 's(emantic)-selection'. He then continues,

> If we succeed in eliminating recourse to c-selection as well as phrase structure rules, thus reducing syntactic representations at D-structure to projections of semantic properties of lexical items, it will follow that the complement of any lexical head in a syntactic representation must be s-selected by it, because there is no other way for the position to exist. For example, there cannot be such sentences as (68), where V is a verb that does not s-select an object and *there* is a pleonastic element... lacking any semantic role...

John [$_{VP}$V there] (68)

... Similarly, we cannot have "raising to object" to yield (70ii) (with *e* the trace of *Bill*) from the D-structure (70i):

*i*  John [$_{VP}$believes *e* [$_S$Bill to be intelligent]]     (70)

*ii* John [$_{VP}$believes Bill [$_S$*e* to be intelligent]]

The verb *believe* s-selects only a proposition. Therefore, in (70i) the position occupied by *e* cannot exist at D-structure, because it is not s-selected by *believe*. [pp. 90–1]

This line of reasoning is part of the more general theory outlined in Chomsky (1986; 1989) emphasizing the importance of 'economy of representation' and 'full interpretation'. The leading idea of this approach is that symbols cannot appear in a representation at a linguistic level unless they have significance at that level of representation. It was this concept that formed the background for the expletive replacement analysis discussed above with respect to Uriagereka's (53)–(54). The pleonastic element *there* is replaced at LF because it has no significance at this level, being semantically empty. Now given that D-structure is "an abstract representation of semantically relevant grammatical relations..." [Chomsky (1986, p. 67)], Chomsky's conclusion about raising would seem to follow. The empty NP in his (70)ii above is not s-selected, has no semantic import, and therefore cannot appear at a level of representation that is devoted to representing s-selection relations. Ultimately, though, there is an asymmetry that must be stipulated, since this line of reasoning would lead to the conclusion that not only non-thematic objects, but also non-thematic subjects, are precluded at D-structure. That is, it would disallow even subject raising into subject position, or the NP preposing portion of passive, or, for that matter, D-structures with pleonastic *it* or *there*, all of which are well-motivated internal to Chomsky's theory. Since there is no evident semantic difference between pleonastic subject positions and pleonastic object positions, we are in the position of essentially stipulating either that the former are allowed or that the latter are disallowed. And the principled nature of Chomsky's recent theory makes such a stipulation rather difficult.

Postal and Pullum (1988) consider some of these same conceptual questions, and a related empirical question: Are pleonastic objects in fact impossible? They cite a variety of examples, including the following ones, indicating that expletives are possible in object position.

(73) I dislike it that he is so cruel

(74) I didn't suspect it for a moment that you would fail

(75) I regret it very much that we could not hire Mosconi

(76) I resent it greatly that you didn't call me

(77) I don't mind it very much that he did that

All of these are fully acceptable, and in all of them, the *it* is reasonably regarded as an expletive. And if pleonastic objects are allowed, Postal and Pullum argue, there is no principled basis for rejecting raising to object position. This reasoning seems sound, but the actual patterning of facts is surprisingly discordant. In particular, there is very little correlation between the verbs that take expletive objects and those that take infinitival complements with overt subjects. The verbs in (73)–(77), for example, range from marginal to completely unacceptable in 'raising' contexts:

(78) ??I dislike him to be so cruel.

(79) ?*I didn't suspect you to have failed.

(80) *I regret them not to have hired Mosconi.

(81) *I resent you not to have called me.

(82) *I don't mind him to have done that.

Conversely, Postal's best instances of B-raising verbs, *believe*, *prove*, *find*, and *show*, are not particularly comfortable with *it* objects:

(83) I believe (??it) that John left.

(84) I will prove (?*it) that Mary is the culprit.

(85) They have found (*it) that there is a prime number greater than 17.

(86) I will show (*it) that the Coordinate Structure Constraint is valid.

Given that only some verbs allow expletive objects, and given that only some verbs appear in raising configurations, by Postal and Pullum's argument one would expect these two classes of verbs to converge. But it is clear that they do not. In fact, most of the best instances of expletive objects occur with factive verbs, in the sense of Kiparsky and Kiparsky (1970), while, as the Kiparskys observed, raising is generally not permitted with factives. Thus, while Postal and Pullum's examples of expletive objects potentially provide a conceptual basis for allowing raising to object, they provide little if any empirical basis.

There are two further theoretical questions that must be addressed. The first specifically involves the Condition C effect in (17) and (23) above. Since in this instance, the relevant phenomenon is a filtering effect, rather than a licensing effect as with polarity *any*, binominal *each*, reciprocals, it is crucial that the raising process be obligatory. If it were optional, it could simply refrain from applying, and there then should be no detectable noncoreference phenomenon. This is significant since we assume, following Chomsky and Lasnik (1977), that obligatoriness is not simply a stipulated property of transformational operations, but rather, must follow from deeper principles. Note that under Chomsky's approach, while the level of application was argued to be wrong, obligatoriness is straightforward. The Case of an accusative NP would not be appropriately licensed if it did not raise to SPEC of AGR-O. It is less clear under the classic transformational account. Interestingly, Postal and Pullum suggest an answer that is Case based, much like the one we just sketched, conjecturing that raising is necessary in order for the accusative NP to be close enough to the verb that assigns case to it: 'the transclausal boundary Case-marking alternatives to Raising-to-Object analyses violate what would otherwise be a possible restrictive constraint on Case marking' [p. 666].

The final theoretical question was alluded to earlier. We noted that with respect to all of the paradigms considered, the subject of the infinitive was behaving like an object of the higher verb. We further observed that it was unclear why even true objects were behaving the way they were, since all of the paradigms involved c-command phenomena, and objects do not obviously c-command adjuncts. Here, again, an approach in terms of SPEC of AGR-O could (apart from the question of level of applicability) give exactly the right structural relations. The SPEC of AGR-O c-commands everything in, or adjoined to, VP.

In summary, we have seen empirical evidence that raising takes place by S-structure. But, at the same time, some of the specific formal properties of raising seem more readily explicable under the LF SPEC of AGR-O approach. It remains to be seen how this conflict can be resolved.

## References

Bach, E. (1974) *Syntactic Theory*, Holt, Rinehart and Winston, New York.
Bach, E. (1977) "Review Article on *On Raising: One Rule of English Grammar and its Theoretical Implications*," Language 53, pp. 621–54.
Barss, A. (1986) "Chains and Anaphoric Dependence: On Reconstruction and its Implications," PhD Dissertation, MIT.
Bresnan, J. (1972) "Theory of Complementation in English Syntax," PhD Dissertation, MIT.
Chomsky, N. (1973) "Conditions on Transformations," in S. R. Anderson and P. Kiparsky, eds, *A Festschrift for Morris Halle*, Holt, Rinehart and Winston, New York.
Chomsky, N. (1981) *Lectures on Government and Binding*, Foris Publications, Dordrecht.
Chomsky, N. (1986) *Knowledge of Language: Its Nature, Origin, and Use*, Praeger, New York.
Chomsky, N. (1989) "Some Notes on Economy of Derivation and Representation," *MIT Working Papers in Linguistics* 10, pp. 43–74.
Chomsky, N. and H. Lasnik (1977) "Filters and Control," *Linguistic Inquiry* 11, pp. 1–46.
Kiparsky, P. and C. Kiparsky (1970) "Fact," in M. Bierwisch and K. E. Heidolph, eds, *Progress in Linguistics*, Mouton, The Hague.

Langacker, R. W. (1969) "On Pronominalization and the Chain of Command," in D. A. Reibel and S. A. Schane, eds, *Modern Studies in English*, Prentice-Hall, Englewood Cliffs, New Jersey.

Lasnik, H. (1976) "Remarks on Coreference," *Linguistic Analysis* 2, pp. 1–22.

Lasnik, H. (to appear) [1992] "Two Notes on Control and Binding," in R. K. Larson, et al., eds, *Control and Grammar*, Kluwer Academic Publishers, Dordrecht.

Lasnik, H. and M. Saito (1990) *Move-α*, forthcoming from MIT Press, Cambridge, Massachusetts [pub. 1992 as *Move-α: Conditions on its Application and Output*].

McCawley, J. D. (1988) "Review Article on *Knowledge of Language: Its Structure, Origin, and Use*," Language 64, pp. 355–65.

May, R. (1977) "The Grammar of Quantification", PhD Dissertation, MIT.

Pesetsky, D. (1982) "Paths and Categories," PhD Dissertation, MIT.

Postal, P. M. (1974) *On Raising: One Rule of English Grammar and its Theoretical Implications*, MIT Press, Cambridge, Massachusetts.

Postal, P. M. and G. K. Pullum (1988) "Expletive Noun Phrases in Subcategorized Positions," *Linguistic Inquiry* 19, pp. 635–70.

Rosenbaum, P. S. (1967) *The Grammar of English Predicate Complement Constructions*, MIT Press, Cambridge, Massachusetts.

Safir, K. and T. Stowell (1988) "Binominal Each," *NELS* 18, pp. 426–50.

Saito, M. (1986) "LF Effects of Scrambling," Princeton Workshop on Comparative Grammar.

Saito, M. (1989) "Scrambling as Semantically Vacuous A'-Movement," in M. R. Baltin and A. S. Kroch, eds, *Alternative Conceptions of Phrase Structure*, University of Chicago Press, Chicago.

Uriagereka, J. (1988) "On Government," PhD Dissertation, University of Connecticut.

## 2  Discussion of Lasnik and Saito (1991)

In their paper, Lasnik and Saito (L&S) cite five arguments for the raising analysis, all of which involve demonstrating the different properties of subjects of embedded infinitival versus tensed complements of RtoO predicates. It turns out that in each instance the difference can be attributed to the infinitival subject residing higher in the Phrase Structure than the subject of the tensed complement, and in each instance the infinitival subject patterns with direct objects. As shown in previous chapters, these are the classic types of arguments that have been put forward for Raising. In fact, three of the arguments cited are resurrected from Postal (1974) – the scope of *few*, pronominalization, and binomial *each*. L&S add to this the behavior of reciprocal binding and licensing negative polarity items. In each of these cases, the infinitival subject must c-command a matrix clause dependent to account for the contrast; this, of course, necessitates that the subject also be a matrix clause dependent. Thus, L&S propose that just as direct objects must move to Spec,AgrOP for Case checking, the infinitival subject also moves to Spec,AgrOP for Case checking. Accordingly, (1) has a derivation like that in (2), ignoring for the sake of clarity movement in the embedded clause.[1]

(1) Chris believes Terry to have left.

(2)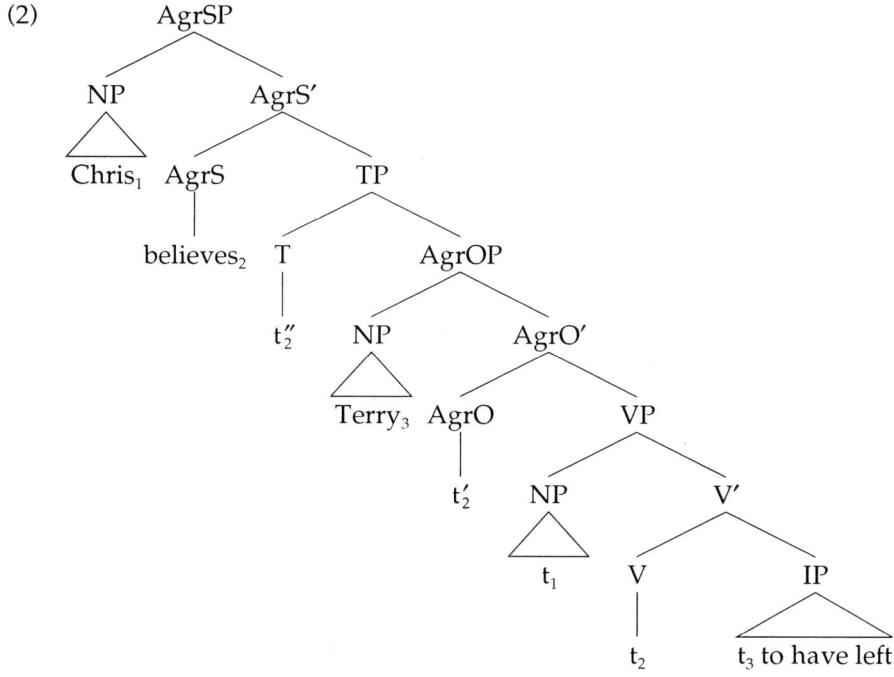

In (2), *Terry* has moved into Spec,AgrOP from its complement clause position.

Among the evidence L&S adduce for the raising analysis is Postal's argument from pronominalization. Recall from chapter 3 and L&S's discussion of Postal's argument regarding the restriction that a pronoun may not (c-)command its antecedent, which, as L&S point out, would be a violation of principle C of the Binding Theory. Specifically, the ungrammaticality of (3) (= &S's (16)) as opposed to (4) (= & S's (15)) results from the fact that *him* c-commands *Bob*; thus an R-expression is illicitly bound.

(3) *Joan believes him$_i$ to be a genius even more fervently than Bob$_i$ does.

(4) Joan believes he$_i$ is a genius even more fervently than Bob$_i$ does.

Recall also from chapter 5 and L&S's discussion that Bresnan (1976) suggests that the ungrammaticality of (3) is due not to any c-command relation between *him* and *Bob* but to the ungrammaticality of the source for (3). The sentence in (3) includes VP ellipsis, and if the elided VP is restored, the sentence is still ungrammatical (5) (= &S's (17)).

(5) *Joan believes him$_i$ to be a genius even more fervently than Bob$_i$ believes him$_i$ to be a genius.

Crucially, (5) is ungrammatical because the sentence of comparison *$Bob_i$ believes $him_i$ to be a genius* is ungrammatical, and thus the ungrammaticality of the source of (3) could itself well account for the ungrammaticality of (3). However, L&S are able to rescue the pronominalization argument. When they replace the NP *Bob* with *Bob's mother*, as in (6) (= &S's (23) and (7) (= &S's (22)), the effects noted in (3) and (4) are replicated.

(6) ?*Joan believes $him_i$ to be a genius even more fervently than Bob's $mother_i$ does.

(7) Joan believes $he_i$ is a genius even more fervently than Bob's $mother_i$ does.

The ungrammaticality of (6) cannot be attributed to the fact that the source sentence with the elided VP restored is ungrammatical inasmuch as *Bob's$_i$ mother believes $him_i$ to be a genius* is a perfectly well-formed sentence. What is more, the ungrammaticality of (6) is comparable to the ungrammaticality of L&S's (24), in which *him* is the object of *believe*. Thus, the infinitival subject of the RtoO structure (6) patterns like an object (and one of Bresnan's stronger criticisms of Postal's arguments for Raising dissolves).

All five of L&S's arguments for the high position of the infinitival subject in the tree involve interpretation. As such, these data only provide evidence that the subject has raised to this position by LF, the level of interpretation. Therefore, as L&S indicate, this means that the data are indeterminate regarding whether the movement is overt movement occurring before Spell-Out or covert occurring after Spell-Out. Here, L&S seem to be of two minds. In section 3, they consider various binding phenomena that hint at the possibility that movement must occur in the overt syntax. To take one example, L&S argue that the grammaticality of (8) (= L&S's (47)) and the ungrammaticality of (9) (= L&S's (48)) indicate that anaphor binding must be allowed to occur by S-structure (Spell-Out).

(8) $John_i$ wonders which picture of $himself_i$ Mary showed to Susan.

(9) *$John_i$ wonders who showed which picture of $himself_i$ to Susan.

The sentence in (8) is grammatical because *which picture of himself* moves to Spec,CP of the lower clause before Spell-Out and in this position can be licitly bound by *John*. If binding were an LF phenomenon, (9) should be equally grammatical. This is because the NP *which picture of himself* moves to Spec,CP of the lower clause at LF for proper interpretation of its scope. In that position, it should be possible for *John* to bind the anaphor *himself* here just as it does in (8). However, (9) is ungrammatical. This ungrammaticality is explained if, as L&S state, "anaphors must be licensed at a level prior to LF," i.e., they must be bound before Spell-Out. The ungrammaticality of (9) is evidence for this since pre-Spell-Out *which picture of himself* is in object position of the embedded clause and thus cannot be licitly bound by *John*. Granting this, anaphor binding provides evidence for overt movement of the subject. As (10) (= L&S's (49)) shows, the infinitival subject *the defendants* may bind the anaphor *each other* in the matrix clause; therefore, it must have moved to Spec,AgrOP prior to Spell-Out.

(10) ?The DA proved [the defendants$_i$ to be guilty] during each other's$_i$ trials.

As (11a) shows, if *the defendants* moves to Spec,AgrOP pre-Spell-Out, it c-commands the anaphor *each other* in the prepositional phrase, while as (11b) shows, if it remains in the embedded clause at Spell-Out, it does not c-command the anaphor.

(11)  a.   ... proved$_j$ [$_{AgrOP}$the defendants$_i$ [$_{VP}$t$_j$ [$_{AgrSP}$t$_i$ to be guilty] during each other's$_i$ trials]]

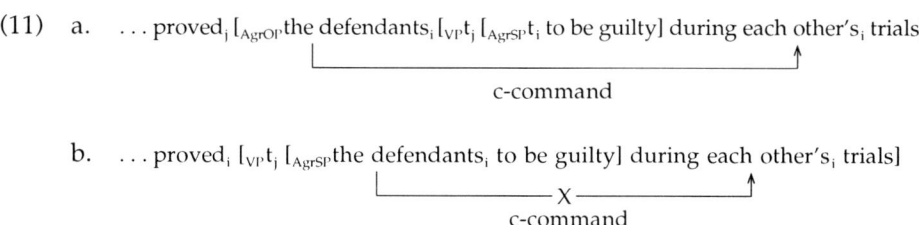

c-command

   b.   ... proved$_j$ [$_{VP}$t$_j$ [$_{AgrSP}$the defendants$_i$ to be guilty] during each other's$_i$ trials]

——X——
c-command

At the same time, L&S appear to be somewhat less than convinced by their own empirical evidence. While asserting that there is "some reason to believe that the raising operation . . . is an independent S-structure operation," L&S nonetheless take very seriously Chomsky's (1989, 1992) position that movement to Spec,AgrOP is an LF operation in English. They appear to see the tension between the empirical evidence and the theoretical position as requiring caution and conclude that "it remains to be seen how this conflict can be resolved."[2] As we will see in section 3, Runner (1995) argues strongly for overt Raising, citing arguments of Postal's from adverbs not considered by L&S as well as data he adduces from quantifier float.

Despite any equivocation about when Raising occurs, L&S are clear about the fact that the infinitival subject has the properties of an object. Furthermore, while L&S take the position that non-thematic object positions exist, citing the evidence in Postal and Pullum (1988) (see chapter 9), within the Minimalist framework there is no reason to believe that Raising is to an argument position. What L&S have shown is that the infinitival subject ultimately occupies the same position as the accusative object. But, as they argue, even thematic objects of the verb must raise out of the VP to be in an appropriate structural configuration to license negative polarity items in VP adjuncts, as in (12) (= L&S's (30)).

(12) The DA accused none of the defendants during any of the trials.

If the object *none of the defendants* remained in its VP-internal position at LF, it would not c-command the NPI *any* in the PP adjunct, as is obvious in (13).

(13)

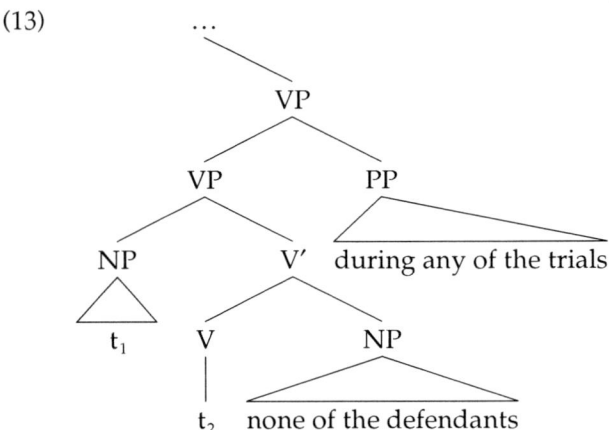

However, if the object moves to Spec,AgrOP by LF, the appropriate c-command relation is established, as in (14).

(14)

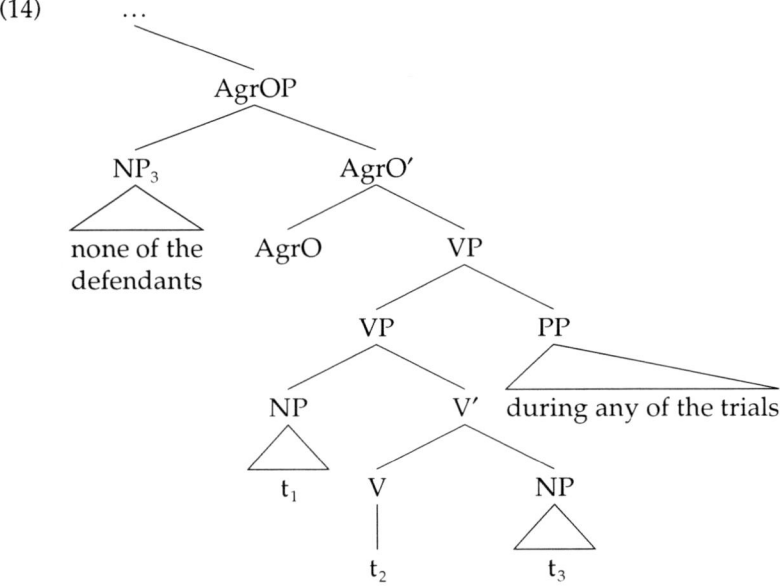

Thus, under L&S's proposal, RtoO infinitival subjects like objects in general are derived objects, that is, in the course of the derivation both types of arguments move into the same Spec,AgrOP position. In this way, the current analysis is equivalent to others that precede it in asserting that these infinitival subjects are final objects.[3]

## 3  Evidence for overt movement: Runner (1995)

While L&S are equivocal about whether movement to Spec,AgrOP is overt or covert, a number of others took up the issue, all concluding that the movement is indeed overt (Koizumi 1993, 1995; Runner 1995; Ura 1993). Here we focus on Runner (1995), who devotes the most energy to arguing strongly for overt movement, explaining that the central claim of his dissertation is that "direct objects in English move overtly to a Case position external to VP" (1995:vii).

After arguing extensively that direct objects in English move to Spec,AgrOP in overt syntax, Runner turns his attention to RtoO structures. He examines particularly closely evidence bearing on the surface position of the infinitival subject. He provides conceptual evidence in addition to empirical evidence. In developing his conceptual argument, Runner notes that if the RtoO subject did not move to Spec,AgrOP until after Spell-Out there would be no account for why RtoO passive and unaccusative subjects occur before the verb. Minimalist assumptions about the thematic position of passive and unaccusative subjects parallel the GB analysis – they occur postverbally, in the thematic object position. Thus, the structures in (15b) and (16b) underlie (15a) and (16a).

(15) a. Laverne believes Shirley$_i$ to have been arrested t$_i$.    [= Runner 1995: (18)]
    b. Laverne believes [to have been [$_{VP}$arrested Shirley]]

(16) a. Richie expects Ralph$_i$ to arrive t$_i$ at nine.    [= Runner 1995: (19)]
    b. Richie expects [ to [$_{VP}$arrive Ralph at nine]]

As Runner points out, if the accusative Case feature in English is weak and movement to Spec,AgrOP occurs at LF, there is no explanation for why the RtoO subject precedes the infinitive rather than remaining in situ. Under the overt movement analysis, *Shirley* in (15a) and *Ralph* in (16a) precede the infinitive precisely because they have moved to Spec,AgrOP before Spell-Out for Case checking.[4]

In presenting the case for overt movement, Runner resurrects two arguments from Postal regarding the placement of adverbs in RtoO structures. First, Runner notes that if raising does not occur until LF, there would be no account for why the adverb *very strongly* in (17b) cannot precede the RtoO subject.

(17) a. I believe very strongly that Tony is honest.
    b. *I believe very strongly Tony to be honest.

Since adverbs can clearly precede clausal complements (16a), if *Tony* were in the embedded clause at Spell-Out, (17b) should be perfectly grammatical. However, (17b) is parallel to adverb placement with objects; that is, the adverb may not intercede between the verb and its object, (18).

(18) *I believe very strongly Tony's assertion.

If both the object *Tony's assertion* in (18) and the RtoO subject *Tony* in (17b) raise to Spec,AgrOP in overt syntax, the ungrammaticality of (18) and (17b) is expected.

The second of Postal's arguments that Runner cites is also from adverbs. As was discussed in chapter 3, section 1, the adverb *foolishly* has different scope possibilities in the sentences in (19). (Again, these examples are from Postal 1974.)

(19) a. I believed that Nixon, foolishly, was interested in ending the war.
b. I believed Nixon, foolishly, to be interested in ending the war.

In (19a), the adverb unambiguously modifies the embedded clause with the approximate meaning "it was foolish of Nixon to be interested in ending the war." In (19b), on the other hand, the interpretation of the adverb is ambiguous. It can either have the same meaning as in (19a) or it may modify the matrix clause, in which case it has the approximate meaning "it was foolish of me to believe that Nixon was interested in ending the war." As Runner points out, these facts provide direct evidence for overt movement to Spec,AgrOP (in just the same way they provided evidence of Raising for Postal). If at Spell-Out *Nixon* were still a dependent of the embedded clause, the adverb *foolishly* would also necessarily be an embedded dependent and (19b) should have only the meaning of (19a). However, with the subject in Spec,AgrOP it is possible for the adverb to be either a constituent of the embedded clause, adjoined to the left edge, or a constituent of the matrix clause, adjoined to the right, giving it matrix scope. Postal's Adverb II argument thus provides evidence for overt movement.

Runner also provides his own novel argument for overt movement based on ordering restrictions on adverbs and floated quantifiers. Leaving aside the details of the argument here, Runner notes that in finite clauses a sentential adverb such as *probably* can naturally precede the floated quantifier *all* (20a) but not follow it (20b).

(20) a. The boys probably all will leave after the movie.
b. ?*The boys all probably will leave after the movie.

Runner notes that the same ordering effects obtain in non-finite clauses.

(21) a. It would worry Martha for [the boys all to leave].
b. ?It would worry Martha for [the boys probably to leave].

(22) a. ?It would worry Martha for [the boys probably all to leave].
b. *It would worry Martha for [the boys all probably to leave].

As he notes, *probably* is not an entirely felicitous adverb in non-finite clauses (thus the judgment of (21b)), so it is the contrast between (22a) and (22b) that is the focus. While (22a) is somewhat questionable, (22b) is significantly worse. This, then, parallels the facts in (20). In both (20) and (22) *the boys* is in Spec,AgrSP, as is expected of subjects in English. Thus, one can conclude that the appropriate ordering is subject–*probably*–*all*. Now, Runner reasons, if raising is covert and the RtoO subject is in an embedded Spec,AgrSP at Spell-Out, it is predicted that the order subject–*all*–*probably*–*to* should be ungrammatical, just as in (22b). However, this order is indeed possible, as (23) illustrates.

(23) John expects the boys all probably to have left.

Under Runner's analysis of the positions of *probably* and *all* in the tree structure (the details of which will not concern us here), the unanticipated ordering found in (23) can be accounted for if the RtoO subject moves overtly to Spec,AgrOP. This is because the quantifier *all* can reside in the Spec,AgrSP vacated by the RtoO subject, a position that precedes the adverb.

Runner's last argument for overt movement is based on the interaction of particle verbs and RtoO. As is well known, the direct object of a particle verb can appear either following the particle (24a) or preceding it (24b).

(24) a. The operator looked up the number.
     b. The operator looked the number up.

Following Johnson's (1991) analysis, Runner assumes that the two structures in (24) illustrate the two possibilities available for particle verbs: (i) the particle moves with the verb up the tree or (ii) the verb moves alone, stranding the particle. Assuming overt movement of object, he gives the following structures for (24a,b):

(25) a. The operator$_i$ [[looked up]$_j$ [$_{AgrOP}$the number$_k$ [$_{VP}$t$_i$ t$_j$ t$_k$]]].
     b. The operator$_i$ [[looked]$_j$ [$_{AgrOP}$the number$_k$ [$_{VP}$t$_i$ [t$_j$ up ] t$_k$]]].

Crucially, the verb–object–particle order is possible only because the object has moved overtly to Spec,AgrOP. If Raising is overt movement, it is predicted that RtoO structures should show a similar effect, which is indeed the case. Citing Johnson (1991), Runner shows that the RtoO subject can either follow (as in (26a)) or precede (as in (26b)) the particle *out* in the verb *make out*.[5]

(26) a. Mikey made out George to be a liar.
        Mikey$_i$ [[made out]$_j$ [$_{AgrOP}$George$_k$ [$_{VP}$t$_i$ t$_j$ [$_{AgrSP}$t$_k$ to be a liar]]]].

     b. Mikey made George out to be a liar.
        Mikey$_i$ [[made]$_j$ [$_{AgrOP}$George$_k$ [$_{VP}$t$_i$ [ t$_j$ out] [$_{AgrSP}$t$_k$ to be a liar]]]].

If *George* were to remain in situ until LF, the only way to account for the fact that the particle *out* follows the NP in (26b) would be by lowering the particle into the embedded clause in overt syntax, a move disallowed by the theory. Thus, the particle verb facts provide additional evidence for the overt movement analysis.

## 4 Neo-ECM

Recall that there are languages such as Bauan Fijian, Kipsigis, Niuean, and others in which complements in apparent RtoO structures are finite rather than non-finite. To handle these cases, Massam (1985) proposed ECM analyses in which dependents of the embedded clause move to Spec,CP for Case and may optionally raise from that position to an argument position in the matrix clause. Thus, we saw in chapter 9 that Massam proposed that the Bauan Fijian sentence in (27a) has the structure in (27b).

(27) a.  Au   a    vinakati iko    mo         mokuti Timoci.
         1SG  PST  want     you    SUB.2SG hit         T
         'I wanted you to hit Timothy.'
    b.  Au$_j$ a vinakati [$_{CP}$iko$_i$ [$_{CP}$mo mokuti Timoci t$_i$ ]] pro$_j$

In (27) *iko* 'you' moves from its embedded subject position $t_i$ to Spec2,CP (a special second Spec,CP position), where it is assigned accusative Case by the matrix verb *vinakati* 'want.' Note that subjects are clause-final in Fijian, Spec,CP precedes the head, and agreement clitics such as *au* 'I' are coindexed with a *pro* in subject position. Additionally, Bauan Fijian includes the option of moving an element from Spec2,CP into an argument position in the higher clause. This is exemplified by (28a), which has the structure in (28b).

(28) a.  Au   a   tukuni       ni'u        a   mokuti Mere.
         1SG  PST say.PASS SUB.1SG PST hit    M
         'I was said to have hit Mary.'
    b.  Au$_j$ a tukuni [$_{CP}$t$_i$ [$_{CP}$ni'u a mokuti Mere t$_i$ ]] pro$_i$

In (28b), the first person singular pronoun, realized as *au* here, moves from its subject position in the embedded clause to Spec2,CP of the complement clause and then on to subject of the matrix clause. Recall also from the discussion in chapter 9 that the movement from an A'-position to an A-position is an example of improper movement, ruled out by a prohibition on an application of A-movement to the output of A'-movement.

In his MIT dissertation, Bruening (2001b) revisits Massam's analysis. On the basis of data largely from Passamaquoddy, Bruening (2001a, 2001b, 2002) proposes two analyses which he claims can account for a range of apparent RtoO structures in many languages. One analysis, schematized by the structure in (29), can be roughly characterized as movement to Comp (Spec,CP), and the other, which includes the structure in (30), as movement from Comp.

(29)  [ ... V (NP) [$_{CP}$NP$_i$ [ ... t$_i$ ... ]]]        Movement to Comp

(30)  [ ... V (NP) NP$_i$ [$_{CP}$t$_i$ [ ... pro$_i$ ... ]]]    Movement from Comp

Bruening proposes the movement to Comp analysis for Passamaquoddy (and other languages) on the basis of the moved element being on the left edge of the clause and the fact that the trace of movement behaves as a bound variable. Movement from Comp is posited since the moved NP has no apparent thematic role in the matrix clause but must be in a sufficiently local position to be able to move into a matrix argument position. The movement to Comp structure in (29) is precisely the structure Massam proposes for the Bauan Fijian example in (27), a typical A'-movement. The structure in (30) is a cross between Massam's analysis of (28) and the structure proposed for Madurese and Cebuano in chapter 10. It shares with Massam's analysis the movement of an element from Spec,CP to an argument position in a higher clause, and it shares with the analysis of Madurese the fact that the element in the matrix clause binds a pronoun in the embedded clause.

Applying Bruening's analyses to the Bauan Fijian data, (27a) would have the same structure as in (27b), while (28a) would have the structure in (31).

(31)  Au$_i$ a tukuni [$_{CP}$t$_i$ [$_{CP}$ni'u a mokuti Mere pro$_i$ ]] pro$_i$

The only difference here is that while the trace in Spec,CP in (28b) binds a trace, the trace in (31) binds a pronoun. The theoretical advantage of (31) over (28b) is that Bruening has been able to eliminate the improper movement that exists in Massam's analysis. However, in Massam's proposal (27a) and (28a) share an analysis, and (28) is simply a continuation of the movement of the embedded dependent; that is, (27) and (28) have analyses clearly related to each other. This is not so in Bruening's analysis. In Bruening's proposal, the analyses are formally unrelated: in movement to Comp the element in Spec,CP binds a trace, and in movement from Comp the element generated in Spec,CP binds a pronoun. Additionally Bruening stipulates in the movement from Comp analysis that if an element is generated (merged) in the embedded Spec,CP position, it must move to an argument position in the higher clause. Under Bruening's proposal, the fact that the class of predicates governing movement to Comp is exactly the same as the class of predicates governing movement from Comp is purely accidental, a shortcoming not shared by Massam's proposal.

As part of his explication, Bruening analyzes the same type of Japanese RtoO structure discussed in chapter 10. It is instructive here to evaluate this analysis in the context of other approaches that have arisen to Japanese RtoO constructions in the Minimalist literature.

## 5 Neo-"a variety of previous approaches": Raising in Japanese redux

Recall from chapter 10, section 3, that Japanese RtoO constructions are typified by the following paradigm, with examples repeated from Kuno (1976).

(32) a. Yamada wa Tanaka ga baka da to        [= Kuno 1976: (17a)]
         TOP           NOM    fool is COMP
      omotteita.
      thought
      'Yamada thought Tanaka to be a fool.'
    b. Yamada wa Tanaka o baka da to         [= Kuno 1976: (17b)]
         TOP           ACC    fool is COMP
      omotteita.
      thought
      'Yamada thought Tanaka to be a fool.'

There was, and there still is, a general consensus that the matrix verb *omotteita* 'thought' takes a CP complement in both (32a) and (32b), and that *Tanaka ga* in (32a) is inside the CP at Spell-Out. The relevant structure of (32a) would be assumed to be something like (33).

(33)  Yamada wa [$_{CP}$Tanaka ga baka da to] omotteita.

As for (32b), recall from chapter 10 that there was (and there still is) disagreement as to the derivational status of *Tanaka o*. Kuno (1976) argued in favor of a traditional RtoO analysis in which the accusative nominal is the underlying subject of the embedded clause and the surface object of the matrix verb. Marantz (1983) and Saito (1983) took the position that the accusative nominal is base generated as an object of the higher clause. And Sells (1990) proposed that the accusative nominal is assigned accusative Case inside the embedded clause and that it optionally moves (via scrambling) into the matrix clause.

Kuno's and Sells's analyses were seen to address the broadest range of empirical data, and were exemplars of the two main approaches to this construction, RtoO, and ECM.[6] Each of these two approaches brings along with it a particular set of problems. For an RtoO analysis, the two confounds are (i) how to account for A-movement across a CP boundary, and (ii) how to avoid double Case marking of the raised NP. For an ECM analysis, there is the inverse issue of managing Case assignment across a CP boundary, as well as explaining the substantial evidence that the accusative nominal can indeed be outside the embedded clause. As will be seen in this discussion, some of the solutions to these problems are familiar, as are the analyses themselves. We will consider, in turn, analyses offered in Hiraiwa (2001), Bruening (2001a, 2001b, 2002), Tanaka (2002), and Harada (2003).

Hiraiwa (2001) presents two types of evidence that Raising, while possible, is not obligatory. That is, he tries to show that the accusative nominal in (32b) can remain inside CP. Example (34) is adapted from Hiraiwa (2001:12b).

(34)  Yamada ga    [$_{CP}$sono sigoto ni    Tanaka ga/o      muitenai
      NOM         the job      DAT         NOM/ACC  is.not.suitable
      to]   omotta
      COMP  thought
      'Yamada thought Tanaka is not suitable for the job.'

In (34), the phrase *sono sigoto ni* 'for the job' is an argument of the embedded predicate *muitenai* 'is.not.suitable,' and is arguably within the embedded CP (although scrambled in this instance to the left of the matrix subject). The grammaticality of *Tanaka o* in this purportedly CP-internal position is taken as evidence that the accusative nominal need not be raised.

A second class of evidence introduced by Hiraiwa concerns multiple cleft constructions. These are constructions in which two phrases are simultaneously clefted, resulting in an expression something like 'It is Tanaka, for the job, that Yamada thought to be unsuitable.' As reported in Koizumi (1995), a restriction on multiple cleft constructions is that the clefted phrases must be clausemates. Hiraiwa shows that *Tanaka o* may be clefted with either *Yamada ga* or *sono sigoto ni*. In contrast, *Yamada ga* may not be clefted with *sono sigoto ni*. The impossibility of this last combination is attributed to the matrix subject and the embedded dative phrase not being clausemates. The grammatical clefting of *Tanaka o* with either the embedded dative phrase or the matrix subject is taken by Hiraiwa as evidence of the optionality of Raising.

Hiraiwa's analysis of this construction is in the tradition of ECM. He relies on the long-distance operation of AGREE in addition to MOVE, proposing that "syntactic raising...in ECM [constructions] is optional in Japanese; a pure AGREE suffices for Case-checking" (Hiraiwa 2001:73). In proposing optional movement of the accusative NP, and delinking this movement from the assignment/checking of accusative Case, Hiraiwa's solution echoes that of Sells (1990).

Bruening (2001a, 2001b, 2002) also takes up Japanese RtoO constructions, and as seen in the previous section, proposes multiple derivations rather than optional movement. For cases in which the accusative nominal appears to have remained in the embedded clause, Bruening proposes a neo-ECM analysis, in which this nominal has moved from its initial IP/TP internal position into Spec,CP as shown in (29). To account for those instances in which the accusative nominal shows signs of being outside of the embedded clause, Bruening's proposal is depicted in (30). There, the accusative nominal is base-generated in Spec,CP, binds a null pro in IP/TP, and moves into the matrix clause.[7]

Tanaka (2002) takes issue with both Hiraiwa's and Bruening's accounts, finding problematic some of the grammaticality judgments that both bring to bear in their assertion that the accusative nominal may remain within the embedded clause. Tanaka recalls Kuno's arguments in favor of Raising, and introduces some additional facts. For instance, he notes (as pointed out in Saito 1985 and Sells 1990) that scrambling the embedded clause in front of the raised object results in a proper binding condition violation. Example (35) is repeated here from chapter 10, example (86).

(35) a. [Tanaka o]$_1$ Yamada wa [t$_1$ tensai da to] omotteita
            ACC           TOP      genius is COMP thought
    'Tanaka, Yamada thought him to be a genius.'
b. *Yamada wa [t$_1$ baka da to]$_2$ [Tanaka o]$_1$ t$_2$ omotteita
     TOP     fool is COMP         ACC   thought
   (Yamada thought Tanaka to be a fool.)

Example (35b) is held to be ungrammatical because the raised NP *Tanaka o* does not c-command, and hence does not properly bind, its trace. Proposing that RtoO constructions in Japanese do indeed involve Raising, Tanaka asserts that A-movement goes through Spec,CP. Relying on Chomsky's (1998, 1999) notion of "phase," Tanaka treats Spec,CP as a generic "escape hatch" for movement. Without additional stipulations though, Spec,CP is an A'-position, out of which A-movement would be prohibited. Tanaka's solution to this is to propose that particular lexical items (RtoO verbs in this case) select a CP "whose head can license an A-position in its edge [that is, in Spec,CP]" (Tanaka 2002:651). In this respect, Tanaka's solution is dependent on the sort of lexical diacritic particular to raising verbs that was first discussed here in chapter 2 (see note 5 there).

Harada (2003) presents an approach to Japanese RtoO constructions that is rather distinct from the three discussed here above. Recalling the observations of Sells 1990 (see chapter 10, section 3, "Alternative analyses"), Harada notes that RtoO constructions are limited to "adjectival predicates" (that is, adjectives and adjectival nouns). As she observes, neither Hiraiwa (2001) nor Bruening (2001b) appear to offer a straightforward way to account for this fact. Harada takes the position that the accusative nominal in an RtoO construction is unambiguously outside of the embedded clause at Spell-Out, proposing a surface structure that would be consistent with the application of Raising. However, Harada does not propose Raising (or any movement operation per se). Instead, she adopts a morphosyntactic operation of Predicate Agglutination (PA), proposed in Kuroda (1992). For Harada, this operation is a morphological concatenation of "a predicate stem and its suffixes" and can apply to adjectival predicates either before or after Spell-Out (in the case of verbal predicates, concatenation is presumed to apply only after Spell-Out). It is the operation of concatenation pre-Spell-Out that results in the RtoO structure of (32b).

(36)   Yamada wa Tanaka o baka-da-to omot-te i-ta

In (36), the hyphenated forms are predicates that have undergone Predicate Agglutination (PA), and the (pre-Spell-Out) application of PA to *baka-da-to* before it can license nominative Case on the embedded subject *Tanaka* results in this NP getting accusative case in the matrix clause.

While this analysis does explain many of the traditional data paradigms associated with this construction, it is not without problems. First of all, it creates a post- and pre- Spell-Out option for PA that appear to be at odds with Kuroda's own proposal. For Kuroda (1992:254), PA is a predicate raising operation that combines an "embedded predicate and the matrix predicate (the raising trigger) . . . into the unmistakable unit of a phonological word." This description makes it rather clear that the operation is intended only to apply pre-Spell-Out, in order for it to serve as input to the PF interface. Further, where Kuroda fashions PA as an operation that merges distinct predicates, Harada treats it as a more general operation that merges any given predicate with its following functional heads (e.g., affixes and complementizers).

There are data issues as well. In proposing a solution that does not involve movement, Harada's explanation for the ungrammaticality of (35b) cannot appeal to principles such as the proper binding condition, and it is accordingly less than straightforward and relies on some fairly subtle interpretations of quantifier scope such as reported in Takano (2002). It is further the case that (in contrast to Sells 1990, Hiraiwa 2001, and Bruening 2001b) no clear explanation emerges from Harada's analysis for the failure of the accusative nominal to undergo passive, as reported in chapter 10, section 3, "The exceptional properties of Japanese RtoO constructions."

Finally, it is worth noting that Harada critiques Sells's lexical exceptional Case account of the accusative nominal in Japanese RtoO, and insists on attributing the accusative Case licensing to the matrix clause. This criticism takes three forms. First, Harada claims (referring again to quantifier scope interpretations reported in Takano 2002) that the accusative nominal does not exhibit certain narrow-scope interpretations that would be predicted if it were in the embedded clause. Second, she objects to Sells's treatment of accusative as a variety of inherent (that is, lexical) Case. And finally, she asserts that Sells is incorrect in claiming that RtoO embedded predicates must be unaccusative, citing RtoO constructions containing two-place embedded adjectival predicates such as *kirai* 'dislike.'[8]

(37) Taroo wa Hanako o ninzin ga kirai da  [= Harada 2003: (61)]
TOP ACC carrot NOM dislike is
to omotteita.
COMP thought
'Taro thought that Hanako dislikes carrots.'

Harada's analysis thus resuscitates an approach similar in some ways to that of Marantz (1983), while being far more explicit about its empirical coverage and theoretical consequences.

To be fair to the several authors cited here above, each has endeavored to extend – and succeeded in some measure in extending – the empirical domain that any treatment of Japanese RtoO must cover. At the same time, it does not appear that any one of these analyses is able to explain all the important facts. Thus, while the face of syntactic theory is substantially changed from the 1980s, the innovations of the Minimalist and other programs have not thus far brought about a clear resolution to the problem of accounting for Japanese RtoO. There is still good evidence that the accusative nominal might be inside the embedded clause, as well as substantial evidence that it is not. And it is still clear that Japanese RtoO is not only restricted to a certain class of matrix raising trigger verbs, but is also constrained by the lexical category and argument structure of the embedded predicate itself. The successful analysis will need to accommodate all these facts, regardless of the theoretical devices brought to bear.

### Notes

1 It is important to note that L&S's derivation is distinct from that in Chomsky (1989, 1992), where he proposes that movement of an object to check an accusative Case feature is covert. For their part, L&S analyze RtoO as potentially being overt, i.e., accomplished by Spell-Out, on the basis of the evidence discussed at the end of this section.

2 One complication that L&S do not take note of is the issue of verb movement. As was discussed in chapter 11, section 1, Pollock (1989) provides extensive evidence that verb movement in English is covert (in contrast with verb movement in French).

Now if L&S are correct about RtoO being overt (and about the landing site of the raised infinitival subject), then they would also have to assume overt raising of the verb, since it precedes the RtoO nominal at Spell-Out. This would presumably require a reassessment of Pollock's evidence to the contrary. It was just this problem of verb movement that led to L&S not endorsing overt movement to Spec,AgrOP in their paper (Lasnik, p.c.). Since then, Lasnik (1999b, 2001) has come down firmly on the side of overt movement to Spec,AgrOP when the structure includes AgrO, which he argues is optional in some cases.

3   In work contemporaneous to L&S, Johnson (1991) arrives at a very similar analysis. In Johnson's analysis all objects raise from their position as sisters of V into a Spec,VP position at the same time as the V moves to AgrO, and objects are assigned Case by the verb, as in (i).

(i)   ... [$_{AgrOP}$accused$_j$ [$_{VP}$none of the defendants$_i$ [$_{VP}$ [$_{V'}$t$_j$ t$_i$ ] during any of the trials]]]

RtoO subjects are treated in exactly the same manner, raising from subject position in an embedded IP to Spec,VP, where they are assigned Case. While Johnson's analysis of objects pre-dates L&S's analysis of RtoO, it is not fully couched in terms of the Minimalist Program and does not focus on RtoO; therefore, we have chosen to focus on L&S's analysis.

4   As Runner points out, it would be possible to account for the position of the infinitival subject in (15a) and (16a) by positing some special strong feature for infinitival T that must be checked, thus motivating overt movement. However, such a move is obviously ad hoc and would violate the principle of Greed, since the movement would not be motivated by any need to check any feature of the infinitival subject.

5   Postal (1974:412–16) gives essentially the same argument in his chapter 12 when he cites (i) as showing that the embedded subject must raise to object in order for it to precede the particle *out* in *figure out*.

(i)   I figured it out to be more than 300 miles from here to Tulsa.

However, there Postal considers the argument to be equivocal for a variety of reasons.

6   While Sells's (1990) analysis is not strictly an ECM analysis as it is traditionally understood in GB terms, it is, literally, an "exceptional Case marking" analysis in that it involves the accusative nominal getting exceptional Case lexically.

7   Idan Landau (p.c.) suggests that the inability of the RtoO nominal to undergo passive (as shown in example (75) in chapter 10) is explicable on the assumption that the accusative nominal has raised out of the complement VP into Spec,CP (which is the account provided in Landau 2002 for the unacceptability of *There was prevented from being a riot.*). The reason for this is that, for Landau and others, A-bar movement into Spec,CP cannot be followed by A-movement (such as passive). It is unclear whether Bruening would restrict movement to/from Spec,CP in this fashion (that is, whether he would consider a nominal "generated" in Spec,CP to be available for A-movement/passive).

8   It is beyond the scope of this discussion to comment on quantifier scope and radical reconstruction effects or on particular theory-internal conceptions on structural/inherent Case. However, the example given in (37) does deserve a comment. While Sells's claim regarding the unaccusativity of embedded RtoO predicates has not been conclusively proven, Harada's counterexample is only apparent. Contrary to Harada's assertion, it is not the case that all unaccusatives are monadic (one-place)

predicates. In Belletti (1988) and Belletti and Rizzi (1988), substantial evidence is presented to show that certain two-place predicates, namely "psych-verbs," take EXPERIENCER and THEME arguments, and are unaccusative in Italian and some other languages. Given that *kirai* 'dislike' falls squarely into the semantic domain of a psychological predicate, it is certainly plausible that it might be unaccusative (if Japanese psych-verbs are generally so). Sells's claim thus remains to be disproven.

# CHAPTER 13

# THE SEPARATION/ UNIFICATION OF RAISING AND CONTROL

*As we have seen, straightforward explanations are forthcoming for all of these properties of PRO (with some exceptions, as noted, to which we will return) if we assume the projection principle and the analysis of S as NP–INFL–VP, assumptions which seem near optimal.*

Chomsky (1981:71)

## 1 The origins of the Raising/Control distinction

From Standard Theory through Minimalism as laid out in Chomsky (1995), Chomskyan theory has maintained a clear distinction between Raising and Control. Within Standard Theory, as exemplified in Rosenbaum (1967) and much of Postal's (1974) framework, Deep Structure is assumed to be the level from which semantic representation is constructed. Therefore, synonymous sentences are assigned the same Deep Structure. As shown in chapter 2, in Rosenbaum's analysis, sentences such as those in (1) are both derived from the same Deep Structure, which is something along the lines of that in (2).

(1) a. Everyone believed Robin to be polite.
 b. Everyone believed that Robin is polite.

(2) everyone believed [$_{NP}$it [$_S$Robin be polite]]

Differences in the Surface Structure relate to differential applications of the complementizer insertion rule, pronoun replacement, and other transformations. (1a) is derived from (2) when the *for-to* complementizer is inserted, the *for* complementizer is deleted, and *Robin* replaces the pronoun *it*. (1b) is derived by inserting the *that* complementizer followed by other minor transformations. Likewise, sentences having both non-finite and finite complements with a control predicate such as *persuade*, as in (3), share the same deep structure (4).

(3) a. Barnett persuaded the doctor to examine Tilman.
    b. Barnett persuaded the doctor that she should examine Tilman.

(4) Barnett persuaded [$_{NP}$the doctor] [$_S$[$_{NP}$the doctor] examine Tilman]

Again, differences in the surface manifestations in (3) result from different applications of transformations. (3a) results from inserting the *for-to* complementizer into the Deep Structure in (4) and applying Equi NP Deletion. The derivation of (3b) from (4) begins with the insertion of *that* into the Deep Structure and subsequent pronominalization of the embedded subject.

It is clear that sentences with tensed complements of verbs like *believe* and *persuade* must have different Deep Structures because the sentences surface with a different number of arguments – *believe* has only an S complement, while *persuade* has both an NP complement and an S complement. Thus, the Deep Structures for (1b) and (3b) must differ at least in this regard. Under the Standard Theory assumption that synonymous sentences have the same Deep Structure, the raising and control counterparts must share the deep structure of the corresponding sentences with tensed complements. Clearly then, Raising and Control had to have different Deep Structures, even if the surface strings appear to be identical.

The structural differences, which followed solely from these theoretical assumptions about the relationship of Deep Structure and semantic interpretation, appeared to correlate with empirical differences between Raising and Control. So, as set out in chapter 1, raising structures and control structures differ with respect to thematic role assignment (5), embedded passive (6), selectional restrictions (7), pleonastic subjects (8), and idiom chunks (9).

(5) *Thematic role assignment: one role for raising NP, two for control NP:*
    a. Barnett believed the doctor to have examined Tilman. (*doctor* is agent only)
    b. Barnett persuaded the doctor to examine Tilman. (*doctor* is agent and persuadee)

(6) *Embedded passive: active/passive synonomy with Raising but not Control:*
    a. Barnett believed Tilman to have been examined by the doctor. (synonymous with (5a))
    b. Barnett persuaded Tilman to be examined by the doctor. (not synonymous with (5b))

(7) *Selectional restrictions: raising structures mirror selectional restrictions of embedded verbs, control structures do not:*
    a. Barnett believed the rock to be granite.
    b. #Barnett believed the rock to understand the issues of the day.
    c. #Barnett persuaded the rock to be granite.
    d. #Barnett persuaded the rock to understand the issues of the day.

(8) Pleonastic subjects: possible with Raising but not Control:
   a. Barnett believed there to be a unicorn in the garden.
   b. *Barnett persuaded there to be a unicorn in the garden.

(9) Idioms: idiomatic meaning preserved in Raising but not Control:
   a. Tina believed the cat to be out of the bag by now.
   b. ?Tina persuaded the cat to be out of the bag.

Thus, within Standard Theory, there seemed to be firm justification for distinguishing Raising from Control. And this thinking persists through each of the later instantiations of the theory up through Minimalism.

However, for many working outside the Chomskyan framework as narrowly conceived, Raising and Control were not distinguished syntactically. As we saw in chapter 5, in his review of the Chomsky–Postal debate, Bach (1977) sets out what he calls the "No-Rule Hypothesis." In this analysis, neither Raising nor Control is derived transformationally, both simply having a structure in which the complement clause is generated as a subjectless VP rather than a clause. Thus, the initial and final structure associated with the RtoO and object control constructions is as in (10).

(10) a. Barnett [$_{VP}$believed [$_{NP}$the doctor] [$_{VP}$to have examined Tilman]]
    b. Barnett [$_{VP}$persuaded [$_{NP}$the doctor] [$_{VP}$to examine Tilman]]

Bach asserts that the difference between Raising and Control in this analysis is a matter of semantic interpretation rather than syntactic derivation. Semantic rules, which go unformulated in Bach (1977), ensure that in (10a) *the doctor* is interpreted only as the agent of the predicate *examine*, while in (10b) *the doctor* is interpreted as both the agent of *examine* and the persuadee.

Bach's is by no means the first or only proposal that assigns the same syntactic representation to Raising and Control. Brame (1976) proposes just such a VP analysis, building on Bresnan's (1971) analysis of *tough* constructions. Bresnan (1971) proposes that in Deep Structure the infinitival complement of a predicate such as *tough* can be a bare VP and not a clause, assigning to (11a) the structure in (11b) rather than that in (11c), as was assumed in many Standard Theory accounts.

(11) a. It will be tough for at least some students   [= Brame 1976:73 (2b)]
        to be in class on time.
    b. it will be tough [$_{PP}$for at least some       [= Brame 1976:73 (2d)]
        students] [$_{VP}$to be in class on time]
    c. it will be tough [$_S$for for at least some      [= Brame 1976:73 (2c)]
        students to be in class on time]

On the basis of this idea, Brame argues that the infinitival complements in both raising and control structures should also be analyzed as VP. Focusing on the Standard Theory analysis of Equi NP Deletion (Control), Brame argues that an analysis which includes the Equi NP Deletion transformation requires at least seven ad hoc stipulations and/or theoretical devices that are unnecessary if the complement is taken to be a VP. Among Brame's objections are the need to make Equi obligatory for some predicates while it is optional for others and the need to make Raising optional rather than obligatory for some predicates.

Brame notes that, when they select infinitival complements, *try* and *persuade* require Equi to apply. Thus, while (12a) and (13a) are grammatical, (12b) and (13b) are not.

(12) a. John tried to leave. [= Brame 1976:93 (25b)]
b. *John tried for Mary to leave. [= Brame 1976:94 (26a)]

(13) a. John persuaded Mary to leave [= Brame 1976:96 (27b)]
b. *John persuaded Mary for Harry to leave [= Brame 1976:96 (28a)]

A number of different devices had been proposed to account for the obligatory application of Equi for infinitival complements with these predicates, all of which Brame claims add to the complexity of the theory.[1] Brame argues that the possibility of a grammatical (12b) and (13b) arises only on the assumption that the infinitival complements must be S. If these infinitivals are S complements, then they should contain subject positions, and it should be possible to fill these subject positions with any NP in Deep Structure. If this happens and Equi is not applied, then (12b) and (13b) would indeed be completely grammatical. Thus, the assumption that infinitivals are S complements requires that some mechanism be devised making Equi obligatory with infinitival complements of *try* and *persuade*. However, Brame asserts, if *try* and *persuade* were instead assumed to subcategorize for infinitival VP rather than infinitival S, then these structures would never be generated, and identifying individual lexical items as obligatorily undergoing a specific transformation would be unnecessary.[2] In this way, the apparent obligatory nature of Equi with these predicates can be reduced to their subcategorization frames: *try* subcategorizes for a VP complement and *persuade* for NP and VP complements.

Brame also notes that under the Equi analysis, Raising must be made optional for predicates such as *expect*, given the sentences in (14).

(14) a. Sally expects herself to become rich some day. [= Brame 1976:97 (36)]
b. Sally expects to become rich some day.

Assuming base-generated infinitives, the Deep Structure for the sentences in (14) would be:

(15) Sally$_i$ expects [$_S$Sally$_i$ to become rich some day] [= Brame 1976:97 (37)]

According to Brame, (14a) is derived if Raising applies and (14b) applies if it does not. As we have seen, *expect* is somewhat unusual in this regard: other RtoO predicates such as *believe* do not admit both the raising option and the control option. Brame argues that once again these facts can be handled as subcategorization facts. Assuming a raising analysis, the possibilities in (14) follow from the fact that *expect* subcategorizes for both infinitival VP (resulting in (14b)) and infinitival S (resulting in (14a)), unlike a verb such as *believe*, which can only take an infinitival VP complement and not an infinitival S complement.[3]

Much later in his discussion, Brame goes on to argue against transformational derivations for a number of structures, including Passive and Raising. He argues that adopting the VP analysis for Equi, in fact, makes a VP analysis for Raising more attractive as well. Thus, Brame ultimately concludes that Raising and Control are not distinguished at Deep Structure, with raising and control predicates having the subcategorization frames in (16).

(16) a. RtoS, Subject Control: *try/seem*      [ ____ VP]
      b. RtoO, Object Control: *persuade/believe* [ ____ NP VP]

While Brame's may be one of the first analyses in the general generative framework to treat Raising and Control as structurally identical, his is certainly not the only such proposal. Bresnan (1978) adopts a similar approach, where she posits the category VP' for subjectless infinitival complements. In her proposal, she claims – contra her position in Bresnan (1976) (see chapter 5) – that the surface structure for Raising and Control is the same: V (NP) VP', as in (17).

(17) a. Sandy appeared [$_{VP'}$to be nice]
      b. Sandy tried [$_{VP'}$to be nice]
      c. Dana expected [$_{NP}$Sandy] [$_{VP'}$to be nice]
      d. Dana persuaded [$_{NP}$Sandy] [$_{VP'}$to be nice]

Since Bresnan proposes (for reasons outside of present considerations) that there are no transformations such as Passive, Raising, and Equi, there is no Deep-Structure–Surface-Structure distinction. This means that the bracketings in (17) are the constituent structures for these sentences. According to Bresnan the sole difference between raising and control structures relates to semantic differences between the matrix predicates involved. Thus, for instance, although both *expect* and *persuade* take NP and VP' complements, *persuade* assigns a thematic role to its NP complement and *expect* does not. In both instances, however, the subcategorized matrix NP is associated with the argument structure of the embedded predicate through identical specifications in the lexical entries of *expect* and *persuade*.

Bresnan (1982), which sets out the Lexical Functional Grammar analysis of Raising and Control, includes, to all intents and purposes, the same analysis. In fact, a large number of non-Chomskyan frameworks take raising and control structures to be structurally isomorphic. These include Generalized Phrase Structure Grammar (Gazdar et al. 1985), Head-Driven Phrase Structure Grammar (Pollard and Sag 1994), and Categorial Grammar (Jacobson 1992), to mention a few. In each of these proposals the distinction between Raising and Control is taken to arise from a semantic property of the predicates involved.

So, while there has been a bright line dividing Raising and Control in the Chomskyan tradition as narrowly construed, there have been a sizeable number of proposals that explicitly reject this position.

## 2 The 1980s arguments for and against a syntactic Raising and Control distinction

With the introduction of GB theory, there was a clear and present need to support the analysis of Control that had been developed in Chomsky and Lasnik (1977). The Projection Principle and θ-criterion could not accommodate a VP-complement analysis of control structures, since such an analysis would require the assignment of two semantic roles to a single NP. Koster and May (K&M) (1982) came forward to argue in favor of an S' (i.e., [$_S$PRO to VP]) analysis for all bare infinitives in opposition to the VP or VP' analyses, such as proposed in Brame (1976) and Bresnan (1971, 1978). The alternatives are illustrated here in (18).

(18) a. John tried [$_{VP'}$to [$_{VP}$leave the country]]  [Bresnan 1978]
 b. John$_1$ tried [$_S$PRO$_1$ to [$_{VP}$leave the country]] [Koster and May 1982]

K&M's argumentation takes the following form: they first consider some of the empirical arguments used in Brame (1976) and Bresnan (1971, 1978); they next discuss the complications that a VP' analysis poses for the Phrase Structure (PS)-component of the grammar; and finally, they present their own empirical and theoretical arguments in favor of PRO and an S' analysis.

In confronting Brame's and Bresnan's analyses, K&M take up in turn the VP' account of *tough* constructions and the VP' account of Equi clauses.[4] In this regard, K&M take the position that while the arguments against Equi NP Deletion are still compelling, these arguments do not provide any conclusive evidence in favor of a subjectless VP', as in (18a), over a null-subject S', as in (18b).

All things being thus far somewhat equal, K&M next examine the implications of the VP' analysis for the PS rules of the grammar. While such an analysis may be simpler at some level, they argue that it would require a doubling of the rules that introduce sentential complements. Alongside the separately necessary PS-rule (19a), the grammar would also include (19b).

(19) a. VP → V S'
 b. VP → V VP'

This augmentation of the PS-rules would affect complement rules for the categories N, A, and P, in addition to V, since all four categories cooccur with both tensed and infinitival sentential complements.[5]

The empirical arguments that K&M present for their analysis include specific evidence for analyzing the complements of control verbs (e.g., *want*) as sentential, along with evidence that bare infinitives generally are best analyzed as clauses. As an example of the former, K&M (1982:132) argue that control complements cannot be VP' on the basis of pseudocleft facts. They present the contrast in (20) to show that VPs, as opposed to sentences, cannot be the focus of pseudocleft constructions.

(20) a. What he wanted was [s'for Bill to see      [= K&M 1982:(64b)]
       Monument Valley]
    b. *What he wanted for Bill was [vpto see      [= K&M 1982:(65b)]
       Monument Valley]

In (20a), the entire infinitival sentence *for Bill to see Monument Valley* is pseudoclefted. In (20b), though, the infinitival constituent *to see Monument Valley* cannot be pseudoclefted and leave behind its complementizer and subject *for Bill*. K&M then demonstrate that the same infinitival constituent can be pseudoclefted when the infinitival subject is not overtly expressed.

(21) What he wanted was [??to visit Monument Valley]      [= K&M 1982:(66)]

According to K&M, if bare infinitives are VP or VP' constituents, then (21) should be as ungrammatical as (20b). So, the grammaticality of (21) supports their contention that the phrase *to visit Monument Valley* is an S' with a covert subject NP.

In their argument for an S' analysis of bare infinitives, K&M also appeal to coordination facts and the distribution of anaphors. Among the constraints assumed to pertain to coordination at this time was one that required conjuncts to be of the same category (Radford 1981:60). It is this constraint which was assumed to rule out (22c), where the conjuncts are NP and PP.[6]

(22) a. I wrote [NPa postcard]
    b. I wrote [PPwith a crayon]
    c. *I wrote [NPa postcard] and [PPwith a crayon]

On this basis, K&M (1982:133) present data showing that bare infinitives can be conjoined with full clauses.

(23) a. [to write a novel] and [for the world to give it critical acclaim] is John's dream
    b. John expected [to write a novel] but [that it would be a critical disaster]

On their presumed premise that only like categories may be conjoined, they claim that *to write a novel* must also be an S' in (23a) and (23b).

A more theory-dependent argument put forward in support of the S' status of bare infinitives concerns the binding theory and the distribution of anaphors. Here, K&M (1982:137) note that bare infinitives can have reflexive objects despite the fact that they have no overt antecedent locally. Accordingly, we find examples such as (24).

(24) a. John said [that it was easy [to shave himself]]
    b. [to hurt oneself] is foolish

In (24a), the c-commanding antecedent of *himself* is not local (i.e., is outside of its governing category) and in (24b) the reflexive *oneself* has no overt antecedent at all. If bare infinitives are VP or VP', then these clauses violate principle A of the binding theory and should be ungrammatical. However, if they are S and contain PRO, as in (25), then binding theoretic concerns are satisfied.

(25) a. John$_1$ said [that it was easy [$_S$PRO$_1$ to shave himself$_1$]]
    b. [$_S$PRO$_1$ to hurt oneself$_1$] is foolish

The structures in (25) satisfy the local binding constraint on anaphors and thus account for the grammaticality of (24) under the assumptions of GB theory.

Culicover and Wilkins (C&W) (1986) challenge the need for a grammatical category PRO and the S' analysis of Control. Their preliminary assumptions, as laid out at the beginning of the article, involve dispensing with Chomsky's Projection Principle and with his version of the θ-criterion. In place of these, they introduce a set of formal mechanisms, including something called "R[ole]-structure" that maps semantic relations from predicates to their arguments. Among the important aspects of their system is its ability to map thematic roles (via coindexation) from a head onto arguments that are outside of the maximal projection of the relevant head. Thus, for them, R-structure allows *John* to be the THEME of *nude* in (26), without the need for any syntactic argument position within the AP projected by *nude*.

(26) [John$_1$ [[ate the meat] [$_{AP}$nude$_1$]]]

In (26), the coindexation rule assigns an identical index to the R-structures of *John* and *nude* on the basis of (i) *nude* not bearing a grammatical relation to the verb *eat* and (ii) *nude* being high enough in the structure relative to *John*. The coindexation facilitates *John* being interpreted as the THEME of *nude*. Next, they show how the indexing mechanisms handle the R-structure of raising and control clauses in which an infinitival VP has a matrix NP as its subject. All such constructions have the constituent structure and indexation exemplified in (27), where the differences between raising and control constructions are handled in the R-structure of the sentence.

(27) a. John convinced Bill$_1$ [$_{VP}$to be nice]$_1$
    b. John believed Bill$_1$ [$_{VP}$to be nice]$_1$

In (27a), *Bill* has the THEME role with respect to *convinced*, and *to be nice* is its GOAL. Coindexation allows *Bill* to be further interpreted as the THEME of the VP predicate *to be nice*. In (27b), *Bill* is assigned no role by *believe* but is interpreted as the THEME of the VP predicate *to be nice* via coindexation. Coindexation of the NP and VP further allows them to be interpreted together as a propositional THEME of the main verb *believe*.

Following the presentation of their formal account of bare infinitival constructions, C&W (1986:140–6) present arguments against the postulation of PRO and challenge the arguments given in K&M (1982) for the S' structure of subjectless infinitives.

As an example of the first sort, C&W examine the phenomenon of (verb) gapping, presenting contrasts such as in (28).

(28) a. I believe Mary to be rich, and Bill *(believes)    [= C&W 1986:(36a)]
   Sam to be poor.
   b. John wants to eat the beans, and Mary (wants)  [= C&W 1986:(36b)]
   to eat the potatoes.

According to C&W's judgments, (28a) is ungrammatical without the overt verb *believes* in the second clause (i.e., it cannot be gapped), while the ellipsis of *want* in the second clause of (28b) is permissible.[7] Recall that the GB analysis of (28a) is ECM, and so under a standard GB account of ECM and Control, both *believe* and *want* are followed by S-like complements, as in (29).

(29) a. I believe [$_S$Mary to be rich] . . .
   b. John$_1$ wants [$_S$PRO$_1$ to eat the beans] . . .

C&W here take advantage of this by claiming that if verb gapping is not licensed before the [NP to VP] constituent in (28a), then it should not be licensed in (28b) either, unless the postverbal constituent is not [NP to VP]. Thus, the grammaticality of gapping in (28b) contrasted with (28a) is taken by them to be evidence for a VP analysis of *to eat the beans*.[8] They present a number of additional empirical arguments against PRO, some of which are readily explained through application of GB's Case theoretic principles (and in this regard C&W are somewhat unfair in not taking the PRO Theorem on its own terms).

C&W next turn to a direct response to K&M (1982). Among other things, they take issue with K&M's characterization of VP complementation vis-à-vis the PS-component of the grammar. They refute K&M's claim that the VP analysis would entail a doubling of complement rules, claiming that both VP and S are projections of a [+V] category and that (19) and other similar rule pairs could be replaced by the very general complementation rule given here in (30).

(30)  $X^{max} \rightarrow X \; [+V]^{max}$              [= C&W 1986:144 (50)]

C&W also take issue with the empirical arguments presented in K&M (1982). Recall, for example, the contrast between (20b) and (21), repeated here in (31).

(31) a. *What he wanted for Bill was [$_{VP}$to see    [= K&M 1982:(65b)]
   Monument Valley]
   b. What he wanted was [$_{??}$to visit Monument    [= K&M 1982:(66)]
   Valley]

According to K&M, VPs as in (31a) cannot be pseudoclefted. The infinitival constituent in (31b) must therefore be an S' rather than a VP. But C&W show that some VPs can indeed be pseudoclefted, as (32) shows.

(32) a. What he did was [$_{VP}$feed the ducks]   [= C&W 1986:(52a)]
     b. What he wanted to do was [$_{VP}$feed the ducks]   [= C&W 1986:(52b)]

Given these data, K&M's claim appears much less conclusive. Similarly, recall that K&M used coordination facts to argue for an S' analysis of subjectless infinitives, such as in (23b), repeated here in (33). In (33), *to write a novel* is claimed to be an S' because it is coordinated with the clearly S' category *that it would be a critical disaster*.

(33) John expected [to write a novel] but [that it would be a critical disaster]

However, once again, C&W (1986:145) argue that the evidence is inconclusive, showing that conjunction is not restricted to like categories, as in (34).

(34) a. John hopes [$_{S'}$for Mary to leave] and [$_{PP}$for a miracle]
     b. I believe [$_{NP}$your answer], and [$_{S'}$that you believe what you are saying]
     c. [$_{S'}$That you were here last night], and [$_{NP}$John's reaction when you told him], surprised me.

Example (34a) has coordination of S' and PP, (34b) has NP and S', and (34c) has S' and NP. Finally (here), with respect to K&M's anaphora arguments (see examples (24) and (25) above), C&W state: "even if PRO unproblematically explains the relevant aspects of anaphora and coreference, this does not affect our claim that PRO is not a syntactic element. A theory can perfectly well use PRO . . . at LF . . . without incorporating it into strictly syntactic levels" (C&W 1986:146).

These two articles are both partly successful in attaining their goals. Koster and May (1982) and Culicover and Wilkins (1986) are able to demonstrate that their analyses of controlled subjectless infinitives (S' and VP', respectively) are conceptually plausible. However, beyond that, neither article is really able to prove on the basis of conclusive empirical evidence that its analysis is conceptually necessary. So we are left with a standoff, a debate whose conflicting claims are inextricably tied to distinct sets of preliminary assumptions. Given this lack of resolution, it is perhaps instructive to understand how these conceptually distinct and unresolvable analyses follow from slightly different assumptions regarding the mapping from thematic roles to syntactic positions.

## 3 The role of thematic–syntactic mapping in constraining analyses

In the literature, one finds a range of assumptions regarding the mapping from semantic roles to syntactic argument positions. One type of assumption that plays a key role in helping to determine the permissible analyses for raising and control constructions is whether role-to-position mapping is constrained to be one-to-one, allowed to be one-to-many, or allowed to be many-to-one – that is, whether each semantic role must be correlated with one syntactic position (one-to-one), whether a semantic role may be distributed over more than one syntactic position (one-to-many), or whether two or more semantic roles may be assigned to the same syntactic position (many-to-one).

Chomsky's (1981) θ-criterion has the appearance of adopting the most restrictive (one-to-one) view, nearly claiming that a syntactic argument position must be (i) assigned at least one thematic role and (ii) assigned no more than one thematic role. Actually, the θ-criterion would be an idealization of the one-to-one mapping, since Chomsky speaks not of "argument positions" but of "A-positions," which he defines as follows: "An A-position is one in which an argument such as a name or a variable may appear in D-structures; it is a potential θ-position. The position of subject may or may not be a θ-position, depending on the properties of the associated VP. Complements of X' are always θ-positions, with the possible exception of idioms" (Chomsky 1981:47). As we have seen, the GB analyses of passive and RtoS crucially depend on a non-thematic subject position for an NP to move to. Under Chomsky's assumption that complement positions are "always θ-positions," the first half of the θ-criterion rules out non-thematic object complement positions of the sort that would be necessary under certain implementations of the RtoO analysis of *believe* verbs, and leads directly to the necessary assumption of the ECM analysis in (35a).

(35) a. I believe [$_S$Mary to be nice]
     b. John$_1$ wants [$_{S'}$PRO$_1$ to eat the anchovies]

The second half of this restriction forces the adoption of a controlled PRO analysis of subjectless infinitival complements of *want*, as in (35b). The θ-criterion precludes, a priori, any analysis in which the matrix subject *John* would be directly assigned the subject thematic roles of both *want* and *eat*. Even though the θ-criterion must be relaxed to allow non-thematic subjects, it still precludes their being assigned multiple thematic roles. For GB theory, then, θ-criterion restrictions (i) and (ii) apply within the VP, and θ-criterion restriction (ii) also applies VP-externally.

Derivational approaches to raising and control constructions such as in Postal (1974) implicitly allow a syntactic argument position to be non-thematic (have less than one thematic role). Put differently, they allow a single semantic argument to be distributed over multiple syntactic positions in the derivation, i.e., one-to-many. By taking the position that non-thematic syntactic positions may be projected both VP-internally and VP-externally as in (36), RtoS and RtoO analyses are sanctioned.

(36) a. [$_{NP}$ ] [$_{VP}$seems [$_S$Mary to be nice]]
     b. John [$_{VP}$believes [$_{NP}$ ] [$_S$Mary to be nice]]

Thus, by allowing any argument position to have zero or one thematic role, the analyses of *seem* and *believe* complements can be unified. At the same time, it is assumed in such frameworks that each argument position corresponds to at most one thematic role, and for this reason, control constructions are assumed to involve additional underlying NP positions, as in (37), that are deleted (e.g., by Equi NP Deletion) at surface structure.

(37) a. Mary [$_{VP}$tried [$_S$Mary to be nice]]
    b. John [$_{VP}$convinced Mary [$_S$Mary to be nice]]

Conceptually, as regards constraints on thematic role assignment, the Equi approach is analogous to the GB analysis of Control, the key difference being that the second instance of *Mary* in each of (37a) and (37b) would be PRO underlyingly in the GB account.

The principle aim of base-generated, non-derivational frameworks such as LFG, Categorial Grammar, GPSG, and HPSG is to do away with the derivational component of syntax, i.e., to proscribe movement operations. Partly as a consequence of this, they must maintain the least restricted view of thematic role assignment. In these approaches, not only can argument positions fail to be assigned thematic roles (i.e., one-to-many), but they may also be assigned more than one thematic role (i.e., many-to-one). It should be noted at the outset that the distribution of expletive arguments, which are crucial in a derivational RtoS and RtoO account of *seem* and *believe* verbs, plays no role in a non-derivational analysis of these (as in (38), where the interpretation of coindexed elements has the interpretation described in section 2) since such an analysis would not posit movement and would therefore have no need for non-thematic NP positions as movement landing sites.

(38) a. Mary$_1$ [$_{VP}$seems [$_{VP}$to be nice]$_1$ ]
    b. John [$_{VP}$believes Mary$_1$ [$_{VP}$to be nice]$_1$ ]

It is the assumption that a single argument position may bear multiple thematic roles which underlies the sanctioning of the VP analysis of control clauses, and the unification of the syntax of raising and control complements.

(39) a. Mary$_1$ [$_{VP}$tried [$_{VP}$to be nice]$_1$ ]
    b. John [$_{VP}$convinced Mary$_1$ [$_{VP}$to be nice]$_1$ ]

The only distinction between the sentences in (38) and those in (39) is that in the latter *Mary* has an extra thematic role from the matrix verb.

As a final point in this discussion, it is important to take note of the empirical status of these different conceptualizations of thematic role–argument structure mapping. The most restrictive view, that of Chomsky's θ-criterion and Extended Projection Principle in which non-subject expletives are not possible, is empirically unsustainable. Not only can a subject NP have no thematic role, but non-thematic NPs are found in verb complement and prepositional complement positions. As noted in chapter 9, Postal and Pullum (1988) provides a robust set of diagnostics demonstrating that subject, object, and object of preposition expletives, as shown here in (40), all have the same syntactic status.

(40) a. It seems that Gerry can't drive.        Subject expletive
    b. I regret **it** very much that you        Direct object expletive
       were unable to get seats.
    c. You can depend upon **it** that           Object of preposition expletive
       Ralph will be late.

While allowing syntactic arguments to have zero or one thematic roles is an empirical necessity, the need to allow arguments to have more than one thematic role is not. There is no clear and conclusive set of empirical arguments that would enable one to decide between the VP' and S' analyses of the *convince* complement in (41).

(41) a. John [$_{VP}$convinced Mary$_1$ [$_{VP}$to be nice]$_1$ ]
    b. John [$_{VP}$convinced Mary$_1$ [$_{S'}$PRO$_1$ to be nice] ]

Both analyses claim *Mary* to be the object of *convinced*, and where one manages the thematic role assigned by *to be nice* by indexation of the VP' and the coindexation of *Mary* with this VP', the other claims the thematic role to be assigned normally to a null subject position and provides for the coindexation of *Mary* with this null subject. The analysis in (41a) then provides a more uniform account of a wider range of constructions and does away with syntactic derivations, at the cost of weakening restrictions on thematic role mapping. The analysis in (41b) maintains a more restricted principle of thematic role mapping, but sacrifices uniformity of syntactic structure across Raising and Control. The conclusions in either case appear to be motivated as much by conceptual preferences as by anything else.

## 4  The collapse of the Raising/Control distinction in Minimalist theory

The Minimalist abandonment of the ECM analysis of *believe* verbs is an important theoretical step away from keeping the analyses of Raising and Control separate in that framework. As we have seen, the GB analysis of infinitival complements of *believe* and *persuade* verbs required the postverbal NP of the former to be part of the infinitival complement at all levels of structure, in contrast with the postverbal NP in the *persuade* case, which was held to be base generated as a sister of the verb. Example (42) reviews the relative position of the object pronoun *him* in both of these constructions, leaving aside the status of null categories.

(42) a. John believes [him to be nice]
    b. John persuaded him [to be nice]

With the Neo-RtoO account presented in Lasnik and Saito (1991), the object pronoun in (42a) is now taken to raise into a surface position outside of the infinitival complement. Whether the movement of this category is overt (i.e., moved by Spell-Out) or covert is of little consequence here, since at LF both structures would now have *him* in a position outside of the infinitive, as in (43).

(43) a. John believes him [to be nice]
    b. John persuaded him [to be nice]

In the Neo-RtoO account, it is important to recall that the landing site for movement of *him* in (43) is Spec,AgrO. In (43a), *him* moves from a position inside the infinitival complement into Spec,AgrO of the matrix clause. In (43b), *him* moves from the object position of the matrix verb *persuade* into Spec,AgrO of the matrix clause.[9] The differences in the derivation of the pronoun in the two contructions, relative to the infinitival clause and its containing VP, is shown in (44).

(44) a. Neo-RtoO: [$_{AgrOP}$him$_1$ ... [$_{VP}$ ... [t$_1$ to be nice]]]
    b. Control:   [$_{AgrOP}$him$_1$ ... [$_{VP}$ ... t$_1$ ... [PRO$_1$ to be nice]]]

Here we see that, at LF at least, the difference between the two structures reduces to whether *him* is coindexed with a single NP-trace (44a) or an NP-trace and a PRO (44b). At this stage, with *him* and *to be nice* derived into separate constituents in both cases, the difference between raising and control constructions now reduces to distinctions in the number and type of null categories involved in each structure.

It is no surprise that this state of affairs led directly to Minimalist proposals for doing away with the Raising/Control distinction.[10] Hornstein (1999) proposes doing away with the θ-criterion (at least that part which constrains a single argument from having more than one semantic role). Arguing that PRO can be dispensed with as a separate type of null category, he suggests that Control is like Raising in involving movement alone. In place of the PRO in (44b), then, he would have another NP-trace, as in (45).[11]

(45) a. Neo-RtoO:           [$_{AgrOP}$him$_1$ ... [$_{VP}$ ... [t$_1$ to be nice]]]
    b. "Control" as movement: [$_{AgrOP}$him$_1$ ... [$_{VP}$ ... t'$_1$ ... [t$_1$ to be nice]]]

Under Hornstein's account, *him* would be inserted into the derivation as the subject of the infinitival clause in both raising and control structures. In the RtoO case, it would move directly to a functional projection, but in the control case, it would move through the position labeled t'$_1$, picking up an extra semantic role along the way. The discussion that follows takes a closer look at the Hornstein (1999) analysis, and considers objections to it laid out in Culicover and Jackendoff (2001) and Jackendoff and Culicover (2003) as well as responses to those objections in Boeckx and Hornstein (2003).

## *Control is movement*

If Raising and Control are to be unified, then there are two paths that one might take. Either Control is to be analyzed as a kind of Raising (that is, they both involve syntactic, e.g., movement, operations), or Raising should be analyzed as a kind of Control (that is, they both involve interpretive, e.g., LF, computations). We will examine the first path, followed in Hornstein (1999) (see Hornstein 1997 for an earlier version of this analysis), keeping an eye on the alternative as we go along. The position taken in Hornstein (1999) is that two residual concepts of GB syntax should be questioned and ultimately dispensed with: (i) the θ-criterion and (ii) the control module, including the PRO Theorem.

With regard to the first of these, Hornstein claims that the Minimalist Program implicitly retains the θ-criterion, which renders the abolition of D-structure "less radical" than it first appears. Chomsky (1995) restricts θ-role assignment to the initial merger of a given NP into the derivation and claims that θ-roles are not features that can be checked. Chomsky thus maintains the GB-like principle of limiting argument insertion to the foot of a given chain and the prohibition on movement into θ-positions. Noting that these assumptions about θ-roles are critical to keeping separate the analyses of Raising and Control, Hornstein suggests that they might profitably be set aside.

With respect to the control module and PRO, Hornstein says that they are both problematic for Minimalist theory, and that they both complicate the grammar. On the control module, Hornstein derides the principles that determine the interpretation of controlled PRO as being unsettled and unsatisfying empirically, suggesting that "control theory has not been one of the bright stars in the GB firmament" (Hornstein 1999:72). On PRO itself, Hornstein notes that Minimalist theory cannot cope with the PRO Theorem, i.e., PRO being a [+anaphoric, +pronominal] null pronoun that must be ungoverned (see chapter 8, section 6). Since the MP has no theory of government, the PRO Theorem as it exists in GB theory cannot be maintained.

The need to replace the PRO Theorem is acknowledged in Chomsky and Lasnik (1993), wherein they propose that PRO is indeed a Case-marked category, receiving "null Case" from non-finite T.[12] Their proposal is motivated in part by the fact that PRO is assumed to move out of non-Case-marked positions, as in (46a), and to not be able to move out of Case-marked positions, as in (46b).

(46) a. we never expected [PRO$_1$ to be found t$_1$ ]  [= Chomsky and Lasnik 1993:(309)]
 b. *it is unfair [PRO$_1$ to talk about t$_1$ ]  [= Chomsky and Lasnik 1993:(311b)]

Compare (46) with (47), which contains an overt NP in the embedded subject position.

(47) a. we never expected that [John$_1$ would be found t$_1$ ]
 b. *it is unfair for [John$_1$ to talk about t$_1$ ]

In both (46) and (47), the grammatical sentences involve movement out of a non-Case-marked position (object of a passive verb), and the ungrammatical sentences involve movement out of a Case-marked position (object of a preposition). In this regard, the movement of PRO appears to be analogous to that of Case-bearing overt NPs. Examining (46) more closely, (46a) might be explained on the premise that PRO must be ungoverned and that government applies at S-structure (i.e., Spell-Out), since the position of the trace is still governed even though it is not Case marked. However, if that explanation is adopted, then the ungrammaticality of (46b) is yet more confounding, since PRO has moved there out of a governed, Case-marked position into an ungoverned one. To put it simply, if movement of PRO rescues (46a) from ill-formedness, why can't it also rescue (46b)? Consider (46b) and (48).

(48)  it is unfair [PRO to talk about John]     [= Chomsky and Lasnik 1993:(311c)]

Since the landing site for PRO in (46b) is legitimate, as (48) demonstrates, the ungrammaticality of (46b) must only result from its having moved out of a Case-marked position (which makes little sense if PRO is required not to bear Case, among other things). It is at this juncture that Chomsky and Lasnik offer the "null Case" proposal, in which PRO is only able to move from a Caseless position into a position in which null Case is assigned, i.e., the Spec,IP of an infinitival clause.

Hornstein levels several criticisms at the null Case proposal. First of all, he contends that it is conceptually inelegant, insofar as null Case is designed to be assigned to only one class of (null) expressions and is assigned by only one kind of T. As he puts it, the hypothesis is "constructed to exactly fit the observed facts." This said, it does not serve to simplify the theory, since a control module, specifying the denotation/construal of PRO (e.g., coindexation), is still required. Among other things, Hornstein also notes that null-Case-marked PRO does not block *wanna* contraction, as seen here in (49).

(49)  a.  I want [PRO to win]           → I wanna win
      b.  I$_1$ am going [t$_1$ to win]      → I'm gonna win
      c.  who$_1$ do you want [t$_1$ to win] → *who do you wanna win

Since *wh*-traces (as in (49c)) are distinguished from NP-traces (as in (49b)) in that the former are Case marked (here by the matrix verb *want*), PRO behaves in this instance like a non-Case-marked null category.

Hornstein's proposed alternative involves teasing apart the distribution of Obligatory Control (OC) PRO, as in (50a), and Non-Obligatory Control (NOC) PRO, as in (50b).

(50)  a.  I convinced him$_1$ [PRO$_1$ to study hard]
      b.  I convinced him that [PRO$_{arb}$ studying hard] is the best plan

Rather than treat PRO generally as a [+anaphoric, +pronominal] category, Hornstein argues that PRO is ambiguous, that PRO$_{arb}$ is a pure pronominal, and (on the basis of facts reported in Lebeaux 1985, Higginbotham 1992, and Fodor 1975) that controlled PRO is an anaphor. We will focus here on the arguments for OC PRO being classed as an anaphor, with data repeated from Hornstein (1999).[13] In each case below, OC PRO can be contrasted with NOC PRO.

(51)  a.  *It was expected PRO to shave himself.      [= Hornstein 1999:73 (4)]
      b.  *John$_1$ thinks that it was expected PRO$_1$ to shave himself.

  c. *John$_1$'s campaign expects PRO$_1$ to shave himself.
  d. John$_1$ expects PRO$_1$ to win and Bill does too. (Bill expects Bill/*John to win)
  e. Only Churchill$_1$ remembers PRO$_1$ giving the BST speech.

Like an anaphor, OC PRO must have a local, c-commanding antecedent. (51a) is ill-formed because OC PRO has no antecedent, (51b) is out because the intended antecedent, *John*, is not in the same clause, and (51c) is ungrammatical because the intended antecedent, *John*, does not c-command PRO. In (51d), PRO entails a "sloppy" interpretation with VP ellipsis, and is like an anaphor in this regard (compare (51d) and (52)).

(52) a. John$_1$ expects himself$_1$ to win and Bill does too. (Bill expects Bill/*John to win)
  b. John$_1$ expects that he$_1$ will win and Bill does too. (Bill expects Bill/John will win)

In both (51d) and (52a), the sentence can only mean that 'John and Bill each expect to win.' In (52b), where the embedded clause has a pronoun, the sentence is ambiguous; it can mean that 'John and Bill each expect to win' or that 'John and Bill both expect John to win.' Similarly, (51e) is restricted to an interpretation in which only Churchill could have this memory, consistent with the interpretation obtained with a bound anaphor as in (53a), but not with a coreferential pronoun as in (53b), where Churchill among others could potentially have the memory that he gave said speech.

(53) a. Only Churchill$_1$ remembers himself$_1$ giving the BST speech. [= (51e)]
  b. Only Churchill$_1$ remembers that he$_1$ gave the BST speech. [≠ (51e)]

 If Hornstein is correct about OC PRO being an anaphor, then there would be little to distinguish it from traces of NP-movement. If government is set aside (as Hornstein proposes), then both OC PRO and NP traces are [+anaphoric, −pronominal] null NPs, can occur in a θ-position, and are not Case marked. The only remaining difference between them is that OC PRO is coindexed with a θ-marked position, and NP-trace is coindexed with a non-θ-position, as (54) shows.

(54) a. Toni$_1$ tried [PRO$_1$ to leave]
  b. Toni$_1$ appeared [t$_1$ to leave]

That is, the pair of elements <Toni$_1$, PRO$_1$> in (54a) has two θ-roles, while the pair of elements <Toni$_1$, t$_1$> in (54b) has one. Thus, once the θ-criterion has been dismissed (for the reasons noted above), the syntactic derivation of RtoS and Subject Control are largely identical. The derivations in (55) illustrate Hornstein's analysis, utilizing the MP Copy and Merge conceptualization of movement as explained and illustrated in chapter 11, examples (20) and (21). In these representations, below, all copies of the movement operation are shown with the understanding that only the highest copy is pronounced at Spell-Out.

(55)  a.  [IPToni [VPToni tried [IPToni to [VPToni leave]
      b.  [IPToni [VPappeared [IPToni to [VPToni leave]

In (55a), a control construction, *Toni* merges with *leave*, checking the verb's θ-role, moves to Spec, IP to check the D-feature of the lower IP, moves to Spec of the higher VP to check the θ-role of the verb *tried*, and then moves to Spec of the higher IP to check its D-feature and to check its own Case. The matrix subject having multiple θ-roles is what distinguishes a control structure (55a) from a raising construction (55b). The derivation of the raising construction in (55b) is pretty much the same, except for *Toni* not moving to Spec of the higher VP, since *appeared* has no subject θ-role to check. Thus, in (55b) the matrix subject only has a single θ-role acquired in the lower clause.

While the approach advocated by Hornstein has a certain appeal, it is not without serious problems. Some of these are elaborated by Landau (2003). For example, he notes that Hornstein's "Control is movement" approach presents no obvious way to block the propagation of Control across a passive matrix verb (this having been pointed out previously in Brody 1999). To illustrate, (56a) with the control verb *hope* is ungrammatical in contrast with (56b) with the raising verb *expect*.

(56)  a.  *John was hoped to win the game.      [= Landau 2003:(5a)]
      b.  John was expected to win the game.    [= Landau 2003:(6a)]

Hornstein's account of (56b) would have John moving directly from the embedded IP into the subject position of the matrix IP, skipping over the matrix VP since there is no θ-role for it to acquire there. This is shown here in (57), which is comparable to (55b).

(57)  [IPJohn was [VPexpected [IPJohn to [VPJohn win the game]

In principle, there is nothing to rule out the generation of (56a) on the same principles, with a derivation such as shown in (58).

(58)  [IPJohn was [VPhoped [IPJohn to [VPJohn win the game]

Hornstein's (2000) solution to this problem, as Landau points out, is supported by some rather dubious grammaticality judgments. Appealing to Chomsky's (1998) notion of "phase," Hornstein assumes that CPs are phases and that movement out of a complement is not possible if the complement is a CP at the point that movement occurs. In other words, A-movement out of IP complements is generally permissible, and A-movement out of CP complements is in principle not permissible. Noting that control verbs such as *hope* and *try* are assumed to take CP complements, Hornstein suggests that complementizer deletion ("incorporation" in his terms) can "void the CP phase derivationally," allowing the derivation of (54a) in the manner shown in (55a). In the case of (56a), Hornstein proposes that complementizer incorporation/deletion is prevented from applying to the complements of passive verbs, that their complements must remain CP phases, and therefore that A-movement out of the complement of *was hoped* is not possible and that (56a) is not derivable. In support of his suggestion, Hornstein (2000:137 (13)) claims that the deletion of a complementizer after a passive verb is unacceptable, providing the following contrast.

(59) a. John fervently believes (that) there's a man here.
 b. It's fervently believed ??(that) there's a man here.

Unfortunately, the judgments presented in (59) are far from certain, and it is not difficult to construct passive sentences in which deletion of an embedded complementizer is perfectly natural.

(60) It was assumed (that) he got on an 8:33 express after leaving the office at 8:00.

To the extent that (60) is acceptable without *that*, Hornstein's movement analysis of Control still overgenerates ungrammatical sentences such as (56a).

Landau goes on to identify other theory-internal problems for Hornstein's analysis, which are beyond the scope of this discussion. The next section of this chapter takes up an earlier critique of Hornstein's analysis, from Culicover and Jackendoff, in which they claim any syntactic approach to Control to be fundamentally misguided.

## Control is not movement

Culicover and Jackendoff (C&J 2001) and Jackendoff and Culicover (J&C 2003) present a case against Hornstein's unified syntactic approach to Control and Raising.[14] While approving of Hornstein's (and the MP's) overarching goals of eliminating "certain formal syntactic devices" (e.g., the θ-criterion and PRO), they contend that the program has not gone far enough and that, like the non-derivational generative approaches of HPSG and LFG, it should "eliminate the binding relation in syntactic structure" altogether. That is, while C&J are sympathetic to the idea that raising and control clauses have the same syntactic structure, they see no reason for any sort of movement operations or linked NP positions in either case to derive the interpretation of such constructions. The derivations proposed by Hornstein such as in (55) would just as well be replaced by something like (61), which is much the same analysis proposed in Bach (1977) (see chapter 5, section 3).

(61) a. [$_{IP}$Toni [$_{VP}$tried [$_{VP}$to leave]
 b. [$_{IP}$Toni [$_{VP}$appeared [$_{VP}$to leave]

According to C&J, both *try* and *appear* "project their subject argument downward into the argument structure of the complement" VP *to leave*. The difference between them rests on the fact that only the former assigns an independent θ-role to its subject. C&J's arguments against a movement account of Control take two forms. First, they challenge many of the empirically based arguments in favor of collapsing PRO and NP-trace, and second, they present motivations for a semantic account of those control phenomena. Only a few points will be discussed here.

For instance, on the issue of treating PRO as an anaphor, Hornstein notes that OC clauses can often be paraphrased by replacing PRO with a reflexive, as in the grammatical (62a). The ungrammatical (62b) also shows the alignment of OC PRO and the reflexive anaphor in that they are both blocked when not c-commanded by their antecedent/controller.

(62) a. John$_1$ expects PRO$_1$/himself$_1$ to win
     b. *John$_1$'s campaign expects PRO$_1$/himself$_1$ to win

But C&J note that this ignores the fact that *expect* is both a subject control verb and an RtoO verb, as (63) shows, and that the same point could not be made with any other pure control predicate. Compare (63) and (64).

(63) a. John expects PRO/himself/Fred to win     [= C&J 2001:495 (6)]
     b. John expects there to be trouble.

(64) a. John tried PRO/*himself/*Fred to win     [= C&J 2001:496 (7)]
     b. *John tried there to be trouble.

From an examination of the many different varieties of control phenomena presented in J&C (2003), it appears that Hornstein's OC and NOC categorization oversimplifies the picture and leaves a significant number of distinctions among control predicates unaccounted for.[15]

Another problem for Hornstein, according to C&J (2001), stems from his attempt to account for the determination of subject vs. object control in terms of syntactic proximity of the controller to the controlled subject position. Hornstein takes up Rosenbaum's (1970:26–8) Minimal Distance Principle (MDP) which selects as controller "the NP closest in the tree to the infinitival." All other things being equal, the MDP predicts that intransitive control verbs are Subject Control and that transitive control verbs are Object Control, the matrix object being "closer" to the controlled subject than the matrix subject. On this view, control predicates like *promise* are highly marked, since they are transitive and the matrix subject, which is more distant, controls the complement subject. Hornstein claims that the MDP is simply an instance of the more general Minimal Link Condition (MLC, the principle that requires "shortest moves": Chomsky 1995:264). As we see directly below, by incorporating the MDP into a larger syntactic model, Hornstein has perhaps created an insoluble problem for a syntactic account of Control.

First, as C&J note, the *promise* class is not as restricted as one might think. While *promise* and *vow* might be the only transitive subject control verbs, there are many such nominals (including *offer, guarantee, obligation, agreement,* and *contract*) as shown in (65).

(65) John's agreement/contract with Susan to take   [= C&J 2001:504 (32b)]
care of himself/*herself

There are also a number of predicates (e.g., *contract with* and *arrange with*) that permit both subject and object control.[16]

(66) John$_1$ contracted with Susan$_2$ to $_{1/2}$take care of   [= J&C 2003:(43a)]
himself/him.

Note that there are many more "highly marked" predicates than one might desire to have, especially if the MDP, rather than being a descriptive observation, is an epiphenominal result of a deeper principal of syntactic markedness (MLC). Also note the problems posed by the fact that some predicates are agnostic about which argument is the controller. If the noun *contract* violates the MLC by allowing Subject Control, how is one to account for the verb *contract with* which allows either subject or Object Control?

The second problem for the MDP/MLC account is that it makes the wrong predictions regarding Control into adjunct clauses, which always have Subject Control. Consider (67).

(67) John flattered Mary without compromising   [= C&J 2001:498 (15a)]
himself/*herself.

According to Rosenbaum (under his MDP), *John* controls into the adjunct clause because the adjunct clause is outside the VP and closer to the subject. Subject control would be predicted if the *without* clause is higher than the VP. However, Hornstein adopts a Minimalist theoretic approach to the placement of adjuncts, placing them inside the VP as in (68).

(68) John [$_{VP}$read every book$_1$ without   [= Hornstein 1999:88 (38)]
reviewing it$_1$]

According to Hornstein, *every book* can only bind *it* if it c-commands the pronoun at LF. This would entail, with regard to (67), that both *John* and *Mary* must c-command the *without* clause at LF (and that *Mary* is the closer potential controller). While Hornstein does show how *John* can be derived as a controller for *without compromising himself*, he does not show (as C&J point out) why *Mary* cannot be so.

PP-internal controllers appear to pose yet another problem for Hornstein's movement account of Control (and for that matter for any account that relies on PRO being c-commanded by its controller). A limited number of verbs (such as *plead* and *pray*) and a great number of nominals (such as *reminder* and *order*) allow the object of a preposition to control the subject of an infinitival clause, as seen in (69).

(69) a. John prayed [_PP_ to Athena] to take care      [= C&J 2001:509 (47b)]
of herself/*himself
  b. John's reminder [_PP_ to Susan] to take care of herself/*himself

In these cases, it is not clear how (under the movement account) the subject of the infinitival clause could possibly move into a PP headed by *to*. Even if the θ-criterion is dispensed with, the moved NP would presumably fail to c-command its original position within the complement clause.[17]

## Control is not *not movement*

Boeckx and Hornstein (2003) (B&H) is a direct response to C&J (2001), taking issue with their overall rejection of syntactically based accounts of Control, challenging their assessment of the *promise* class of control predicates (the violators of the MDP), and rejecting the conflation of control verbs and control nouns. B&H claim that, while the Hornstein (1999) movement account of Control may ultimately not be the correct one, some syntactic account is to be preferred over a purely semantic/thematic analysis such as C&J propose.

As B&H put it, there are two important issues to contend with in explaining the grammar of control structures. One of these issues concerns explaining the distribution of the controllee, i.e., the distribution of PRO in previous accounts. The other concerns identifying the controller, and explaining its relation to the controllee. With respect to the first, B&H assert that there is basic agreement that the restricted distribution of controllees (to the subject position of a dependent clause) is a syntactic rather than a semantic matter. That controlled clauses are always non-finite is a syntactic fact, not a semantic one.

As regards the second issue, predicting which element of the matrix clause will be the controller, B&H acknowledge that semantic considerations play a large role in this. But they insist that reducing control theory to a thematically coded catalogue of possible controllers (as they claim C&J would have it) should be a methodological "last resort," given the syntactic generalizations that are so salient. Such a thematic approach will have little to say about the distribution of controllers to the extent that they correlate to grammatical categories rather than semantic ones. In this regard, the case of controlled adjunct clauses is illustrative.

(70) a. John flattered Mary after embarrassing himself/*herself.
  b. Mary was flattered by John after embarrassing herself/*himself.

In (70), the controller of the adjunct clause must be the subject of the sentence, regardless of its thematic role. Now, as B&H point out, "adjuncts are by definition unselected, a-thematic material," and the *after* clause in (70) is not thematically related in any way to the matrix sentence. In this situation, a semantic account like C&J's, which explains the control relation in terms of semantic relations and dependencies, would seem to have nothing to say about the restriction of the controller to the subject of the matrix clause. So while Hornstein's (1999) account itself might not adequately explain the inability of *Mary* to be the controller in (67) and in (70a), it is clear to B&H that the account for the distribution of adjunct controllers ought to be a syntactic one, and historically (starting with Rosenbaum 1970) accounts for this construction have been so.

B&H take up C&J's criticism of the MDP/MLC as a condition on the distribution of controllers, which predicts that transitive control verbs should all be Object Control. While agreeing that the control properties of *promise* and a few other predicates do indeed place an explanatory burden on their account, B&H assert that the MDP/MLC view turns out to be superior once all factors are considered. The assertion that *promise* is syntactically marked as a control verb in being transitive and determining Subject Control turns out to be well-founded when factors such as L1 acquisition and speaker variation are considered. B&H note that Carol Chomsky (1969) showed that children acquire the subject control property of *promise* later than the object control property of verbs like *persuade*, and that Courtenay (1998) claims that many adult speakers never acquire subject control for transitive *promise*, treating it instead as an object control verb or disallowing it from taking an NP object when it is control, e.g., *I promised (*Kate) to leave*. Taken together with the general scarcity of transitive subject control verbs, these facts support the conclusion that they are indeed highly marked. The MDP/MLC account (or something like it), B&H assert, would have something to say about this, where a purely semantic account would not.[18]

Finally, B&H dispute the significance of C&J's appeal to Control within nominalizations. As B&H point out, there is general agreement among them that Control in nominalizations behaves differently from control in VPs, and that the movement theory of Control does not fare as well when the control clause is a nominalization. For C&J, this is evidence against a movement account, in that for them a semantic account that can explain the distribution of both verbal and nominal control structures is to be preferred over an account that can only handle one of these. B&H, for their part, point out that verbal and nominal structures exhibit significant differences with respect to their assignment of thematic roles. For instance, a *by*-phrase within a nominalization can only have an agentive meaning, while *by*-phrases are not so restricted in VPs. Consider (71).

(71) a. The house was encircled by the trees. [= B&H (8)]
 b. the encirclement of the house by the trees

In (71a), the phrase *by the trees* need not have an agentive interpretation, while in (71b) it must be agentive. These and other facts (such as the impossibility of preserving idiomatic readings in nominalizations; e.g., *John's letting of the cat out of the bag*) lead B&H to reason that if the thematic properties of verbal and nominal phrases are distinct, then so might be their syntax. In fact, as they point out, the syntax of Raising is distinct in nominalizations – it does not apply. So contrasting with (72a), an RtoS clause, we find its nominal analogue to be ill-formed.

(72) a. John appears to be polite.
 b. *John's appearance to be polite. (cf. the appearance to be polite)

B&H go on to sketch an explanation for why Control, but not Raising, is possible in nominalizations. However, the adequacy of their solution notwithstanding, they do successfully demonstrate the need for caution in assuming (as C&J do) that grammatical analyses should be indistinguishable across categories, and for caution in asserting a priori the superiority of any account that unifies verbal and nominal instances of Control.[19]

The conclusion reached in comparing these accounts is that a purely syntactic account of Control is most likely unattainable, but that a purely semantic account inevitably leaves some important issues without an explanation. Even if we take Hornstein's point about it not being necessarily desirable to conflate nominal and verbal cases of Control, there are cases such as (69), repeated here, which seem to defy any attempt to render the controller–controllee relation in configurational terms (i.e., as requiring c-command).

(69) a. John prayed [$_{PP}$to Athena] to take care of herself/*himself      [= C&J 2001:509 (47b)]
  b. John's reminder [$_{PP}$to Susan] to take care of herself/*himself

At the same time, it is clear that syntactic constraints must also determine the choice of controller, independent of thematic considerations. As (70), repeated here, shows, either the agent or theme of *flatter* may control into an adjunct clause, but only from subject position.

(70) a. John flattered Mary after embarrassing himself/*herself.
  b. Mary was flattered by John after embarrassing herself/*himself.

While Hornstein's particular account fails to rule out *Mary* as a controller (as pointed out in C&J 2001), a syntactic analysis is certainly warranted (and some version of the MDP combined with the correct analysis of adjunct clauses might to be able to accomplish this). A purely thematic account of control does not appear to offer any clear way to encode the syntactically based constraints observed here.

## 5 Back to empiricism

The first section of this chapter examined some of the empirical reasons for keeping Raising and Control separate, and then surveyed some of the theory-dependent arguments for either maintaining or eliminating the distinction. The debate outlined in section 4 is a skirmish between a view of grammar that seeks to unite the raising and control phenomena under the banner of syntactic analysis and a view that prefers to analyze both in terms of thematically based lexical conceptual structure (LCS). Overall, then, it would appear that the decision of whether to separate or merge one's account of Raising and Control, and whether to attribute their properties to syntactic or semantic components of the grammar, is to some extent a matter of theoretical predisposition. However, it is fair to ask whether the answers to these questions turn entirely on theoretical predispositions, or whether there might be an empirical basis for determining, if not the best analysis of these, then at least what module of the grammar is involved and whether there is an independent basis for the Raising/Control distinction. The remainder of this chapter will try to review some of the empirical bases for the separation of Raising and Control, leaving a fully detailed analysis of each for another day.

Unified analyses of Raising and Control are principally concerned with accounting for the distribution of the controller or raisee (e.g., case, semantic role assignment, surface constituency, etc.). Many of these are described in section 1 of this chapter. But one does not have to look far to find differences between the two constructions that have little to do with the controller or raisee itself. Recall from note 12 of this chapter, that the infinitival complement of a control verb, as opposed to that of a raising verb, is specified for a tense that Bresnan calls "unrealized future" (see Bresnan 1972 and Stowell 1982). The difference is illustrated here in (73).

(73) a. Bill believed himself to be the smartest.
     b. I persuaded John to win the race.

As Stowell (1982:566) notes, "there is an understood present tense in . . . [the RtoO sentence (73a), and] an understood future tense in . . . [the object control sentence (73b)]." The fact that the tense of the complement infinitival clause is determined by the matrix verb provided some of the motivation for Martin's (2001) null Case analysis of PRO, in which RtoO infinitives are claimed to be [−tense, −finite] and Control infinitives are [+tense, −finite]. While Hornstein's critique of the null Case proposal for PRO may be valid, his proposed alternatives in which Raising and Control are conflated leaves "the tense of infinitives" unexplained.

Landau (2003: section 5) illustrates some of the differences between raising and control constructions, several of which appear to hold cross-linguistically. First, control complements may sometimes be introduced by complementizers, while raising complements never are.[20] It is for this reason that analyses of Raising and Control have often presumed raising complements to be IPs and control complements to be CPs.

Second, RtoS predicates, such as *appear*, are found to pattern with unaccusative verbs, in contrast with subject control predicates, such as *try*. Consider the *en* cliticization contrast noted in Ruwet (1991), repeated here. In (74), a raising construction, *en* cliticization is grammatical.

(74) a. L'auteur de ce livre semble être génial.
        'The author of this book seems to be brilliant.'
     b. L'auteur semble **en** être génial.
        'The author of it seems to be brilliant.'

On the contrary, *en* cannot cliticize to the embedded verb in a control construction, as in (75b).[21]

(75) a. L'auteur de ce livre prétend être génial.
 'The author of this book claims to be brilliant.'
 b. *L'auteur prétend en être génial.
 (The author of it claims to be brilliant.)

Similar distinctions in the distribution of clitics arise in Italian, Landau points out; Rizzi (1986) has shown that the reflexive clitic *si* cannot be part of a chain involving NP-movement [*NP$_1$ ... si$_1$ ... t$_1$], such as in passives and unaccusatives. Raising and control constructions are found by Rizzi to differ in this regard. Raising patterns as an NP-movement construction, disallowing the reflexive clitic, while Control patterns with other non-movement constructions, allowing it.

Other evidence cited in Landau (2003) includes: (i) the distribution of *each*, for which it is shown in Burzio (1981) and Chomsky (1981) that "control 'breaks' the association of *each* with a lower NP, but raising does not"; (ii) a case mismatch exhibited between controllers and floating quantifiers in Icelandic, which does not appear in raising constructions (Sigurðsson 1991); and (iii) the existence of partial control, as reported in Landau (2000). With respect to this last, Landau (2000: ch. 2) discusses instances of Control in which the controller is singular and the controllee denotes a group that includes the controller. This phenomenon, first discussed in Lawler (1972), is illustrated in (76).

(76) The chair$_1$ preferred [PRO$_{1+}$ to gather at 6]   [= Landau 2003:(40a)]

Constructions such as (76), where PRO and its controller do not have the same denotation, seem to defy any movement account of Control. Further, as Landau points out, "there is no partial raising." Finally, turning back to the issue of Control in nominalizations, it would be fair to say that if C&J are right about Control being semantic and B&H are right about there being no raising in nominalizations, then Control and Raising cannot be unified under either a syntactic Hornstein-type account or a semantic C&J-type account.

What the reader can conclude from the evidence presented in this section is that there is a great variety of empirical evidence that must be taken into account in shaping any analysis of Raising and Control.[22] These data seem to present potentially insurmountable obstacles to the formulation of a unified account of these two constructions, whether the account is syntactic or semantic in its orientation. Ultimately, for any lasting progress to be made in the understanding of these phenomena, empirical considerations must play a greater role than theory-internal ones, and those who ignore the data do so at their own peril.

## Notes

1 These include Lakoff's (1970) "positive absolute exceptions," Perlmutter's (1968) "deep structure constraints," and others.
2 Note that Brame's (1976) analysis predates VP-internal subject hypotheses by at least several years. Accordingly, the standard assumption at the time was that

3   there is no subject position in a VP, and if the complements are VPs then the excrescent subjects (*Mary* in (12b) and *Harry* in (13b)) could not be generated.
3   At this point in his discussion, Brame assumes a raising analysis, a position he will eventually abandon, making his argument initially for a VP analysis of Control only. However, his overarching goal is to show that if one assumes all infinitival complements are S, one encounters problems that do not face an analysis in which control complements are VP. Therefore, this is not a position that is inconsistent with his eventual claim that all infinitival complements are VP.
4   The portion of their article that is concerned with the proper analysis of *tough* constructions is beyond the scope of this chapter.
5   K&M's discussion of VP' and PS also takes up the issue of whether VP' can be considered a "maximal projection" and whether VP' and S' would be assumed to be projections of the same head (INFL). Since much of this discussion relies on conceptions of PS that are no longer relevant, it is excluded from discussion here.
6   As is noted in Sag et al. (1985), the coordination of unlike categories is not prohibited in principle, as (i) shows, and such apparent effects have a more complex explanation.

   (i)   George was [$_{AP}$healthy] and [$_{PP}$of sound mind]

   See also Chametzky (1987) and Bayer (1996).
7   Idan Landau (p.c.) points out that key data in C&W's gapping argument do not form a minimal pair. Consider (i) and (ii).

   (i)  a.  I believe Mary to be rich, and Bill *(believes)       [= C&W 1986:(36a)]
            Sam to be poor.
        b.  I persuaded Mary to be nice, and Bill *(persuaded) Sam to be rude.

   (ii) a.  Mary appears to be rich, and Bill (appears) to be poor.
        b.  John wants to eat the beans, and Mary (wants)          [= C&W 1986:(36b)]
            to eat the potatoes.

   It is clear from these facts that gapping is not possible when the raising/control verb is transitive, and that the distinction between Raising and Control does not play the part that C&W say it does.
8   It is worth noting here that under an RtoO analysis of (28a), the impossibility of gapping would have a different explanation. Note first that gapping is less felicitous when a verb is followed by two arguments than when it is followed by one. Consider (i).

   (i)  a.  Mary told a joke, and Larry (told) a story.
        b.  Mary told Arthur a joke, and Larry *(told) Kevin a story.

   In (ib), the ellipsis of *told* appears to be blocked when it is followed by two constituents (NPs in this case). Under an RtoO analysis of (28a), the ellipsis of *believes* in the second conjunct is ill-formed for the same reason (i.e., *Sam* and *to be poor* do not form a surface constituent). In this view, C&W's gapping argument against analyzing the subjectless infinitive as an S' evaporates.
9   Keep in mind that, Postal and Pullum (1988) notwithstanding, the Neo-RtoO analysis preserves the Projection Principle and the θ-criterion, since the landing site for all derived objects is in a functional projection.

10 Not all minimalist proposals have tended in this direction. Rooryck (2000), for example, examines the empirical contrasts between French and English raising and control constructions (building on observations in Ruwet 1991), and points to the formal problems arising from trying to adapt an ECM account to Minimalist assumptions. His analysis of Raising and Control proposes uniform (CP) complementation for both constructions and an "ECM-RtoO" derivation for the raising cases. Raising (but not Control) first involves movement of the entire embedded AgrSP complement into the Spec of its containing CP, as in (i), thereby permitting subsequent movement of the embedded subject to the matrix Spec,AgrOP.

(i) Barnett believed [$_{CP}$[$_{AgrSP}$the doctor to have examined Tilman]$_1$ [C$^0$ t$_1$]]

In contrast, Control is claimed not to have movement of AgrSP to Spec,CP.

11 Actually, Hornstein (1999) operationalizes movement using the MP model of Copy and Merge, and thus, the NP traces shown here are not quite consistent with those assumptions. Nevertheless, the contrast between (44) and (45) faithfully illustrates the conceptual change that Hornstein proposes.

12 Further elaboration of this notion, with additional arguments, can be found in Martin (2001). Martin's presentation refines the notion of "null Case," connecting it to [+tense] infinitival clauses (i.e., those associated with control structures).

(i) a. Sheila believes [he is nice]
    b. Sheila$_1$ wants [PRO$_1$ to be nice]
    c. Sheila believes [him to be nice]

It has been shown in Bresnan (1972) and Stowell (1982) that the infinitival complement of a control verb (as opposed to that of a raising verb) is specified for a tense that Bresnan calls "unrealized future." Taking up these observations, Martin proposes that RtoO infinitives differ from control infinitives in that only the latter assign "null Case" to PRO, while the former assign no Case at all (opening the way for an ECM or RtoO analysis of these). Thus, for Martin, [+tense, +finite] checks nominative Case (ia), [+tense, −finite] checks null Case (ib), and [−tense, −finite] does not check Case at all (ic).

Independent of but contemporaneous with the null Case proposal, Wyngaerd (1994) offers an analysis in which PRO is assigned nominative Case by the [−tense] I node, requiring elaboration of the representation of verb agreement. We do not take up this intriguing proposal here.

13 Other ways in which OC PRO is distinguished from NOC PRO include the inability to have a split antecedent, as in (ia), and the restriction of (ib) to a reading in which *the unfortunate* has expectations only about himself or herself getting a medal.

(i) a. *John$_1$ told Mary$_2$ PRO$_{1+2}$ to wash themselves/     [= Lasnik 1999a:(4e)]
       each other.
    b. The unfortunate$_1$ expects PRO$_{1/*ARB}$ to get     [= Lasnik 1999a:(4f)]
       the medal.

NOC PRO constructions, in contrast, allow split antecedents and the interpretations are not so restricted.

(ii) a. John$_1$ told Mary$_2$ [that [PRO$_{1+2}$ washing     [= Lasnik 1999a:(6e)]
        themselves/each other] would be fun]

b. The unfortunate₁ believes [that [PRO₁/ARB getting   [= Lasnik 1999a:(6f)]
the medal] would be boring.

14 Where C&J (2001) is primarily a response to Hornstein (1999), J&C (2003) articulates a much more fully developed semantic treatment of the many types of Control in English (inclusive of both verbal and nominal clauses), as well as of the semantic factors that can shift Control from what a given lexical predicate might otherwise entail. The discussion here focuses primarily on the debate between Hornstein and C&J and does not attempt to do justice to the content of J&C (2003).

15 In addition to the traditional subject (e.g., *promise*) and object (e.g., *persuade*) classes of control verbs, J&C (2003) also takes up, among other things, (i) the issue of "free, nearly free, and unique control"; (ii) the fact that control verbs such as *urge* must take "actional"/volitional complements (e.g., *to dance*), while others such as *hope* can take "situational"/non-volitional complements (e.g., *to grow tall*); (iii) the *shout* and *ask* classes of control verbs; and (iv) partial control.

16 The index "1/2" in front of the verb *take care* in (66) is intended by C&J to identify the subject of the infinitival VP, which in this case can be either *John* or *Susan*.

17 Manzini and Roussou (2000) offer a Minimalist account of Control that appears to be essentially a syntactic operationalization of a semantic account. Eschewing overt movement of DP phrases, they assert the theoretical superiority of F(eature)-movement in its place in contexts where A-movement has traditionally been assumed. Their analysis of a control sentence such as (i) involves such mechanisms.

(i)  [IP John I [VP tried [IP to [VP leave]]]]    [= Manzini and Roussou 2000:422 (27)]

The derivation of (i), they claim, involves a matrix DP *John* "directly merged into the [Spec, I] position to lexicalize the D-feature of I." The control interpretation is achieved on account of the subject DP attracting "[the theta features of?] both the matrix V and the embedded V." Looking past the theory-internal details of this analysis, though, it is difficult to discern a clear difference between it and something that might be put forward by C&J (2001) or, for that matter, by Bach (1977).

18 B&H propose a syntactic account for the subject control property of *promise*, claiming that it fails to be Object Control like other transitive control verbs because its nominal object is actually contained within a PP headed by a null P. Their analysis is given in (i).

(i)  John promised [PP P_null Mary] [to leave early]    [= B&H (5a)]

In (i), *Mary* cannot control into the infinitival clause because it does not c-command it. While this analysis (based on work presented in Boeckx 1999, 2002) does in fact provide a syntactic explanation for the difference between *promise* and *persuade*, it is not without flaws. Most notably, it undermines any potential syntactic explanation for why the objects of prepositions in (69) are indeed able to control into the adjacent infinitive. So, while the solution is rather creative, it cannot ultimately be correct.

19 The "Control as movement" approach of Hornstein (1999) and Boeckx and Hornstein (2003) has also been shown to yield quite insightful solutions to seemingly intractable data. One compelling example of this is found in Polinsky and Potsdam's (P&P) (2002) analysis of "backward Control" in Tsez. This Nakh-Daghestanian language of the Caucasus has a control construction in which the controller surfaces

as the overt subject of the embedded clause, and the controllee is a null matrix subject. The construction is exemplified in (i), where ERG(ative) case on *kidbā* 'girl' is an indication that it is a surface subject of the embedded clause.

(i)  Δ$_{i/*k}$ [kidbā$_i$  ziya       bišra]   yoqsi           [= P&P 2002:246 (2)]
     girl.ERG cow.ABS feed.INF began
     'The girl began to feed the cow.'

The "silent element Δ [i.e., the null matrix subject] is obligatorily coindexed with the subject of an infinitival complement clause" (P&P 2002:246). P&P present substantial evidence for the null matrix subject and for its being (backward) controlled by the subject of the complement clause. Evidence comes from, among other sources, the distribution of depictive phrases such as *sixoli* 'alone' and reflexive binding.

P&P (2002:258–9) show that depictives must be c-commanded by the phrase that they modify. The appearance of *sisxoli* in (ii) is evidence for the existence of the null-controlled matrix subject, since only the c-commanding null subject Δ could license its appearance before the embedded subject *kidbā*.

(ii) Δ$_i$ sisxoli [kidbā$_i$  ziya       bišra]   yoqsi           [= P&P 2002:259 (36a)]
     alone    girl.ERG cow.ABS feed.INF began
     'The girl$_i$ alone$_i$ began to feed the cow.'
     *'The girl began to feed the cow$_i$ alone$_i$.'

If 'girl' in (ii) were to have ABS(olutive) case, *kid* 'girl.ABS,' indicating that it is the surface subject of *yoqsi* 'began,' the sentence would be ungrammatical, as *sisxoli* 'alone' would then precede the matrix subject.

Similarly, reflexives must have a local antecedent, and (iii) supports their claim for a null controllee in the matrix clause. The dative reflexive *nesā nesir* is clearly a dependent of the matrix clause and could only have the null subject Δ as an antecedent.

(iii) Δ$_i$ nesā nesir$_i$ [irbahin-ā$_i$  halmaɣ-or  ɣutku       [= P&P 2002:259 (36a)]
      REFL.DAT            Ibrahim.ERG friend-DAT house.ABS
      rod-a]   Ø-oq-si
      make-INF AGR-begin-PAST.EVID
      'Ibrahim began, for himself, to build a house for his friend.'

P&P propose a movement analysis of this control construction, adopting the assumptions made in Hornstein (1999) regarding the possibility of a DP having multiple θ-roles. They claim that this movement in Tsez is covert, i.e., accomplished after Spell-Out. That is, *irbahin* moves from subject position of the embedded clause into the matrix subject position by LF.

20  Note, however, that this generalization depends on proving that purported Raising in Japanese, and other languages, is not truly Raising (see the relevant discussion above in chapters 10 and 12).
21  The reader may recall as well that Ruwet cast some doubt upon the *en* cliticization test as a diagnostic for Raising, finding that *en* cliticization on the embedded verb is only possible when the subject is non-human. However, Landau (2003:note 16) points out that not all speakers of French have this restriction, and that for those who do not have it, the *en* cliticization test is a reliable diagnostic of unaccusativity and of Raising.

22 Advances in psycholinguistic methodology may bring a new type of evidence to bear on this issue. In recent work, Featherston et al. (2000) report a significant difference in the Event-Related Potentials (ERPs) elicited at the empty subject positions in German raising constructions vs. control constructions. They hypothesize that the difference in ERPs provides evidence for the difference in processing the empty categories at this site, specifically a trace vs. PRO. Whether or not such a result can be replicated or even sustained, experimental data of this kind may provide additional evidence for distinguishing Raising from Control.

# REFERENCES

Abney, Steven. 1987. The English noun phrase in its sentential aspect. MIT dissertation.
Aissen, Judith L. 1979. Possessor ascension in Tzotzil. In Laura Martin, ed., *Papers in Mayan linguistics*, 89–108. Columbia, MO: Lucas Brothers.
Aissen, Judith L. 1990. Towards a theory of agreement controllers. In Paul M. Postal and Brian D. Joseph, eds, *Studies in relational grammar 3*, 279–320. Chicago: University of Chicago Press.
Akatsuka-McCawley, Noriko. 1972. On the treatment of Japanese passives. *Proceedings of the Chicago Linguistic Society (CLS)* 8.259–70.
Akmajian, Adrian, and Frank Heny. 1976. *An introduction to the principles of transformational syntax*. Cambridge, MA: MIT Press.
Allen, Barbara J., Donald G. Frantz, Donna B. Gardiner, and David M. Perlmutter. 1990. Verb agreement, possessor ascension, and multistratal representation in Southern Tiwa. In Paul M. Postal and Brian D. Joseph, eds, *Studies in relational grammar 3*, 312–83. Chicago: University of Chicago Press.
Andrews, Avery. 1982. The representation of case in Modern Icelandic. In Joan Bresnan, ed., *The mental representation of grammatical relations*, 427–503. Cambridge, MA: MIT Press.
Aoun, Joseph. 1979. On government, Case-marking, and clitic-placement. Unpublished MS, MIT.
Bach, Emmon. 1977. Review article on Postal, *On raising: One rule of English grammar and its theoretical implications*. *Language* 53.621–54.
Baker, Mark C. 1988. *Incorporation: A theory of grammatical function changing*. Chicago: University of Chicago Press.
Bayer, Samuel. 1996. The coordination of unlike categories. *Language* 72.579–616.
Bell, Sarah J. 1976. Cebuano subjects in two frameworks. MIT dissertation.
Bell, Sarah J. 1983. Advancements and ascensions in Cebuano. In David M. Perlmutter, ed., *Studies in relational grammar 1*, 143–218. Chicago: University of Chicago Press.
Belletti, Adriana. 1988. The Case of unaccusatives. *Linguistic Inquiry* 19.1–34.
Belletti, Adriana, and Luigi Rizzi. 1988. Psych-verbs and θ-theory. *Natural Language and Linguistic Theory* 6.291–352.
Bobaljik, Jonathan David, and Dianne Jonas. 1996. Subject positions and the roles of TP. *Linguistic Inquiry* 27.195–236.
Boeckx, Cedric. 1999. Conflicting c-command requirements. *Studia Linguistica* 53.227–50.

Boeckx, Cedric. 2002. Patterns of subject raising across experiencers. Unpublished MS, University of Illinois, Urbana-Champaign.

Boeckx, Cedric, and Norbert Hornstein. 2003. Reply to "Control is not movement." Unpublished MS, University of Connecticut and University of Maryland.

Bowers, John. 1993. The syntax of predication. *Linguistic Inquiry* 24.591–656.

Brame, Michael. 1976. *Conjectures and refutations in syntax and semantics*. Amsterdam: North-Holland.

Bresnan, Joan. 1970. On complementizers: Towards a syntactic theory of complement types. *Foundations of Language* 6.297–321.

Bresnan, Joan. 1971. Sentence stress and syntactic transformations. *Language* 47.257–81.

Bresnan, Joan. 1972. Theory of complementation in English syntax. MIT dissertation.

Bresnan, Joan. 1976. Nonarguments for raising. *Linguistic Inquiry* 7.3–40.

Bresnan, Joan. 1978. A realistic transformational grammar. In Morris Halle, Joan Bresnan, and George A. Miller, eds, *Linguistic theory and psychological reality*, 1–60. Cambridge, MA: MIT Press.

Bresnan, Joan. 1982. Control and complementation. *Linguistic Inquiry* 13.3–40.

Bresnan, Joan. 1994. Locative inversion and the architecture of Universal Grammar. *Language* 70.72–131.

Brody, Michael. 1999. Relating syntactic elements: Remarks on Norbert Hornstein's "Movement and chains." *Syntax* 2.210–26.

Bruening, Benjamin. 2001a. Raising to object and proper Movement. Unpublished MS, University of Delaware.

Bruening, Benjamin. 2001b. Syntax at the edge: Cross-clausal phenomena and the syntax of Passamaquoddy. MIT dissertation.

Bruening, Benjamin. 2002. Raising to Object and Improper Movement. Paper presented at the 21st meeting of the West Coast Conference on Formal Linguistics (WCCFL 21). University of California, Santa Cruz.

Burzio, Luigi. 1981. Intransitive verbs and Italian auxiliaries. MIT dissertation.

Burzio, Luigi. 1986. *Italian syntax: A Government-Binding approach*. Dordrecht: D. Reidel.

Chametzky, Robert. 1987. Coordination and the organization of a grammar. University of Chicago dissertation.

Chomsky, Carol. 1969. *The acquisition of syntax in children from 5 to 10*. Cambridge, MA: MIT Press.

Chomsky, Noam. 1965. *Aspects of the theory of syntax*. Cambridge, MA: MIT Press.

Chomsky, Noam. 1970. Remarks on nominalization. In Roderick Jacobs and Peter Rosenbaum, eds, *Readings in transformational grammar*, 184–221. Waltham, MA: Ginn.

Chomsky, Noam. 1971. Deep structure, surface structure, and semantic interpretation. In Danny Steinberg and Leon Jakobovits, eds, *Semantics: An interdisciplinary reader in linguistics and psychology*, 183–216. Cambridge: Cambridge University Press.

Chomsky, Noam. 1973. Conditions on transformations. In Stephen Anderson and Paul Kiparsky, eds, *A festschrift for Morris Halle*, 232–86. New York: Holt, Rinehart, and Winston.

Chomsky, Noam. 1977. On *wh*-movement. In Peter Culicover, Thomas Wasow, and Adrian Akmajian, eds, *Formal syntax*, 71–132. New York: Academic Press.

Chomsky, Noam. 1980. On binding. *Linguistic Inquiry* 11.1–46.

Chomsky, Noam. 1981. *Lectures on Government and Binding*. Dordrecht: Foris. Reprinted 1993, Dordrecht: Mouton de Gruyter.

Chomsky, Noam. 1982. *Some concepts and consequences of the theory of Government and Binding*. Cambridge, MA: MIT Press.

Chomsky, Noam. 1986a. *Barriers*. Cambridge, MA: MIT Press.

Chomsky, Noam. 1986b. *Knowledge of language: Its nature, origin, and use.* New York: Praeger.
Chomsky, Noam. 1989 [1991]. Some notes on economy of derivation and representation. In Itziar Laka and Anoop Mahajan, eds, *Functional heads and clause structure. MIT Working Papers in Linguistics 10*, 43–74. MIT Department of Linguistics and Philosophy. Reprinted 1991 in Robert Freidin, ed., *Principles and parameters in comparative grammar*, 417–54. Cambridge, MA: MIT Press. Reprinted with minor revisions in Chomsky 1995 (pp. 129–66).
Chomsky, Noam. 1992 [1993]. A minimalist program for linguistic theory. *MIT Occasional Papers in Linguistics 1.* Cambridge, MA: MIT Department of Linguistics and Philosophy. Reprinted 1993 in Kenneth Hale and Samuel J. Keyser, eds, *The view from Building 20: Essays in honor of Sylvain Bromberger*, 1–52. Cambridge, MA: MIT Press. Reprinted with minor revisions in Chomsky 1995 (pp. 167–217).
Chomsky, Noam. 1994 [1995]. Bare phrase structure. *MIT Occasional Papers in Linguistics 5.* Cambridge, MA: MIT Department of Linguistics and Philosophy. Reprinted 1995 in Gert Webelhuth, ed., *Government and Binding Theory and the Minimalist Program*, 383–439. Oxford: Blackwell Publishing.
Chomsky, Noam. 1995. *The Minimalist Program.* Cambridge, MA: MIT Press. (Includes Chomsky 1989 [1991], Chomsky 1992 [1993], and Chomsky and Lasnik 1993 [1995].)
Chomsky, Noam. 1998 [2000]. Minimalist inquiries: The framework. *MIT Occasional Papers in Linguistics 15.* Cambridge, MA: MIT Working Papers in Linguistics. Reprinted 2000 in Roger Martin, David Michaels, and Juan Uriagereka, eds, *Step by step: Essays on minimalist syntax in honor of Howard Lasnik*, 89–155. Cambridge, MA: MIT Press.
Chomsky, Noam. 1999 [2001]. Derivation by phase. *MIT Occasional Papers in Linguistics 15.* Cambridge, MA: MIT Department of Linguistics. Reprinted 2001 in Michael Kenstowicz, ed., *Ken Hale: A life in language*, 1–52. Cambridge, MA: MIT Press.
Chomsky, Noam, and Howard Lasnik. 1977. Filters and Control. *Linguistic Inquiry* 8.425–504.
Chomsky, Noam, and Howard Lasnik. 1993 [1995]. The theory of principles and parameters. In Joachim Jacobs, Arnim von Stechow, Wolfgang Sternefeld, and Theo Vennemann, eds, *Syntax: An international handbook of contemporary research*, 506–69. Berlin: Walter de Gruyter. Reprinted with minor revisions in Chomsky 1995 (pp. 13–127).
Chung, Sandra. 1976. On the subject of two passives in Indonesian. In Charles Li, ed., *Subject and topic*, 57–98. New York: Academic Press.
Cole, Peter, and Gabriella Hermon. 1981. Subjecthood and islandhood: Evidence from Quechua. *Linguistic Inquiry* 12.1–30.
Courtenay, Karen. 1998. Summary: Subject control verb *promise* in English. http://www.linguistlist.org/issues/9/9-651.html
Culicover, Peter, and Ray Jackendoff. 2001. Control is not movement. *Linguistic Inquiry* 32.493–512.
Culicover, Peter, and Wendy Wilkins. 1986. Control, PRO, and the projection principle. *Language* 62.120–53.
Davies, William D. 1981. Possessor ascension in Choctaw. *NELS* 11.38–57.
Davies, William D. 1986. *Choctaw verb agreement and universal grammar.* Dordrecht: D. Reidel.
Davies, William D. 1988. The case against functional control. *Lingua* 76.1–20.
Davies, William D. 1990. Javanese evidence for Subject-to-Object Raising. In Katarzyna Dziwirek, Patrick Farrell, and Errapel Mejias-Bikandi, eds, *Grammatical relations: A cross-theoretical perspective*, 95–108. Stanford: CSLI.

Davies, William D. 2001. Against raising in Madurese (and other Javanic languages). *Proceedings of the Chicago Linguistic Society (CLS)* 36.57–69.

Davies, William D., and Stanley Dubinsky. 1999. Sentential subjects as complex NPs: New reasons for an old account of subjacency. *Proceedings of the Chicago Linguistic Society (CLS)* 34.83–94.

Davies, William D., and Stanley Dubinsky. 2001a. Functional structure and a parameterization of subject properties. In William Davies and Stanley Dubinsky, eds, *Objects and other subjects: Grammatical functions, functional categories, and configurationality*, 247–79. Dordrecht: Kluwer Academic.

Davies, William D., and Stanley Dubinsky, eds. 2001b. *Objects and other subjects: Grammatical functions, functional categories, and configurationality*. Dordrecht: Kluwer Academic.

Davies, William D., and Stanley Dubinsky. 2003. On extraction from NPs. *Natural Language and Linguistic Theory* 21.1–37.

Dowty, David. 1982. Grammatical relations and Montague Grammar. In Pauline Jacobson and Geoffrey K. Pullum, eds, *On the nature of syntactic representation*, 79–130. Dordrecht: D. Reidel.

Dowty, David. 1985. On recent analyses of the semantics of control. *Linguistics and Philosophy* 8.291–331.

Dubinsky, Stanley. 1985. Japanese union constructions: A unified analyis of -*rare* and -*sase*. Cornell University dissertation.

Dubinsky, Stanley. 1992. Case assignment to VP-adjoined positions: Nominative objects in Japanese. *Linguistics* 30.873–910.

Dubinsky, Stanley. 1997. Predicate union and the syntax of Japanese passives. *Journal of Linguistics* 33.1–37.

Dubinsky, Stanley. 1999. Easy clauses to mistake as relatives: The syntax of English postnominal infinitives. *Western Conference on Linguistics (WECOL) 1998* 10.108–19.

Dubinsky, Stanley, and Carol Rosen. 1987. *A bibliography on Relational Grammar through May 1987 with selected titles on Lexical-Functional Grammar* (1st edn 1983.). Bloomington, IN: Indiana University Linguistics Club.

Emonds, Joseph. 1970. Root and structure preserving transformations. MIT dissertation.

Emonds, Joseph. 1976. *A transformational approach to English syntax: Root, structure preserving, and local transformations*. New York: Academic Press.

Emonds, Joseph. 1978. The verbal complex V'-V in French. *Linguistic Inquiry* 9.49–77.

Emonds, Joseph. 1985. *A unified theory of syntactic categories*. Dordrecht: Foris.

Featherston, Samuel, Matthias Gross, Thomas F. Münte, and Harald Clahsen. 2000. Brain potentials in the processing of complex sentences: An ERP study of control and raising constructions. *Journal of Psycholinguistic Research* 29.141–54.

Fillmore, Charles. 1968. The case for case. In Emmon Bach and Robert Harms, eds, *Universals in linguistic theory*, 1–87. New York: Holt, Rinehart, and Winston.

Fodor, Jerry. 1975. *The language of thought*. New York: Thomas Y. Crowell.

Franco, Jon. 1993. On object agreement in Spanish. University of Southern California dissertation.

Gazdar, Gerald, Ewan Klein, Geoffrey K. Pullum, and Ivan Sag. 1985. *Generalized Phrase Structure Grammar*. Cambridge, MA: Harvard University Press.

Gibson, Jeanne. 1980. Clause union in Chamorro and in universal grammar. UCSD dissertation. Published 1992, New York: Garland Press.

Gordon, Lynn. 1980. Raising in Bauan Fijian. Unpublished MS, UCLA.

Grimshaw, Jane. 1979. Complement selection and the lexicon. *Linguistic Inquiry* 10.279–326.

Gruber, Jeffrey. 1965. Studies in lexical relations. MIT dissertation. Reprinted 1976 in Gruber, *Lexical* Structures in Syntax and Semantics. Amsterdam: North-Holland.

Guilfoyle, Eithne, Henrietta Hung, and Lisa Travies. 1992. Spec of IP and Spec of VP: Two subjects in Austronesian languages. *Natural Language and Linguistic Theory* 16.547–93.

Harada, Naomi. 2002. Licensing PF-visible formal features: A linear algorithm and Case-related phenomena in PF. University of California-Irvine dissertation.

Harada, Naomi. 2003. Raising to object is NOT an edge phenomenon. Paper presented at the January 2003 Annual Meeting of the Linguistics Society of America, and unpublished MS, ATR International.

Harada, S. I. 1973. Counter equi NP deletion. *Bulletin of the Research Institute of Logopedics and Phoniatrics* 7.113–47. Tokyo: University of Tokyo.

Harris, Randy Allen. 1995. *The linguistic wars*. Oxford: Oxford University Press.

Hermon, Gabriella. 1984. *Syntactic modularity*. Dordrecht: Foris. Published version of 1981 University of Illinois dissertation "Non-nominative subject constructions in the Government and Binding framework."

Higginbotham, James. 1992. Reference and control. In Richard K. Larson, Sabine Iatridou, Utpal Lahiri, and James Higginbotham, eds, *Control and grammar*, 79–108. Dordrecht: Kluwer Academic.

Higgins, Roger. 1981. Proleptic objects and verbs of perception in Zacapoaxtla Nahuat. *Texas Linguistic Forum* 18.69–88.

Hiraiwa, Ken. 2001. Multiple agree and the defective intervention constraint in Japanese. *Proceedings of the HUMIT 2000. MIT Working Papers in Linguistics* 40, 67–80.

Hornstein, Norbert. 1997. Control in GB and Minimalism. *Glot International* 8.2.3–6.

Hornstein, Norbert. 1999. Movement and Control. *Linguistic Inquiry* 30.69–96.

Hornstein, Norbert. 2000. On A-chains: A reply to Brody. *Syntax* 3.129–43.

Huck, Geoffrey J., and John A. Goldsmith. 1995. *Ideology and linguistic theory: Noam Chomsky and the deep structure debates*. London: Routledge.

Jackendoff, Ray. 1969. Some rules of semantic interpretation for English. MIT dissertation. Revised and published as Jackendoff 1972.

Jackendoff, Ray. 1972. *Semantic interpretation in generative grammar*. Cambridge, MA: MIT Press.

Jackendoff, Ray. 1976. Toward an explanatory semantic representation. *Linguistic Inquiry* 7.89–150.

Jackendoff, Ray. 1977. *X-bar syntax: A study of phrase structure*. Cambridge MA: MIT Press.

Jackendoff, Ray. 1995. The architecture of the language faculty: A neominimalist perspective. MS, Brandeis University. Published 1998 in Peter Culicover and Louise McNally, eds, *The limits of syntax*, 19–45. San Diego: Academic Press.

Jackendoff, Ray, and Peter Culicover. 2003. The semantic basis of Control in English. *Language* 79.517–56.

Jacobson, Pauline. 1992. Raising without movement. In Richard K. Larson, Sabine Iatridou, Utpal Lahiri, and James Higginbotham, eds, *Control and grammar*, 149–94. Dordrecht: Kluwer Academic.

Jake, Janice. 1985. *Grammatical relations in Imbabura Quechua*. New York: Garland Publishing. Published version of 1983 University of Illinois dissertation.

Jake, Janice, and David Odden. 1979. Raising in Kipsigis. *Studies in the Linguistic Sciences* 9.131–55.

Johnson, David, and Shalom Lappin. 1996. A critique of the Minimalist Program. MS, IBM Watson Research Center and University of London. Published 1997 in *Linguistics and Philosophy* 20.273–333.

Johnson, David, and Paul M. Postal. 1980. *Arc Pair Grammar*. Princeton, NJ: Princeton University Press.

Johnson, Kyle. 1991. Object positions. *Natural Language and Linguistic Theory* 9.577–636.

Joseph, Brian D. 1976. Raising in Modern Greek: A copying process? In Judith Aissen and Jorge Hankamer, eds, *Harvard Studies in Syntax and Semantics* II.241–78.

Kaplan, Ron, and Joan Bresnan. 1982. Lexical Functional Grammar: A formal system for grammatical representation. In Joan Bresnan, ed., *The mental representation of grammatical relations*, 173–281. Cambridge, MA: MIT Press.

Katz, Jerrold, and Paul Postal. 1964. *An integrated theory of linguistic descriptions*. Cambridge, MA: MIT Press.

Kay, Martin. 1983. *Unification Grammar*. Technical report. Palo Alto, CA: Xerox Palo Alto Research Center.

Kayne, Richard. 1981. On certain differences between French and English. *Linguistic Inquiry* 12.349–71.

Kayne, Richard. 1989. Facets of Romance past participle agreement. In Paola Benincà, ed., *Dialect variation and the theory of grammar*, 85–103. Dordrecht: Foris.

Keenan, Edward, and Bernard Comrie. 1977. Noun phrase accessibility and universal grammar. *Linguistic Inquiry* 8.63–99.

Kimenyi, Alexandre. 1980. *A relational grammar of Kinyarwanda*. UC Publications in Linguistics 91. Berkeley: University of California Press.

Kitagawa, Yoshihisa. 1986. Subjects in Japanese and English. University of Massachusetts dissertation.

Koizumi, Masatoshi. 1993. Object agreement phrases and the Split VP Hypothesis. In Jonathan Bobaljik and Colin Phillips, eds, *Papers on case and agreement I*, 99–148. MIT Working Papers in Linguistics, vol. 18.

Koizumi, Masatoshi. 1995. Phrase structure in minimalist syntax. MIT dissertation.

Koster, Jan, and Robert May. 1982. On the constituency of infinitives. *Language* 58.116–43.

Kotzoglu, George. 2002. Greek "ECM" and how to control it. *Reading Working Papers in Linguistics* 6.39–56.

Kratzer, Angelika. 1994. The event argument and the semantics of Voice. Unpublished MS, University of Massachusetts.

Kratzer, Angelika. 1996. Severing the external argument from its verb. In Johan Rooryck and Laurie Zaring, eds, *Phrase structure and the lexicon*, 109–38. Dordrecht: Kluwer Academic.

Kroeger, Paul. 1993. *Phrase structure and grammatical relations in Tagalog*. Stanford: CSLI.

Kuno, Susumu. 1972. Subject Raising in Japanese. *Papers in Japanese Linguistics* 1.1.

Kuno, Susumu. 1973. *The structure of the Japanese language*. Cambridge, MA: MIT Press.

Kuno, Susumu. 1976. Subject Raising. In Masayoshi Shibatani, ed., *Syntax and Semantics 5: Japanese Generative Grammar*, 17–49. New York, Academic Press. Revised version of 1972. Subject Raising in Japanese. *Papers in Japanese Linguistics* 1.1.

Kuroda, S. Y. 1988. Whether we agree or not: A comparative syntax of English and Japanese. *Lingvisticae Investigationes* 12.1–47. Also in William Poser, ed., *Papers from the Second International Workshop on Japanese Syntax*, 103–43. Stanford: CSLI.

Kuroda, S. Y. 1992. Movement of noun phrases in Japanese. In S. Y. Kuroda, *Japanese syntax and semantics*, 253–92. Dordrecht: Kluwer Acedemic.

Lakoff, George. 1967. Deep and surface grammar. Unpublished MS, Harvard University.

Lakoff, George. 1970. Global rules. *Language* 46.627–39.

Lakoff, George. 1971. On Generative Semantics. In Danny Steinberg and Leon Jakobovits, eds, *Semantics: An interdisciplinary reader in linguistics and psychology*, 232–96. Cambridge: Cambridge University Press.

Landau, Idan. 2000. *Elements of Control: Structure and meaning in infinitival constructions*. Dordrecht: Kluwer Academic.

Landau, Idan. 2002. (Un)interpretable Neg in Comp. *Linguistic Inquiry* 33.465–92.

Landau, Idan. 2003. Movement out of control. *Linguistic Inquiry* 34.471–98.
Landau, Idan. To appear. The scale of finiteness and control. *Natural Language and Linguistic Theory*.
Larson, Richard. 1988. On the double object construction. *Linguistic Inquiry* 19.335–91.
Lasnik, Howard. 1993. Lectures on Minimalist Syntax. *University of Connecticut Working Papers in Linguistics. Occasional Papers 1*. Storrs, CT: University of Connecticut Department of Linguistics.
Lasnik, Howard. 1995. Case and expletives revisited. *Linguistic Inquiry* 26.615–33.
Lasnik, Howard. 1999a. Chains of arguments. In Samuel Epstein and Norbert Hornstein, eds, *Working Minimalism*, 189–215. Cambridge, MA: MIT Press.
Lasnik, Howard. 1999b. *Minimalist analysis*. Oxford: Blackwell Publishing.
Lasnik, Howard. 2001. Subjects, objects, and the EPP. In William D. Davies and Stanley Dubinsky, eds, *Objects and other subjects: Grammatical functions, functional categories, and configurationality*, 103–21. Dordrecht: Kluwer Academic.
Lasnik, Howard, and Mamoru Saito. 1991. On the subject of infinitives. *Proceedings of the Chicago Linguistic Society (CLS)* 27.324–43.
Lawler, John. 1972. A problem in participatory democracy. Bloomington, IN: Indiana University Linguistics Club.
Lebeaux, David. 1985. Locality and anaphoric binding. *Linguistic Review* 4.343–63.
Lees, Robert B. 1960. *The grammar of English nominalizations*. The Hague: Mouton.
Lefebvre, Claire, and Pieter Muysken. 1982. Raising as move Case. *Linguistic Review* 2.161–210.
Lightfoot, David. 1976. The theoretical implications of subject raising. *Foundations of Language* 14.257–86.
Manzini, Maria Rita. 1983. On Control and control theory. *Linguistic Inquiry* 14.421–46.
Manzini, Maria Rita, and Anna Roussou. 2000. A minimalist theory of A-movement and control. *Lingua* 110.409–47.
Marantz, Alec. 1983. Raising and category types in Japanese. In Yukio Otsu, Henk van Riemsdijk, Kazoku Inoue, Akio Kamio, and Noriko Kawasaki, eds, *Studies in generative grammar and language acquisition*, 29–47. Tokyo: Department of Linguistics, International Christian University.
Marantz, Alec. 1984. *On the nature of grammatical relations*. Cambridge, MA: MIT Press.
Marantz, Alec. 1995. The Minimalist Program. In Gert Webelhuth, ed., *Government and Binding Theory and the Minimalist Program*, 349–82. Oxford: Blackwell Publishing.
Marantz, Alec. 1997. No escape from syntax: Don't try morphological analysis in the privacy of your own lexicon. *Proceedings of the 21st Annual Penn Linguistics Colloquium. University of Pennsylvania Working Papers in Linguistics (PWPL)* 4.2, 201–25. Philadelphia: University of Pennsylvania Department of Linguistics.
Martin, Roger. 2001. Null Case and the distribution of PRO. *Linguistic Inquiry* 32.141–66.
Massam, Diane. 1985. Case theory and the projection principle. MIT dissertation.
Massam, Diane. 2001. On predication and the status of subjects in Niuean. In William D. Davies and Stanley Dubinsky, eds, *Objects and other subjects: Grammatical functions, functional categories, and configurationality*, 225–46. Dordrecht: Kluwer Academic.
McCawley, James. 1970. English as a VSO language. *Language* 46.286–99.
McCawley, James. 1982. *30 million theories of grammar*. London: Croom Helm.
McCloskey, James. 1991. Clause structure, ellipsis and proper government in Irish. *Lingua* 85.259–302.
McCloskey, James. 1997. Subjecthood and subject positions. In Liliane Haegeman, ed., *Elements of grammar: Handbook of generative syntax*, 197–235. Dordrecht: Kluwer Academic.

McCloskey, James. 2001. The distribution of subject properties in Irish. In William D. Davies and Stanley Dubinsky, eds, *Objects and other subjects: Grammatical functions, functional categories, and configurationality*, 157–92. Dordrecht: Kluwer Academic.

Moore, John. 1998. Turkish copy-raising and A-chain locality. *Natural Language and Linguistic Theory* 16.148–89.

Moravcsik, Edith, and Jessica Wirth. 1980. *Current approaches to syntax*. Syntax and Semantics 13. New York: Academic Press.

Neidle, Carol. 1982. Case agreement in Russian. In Joan Bresnan, ed., *The mental representation of grammatical relations*, 391–426. Cambridge, MA: MIT Press.

Newmeyer, Frederick. 1969. English aspectual verbs. University of Illinois dissertation. Published as Newmeyer 1975.

Newmeyer, Frederick. 1975. *English aspectual verbs*. The Hague: Mouton.

Newmeyer, Frederick. 1986. *Linguistic theory in America*. New York: Academic Press. 2nd edn.

Newmeyer, Frederick. 2001. Grammatical functions, thematic roles, and phrase structure: Their underlying disunity. In William D. Davies and Stanley Dubinsky, eds, *Objects and other subjects: Grammatical functions, functional categories, and configurationality*, 53–75. Dordrecht: Kluwer Academic.

Nuñes, Jairo. 1995. The copy theory of movement and linearization of chains in the Minimalist Program. University of Maryland dissertation.

Perlmutter, David M. 1968. Deep and surface constraints in syntax. MIT dissertation.

Perlmutter, David M. 1970. The two verbs "begin." In Roderick Jacobs and Peter Rosenbaum, eds, *Readings in transformational grammar*, 107–19. Waltham, MA: Ginn.

Perlmutter, David M., and Paul M. Postal. 1977. Toward a universal characterization of passivization. *BLS* 3.394–417. Revised version 1983 in David M. Perlmutter, ed., *Studies in Relational Grammar 1*, 3–29. Chicago: University of Chicago Press.

Perlmutter, David M., and Paul M. Postal. 1983a. Some proposed laws of basic clause structure. In David M. Perlmutter, ed., *Studies in relational grammar 1*, 81–128. Chicago: University of Chicago Press.

Perlmutter, David M., and Paul M. Postal. 1983b [1972]. The Relational Succession Law. In David M. Perlmutter, ed., *Studies in relational grammar 1*, 30–80. Chicago: University of Chicago Press.

Perlmutter, David M., and Paul M. Postal. 1984a. Impersonal passives and some relational laws. In David M. Perlmutter and Carol Rosen, eds, *Studies in relational grammar 2*, 126–70. Chicago: University of Chicago Press.

Perlmutter, David M., and Paul M. Postal. 1984b. The 1-advancement Exclusiveness Law. In David M. Perlmutter and Carol Rosen, eds, *Studies in relational grammar 2*, 81–125. Chicago: University of Chicago Press.

Pesetsky, David. 1997. Optimality Theory and syntax: Movement and pronunciation. In Diana Archangeli and D. Terence Langendoen, eds, *Optimality Theory: An overview*, 134–70. Chicago: University of Chicago Press.

Polinsky, Maria, and Eric Potsdam. 2002. Backward control. *Linguistic Inquiry* 33.245–82.

Pollard, Carl, and Ivan Sag. 1987. *Information based syntax*. CSLI Lecture Notes 13. Stanford: CSLI.

Pollard, Carl, and Ivan Sag. 1994. *Head-driven Phrase Structure Grammar*. Chicago: University of Chicago Press.

Pollock, Jean-Yves. 1989. Verb movement, universal grammar, and the structure of IP. *Linguistic Inquiry* 20.365–424.

Poser, William. 1983. What is the double-*o* constraint a constraint on? Paper presented at the Second West Coast Conference on Formal Linguistics, Los Angeles.

Postal, Paul M. 1966. A note on "understood transitively." *International Journal of American Linguistics* 32.90–3.
Postal, Paul M. 1969. Review of McIntosh and Halliday, *Patterns of language*. *Foundations of Language* 5.409–26.
Postal, Paul M. 1970. On coreferential complement subject deletion. *Linguistic Inquiry* 1.439–500.
Postal, Paul M. 1971. *Cross-over phenomena*. New York: Holt, Rinehart, and Winston.
Postal, Paul M. 1972. The best theory. In Stanley Peters, ed., *Goals of linguistic theory*, 131–70. New York: Holt, Rinehart, and Winston.
Postal, Paul M. 1974. *On Raising: One rule of English grammar and its theoretical implications*. Cambridge, MA: MIT Press.
Postal, Paul M. 1977. About a "nonargument" for raising. *Linguistic Inquiry* 8.141–54.
Postal, Paul M., and Geoffrey K. Pullum. 1988. Expletive noun phrases in subcategorized positions. *Linguistic Inquiry* 19.635–70.
Potsdam, Eric, and Jeffrey Runner. 2001. Richard returns: Copy Raising and its implications. *Proceedings of the Chicago Linguistic Society (CLS)* 37.453–68.
Prince, Alan, and Paul Smolensky. 1993. *Optimality Theory: Constraint interaction in generative grammar*. New Brunswick, NJ: Rutgers University Center for Cognitive Science.
Pullum, Geoffrey K. 1991. Citation etiquette beyond Thunderdome. In Pullum, *The great Eskimo vocabulary hoax and other irreverent essays on the study of language*, 147–58. Chicago: University of Chicago Press.
Pullum, Geoffrey K. 1996. Nostalgic views from Building 20. Review article on *The view from Building 20: Essays in linguistics in honor of Sylvain Bromberger*, eds Kenneth Hale and Samuel Jay Keyser. *Journal of Linguistics* 32.137–47.
Pylkkänen, Liina. 2001. Root-selecting, verb-selecting and VoiceP-selecting causatives. Paper presented at the North East Linguistic Society (NELS) 32nd Annual Meeting, CUNY Graduate Center and New York University, New York City, NY.
Pylkkänen, Liina. 2002. Verbal domains: Causative formation at the root, category and phase levels. Paper presented at the Linguistic Society of America Annual Meeting, Hyatt Regency San Francisco Hotel, San Francisco, CA.
Radford, Andrew. 1981. *Transformational syntax: A student's guide to Chomsky's Extended Standard Theory*. London: Cambridge University Press.
Rizzi, Luigi. 1986. On chain formation. In Hagit Borer, ed., *The syntax of pronominal clitics*. *Syntax and Semantics 17*, 65–96. New York: Academic Press.
Rizzi, Luigi. 1990. *Relativized minimality*. Cambridge, MA: MIT Press.
Rizzi, Luigi. 1991. Residual verb second and the Wh-Criterion. *Technical Reports in Formal and Computational Linguistics* 2, University of Geneva. Reprinted in Adriana Belletti and Luigi Rizzi, eds, *Parameters and functional heads*, 63–90. Oxford: Oxford University Press.
Rogers, Andy. 1971. Three kinds of physical perception verbs. *Proceedings of the Chicago Linguistic Society (CLS)* 7.206–22.
Rogers, Andy. 1972. Another look at flip perception verbs. *Proceedings of the Chicago Linguistic Society (CLS)* 8.303–15.
Rogers, Andy. 1974. A Transderivational Constraint on Richard? *Proceedings of the Chicago Linguistic Society (CLS)* 10.551–8.
Rooryck, Johan. 2000. *Configurations of sentential complementation*. London: Routledge.
Rosen, Carol. 1981. The relational structure of reflexive clauses: Evidence from Italian. Harvard dissertation. Published 1988 in the *Outstanding Dissertations in Linguistics* series, Jorge Hankamer, ed. New York: Garland Publishing.
Rosenbaum, Peter S. 1967. *The grammar of English predicate complement constructions*. Cambridge, MA: MIT Press.

Rosenbaum, Peter S. 1970. A principle governing deletion in English sentential complementations. In Roderick Jacobs and Peter Rosenbaum, eds, *Readings in transformational grammar*, 20–9. Waltham, MA: Ginn.

Ross, John R. 1967. Constraints on variables in syntax. MIT dissertation.

Rouveret, Alain, and Jean Roger Vergnaud. 1980. Specifying reference to the subject: French causatives and conditions on representations. *Linguistic Inquiry* 11.97–202.

Runner, Jeffrey. 1995. Noun phrase licensing and interpretation. University of Massachusetts dissertation.

Ruwet, Nicolas. 1991. *Syntax and the human experience*. Chicago: University of Chicago Press. Translation (by John Goldsmith) and republication of 1982 MS.

Sag, Ivan, Gerald Gazdar, Thomas Wasow, and Steven Weisler. 1985. Coordination and how to distinguish categories. *Natural Language and Linguistic Theory* 3.117–72.

Saito, Mamoru. 1983. Comments on the papers on generative syntax. In Yukio Otsu, Henk van Riemsdijk, Kazoku Inoue, Akio Kamio, and Noriko Kawasaki, eds, *Studies in generative grammar and language acquisition*, 79–89. Tokyo: Department of Linguistics, International Christian University.

Saito, Mamoru. 1985. Some asymmetries in Japanese and their theoretical implications. MIT dissertation.

Schachter, Paul. 1976. The subject in Philippine languages: Topic, actor, actor-topic, or none of the above. In Charles N. Li, ed., *Subject and topic*, 491–518. New York: Academic Press.

Seiter, William J. 1983. Subject–Direct Object Raising in Niuean. In David M. Perlmutter, ed., *Studies in relational grammar 1*, 317–59. Chicago: University of Chicago Press.

Sells, Peter. 1990. Is there Subject-to-Object Raising in Japanese? In Katarzyna Dziwirek, Patrick Farrell, and Errapel Mejías-Bikandi, eds, *Grammatical relations: A cross-theoretical perspective*, 445–57. Stanford: CSLI.

Shibatani, Masayoshi. 1978. Mikami Akira and the notion of "subject" in Japanese grammar. In John Hinds and Irwin Howard, eds, *Problems in Japanese syntax and semantics*, 52–67. Tokyo: Kaitakusha.

Shibatani, Masayoshi, and Sandra A. Thompson, eds. 1996. *Grammatical constructions: Their form and meaning*. Oxford: Clarendon Press.

Shieber, Stuart. 1986. *An introduction to unification-based approaches to grammar*. Stanford: CSLI.

Shieber, Stuart, Hans Uszkoreit, Fernando Pereira, Jane Robinson, and Mabry Tyson. 1983. The formalism and implementation of PATR-II. In Barbara J. Grosz and Mark Stickel, eds, *Research on interactive acquisition and use of knowledge*, technical report 4, 39–79. Final report for SRI Project 1894. Menlo Park, CA: SRI International.

Sigurðsson, Halldór Ármann. 1991. Icelandic Case-marked PRO and the licensing of lexical arguments. *Natural Language and Linguistic Theory* 9.327–63.

Son, Min-Jeong. 2003. A unified syntactic account of morphological causatives in Korean. Paper presented at the 13th Japanese/Korean Linguistics Conference, Michigan State University, August 1–3.

Sportiche, Dominique. 1988. A theory of floating quantifiers and its corollaries for constituent structure. *Linguistic Inquiry* 19.425–49.

Sportiche, Dominique. 1996. Clitic constructions. In Johan Rooryck and Laurie Zaring, eds, *Phrase structure and the lexicon*, 213–76. Dordrecht: Kluwer Academic.

Stowell, Tim. 1982. The tense of infinitives. *Linguistic Inquiry* 13.561–70.

Takano, Yuji. 2002. Nominative object in Japanese complex predicate constructions: A prolepsis analysis. Unpublished MS, Kinjo Gakuin University. Pub. 2003 as "Nominative objects in Japanese complex predicate constructions: A prolepsis analysis." *Natural Language and Linguistic Theory* 21.779–834.

Tanaka, Hidekazu. 2002. Raising to object out of CP. *Linguistic Inquiry* 33.637–52.
Travis, Lisa deMena. 1984. Parameters and effects of word order variation. MIT dissertation.
Travis, Lisa deMena. 2001. Derived objects in Malagasy. In William D. Davies and Stanley Dubinsky, eds, *Objects and other subjects: Grammatical functions, functional categories, and configurationality*, 123–55. Dordrecht: Kluwer Academic.
Ura, Hiroyuki. 1993. On feature-checking for *wh*-traces. Object agreement phrases and the Split VP Hypothesis. In Jonathan Bobaljik and Colin Phillips, eds, *Papers on case and agreement I*, 243–80. MIT Working Papers in Linguistics, vol. 18.
Uszkoreit, Hans. 1986. Categorial Unification Grammar. *Proceedings of COLING-86*, 187–94.
van Riemsdijk, Henk, and Edwin Williams. 1986. *Introduction to the theory of grammar*. Cambridge, MA: MIT Press.
Wechsler, Stephen, and I Wayan Arka. 1998. Syntactic ergativity in Balinese: An argument structure based theory. *Natural Language and Linguistic Theory* 16.387–441.
Wells, Rulon. 1947. Immediate constituents. *Language* 23.81–117.
Williams, Edwin. 1980. Predication. *Linguistic Inquiry* 11.203–38.
Williams, Edwin. 1981. Argument structure and morphology. *Linguistic Review* 1.81–114.
Wyngaerd, Guido Vanden. 1994. *PRO-legomena: Distribution and reference of infinitival subjects*. Berlin: Mouton de Gruyter.
Zagona, Karen. 1982. Government and proper government of verbal projections. University of Washington dissertation. Revised and published as Zagona 1988.
Zagona, Karen. 1988. *Verb phrase syntax: A parametric study of English and Spanish*. Dordrecht: Kluwer Academic.
Zidani-Eroğlu, Leyla. 1997. Exceptionally case-marked NPs as matrix objects. *Linguistic Inquiry* 28.219–30.

# NAME INDEX

Inasmuch as Noam Chomsky and Paul Postal play such central roles in theory development and the description of Raising and Control and their names appear with such frequency throughout the foregoing pages, including them in this index would provide results of little assistance to those specifically interested in their work. And so their names do not appear here. We hope this causes the reader no inconvenience.

Abney, Steven, 276
Aissen, Judith, 109n, 126, 134
Akatsuka-McCawley, Noriko, 263
Akmajian, Adrian, 18, 143n
Allen, Barbara, 134
Andrews, Avery, 54, 101
Arka, I Wayan, 244
Aronoff, Mark, 141n

Bach, Emmon, 43, 46, 64, 75n, 89, 98–102, 103n, 113n, 212, 265, 301, 310, 311, 334, 350, 360n
Baker, Charles, 39n, 64n, 68
Baker, Mark, 136n
Barss, Andrew, 308
Bayer, Samuel, 358n
Bell, Sarah, 134, 243, 280
Belletti, Adriana, 331n
Berman, Arlene, 110
Besten, Hans den, 145
Bever, Thomas, 139
Bobaljik, Jonathan, 282, 294
Boeckx, Cedric, 345, 353–5, 360n
Bowers, John, 296n
Brame, Michael, 141, 146n, 335–7, 357n, 358n
Bresnan, Joan, 2, 64n, 67–8, 76, 89–98, 100, 102, 112n, 113n, 139, 141n, 212–22, 292, 310, 312, 317, 318, 334–7, 356, 359n

Brody, Michael, 349
Bruening, Benjamin, 299, 324–8, 330n
Burzio, Luigi, 185, 277, 278, 357

Chametzky, Robert, 358n
Chomsky, Carol, 354
Chung, Sandra, 244
Clahsen, Harald, 362n
Cole, Peter, 176, 200, 208, 209n, 210n, 211n, 222, 223n, 230, 234, 235
Comrie, Bernard, 124
Courtenay, Karen, 354
Culicover, Peter, 67n, 143n, 339–41, 345, 350–5, 360n

Dougherty, Ray, 62n, 66, 69, 70n, 141
Dowty, David, 10, 277

Emonds, Joseph, 63, 68, 82–3, 85, 88n, 113n, 116n, 156, 181, 199n, 280, 291

Fauconnier, Gilles, 118n
Featherston, Samuel, 362n
Fiengo, Robert, 143n, 148n
Fillmore, Charles, 14, 178
Fodor, Jerry, 64n, 139, 140, 152, 347
Franco, Jon, 286

# Name Index

Gaatone, David, 118n
Gazdar, Gerald, 292, 297, 336
George, Leland, 47, 91, 92, 209n, 219, 323, 358n
Gibson, Jeanne, 57
Goldsmith, John, 2
Gordon, Lynn, 242n
Grimshaw, Jane, 160, 291
Gross, Matthias, 362n
Gross, Maurice, 113n
Gruber, Jeffrey, 178

Hankamer, Jorge, 46n
Harada, Naomi, 326, 328–9, 330n
Harada, S. I., 267
Harbert, Wayne, 210n
Harris, Randy, 2, 367
Helke, Michael, 70n, 73n
Heny, Frank, 18
Hermon, Gabriella, 176, 200, 208, 209, 210n, 211n, 222, 223n, 230, 233–5, 242n, 262
Higginbotham, James, 347
Higgins, Roger, 113, 116n, 249
Hiraiwa, Ken, 299, 326, 327, 328
Hornstein, Norbert, 199n, 345–57, 359n, 360n, 361n
Huck, Geoffrey, 2
Hust, Joel, 146n

Jackendoff, Ray, 69n, 88n, 141n, 143n, 144n, 146n, 156, 178, 277, 297n, 345, 350–5, 360n
Jacobson, Pauline, 209n, 336
Jake, Janice, 56, 210n, 222, 223n, 233
Johnson, David, 127, 291, 292, 297n
Johnson, Kyle, 299, 323, 330n
Jonas, Dianne, 282, 294
Joseph, Brian, 56, 93, 94, 165, 246

Kajita, Masaru, 113n
Kaplan, Ron, 292
Katz, Jerrold, 64n, 67, 68, 140
Kay, Martin, 292
Kayne, Richard, 37n, 40n, 62n, 92, 118n, 144n, 151n, 176, 200–8, 236, 241n, 285
Keenan, Edward, 124
Kimenyi, Alexandre, 133–4
Kiparsky, Carol, 62, 111n, 314
Kiparsky, Paul, 62, 111n, 314
Kitagawa, Yoshihisa, 278

Klein, Ewan, 297, 336
Koizumi, Masatoshi, 286, 326
Kornfilt, Jaklin, 209n, 219
Koster, Jan, 337, 341
Kotzoglu, George, 270n
Kratzer, Angelika, 296n
Kroeger, Paul, 243, 252
Kuno, Susumu, 34, 129, 254–69, 270n, 271n, 325–7
Kuroda, S. Y., 278, 328

Lakoff, George, 26, 30, 90, 161, 291, 357n
Landau, Idan, 330n, 349, 350, 356, 357, 358n, 361n
Langacker, Ronald, 42n, 302
Langendoen, D. Terrence, 139
Lappin, Shalom, 291, 292, 297n
Larson, Richard, 283, 285, 316
Lasnik, Howard, 49n, 50n, 62n, 74, 75, 93, 106, 129, 137, 143n, 144, 148n, 178, 179, 183, 204, 222, 241n, 273, 296, 297n, 299, 300, 302, 308, 309n, 316–20, 330n, 337, 344, 346–7, 359n, 360n
Lawler, John, 357
Lebeaux, David, 199n, 347
Lees, Robert, 20, 29n
Lefebvre, Claire, 242n
Lightfoot, David, 102n

Maling, Joan, 46n
Manzini, Maria Rita, 360
Marantz, Alec, 262, 265–7, 271n, 277, 290, 292, 296n, 297n, 326, 329
Martin, Roger, 249, 356, 359n
Massam, Diane, 237–41, 242n, 266, 296, 323–5
May, Robert, 143n, 209, 309, 310, 337, 341
McCawley, James, 27, 30, 40n, 58n, 105, 110, 112, 113n, 124, 263, 312
McCloskey, James, 277–8, 282, 296
Moore, John, 246
Moravcsik, Edith, 105
Münte, Thomas, 362n
Muysken, Pieter, 242n

Neidle, Carol, 102
Newmeyer, Frederick, 16n, 160

Odden, David, 56
Otero, Carlos, 145n

Perlmutter, David, 9, 16n, 58n, 59n, 105–8, 111n, 125, 130–4, 138, 161, 222, 296n, 357n
Pesetsky, David, 160, 172n, 222, 312
Peters, P. Stanley, 64n, 141
Polinsky, Maria, 360–1n
Pollard, Carl, 292, 336
Pollock, Jean-Yves, 280–2, 285, 296n, 329n, 330n
Poser, William, 267
Potsdam, Eric, 246, 360n, 361n
Prince, Alan, 138n, 291, 292
Pullum, Geoffrey, 16n, 199n, 209n, 235–6, 291, 297, 313–15, 319, 336, 343, 358n
Pylkkänen, Liina, 296n

Quícoli, António, 119n, 123n, 144

Radford, Andrew, 338
Reinhart, Tanya, 143n
Ritchie, Robert, 141
Rizzi, Luigi, 198n, 286, 297n, 331n, 357
Rogers, Andy, ix
Rosen, Carol, 109n, 126, 130, 131
Rosenbaum, Peter, 1, 5, 17, 20–7, 30, 59n, 60, 78, 81, 82, 84, 88n, 94, 111n, 112, 113n, 198, 300, 301, 332, 351, 352, 354
Ross, John R., 26, 30, 38, 42n, 46n, 62n, 64, 66n, 80, 82, 90, 110n, 111n, 113n, 135n, 138n, 143, 199, 248
Roussou, Anna, 360n
Rouveret, Alain, 184
Runner, Jeffrey, 246, 286, 299, 319, 320, 321, 322, 323, 330n
Ruwet, Nicolas, 12, 13, 14, 113n, 118n, 356, 359n, 361n

Safir, Ken, 305
Sag, Ivan, 292, 297, 336, 358n

Saito, Mamoru, 93, 255, 262, 265–7, 269, 273, 299–300, 307, 308, 316–20, 326–7, 344
Schachter, Paul, 278–9
Seiter, William, 52–3
Sells, Peter, 255, 262, 267–9, 326–9, 330n, 331
Shibatani, Masayoshi, 176n, 262, 268, 271n
Shieber, Stuart, 292, 298
Sigurðsson, Halldór, 357
Smolensky, Paul, 291, 292
Son, Min-Jeong, 296n
Sportiche, Dominique, 278, 286
Stowell, Tim, 305, 356, 359n

Takano, Yuji, 328, 329
Tanaka, Hidekazu, 254–6, 258–65, 268–70, 325–8
Thompson, Sandra, 176n, 209n
Travis, Lisa, 97, 278, 296n

Uriagereka, Juan, 309, 313
Uszkoreit, Hans, 292

van Riemsdijk, Henk, 299
Vergnaud, Jean, 184

Wasow, Thomas, 143n
Wechsler, Stephen, 244
Wells, Rulon, 172n
Wilkins, Wendy, 339, 341
Williams, Edwin, 138n, 199n, 209n, 277, 299
Wirth, Jessica, 105

Zagona, Karen, 278
Zidani-Eroğlu, Leyla, 299

# SUBJECT INDEX

Ø-complementizer, see null
   complementizer, Ø-
   complementizer

A-bar-position, see A'-position
A-bound, 187, 189
   see also binding theory
A-chain, see chain
A-over-A Principle, 64–7, 79, 87n, 88n,
   142, 163, 164
A-position, 183, 187, 240–1, 324, 342
a-structure (in LFG), 101–2
A'-bound, 187
   see also binding theory
A'-chain, see chain
A'(A-bar)-position, 183, 187, 205, 235,
   240, 269, 324, 333n
absolutive case, 52, 53, 108
Accessibility Hierarchy, 124
adequacy
   descriptive adequacy, 46, 140–1,
     154–5
   explanatory adequacy, 46, 140–1,
     154–6, 290
   observational adequacy, 154–5
advancement, 130
Adversative Passive, see passive,
   Adversative Passive
Agr projections, 282–6
   Agr, 280, 282, 294–5
   AgrIO, 286
   AgrO, 285–6, 290, 294, 299, 306, 307,
     330n, 359n
     and overt movement, 316–23

AgrS, 285–6, 290, 294, 295, 299, 306,
   317, 319, 359n
*alone*-final NPs, 40–1
arc, 126–7
Arc Pair Grammar, 292
argument-chain, see chain
argument structure, 181–2, 277, 336, 343
   see also a-structure
ascension, 110–15, 125–6, 136n
Austronesian languages, 243, 254, 278,
   280
   Balinese, 243–4
   Cebuano, 134, 243, 251–3, 270, 280,
     325
   Chamorro, 57, 59n, 107
   Fijian, 238–40, 242n, 246, 323–5
   Indonesian, 243–4, 251, 270
   Javanese, 127, 128, 130, 243, 244, 251,
     270n
   Madurese, 131, 159, 176, 244–54, 259,
     270, 325
   Niuean, 52, 59, 107, 238–40, 242n, 246,
     323
   Tagalog, 243, 251, 252, 278–9
Auxiliary Inversion, see Subject–
   Auxiliary Inversion

Balinese, see Austronesian languages,
   Balinese
bare phrase structure, 294–5
bare VP, see VP analysis of infinitives
*Barriers* framework, 237, 275
Bauan Fijian, see Austronesian languages,
   Fijian

binding theory, 178, 179, 186–9, 196, 198n, 240, 317, 338–9
  binding principles
    principle A, 188–9, 191, 192, 196, 198n, 339
    principle B, 188–9, 196, 204, 269, 303
    principle C, 303, 307, 314, 317
  binding theory (formulated), 187
binominal *each*, 305, 306, 311, 314, 316
Biuniqueness Condition, 233
bounding nodes, *see* subjacency, bounding nodes
bounding theory, *see* subjacency, bounding theory

c-command, *see* command, c-command
c-selection, *see* selection, c-selection
c-structure (in LFG), 101–2
Case theory, 178, 179, 183–6, 205, 212
  Case checking, 316, 321
  Case Filter, 179, 183–6, 191, 204, 240
    Case Filter (formulated), 184
  Case transmission, 206, 208
  inherent Case, 233, 330n
  null Case (analysis of PRO), 346–7, 356, 359n
Categorial Grammar, 100, 155, 336, 343
Categorial Unification Grammar, 292, 373
category selection, *see* selection, c-selection
Cebuano, *see* Austronesian languages, Cebuano
chain (argument or NP), 182, 186, 189, 205, 346, 357
Chamorro, *see* Austronesian languages, Chamorro
$C_{HL}$, 287, 288, 297n
Choctaw, 126–7, 130, 134
chômeur, 128, 131–5
clause-bounded (rule/transformation), 25–6, 70, 211, 219
clausemate condition, 25–6, 60, 79, 85–7, 186–7
cleft, 40n, 326–7
  pseudocleft, 50–1, 66, 338, 340
CNPC, *see* Complex NP Constraint
command, 42–6, 92–3, 143, 302–5
  c-command, 180, 187, 199n, 303–5, 308–10, 315, 317, 319, 320, 351–5, 360n, 361n

COMP, 64, 67–8, 76, 139, 148, 199n, 275, 276
  movement to, 80–1, 183, 192
  COMP escape hatch, 80, 81
complementizer
  Complementizer Incorporation, 350
  Complementizer Insertion, 18, 21–4, 27, 82, 332
  Complementizer Substitution Universal, 64, 66, 76
  null complementizer, 150, 172n, 199n, 204, 205
  prepositional complementizer, 22, 162, 195, 201, 208, 230, 236
  prepositional null complementizer, 204–5
Complex NP Constraint (CNPC), 80, 248
Complex NP Shift, *see* Heavy NP Shift
conditions A, B, and C, *see* binding theory
Conjunct Movement, 37
construal, rules of, 143–50, 156, 157, 165–7, 171, 173n, 178
control nouns, 353
Coordinate Structure Constraint (CSC), 248, 252, 314
Copy, 287, 288, 289, 359n
Copy Raising, 56, 246, 252
copy theory of movement, *see* Move, copy theory of movement
CP deletion and transparency, *see* S′-deletion or transparency
CSC, *see* Coordinate Structure Constraint
cycle, transformational, 75
  cyclic, 26–7, 121
  last cyclic, 26
  postcyclic, 26–7, 111
  strict cyclicity, 75–6
cyclic node, 65, 80
cyclic rule, 26, 76, 109, 110, 111, 121, 143

Dative Movement (Dative Shift), 20, 25, 130, 131
Dative Shift, *see* Dative Movement
Demotion, 130
descriptive adequacy, *see* adequacy
disjoint reference, 214–15, 224–7, 230, 241n, 307, 308
  *see also* binding theory, principle B
double *o* constraint (double object constraint), 267

double object constraint, *see* double *o* constraint
Doubly Filled Comp, 202, 276

economy of representation, 313
economy principles, 288, 291, 292
   Enlightened Self-Interest, 297n
   Greed, 287, 289, 292, 330n
   Last Resort, 289, 291, 292, 353
   Least Effort, 286, 287
   Minimal Link Condition (MLC), 351–4
   Procrastinate, 287, 289, 290, 292, 297n
   Shortest Move, 287, 290, 292, 297n
ECM, *see* Exceptional Case Marking
ECP, *see* Empty Category Principle
embedded passive as argument for raising, 5, 6, 7, 333
Empty Category Principle (ECP), 248, 286
   Proper Binding Condition, 269, 327, 328
empty complementizer, *see* null complementizer, empty complementizer
*en*-cliticization, 12–13
Enlightened Self-Interest, 297n
EPP, *see* Extended Projection Principle
Equi NP Deletion, 24–5, 139, 206, 334–5, 336–7, 342–3
   in Quechua, 222–3
   in Relational Grammar, 134–5
   vs. control in REST, 150–2, 169–70
ergative analysis, *see* unaccusative
ergative case, 52–3
Exceptional Case Marking (ECM), 193–5, 200, 208, 230–9, 241n, 244–5, 255, 261–7, 270n, 299, 323–7, 330n, 359n
existential *there*, *see* pleonastic elements, existential *there*
experiencer subject, 224, 225, 228
   accusative experiencer, 212, 221–8
   desiderative experiencer, 221–8
   lexical experiencer, 221–8
explanatory adequacy, *see* adequacy
expletive objects, *see* pleonastic elements, pleonastic objects
expletive subjects, *see* pleonastic elements, pleonastic subjects
Extended Projection Principle (EPP), 182, 185–6, 190, 196, 277, 290, 296n, 343

external argument, 197, 284
   external θ-role, 278, 295, 297n
   VP-external semantic role, 280
Extraposition, 21–4, 26–7, 30, 85, 90–1, 231–3

factive, 314
Feature Checking, 289–90, 294
Fijian, *see* Austronesian languages, Fijian
filter, 129, 137–40, 145, 151, 160–5, 171, 172n, 173n, 178, 179
   surface filter, 137–40, 147, 152
Final 1 Law, 130–1, 133, 296n
*for* deletion, 49, 170, 195, 206–7
*for-to* filter, 151, 159, 163, 170, 201
French, *see* Romance languages, French
Full Interpretation, 286, 290–2, 313
functional projection, 275, 286, 296n, 297n, 345, 358n
   *see also* AGR projections; NegP; TP; vP
functional structure, 280–2
Functional Unification Grammar, 292

gapping, 37, 51, 199n, 340, 356, 358n
Generalized Phrase Structure Grammar (GPSG), 100, 292, 297n, 336, 343
Generative Semantics, 1, 2, 291, 292
gerund(ive)s, 25, 33, 45–6, 92, 94–8, 149, 196, 235
global rule, 141, 291
government theory, 180–1, 191, 193, 195–6, 205–6, 208, 231–4, 346
   governing category, 188–9, 191–2, 195–6, 198n, 339
   governing category (defined), 188
   government (defined), 180
GPSG, *see* Generalized Phrase Structure Grammar
grammatical theories, *see* Arc Pair Grammar; Categorial Grammar; Categorial Unification Grammar; Functional Unification Grammar; Generalized Phrase Structure Grammar; Generative Semantics; Head Driven Phrase Structure Grammar; Lexical Functional Grammar; Montague Grammar; Optimality Theory
Greed, 287, 289, 292, 330n

Head Driven Phrase Structure Grammar (HPSG), 100, 292, 343, 350
Head Movement Constraint (HMC), 296n
Heavy NP Shift (Complex NP Shift), 31–3, 41, 89–91, 96–8, 102n
HMC, see Head Movement Constraint
host of ascension, 111, 114–15, 121, 122, 136n
HPSG, see Head Driven Phrase Structure Grammar

Icelandic, 54, 55, 101, 103n, 107–8, 236–7, 239, 282, 294
identity, see sloppy interpretation
idioms as argument for Raising, 8–10, 14–15, 30, 94, 247, 301, 333
improper movement, 240–1, 324–5
Inclusion Constraint, see Unlike Person Constraint
Indonesian, see Austronesian languages, Indonesian
inherent Case, 233, 330n
Insertion Prohibition, 64, 69, 75
interpretive semantics, 1, 2
islandhood, 208–16, 219, 221, 226
*it*-Replacement, see Pronoun (*it*) Replacement
Italian, see Romance languages, Italian

Japanese, 129, 130, 134, 176, 243, 254–68, 270n, 271n, 278, 280, 307, 325, 327–9, 331n, 361n
Javanese, see Austronesian languages, Javanese

Kinyarwanda, 133–4
Kipsigis, 56, 59n, 238–40, 246, 323

Last Resort, 289, 291–2, 353
Least Effort, 286–7
lexical feature or diacritic, 23, 29n, 328
Lexical Functional Grammar (LFG), 100–2, 103n, 106, 125, 135, 266, 292, 343, 350
lexical redundancy rule, 61
lexical theory or lexicalism, 60
LF, see Logical Form
LFG, see Lexical Functional Grammar
light v, see vP
Locative Inversion, 96–8

Logical Form (LF)
  in government and binding theory, 178, 179
    and the Projection Principle, 181–2
    and θ-theory, 182–3
  in the Minimalist Program, 287, 290–2, 297n
    and movement to Spec,AgrO, 306–10, 318–20, 321–3
  in REST, 141–2, 145, 146, 156
    and NP-movement, 157–8

Madurese, see Austronesian languages, Madurese
MDP, see Minimal Distance Principle
Merge, 287, 288, 291
meteorological *it*, see pleonastic elements, meteorological *it*
Minimal Distance Principle (MDP), 351–5
Minimal Link Condition (MLC), 351–2, 354
MLC, see Minimal Link Condition
Montague Grammar, 100
Move, 288, 289, 290
  copy theory of movement, 288
Move-α, 179, 183, 189, 216, 316
move NP, 146, 158, 167–8
  NP-movement, 183, 184–6, 189, 198n

negative clitic *ne*, 202
negative evidence, 159
negative polarity (item), 304, 306, 309–11, 319
NegP, 280–1
Niuean, see Austronesian languages, Niuean
NOC, see non-obligatory control
NOC PRO, 199n, 347, 359n
nominative absolutes, 33
non-lexical categories, 18
  see also functional projection
non-obligatory control (NOC), 199n, 347, 351, 359n
*not*-initial NPs, 35–40
NP-chain, see chain
NP-movement, see move NP, NP-movement
[$_{NP}$ NP tense VP] filter, 158, 169
[NP to VP] filter, 162–9, 171

NP-trace, 189, 209, 348
null Case (analysis of PRO), 346, 347, 356, 359n
null complementizer, 150, 172n, 199n, 204, 205
   empty complementizer, 197, 206, 208
   prepositional null complementizer, 204–5
   Ø-complementizer, 164
numeration, 287, 288, 295

object agreement, 56, 213, 239, 306
Object Raising, see tough-movement
obligatory control (OC), 138–9, 147–50, 152, 165–7, 170, 196–7, 199n, 347
   OC PRO, 199n, 347–8, 351, 359n
observational adequacy, see adequacy
OC, see Obligatory Control
Opacity Condition, 224
Optimality Theory (OT), 172n, 291–2
OT, see Optimality Theory

particle verb, 323
partitive clitic en, see en-cliticization
passive, 18–21, 25, 43–4n, 54–5, 63, 65–9, 79, 83, 85–6, 121–2, 128–9, 157–8, 185–6, 189, 205–7, 261–4, 328, 330n, 346, 349–50
   Adversative Passive, 263–4
   embedded passive as argument for raising, 5–7, 10, 333
   Passive transformation, 18–19, 65–69, 128
   Second Passive transformation, 20
PF, see Phonetic Form
phase, 327, 349
Phonetic Form (PF), 177–9, 195, 287–9
   Universal Phonetics (UP), 141–2, 145–6, 156–7
pleonastic elements, 4, 30, 131, 168, 183, 199n, 312–14, 333
   existential there, 7–8, 14, 20, 301
   meteorological it, 8–9
   pleonastic objects (expletive objects), 235, 313–14
   pleonastic subjects (expletive subjects), 7–8, 10, 15, 182, 313, 333–4
pleonastic objects, see pleonastic elements, pleonastic objects

pleonastic subjects, see pleonastic elements, pleonastic subjects
Portuguese, see Romance languages, Portuguese
Possessor Ascension, see Possessor Raising
Possessor Raising (Possessor Ascension), 126, 133–4, 136n
postcyclical, see cycle, transformational
PP-internal controller, 352
PR, see Pronoun (it) Replacement
Predicate Agglutination, 328
PredP, 297n
prepositional complementizer, 22, 162, 195, 201, 208, 230, 236
   prepositional null complementizer, 204–5
principles A, B, and C, see binding theory, binding principles
principles of economy, see economy principles
PRO Theorem, 196, 199n, 204, 340, 346
pro-drop, see Subject Deletion
Procrastinate, 287, 289, 290, 292, 297n
Projection Principle, 181–2, 194, 277, 282, 291, 332, 337, 358n
   formulated, 181
   see also Extended Projection Principle
Pronominalization Constraint, 42–6, 92–3, 302–3, 311
Pronoun Deletion, 21–2, 29n, 161
Pronoun (it) Replacement (PR), 22–3, 25–7, 71, 85, 88n, 332
Proper Binding Condition, see Empty Category Principle, Proper Binding Condition
pseudocleft, see cleft, pseudocleft
pseudo-passive, 67–8
psych-verb, 331n

quantifier, 157, 161, 171, 179, 322–3
   interpretation of, 156, 157, 171, 179
   quantifier float, 53–4, 278, 319
   quantifier lowering, 310
   quantifier raising (QR), 179, 307
   quantifier scope, 257, 302, 328–9, 330n
Quechua, 103n, 208, 209–36, 262
quirky case, 54–5, 236
QR, see quantifier, quantifier raising

R-structure (Role-structure), 339
reciprocal, 25–6, 84, 94, 143, 144, 186, 189, 210, 215–16, 224–5, 304, 309, 311
   Reciprocal Formation, 25, 215
   see also binding theory, binding principles, principle A
recoverability of deletion, 64
reflexive, 19, 25, 79–80, 83–4, 168, 186–9, 211, 215, 224, 230, 257, 308
Reflexive Deletion, 151
Reflexivization transformation, 19, 25–6, 215, 224, 301
   see also binding theory, binding principles, principle A
Relational Network (RN), 127–9
relativized minimality, 297n
Right Node Raising (RNR), 46–50, 93, 99
RN, see Relational Network
RNR, see Right Node Raising
Role-structure, see R-structure
Romance languages, 118
   French, 12, 13, 110, 113, 118–19, 122, 128, 176, 200–8, 236, 278, 280–1, 329n, 359n, 361n
   Italian, 130, 202, 331n, 357n
   Portuguese, 110, 119, 154
   Spanish, 37, 161, 210
rule feature, see lexical feature or diacritic
rules of construal, see construal, rules of

S'-deletion or transparency (also CP deletion), 192–5, 197, 198, 199n, 204, 206–8, 232, 233, 235–7, 241n, 262, 312
s-selection, see selection, s-selection
scrambling, 146, 256, 267, 269, 307, 326–7
Select, 287, 288
selection
   c-selection (category selection), 160, 312
   s-selection (semantic selection), 160, 312, 313
selectional restrictions, 6–7, 159–60, 333
semantic role, see thematic role
semantic selection, see selection, s-selection
Sentential Subject Constraint, 80
Shortest Move, 287, 290, 292, 297n
SIC, see Subject Island Condition

sloppy interpretation (identity), 348
Spanish, see Romance languages, Spanish
SPEC2, 239–40, 241n, 266, 324
Spec-Head, 286, 289, 306
Specified Subject Condition (SSC), 70–7, 79–80, 87n, 149, 179, 198n, 209, 302
   Formulated, 70
Spell-Out, 287, 318–19, 321–2
SSC, see Specified Subject Condition
stratal diagram, 128, 132
Stratal Uniqueness Law, 131–2
stratum, 127–8, 131–2
Strict Cycle Condition, 76
string vacuous movement, 24, 26–7, 83, 88n, 96
strong feature, 290, 295, 330n
structure preservation, 82–3, 88n, 156, 157, 181, 199n, 231
structure sharing, 101–2, 103n, 135, 266–7
subjacency, 60, 80–3, 88n, 183
   bounding nodes, 81–2, 183
   bounding theory, 177–9, 183, 198n
Subject–Auxiliary Inversion (Auxiliary Inversion), 4, 20, 75–6
Subject Deletion (pro-drop), 161
Subject Island Condition (SIC), 213, 226–8, 241n
subjectless VP, see VP analysis of infinitives

Tagalog, see Austronesian languages, Tagalog
tense phrase, see TP
Tensed-S Condition (TSC), 69–70, 73–6, 79–81, 87n, 149, 167–8, 179, 198n, 211–12
   formulated, 69
*that*-trace filter, 160
thematic role (semantic role), 4–5, 277–8, 341–4
   see also θ-theory, θ-role
thematic structure, 4–5, 178, 195
*there*-insertion, 20, 28, 130
   see also pleonastic elements
θ-theory, 181–3, 194
   θ-criterion, 194, 266, 277, 282, 337, 339, 342–3, 345–6, 358n
   formulated, 182
θ-role, 348–9, 361n
Topicalization, 25–6, 79, 80, 111, 271n

*tough*-movement (Object Raising), 111–20, 125, 126, 135n, 334, 337, 358n
TP (tense phrase), 280–2, 285, 294, 306, 317, 327
transformational cycle, *see* cycle, transformational
TSC, *see* Tensed-S Condition
Tsez, 360–1n

unaccusative, 16n, 133, 184–6, 189, 268, 284–5, 288, 296n
Unaccusative Advancement, 131, 133
unergative, 16n, 284, 296n
Universal Phonetics (UP), *see* Phonetic Form, Universal Phonetics
Unlike Person Constraint (Inclusion Constraint), 73–4, 86–7
UP, *see* Phonetic Form, Universal Phonetics

V-initial analysis, *see* VSO Hypothesis
VoiceP, 296–7n
vP (light v), 268, 283–4, 295, 296n
VP analysis of infinitives (VP′), 334–1, 343–4, 358n
VP-external subject, 277, 282
VP-internal subject, 278–80, 282–6, 357n
VP-shell, 283
VP′, *see* VP analysis of infinitives
VSO Hypothesis (V-initial analysis), 27–8, 30, 58n, 108, 110, 113

weak feature, 290
*wh*-movement, 75–7, 80–2, 87n, 135n, 183, 192, 198n, 199n, 204–5, 222–4, 241n

X-bar theory, 144, 156–7, 292